T5-CQC-089

UNDERSTANDING MANTRAS

SUNY Series in Religious Studies
Robert Cummings Neville, Editor

UNDERSTANDING MANTRAS

Harvey P. Alper, Editor

State University of New York Press

Published by

State University of New York Press, Albany

© 1989 State University of New York

All rights reserved

Printed in the United States of America

No part of this book may be used or reproduced
in any manner whatsoever without written permission
except in the case of brief quotations embodied in
critical articles and reviews.

For information, address State University of New York Press,
State University Plaza, Albany, N.Y., 12246

Library of Congress Cataloging-in-Publication Data

Understanding mantras.

(SUNY series in religious studies)
Bibliography: p.
1. Mantras. I. Alper, Harvey P., 1945– .
II. Series.
BL1236.36.U53 1988 294.5'37 87-6481
ISBN 0-88706-598-8

10 9 8 7 6 5 4 3 2 1

CONTENTS

INTRODUCTION

An ocean, verily, is the Word.

Pañcaviṃśa Brāhmaṇa 7.7.9

He lifts the lifewand and the dumb speak.
—Quoiquoiquoiquoiquoiquoiquoiq

"Shem the Penman," *Finnegan's Wake*

THIS VOLUME OF ESSAYS AND bibliography has been assembled in order to focus attention on the Hindu mantra, a common and vital but troubling feature of Indian culture that more often has been taken for granted than made the object of sympathetic and systematic reflection. The volume is exploratory not definitive. It may, I trust, be used as a general introduction to the Hindu mantra and its study, but it does not offer any comprehensive survey, nor does it deal with the use of mantras and mantralike formulas in non-Hindu settings or in those portions of Asia beyond India where Indian culture has penetrated. It is my conviction that the essays collected here speak eloquently for themselves and need no brief content summaries in this Introduction. Rather, I shall set the stage for reading the essays by indicating quite schematically some of the themes and issues in mantric studies that the essays themselves raise.

MANTRAS: WHY THEY MATTER AND WHY THEY PERPLEX US

In 1984, Sri Satguru Publications in Delhi brought out an English translation of Mahīdhara's *Mantramahodadhi,* a sixteenth century synthetic treatise on Mantraśāstra. Prior to the book's Introduction the publishers insert a "warning" in which they disclaim responsibility—ethically and, I suppose, legally—for the consequences that ensue when mantras are used unsuccessfully or irresponsibly.

> If any person on the basis of Yantras as provided in this book commits any nefarious acts which causes loss, etc., to anybody then for his actions the authors/editors/translators, printer and publisher will not be responsible in any way whatsoever.

> The Mantras/Yantras as provided in this book if are tried by anybody and is not crowned by success, which entirely depends on Sadhaka, the author/editors/translators, printer and publisher will not be responsible in any way for such failures.
>
> The Mantras/Yantra be practiced and used for the help, good cause and service of Mankind. These should not be used for any nefarious means, the responsibility of such actions will be only that of the Sadhaka.

Is this disclaimer meant seriously? Does the publisher fear being sued by someone who believed that he had been harmed by the use of a mantra? Might a disgruntled devotee haul his guru into small claims court because the mantra the latter had imparted did not perform as advertised? Perhaps not, yet this disclaimer underscores the fact that belief in the efficacy of mantras is a commonplace of Indian culture, today as in the past. It further suggests the difficulty of approaching Mantraśāstra from a perspective at once modern and sympathetic.

For India, mantras are real, palpable, mental artifacts to be revered and mastered, to be used or misused. While the significance of mantras is not exclusively religious, mantras obviously play a pivotal role in the religious realm. Instead, the history of the religious life of the Indian people might plausibly be read as a history of mantras. To be sure, there must always have been individuals who were sceptical about mantras. The extent of such scepticism in the past is difficult to gauge, but it could not have been great.* The possibility of the successful use of mantras was, and is, simply a common part of the Indian mentality.

This centrality of mantras in the common life of the Indian people is indicated, for example, by the observation in the *Rājataraṅgiṇī* that, in twelfth century Kaśmir, the crops in the fields were protected from Nāgas by māntrikas, "guards who exercised their function by means of mantras" (cited in Gonda [1963b] 1975b, IV:268). The general repute in which mantras have been held is expressed with uncanny force by as "secular" a text as the *Arthaśāstra* (perhaps third–fourth century A.D.), which holds that "a mantra accomplishes the apprehension of what is not or cannot be seen; imparts the strength of a definite conclusion to what is apprehended, removes doubt when two courses are possible, [and] leads to inference of an entire matter when only a part is seen" (Gonda [1963b] 1975b, 260, citing 1.15.20).

The difficulty we have understanding and explaining mantras may be highlighted by considering the place of Mantraśāstra in India as analogous (but it is *not* identical) to the place of prayer in the West. Among the monotheistic religions of the West, prayer has long been understood

---

**The temptation to interpret the Kautsa controversy as evidence of religious or philosophical scepticism would seem to be misplaced.*

as conversation with God; it has long been taken as the paradigmatic form of religious utterance. The most common form of prayer has been petition, but the most prestigious form often have been considered to be praise, thanksgiving, and adoration, forms of religious discourse lacking practical ends. (This is especially true of the Jewish and Muslim traditions and of Christian monasticism.) Recently, a number of theologians and social scientists have suggested that narrative (story) rather than prayer (conversation) plays a primal role in shaping human religious life. Both prayer and story are ways in which human beings use language to domesticate the enormity of the cosmos, bringing it into scale with the human dimension, and both are fundamentally personalistic. Whatever their importance might be elsewhere, it is arguable that in India neither prayer nor story is the paradigmatic form of religious utterance. It is mantra.*

Most of us who study mantras critically—historians, philosophers, Sanskritists—take the Enlightenment consensus for granted. We do not believe in magic. Generally, we do not pray. If we do pray, we try to do so in a universalistic idiom. We do not ask openly for mundane, temporal goods. If we prayed for the latter and if our prayers were answered, many of us would be incredulous and deeply embarrassed. In contrast to prayer and story, mantra is impersonal. In contrast to the most "desirable" forms of prayer, it is often practical. According to the standards of modern science, mantras are irrational. Mantraśāstra thus shares neither the prestige of modernity nor the lingering prestige of traditional Western religion. Perhaps for this reason it has fallen through the cracks of Indology. As an impersonal, often practical form of religious utterance, yet associated with a sophisticated civilization, mantra invites special attention.

DEFINITION

Earlier studies of mantra often began by proposing formal or informal definitions. An enumeration of these definitions is beyond the scope of this introduction and, in any case, would serve little purpose. But, one should note the heterogeneity of the various definitions. Gonda (1963b) and Bharati (1965) represent the two poles.

Gonda treats definition quite informally and tends to use it to describe the understanding of mantra in whatever text or secondary source with which he happens to be dealing. Therefore, it is not unusual for him to move effortlessly through a series of "definitions" within a few pages. Gonda ([1963b] 1975, IV:251) first focuses on the Veda and defines mantra "provisionally and for practical purposes" as "a general

**Coburn (1984b, 450, n. 10) surely is correct in qualifying the suggestion that story is the paradigmatic form of religious utterance. The primacy of mantra is implicit in the first category of Coburn's fivefold typology (p. 452).*

name for the formulas, verses or sequences of words in prose which contain praise . . . , are believed to have magical, religious, or spiritual efficiency, are recited, muttered or sung in the Vedic ritual and which are collected in the methodically arranged corpora of Vedic texts." He immediately qualifies this by adding that the word applies to "comparable 'formulas' of different origin used in the post-vedic cults." Focusing on practical morality (*daṇḍanīti*), Gonda (p. 259) offers a second definition of mantra as "consultation, resolution, advice, counsel, design, plan, secret." Moving on to classical Hinduism (p. 271), he offers a third definition, notable for its anthropological and heuristic breadth: In the religious practice of the Hindu age, as well as earlier, the term *mantra* "covers also all potent (so-called magical) forms of texts, words, sounds, letters, which bring good luck to those who know or 'possess' them and evil to their enemies." By the very next page, Gonda has moved on to another, Tantric, context and defines mantra as "a power (*śakti-*) in the form of formulated and expressed thought."

Bharati's strategy (1965, 105–11) could not be more divergent. After surveying attempts at a definition of mantra by scholars such as Bhattacharya, Eliade, von Glasenapp, Govinda, Guenther, Majumdar, Woodroffe, and Zimmer, he offers his own succinct, formal definition: "A *mantra* is a quasi-morpheme or a series of quasi-morphemes, or a series of mixed genuine and quasi-morphemes arranged in conventional patterns, based on codified esoteric traditions, and passed on from one preceptor to one disciple in the course of a prescribed initiation" (p. 111).

Whatever the advantages of such informal and formal definitions, generally speaking, the essays in this volume do not find the problem of definition a profitable point of departure. A loose working consensus, however, may be discerned in the way many of them take the scope of the term *mantra*. First, they assume that a mantra is whatever anyone in a position to know calls a mantra.* Second, they usually assume that the term and the phenomenon are not coextensive. Third, they recognize that, as far back as the evidence goes, there has been a large family of Indic terms—e.g., *brahman, stobha, bīja, kavaca, dhāraṇi, yāmala*—employed in various traditions and periods to name especially potent "words" and "sounds." Sometimes, these terms have been used with overlapping or roughly synonomous meanings, often they have been used with technical precision. When they are used technically, their exact force and meaning can be determined only through an exegesis that is text and tradition specific. Finally, there is a recognition that the

**In this they stand in the company of Sāyana, the sixteenth century exegete, who stipulated that a mantra is best defined as that which the priests who are performing a sacrifice call a mantra:* yājñikasamākhyānasya nirdoṣalakṣaṇatvāt *(Sontakke and Kashikar 1933, 1.16). Sāyaṇa is ultimately following Prabhākara's position (cf. Jha [1942] 1964, 160, and Murty 1959, 26).*

precision of the texts cannot be read into social usage without caution. On the popular level, words such as *mantra* long ago acquired a broad, if imprecise meaning.

HISTORY

Jan Gonda has long championed the view that certain continuities in Indian culture undergird and facilitate the admittedly real discontinuities. Thus, it can be no surprise when he quotes a long passage discussing mantra from the twentieth century neo-Hindu mystic Śrī Aurobindo and comments, "The survey of the Vedic uses of the term [mantra] will show that the essence of [Aurobindo's interpretation] is indeed already characteristic of the mantras of the Vedic period,—one of the numerous indicia of the agelong continuity of Indian religious thought" ([1963b] 1975, IV:253). Such generalizations are dangerous, for they tend to reify traditional Indian culture and suggest that it was an unchanging monolith. Nonetheless, my study of mantra leads me to conclude that Gonda is correct in some large measure. The history of Mantraśāstra strikes me overwhelmingly as a set of variations on a theme: The further afield, the more "rococo," the development gets, the more it reaffirms its original character. In this, it might be apt to compare the history of Mantraśāstra to the development of a *rāga*. In the realm of mantra there has been forward movement; there has been no revolution.

The essays in this volume present diverse evidence of historical change and historical continuity. Quite naturally, readers will form their own judgments concerning the import of this evidence. It might, however, be useful to draw attention to three points that relate directly to the assessment of the balance between continuity and discontinuity in Mantraśāstra. (1) The historical origin of the mantra is not easily reconstructed on the basis of the surviving documents. Nonetheless, as Findly shows, the ṚV itself contains evidence of a fundamental transformation that created the mantra as the tradition subsequently knew it. In other words, the journey from poetic inspiration to ritual utilization is noticeable from the start. (2) The evidence presented by Staal, and Wheelock, underlines the historical continuity of mantra from the period of SV to the Tantras. The parallel between Vedic and Tantric deformations of ordinary, otherwise linguistically meaningful, sentences is particularly suggestive. In a sense, the patterned repetitions of *japa* are the theistic and meditative correlates of the ritual deconstruction of the texts in the tradition of Brahmanic sacrifice. (3) Several of the essays that deal with classical Hinduism—Oberhammer, Gupta, and especially Rocher—underscore the difficulty of drawing hard and fast distinctions between different periods of mantras. The distinction between Vedic, Purāṇic, and Tantric mantras must be considered one of those pious organizational fictions in which Indian culture, like most cultures, abounds.

FUNCTION

As a tool of human intentionality, mantras are protean. They are used in an astonishing variety of contexts, for a plethora of purposes, with a multitude of informing emotions, and by the widest variety of individuals. Gonda ([1963b] 1975b, IV:250) nonetheless asserts that the term *mantra* has "kept a definite semantic kernel." Many scholars might *feel* that this judgment is correct, yet neither Gonda nor anyone else has really demonstrated exactly the limits and content of this semantic kernel. Lurking behind our sense of the commonality of mantras one can sense the instinctive conclusion of the rationalist. After all, nothing really distinguishes one magic formula from another: Whether one is trying to hail a taxi in New York during rush hour, trying to post a package overseas from an Indian post office, or even trying to dodge the explosions while crossing a minefield, reciting a mantra—any mantra—will be as ineffective as reciting anything else.

The tradition, in contrast, takes for granted that mantras are anything but arbitrary and interchangeable. Each of them is understood to be a finely honed instrument for exercising power, a tool designed for a particular task, which will achieve a particular end when, and only when, it is used in a particular manner. Mantras, according to this view, are as distinct from each other as are hammers from screwdrivers. More critically, they are taken to be as distinct from each other as are individuals. This conviction is illustrated, for example, by the Pāñcarātra conviction that "each letter of the *mātṛkā* is in its own right a mantra *with a distinct personality*" (Gupta, this volume, italics mine), by the proliferation of different sorts of initiations (*dīkṣās*), as well as by the well-known proclivity of certain devotees to collect gurus the way some Americans collect baseball cards.*

It is clear that mantras are understood by the tradition as polyvalent instruments of power. Debating what really counts as a mantra and what defines it as a mantra is unlikely to yield interesting results. Listing all of the situations in which mantras may be used may or may not be theoretically possible.** In any case, it is impractical without more computer time than impecunious Sanskritists are likely to command. How-

**For example, Bharati (1965, 197, n. 3) cites a story from the SkandaP, in which a monk acquired thirty-three different* dīkṣas *that were imparted by no less than thirty-three gurus, one of whom was a crow.*

***The tradition seems to hold that the number of mantras is finite but very large. Hence, it ought to be theoretically possible to provide an exhaustive list of the contexts in which they may be used, but I would demur. Although the tradition characteristically denies this, an infinity of new mantras may be created, just as one may create an infinity of new sentences in a natural language.*

ever, it is possible to get a handle on the sorts of situations in which mantras characteristically are used. Many scholars have suggested the need for classifying the intented force of mantric utterance. Gonda ([1963b] 1975b, IV:249) speaks of mantras being "invocatory," "evocatory," "deprecatory," and "conservatory." Bharati (1965, 111 ff) more cogently proposes a threefold division of the purpose of mantric utterance: "propitiation," "acquisition," and "identification." Many other schemes of classification have been proposed, but none has yet won general acceptance.

Perhaps foolishly, I wish to enter this fray by suggesting a simple foursided grid (see Figure 1) in whose terms any particular use of a mantra might be placed *for the purpose of comparison.* The grid has two scales, each of which is understood as a continuum. It is my conviction that few if any mantric utterances would ever exemplify a single, "pure" character. Human life is too complex and too rich for that to be the case. Placement of a particular mantra within this continuum, thus, is meant to suggest its relative character.

The horizontal scale shows intentionality. Towards the left pole I place mantras uttered predominantly to achieve some specific practical goal; e.g., the disovery of lost cattle, the cure of impotence or barrenness, a passing grade on a university examination. Towards the right pole I place mantras uttered predominantly to achieve some transcendental goal; e.g., escape from *saṃsāra,* the diminution of the effect of bad karma, transportation to the realm of the god to whom one is devoted. The left pole I label *quotidian;* the right pole I label *redemptive.* By the

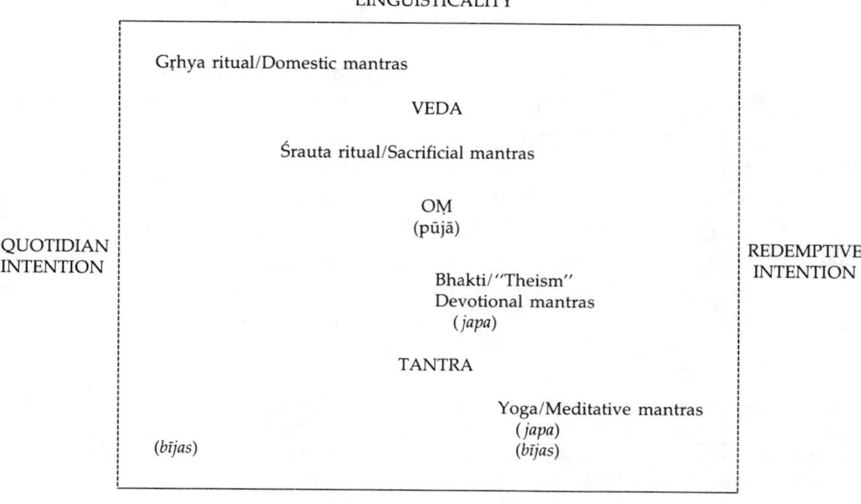

Figure 1. Grid for Comparing Mantras

former term, I designate purposes informed by the need to cope with the multitudinous dilemmas *of daily life*. By the latter term, I designate purposes informed by the desire to cope with the human condition *as a whole*. I choose these terms precisely to avoid more common terms that already carry a heavy burden of connotations.*

The vertical scale shows linguisticality. Towards the top I place mantras that are entirely intelligible as sentences in an ordinary language; e.g., the Gāyatrī. Towards the bottom pole I place mantras that, however they may be decoded, are in no way intelligible as ordinary language in themselves; e.g., *bīja* mantras. Here, too, it seems to me that there is a continuum, rather than an absolute distinction. If one takes the ritual and social context of Mantraśāstra into consideration, all or most mantras may be understood to share the characters of both linguisticality and alinguisticality.

The placement of items in Figure 1 suggests how a grid might be employed to situate both classes and particular instances of mantric utterance for comparison. Thus, it seems to me, that mantras used in the domestic (*gṛhya*) ritual typically are quotidian and linguistic in comparison to those use in Tantra, which tend to be characteristically redemptive and alinguistic. Conversely, it seems to me that the mantras used in the Śrauta ritual and devotionally show a high degree of variation in terms of both the intentions with which they are used and their linguisticality. In any case, I shall not attempt to argue my particular historical judgments here; I merely wish to suggest a procedure for classification that readers might test against the evidence presented in this volume.

METHOD

The reader will find no methodological manifesto in this volume. There is no unanimity among the contributors concerning the description and classification of mantras or the most fruitful way to study them. Rather, the consensus is that mantras merit study and that this study will yield the most interesting results if informed by careful method, be that method anthropolgoical, historical, philological, or philosophical. Moreover, certain themes and issues recur as leitmotifs through the essays. In the remainder of the Introduction, I shall draw attention to some of these recurring motifs. Among them, two are fundamental: the

---

*Quotidien, *of course, is a common French adjective for daily. Its use in this context was suggested to me originally by the subtitle of Brunner (1963). I cannot take the space for a full justification of this nomenclature here. Suffice it to say that I have attempted to avoid invoking the hackneyed Western distinction between magic and religion and to propose a terminology compatible with other distinctions that have been proposed to classify diverging sorts of Hindu religious life; e.g., Mandelbaum's distinction between transcendental and pragmatic (see Mandlebaum 1966 and cf. Goudriaan and Gupta 1981, 112 ff).*

question of whether mantras are instances of language and, if so, what sort of linguistic utterance are they; and the question of whether and, if so, how mantras function as instruments of religious transfiguration.

There can be no doubt that Jan Gonda's (1963b) essay, "The Indian Mantra," remains the single most important contribution to the study of the subject. In many regards, it is a model of Indological synthesis, ranging widely over the available primary and secondary sources. All the contributors to this volume remain indebted to it; many of us remain under its spell. Nonetheless, without wanting to appear ungrateful, it should be said that, upon close reading, the essay's Indological strengths are not matched by methodological acumen. Many researchers have recognized that the mere enumeration of mantras will never suffice. The need for systematic, critical reflection on mantra emerges from Indology itself. The importance of supplementing Indological inquiry with broader, more searching sorts of analysis has been noted, for example, by Padoux. The need for philosophical precision in studying mantras was passionately asserted by Bharati twenty years ago. This volume has evolved partially in response to the call of these two scholars.

Padoux's remarks (1978b, 238 f) merit citation:

> All the [Indological] researches [previously mentioned], important as they are, still do not suffice for a complete understanding of the problem of *mantra,* if only because they remain on the surface: they limit themselves to reporting what different texts, schools, authors, say on the subject. They report a discourse, they contribute to clarify it, they unveil its relations to other discourses, or its historical origins and developments, but they do not *explain* it: what really *are mantra-s?* How do they "function"? What can one say about the mantric phenomenon as a peculiar type of human praxis and discourse? Those, indeed, are the most important problems.

How might one achieve such comprehensive understanding of the context, character, and significance of mantric utterance? Judging by many of the essays in this volume—for example, those of Alper, Coward, Findly, Staal, Taber, and Wheelock—there seems to be a general conviction that progress in understanding and explaining mantras depends upon filtering the results of philological-historical analysis through the critical sieve of philosophy.* In this we all heed Bharati's recommendation (1965, 102 f) that mantra be examined with the tools of analytic philosophy.

In subjecting mantra to philosophical scrutiny, one crux stands out

**It is, I am convinced, equally important to collate the examination of texts with anthropological field reports that examine how mantras, in fact, are used. A companion volume bringing such inquiries together and subjecting them to philosophical reflection would be useful.*

as central: Should the indigenous interpretative tradition be taken seriously *as interpretation?* To be sure, everyone recognizes that the analyses of mantra by Indian theoreticians can be studied in themselves, as primary sources. The question is whether their work helps us explain and understand the phenomenon itself? The issue will be drawn clearly for the reader by contrasting the analyses of Taber, Coward, and Alper, on the one hand, with that of Staal, on the other. The former—dealing respectively with Śabara, Bhartṛhari, and Kṣemarāja—answer the question affirmatively; Staal answers with an emphatic no.

IS MANTRA LANGUAGE?

The most fundamental discussion running through these pages concerns the linguisticality of mantras. In the past decade or so, a series of studies by McDermott, Staal, and Wheelock have focused attention on this issue. Far from leading to a new concensus, their work demonstrates radical—seemingly irreconcilable—differences in evaluating the nature and function of mantra. In my own judgment, this volume makes two significant contributions to mantric studies: taken together, the essays make this difference of interpretation apparent; and they do so in a manner which shows that only rigorous philosophical reflection can establish whether a problematic sort of utterance—and there isn't even agreement whether a mantra counts as an "utterance"—such as mantra is senseless mumbo jumbo (cf. Bharati 1965, 102).

The key question is raised forcefully by comparing the position of Staal with those of Wheelock and Alper.* Staal's approach is alinguistic, essentially. Largely, he assimilates mantra to ritual. This contrasts dramatically with the speech act analyses of Wheelock and Alper, both of whom take for granted that mantric utterance is a form of language.

Staal's argument has developed over a number of years and has been expressed in a number of publications. For this reason, in addition to its historical and philosophical sophistication, it is difficult to do justice to it in a few sentences. Nevertheless, a schematic outline might help the reader compare it with that of his opponents.** Staal's point of departure is an observation that is unexceptionable at face value: "Mantras are bits and pieces from the Vedas put to ritual use." This is the linch pin of Staal's position, from which the remainder of his analysis is logically deducible. He observes that the raison d'être of mantras, that context without which they are not mantras, is Vedic ritual. Period. He continues by asking what mantras are like and responds with analogies taken exclusively from alinguistic phenomenon: "mantras are like mu-

---

**As suggested above, the approach taken and/or the conclusions reached in the essays of Coward, Findly, and Taber might also be contrasted with Staal's alinguiticality thesis.*

***I shall not attempt to trace the development of Staal's position through his work; however, see the relevant items in the Bibliography.*

sic," like the nattering of infants and madmen, like the patterned song of birds. He concludes, "there is every reason to accept as a well established fact that mantras, even if they consist of language, are not used in the manner of language."*

Although a majority of the contributors to this volume, including me, hold that mantra generally is a linguistic phenomenon, Staal's case should not be dismissed out of hand. His work on ritual, language, and mantras cumulatively makes a distinguished contribution to our understanding of Indian culture. He has proposed a general theory and established a prima facie case. He is the *pūrvapakṣin;* if one thinks his position incorrect, then one is obligated to demonstrate it.

Can Staal's position be refuted? Not as easily as one might imagine. The most obvious refutation turns out to be no refutation at all. If one merely points to the fact that some, I would say many, mantras may be translated into a natural language other than Sanskrit, Staal might easily respond: This apparent translatability misses the point. Even if the words used in a mantra are otherwise translatable, even if they otherwise amount to a sentence, a mantra *qua mantra* is untranslatable. Its apparent linguistic meaning is adventitious to its function as a mantra.

Moreover, it must be admitted that none of the advocates of the linguistic thesis argue for it directly in this volume; we all assume it. Staal's work certainly shows that this is not sufficient. To show that Staal is in some large measure incorrect someone must produce a well-reasoned argument that demonstrates that mantra should count as language. Unless and until that is done, it is futile to try to demonstrate that the utterance of a mantra is a particular act of speech.

On the one hand it is true that from the start mantras have been associated with special "words" (noises, sounds), such as *svāhā,* that have no meaning in ordinary language. This strongly suggests that some mantras, or all mantras in some sense, are abracadabra words. It is further the case that there is no apparent correlation between the context or use of a mantra and its being, in part, linguistically meaningful. Finally, there can be no doubt that, while languages are preeminently instruments of public communication, one of the most characteristic uses of mantra is the esoteric mental repetition of *japa.*

Against this one might observe that the evidence Staal marshals is selected to illustrate his thesis, naturally enough. Other evidence might be assembled that, if not refute it, would call it into question, or at least, suggest that the alinguisticality thesis, in its pure form, requires modification. After all, some mantras are or contain sentences. Whether one

---

**Staal's interpretation of mantra as meaningless, as a practical matter, is tied to his theory of ritual as meaningless. They are correlated but do not entail each other, I believe. The thesis that ritual is meaningless does entail that mantras, as ritual, are meaningless. On the other hand, one might argue that while ritual in general is meaningful, mantras are an instance of meaningless ritual. Similarly, Staal's historical speculation, his hypothesis that "mantras are the missing link between ritual and language," is compatible with his analysis of mantra but not entailed by it.*

classifies them as prayers, they accurately express the intention of a speaker. Gonda ([1963b] 1975, IV:267), for example, translates a mantra drawn from BrahamP 56.72 f: "Save me who am immersed in the sea of mundane existence, swallowed by evil, senseless, O thou who art the destroyer of the eyes of Bhaga, O enemy of Tripura, homage to Thee!"* As this example illustrates, the tradition of overtly meaningful mantras by no means disappears with the Vedic *Saṃhitās*. Indeed, numerous examples of meaningful mantras, used with either quotidian or redemptive intention, can be found in a wide variety of texts. See, for example, C. M. Brown (1974, 45) for a mantra to be recited over a human being prior to his sacrifice and Goudriaan and Gupta (1981, 79 f) for a propitiatory mantra to Śivā (the jackal, the word is feminine, is understood as a manifestation of Śakti), which must contain the sentences "Take, take!" "Devour, devour!" "Create success for me!" and "Destroy, destroy; kill, kill my foes!"

Where does this leave one? Judging by the essays in this volume, both the linguisticality and the alinguisticality of mantras is arguable. There is no open and shut case; neither is established. Hence, the vertical pole in Figure 1 must take into account this argument.

MANTRAS AS RELIGIOUS INSTRUMENTS

The thesis that mantras are instruments of fundamental religious transformation is curiously hybrid and, therefore, curiously problematic. It argues that the utterance of a mantra is an instance of language, but language of so peculiar a sort that it shares some of the characteristics of alinguisticality. Scholars with positions as diverse as Renou and Bharati—and, in this volume, Padoux, Wheelock, and Alper—accept versions of this thesis. It is safe to predict that more shall be said about it in the future.

To Bharati (1965, 102), for example, "*mantra* is meaningful not in any descriptive or even persuasive sense, but within the mystical universe of discourse." According to him, this means that mantric discourse is "verifiable not by what it describes but by what it effects"; that is, "if it creates that somewhat complex feeling-tone in the practising person, which has found its expression in the bulk of mystical literature such as tantra, then it is verified." In other words, it can be verified only by "its emotive numinous effect as well as in the corroboration of such effects in religious literature."

Such an assertion fits well with our preconceptions about the mystical. We have been mesmerized by the ineffability, the alinguisticality, of religious experience. For the modern, especially the Protestant, West, religion is preeminently an inner state of consciousness, a "raw feel" of

**He comments that it is to be uttered when one immerses one's head in the temple pool of Śiva built by the sage Mārkaṇḍeya in Benares.*

the numinous, a sensation that is by definition private. William James characteristically observes, "The handiest of the marks by which I classify a state of mind as mystical is negative. The subject of it immediately says that it defies expression, that no adequate report of its contents can be given in words" (1902, 371).

Time and again, we have taken the religions of the East as holding paradigmatically that the ultimate (Brahman, Nirvāṇa, Tao, or whatever) is *eo ipso* beyond words. Of course, certain strands of Indian spirituality say just that. Coburn (1984b, 446) remarks that for some strata of Indian society simply hearing, not understanding, the cultured Sanskrit language "bordered on being a numinous experience." If this is an exaggeration, it contains more than a grain of truth. Neither the social prestige nor the religious repute of mantras depend upon their meaningfulness. As Coburn (1984b, 445) says "the holiness of holy words is not a function of their intelligibility." On the contrary, sometimes it seems as if sanctity is "inversely related to comprehensibility."

Granted, this is often the case. There is, however, a counter-balancing theme within South Asian spirituality: that the ultimate is essentially linguistic. From this emerge the mundane conversations of human beings. As the essays by Coward and Alper in this volume indicate, this theme is especially well represented in some of the traditions that portray the ultimate as *Vāc* or that teach a Tantric *sādhanā.** Perhaps, this should not surprise us. The intellectual elite of the West has been fixated on counting, that is, on mathematics, as *the* model for true knowing. In contrast, the Indian elite has been fixated on linguistics, that is, on speaking. This can be seen scholastically in the preeminence of Pāṇini; it can be seen epistemologically in the preoccupation with *śabda* (verbal authority); it can be seen socially in the prestige of the guru; it can be seen ritually in the centrality of the mantra.

I hope that it is not out of place for me to close this introduction by expressing the hope that this volume will both help establish the academic importance of studying mantras and win a sympathetic hearing for them. India is not merely, or even principally, the land of Vedānta. It is not merely, though it indeed is, the land of Viṣṇu and Śiva. Ritually, it is the land of the mantra. To know and love Indian religious life means coming to terms with mantric utterance.

The fact that mantras cannot be readily classified as linguistic or alinguistic challenges our conception of mysticism. The fact that they are not readily classifiable as prayers or spells further challenges our conception of religious language. As some philosophers of religion have

---

**I am not certain whether the same divergence occurs in the Buddhist tradition. S. Dasgupta (1962, 21f.) cites the argument in Vasubandhu's* Bodhisattvabhūmi *that meaninglessness is the real meaning of mantra. Gonda ([1963b] 1975b, 300) adds that Vasubandhu teaches that expressly meaningless syllables "enable the initiate to understand by pure intuition, that the nature of the dharmas is meaningless and to bring about the revolution of a unique and immutable transcendental meaning which is the real nature of all."*

realized, the extraordinary diversity of religious life has been "disguised" by the "poverty of examples" with which Western scholars have typically chosen to deal (Sherry 1977, 108, 50). Christian thinkers have rarely ventured beyond monotheism; anthropologists have focused largely on the animistic or magical language games of tribal peoples. Curiously, left to the side have been the articulate, rational polytheisms of India and China.

An understanding of religious language in general is not possible. If I may use Wittgensteinian jargon, every historical tradition draws together a family of language games and forms of life. Ultimately, the challenge of this diversity is existential. Hacker (1972, 118), referring to the category of *Gedankenrealismus,* comments, "From ancient times there has been in India the conviction that mental representations, if reaching a high degree of intensity, are capable of bringing about a reality not only on the psychological level but even in the domain of material things." It is a simple matter to dismiss this as primitive, but one ought to think twice before doing so.

Mantras are many-sided instruments. Surely, they may be understood in many ways. Like so many religious phenomena, they are anodyne. They are meant to soothe us, to convince us that, all appearances to the contrary, we really are in control of the universe. But, mantras are not merely instruments of consolation; they are one of the structural pivots around which a mature and sophisticated society has organized its life. Traditional Indian society is predicated on its belief in the efficacy of the well-spoken human word and the well-made ritual gesture. May we explain mantras scientifically at the same time that we appreciate them personally? If so, perhaps we shall open up a new perspective, both on the variety of Indian religious life and on humanity's capacity to give voice to that beyond which there is nothing more.

CHAPTER 1

Mántra kaviśastá: Speech as Performative in the Ṛgveda

Ellison Banks Findly

AS THE LATE VEDIC AND classical Sanskrit tradition develops, one of the increasingly central concepts is mantra as "eine 'traditionelle Formel', deren Würde eben darin besteht, dass sie von den Weisen der Vorzeit her überliefert ist" [a 'traditional formula' whose value consists precisely in the fact that the sages of the primeval past have handed it down] (Thieme 1957b; 68–69). The extended use of this term in later literature, and of the concept throughout the varieties of the Hindu experience (cf. Gonda 1963b), might lead one to suppose a substantial foundation for mantra in the very early literature. While the philosophic and psychological bases for mantra, in fact, do become well defined in the course of the Ṛgveda, and the argument for this will be central to this paper, the term itself is an uncommon, often unclear commodity until well into the Upaniṣadic era.[1]

In the Ṛgveda itself, we find twenty-one references to mantra as well as single references to *mantrakṛ́t* and *mantraśrútya*.[2] Although not confined to the hymns of one deity;[3] three quarters of the mantra references are found in Books 1 and 10. Following the findings of scholars who have investigated the literary strata in the Ṛgveda (i.e., Arnold 1905; Belvalkar 1922, 16; Chattopadhyaya 1985, 32; Macdonell, 1900, 34ff.; and Oldenberg 1888, 221–22, 232), I suggest, then, that the development of the term *mantra* may belong to a younger period of Ṛgvedic composition.[4]

Given this overall paucity of references, one could argue further that mantra is not only a late Ṛgvedic concept but, perhaps, an insignificant one as well. Following this line of reasoning, that is, that silence or at least vague and irregular murmurings denotes inconsequence, however, mantra could be shown to attain prominence only after the other elements of the *śrauta* system. And this, of course, is not the case. In general, inattention to a term in the Ṛgveda does not always mean inattention to the corresponding concept. And, in this instance, I will argue, mantra is a development central to Ṛgvedic thought, which takes place at a peak period of creativity and which bridges the transition from the earlier, more theistic sensibilities to the later, increasingly ritualistic concerns.[5]

While the focus of this paper will be an investigation of how Ṛgvedic thinkers conceived of the term *mantra,* it cannot be confined only to those places in the text where mantra appears. Rather, the investigation must be expanded to include other psychological and philosophic contexts, especially those involving ritual speech, which might have given rise to a notion of mantra, particularly as it is *kaviśastá,* 'pronounced by the seers.' Organizationally, then, I will begin with the descriptive contexts of the word and move backward to what I postulate might have been an earlier phase of Ṛgvedic thought, thereby showing changes that the development of mantra brought about, or reflected, in the early speculations about speech, ritual, and otherwise. While this necessarily means deciphering chronological layers within the Ṛgveda, I am less concerned with pronouncing certain hymns or parts of hymns early or late than with tracing briefly those types of changes in Ṛgvedic thought that facilitated the rise of the notion of mantra. Proceeding this way, I follow the line of thinking that finds one of the clearest, most retrievable "chronologies" of the Ṛgveda to be the development of its religious thought (i.e., Chattopadhyaya 1935, 35; Thieme 1975a, 53).

An underlying concern of this discussion will be that the changes represented by mantra have implications not only for abstractions of Ṛgvedic philosophy, but also for understanding those who composed and uttered the words that proved to be so efficacious in religious life. If ritual speech is performative speech, as I will argue and as most now understand it, then it behooves me to mention both the theory of how speech operates in the Vedic *śrauta* system, as is done most commendably later in this volume, and, more importantly for the Ṛgveda, those who are speaking (i.e., the priests) and their vision of and relationship with whatever "transcendent other" empowers their speech to be performative in the first place. While later mantric material, as used in the developed *śrauta* system, derives its primary power from its associative role in building layer upon layer of analogy in the complex matrix of the ritual world (Heesterman 1964, 12–14; 1967, 22ff.), early Ṛgvedic material, though it also uses analogy albeit in a more rudimentary and clumsy fashion, derives its primary power from the poet's accessibility and eloquent insight into the divine mysteries. The development of the notion of mantra, then, falls late in this period, as those attuned to the changing religious sensibilities moved away from the poetic insight born of the face-to-face contemplation of god to the complex detailing of the mechanics of ritual.[6] We will argue, then, that the term *mantra,* as developed in the late Ṛgvedic era, represents a new view of ritual speech, which is performative and agentive and, perhaps more importantly, a move away from the earlier focus upon the internal person and personality of the priest, whose self-image and sense of vocational identity were so bound up with his personal skills of eloquence and his feeling of self-worth vis-à-vis god. The new view of speech, which supplants the creatively eloquent insight, is the known formula that, because of its traditional status, would effectively perform in the ritual context.

THE POWER OF MANTRA

In his article on *bráhman,* Thieme raises the question of why there are so many words in the Ṛgveda for ritual speech (1952, 101). We find, for instance, *dhī́, vā́c, mántra, ukthá, stóma, gír* and *bráhman* which variously describe those things which are spoken, sung or heard at the ritual. Thieme argues, and rightly, that the Ṛgvedic poets have a clear sense of the meaning of each of these words, never randomly picking from the group but consistently applying the right word to the appropriate situation (1952, 101). The rightness of a word, he maintains, depends upon what about ritual speech the poets are trying to express: "Der Hymnus heisst hier *bráhman,* weil er als Formulierung dichterisch geformt ist, *gír,* weil er als Lied gesungen, *ukthá* weil er als Rezitation gesprochen, und *mánman,* weil er als Inhalt gedacht wird" (The hymn is called *bráhman* because it is composed as poetic formulation, *gír* because it is sung as song, *ukthá* because it is spoken as recitation, and *mánman* because it is reflected upon as meaning) (1952, 103). Given the assumption, then, that there are specialized terms for the various aspects of Ṛgvedic speech, what aspects are associated with mantra?

In examining those few Ṛgvedic passages that mention mantra, one theme stands out clearly: Mantra has power and the source of that power is the truth and order that stands at the very center of the Vedic universe (Gonda 1963b, 257ff.). The pure power encapsulated in a mantra and released upon its utterance can work for or against whoever uses it. Should the user, or beneficiary, of mantra speak out of spite, malice, or ignorance, the power unleashed by the event can be frightening, harmful, or even fatal. For instance, in the hands of a priest who has been duped out of his sacrificial fee by a niggardly patron (Geldner 1951, 1.206n), the mantra can prove terrifyingly dangerous:

> When, Agni, the malicious, greedy skinflint
> hurts us [priests] with his duplicity,
> let the mantra fall back on him as an oppressive [curse]!
> He shall be done in by his own unholy speech. (1.147.4)

Here the mantra, whose negative power derives its very energy and validity from the normative ritual context, as appears to be true for mantra throughout the Ṛgveda,[7] is used outside the normative ritual context, much like black magic, as revenge against someone who has violated the rules and customs of the ritual by reneging on a contract.

The *dur°* of "unholy speech" (*duruktá*) gives less a sense of ignorant or foolish speech than the implication of blasphemous and even maliciously intended speech. Mantra, then, sets negative avenging power against speech that, similarly, is intended to do harm. Moreover, the violator's "duplicity" (*dvayá*) implies a breach of promise, a setting of false action against true, which flies directly in the face of mantra's close association with the foundation of Ṛgvedic thought, *ṛtá*.

In a second passage, from a hymn to Mitra and Varuṇa, mantra is called raging (*ṛ́ghāvat*), a term normally reserved for the battles and deeds of the Indra context.[8] The description of mantra by such a strong word establishes quite clearly both the great strength of mantra's power and, again, its pursuing and avenging qualities, which can be counted on to carry out the policing commands of the user. That the implicated victims of the mantra are called god-revilers (*devaníd*) further testifies to mantra's combative, almost sorcerous, abilities against powerfully malicious speech. Indeed, mantra comes to be seen as the most potent weapon, verbal or otherwise, in the on-going warfare among the varying religious persuasions. Finally, I must note the clear distinction this verse draws between the realms of truth and falsehood. Mantra here and elsewhere, is a martial arm for the policy-making upholders of truth (Renon 1949b, 268–69), empowered to seek out and destroy the hostile pursuers of all that is untrue:

> And that much was not known by these [men].
> The raging mantra pronounced by the seers is true:
> The powerful four-cornered [*vájra*] slays the three-cornered
> [weapon of the gods' enemies].
> The god-revilers were the first to age. (1.152.2)

Not only does the power of mantra have clearly designed policing powers against Vedic enemies, it also is so highly charged that, unless properly and carefully handled, it can fall back upon and burn its handler. For this reason, the composer of a mantra receives only the highest admiration, even, as here, when that admiration is from the gods:

> These [poets] have surpassed all with their skills,
> who bravely fashioned a choice mantra,
> who, most attentive, promoted the clans,
> and who took note of this truth of mine. (7.7.6)

Agni praises that poet whose courage is great enough and skill refined enough to create a mantra so true, so fine, that its powerful energy can not possibly turn back on him. A well-made mantra, in fact, will not only not harm the poet but, indeed, serve as an amulet to protect him from all danger. This protection, of course, receives its force from the mantra-maker's ties with the powers that be:

Place an ungarbled, well-set and elegant mantra
among the [gods] worthy of worship!
For the many assaults will not overtake him
who has come into Indra's favor by his deeds. (7.32.13)

Pure power, then, whether it be avenging, protective, or even highly potential but neutralized seems to be at the basis of mantra (Gonda 1941, 287), a conception affirmed in the Atharvaveda[9] and amplified in later literature. The bases of this power, like the power itself, are defined clearly though scantily in the text. From an examination of the passages, it becomes clear that the sources of mantric power are twofold, the first pertaining to its form and the second to its content, and both are readily accessible to the skilled, initiated seer.

Mantra is empowered, first, by the formal elements of its own composition. In 7.32.13ab just quoted, *mántram ákharvaṃ súdhitaṃ supéśasaṃ dádhāta yajñíyeṣv ā́*, reflects the qualities most prized by poets in their language. "Ungarbled, well-set and elegant" indicate the high standards in use for forms of speech, which once thus composed are that much more assured of potency in and out of the ritual. Some see here an early reference "to what must have been a sacral poetics" in force (Johnson 1980, 144n) governing the productivity of ancient contests. That there must have been such rules is clear, rules regulating, at least, the general quality of eloquence, if not every detail. Confirmation of this comes from yet another mantra passage in which speech, in order to effectively extract blessings from the gods, must be both "pleasing" (*śambhū́*) and "unrivalled" (*anehás*), that is, matchless or perfect:

We want to pronounce that mantra at the ceremonies, gods,
which is pleasing and unrivalled.
And so the men have willingly taken up this speech
that they will attain all riches from you. (1.40.6)

A perfect mantra, here called speech (*vā́c,* 6c), must be so exquisitely rendered that it conforms impeccably, we presume, to rules of poetry such as those suggested by 7.32.13. This perfect conformation to poetic standards then constitutes the formal structure by which mantra is empowered.

It is empowered, secondly and more consistently in the Ṛgveda, by the substantial elements of its truth. Over and over, the poets remind their audience that the power released from the pronunciation and repetition of a mantra is due to the fact that the mantra is true. Mantra's ties to *ṛtá,* the transcendent truth of the cosmic and human orders, is clear. In whatever Indra does by his own counsel (mantra), he is truthful (*ṛtávan*) (3.53.8d); all the gods who promote the truth (*ṛtāvṛ́dh*) will be favorable if invited to the ritual with mantras (6.50.14cd); and a choice mantra to Agni will necessarily capture the truth (*ṛtá*) known by and essential to the god of fire (7.7.6bd). Mantras, however, are not just in harmony with the truth moving through the cosmos, but are in and of themselves also truthful (*satyá*). In securing the spheres of cosmic activity, Agni stayed the heavens with truthful (*satyá*) mantras (1.67.5); and the mantra that makes known a secret ordinarily hidden from man is true (*satyá*) (1.152.2b). The power of the mantra, then, depends not only upon well-tended form, but also upon attunement with a metaphysical reality that, for the most part, is separate from man.

This attunement, however, even though it bespeaks a realm normally beyond man, is not brought about by a miraculous display of the divine but by an internal searching in the body's own organ of insight, the heart. Already in the Ṛgveda, it has become a consistent belief that the revelation of ultimate truth is not a matter of extraordinary experience dependent upon a deus ex machina. The internalization of the revelatory event (that is, the elevation of the self as the material and instrumental cause as well as the prefigurative result of final wisdom) is a development already well underway in the Ṛgveda itself, and one which becomes especially allied with the notion of mantra. Mantra is true if—and only if—it is formulated with the deepest, most profound understanding possible, that is, with insight arising from the heart (Gonda 1963b, 251–52). And, if it is indeed fashioned from the heart, the theory goes, it will in some way touch upon the riddles of the world in which man lives, giving power over those things that remain mysterious. When well pronounced, a true mantra, then, will hit its mark at all levels of intention:

> We would pronounce this mantra well
> which was well fashioned for him from the heart;
>   he will understand it, to be sure:
> By the power of his Asura-strength,
> the lord[10] Apāṁ Napāt created all creatures. (2.35.2)

The mantra of ab, which was well-fashioned (*sútaṣṭa*) in the heart (*hṛ́d*), indicates the truth that is captured in cd: Apāṁ Napāt, a form of Agni, has given life to all creatures by his light and warmth. This revelation, the humanizing and civilizing aspects of fire, though clearly sparked by external experience, has come to fruition only after internal meditation has been given expression by the self-styled skills of the poet.

Mantras formulated in the heart are true not just because they capture the truth of some cosmological occurrence but because they themselves have participated, and continue to participate, in these same cosmological events. In the following verses, again addressed to Agni, the poet points to what is true about the ritual fire. Somehow Agni is responsible for the proper maintenance of the cosmos that, incidentally, he has done with truthful mantras. Mantras not only capture the truth with their insight, well formed and from the heart, they *are* the truth, they have actually participated in the primordial revelation of truth, and they therefore become essential to truth's preservation. Because of this participatory role played by mantra in the original events of creation, the implication is that if the priest were to pronounce the right mantra he would repeat the same primordial, life-preserving acts originally and continually performed by Agni with mantras:

3–4. Holding all manly powers in his hand,
he set the gods to trembling as he descended to his hiding place.
There thoughtful (*dhiyaṃdhā́*) men find him
whenever they pronounce (*śaṁs*) mantras formulated in their hearts.

5–6. Like an unborn [god] he fortifies the earth floor,
he stays the heaven with truthful mantras.
Protect the cherished tracks of the cows [of dawn]!
All our lives, Agni, you go from hiding place to hiding place. (1.67.3–6)

Like much in Agni mythology, the central concern here, and therefore the core of the insightful mantra, is Agni's role in the daily retrieval of the sun out of darkness and in the preservation of the sun's route across the sky(6). Because of their original, central role in making the broad space between heaven and earth(5) *and* because of their power, apparently singular among the elements of ritual, to bring Agni from his hiding place (i.e., in the kindling of the firesticks and the appearance of the sun over the morning horizon), mantras have a doubly potent claim to truth.

As Kuiper (1960, 248) pointed out and as suggested by these verses, of all the gods, Agni, because of his secret hiding place, is the god of insight and inspiration. As the fire visible to man on earth, Agni links the worshipper to the fiery mysteries of the cosmic recurrence of the sun and the dawn. Because he gives rise to the sun every morning by the magical power of ritual analogy, Agni is thought to reside in the place of eternal life, the place from which the world is constantly maintained.[11] Agni has and gives insight, the revelatory insight of the mantra, because he alone knows the secrets of world continuity. The following hymn, 4.11, describes Agni's relationship to speech that is well-formed and insightful and, therefore, immensely powerful:

1. Your delightful countenance, mighty Agni,
shines out next to the [daytime] sun.
Bright to look at, it is also seen at night.
On your body, there is glossy food [i.e., butter] to see.

2. Release the insight (*manīṣā́*) to the singer, Agni
   through inspiration as through a canal, when you, of strong stock are praised!
   Inspire us to that rich thought (*mánman*), most noble,
   which you with all the gods would most graciously accept, brilliant one!

3. From you, Agni, come poetic gifts, from you insights (*manīṣā́*),
   from you choice hymns.
   From you comes richness, ornamented by sons,
   to the properly devout and pious mortal.

4. From you comes the battle horse of special power, who wins the prize,
   who bestows superiority and has the courage of truth.
   From you the god-sent, joy bringing prize,
   from you the swift, quick steed, Agni!

5. You, Agni, with the eloquent tongue
   god-serving mortals seek out as the first god, immortal!
   to win with prayers (*dhī́*) him who wards off hostility,
   the domestic, insightful lord of the home.

6. Dull-mindedness (*ámati*) is far from us, far away anxiety (*áṁhas*),
   far-away all injurious thought (*durmatí*), whenever you watch over [us].
   By night, Agni son of strength, you are auspicious
   to the one you accompany for well being (*svastí*), god!

This hymn is significant for two reasons. First, it clearly delineates Agni as the vital energy at the center of the mysterious cosmos [''your . . . countenance shines out next to the sun'' (1ab) and yet is better than the sun because it shines out at night (1c)], but also as the god who is most intimate with man [''the domestic . . . lord of the home'' (5d), ''the one you accompany for well being'' (6d)]. Moreover, the poet sees Agni as the god responsible for all the insight, all the inspiration, and all the poetic gifts man can ever hope to have. From verse 3, the hearer would suppose that man could not think, imagine, speak, or sing without the bounty of tongues bestowed by Agni. Divine wisdom and fine prayer are gifts to man only through the grace of god. Second, and more important for us, however, is the continuous association in this hymn, and others, of the forms of insight that penetrate the universe and that the poet can turn to proper ritual use with words derived from the root *man*. Although the term *mantra* is never used here, and may in fact not have been a common term at the time of the composition of this hymn, there is a consistent alliance between Agni as the source of insight and the expression (Upadhyaya 1961, 23ff.) of that insight in an inspired thought, denoted either by *manīṣā́* or *mánman* (Sharma 1972). Moreover, these thought-forms won from Agni would seem to be effective in warding off hostility (*dvéṣas*), a theme reminiscent of the powers of the legitimate mantra. Note here, however, that 5c says that Agni and not the prayers actually wards off hostility; while in the passages specific for mantra (1.147.4; 1.152.2), it is the mantra itself that is empowered to protect. This may indicate, during the development of the Ṛgveda, a shift in the locus of power from the gods themselves to the religious mechanics of men. Still, from this hymn, and particularly from 1.67.3–6, I can designate Agni, and especially *ṛtá* and *satyá,* as the primary sources of power behind mantra's ability to protect and defend.

"PRONOUNCED BY THE SEERS"

This shift in power away from the gods and into the elements of ritual technique brings to the forefront the second major theme associated with *mántra,* that it is *kaviśastá,* "pronounced by the seers." If we were to look through the Ṛgveda, paying particular attention to the words for "word(s)," one clear and acute observation would be that many of the words for ritual speech have associated with them corresponding designations for a specialized priest.[12] As Thieme says, "als *brahmán* 'Dichter' . . . ist Vasiṣṭha durch ein *bráhman,* ein Gedicht, entstanden" (through a *bráhman,* a poem, Vasiṣṭha has emerged . . . as a *brahmán,* a poet) (1952, 115). We would understand the identity of the poet-priest, then, to be defined by his relation to the word. The configuration of the office and of the self-perception of a religious official would be bound by the specific demands made upon him by his specialized type of speech. The figure of the priest is central, limited only by what he must do with the ritual word. In the case of mantra, however, two very interesting deviations from this pattern occur.

First, there appears to be no priestly specialization associated exclusively with mantra. This may be due to the special role of the word itself, which seems to have reference not to a particular ritual function but to the theoretical foundations of ritual speech as a whole; that is, mantra seems to be not a functionally defined type of speech but, rather, a theoretical formulation about speech. If this is the case, then, it becomes clear why mantra survives as a key term in the classical tradition:[13] it is unspecialized in use yet theoretical in implication and, thus, perfectly suited to a complex ritual that has become increasingly dependent upon a sophisticated understanding of language.

Second, the Ṛgvedic mantra does not belong to a system centered on the religious officiant, whose boundaries are defined only by what is required of him with words, but to an exceptional structure, peculiarly adapted to the vision of *mántra,* centered on the word, whose boundaries are defined only by what is done with it by the poet-priest. The qualifying phrase for mantra, then—a theme equally as important as mantra's power—becomes *kaviśastá* (pronounced by the seers), a phrase used three times[14] of mantra and twice[15] of Agni and amply supported for mantra by the remaining vocabulary of its verses.

Lacking association with a particular ritual function and, therefore, with a particularized ritual priest, mantra becomes attracted into the realm of the *kaví,* a functionary with a broad and varied base in the Ṛgveda, whose parameters are especially conducive to the emergent conception of mantra. Renou's understanding of the office of *kaví* draws upon the following elements: (1) god or man, a *kaví* can unravel the intricacies of an enigma, the central task of what he believes is the Vedic word contest; (2) composition of a hymn is only a part of a *Kaví's* activity, for he also works manually and orally at the ritual; and (3) when applied to gods, *kaví* refers primarily to Agni and Soma as the two gods most closely allied with the ritual (Renou 1953, 180–83; Velankar 1966, 253). Velankar's critique of Renou, following that of Bhawe (1959, 29–30), deemphasizes the ritual role of the *kaví,* saying that the primary intent of the term is to designate an individual "who had an intuitional knowledge of cosmic matters, being gifted with a vision owing to which he could have a direct acquaintance with such events and personalities as were associated with the creation" (p. 253). Because the ritual is only a symbolic replication of the creation, he argues, knowledge of all matters concerning ritual is secondary for the *kaví* (p. 253).

An examination of Ṛgvedic material on the *kaví,* however, supports both claims. *Kaví* appears to be a general title given to priests as composers and singers of songs. Most important, it seems to be a name that singles out the peculiar quality of revelatory insight: *Kavís* tremble with inspiration (*vípra*);[16] they know the truth (*ṛtajñá*);[17] they work with prayers (*dhí*),[18] ideas (*mánman*),[19] poetic gifts (*kā́vya*),[20] insights (*manīṣā́*),[21] hymns (*ukthá*),[22] poems (*matí*),[23] and thoughts (*mánas*);[24] they are wise (*dhī́ra*);[25] their insight comes from the heart (*hṛ́d*);[26] they bring forth secrets (*niṇyá*);[27] and they have grapsed those things grounded in the highest laws (*vratá*).[28] There also is a ritual component, however: Their words must show a specific knowledge of appropriate meter (*chándas*);[29] they must spread the ritual threads (*tántu*);[30] and they must make pure the Soma.[31] The roles of the *kaví,* then, appear to be twofold—wise ones whose words are filled with intuitional knowledge and technical masters of the sacred ritual—neither of which is exclusive of the other, of course. One thing is clear throughout, however, that the *kaví* is associated with speech: speech that has insight, and speech that is spoken out loud.

From an investigation of the mantra passages, the point of entry into the *kaví* arena seems, surprisingly, to be less the focus on insight than the focus on pronunciation. As Thieme says, *mántra* "hat eine Wirkung . . . die bedingt ist nicht so sehr durch ihren Inhalt als durch ihre Form, die in peinlich Korrekter Aufsagung gewahrt werden muss" (mantra has an effect . . . that is conditioned less through its content than its form, a form that must be safeguarded through scrupulously correct recitation) (1957b, 69). If this, in fact, is the case, then mantra belongs to the *kaví* system primarily on its active levels, that is, on those levels in which the insight bears fruit in ritual performance. However, this would not preclude participation in the *kaví's* gathering of insight, given the inner consistency and necessary dependency of all elements in the *kaví* system. The following verse, in fact, with its designation of Agni, the god of insight, as *kaví* and as a god invited to the ritual with mantras, firmly allies the mantra to this insightful level of *kaví* activity:

> Vaiśvānara shining all the time,
> Agni the *kaví,* we call with mantras;
> the god who by his greatness embraces both broad [worlds],
> the one above as well as below. (10.88.14)[32]

Nevertheless, as suggested here and as the definitive *kaviśastá* makes clear, the specific relation between *mántra* and *kaví* is active, belonging primarily to the performative realm of the seer in ritual. Because of *kaviśastá,* we now ask of mantra not only what does it do—it has power and uses that power to protect and defend—but how does one use it? How does one make that power effective? The answer to this is clear. To make mantra work one pronounces it. In the proper and appropriate ritual context, mantra goes into effect only when it is spoken out loud in as clear and precise a manner as possible. Three times out of twenty-one, for instance, the priest says *mántraṃ vocema*[33] (we would pronounce the mantra); once *mántrair agníṃ kavím áchā vadāmaḥ* (we call Agni the seer with mantras);[34] and once Brahmanaspati speaks (*vadati*)[35] the mantra meant as praise. Moreover, in addition to the three times mantra is "pronounced by the seer" (*kaviśastá*), it is also pronounced (*áśaṁsan*)[36] by thoughtful men in search of Agni. Sharma (1979), following Pāṇini, goes so far as to theorize that the root *man-a* is a substitute for *mnā* (to rote, to utter), the latter being a contracted form of the former, and that the primary sense of *man-a* is not "to think" but "to speak, to utter" "originally used in the exclusive sense of loud recitation or repeated recital of the sacred text" (p. 138). This interpretation would certainly confirm our understanding of mantra in the Ṛgveda as something that must be pronounced to have power but does not necessarily concur with other interpretations of derivatives of *man* (Upadhyaya 1961).

It would seem, then, that *kaviśastá* is a definitive attribute of mantra in two ways. First, it draws the "priestless" mantra into the realm of a clearly defined religious functionary, one who is operative on both the contemplative and the active levels. And, although mantra seems to belong primarily to the ritual activity of the *kaví,* it also participates in the *kaví's* insight, given that the other two references of *kaviśastá* are to Agni, the god of insight. Second, and more important, however, *kaviśastá* underscores the pronunciation of mentra as essential to its effectiveness. In fact, the Ṛgveda even says as much: Without pronunciation, mantra is powerless. Despite the nonritual, even nonreligious context of the following verse, for example, an admonition by Purūravas to the beautiful Urvaśī, the vision of what should be done with mantra for one to receive its benefits is clear:

> If these mantras of ours remain unspoken
> they will bring no joy, even on the most distant day.
> (10.95.1cd)[37]

The necessity of its pronunciation and the concomitant assurance of its power fit firmly within a third and final aspect of mantra, its agency. By composition mantra is an agent noun, though, as Wackernagel pointed out (1954, 703, 708), it does not necessarily follow the pattern established for its class. Unlike *kṣé-tra* (field), *pā́-tra* (cup) *vás-tra* (garment), *khan-í-tra* (shovel), and *dáṃṣ-tra* (tusk), which have the general sense of a means or instrument for performing the task designated by the root, *mán-tra* belongs to a much smaller group of nouns, which includes *tán-tra* (warp) and *dáttra* (gift), whose instrumental designation is understood only indirectly. The primary meaning of these words seems to have been much like a past participle: what is stretched; what is given; what is thought or spoken. If this is the case, it would account for the instances where mantra refers most clearly to advise or counsel. The instrumental understanding of mantra, however, even if secondary, is clearly the predominant one in the Ṛgveda,[38] arising most likely by analogy to the larger, first class mentioned earlier. Seen in time, then, as a real agent noun, mantra becomes a classic term in later tradition to designate a peculiar kind of instrumentality. As Thieme says,

> er is das . . . Instrument (*-tra*) der durch das Element *man-* benannten Handlung, also das Instrument des Denkens, des Erkennens: ein "formulierter Gedanke," den man sprachlich vortragen kann, der dem Dichter hilft in seinen Reflexionen und Meditationen fortzufahren.
>
> (it is the . . . instrument (*-tra*) of the activity designated by the root *man-*, therefore the instrument of thought, of mental perception (*erkennen*); a "well-formulated idea" (*formulierter Gedanke*) that may be executed verbally to help a poet continue his reflection and meditation.) (1957b, 60)

If Thieme is right and this is the peculiar cast to the agency of mantra that we must follow, then how do we relate mentra as "the vehicle for thinking, for reflecting" to its two contextual understandings in the Ṛgveda?

The key lies in rethinking the relationship between these two themes underlying mantra. Speech has power *and* is pronounced. Somewhere in the development of the concept of mantra, the seers put these two notions together, formulating a theory that would be seminal for centuries to come. Speech has power *because* it is pronounced. If speech's effectiveness is due to its being pronounced, then its pronunciation must be seen as a performative act, as an act that sets in motion a whole matrix of power and thereby gets results. The result most desired by the religiously sensitive in Vedic times is insight, contemplative insight, into the mysteries of the human and the divine. Then, I argue, mantra, as "the vehicle for reflection," is the seers' formulation of a theory about speech itself, a word whose very structure captures the new understanding that speech "can do" and that what speech can do best is open the channels of the heart to the gods, so that inspiration can be claimed by the very user of the word. However, what the seers demand for this mantra the very vehicle for inspiration, is that it be spoken properly and that its potential for all manner of power be recognized.

Mantra, then, is formulated as an unspecialized term that incorporates the Ṛgvedic seers' growing sense that their words in ritual actually do something. As "Zaubersprüche" (Thieme 1957b, 69), mantras, from their very conception in the Ṛgveda, are classical examples of what are now called speech acts. In *How to Do Things with Words,* Austin (1965) outlines the two essential elements of the performative utterance. First, it does not describe or report anything at all and, therefore, is not thought to be true or false; and second, that the uttering of the sentence is, or is part of, the performance of an action, an action that, again, would not normally be described just as saying something (p. 5). Of these two elements, the second is clearly appropriate for mantra. That to say a mantra is to do something more than just to say something is obvious from the consistent association of mantra with powerful effects and, less directly, from the essential requirement that a mantra be pronounced. The first element, however, is more problematic. In the first place, Ṛgvedic seers are emphatic that the basis for the mantra's power is its truth (*ṛtá, satyá*) and that it be formulated by thoughtful, reflective men from their hearts. Second, although mantras from the later Indian tradition, more often than not, can be of a nonsensical nature (Tambiah 1968a, 178ff.), the Ṛgvedic context for mantra, scanty though it be, implies that, at least in this period, a mantra must have meaning (e.g., 1968a, 2.35.2: "May we pronounce that mantra well which was well-fashioned for him from the heart; he will understand it, to be sure."). In fact, the original sense of the word, "a vehicle for reflection," could be taken as the very indication that by using the tool of mantra one begins to reflect upon something, that content and meaning are integral to the opening of the channels between men and the gods.

Austin, however, goes on to describe any number of conditions that qualify the performative utterance and that most appropriately describe the Ṛgvedic conception of *mántra:* (1) that there be "an accepted conventional procedure having a certain conventional effect, that procedure to include the uttering of certain words by certain persons in certain circumstances"; (2) that "the particular persons and circumstances in a given case must be appropriate for the invocation of the particular procedure invoked"; and (3) that "the procedure must be executed by all participants both correctly and completely" (1965, 14–15). There is no need to describe the details of the classical *śrauta* system here, even as it might have been known to the Ṛgveda; it will be sufficient to note that the rules and conventions of this system, into which mantra fits most clearly, amply support the conditions for correct procedure formulated by Austin. The first condition describes the need to have the utterance heard by someone and understood by him and others in the context (Austin 1965, 22)—that the mantra must be pronounced (*vad, vac, śaṁs*) and that in almost all cases it is to be heard by the gods. (And, I presume, that following the later ritual, it must also be heard by the other priests and the patron.) The second condition prescribes a certain person be designated as the invoker of the utterance (Austin 1965, 34–35)—that the mantra is peculiarly allied with the *kaví.* And, the third condition requires that the form of the utterance, particularly its grammar, meet set requirements and be complete (Austin 1965, 67–93)—that the mantra must be "ungarbled, well set, and elegant" (7.32.13ab) as well as "perfect" (1.40.6b).

Following generalized rules such as those just listed, the power of the word as a performative utterance becomes crystallized in the notion of mantra. No other term for ritual speech in the Ṛgveda is seen to express as clearly the agentive quality of speech as much as mantra, where the priest's growing sensitivity to the pure power of pronounced speech, as an instrument for the insight already deemed so central, is finally put into concrete form. Although the Ṛgveda knows other agent nouns for ritual speech—e.g., *stotrá* (song of praise) (*nítyastotra, priyástotra, marútstotra*) (Wackernagel 1954, 703)—it is in mantra where the agent suffix comes to be so significant philosophically. Mantra is the tool, the mechanism, for yoking the reflective powers of the seer into the machinery of ritual (Tambiah 1968a, 175–76). Although, in later times, the focus of mantra really becomes that of a key to meditation, a key to the establishment and maintenance of divine accessibility, the earlier formulation, at least as bound by the context of the Ṛgveda, focuses primarily upon the qualities of its use by the religious functionary: the power released upon pronunciation.

THE POWER OF SPEECH

The view of speech captured in the word *mantra* differs considerably from the view of speech known to an earlier period. This suggestion is based upon the rarity in the Ṛgvedic mantra system of a number of things apparently central to the understanding of religious consciousness, especially to the formation of religious language. For instance, we have in the mantra system, especially in the designation mantra *kaviśastá,* an indication that the word is preeminent, not the speaker. We do not get, for instance, the senseless **kaví mantraśastá* (the seer pronounced, by/with a mantrá[39]), nor do we get the more plausible **kaví mantraśaś* (cf., *ukthaśaś*) (the seer pronouncing the mantra); in both of which cases the speaker could be seen as preeminent over the word. We do, however, get the *hapax mantrakṛ́t* in a Soma hymn—"Ṛṣi Kaśyapa, strengthening your songs (*gír*) through the praises (*stóma*) of the mantra-makers" (9.114.2ab)—as well as the *hapax mantraśrútya* in an Indra hymn—"We neglect nothing, O gods, we conceal nothing, we go forth mindful of your counsel" (10.134.7ab)—but neither fits neatly into a system supportive of the centrality of any single religious functionary.

Remembering the importance of the development of thought in the Ṛgveda (Chattopadhyaya 1935, 35), and ever mindful of the need to uncover the *religious* persuasions of the Ṛgvedic world (Thieme 1957a, 53–54), we must now turn back to a type of religiosity that, I argue, is earlier than that of mantra and yet necessary to it; necessary not only historically, as one thing naturally gives rise to another, but logically as well, for the mantra system, as emergent in the late Ṛgveda, makes much more sense when seen as dependent upon an older, more personalized and theistic type of religiosity. One way of getting at this developmental process is to see not only what has changed in the view of speech but, perhaps more significant here, what might have been left out as mantra emerged.

In his discussions of *bráhman,* Thieme makes a distinction between the *Formel* and the *Formulierung*:

> Die Formel ist ihrem Wesen nach überkommen, ihre Wirkung beruht darauf, dass sie in bewährter Weise wiederholt wird. . . . Die Formulierung wirkt, wenn sie neu ist. . . . Die Formel ist anonym, die Formulierung gehört dem Individuum. . . . Die Formel ist eine anerkannte Grösse, aber die Formulierung kann misslingen, sie ist dem Tadel ausgesetzt.
>
> (The formula (*Formel*) is traditional in character, its effects depend on the fact that it is repeated in a time-tested manner. . . . The formulation (*Formulierung*) works when it is new. . . . The formula is anonymous, the formulation belongs to the individual. . . . The formula is a known

quantity, but the formulation may miscarry, it is exposed to criticism.) (1952, 102–103)

This classic contrast between tradition and novelty, between anonymity and individuality, between recognized powers and uncertain potentials, neatly fits Thieme's vision of the movement from *bráhman* (formulation) to mantra (formula)[40] (cf., Renou 1949b, 268). It also supports the view that the Ṛgveda covers a very large period, moving from simple ritualistic concerns to highly complex and developed liturgical procedures (Bergaigne 1889, 6–17; Renou 1962). If we are to assume, then, that indeed there is a development in the Ṛgveda, what would characterize this "earlier phase" out of which mantra emerges?

We saw that in the mantric conception of speech the locus of power is in its pronunciation by a religious functionary. Although the pronouncer is important here, he is seen less as a person and more as a vehicle, more as a tool through whom the mantra is empowered. This depersonalization of the priest, however, has not always been the case, for substantial portions of the Ṛgveda preserve a highly developed sense of priestly individuality. If we look closely, we discover that this strong sense of self is dependent upon the priest's relation to his own speech, speech that is religious but not necessarily ritualistic. I will argue, then, that the very centrality of uttered speech seen in the mantric system must have arisen out of an earlier system in which the person of the priest was central but where his centrality depended precisely upon the quality of his speech.

That speech—that possession of beautiful speech—was the key to a positive priestly self-image—the key by which the priest could measure his vocational effectiveness—is brought out most clearly in the story of the priest Viśvāmitra's return to power, hinted at in 3.53.15–16:

15. Sasarparí speech, given by Jamadagni,
roars loudly as she banishes dull-mindedness (*ámati*).
The daughter of Sūrya spreads out to the gods
her aging, immortal fame.[41]

16. Sasarparī speech brought them [Viśvāmitra's Kuśikas] quick fame
among the families of the five peoples.
Now on my side,[42] she gives new life
whom the Palastis and Jamadagnis gave me.

According to later tradition, Viśvāmitra was defeated by a Vasiṣṭha in a verbal contest at a sacrifice of King Sudās. The Jamadagnis then gave him Sasarparī speech, "poetry personified" according to Bhawe (1950, 19ff., 27), which he mastered over a period of time. When he had learned this new art of speaking, Viśvāmitra once again took a place of honor among the Vedic peoples (Geldner 1951, 1.394n). The gift of powerful and beautiful speech, which brought new life to Viśvāmitra and his family and a reaffirmation of priestly vocation among the peoples before whom they had previously lost face, stands in direct contrast to one of the things most feared by Vedic man, *ámati* or "dull mindedness." In its fifteen or so appearances in the Ṛgveda, *ámati* consistently refers to a lack of thought or inspiration, a poverty of ideas or spirit, before which the seer trembles and against which he pleads to the gods for protection. Inability to provide acceptable ritual speech appears to mark the seer as unfit and, in many cases, to deprive him of the benefits of his priestly vocation. Consistently, *ámati* is the absence of *matí*, a thought formulated into a prayer that has come particularly from those who are inspired (*vípra*)[43] and who speak from the heart (*hṛ́d*).[44] As "no thought" or "no appropriate thought," *ámati* is sometimes found in conjunction with another fear of Vedic man, *durmatí* or "evil thought, evil intention," a more complex concept that can result as much in physical danger as it can in a lack of grace from the gods. *Durmatí*, though clearly located in the mind, is a less cerebral concept than *ámati*, however, whose implications seem to bear purely upon soteriology; for *durmatí* stands in contrast not to *matí* but to *svastí*, well being in a broad sense, physical as well as psychological. We must remember in this context, then, 4.11.6, in which the seer (as he does in many places in the Ṛgveda) states his expectations of a relationship with god:

> Dull mindedness (*ámati*) is far from us, far away anxiety (*áṁhas*),
> far away all injurious thought (*durmatí*), whenever you watch over (us).
> By night, Agni son of strength, you are auspicious
> to the one you accompany for well being (*svastí*), god!

As we saw in 3.53.15–16, the priest is possessor and manipulator of ritual speech, a function that defines his vocational identity as well as his psychological well being and that would not be his should he be overcome by *ámati*. It is not just the possession of ritual speech, however, that is the magical key to the priestly office. Rather, it is the infusion of this speech by eloquence, and eloquence is defined in a very peculiar way. As noted earlier, to be eloquent with the gifts of a true *kaví* means not simply to be able to use meter, syntax, ritual vocabulary, and mythical analogy correctly, but to use them with authority, to make what is true on a cosmic scale true and effective on the human scale. To be eloquent means that one's words must have validity and, to have validity, they must have insight, for without insight into the truth, words will fall short of their mark (Kuiper 1960, 254).

Almost from the beginning, this eloquence was defined quite strictly, by the communal standard of peer opinion, as it judged ritual effectiveness, setting the measure of beautiful speech. Whatever the specific context might have been, it is clear that the priestly poets competed against each other in word duels in which contestants had to rely upon the "mental quickness in the heart" (10.71.8) (Kuiper 1960, 280) hoping, of course, that *ámati* would be far, far away. Whether these contests were secular "matches of artistic dexterity and literary cleverness" (Thieme 1957a, 53) as Geldner (1951), Renou (1955–69, 1.1–27), and to some extent Johnson (1980, 3–25) think or, more likely, "contests of rivaling ritual performances and of rivaling word power accompanying rivaling rites" as Thieme (1957a, 53), Schmidt (1959, 446–47), and Kuiper (1960, 217–23) argue, they appear to have been quite fierce and quite important to the career of the poet-priest, for not only were material prizes at stake, but social standing and jobs as well. Note hymn 7.23:

1. The formulations (*bráhman*) rose up in competition.
   Ennoble Indra at the verbal contest, Vasiṣṭha!
   He, who by his might is spread out over all [worlds],
   will listen favorably to the words of someone as good as me.

2. The gods' own cry has been raised, Indra,
   which the strong will command at the contest;
   for amongst ordinary people the length of one's own life is not known.
   So help us over these anxieties (*áṁhas*)!

3. In order to yoke up the wagon, seeking cow-booty, with bays
   the formulations (*bráhman*) approached him who relished them.
   Indra pushed both worlds apart with his greatness,
   slaying the [otherwise] unconquerable powers of resistance.

4. The waters swell up, which had been barren like cows.
   Your singers, Indra, have arrived at truth.
   Come [swiftly] like Vāyu to our teams,
   for you portion out the prizes according to [the merits of] the prayers.

5. Let these intoxicants intoxicate you, Indra,
   the high-spirited, who gives bounty to the singer,
   for you alone among the gods have compassion for the mortals.
   Enjoy yourself, hero, at this drinking fest of ours.

6. Thus the Vasiṣṭhas praise Indra with songs,
   the bull armed with the cudgel.

Praised let him give us blessings of sons and cows!
Protect us always with your blessings!

Following Kuiper's exegesis of this hymn (1960, 271), we know that it describes a ritual contest between priestly poets. This contest is likened to a real battle, with the competition being primarily for social prominence based upon ritual effectiveness. Line 1b indicates the presence of at least one representative of the Vasiṣṭha family, although it is not clear from the hymn what is the range of contestants, just the Vasiṣṭhas or a broad spectrum of priestly families. Lines 1bcd suggest that Indra is to receive all entries and be the final judge, although from 1d there seems to be no question as to the winner. By the beginning of the hymn, it is clear that the formulations have been sent to the gods (1a, 2a), the prizes put up (2b), and the question raised about which the poets must be wise (2c, this will be discussed later). By the end of the hymn, the Vasiṣṭhas seem confident of their eloquence and of receiving the prizes due them.

In 2d, we are told of the central anxiety of the poets, the central issue, therefore, to be answered at these contests. According to Kuiper's theory, this *áṁhas* refers to the darkness and death associated with the ending of the old year and the beginning of the new, when the sun appears after a long period of winter darkness at the spring equinox (Kuiper 1960, 218ff.; cf., Gonda 1941, 286). Following, as it does, however, a concern over the length of one's own life (that is, how many equinoxes one will see), I suggest that this anxiety is due less to a concern whether the year will begin again than to one about extending individual lives as long as possible. Gonda finds in *áṁhas* a family of ideas that stands in direct opposition to the idea "of 'broadness' expressed by *uru-* and its family" (1957, 40), a reference to narrowness, to limits, to boundaries, much like the German *enge*. An investigation of *áṁhas* passages shows that it is something afflicting man primarily, and that man continually needs to be protected and freed from it. The particular concerns of the Vedic singers in *áṁhas* seem to be threefold: concern about social standing (free us from the reproach of our fellows); concern about external dangers (free us from warfare and allow our animals to roam free); and concern about long life (free us from the fear of living less than a hundred autumns). Given a slightly philosophic interpretation, Gonda's view of *áṁhas* as narrowness would certainly fit the subject matter of all three categories, but the *áṁhas* passages seem to emphasize less the specifics of such categories than the heightened sense of concern *about* these specifics. I argue, then, that *áṁhas* refers not only to physical needs and dangers but, more importantly, to their psychological ramifications; that is, to the anxieties about these needs and dangers. Vedic man wanted freedom from anxiety about trouble as much as he did from trouble itself.

Nevertheless, as Kuiper has suggested, it is clear that for some sort of *áṁhas*-relieving insight contestants will win prizes (2b, 4d, 5b) of cows

(3a, 6c), sons (6c) and social prominence, if the entries please Indra (1d, 4d, 5c). And, pleasing Indra involves offering the intoxicating Soma (5a), truthfully (and reverently) recounting Indra's great deeds, and, most important, reaffirming the divine and immortal status of the gods and thereby indicating that one, in contrast, has come to terms with one's own mortality (2c, 5c). The insight by which prizes are won, then, must involve the acceptance of human mortality (that is, of living for a finite number of equinoxes); for divine rewards could only be given to men for whom the cosmos has a proper hierarchical order. That the insightful entries that won prizes at these contests were in time, in fact, called *mantras* is attested in the following verse to the Aśvins:

> May we succeed with our song of praise (*stóma*), may we win
> the prize.
> Come here by wagon to our mantra you two,
> to the cooked sweetness, like a treasure among the cows.
> Bhūtāṁśa has just fulfilled the wish of the Aśvins. (10.106.11)

As suggested in 7.23.1c, 3cd, and 4a, competition at ritual contests involved a second kind of insight as well, insight into the secret workings of the cosmos. In 6.9, a hymn to Agni Vaiśvānara and "a rare, intensely personal account of one poet's experience of the contest and the exaltation he attains as a result of Agni's inspiration" (Johnson 1980, 12), the poet reveals what he has learned about Agni and the continuity of the days: knowledge, he tells us, that he is afraid to make known for fear of upstaging his elders:[45]

1. The dark day and the bright day, the two realms of space,
revolve by their own wisdom.
Agni Vaiśvānara, just born,
pushed back the darkness with his light like a king.

2. I do not know how to stretch the thread nor weave the cloth,
nor what they weave when they enter the contest.
Even so, whose son would speak fine words here,
thereby surpassing an inferior father?

3. *He*[46] knows how to stretch the thread and weave the cloth;
he will speak fine words correctly.
Who understands this [wisdom] is the protector of
immortality;
though he moves below, he still sees higher than any other.

4. This is the first Hotar. Behold him!
This is the immortal light among the mortals.

This is he who was born and firmly fixed,
the immortal, growing strong in body.

5. He is the light firmly planted for all to see
the thought (*mánas*) fastest of those flying between [the two worlds].
All the gods, like minded and like willed,
come together from all sides, as they should, to the one source of inspiration.

6. My ears fly open, my eye opens out,
beyond to this light set in my heart.
My mind (*mánas*) flies up, straining into the distance.
What shall I say? What shall I think (*manişye*)?

7. All the gods bowed to you in fear, Agni,
as you stood there in darkness.
May Vaiśvānara bring us help!
May the immortal bring us help!

This hymn, intended as one of profound insight, reveres Agni Vaiśvānara as the light of the world and the inner light of inspiration and is, as Johnson says, "one of the earliest recorded milestones of Indian mysticism" (1980, 19). In verse 1, the poet describes his discovery of the cosmic mystery of light and darkness, that they are meant to alternate, and do so consistently and by their own conscious powers when the Vaiśvnara form of Agni is ennobled to victory. Hidden behind the description of the light of Agni as the ritual fire at dawn is the implication that Agni's light as insight (that is, the inner light in the heart of man) has victoriously overcome the darkness of ignorance.

The real theme of the hymn, however, appears in verse 2, as the young poet awaiting his turn watches the others enter the contest ground (2b). Here he betrays his lack of confidence in his own abilities to succeed in the impending competition. He is not sure, first, how to "stretch the thread"; that is, how to describe the theoretical and hence theological bases of the sacrifice whereby he would capture the insight of sacrificial theory in compact and eloquent speech. Second, he is afraid of composing words more eloquent than another, particularly his father, who may also be his teacher, thereby upsetting the social (and philosophical) structure of traditional learning.[47]

With verse 3, we move into the layered meaning of the ritual world, as its subject, following O'Flaherty (1981, 116), is understood as both Agni and the inspired poet. When understood as Agni, lines ab describe the fire god as the foremost priest of the ritual, whose knowledge of appropriate procedure, and particularly of eloquent and insightful speech, is surpassed by none. The riddle of Agni is then exposed in line d, where he is understood as the fire at dawn who brings the sun, the fire who can protect immortality because he is an ever-renewable resource and the key to the perpetually recurring sun. When understood as the inspired poet, lines ab describe a successful contestant in the competition, whose ritual knowledge and verbal skills are now capable of sustaining the cosmos; the immortality of line 3d is the immortality of the worlds as ensured by the ritual and, by implication, the immortality of man as well. The layers of meaning in line 3d, then, are threefold: Agni as fire below and sun above; the bright young poet who has surpassed his aging elders in wisdom; and the earthly mortal who has penetrated the mysteries of his immortal gods. In all three cases, though, an insightful vision is central to this verse (Johnson 1980, 123).

Verse 4 makes clear that the insight needed at this ritual contest has to do with the peculiarity of Agni as god. He is an immortal among the mortals, who, as line 5b tells us, is the messengerial embodiment of thought flying quickly between the two worlds, continually bonding the contract between men and gods, as well as the central source of insight that upholds the divine world (5d). The experience climaxes in verse 6, where the young poet receives insight from Agni and describes his deathlike experience of contemplation in detail. All his senses open out as he discovers the knowledge already firmly fixed in his heart. As he increasingly interiorizes his experience, his mind conversely seems to wander into the far unknown, "indicating his absorption in a state of speechless wonder" (Johnson 1980, 20–21) and giving rise to the rhetorical questions of 6d (Thieme 1957a, 53). In verse 7, finally, homage is paid to the distant but not capricious god of fire, who has as absolute a control over light and warmth as he does over the vision into the unknown.

The priestly competition, then, is the vehicle by which the seer's identity is established, an identity based as much upon his ability to play with words as it is upon his powers of infusing them with an inspiration that is ritually effective. I have been suggesting for some time, moreover, what the content of this insight might be and must now speak directly about the referent of clear and effective ritual speech. If the place where insight is measured is the ritual contest, then the standard by which it is measured is the ability to formulate ultimate questions and, more important, to supply some kind of resolution to them. What, then, are the subjects of these riddles, these perplexing questions, that the priest must solve by his eloquent use of the word? To be "true," it seems, eloquent speech must correctly describe one of three things: the cosmic mysteries of the universe; the mysteries of human life; and/or the ritual symbolism by which these mysteries are expressed, understood, manipulated, and put to use beneficial for man. As we have seen, the cosmic mysteries about which the seer must have insight center around the great deeds of the gods, particularly (1) the central role Agni plays in the life of the creatures (2.35.2) and in regulating the procession of days

(6.9.1) by his swift travels between each world (6.9.5), and (2) the importance of Indra in overcoming the powers of resistance (*vṛtrā́ni*) (7.23.3), which Kuiper believes is repeated over again in the verbal context (1960, 251).

In the following hymn, 4.5,[48] again to Agni Vaiśvānara, the poet reports on a contest in which he has participated successfully and reveals the secrets of the ritual in a symbolism that is understood to explain the cosmic mysteries:

1. How can we of one mind reverence
the gracious Agni Vaiśvānara?
With great high growth
he stays the great light like a post the dike.

2. Do not belittle the autonomous god
who gave me this gift, for I am an ignorant mortal
while he is the clever immortal,
the wise, most virile Vaiśvānara, the youthful Agni.

3. The mighty, thousand-semened bull with sharp horns
has a great song with double tone.
As one reveals the hidden track of a cow,
Agni has declared the inner meaning (*manīṣā́*)[49] to me.

4. The sharp-toothed but benevolent Agni
shall chew them thoroughly with his hottest flame,
who violate the institutes of Varuna,
the precious, firm [laws] of attentive Mitra.

5. Willful like brotherless maidens,
wicked like cuckolding wives,
evil, lawless (*ánṛta*), and truthless (*asatyá*),
they were born for this deep place.[50]

6. Who then am I, clarifying Agni,
that upon me who does not violate [the institutes],
you have boldly laid, like a heavy burden, this insight
(*mánman*) so high and deep,
this new question with seven meanings for the offering?

7. May our meditation, cleansing with its ritual insight,[51]
reach him who consistently remains the same:
once the precious substance of the cow is in the leather skin
of ritual food,
the orb of the sun will break over the tip of the earth.

8. What part of this speech of mine should I declare?
They speak covertly about the secret riddle in the depths:
when they have unlocked the mystery of the dawns like a door,
[Agni] protects the dear tip of the earth, the place of the bird.

9. This is that great face of the great [gods]
which, leading, the cow of dawn shall follow.
I found it shining secretly in the place of truth (*ṛtá*)
going quickly, quickly.

10. Then, his mouth shining in the presence of his parents,
he thought (*ámanuta*) of the dear, hidden substance of the cow.
In the farthest place of the mother, facing the cow,
the tongue of the bull, of the extended flame [went forth].

11. I speak humbly about the truth when asked,
trusting in you Jātavedas, if this is all right.
You rule over all this richness
which is in heaven and on earth.

12. Of this, what richness is ours, indeed what treasure?
Tell us, Jātavedas, as the one who knows!
The farthest end of this, our way is hidden.
We went, as it were, finding fault with the wrong road.

13. What is the signpost? What is the direction? What is the goal?
We want to reach it like race horses the victory prize.
When will the dawns, the divine wives of immortality
spread [their light] over us with the color of the sun?

14. Those with their weak, trifling words,
with their paltry retorts, who leave one disappointed,
what can they say here now, Agni?
Unarmed, let them fall into oblivion.

15. The face of the god, of this bull kindled into splendor,
shone in the home.
Clothed in white, beautiful in form,
rich in gifts, he shone like a dwelling full of riches.

Dedicated to and revelatory about Agni Vaiśvānara in the priestly contest, hymn 4.5 begins with the poet's feeling of unworthiness about reverencing Agni. How can man offer anything to Agni when the god gives us so much, especially the light/insight that maintains the cosmos.

This self-depreciating theme continues into verse 2 where the poet speaks again to the vast abyss between god and man, emphasizing both man's ignorance in the face of Agni's wisdom (Renou 1955–69, 2.55–56) and man's mortality in the face of Agni's freedom from all boundaries, particularly that of death.[52] The psychological implications of this verse are magnificent. On the one hand, the poet is genuinely fearful of his ignorance and his ritual ineffectiveness as he enters the contest, and on the other, he knows that pride and arrogance before the god who must be pleased would be an unforgivable error. Having prepared Agni with a description of man's own inadequacies, in verse 3, the poet focuses on the insight of the eloquent Agni, the primordial priest, whose ritual song (*sā́man*) penetrates the inner meaning (*manīṣā́*) of the cosmic mysteries that surround the symbolism of the cow (O'Flaherty 1981, 113) and that, because of his praise of the god, are now available to the contestant. In verses 4 and 5 we get the hymn's first references to the poet's opponents in the contest, who are characterized above all else as violating the established laws of truth (*ṛtá, satyá*) for which they will be destroyed, literally and figuratively, by the insight of Agni. Why, the poet than asks in verse 6, if l stand in such good stead in relation to others, must I have such a difficult puzzle to untangle in the contest, a new puzzle (cf. Renou (1955–69, 2.57) that has a multitude of difficult meanings for the ritual?

Beginning in verse 7 the content of the secret is revealed. In lines 7ab, the poet tells a truth about Agni (that he is perpetual) and hopes that this truth born of the poet's meditation may be effective. Lines 7cd suggest the symbolism used to describe the cosmic mysteries. Ritual foods and implements, when properly prepared and manipulated, stimulate and perpetuate the proper functioning of the natural world.[53] In verse 8, the poet asks out loud what part of his understanding he should make known (Renou 1955–69, 2.58), that same understanding coveted secretly by more advanced poets about the magical mysteries of the dawn, a riddle whose key lies in the nature of Agni and the sun as described in verse 9: that the fire on the ritual ground is identical with the sun and that, when kindled, Agni as sun will rise up out of his eternal hiding place in the seat of truth to take his place in the sky. Having discovered the secret, and indeed having even experienced the sun in the secret hiding place (9cd), the poet continues with his revelation about Agni and the ritual process in verse 10 (O'Flaherty 1981, 113; Johnson 1980, 35–37), and in 11–12ab goes directly to Agni, this time in his Jātavedas (more intimate) form, to broach, as is appropriate with this god (Findly 1981), the subject of material reward for "his devotion and proper action in the contest" (Johnson 1980, 24). The next four lines (12cd–13ab) reveal the poet's concern for the rules governing performance and the determination of success at the contest (Geldner 1951, 1.423–26; Renou 1955–69, 2.58–59). Hopeful as he is of winning, he is not sure what to do nor how to discriminate between right and wrong attempts. Lines 13cd are again a revelation of the secret of the cosmic mysteries of dawn but allude as well to the light of wisdom hoped for by the aspiring poet as he moves on, in verse 14, to speak out against his ignorant, unsuccessful opponents in the contest. Finally, in verse 15, the poet describes the Agni of his visionary experience and, in so doing, presents a closing praise of him as the god from whom the desired prizes come.

The truth of the eloquent speech in this hymn fits two of the three categories suggested earlier: the cosmic mysteries of the universe and the ritual symbolism and technique by which these mysteries are made effective. That the riddle of the mystery of dawn is intricately tied to the liturgical symbolism that would make it true is based upon the centrality of Agni. By a visionary experience given by Agni, the poet comes to see not only that the content of the secret is the manifold identity of Agni, but also that Agni himself is the keeper of this secret, as well as the rewarder of the wise and chastiser of the ignorant. Cosmic secrets, tied as they are to the knowledge of their ritual expression and manipulation, in this way, are the source of great *áṁhas,* but another secret is even more fearful and anxiety producing, that connected with the mystery of human life. We have already seen that there is great *áṁhas* about the length of one's own life, the most important secret not known to man (7.23.2cd), and that in this horrible abyss between finite, mortal man and the infinite, immortal gods, only Agni, who knows both worlds, has insight into this anxiety and, therefore, ultimately can be compassionate to man. Coming to terms with the finite dimension of man, I argue, is the kernel of insight in Ṛgvedic thought, and successful resolution of this problem (that is, a true formulation about human mysteries) is what, in fact, empowers ritual speech, even that ritual speech called mantra, to defeat Vedic enemies:

> And that much was not known by these [men].
> The raging mantra pronounced by the seers is true:
> The powerful four-cornered (*vájra*) slays the three-cornered
> [weapon of the gods' enemies].
> The god-revilers were the first to age. (1.152.2)

From a Mitra and Varuṇa hymn, this verse contrasts the position of truth with that of falsehood and places the power of mantra squarely on the side of truth. Although the riddle of line c is significant in understanding cosmic victories (Geldner 1951, 1.210; Johnson 1980, 6, 83–87), it is not as central to my argument as is line d, with its pronouncement of punishment to the ignorant and implicit reward to the wise—those who can formulate and speak a true mantra have in their power the key to longevity and even, perhaps, to immortality.

We have seen that the secrets embedded in ritual speech are a response to a profoundly felt *áṁhas* about certain mysteries. The continuing need to respond to this *áṁhas,* I now argue, is one of the keys (note 1.152.2 just quoted) to the emergent notion of mantra: The priest can respond to *áṁhas* only if his weapon is extremely powerful. That mantra is specifically tied to victory over anxiety is clear from the following lines addressed to Agni:

> You take pleasure in him who presents the offering *to ensure certainty* (*avṛká*),
> in the mantra of the singer [composed] with insight (*mánas*). (1.31.13cd)

The concept of *áṁhas,* then, is what makes the development of mantra so important, for, in the end, the reason speech must be performative is to carry man beyond the boundaries of death.

I now turn briefly to the final element in the classic religious matrix of the Ṛgveda, the source of that insight central to eloquent speech that is the face-to-face relationship with god. Embedded in the large corpus of primarily ritualistic hymns, there is still extant a number of hymns, many from Book 7, that preserve a highly personal, intimate, and immediate focus upon man's relationship with god (Dandekar 1969; 1970). These hymns make clear that, in order to have insight, the priestly poet must have a right and true relationship with his god, which can then be mediated by the spoken word.[54] Vasiṣṭha's hymn 7.88 to Varuṇa is a good example of the intimate and "in confidence" communication that can exist between a poet and his god. As he is praying to Varuṇa, Vasiṣṭha relates the secret of heaven (light and darkness) that has been demonstrated to him and how, because of this, he has been made a *ṛ́ṣi* (seer) and *stotṛ́* (singer). This relationship, which was once quite friendly, however, has now become a thing of the past for, because of some sin for which Vasiṣṭha can give no accounting, the judgment of Varuṇa has come between them. Vasiṣṭha asks, as the hymn closes, for Varuṇa to take the judgmental noose from around his neck and restore the intimacy of earlier times.

1. Vasiṣṭha, present a pure, most agreeable prayer (*matí*)
   to the gracious Varuṇa,
   who will then turn hither the lofty bull [sun],
   bearing a thousand gifts and worthy of worship.

2. "And now having come into sight of him (Varuṇa),
   I think (*maṅsi*) the face of Varuṇa is Agni's.
   May the overseer lead me to the sun [closed up] in the crag
   and the darkness, to see the spectacle.

3. "Whenever we two, Varuṇa and I, board the boat
   and steer out into the middle of the ocean,

whenever we skim across waves of the waters,
we will swing in the swing and sparkle."

4. Varuṇa set Vasiṣṭha in the boat.
The inspired master made him a seer, a singer, through his great powers
for all the auspicious times of the days,[55]
for as long as the heavens, for as long as the dawns shall last.

5. "What has become of those friendly relations of ours,
when of old we could get together without hostility?
I used to go to your house on high,
to your thousand-doored home, autonomous Varuṇa!

6. "As when a steady companion who has sinned against you
remains your friend because he is dear, Varuṇa,
so may we sinners not pay penalty to you, avenger!
Inspired one, extend protection to your singer!

7. "Abiding in these firm abodes,
may Varuṇa release the noose from us,
winning support from the lap of Aditi.
Protect us always with your blessing!"

Vasiṣṭha has been made a seer through Varuṇa's great powers (4b), based upon his promise as an insightful singer and composer of the excellent prayer (*matí,* 1a). Having been made a seer entitles Vasiṣṭha to the special company of Varuṇa (3) and to a relationship of divine friendship (6, 7) experienced only by the privileged few. According to Dandekar, in fact, "The personal relationship which Vasiṣṭha claimed with Varuṇa unmistakably reminds one of the classical relationship between a *bhakta* and the God" (1970:79). To remain in this friendship, in this *bhakti*-like relationship, Vasiṣṭha must follow *ṛtá* (7c) and refrain from sin (6), otherwise the noose which prevents the freedom for peace and progress, and which makes death more imminent, will be his forever. At the core of this relationship, facilitated and renewed at each religious moment by the *matí* 'prayer', is the opportunity to contemplate (*man*) the face of god and win, thereby, insight into the mysteries.

FROM CONTEST TO RITUAL

Out of this religious matrix, which focuses on the insightful and eloquent speech arising from a seer's intimate and personal relationship with god (i.e., from a face-to-face contemplation of the divine), arises the view of speech as agentive, the notion of mantra that is powerful precisely because it is *kaviśastá.* In the classical Ṛgvedic system, it is the intimate relationship between man and god that is the source of power, because this relationship allowed man to tap the power of *ṛtá* and *satyá*, newly accessible to man once the relationship with god was established. In the subsequent system into which mantra fits, however, the source of power is that it is pronounced, not necessarily that it is born of insight or that it is particularly eloquent (for these things, though sometimes stated outright, are more often than not simply assumed), but that it is spoken out loud in a particular way in a particular context. With mantra, speech has become an event, both on the particular ritual level around the fire hearths and on the cosmic level whereby it analogically sets into motion the powerful mythic life of the gods. As the seer is transformed from a poet who thinks upon the divine to a priest who makes effective the ritual, mantra becomes the new and conscious designation of speech as performative.

The new focus on the power of speech and the shift in the source of this power from the intimate relationship with god to the pronunciation in ritual, which we find in the rise of mantra, does not mean an abrupt break in tradition, however. The word *mantra*, in fact, is clearly intended to be a continuation of the earlier "insight tradition." Note, for instance, that many of the standard words for insight and insightful prayer come from *man* (*matí, mánas, manīṣā́, mánman*) and that *man* is often used to describe the contemplation of the face-to-face relationship with god. It is no accident, then, that the word for agentive speech be based upon this tradition of powerful insight. The Ṛgvedic poet is explicit, in fact, that mantra be inspired and that it have communicable meaning: "May we pronounce that mantra well that was well fashioned for him from the heart; he will understand it, to be sure" (2.35.2ab). Moreover, the power of mantra is clearly to be a response to the old anxieties of Vedic man, for it is "to ensure certainty" (1.31.13) and to "bring joy on the most distant day" (10.95.1d). Added to this are the implications that mantra is a familiar term amongst those participating in verbal contests (10.106.11ab) and that the context of mantra in the Ṛgveda supports the very basic concerns of these contests (e.g., 2.35.2; 7.7.6; 7.32.13).

Nevertheless, the focus on power and pronunciation in mantra indicates a new emphasis on ritual effectiveness, and I argue, that, while by design the mantra system rests upon and in fact participates in this earlier stratum of insight and eloquence, it has already moved on to reflect the issues that become central in the *Brāhmaṇas*, the expanding of the techniques and analogical referents of the liturgical complex and the very divinization of ritual itself. Note 10.50.6 to Indra:

> You have made all these Soma-fests efficacious,
> which you, son of strength, have appropriated for yourself.
> According to your wish, to your command, the beaker lasts continually,
> as does the worship, the mantra, the uplifted formulation, the speech (*vácas*).

The emergence of the notion of *mántra,* then, stands at a pivotal point in the development of Ṛgvedic thought, incorporating key elements of matrices before and after. The following verse, 1.74.1, neatly summarizes this threshold nature of mantra. Mantra is a speech act (1b), belonging with the increasing centrality of ritual as a conception and as an act (1a), which has its foundation, nevertheless, in the earlier insight structures where empowerment comes primarily from meaningful communication with the divine (1c):

> Undertaking the ceremony
> we would pronounce a mantra to Agni
> who hears us in the distance.

NOTES

1. Note, for instance, the listings in Vishva Bandhu's (1935–76) *A Vedic Word-Concordance,* where the Ṛgveda and the Śatapathabrāhmaṇa contain the majority of citations in an already short list of references (1.4, 2441; 2.2, 776; 3.2, 639–41).

2. The situation is even bleaker in the Atharvaveda. There, in addition to references requoted from the Ṛgveda, e.g., Śau.6.64.2 (=RV.10.191.3), 18.1.60 (=RV.10.14. 4), and 20.59.4 (=RV.7.32.13), only a few new references appear, i.e., 2.7.5 and 5.20.11.

3. In fact, there is a fairly even spread over most of the major Ṛgvedic deities, with perhaps the highest proportion found in Agni hymns.

4. According to Belvalkar's (1922) study, the 3.53.8 and 6.50.14 mantra references may be late as well (pp. 17, 21, 25).

5. Furthermore, one could argue that the history of the use of the term *mantra* is the mirror opposite of that of *bráhman,* the really significant term for ritual speech in the Saṁhitas and Brāhmaṇas (Renou 1948–49; Gonda 1950; Thieme 1952). As the concept of brahman decreases in significance, that of mantra increases. This suggestion is borne out by the evidence of Bandhu's (1935–76) concordance (1.4, 2291–95, 2441; 2.2, 727–29, 776; 3.2, 583ff., 639–41).

6. This suggestion is supported by Dandekar's theory of the replacement of an ancient cult of Varuṇa by a new one dedicated to Indra early in the development of Ṛgvedic thought (Dandekar 1969, 237–38; 1970, 77).

7. That mantra cannot be understood outside its use in the ritual is clear from RV.1.40.5; 1.74.1; 10.50.6; and 10.88.14.

8. The other three references are RV.3.30.3b (of Indra who performs powerful deeds among mortals), 4.24.8a (of a stormy ritual contest over which Indra has presided and out of which Vāmadeva emerges the winner), and 10.27.3c (of an undetermined type of conflict, though presumably a regular battle). On the

last, Indra's complaint is that it is only when the battle is "raging" does man call on him.

9. Śau.2.7.5 and 5.20.11.

10. O'Flaherty takes *aryás* as an acc. pl. modifying *bhúvanā*, "noble creatures" (1981, 105).

11. Note that for the Vedic world, the place of this truth is not way off out there but deeply hidden somewhere down here. We might speculate that the initial Vedic focus on the depths of the earth rather than the heights of the sky is responsible for the eventual internalization of the transcendent yet deeply hidden truth of the world initially associated with Agni.

12. Note, for instance, the association of *brahmán* (formulator) with *bráhman* (formulation); *hotṛ́* (invoker) with *háva, hávana, havás, hávīman, hávyā, hótrā, hóman* (invocation); *udgātṛ́* (Sāman singer) with *gātú, gāthá, gā́thā, gāyatrá, gā́yas* (song) (N.B. *gír*); *praśāstṛ́* (director ?) with *práśasti* (praise), *praśā́sana, praśís* (command), *śáṁsa, śásā, śastí* (praise); *upavaktṛ́* (caller) with *upavāká* (speech), *vákman* (invocation), *vácas* (word); and *prastotṛ́* (Sāman singer) with *prástuti* (praise), *stút, stotrá, stóma, stutí* (song of praise). Names like *agnídh* (fire kindler), *adhvaryú* (ritual celebrant), *néṣtṛ* (leader), *puróhita* (house priest), and *potṛ́* (purifier), however, are not directly related to ritual speech.

13. Heesterman's (1964) discussion of the preclassical and classical systems in the Vedic tradition has a bearing on this argument.

14. 1.152.2b; 6.50.14d; 10.14.4c. Cf., 1.67.4 mantra and *śas*.

15. 3.21.4c; 3.29.7b. Cf., 5.1.8b, *kavipraśastá* of Agni.

16. *Kaví* as *vípra*: i.e., 9.84.5; 4.26.1; 10.64.16; 10.114.5; 3.34.7; 1.76.5; 10.112.9; 3.5.1.

17. As *ṛtajñā́*: i.e., 10.64.16. Cf., 2.24.7; 7.76.4; 10.177.2.

18. As *dhī́*: i.e., 1.95.8.

19. As *mánman*: i.e., 1.151.7.

20. As *kā́vya*: i.e., 9.84.5; 8.8.11.

21. As *manīṣā́*: i.e., 6.49.4; 10.124.9; 10.177.2; 10.129.4; 9.72.6.

22. As *ukthá*: i.e., 3.34.7.

23. As *matí*: i.e., 9.97.32; 9.64.10.

24. As *mánas*: i.e., 10.5.3.

25. As *dhī́ra*: i.e., 1.146.4; 3.8.4.

26. As *hŕ̥d*: i.e., 1.146.4; 10.129.4.

27. As *niṇyá*: i.e., 4.16.3.

28. As *vratá*: i.e., 10.114.2.

29. As *chándas*: i.e., 10.114.5. Cf., 10.114.6; 10.124.9.

30. As *tántu*: i.e., 1.164.5. Cf., 10.5.3.

31. Soma: i.e., 9.74.9.

32. Johnson (1980) elaborates on the role of Agni in this hymn as "the inner light of divine inspiration dwelling in the heart," the focal point of meditation for poets called upon to participate in what he calls "the sacrificial symposium" (pp. 7–8). If this hymn, in fact, describes such a verbal contest, verse 14 is central, as it names the invitatory verses to the patron deity, Agni Vaiśvānara, mantras.

33. 1.40.6ab; 1.74.1b; 2.35.2b.

34. 10.88.14b.

35. 1.40.5b.

36. 1.67.4.

37. d following O'Flaherty (1981, 253). Thieme: "Nicht werden uns diese Gedanken (= Die Gedanken, die wir im Sinne haben), [wenn sie] unausgesprochen [bleiben], später Freude schaffen" (1957b, 70). Eggeling: "Untold, these secrets of ours will not bring us joy in days to come" (These thoughts (=that we intend) will not create joy for us later, [if they remain] unpronounced) (1982–1900, SB.11.5.1.6, 70–71).

38. I am indebted to Dr. Stephanie Jamison for calling my attention to the verb *mantráy* here, which would confirm an instrumental or performative interpretation of *mántra*, with meanings such as I swear or I promise.

39. Again, I am grateful to Dr. Jamison for pointing out that *mantra* would have to be in an instrumental relation to the past participle as second member and that this hypothetical phrase could not mean, for instance, "the seer by whom the *mántra* is pronounced." See her 1979 discussion of such compounds (198–99, n. 8).

40. Of course, this would not preclude the overlapping of periods in which both these terms enjoyed use. Note, for instance, the conjunction of mantra and *bráhman* in 10.50.4 (and 6); Johnson, in fact, treats them as interchangeable terms (1980, 84).

41. Bloomfield discusses 10.85.12 in which Sūryā "mounted her mind-car," an image in which "You mount your mind or wish-car and reach your destination, that is to say, the object of your desire" (1919, 281). This use of the mind may be prefigured here, and certainly is corroborated by the term *mantra*. On

Sūryā as goddess of speech, see Bhawe's discussion of the muse of poetry (1950, 19–27).

42. Following Geldner 1951, 1.394–95.

43. *Vípra*: i.e., 3.30.20; 3.5.3; 7.66.8; 7.78.2.

44. *Hṛ́d*: i.e., 3.39.1; 3.26.8.

45. The translation of this hymn benefitted greatly from the work of O'Flaherty (1981, 115–17).

46. Agni or the inspired poet.

47. Johnson's interpretation of the sequence of events as represented in 2cd is complicated. Since the exact structure of these "sacrificial symposia" does not bear directly upon the argument here, I will simply reproduce his translation: "Indeed whose [companion] will be the 'son' to respond [correctly to the *bráhmans*] which are to be explained here at the prior position [placed into competition] by the 'father' [sitting] at the later position?" (1980, 18). I still am not convinced by his discussion of this verse (149–150), as the fear of upstaging an elder fits so well syntactically and contextually and is a much simpler solution.

48. Again, I am indebted to O'Flaherty in a number of places here (1981, 112–15).

49. Cf., Upadhyaya (1961) and Johnson (1980, 22) on the referent of this word.

50. One of the few references to a hell found in the Ṛgveda. Cf., 7.104.3, 11, 17 (Macdonell, 1897, no. 75). Note, however, Johnson's unusual understanding of lines cd as "Faced with the difficult *bráhman*, the poet at first paranoically thinks that such evil competitors . . . have posed the enigma (5cd), the *padám* . . . *gabhīrám* (profound phrase), so that it will be impossible for him to understand" (1980, 22).

51. Cf., Johnson's discussion of *krátu* here and elsewhere (1980, 145).

52. Note here Gonda's (1957) discussion of *áṁhas* as essentially descriptive of a "narrowness" around man.

53. The discussions in both Johnson (1980, 34–35) and O'Flaherty (1981, 113) are extensive and complicated, perhaps overly so if lines cd are understood within the context of ritual magic at dawn. Johnson's discussion, particularly, lacks a ritual focus that is essential here; while he is right about the experience of insight, he is often silent about the content of that insight, which, more often than not, is a description and explanation of ritual analogues.

54. Compare the material in Brown (1968a, 206–207) where Dīrghatamas gets his knowledge from a transcendental vision with Vāc as its source.

55. A reference to the regular progression of the ritual calendar and to the establishment of Vasiṣṭha as ritual practitioner par excellence.

CHAPTER 2

Vedic Mantras

Frits Staal

THIS ARTICLE CONSISTS OF TWO parts. The first part (pages 48–59) presents the evidence in the form of six mantras, provided in their original Vedic, with a translation and a discussion of the context in which they occur and are used. The second part formulates conclusions drawn from this evidence. There are three sections: the first (pages 59–66) deals with the distinction between Vedic and Tantric mantras; the second (pages 66–70) compares mantras with speech acts; and the third (pages 70–85) discusses the relations between mantras and language.

THE EVIDENCE

Vedic Mantras are bits and pieces of the Vedas put to ritual use.* In the earlier ritual literature (e.g., in the Śrauta Sutras and in the Yajurveda itself), mantras are distinguished from *brāhmanas,* or interpretive passages that elucidate and interpret the ritual use of mantras. In the later ritual literature (e.g., in the Mīmāṃsā), mantras are distinguished from *vidhis,* or injunctions that prompt to ritual acts. Mantras occur in each of the four Vedas. They belong to different kinds of Vedic utterances, such as *ṛc,* "verse (from the Ṛgveda)," *sāman* "chant or melody (from the Sāmaveda)," *yajus,* "formula (from the Yajurveda), generally muttered," and *nigada* "formula (from the Yajurveda), generally spoken loud."

**Although this article is addressed primarily to Indologists and scholars of religion, the material also is of interest to linguists and philosophers. In order not to make the exposition unpalatable to its intended audience, I have not tried to adhere to standards of rigor and sophistication considered commendable in linguistics and philosophy. All the same, I have benefitted from comments by Yuki Kuroda and Steve Yablo.*

Before discussing mantras in general, it will be helpful to consider some examples. I shall list six of these, in the original Sanskrit, along with translations or with what I shall refer to as translatory meanings. I have omitted accents even though they are considered part of the mantras. Afterward I shall discuss these mantras in detail, one by one, and derive some general conclusions.

1. *agnīñ . . .*
   agnīñ jyotiṣmataḥ kuruta / dīkṣita vācaṃ yaccha / patni vācaṃ yaccha/
   (Kindle the fires! Consecrated one, control your speech! Wife, control your speech!)
   (*Baudhāyana Śrauta Sūtra* 6.6)

2. *mitro na ehi . . .*
   mitro na ehi sumitradhā / indrasyorum ā viśa dakṣiṇam / uśann uśantaṃ śyonaḥ śyonam/
   (Come to us as a friend, making good friends. Enter the right thigh of Indra; you willing, it willing, you gracious, it gracious)
   (*Taittirīya Saṃhitā* 1.2.7.1 f)

3. *yo'sman dveṣṭi . . .*
   yo'sman dveṣti yaṃ ca vayaṃ dviṣma / idam asya grīvā api kṛntāmi /
   (He who hates us and whom we hate, here I cut off his neck!)
   (*Taittirīya Saṃhitā* 1.3.1.1 c)

4. *devasya tvā savituḥ . . .*
   devasya tvā savituḥ prasave'śvinor bāhubhyām pūṣṇo hastābhyām agnaye jyuṣṭaṃ nirvapāmy agnīṣomābhyām/
   (On the impulse of the God Savitṛ, with the arms of the Aśvins, with the hands of Pūṣan, I offer you dear to Agni, to Agni and Soma.)
   (*Taittirīya Saṃhitā* 1.1.4.2 m)

5. *indra juṣasva . . .*
   indra juṣasva pra vahā yāhi śūra haribhyām / pibā sutasya mater iha madhoś cakānaś cārur madāya // indra jaṭaraṃ navyo na pṛṇasva madhor divo na / asya sutasya svarṇopa tvā madāḥ suvāco aguḥ // indras turāṣaṇ mitro vṛtraṃ yo jaghāna yatīr na / bibheda valaṃ bhṛgur na sasahe śatrūn made somasya //
   "Indra enjoy—drive on,
   come, hero—with your two steeds,
   drink of Soma—like a sage,

loving the sweet, pleased with inebriation!
Indra, your belly—like one to be praised,
fill it with sweet—like heavens,
with pressed Soma—like paradise,
well-spoken inebriants have gone to you!
Indra fast conquering—like a friend,
killing the demon—like ascetics,
he split the cave—like Bhṛgu,
he conquers his enemies inebriated with Soma!"

(*Atharvaveda* 2.5.1–3)

6. *hā bu hā bu hā bu . . .*

hā bu hā bu hā bu bhā bhaṃ bhaṃ bhaṃ bhaṃ bhaṃ bhā bhaṃ bhaṃ bhaṃ bhaṃ bhaṃ bhā bhaṃ bhaṃ bhaṃ bhaṃ bham/ hā bu hā bu hā bu brahma jajñānaṃ prathamaṃ purāstāt / vi sīmatas suruco vena ā vāt/ sa budhniyā upamā asya vā yi sṭḥāḥ/ satas ca yonim asataś ca vā yi vaḥ / hā bu hā bu hā bu bhā bhaṃ bhaṃ bhaṃ bhaṃ bhaṃ bhā bhaṃ bhaṃ bhaṃ bhaṃ bhaṃ bhā bhaṃ bhaṃ bhaṃ bhaṃ bham/ hā bu hā bu hā vu vā/ brahma devānāṃ bhāti parame vyoman brahma devānāṃ bhāti parame vyoman brahma devānāṃ bhāti parame vyomān//

Here translation becomes more difficult even than in the previous case (5); but it may be attempted, in free fashion, as follows:

(Hey hey hey! BANG bang bang bang bang bang BANG bang bang bang bang bang BANG bang bang bang bang ! Hey hey hey! Born as brahman first in the ea-east, Vena has shone out of the glimmering horizon. He has revealed its highest and lowest positionemes, the womb of being and of non-be-be-ying. Hey hey hey! BANG bang bang bang bang bang BANG bang bang bang bang bang BANG bang bang bang bang bang! Hey hey, hey man! Brahman shines in the highest heaven of the gods brahman shines in the highest heaven of the gods brahman shines in the highest heaven of the gogodeses!)

(*Jaiminīya Araṇyageyagāna* 12.9)

All the expressions in these six examples are mantras or consist of mantras. They are not only very different from each other, but, the further we proceed in the sequence, the more difficult it becomes to provide a "translatory meaning." So let us now review these six once again, one by one, place them in their ritual context, and see what general conclusions can be drawn.

1. *AGNĪÑ . . .*

This mantra is a command, technically called *praiṣārtha*. It belongs to the category *nigada*. It is addressed by the Adhvaryu priest, shouting in a loud voice, to the other priests, the Yajamāna (ritual patron) and the Yajamāna's wife, after the Yajamāna's consecration has taken place. Following the mantra, fuel is added to the fires, and the Yajamāna and his wife "control their speech" (i.e., they pronounce only what is prescribed, but do not chatter; see Staal 1983a [AGNI] I.333). It stands to reason, therefore, to assume that this mantra is an ordinary command, which has been understood as such by those to whom it was addressed. This implies, among other things, that the Adhvaryu priest is the kind of person who has the authority to issue such commands.

2. *MITRO NA EHI . . .*

This mantra is a *yajus,* muttered by the Yajamāna after the Soma plant has been purchased by the Adhvaryu from a merchant. The Yajamāna mutters the first part of the mantra (. . . *sumitradhā*) when the Adhvaryu approaches him with the Soma bundle. He then uncovers his right thigh, places the bundle on it, and recites the remainder of the mantra (Caland & Henry 1906, I.46; Kashikar & Dandekar 1958–73, II, Sanskrit Section; I.50). Here no command is given or followed. The mantras accompany an act or acts and may be interpreted as comments on that act or on those acts.

3. *YO'SMĀN DVEṢṬI . . .*

This mantra, which is recited frequently, has a purely ritual use: It is recited when the soil within a ritual enclosure is prepared with the help of the *sphya,* a wooden knife. One of the *brāhmaṇas* associated with this mantra provides it with an interpretation that is a rationalization, as is usual: The enemy has to be excluded from the altar, for making the altar is a cruel act. "Let him think of anyone he hates; he does truly inflict trouble upon him!" (*Taittirīya Saṃhitā* 2.6.4.4). Another brāhmaṇa comments, "There are two persons: one whom he hates, and one who hates him. Surely, he should cut off the necks of both, successively" (*Taittirīya Saṃhitā* 6.1.8.4; cf. Staal 1983a, I.104).

When I call such interpretations *rationalizations,* I do not intend to deny that there were real enemies in Vedic times, whose necks could be, or actually were, cut off. There is ample evidence for battles, sometimes intruding on ritual (see, e.g., Heesterman 1962). Such a background is reflected in the "translatory meaning" of the mantra and points to one of its possible origins. However, the meaning of a mantra is its ritual use. In ritual terms it means that the soil is scratched with the *sphya*. The authors of the brāhmaṇas are aware of these ritual uses, but they go willfully beyond them, invoking anything that strikes their fancy, contradicting themselves, giving vent to their adventitious and often infantile wishes—not unlike some contemporary theorists of ritual.

4. *DEVASYA TVĀ SAVITUḤ . . .*

This mantra is recited frequently throughout all ritual performances. It accompanies and indicates an offering (*nirvāpa*). The first three phrases (through *hastābhyām*) occur at the beginning of many other mantras (see Bloomfield 1906, 492–94). Characteristically, the *brāhmaṇas* are unhelpful; e.g., "He says 'On the impulse of the God Savitṛ' when he takes the sword, for impelling. He says 'with the arms of the Aśvins' because the Aśvins were the Adhvaryus of the Gods. He says 'with the hands of Pūṣan,' for restraint" (*Taittirīya Saṃhitā* 2.6.4.1). All of this is vacuous because there need not be a sword, there is always one Adhvaryu already, there is no need or clear use of impelling or restraint. However, there always is an offering.

That the ritual meaning is only "offering" is obvious from a discussion in the *Mīmāṃsāsūtra* (2.1.46). The purpose of this discussion is to establish that mantras always consist of a single sentence because they express a single meaning (*arthaikatvād ekaṃ vākyam*). The commentator Śabara elucidated this as follow, "The sūtra is explained because mantras fulfil a single purpose. *Devasya tvā* . . . , for example, indicates 'offering.' The words that comprise the mantra express precisely this, and therefore consist of a single sentence" (*ekaprayojanatvād upapannam / yathā tāvad devasya tveti nirvāpaprakāśanam / tasya viśiṣṭasya vācaka etāvān padasamūhas tadvākyam*).

5. *INDRA JUṢASVA* . . .

These mantras are curious, to say the least, and they may well have been composed under the influence of Soma. This is rare, if not exceptional. In the Ṛgveda, only one hymn (10.119) describes the effects of drinking Soma in detail. Even with respect to this hymn, Brough (1971, 341) judges, "Such a hymn cannot have been composed by a poet under the influence of *soma*: the artifice of its structure excludes this."

I don't know whether this is true, but there are good reasons to doubt it. I knew at least one mathematician who could do mathematics only when he was drunk, not on account of the auspicious inebriation (*sumada*) of Soma, but on account of the evil intoxication (*durmada*) of alcohol. It, therefore, is not unreasonable to suppose that the mantras *indra juṣasva* . . . might have been composed under the influence of Soma, even though they consist of *svarāj* meters—relatively uncommon meters consisting of thirty-four syllables each.

It is such meters that are important in the ritual use of these remarkable mantras. They constitute the material from which ritualists have constructed the beginning of the *śastra* recitation characteristic of an extended Soma ritual, "the sixteenth" (*ṣoḍaśī*). In order to put this in context, it should be recalled that the paradigm or prototype of the Soma rituals is the Agniṣṭoma, which consists of twelve Soma sequences. A Soma sequence is a sequence consisting of a *stotra* chant, a *śastra* recitation, Soma offering to the deities, and Soma drinking by the Yajamāna and his chief priests (Staal 1983a, I.49). In the Agniṣṭoma, there are five such Soma sequences during the morning pressing, five during the midday pressing, and two during the third pressing. From this prototype an extension is constructed by adding three Soma sequences; the resulting Soma ritual is called *ukthya.* When another Soma sequence is added to these fifteen, the "sixteenth" is arrived at. One characteristic feature of this Soma ritual is that its *śastra* recitation should consist in its entirety of *anuṣṭubh* verses, viz., meters that consist of four octosyllabic verses, or 4 × 8 = 32 syllables.

Since the mantras *indra juṣasva . . .* consist of three verses in the *svarāj* meter, and the first verse of a *śastra* recitation is always recited thrice, we have 5 × 34 = 170 syllables at our disposal. If we disregard the syntax and meaning of these verses and concentrate only on counting syllables, we can make use of 160 = 5 × 32 syllables to obtain five *anuṣṭubh* verses, leaving an excess of ten syllables. Such a procedure is in accordance with the general character of Vedic mantras, in which formal features such as meters are of paramount importance. In terms of syntax or "translatory meaning," however, the resulting *anuṣṭubh* verses do not make sense, for they are arrived at by cutting off the last *two* syllables of the first verse and adding them to the beginning of the second (which is a repetition of the first); cutting off the last *four* of the second and adding them to the beginning of the third (another repetition of the first); cutting off the last *six* of the third and adding them to the beginning of the fourth; cutting off the last *eight* of the fourth and adding them to the beginning of the fifth; and cutting off the last *ten* of the fifth and putting them in storage, so to speak. The entire procedure may be pictured as follows:

32 + (2) → 32
30 + (4) → 32
28 + (6) → 32
26 + (8) → 32
24 + (10) → 32
10

To provide a translatory meaning becomes very hazardous, but an idea may be gained from the following:

1. Indra enjoy—drive on,
come hero—with your two steeds,
drink of Soma—like a sage,
loving the sweet, pleased with!

2. Inebriation, Indra enjoy,
drive on, come, hero, with
your two steeds, drink of Soma,
like a sage, loving the sweet!

3. Pleased with inebriation—Indra,
enjoy, drive on, come, hero,
with your two steeds, drink of
Soma like a sage, loving!

4. The sweet, pleased with inebriation, Indra,
your belly, like one to be praised, fill,
it with sweet—like heavens with,
pressed Soma, like paradise well-spoken!

5. Inebriants have gone to you, Indra,
fast conquering like a friend killing,
the demon like ascetics he split,
the cave like Bhṛgu he conquers!"

The remainder—"His enemies inebriated with Soma!"—is used for the beginning of the next part of the *ṣoḍaśi śastra,* which I shall not write out in full, because it results in the same kind of meters, and the same kind of absurdities in terms of syntax and translatory meaning.

Later in the *śastra,* which is very long, use is made of a technique called *viharaṇam* (intertwining or transposition). Its first occurrence is in the construction of two *anuṣṭubh* verses (consisting of 2 × 32 syllables) from intertwining a *gāyatrī* verse (consisting of 3 × 8 syllables) with a *paṅkti* verse (consisting of 5 × 8 syllables):

$$
\begin{array}{r}
3 \times 8 = 24 \\
+ \underline{5 \times 8 = 40} \\
2 \times 32 = 64
\end{array}
$$

The *gāyatrī* verse is Ṛgveda 1.16.1:

ā tvā vahantu harayo vṛṣaṇaṃ somapītaye/
indra tvā sūracakṣasaḥ//
(The tawny horses take you bull to the Soma drinking,
You, Indra, with your sunny eyes!!)

The *paṅkti* verse is Ṛgveda 1.84.10:

Svādor itthā viṣūvato madhvaḥ pibanti gauryaḥ/ yā indreṇa sayāvarīr vṛṣṇā madanti sobhase vasvīr anu svarājyam//
(The gaurī cows drink from the sweet liquid, basic to the ritual,
enjoying themselves with their companion, Indra the bull, to look beautiful; beneficient to his supremacy.)

The intertwining of these two is as follows:

> *ā tvā vahantu harayas* svādor itthā viṣūvataḥ/ *vṛṣaṇaṃ somapītaye* madhvaḥ pibanti gauryo// *indra tvā sūracakṣaso* yā indreṇa sayāvarīḥ / vṛṣṇā madanti sobhase vasvīr anu svarājyo//

In this construction, the portions from the underlying *gāyatrī* verse are in italics, and the portions from the underlying *paṅkti* verse are in Roman. (The *-o* ending is another feature of *śastra* recitation, to which I shall return.)

The translatory meaning can only be guessed at, but the following may convey some of its flavor:

> The tawny horses take from the sweet, basic to the ritual. You bull to the Soma drinking, the gaurī cows drink from the liquid. You, Indra, with your sunny eyes—enjoying themselves with their companion, Indra the bull, to look beautiful; beneficient to his supremacy.

An intoxicated Sanskrit scholar might interpret this as a poetic rendering of a Soma orgy; however, it merely results from the metrical arithmetic of the *viharaṇam* technique. In terms of syntax or translatory meaning, none of these mantras make sense; their ritual meaning, on the other hand, is straightforward and uncontroversial: They constitute a portion of the sixteenth *śastra*.

In the sequel of the "sixteenth recitation" are further cases of *viharaṇam* and also instances where mantras, though recited in regular sequence, are reanalyzed into *anuṣṭubh* meters by counting the syllables of their original meters differently. The reader interested in these exercises can find them in Staal, 1983a, I.661–63, and can listen to them on the accompanying casette. The examples given should be sufficient to illustrate the ritual use and meaning of such mantras.

6. *HĀ BU HĀ BU HĀ BU* . . .

These mantras are chanted by the Udgātā priest of the Sāmaveda after the Adhvaryu has placed a small image of a golden man (*hiraṇmayapuruṣa*) on the lotus leaf that was earlier deposited and buried at the center of the Agni field; later the large bird-shaped altar of the Agnicayana will be constructed there. These chants (see Staal 1983a, I.414–17 and the accompanying cassette), which continue through some of the following rites, consist of four parts, and the mantras we are considering constitute the last chant of the third part. In this third part, there are many chants similar in structure. They start with *hā bu hā bu hā bu* . . . , which is followed by a triple repetition of six syllables, five of them identical, and the first a variation, e.g.,

> *phāt phat phat phat phat phat*
> *hā bu hau hau hau hau hau*
> *kā hvā hvā hvā hvā hvā.*

This is followed, in each case, by a verse, generally from the Ṛgveda, set to music in accordance with a melody (*sāman*), after which there is another round of meaningless syllables and finally a coda (*nidhana*), which is also meaningless.

Such meaningless syllables from the Sāmaveda are called *stobha.* If Vedic mantras are called *bits* and *pieces,* the *stobhas* are the bits. *Stobhas* are very similar to the *bīja*-mantras of later Tantrism, meaningless syllables that sometimes are strung together in sequences called *mantramālā* or *mālāmantra* (mantra garland, cf. Padoux 1978a, 81), but that also may be arranged two dimensionally in *maṇḍalas, cakras,* or deities. The accompanying illustration depicts *bīja*-mantras for Hanumān, the monkey god, also god of the martial arts. His legs, for example, are marked *raṃ raṃ raṃ raṃ raṃ raṃ. . . .* Some of the Vedic *stobhas* are combined into larger mantra sequences with specific structures, not dissimilar to musical structures. These structures may be represented in abstract or algebraic form. The chant *hā bu hā bu hā bu . . . ,* for example, is of the form:

$$P^3\ (QR^5)^3P^3$$
$$X$$
$$P^3\ (QR^5)^3P^2P^*$$
$$Y$$

where a superscript indicates the number of times that a form has to be repeated; for example, P^3 stands for *PPP,* $(QR^5)^3$ stands for *QRRRRRQRRRRRQRRRRR,* etc. To obtain the chant *hā bu hā bu hā bu . . .* from this formula, we substitute *P* for *hā bu; Q* for *bhā; R* for *bhaṃ; X* for *brahma jajñānaṃ; P** for *hā vu vā; Y* for *brahma devānāṃ.*

An abstract representation of this type may seem arbitrary at first sight, but it is not. It is not arbitrary because, by varied substitutions, we are in a position to construct other chants: first, by varying the "language" mantras *X* and *Y*; then by replacing *Q* with *phāt* and *R* with *phat;* or *Q* with *hā bu* and *R* with *hau;* or *Q* with *kā* and *R* with *hvā;* etc. In all these substitutions, *P* and *P** remain the same. But there are other chants where part of the same structure is retained, but *P* and *P** are replaced with, respectively, *u hu vā hā bu* and *u hu vā hā vu vā,* or *hā vu vā* and *hā hā vu vo vā hā yi.* In other words, this abstract representation represents the invariant structure of a number of chants that can be derived by rules of various types.

Mantras For Hanumān

I have provided such abstract structures elsewhere (see Staal 1983b) and mention them in the present context only to illustrate how some ritual chants consist of elaborate structures constructed from single *stobhas*. The ritual meaning of such mantras does not lie in their language or even in their poetic or metrical structure but in the sounds, with their themes and variations, repetitions, inversions, interpolations, and the particular distribution of their elements.

Such meaningless syllables or elements are not confined to the Sāmaveda. In the *śastra* recitations of the Ṛgveda, there are insertions of *-o* or *-om,* as we have already seen, and of *śoṃsavo,* which means something (let us both recite) but which is treated as a similarly meaningless element, occurs in various forms (e.g., *śośoṃsāvo*) and is responded to by the Adhvaryu with such formulas as *othāmo daiva, āthāmo daiva, othāmo daiva made, modāmo daivotho,* and other "bizarres contortions liturgiques," as Caland and Henry (1906, I.232, n. 8) called them. In the *Āśvalāyana* tradition of the Ṛgveda, the Hotā priest murmurs before the beginning of his first *śastra: su mat pad vag de* (Caland & Henry, I.231). Each *śastra* recitation, moreover, has its own peculiarities, which have nothing to do with syntax or translatory meaning. During the noctural rounds in the more advanced Soma rituals, for example, the first quarter verse is repeated in the first round, the second in the second, and the third in the third (see Staal 1983a, I.663–80, II.750–52). In the Sāmaveda chants, the choreography of the mantras becomes richer and more varied. The chants themselves are preceded by *o hṃ,* and certain sequences by *hṃ.* The patterns become so complex that the priests keep track of them by constructing figures, called *viṣṭuti,* with the help of sticks on a piece of cloth (for illustrations see Staal 1983a, I.Figures 48–51). In many melodies (called *gāyatra*), the *udgītha* or second portion of the chant, sung by the Udgātā, is *o vā o vā o vā hṃ bhā o vā.*

In musical chants, the occurrence of such sounds is of course not surprising. Their function is simply to fill out the melody when there is no text. This is found all over the world. The only systematic differences between such melodic insertions are those induced by the phonological structure of the language in which they are inserted. For example, *heisa hopsasa* would not fit in a Vedic or Sanskrit context, but fits quite well in German when sung by Papageno in Mozart's *Zauberflöte*:

> Der Vogelfänger bin ich ja,
> stets lustig, heisa hopsasa!

Heisa hopsasa is reminiscent of the kind of sounds one would use, in German, when addressing a horse or a pack animal. It would be helpful to know what sounds the Vedic Indians used in such circumstances and in other kinds of extraordinary circumstances. Such information would not assist us in explaining the meaning or ritual use of mantras, but it would throw light on their origins and on the associations they may have evoked in ancient India.

CONCLUSIONS

The six types of mantra we have discussed constitute a fairly representative sample of Vedic mantras. Though there are other kinds, these are the types met with most frequently. The reader will have noticed that the first examples are closer to ordinary language in ordinary use, but each next illustration in the sequence is less like ordinary language, more devoid of translatory meaning, and more characteristically "mantra."

This material enables us to derive some general conclusions, which I shall present under three headings: Vedic and Tantric Mantras; Mantras and Speech Acts; and Mantras and Language.

CONCLUSION 1: VEDIC AND TANTRIC MANTRAS

It is not possible to institute a proper comparison between Vedic and Tantric mantras without presenting and discussing a similar body of Tantric material, and this would be beyond the scope of this essay. However, the Vedic material is sufficient to show that certain alleged differences between the two kinds of mantras, in fact, do not exist.

Wheelock (Chapter Three of this volume) says that "the Vedic mantra truthfully *describes* and thereby actualizes a bandhu between ritual object and cosmic entity," and that the Vedic mantra "stands as a *means* to the ends of the sacrifice. The Tantric mantra, on the other hand, as the essence of the ritual procedure, is an object of value *in itself*."

It is clear that these expressions are not applicable to most of the mantras we have considered. Wheelock's terms are obviously inspired by the *brāhmaṇa* literature and not products of his own fancy. However, that does not make them any more relevant. *Brāhmaṇa* interpretations are more fanciful than anything contemporary scholars have yet come up with. Of course, the authors of the *Brāhmaṇas* knew the ritual uses of the mantras (unlike some contemporary scholars), but they tried to go beyond this and interpret these uses. Their attempts, if they are not ad hoc, in general are rationalizations. Most mantras, for example, do not describe nor do they refer to cosmic entities. Moreover, the further we proceed along the entries of our list, the more obvious it becomes that these mantras are ends in themselves. The Udgātā continues to chant long after the golden man has been laid down. There are no specific ritual acts with which any of these mantras are individually associated, and that could explain their occurrence—just as there are no events in the life of Christ that explain any bars or themes in the C major aria "*Geduld!*" for tenor and cello from Bach's *St. Matthew Passion*. Vedic and Tantric mantras, therefore, are not different in terms of the characteristics alleged by Wheelock.

According to Padoux (1963, 296), Śaivite mantras are different from

Vedic mantras because a Vedic mantra is essentially a verse or a group of verses: "un verset ou un groupe de versets." However, as we have seen, this is applicable only to the textual sources of some Vedic mantras. It does not apply to prose mantras, to *stobhas,* or to any of the numerous sounds and noises that pervade the other ritual uses of the Vedas. Moreover, even if a Vedic mantra seems to be a verse, in its ritual use it is not treated as a verse at all. It is treated in the same manner as other sound sequences that never were verses, even to begin with. The counting of syllables that features in the ritual use of (6) *indra juṣasva . . .* is not similar to the counting of syllables that we find in true versification; it is similar to the counting of syllables that is applied to *stobhas* and is typical of their ritual use. Even if *stobhas* are interpreted, as e.g. in *Chāndogya Upaniṣad* 1.13.1–4, the interpretations should not be taken symbolically (as was done by the philosopher Śaṅkara in his commentary on this passage) but should be explained in terms of syllable counting (see Faddegon 1927; Gren-Eklund 1978–79). In other words, in all these mantras, language, whether versified or not, is not treated in the same manner as ordinary language. Vedic and Tantric mantras, therefore, cannot be different on account of the fact that Vedic mantras are "in verse."

A functional difference between Vedic and Tantric mantras may seem to be that the latter are used not only in ritual, but also in meditation. Now, meditation is not so different from ritual as is often assumed and it, too, is alluded to in the Vedas (see, e.g., Staal 1975b, 79). Moreover, a characteristic of meditation, viz., that it is silent, also is applicable to ritual acts. Both Padoux and Wheelock have emphasized the silent use of mantras in Tantric ritual. I shall return to this topic in my final conclusion, but it should be emphasized here that silence plays a very important role in Vedic mantras, too. Many Vedic mantras are *anirukta* (not enunciated), *upāṃśu* (inaudible), and are recited *tuṣṇīm* (in silence), or *manasā* (mentally). The *brahman* priest is in principle always silent. Though all the deities "love what is out of sight" (*parokṣapriyā devāḥ*), Prajāpati is the one who has a special preference for silent mantras and silence (perhaps, because he was not an Aryan deity and most mantras are Aryan imports). True, the Ṛgveda says, "If these mantras of ours remain unspoken/ they will bring no joy, even on the most distant day" (10.95.1; quoted by Findly, Chapter One, page 26). But the use of mantras in Vedic ritual presents a very different picture. Mantras are often transformed, made unrecognizable, hidden, truncated, decapitated, quartered, and reduced until literally nothing is left. I shall not belabor this point since it has been illustrated earlier in this article and dealt with comprehensively in the literature (see especially Renou 1949a and Renou 1954d, with Silburn; compare also Howard 1983).

In terms of the characterizations mentioned, then, it is not easy to make a clear distinction between Vedic and Tantric mantras. In terms of form, the similarities are striking. I am not familiar with comprehensive lists of Tantric mantras, but in the Vedic domain, such lists exist. Leaving aside Bloomfield's monumental *Vedic Concordance*, and concentrating on *stobhas* only, for example, we have the *Stobhānusaṃhāra*, published by Satyavrata Sāmaśramin in the *Bibliotheca Indica* (Volume II, 1874, 519–42) and made accessible by van der Hoogt ([1929] 1930). I shall supply some of the *stobhas* listed in this work in order to give an idea of their forms. The reader can compare them with Tantric mantras, such as those listed by Padoux (1963, 339–61) and Bharati (1965, 119):

ā	*(e)re*	*hā-u*	*iṣ*	*phat*
as	*hā*	*hṃ*	*iṭ*	*pnya*
auhovā	*hahas*	*ho-i*	*kāhvau*	*um*
bhā	*hai*	*hum*	*kit*	*up*
dada	*hā-i*	*hup*	*mṛs*	*vava*
(e)bṛ	*ham*	*hvau*	*nam*	*vo-i*
(e)rā	*has*	*ihi*	*om*	

The stobha *dada* inspired Faddegon to coin the felicitous expression *Ritualistic Dadaism* (Faddegon 1927; cf. Gren-Eklund 1978–79).

Most of these *stobhas* and most of the Tantric *bīja*-mantras are not words of Sanskrit but have been constructed in accordance with the phonological rules for Sanskrit. I have come across two apparent exceptions to this rule, one in the *Stobhānumsaṃhāra* (just quoted in the list), and one discussed by Padoux. The first is *pnya*. I do not believe that *pna-* occurs in Sanskrit in initial position, and neither does *pnya-*. In middle position both are available, e.g., *svapna* (sleep, dream) and *svapnya* (a vision in a dream); the latter occurs in the Atharvaveda, and is rare. Perhaps *pnya* was constructed by a Sāmavedin who heard *svapnya* and mistakenly assumed that this form consisted of the familiar reflexive pronoun *sva-* and a hypothetical *-pnya*.

The unphonological mantra studied by Padoux is certainly not pronouncable: *rkhkṣem*. However, its analysis (Padoux 1963, 356–58) is both pronouncable and clear in Tantric terms, *ra-kha-kṣem*. I, therefore, believe that we are entitled to retain the general conclusion that mantras are constructed in accordance with the phonological rules of Sanskrit.

All natural languages share some phonological properties (see, e.g., Chomsky and Halle 1978, part IV). Are there also universal mantras? It may seem premature to ask such a question since, outside the Vedic realm, mantras have been studied so haphazardly. Moreover, we should exclude historical influences, borrowing and exports: For example, mantras have been exported from Sanskrit into Chinese, Korean, Japanese, or Tibetan. Some of these have been modified to make them fit more comfortably within the phonological structure of the recipient languages. All of them, incidentally, illustrate T. R. V. Murti's view that "Buddhism is Hinduism for export." However, Vedic and Sanskrit have no monopoly in the export of mantras. There are purely Chinese mantras in Taoism and, according to Parpola, the famous mantra OṂ may have been imported into Vedic and Sanskrit from the Dravidian (Parpola 1981).

At present, I have only one possible candidate for a universal mantra: *hṃ* (with its variants *him* and *hum*). This mantra is common in Vedic and Tantric contexts. It is intoned at the beginning of many chants. But is not confined to India, or even Asia. In the *Zauberflöte,* Papageno chants:

> Hm hm hm hm – – – –
> – – – – – – – – –!

Hṃ is not confined to the old world, since, as Paul Attinello informs me, in 1930 the American composer Ruth Crawford-Seeger composed *Chant 1930,* which begins "Hum Hum Hum." The universality of this mantra may be due to its onomatopeoic representation of a kind of heavy breathing. Or, perhaps, the author of a passage of the *Taittirīya Saṃhitā* explained it correctly when referring to the wind:

> *vāyur hiṃkartā*
> (The maker of the sound HṂ is Vāyu)
> (*Taittirīya Saṃhitā* 3.3.2.1 a).

Other candidates for universal mantrahood are *hi* and *ha.* Compare for example the German jingle:

> Unter einen Apfelbaum
> hi ha Apfelbaum
> hatt' ich einen schönen Traum
> hi ha schönen Traum.
>
> (Under an appletree
> hi ha appletree
> I had a wonderful dream
> hi ha a wonderful dream)

Hi and *hay* are common in Peyote songs, which in general consist of meaningless syllables, especially among the Arapaho (see Nettl 1953). *Ha* is also found on Tierra de Fuego. When Waldon and Drayton landed there in 1838 from H.M.S. *Beagle,* "a group of natives took their arms and jumped with them in time to the following song:

> "Ha ma la ha ma la ha ma la ha ma la
> O la la la la   la la la la" (Bowra 1966, 388).

Another possible candidate, OṂ itself, is also akin to breathing. It figures predominantly in *prāṇānyāma* recitations (see Staal 1983a, I.283, 380, Plate 62).

It is often assumed, albeit tacitly, that Tantric mantras are very different from the other mantras of medieval Hinduism. However, there are similarities. The so-called Purāṇic mantras, or mantras prescribed in the Purāṇas, are a case in point. Whereas, they are literally meaningful, unlike the Tantric *bīja*-mantras, they are treated as if they were devoid of meaning. This is shown by the fact that the following mantras (provided with their translatory meaning):

namaḥ śivāya (homage to Śiva)
oṃ namaḥ śivāya (OṂ! Homage to Śiva)
oṃ namo nārāyaṇāya (OṂ! Homage to Nārāyaṇa)
oṃ namo bhagavate vāsudevāya (OṂ! Homage to Lord Vāsudeva)
śrīrāmajayarāmajayajayarāma ([long] live Śrī Rāma, live Rāma, Rāma live!)

are *not* distinguished from each other (as Western scholars are likely to assume) by the different deities to which they refer or by their "translatory meanings," but by the fact that these mantras are, respectively, five-syllabic (*pañcākṣara*), six-syllabic (*ṣaḍakṣara*), eight-syllabic, twelve-syllabic, thirteen-syllabic, etc. (Kane 1930–62, V.1958, 1962, n. 219, 1775). Just like Vedic and Tantric mantras, these Purāṇic mantras are treated not like utterances of language but as if their main characteristic were the number of their syllables. This is both characteristically Indian and characteristically "mantra."

To sum up, it is not possible to make a systematic distinction between Vedic, Tantric, and other Hindu mantras. I have not taken the Buddhist evidence into account, but I am pleased to record that Wayman, despite numerous controversial and ad hoc interpretations, has similarly stressed the continuity between Vedic and Buddhist mantras and has concluded his survey of Budhist Tantric mantras by saying, "It is . . . obvious from the present study that the later religious practices of India, such as the Buddhist *Tantra,* have a profound debt to the Vedic religion" (Wayman 1976, 497).

The Buddhist Yogācāra philosophers made theoretical distinctions also reminiscent of Vedic notions. They distinguish, for example, *arthadhāraṇī,* (meaning(ful)-memorizations), which consist of nouns, words, and phonemes not yet formulated or even expressed mentally, from *mantra-dhāraṇī,* which are similar but more effective: The Bodhisattvas use these to alleviate the afflictions of beings. This distinction implies a difference between *dhāraṇī* and *samādhi* or "concentration": Whereas, the latter is always associated with thinking (*cittasaṃprayukta*), the former, according to these theorists, may be associated with thinking or dissociated from thinking (*cittaviprayukta*). In other words, some *dhāraṇī* are meaningful and others are meaningless, but all are treated similarly and belong to the same category (see Lamotte 1966–76, IV.1857–59). This is clearly similar to the Vedic and Tantric use of mantras, which also is characterized by its independence from the distinction between meaningful and meaningless.

The use of the concept of meaninglessness to refer to certain kinds of mantras is not new. In the *Nirukta* (1.15), an early work of the Vedic period, and again in the *Mīmāṃasāsūtra* (1.2.31–39), reference is made to the doctrine of Kautsa that "mantras are meaningless" (*anarthakā mantrāḥ*; for a fuller discussion see Staal 1967, 24–26, 45–47). This view has always remained the view of a minority, for most Indian commentators and philosophers have tried hard to provide mantras with meaning, even if it meant invoking the improbable or the impossible. I have already referred to the *Brāhmaṇas* with their ad hoc interpretations, contradictions, and rationalizations. In the later literatures of Hinduism and Buddhism, such rationalizations continue to develop, and they tend to become more systematic. They are plentiful in Śankara (referred to in passing, on page 60). In Buddhist philosophy, a distinction is made between explicit meaning (*nītārtha*; Tibetan: *ṅes don*) and implicit meaning (*neyārtha*; Tibetan: *draṅ don*; see, e.g., Murti 1955, 254; Ruegg 1969, 56; 1973, 58). In Buddhist Tantrism, this developed into full-fledged systems of hermeneutics that are similar to the discussions in Hindu Tantrism on *sandhābhāṣā*.

All such systems and concepts derive from metaphysics and are not directly concerned with mantras. Steinkellner (1978b) studied one such system of hermeneutics, due perhaps to Candrakīrti, which distinguishes one literal and three "Tantric" meanings. This system formed the basis for the Guhyasamāja school and was adopted by all Indian and Tibetan exegetes from the eighth century onward. Scholars should note that, as in the case of the *Brāhmaṇas*, nothing is sacrosanct about such interpretations. They are the predictable professional views of philosophers, theologians, priests, and exegetes all over the world. They need not be taken seriously as possible explanations, because they themselves stand in need of an explanation. They do not throw any light on the nature of mantras, for example.

There are more important kinds of evidence that have to be taken into account before we can conceptualize or adequately picture the history of the Indian mantra from Veda to Tantra, Hindu as well as Buddhist. Foremost among these kinds of evidence are the techniques of chanting and recitation in the context of which many mantras developed. The relevance of such evidence is clear in the case of the Sāmavedic *stobhas*, which can only be understood within the context of the chants and melodies (*sāman*) of the Sāmaveda (see, e.g., Staal 1961, Chapter 8). For Buddhist chants, Paul Demiéville has collected the relevant facts in two articles, published with an interval of half a century between them (Demiéville 1930 and 1980). The evidence from chant and recitation (or "hymnology," in the words of Demiéville) is far too rich and varied to be taken into account in the present context; but it demonstrates, among other things, the importance of musical categories for explaining some of the characteristics that distinguish mantras from language. The close relationship between mantras and music partly reflects the general relationship between ritual and music, a topic that also is much too large to consider here (cf. Staal 1984b). All we can do in the present context is emphasize that mantras cannot be understood unless their musical character is taken into account. This explains in turn why mantras cannot be explained wholly or, perhaps, even partly in terms of language.

Before getting involved in discussions and controversies about uses, functions, and meanings—indeed before trying to understand them—a complete inventory of mantras (Vedic, Tantric, Buddhist, and Hindu—whatever labels outsiders have affixed) is an obvious desideratum. On the Vedic side, most of the work has been done in Bloomfield's *Vedic Concordance* and through such works as van der Hoogt 1929, already cited. On the Tantric side, let us express the hope that the task will be undertaken by the workgroup "Equipe de Recherche 249," recently organized by André Padoux under the auspices of the CNRS at Paris. To put lists of mantras in proper perspective, their phonological analysis would have to be undertaken, and the result compared with statistical letter and word approximations of different orders for Sanskrit (such as have been provided for English by Miller & Chomsky 1963, 428–429). All that is needed to carry out the latter task is a good edition of a romanized Sanskrit text (I would recommend, on the Vedic side, Weber's edition of the *Taittirīya Saṃhitā* in *Indische Studien,* Volumes 11 and 12, 1871–1872) and a computer. I am tempted to predict that the result of such work would demonstrate that it is impossible to distinguish among Vedic, Buddhist, Hindu, and Tantric mantras, and that statistical approximations have nothing to do with it. But, who can tell?

Whatever the difficulty of drawing boundaries, it remains a curious fact that monosyllabic mantras of the *stobha* type re-emerged in Tantrism after apparently lying dormant for more than a millenium. It is their popularity that stands in need of an explanation not their occurrence somewhere on the subcontinent, for traditions of Sāmaveda chanting have been handed down without interruption from Vedic times and continue to the present day. Knowledgeable Sāmavedins have always been rare, secluded, orthodox, and reluctant to divulge their art; but we need only assume that one became a Tantric or Buddhist and chanted *stobhas* for the edification or entertainment of his fellow *sādhakas* or monks. Though controversial, this would not be unheard of, for the Buddha himself had on several occasions asked a young novice with a beautiful voice to come to his cell at night and chant. An opportunity for transmission, in such places as Banaras or Kanchipuram, therefore, always was available; that these mantras found their way into meditation is also not surprising, especially in Buddhist monasteries; an explanation is required only for their subsequent diffusion. This will be provided after we have come to understand mantras better.

CONCLUSION 2: MANTRAS AND SPEECH ACTS

The thesis that mantras are speech acts, an idea espoused elsewhere in this volume (Wheelock, Chapter Three; Alper, Chapter Ten), needs clarification before it can be subjected to closer scrutiny. Some such clarification has been provided by Wheelock in an earlier article (Wheelock 1982). Wheelock began his disucssion with Austin's distinction between locutionary, illocutionary, and perlocutionary acts and concentrated on Searle's taxonomy of illocutionary acts as "perhaps the most significant advance over Austin's primitive classification" (Wheelock 1982, 54). In order to clarify this, we shall modify slightly Austin's original formulation into saying that speech acts have three kinds of force: the locutionary, the illocutionary, and the perlocutionary. The illocutionary force of a speech act is concerned with the effect the speaker intends to produce in the hearer. Searle's classifications of speech acts is based on the assumption that all speech acts are concerned with such effects, viz., with *intention.*

Adopting Searle's classification, Wheelock has pointed out that there are several basic differences between "ritual speech acts" and "ordinary speech acts." For example, "the very basic requirement that an ordinary speech event involves a speaker and a hearer is one that is often lacking in ritual speech acts" (Wheelock 1982, 58). And also, "the most essential distinguishing feature of ritual utterances is that they are speech acts that convey little or no information" (ibid.). Wheelock has also referred, with apparent approval, to Tambiah's view that "in ritual, language appears to be used in ways that violate the communication function" (p. 57). Wheelock continues to refer to "ritual speech acts," and he assumes that mantras also are speech acts.

I entirely agree with Wheelock that mantras do not always require a speaker and a hearer and do not necessarily convey information; and with Tambiah that they need not be communicative. But Wheelock could have gone a simple step further and recognized that mantras are not speech acts at all. This follows from Searle's view, because according to Searle, all speech acts involve intention; since all mantras do not, mantras cannot be speech acts. Searle's assumption that all speech acts involve intention is based, in turn, upon his view that all language is communicative, where "communication" includes what has traditionally been regarded as "expression." I believe with Chomsky (1975, 57) that Searle's use of the term is unfortunate, because "the notion 'communication' is now deprived of its essential and interesting character." Searle's views, therefore, do not provide sufficiently solid grounds for concluding that mantras are not speech acts.

Taking *communication* in the traditional sense, as involving a speaker and a hearer (the sense that Tambiah undoubtedly and Wheelock very probably had in mind), it should be obvious that the view that all language is for communication is not a truism. In fact, the rationalist tradition in Western philosophy has never espoused that view but instead propounded that language is a system for the expression of thought (see, e.g., Chomsky 1964, Chapter 1; 1966). We do not have to take sides on this important issue in the present context. All we want to know is what happens to the relationship between mantras and speech acts if we reject the assumption that communication is the only function of language. For example, if the expression of thought is another equally important function of language, or even its main function, it is incumbent upon us to find out whether mantras and speech acts always, sometimes, or ever express thought.

The answers to such questions are not obvious. They can only be reached when the issues are formulated more carefully and precisely. A framework for doing this that is more satisfactory than Searle's has been provided by S.-Y. Kuroda. Kuroda (1975; 1979) distinguishes three functions of language: the communicative, the objectifying, and the objective. The communicative function presupposes the objectifying, which involves intention; and both presuppose the objective, which expresses meaning, but involves neither intention nor communication. Kuroda has argued on purely grammatical grounds that the objective function is found in narrative style, and probably in legal decrees, too. He furthermore has suggested that "the 'magical' use of language in primitive rituals" may have to be understood along similar lines (Kuroda 1979, 16).

If it is true that all language use presupposes such an objective function, the question naturally arises whether mantras do. However, this is clearly not the case, because mantras often have no meaning. We, therefore, arrive once more, and without depending on Searle, at the conclusion that mantras are not speech acts.

It is not only the case that mantras are not speech acts; in the Indian view, a mantra is not even an act, viz., a ritual act (*karman*). That mantras are not acts is obvious from their ritual uses, but it also is explicitly stated in the *Śrautasūtras* and in the Mīmāṃsā. The *Śrautasūtras* formulate the requirement that there should be a 1:1 correspondence between mantras and acts; e.g., *ekamantrāṇi karmāṇi* (acts are accompanied by single mantras) (*Āpastamba Śrautasūtra* 24.1.38). There are exceptions, always formulated explicitly, in accordance with *vacanād ekaṃ karma bahumantram* (when it is explicitly stated, one act corresponds to several mantras) (*Āpastamba Śrautasūtra* 24.1.44). It also is laid down that the beginning of the act should coincide with the end of the mantra, *mantrāntaiḥ karmādīn saṃnipātayet* (*Āpastamba Śrautasūtra* 24.2.1). This topic is taken up in the *Mīmāṃsāsūtra, adhyāya* 12, *pāda* 3, beginning with *sūtra* 25. After discussing the general case, the *sūtrakāra* addresses a number of special cases, and continues in the next *pāda* with a consideration of mantras that do not accompany acts (*akarmasaṃyuktāḥ*: 12.4.1). The discussion ends only to make room for the next topic, a discussion of the complexities arising from the eleven anuses of the *ekādaśinī* ritual (12.4.6).

It is likely that the idea that mantras are succeeded by acts is related to a notion we find elsewhere, viz., that "magical rites" are succeeded by "technical operations." Tambiah has drawn attention to Malinowski's analysis of the relation between Trobriand magic and practical activity, which shows that "the whole cycle of gardening or of canoe building must be seen as one long series of activities which form a regular pattern of $M \rightarrow T$, $M \rightarrow T$, $M \rightarrow T$, $M \rightarrow T$: where M stands for the magical rite and T for the technical operation that succeeds it" (Tambiah 1968, 1985, followed by detailed examples).

As we have seen, even mantras that accompany acts only occasionally refer to those acts. This is further corroborated by the lack of any general term for such mantras. A technical term exists, on the other hand, for *ṛks* that refer to (or address, *abhivad-*) the accompanying act: They are called *rūpasamṛddha* (perfect in form). This often means no more than that the mantra contains a particular word. For example, Ṛgveda 1.74.3 contains the word *ajani* (is born) and is recited when Soma "is born." *Aitareyabrāhmaṇa* 1.16 (3.5) refers to such cases in the following terms, *etad vai yajñasya samṛddhaṃ yad rūpasamṛddhaṃ yat karma kriyamānam ṛg abhivadati,* (the perfection of ritual is when it is perfect in form, viz., when the *ṛk* refers to [addresses] the act that is being performed) (cf. Kane 1930–62, V, Pt. II.1097).

Though mantras are not speech acts, Austin's ideas may throw light on mantras in another respect. Austin originally was interested in performatives, which he contrasted with constative utterances. Later, he arrived at the conclusion that all speech acts exhibit both features or forces. Performatives are speech acts that perform acts in saying something (e.g., promising or baptizing). They cannot be false, but they can go wrong, or be "unhappy." Austin formulated six conditions for the *felicity* of performatives. The first four are

A.1. There must exist an accepted conventional procedure having a certain conventional effect, that procedure to include the uttering of certain words by certain persons in certain circumstances, and further,

A.2. the particular persons and circumstances in a given case must be appropriate for the invocation of the particular procedure invoked.

B.1. The procedure must be executed by all participants both correctly and

B.2. completely (Austin 1962, 14–15).

It is clear from what has been said earlier that mantras are not performatives: They do not perform acts and need not say anything. However, their use is governed by conditions that are similar in part to Austin's four conditions. The chief differences are that mantras need not have an effect, or a visible effect (the Mīmāṃsā thinkers devote much discussion to such *adṛṣṭa* (invisible) effects); what is uttered need not be words; and there need not be more than one person uttering a mantra. It is certainly a necessary condition for the use of mantras, on the other hand, that only the appropriate person can properly use them (e.g., the Adhvaryu priest; see earlier, page 51). In general, only *brahmans* can utter or hear Vedic mantras. Within a given ritual performance, only the appropriate priest can use the prescribed mantras at the proper place and time. In order to be able to discharge this priestly function, a person has to be eligible and elected beforehand. The election of priests constitutes a special ceremony (*ṛtvigvaraṇa*) that takes place at the beginning of a ritual performance (Staal 1983a, I.313–16).

While Austin emphasized, in his illustrations, the appropriateness of the speaker (e.g., a bridegroom saying "Yes, I do," or a person naming a ship), Indian theorists have been equally concerned about persons hearing or receiving mantras as about those who recite or give them. The restrictions in Veda and Tantra are similar, but they are not always the same. No mantras may be learned from books. They can only be learned, at the appropriate time, by eligible students from eligible teachers. Members of low castes, or people beyond the pale of caste (such as outcastes or foreigners) may be punished for hearing Vedic mantras even inadvertently (e.g., by having molten lead poured into their ears). Among Vedic *brahmans,* additional restrictions obtain. The Sāmavedins of Kerala, for example, will not teach their mantras to Ṛgvedins, thereby further endangering the continued existence of their own Veda. In Tantrism (as in Maharishi's Transcendental Meditation), a person is given his own mantra and is not supposed to divulge it at any time.

All such conditions are similar to thoses formulated by Austin—only they go much further. Mantras should be pronounced correctly and completely; but, in addition, they should be recited with the correct degree of loudness, at the correct pitch, and at the correct pace (*Āpastamba Śrautasūtra* 24.1.8–15 translated in Staal 1982 23–24). Moreover, they, or their specifically prescribed portions (e.g., *bhakti* in the Sāmaveda), should be recited in a single breath (see Staal 1983a, I.311, 602, 622). All such requirements that govern the use of mantras resemble the conditions formulated by Austin, but they are more extensive and more stringent than anything that applies to normal use of a natural language, such as English or Sanskrit.

Austin's ideas on the uses of language have been extended considerably and modified by philosophers, linguists, and logicians. A general term sometimes used to refer to this area of investigation is *pragmatics.* I shall adopt the use of this term and extend it so that it can be applied to mantras. We may now formulate a general conclusion: Mantras are subject to much more stringent pragmatic constraints than are natural languages.

As long as we are geared to contemporary theories, fashionable ideas, or anachronisms, we should address the suggestion that mantras are *Sprachspiele* (Chapter Ten of this volume). I believe that it is feasible to defend this view only because Wittgenstein's notion of *Sprachspiel* is exceedingly hazy and flexible. There are few things that *Sprachspiele* are not and cannot do. However, what they are—in short, what prevents anything else from being a *Sprachspiel*—is almost totally unclear. As for myself, I must confess that even in my present state of bewilderment about mantras, I understand them better than *Sprachspiele*. It, therefore, appears to me that to maintain that mantras are *Sprachspiele* is to commit the fallacy of trying to explain obscurum per obscurius.

CONCLUSION 3: MANTRAS AND LANGUAGE

One assumption underlies all discussions on mantras I am familiar with—the assumption that mantras are a special kind of language. I suspect that this assumption is false and shall adduce some reasons in support of this suspicion.

First of all, the domain of mantras is in one sense wider than that of language. Human languages are characterized by properties that fall into four groups: the phonological, syntactic, semantic, and pragmatic. Mantras share with language only phonological and some pragmatic properties. In terms of syntactic or semantic properties, most mantras are not well-formed, as we have seen. It follows from this that the domain of mantras is wider than that of language in the following sense; anything that has certain phonological and pragmatic properties can be a mantra, but it becomes language only if it possesses in addition certain syntactic and semantic properties.

There are things that possess syntactic and phonological properties that are different from language, though they may share semantic properties with language; e.g., mathematical expressions. In mathematics, conditions of well-formedness for terms and formulas correspond to phonological and syntactic properties of natural languages, as in the following examples:

		Well-formed	*Ill-formed*
mathematical:	terms	(a + b)	(a +)
	formulas	(a + b) = c	(a + b)
phonological		*bham*	*hbam*
syntactic		*so gacchati* = he goes	*gacchati tam* = goes him

Other things share semantics, syntax, and pragmatics with natural language, but deviate morphologically and phonologically. An example is the saying popular among Indian logicians:

asmākūnām naiyāyikeṣām arthani tātparyam
śabdani kaś cinta
(Us logickers is intend on meening
whot kare are saund?)

This is not correct, as any student of either Sanskrit or English will recognize. The correct forms are

asmākaṃ naiyāyikānām arthe tātparyam
śabde kā cintā?
(We logicians are intent on meaning,
who cares for sound?)

What we have here differs from mantras in two respects, of which the second is significant in the present context: (1) meaning prevails over form, whereas in mantras form prevails over meaning; (2) this saying is obviously constructed from language, and is parasitic on it, whereas mantras are not obviously constructed from language or parasitic on it.

Similarly, Lewis Carroll's poem in *Through the Looking-Glass,*

Twas brillig, and the slithy toves
  Did gyre and gimble in the wabe:
All mimsy were the borogoves,
  And the mome raths outgrabe—

is phonologically and syntactically similar to English, and its connectives (*and, the, in,* etc.) are English, too; but its "nouns" are not nouns of the English vocabulary. Again, such a poem is obviously constructed in analogy to language, and is parasitic on it—unlike mantras.

It appears likely that mantras are not merely independent of language in a conceptual or logical sense but that they predate language in the development of man in a chronological sense. I have suggested elsewhere (Staal 1979, 1983b) that language is a relatively late acquisition in man, perhaps 100,000 years old, whereas man himself is at least ten times that old. Several facts suggest that ritual is among the important human activities older than language. Animals have rituals similar to human rituals but no language similar to human language (animals have systems of communication, but these differ from language). There are also similarities between the rules of syntax and rules in terms of which certain rituals can be described. Transformational rules, for example, occur in both domains (see Staal 1980; 1984a). Since transformational rules are not widespread in nature or culture, or obvious in any simple sense, this similarity calls for an explanation. These rules of syntax do not smooth the functioning of language but make language more complex and unnatural (see, e.g., Chomsky 1968, 51–53). It stands to reason, therefore, to assume that they are a rudiment of something else, and I have suggested that this something else may be the rules of ritual.

Mantras are defined in terms of ritual and, so, one would expect that they similarly predate language. This expectation is fulfilled. Mantras are in some respects similar not only to language but also to certain sounds animals make, bird songs, for example. Bird songs exhibit structures such as

> *x y x*
> *x y x y*
> *x x y x x y*
> (Thorpe 1966, 353; see also Staal 1985a).

Some such structures are found in language, some in mantras, some in both, and some in neither. The first of these structures, for example, is analogous to the principle of self-embedding in human language. The third exhibits twice the mantra sequence P^2P^* or *hā bu hā bu hā vu vā* we met with earlier (page 50).

Taken by themselves, none of these facts establish conclusively that language developed from mantras or even that mantras predate language, but taken together they become intriguing, and when we combine them with the facts that follow, the probability that such a development took place increases. Another fact may have some bearing on this matter and may be related to the similarities among language, mantras, and bird songs: Birds, like humans, have neural laterization (see Nottebohm 1970).

The development of mantras from language is not easily explained (a point to which I shall return). The development of language from mantras, on the other hand, can be explained by assuming that constraints of a syntactic and semantic nature were imposed on mantras in the course of evolution. Syntactic constraints were already imposed when elaborate structures were constructed from simple *stobhas,* such as we found in the chant *hā bu hā bu hā bu . . .* (6).

The priority of phonological or syntactic over semantic constraints has never been seriously considered because the opposite is always tacitly assumed: Most people take it for granted that language originated with meaning. It is equally possible that meaning was introduced or attached last, as in the following hypothetical scheme of evolution.

I. *Earliest Stage*	*Mantras of Type 1* These are sounds subject to phonological constraints, e.g., *bīja* mantras such as *hiṃ* or *stobhas* such as *bham.*

II. *Intermediate Stage*	*Mantras of Type 2* These are sequences, two-dimensional arrangements, or elaborate constructions of mantras of Type 1, sometimes subject to syntactic constraints, e.g., *hā bu hā bu hā bu bhā bham bham bham* . . . or *huvā yi vācam/ vācaṃ huvā yi/* . . . (*Jaiminīya Araṇyageyagāna* 1.2; Staal 1983a, I.525).
III. *Final Stage*	*Language* These are mantras of Type 2 subject to semantic, further syntactic and different syntactic constraints, e.g., *vācaṃ yaccha* (Control your speech!)

I must leave it to specialists to provide chronological estimates for the duration of the first two stages in this scheme of evolution. The earliest stage represents features that are found among vertebrates and are certainly prehuman. (The term *phonological* in this context refers to any rules that put constraints on the combinations of animal sounds.) The intermediate stage may be anthropoid or characteristic of early man but is probably much older (as suggested by bird song). The final stage corresponds roughly to the last 100,000 years of the development of *homo sapiens*.

In order to evaluate the scheme that I have presented, we need access to many more facts than seem to be available. Animal systems of communication have been widely studied, but we need more information on such topics as the phonology, syntax, and pragmatics of bird song. I have already referred to promising beginnings such as Thorpe 1966; see also Staal 1985a. As I have no expertise in this area, I shall confine myself to such data as have been presented in the present context. This leaves us with plenty of puzzling issues, which stand in need of discussion and clarification.

The first of these issues is raised by an obvious objection that must have occurred to many readers. The mantras I have listed are clearly derived from Sanskrit and not vice versa. How then can the claim be made that language derives from mantras? In order to understand that this claim makes sense, we must recognize a crucial fact that is basic to our entire discussion. The Sanskrit that occurs in these mantras is utilized in an inexplicable and unintelligible fashion, and not in the manner in which a natural language such as Sanskrit is ever normally used. These mantras often say nothing, but even if they say something, they do not say it in the manner in which natural languages say things. Moreover, what is said is not related to nonlinguistic reality in any manner that resembles the normal and usual relationships between language and the world—varied and puzzling as these are. Furthermore, as we have observed on several occasions, these expressions from Sanskrit are used in the same manner in which meaningless mantras (such as *stobhas* and *bīja*-mantras) are used. From the point of view of their ritual use, there is no difference in treatment between mantras we would regard as meaningful and mantras we would regard as meaningless. In the context of a natural language, however, such a state of affairs is inexplicable—nay, unthinkable: The distinction between meaningful and meaningless is fundamental to human language in all its uses. Though believers and scholars may have gotten used to mantras, their use does not, therefore, make sense. Invoking a plethora of religious or other supernatural terms and concepts does not alleviate this unintelligibility.

We have seen that mantras share with language certain phonological and pragmatic properties. But mantras are not used like a special kind of language, such as the language of hunters, carpenters, musicians, or mathematicians. Mantras are used in ritual or meditation to bring about effects that are stated to be "ineffable" and "beyond language." This renders it all the more difficult to conceive of mantras as arising from language.

It may be possible to account for the religious uses of meaningless sounds such as *stobhas* and *bīja*-mantras by some ad hoc hypothesis (e.g., "song, music, dance, and mantras may lead to religious ecstasy"). However, when ordinary expressions of language, such as the mantras exemplified by our illustrations 1 through 5, are used in a manner that is incompatible with their normal linguistic function, it becomes hazardous to even conceive an ad hoc hypothesis. The best we can do is try to explain such uses by assuming that they represent a remnant, vestige, or rudiment of something that existed before language but that was sufficiently similar to language for language to be capable of exercising these inexplicable uses. I believe that this something is mantras. In other words, I am led to assume that there has been a development of *B* (human language) from *A* (mantras), followed by the occasional emergence of functions in *B* that are more easily explained in terms of its predecessor, *A*, than in terms of its successor, *B*.

Such a situation is not rare in biology. The earliest vertebrates were fish, and the wings of birds, as well as the limbs of reptiles and mammals, developed from fins. The primary uses of these body parts are clear: Fins are for swimming, wings for flying, and legs for running. In fact, what we find is extraordinary variation. Crocodiles no longer have fins but use their legs for swimming. The earliest crocodiles, such as *Pelagosaurus*, lived in the open seas. Since their legs and tail did not enable them to swim well, they began to live in and around rivers. So here we have a case of the development of *B* (crocodiles' legs) from *A* (fishes' fins), followed by the emergence of functions in *B* (swimming) that are more easily explained in terms of *A* (fins) than in terms of their successors, *B* (legs).

Another interesting case is penguins. These are birds but they cannot fly. Their wings have developed into flippers that enable them to swim extremely well (20 miles per hour, for example). Walking is difficult for penguins, but they can glide on their bellies on ice over long distances with the help of their flippers. So here we have a development from fins into wings, but the wings are mostly used in the manner in which fins are used, and to some extent in the manner of ski poles. This is like people who use language mostly in the manner of mantras (such people exist, as we shall see).

Humans use their arms and legs as they use their language: the former are generally used for walking, running, grasping, catching, gesticulating, etc., and sometimes, archaically, for swimming; the latter is generally used for speaking or thinking and sometimes, archaically, in the manner in which mantras are used. Numerous parallel developments in other animals, and countless more distantly related cases, therefore, support the hypothesis that human language has developed from mantras and still preserves some rudiments of this mantric background.

There are cases outside religion where people use language entirely or almost entirely in the manner in which mantras are used. This resembles the penguins' use of wings as if they were fins, but in the case of humans, it is either considered regressive and pathological or is actually confined to babies. In 1887, Leopold von Schroeder observed striking similarities between mantras and the utterances of mental patients. Such similarities have been noted and commented on by Eggeling, Keith, and others, but mostly in rhetorical fashion. Von Schroeder (1887, 112–14) was more straightforward and serious. He began his discussion with an illustration of mantras, quoting those that are recited by the Adhvaryu priest when the *ukhā* pot, chief vessel of the Agnicayana, is manufactured. Von Schroeder translated from *Maitrāyaṇi Saṃhitā* 2.7.6, but I shall provide here the parallel passages from *Taittirīya Saṃhitā* 4.1.5 l–q and 6 a–d (see Staal 1983a, I.297–99 and cf. Ikari in Staal 1983a, II.168–77):

l. You are the head of Makha

m. You are the two feet of the ritual.

n. May the Vasus prepare you
with the gāyatrī meter
in the fashion of the Aṅgirases!
You are the earth.

May the Rudras prepare you
with the triṣṭubh meter
in the fashion of the Aṅgirases!
You are the sky.

May the Adityas prepare you
with the jagatī meter
in the fashion of the Aṅgirases!
You are heaven.

May the Viśvedevas, common to all men
prepare you with the anuṣṭubh meter
in the fashion of the Aṅgirases!
You are the directions.

You are the unchanging direction.
Make unchanging in me children,
abundance of wealth,
abundance of cattle, heroism,
and similar things for the yajamāna.

o. You are the waistband of Aditi.

p. May Aditi grasp your hole
with the paṅkti meter
in the fashion of the Aṅgirases!

q. Having fashioned the great ukhā
made of clay as a womb for Agni,
Aditi gave it to her sons saying,
"Fire it!"

a. May the Vāyus make you smoke with the gāyatrī meter
in the fashion of the Aṅgirases!
May the Rudras make you smoke with the jagatī meter
in the fashion of the Aṅgirases!
May the Viśvedevas, common to all men,
make you smoke with the anuṣṭubh meter
in the fashion of the Aṅgirases!
May Indra make you smoke in the fashion of the
Aṅgirases!
May Viṣṇu make you smoke in the fashion of the
Aṅgirases!
May Varuṇa make you smoke in the fashion of the
Aṅgirases!

b. May Aditi, the goddess,
in union with the All-gods,
dig you, trench, in the realm of earth
in the fashion of the Aṅgirases!

c. May the wives of the gods, the goddesses,
united with the Viśvedevas,
put you, ukhā, in the realm of earth
in the fashion of the Aṅgirases!

d. May the Dhīṣaṇās, the goddesses,
united with the Viśvedevas,
fire you, ukhā, in the realm of earth
in the fashion of the Aṅgirases!
May the wives, the goddesses,
united with the Viśvedevas,
fire you, ukhā, in the realm of the earth
in the fashion of the Aṅgirases!

Von Schroeder compared these mantras with the following piece written by a patient and quoted by Th. Güntz (1861; I translate from the German):

First Prayer:
Schiller save his soul and consciousness
Jesus save his soul and consciousness
My mother save her soul and consciousness
van der Velde save his soul and consciousness
Tromlitz save his soul and consciousness
Gerstäcker save his soul and consciousness
Voss save his soul and consciousness
Seume save his soul and consciousness
Körner save his soul and consciousness
Arndt save his soul and consciousness
and save the soul and consciousness of all poets of the book of songs.

Second Prayer:
for all the names that are in Schiller's work.

Third Prayer:
for the soul of my family.

Fourth Prayer:
to destroy my consciousness and my ego.

Von Schroeder also quoted a prose passage from a patient at the hospital Rothenberg near Riga (I translate from the German):

> With humility and affection walk the streets, the indicated, with full knowledge go the streets, which favor going the road with humility, and with deep devotion go the streets, which favor to build the church and keep the peace, which indicated the way which is necessary and desirable for that, build the road with God's desire, buy the peace, and then with good spirit build the church, which is favored, and with good intention gain the stage of learning, which could be desirable for that, with devote endeavor give roses to the institution, build God's church and show his submission with much humility, with much submission and humility try to reach that goal, with much submission try to gain that, and with humility walk the way which is required, make use of God's love, with good intentions lead a good life, with right decision take the road which is required, with good intention go the road which is required, use God's love, with progress go the way, of God's love, build the church, God's love, build the church, God's love, build the church and with good intention, God's love, build the church and with good intent, God's love, build the church" [the last two phrases are repeated about eighty times, and it goes on like that for several pages].

When the psychiatrist asked why he wrote the same thing all the time, the patient answered that he did not know anything else.

Though these writings are pervaded by religious notions, no one would regard them as religiously inspired writing. It is likely that we have here a case of regression to an earlier stage of development: Language is used here in the manner of mantras—Vedic mantras, to be precise, for mainly semantics is affected. *Stobha*-like mantras are probably used by other kinds of patients and in cases of aphasia, to which I shall return.

Mantralike uses of language are also found among babies, and here the recapitulation of phylogeny by ontogeny provides even more striking support for the thesis that language has developed from mantras. Nancy Budwig drew my attention to Ruth Weir's study on the babblings and presleep monologues of a two-and-a-half-year-old child, alone in his crib, talking to himself. Here is an example of what he uttered a few minutes before the onset of sleep:

like like
one like
two like
three four like
monkey's like
up up
light light

turn the light
light
all gone all gone
it's all gone it's all gone
it's not all gone
it's not all
stop it stop it
there (squealing)
yayaya wau wau gigouboubou gigouboubou
now it's all gone
all gone (falsetto)
go go go go
all gone all gone all gone all gone
good luck
that's one
two
go go go go (falsetto)
close the door
gee gee gee gee gee gee (Weir 1970, 128).

The following sequence immediately preceeded sleep, and contains more *stobha*-like elements (I have replaced the phonetic transcriptions by approximate spellings):

yiii (squealing)
I I I
did
gi gi gi gi
the baby the baby the baby
(Baby is crying in the adjoining room)
baby the baby baby (six times)
iii
baby baby baby
bay
baby
bay
happy baby
that's the baby
bay
baby
that's the baby
baby
yaa
aa (squealing)
(SLEEP) (Weir 1970, 197).

Mental patients and children often display features reminiscent of earlier stages of evolution, and that may be referred to as archaic. Religion is generally conservative and characterized by archaic features. It is probable that there are other features of religion that can be interpreted as regressive. Glossolalia, or speaking in tongues, is a related form of regression (see May 1956). Mantras are always archaic. They are often attributed to ancestors or primeval sages (such as the Vedic ṛṣis), or are regarded as eternal or as having originated in a golden age (*kṛtayuga* or *satyayuga*). In Sri Lanka, where demons are similarly primeval, mantras are referred to as the "language of the demons" (*yaksā bāsāva*: Tambiah 1968a, 1977).

The archaic nature of mantras is related to the fact that many mystical phenomena are archaic (cf. Staal 1975b). The mystical state is a state of awareness that can be reached or produced with the aid of mantras, a state of consciousness that is "beyond language" or "ineffable." Mantras give access to this ineffable state. To say with Renou, Padoux, and Wheelock that mantras are beyond the boundary of language, at the highest level of speech "situated beyond language and eventually right to the zone of language," or to say that mantras "point backwards to the source of language, which is the source of all creation itself" (ibid.) is not merely a matter of phenomenological, religious, or spiritual metaphor, or using an apt expression for the right congregation; such expressions should be taken literally as asserting that mantras are the predecessor of language in the process of human evolution.

The mystical state is a prelinguistic state of mind that can be reached when language is renounced, through silence, mantras, or rites. Absence of language accounts for most or all of its allegedly blissful nature. But it also explains certain philosophical and theological ideas and doctrines. An example is the belief that mantras are not only eternal and impervious to transformation but that they fail to effect any transformations. Accordingly, mantras do not transform a person or lead to a new existence; on the contrary, they give access to a state or condition that at all times was already there. This simply means, on our interpretation, that the prelinguistic condition continues to exist beneath a state of awareness now steeped in language—just as our animal nature underlies whatever human characteristics are superimposed on it. Man cannot become an animal; he always already is one. This is formulated analogously in terms of Indian philosophy: No one attains release; everyone is already released, only he or she does not know it. Such ideas are found in the Advaita Vedānta and in the Buddhist Mādhyamika school—the philosophical underpinnings for all the schools of the Tantra. In Budhism, the locus classicus is Nāgārjuna's *Mūlamadhyamakakārikā* 16.8:

> baddho na mucyate tāvad abaddho naiva mucyate
> syātāṃ baddhe mucyamāne yugapadbandhamokṣaṇe

(No one in bondage is released just as
no one who is free is released,
if someone in bondage were to be released
bondage and release would be simultaneous.)

For Vedānta, the locus classicus is Gauḍapāda's *Āgamaśāstra* 2.32:

na nirodho na cotpattir na baddho na ca sādhakaḥ
na mumukṣur na vai mukta ity eṣā paramārthatā
(There is no destruction, no origination,
no one in bondage, no one seeking perfection,
no one desirous of release, no one really released—
this is the highest truth.)*

I have come almost as far as the evidence allows us to go, but there is one more question that may be answered, tentatively, within the framework that we have adopted. Not only do mantras lead to a prelinguistic state, so do rites. Mantras and ritual are both archaic and closely related. The question arises What is their chronological relationship? Is there any reason to believe that one predates the other or are both coterminous?

Though it is tempting to address this issue within a broader perspective (see Staal 1984b; 1985b; 1987; 1988a; 1988b; and 1988c), I shall again confine myself to the kind of data we have been discussing in the present context. A remarkable fact characterizes the history and survival of Vedic ritual in India (cf. Staal 1983a, II, *Preface*). In the course of this history, which has lasted for almost three thousand years, the original Soma has been replaced by substitutes, human and animal heads have been replaced by heads made of gold or clay, animal sacrifices have been abolished, numerous rites have been simplified and abbreviated—but mantras have always been scrupulously preserved. This fact can be accounted for if we assume that mantras, in general, are older than rites and, therefore, are more tenaciously adhered to. Such an assumption does not imply that any specific mantra is earlier than any specific rite. Many fire rites, for example, go back to the dawn of civilization and are much older than the Vedic mantras that accompany these rites in the Vedic fire ritual. The general persistence of mantras beyond rites, however, is made intelligible by the assumption that mantras came before rites in the history of evolution. What this means in zoological or ethological terms is left to specialists to speculate about.

Before I leave the topic of the origin of language, I should make it clear that I regard the evidence in support of the hypothesis that mantras are older than language as extremely strong, if not unassailable. Of course, we cannot prove it: Mantras leave no material evidence. The evidence for the priority of monosyllabic mantras over polysyllabic mantras, viz., for the priority of Stage I to Stage II, is less compelling. It is especially in this area that we need more empirical data, on the songs of

**This theme has been discovered by Madison Avenue: "A vacation to Alaska isn't so much getting away from something as it is getting back to something."*

birds, on growling, miauling, barking, and chirping not only of birds, but—who knows?—of grasshoppers as well. To think that monosyllabics are earlier than polysllabics may be an instance of what might be called the fallacy of atomistic reductionism. On the other hand, there may be serious grounds for such a priority. Apart from the evidence from babbling babies, there is one kind of aphasia, for example, in which the patient is in a position to produce and recognize phonemes, but not words; in another kind, he can produce and recognize words, but not sentences (see Jakobson in Jakobson & Halle, 1960). Such facts suggest the priority of Stage I to Stage II.

We are now in a position to return to the question why monosyllabic mantras of Type I re-emerged in Tantrism after apparently lying dormant for more than a millenium. At this point of our investigation, a curious parallelism should spring to the eye of the unprejudiced observer. Just as mantras are often characterized as a deviation from natural language, Tantrism is often characterized as a deviation from "normal Hinduism." It is a fact that in Trantrism, the basic values of Hinduism are reversed. This explains why Hindus feel uneasy about it. Louis Dumont, who has stressed these "renversements de valeur" ([1966, 342] 1980), has also emphasized that they are expecially characteristic of the left-hand forms, adding, undoubtedly correctly: "mais la forme gauche est pour nous la forme pure" (but for us, the left-hand forms are the pure forms) ([1966, 343]).

An interesting feature of the concept of deviation is that it is a symmetrical relation: If *A* deviates from *B, B* deviates from *A*. If we abandon the narrow perspective of the study of Indian religion and adopt a broader, and also more human, perspective, it cannot fail to strike us that drinking wine, eating meat or fish, and making love are natural things to do. To prohibit such acts is to deviate from the natural—a feature of all orthodox religion, and of orthoprax* Hinduism as well. As we have just seen, it is likely that language is a recent offshoot and, to some extent, a deviation from the biological domain of mantras and ritual. Therefore, it is not surprising that the natural acts espoused by Tantrism are not approached through language (pace scholastic commentaries) but are couched in ritual forms and surrounded by mantras. This constitutes a return to the Veda insofar as all those acts were treated similarly in Vedic times.

For the sake of illustration, let us consider the act of *maithuna*, (coupling). Before the *sādhaka* makes love to his *śakti* (*svīyā*, "his own wife," *parakiyā*, "the wife of another," or *sādhāraṇī*, "one who is common": *Mahānirvāṇatantra* 145, n. 7), he touches the principal parts of the two bodies, his and hers, during a ritual ceremony called *nyāsa*. This consists in the "affixing" of mantras or their pronouncing over these parts of the body. Religious scholars are apt to hypothesize that this is a sanctification or consecration of the body. Eliade understands *nyāsa* as a "ritual

*Orthoprax *means adhering to right practice just as* orthodox *means adhering to right doctrine (see Staal 1959).*

projection of divinities into various parts of the body" (1969 [1954, 215; 1958, 210–211]), and Wheelock (this volume) interprets *nyāsa* as "homage." Since mantras also are regarded as deities or the vehicles of deities, and since Vedic times, deities have been closely associated with the human body, there are always texts that can be quoted in support of such views. However, insofar as they are offered as interpretations, it should be obvious that these formulations explain nothing. Padoux is more careful and nearer the truth when he regards *nyāsa* merely as "imposition d'un mantra" (Index, s.v.). Light is thrown on these curious practices when we interpret the affixing of mantras as a simple return to the biological domain of nature and the body.

The Tantric ceremony of *nyāsa* resembles the Vedic domestic (*gṛhya*) rite prescribed in connection with the first saṃskāra, *garbhādhāna* (impregnation; literally, the placing of the embryo) (see, e.g., Kane 1930–62, II, Pt. I.200–206; Gonda 1980a, 367–68; and Index, *s.v.*). This ceremony, which uses mantras from the Ṛgveda (10.184) and the Atharvaveda (5.25), is related to earlier rites, referred to in *Bṛhad-Āraṇyaka-Upaniṣad* 6.4, that intend to bring about the birth of sons of varying quality, or indeed of a daughter. In all cases, the nature of the child is assumed to depend primarily on the food eaten by the parents prior to the sexual act. The best result (a learned and famous son who recites all the Vedas) is believed to be obtained after the parents have eaten a dish prepared from rice and meat, either veal or beef. Then he approaches her, saying,

> I am *ama*, you are *sā*,
> You are *sā*, I am *ama*,
> I am *sāman*, you are *ṛk*,
> I am heaven, you are earth.
> Come, let us get together
> Deposit seed together
> For a male, a son, riches!

The Upaniṣad continues: "Then he spreads her thighs. 'Spread yourself, heaven and earth!' Inserting his member, placing his mouth upon hers, stroking her three times in the direction in which the hair grows, he says:

> 'Let Viṣṇu prepare the womb,
> Let Tvaṣṭṛ shape the forms,
> Let Prajāpati discharge,
> Let Dhātṛ place the seed in you.
>
> Place the seed, Sinīvāli,
> Place the seed, goddess with flowing hair!
> Let the Aśvin twins place the seed in you,
> The two lotus-garlanded gods.

Golden are the kindling woods
Which the Aśvins use to make fire.
We invoke that seed for you
To bring forth in the tenth month.

As earth is pregnant with Agni,
As heaven is expecting Indra,
As wind is the seed of the skies,
I place the seed in you.'" (cf. Staal 1983a, I.76–77).

Kane, who has translated part of this text (omitting the reference to meat and also omitting, "for reasons of decency," the lines that begin "Then he spread her thighs") remarks: "To modern minds it appears strange that intercourse should have been surrounded by so much mysticism and religion in the ancient sūtra" (Kana 1930–62, II, Pt. I.203). Gonda, who also has translated part of the text (including the sex but excluding the meat) remarks: "This consecratory function manifests itself in a large number of cases in which modern man would not expect it. By pronouncing the proper mantra the sexual act is for instance raised to the rank of a rite resuscitating and wielding that particular part of the universal and omnipresent force which is active in the creation of new human life" (Gonda [1963b, 259] 1975b, 263).

Though such expressions may appeal to certain audiences of "modern men," they cannot serve as an explanation for the use of mantras. They merely are a roundabout formulation of the things that have to be explained, padded with products of free association. Considered within a more sober perspective, the mantras used in this context ("I am *ama*, you are *sā* . . ." and "Let Viṣṇu prepare the womb . . .") are mantras of the same type as *devasya tvā savituḥ* (4). They accompany a single act, impregnation or "placing the seed." The rest is music. This music is part of the structure of mantras we are trying to account for.

Nyāsa is a Tantric not a Vedic rite and, therefore, belongs to a different era. It is tempting to speculate that, by the time we arrive at the Tantric period, mantras are called upon to take away the guilt that centuries of moral disapprobation have attached to parts of the body and to bodily functions. No Hindu can engage in the "five Ms" without experiencing a feeling of guilt. To actually enjoy such activities is possible only if these feelings are overcome. Mantras can effect this because they are natural, like music, dance, and song. They exert a hypnotic influence that signals a breaking away from the tyranny of language and a return to the biological domain of the body. This is manifest in the extraordinary close relationship that exists in Tantrism between the limbs (*aṅga*) of mantras and those of the divine body (Brunner 1986).

In both Veda and Tantra, there is a strong desire for enjoyment, in this world and in the next. In the Veda, this desire is fulfilled partly through begetting sons. In the Tantra, it is fulfilled partly by identifying

Yoga with *bhoga,* "enjoyment." After a period during which ascetism and puritanism were encouraged and prohibitions and restrictions on enjoyment commonly were expressed in Jaina, Buddhist and Hindu treatises, Tantric mantras had a liberating effect and answered a need of the times. The Tantric development turned into a ritual development in which mantras played once again a paramount role. The return from the elaborate mantric compositions of the Vedas to the monosyllabic Tantric mantras of Stage I may be explained by the demands for simplicity, popularity, ease of access, and wide diffusion. In another sense, it represents a return or regression to our prehuman ancestors, aptly symbolized by the nostalgic belief that from the present Kaliyuga, that most debased of eras, there will emerge a new Satyayuga, a Golden Age in which we shall be back in our original condition.

APPENDIX: MOON CHANTS, SPACE FILLERS, AND FLOW OF MILK*

The chants that are the subject of this paper belong to the Agnicayana as performed in the Nambudiri tradition; they therefore resort under the as yet unpublished corpus of the Jaiminīya Sāmaveda. The Agnicayana is connected with sāman chants in two respects: indirectly through the Soma ritual, with which it is always associated; and directly because many chants belong specifically to its own tradition. I will not be concerned with the Soma ritual in the present context, but should briefly refer to the chants that characterize it: the *stotra* chants, which the Nambudiris refer to as *stuti.* Each variety of Soma ritual is defined by a particular sequence of *stotra* chants from the Sāmaveda, coupled with *śastra* recitations from the Ṛgveda. The Adhvaryu recites the formulas that relate these two to each other, and to his own ritual activities. For example, before each *stotra* chant begins, the Adhvaryu hands to the Udgātā two blades of *darbha* grass, also called *stotra,* with the words: *ṛksāmayor upastaraṇam asi mithunasya prajātyai,* (you are the bed for the coupling of *ṛk* and *sāman,* for the sake of procreation). (Baudhāyana Śrauta Sūtra 7.8; cf. Staal 1983a, I.625).

The chants that belong to the Agnicayana tradition itself may be studied from various perspectives. First of all, textually and with special reference to the śrauta sūtras that place them in their ritual context. Asko Parpola has recently undertaken such a study with respect to the Jaiminīya Śrauta Sūtra and its commentary by Bhavatrāta, a Nambudiri who lived in the eighth century A.D. or earlier (Parpola 1983b, 700). Secondly, these chants may be studied from a musical point of view. This has been done, with respect to some Jaiminīya chants of the Agnicayana, by Wayne Howard, in a contribution to the same volume in which Parpola's study appeared (Howard 1982). In the following notes, I shall not be concerned with either textual or musical analysis, but with the structure and distribution of some of these chants. My material is

---

**This appendix is a slightly revised version of a paper originally published in Staal,* Felicitation Volume Professor E. R. Sreekrishna *(Madras: Kalakshetra Publications Press, 1983), 18–30.*

based on recordings and notes obtained from the 1975 performance of the Agnicayana in Kerala, described in detail in Staal 1982a (referred to as AGNI). This distribution and these structures do not always correspond closely to the śrauta texts, as a comparison of the following notes with Parpola's study would demonstrate.

When referring to the unpublished chants of the Jaiminīya Sāmaveda, I have adopted the system of reference used in the manuscripts put at the disposal of Asko Parpola by Itti Ravi Nambudiri, the foremost *sāmaga* of Kerala. In these manuscripts—written down in the Malayalam script, without sound notation, and largely from memory (that of Itti Ravi, his elders, and his pupils)—the Jaiminīya Ārcika is divided into 112, the Grāmageyagāna into 59, and the Araṇyegeyagāna into 25 *ōttus* or "songs". I shall chiefly refer to the chants of the Araṇyegeyagāna, which the Nambudiris call *candrasāmāni,* "moon chants". A reference such as AG 25.7 would thus denote the seventh sāman of the twenty-fifth *ōttu* of the Jaiminīya Araṇyegeyagāna.

The first Agnicayana chants (Staal 1983a, I.410–11) are sung immediately after the Adhvaryu has placed a lotus leaf at the centre of the Field of Agni (*agnikṣetra*) over which the bird-shaped altar will subsequently be constructed. The Udgātā enters, and takes up his position to the west of what will be the tail of the bird, against the northern post of the eastern door of what will later become the Havirdhāna shed. From this position, he sings most of the Jaiminīya chants that characterize the Nambudiri Agnicayana. The first chant is based upon a cryptic mantra of the Taittirīyasaṃhitā (4.2.8.2d), which also occurs in the Atharvasaṃhitā (4.1.1), but not in the Ṛksaṃhitā. The Adhvaryu recites it at the same time, while he places the golden breastplate (*rukma*) which the Yajamāna wore at his consecration to the north of the lotus leaf:

brahma jajñānam prathamam purastād
vi sīmataḥ suruco vena āvaḥ
sa budhniya upamā asya viṣṭhāḥ
gataś ca yonim asataś ca vivaḥ

(Born as brahman first in the east,
Vena has shone out of the glimmering horizon.
He has revealed its highest and lowest positions,
the womb of being and non-being.)

This verse is turned into a chant consisting of the five customary parts (1: *prastāva*; 2: *udgītha*; 3: *pratihāra*; 4: *upadrava*; and 5: *nidhana*) by prefixing and affixing *stobha* elements that will be referred to with the help of capital letters, in the following manner:

A: *huve hā yī*
B: *heṣāyā*

C: *au ho vā*
D: *e ṛtam amṛtam.*

I shall refer to the four lines of the verse of TS 4.2.8.2d with the help of lower case letters: a, b, c, and d, respectively. Then the chant can be represented as follows:

prastāva:	A A B a/	
udgītha:	b/	
pratihāra:	c/	(1)
upadrava:	d A A B C/	
nidhana:	D D D/	

We need to adopt one more convention to interpret this correctly: whenever there is a triple occurrence of a *stobha,* viz., an expression of the form X X X, the final syllable of the third occurrence is lengthened. For example, in D D D, the third occurrence ends in *amṛtām,* and not in *amṛtam.*

Written out in full, the above expressions represent the following chant, which is Jaiminīya Grāmageyagāna 33.9.2:

prastāva:	*huve hā yī huve hā yī heṣāyā/brahma jājñānām prāthāmam purāstāt/*
udgītha:	*vi sīmatās suruco vena ā vāt/*
pratihāra:	*sa budhnyā upamā asya vāyīṣṭhāḥ/*
upadrava:	*sataś ca yonim āsātāś ca vīvaḥ huve hā yī huve hā yī heṣāyā au ho vā/*
nidhana:	*e ṛtam amṛtam e ṛtam amṛtam e ṛtam amṛtām/*

The only feature that is not represented in the formula (1) is the lengthening of certain vowels within the lines a, b, c, and d of the mantra. Of course, further abbreviations of this representation are possible. For example, the sequence A A B may be replaced by W. In that case, the chant becomes

1. W a /
2. b /
3. c / (2)
4. d W C /
5. D D D

The advantage of these representations is that they picture the structure of the chant clearly, and enable us to compare the structures of different chants with each other. Such representations also enable us to express in a simple form differences between different traditions and schools. For example, the corresponding Kauthuma-Rāṇāyanīya chant differs from the above Jaiminīya variety only in that two of the *stobha* elements have different forms: A has to be replaced by

A* *huve hā ī*

and B has to be replaced by:

B*: *hi ṣā yā.*

If these substitutions are made in (1), the result is Kauthuma-Rāṇāyanīya Grāmageyagāna 321.2 (in the edition of R. Nārāyaṇasvāmī Dīkṣita).

From now on, I shall not write out the texts in full, but only represent them by symbolic representations, such as (1) or (2).

The second chant of the Udgātā that accompanies the Adhvaryu's rite with the golden breastplate is a musical composition on a single word: *satya,* (truth). The *stobhas* may be referred to by

E: *ho yi*
F: *hā ā vu vā*
G: *e suvar jyotiḥ*

The chant may then be written as

AG 25.24: *satyom* / *satya* E *satya* E *satya* F / G. (3)

How much more abbreviation or simplification should be resorted to, in a case like this, depends entirely on the occurrence or nonoccurrence of other chants of a similar form: If there are no others, there is no point in abbreviating any further, but if there are, it depends on the degree of similarity between them to what extent further abstraction may be helpful in expressing the structure.

After these relatively modest beginnings, the Udgātā bursts into a much longer sequence of songs. These accompany the deposition by the Adhvaryu of the golden man (*hiraṇmayapuruṣa*) upon the lotus leaf, and continue through several subsequent rites. This sequence consists of four parts (Staal 1983a, I.414–17). The first is called the Great Chant (*mahāsāman*: AG 25.7), and the second consists of seven songs (AG 9.1–7), based upon verses of the Puruṣa hymn of the Ṛgveda (10.90), with changes in the text and in the order of these verses. I shall not analyze these two parts here, because it is not easy to abstract a general structure from them.

The third part begins to exhibit marked regularities, partly obscured by irregularities. It is quite possible that the latter have crept in over the centuries, for these chants have been sung for almost three millenia. This third part consists of nine Moon Chants, AG 12.1–9. Four of these,

AG 12.3–6, consist entirely of *stobhas* and are relatively short. Of the remaining five, three (AG 12.7–9) exhibit the same structure, and two (AG 12.1–2) a very similar pattern. I shall confine myself here to the structure that is the most obvious, and that can be represented in a simple manner with the help of our notation if we adopt one further convention, viz., express repetition of elements by superscripts. For example, instead of writing R R R R R for a fivefold repetition of the element R, I shall write R^5.

The structure of each of AG 12.7–9 may now be represented by

$$\underset{X}{P^3(QR^5)^3P^3}\qquad\qquad (4)$$
$$\underset{Y}{P^3(QR^5)^3\,P^2P^*}$$

The use of parentheses is self-explanatory: Everything within parentheses should be repeated as many times as is indicated by the superscript following the closing parenthesis. Thus, $(QR^5)^3$ stands for QR^5 QR^5 QR^5, or QRRRRRQRRRRRQRRRRR. X represents an underlying mantra, different for each of the three songs, and Y represents the *nidhana,* which consists of the final portion of this mantra and/or a *stobha*. The *stobhas,* which exhibit the invariant structure, are P, Q, and R. Of these, P is the same in the three songs:

P: *hā bu.*

P* is a modification of P, which is used in the final round when P is repeated only once and its third occurrence (like the *amṛtam/amṛtām* we considered before) is replaced by

P* *hā vu vā.*

While the structure of the three chants is the same, the remaining *stobhas,* Q and R, are different, in the following manner:

AG 12.7 has Q: *phāt*
R: *phat*
AG 12.8 has Q: *hā bu*
R: *hau*
AG 12.9 has Q: *bhā*
R: *bhaṃ.*

Written out as far as its *stobhas* are concerned, the last chant, for example, becomes

$$\underset{X}{\textit{hā bu}\ (3\times)\ \textit{bhā bhaṃ bhaṃ bhaṃ bhaṃ bhaṃ}\ (3\times)\ \textit{hā bu}\ (3\times)}$$

hā bu (3 ×) *bhā bhaṃ bhaṃ bhaṃ bhaṃ bhaṃ* (3 ×) *hā bu* (2 ×) *hā vu vā*

Y

In this chant, X happens to be the same mantra TS 4.2.8.2d we have met with before. The structure of AG 12.1–2 deviates to some extent from this pattern (4), but it also possesses the characteristic feature $(QR^5)^3$, in the following manner:

AG 12.1 has Q: *u*
R: *ha*
AG 12.2 has Q: *kā*
R: *hvā*

The fourth and last part of this sequence consists of a single chant, similar to the chant for the lotus leaf (3), but with *puruṣa* as the main *stobha:*

AG 25.25: *puruṣom* / *puruṣa* E *puruṣa* E *puruṣa* F / G (5)

After the *agnikṣetra* has been prepared, the ritual continues with the piling up of the five layers of the altar. The bricks are consecrated by the Adhvaryu on behalf of the Yajamāna, and the Udgātā contributes songs to some of these rites. I shall here consider the sequence of chants that is sung when the "Space Filler Bricks" are consecrated. Most of the bricks are consecrated in a specific order, and are therefore numbered, at least conceptually (cf. Staal 1982, Lecture III). The only exceptions are certain bricks, occurring especially in the intermediate layers (i.e., the second, third, and fourth), that are consecrated without an individual mantra and in any order. These bricks are not consecrated without mantras, but the mantras are the same for each brick. There are three: The first two are called *tayādevatā* and *sūdadohasa*. These are used for the consecration of every brick of the altar. The third is the specific "Space Filler" (*lokampṛṇa*) mantra (TS 4.2.4.4n):

lokam pṛṇa chidram pṛṇā 'tho sīda śivā tvam
indrāgnī tvā bṛhaspatir asmin yonāv asīṣadan

(Fill the space! Fill the hole!
Then sit down in a friendly manner.
Indra, Agni, and Bṛhaspati
have placed you in this womb.)

While the Adhvaryu recites these mantras over the Space Filler Bricks, the Udgātā intones eight Space Filler Chants: AG 24.5–6 and AG

25.32–37. The latter six are of the same form as (3) and (5), but other *stobhas* are substituted in the place of *satya* or *puruṣa*:

§3. AG 25.32: *agna* for Agni
§4. AG 25.33: *vāya* for Vāyu, (wind)
§5. AG 25.34: *sūrya* (sun)
§6. AG 25.35: *candra* (moon)
§7. AG 25.36: *nāka* (vault)
§8. AG 25.37: *śukra* (glow or Venus).

The *nidhana* portions are not always the same. At this point it has become obvious that it would be helpful to express the structure of these chants by representing them by means of a general functional expression, e.g., Ψ (X), defined as follows:

Ψ(X) = "X-*oṃ* / X *ho yi* X *ho yi* X *hā ā vu vā* /"

In this expression, X-*OṂ* is obtained from X by replacing the final *-a* of X by *-OṂ*. The different *nidhana* portions may now be substituted, and all the chants of this form that we have so far considered may be represented as follows:

AG 25.24: Ψ(*satya*) G
AG 25.25: Ψ(*puruṣa*) G
AG 25.32: Ψ(*agna*) *e jyotiḥ*
AG 25.33: Ψ(*vāya*) *e rājā*
AG 25.34: Ψ(*sūrya*) *e bhrājā*
AG 25.35: Ψ(*candra*) *e ā bhrājā*
AG 25.36: Ψ(*nāka*) *e pṛṣṭham*
AG 25.37: Ψ(*śukra*) *e bhrāḷā bhrājā*.

Other chants of this form are sung by the Udgātā on the three occasions (on the first, third, and fifth layers of the altar) when the "perforated pebbles" (*svayamātṛṇṇā*) are deposited at the center by the Adhvaryu in collaboration with the "Ignorant Brahmin" (Staal 1983a, I.419, 461, 505; cf. Staal 1978 and 1982, 42–53). Using our notation, these three chants may be represented as follows:

on the first layer: AG 25.21 Ψ(*bhūra*) G (for *bhū*, earth)
on the second layer: AG 25.22 Ψ(*bhuva*) G (for sky)
on the third layer: AG 25.23 Ψ(*suva*) G (for heaven)

In each of these three cases, G represents again *e suvar jyotiḥ*.

The last sequence of songs I shall consider is chanted after the bird altar has been completed and fully consecrated. It is now vibrating with power, ferocious (*krūra*) and dreadful (*ghora*), and has to be pacified and brought under control. To this end the Adhvaryu, assisted by the Pratiprasthāta, pours a continuous libation of goat milk over the furthest western brick of the northern wing. This brick is chosen because it is eccentric, i.e., far from the center of power, and also because it can be easily approached from different sides (Staal 1983a, I.509 sq.). While performing this oblation, the Adhvaryu recites the famous *Śatarudrīya* or *Rudram* (TS 4.5), which derives its popularity partly from the fact that it was later interpreted within the perspective of Śaiva theism (Gonda 1980b). During this oblation and recitation, the Udgātā chants a sequence of fifty-seven sāmans, together called Flow of Milk (*kṣīradhārā*). These chants last very long and continue after the Rudra ceremonies have been completed. Their complete structural analysis would take up more space than is available here, but I wish to draw attention to two of their most striking features.

I shall first take up the one that appears last. The final seventeen of these fifty-seven Flow of Milk chants have the structure of (3) and (5) we have just considered, and incorporate again the chants we have already mentioned. The others can be represented in a straight-forward manner with the help of our notation in terms of Ψ and G:

§41. AG 25.21 (see page 91)
§42. AG 25.22 (see page 91)
§43. AG 25.23 (see page 91)
§44. AG 25.24 (see page 91)
§45. AG 25.25 (see page 91)
§46. AG 25.26: Ψ (*gaur*) G
§47. AG 25.27: Ψ (*ḷoka*) G
§48. AG 25.28: Ψ (*agner hṛdaya*) G
§49. AG 25.29: Ψ (*dyaur*) G
§50. AG 25.30: Ψ (*antarikṣa*) G
§51. AG 25.31: Ψ (*pṛthivī*) G
§52. AG 25.32 (see page 91)
§53. AG 25.33 (see page 91)
§54. AG 25.34 (see page 91)
§55. AG 25.35 (see page 91)
§56. AG 25.36 (see page 91)
§57. AG 25.37 (see page 91)

In this list, I have only incorporated the representation of the "new" sāmans, viz., sāmans we have not yet met with. The other representations have already been provided. Thus far, the survey of these structures conveys an idea of the distribution of a specific chant structure or melody throughout many sections of the Agnicayana ritual. This structure is like a musical theme that appears and reappears, with variations, at many important junctures of the ceremony.

The second structural feature I wish to discuss occurs earlier in the

Flow of Milk chants: in the ten chants § 18-§ 27 (AG 11.1–10). I shall write out the first of these in full, to clearly exhibit its structure:

> § 18. *hā bu* (3 ×) *aham annam* (3 ×) *aham annādo* (3 ×)
> *ahaṃ vidhārayo* (2 ×) *ahaṃ vidhārayaḥ* / *hā bu* (3 ×)
> *yad varco hiraṇyasya* / *yad vā varco gavām uta*/
> *satyasya brahmaṇo varcaḥ* / *tenamāsaṃ sṛjāmasā yi* /
> *hā bu* (3 ×) *aham annam* (3 ×) . . . *vidhārayaḥ* (as
> at the beginning) / *hā bu hā bu hā vu vā*/
> *e aham annam aham annādo ahaṃ vidhārayaḥ* (3 ×)
> *ahaṃ suvar jyotiḥ*/

This chant incorporates a mantra, *yad varco* . . . , from the Jaiminīya Ārcika (107.34), which also occurs in the Kauthuma-Rāṇāyanīya tradition but is neither found in the Ṛgveda nor in the Yajurveda. The structure of the chant exhibits a special feature that may be represented in a simple fashion if we make use of indexed lower case letters to express elements, as follows:

a_1: *aham annam*
a_2: *aham annādaḥ*
a_3: *ahaṃ vidhārayaḥ*.

The special feature of these chants is that the mantra *yad varco* . . . , which I shall refer to as Y, is *preceded* by the structure:

$$a_1^3 \quad a_2^3 \quad a_3^3$$

and *followed* by the structure:

$$(a_1 \quad a_2 \quad a_3)^3.$$

This feature occurs in all the ten sāmans, but the number of elements need not always be three. Using the following abbreviations:

P: *hā bu*
P*: *hā vu vā*
T: *ahaṃ suvar jyotiḥ*,

the general structure of the ten sāmans is expressed by:

$$P^3\ a_1^3 \ldots a_i^3\ P^3\ Y\ P^3\ a_1^3 \ldots a_i^3\ P\ P\ P^*\ (e\ a_1 \ldots a_i)^3 T.$$

We are now in a position to specify the number of elements (i), and the elements themselves, for each of the ten sāmans, as follows:

§18. i = 3 a_1: *aham annam*
a_2: *aham annādaḥ*
a_3: *ahaṃ vidhārayaḥ*
§19. i = 3 a_1: *ahaṃ sahaḥ*
a_2: *ahaṃ sāsahiḥ*
a_3: *ahaṃ sāsahānaḥ*
§20. i = 1 a_1: *ahaṃ varcaḥ*
§21. i = 1 a_1: *ahaṃ tejaḥ*
§22. i = 4 a_1: *manojait*
a_2: *hṛdayamajait*
a_3: *indrojait*
a_4: *aham ajaiṣam*
§23. i = 4 a_1: *diśanduhe*
a_2: *diśauduhe*
a_3: *diśoduhe*
a_4: *sarvāduhe*
§24. i = 1 a_1: *vayo vayo vayaḥ*

This could alternatively be expressed as

i = 3 a_1: *vayaḥ*
a_2: *vayaḥ*
a_3: *vayaḥ*
§25. Same as §24, but with *rūpam* instead of *vayaḥ*
§26. i = 4 a_1: *udapaptam*
a_2: *ūrddhonabhāṃ syakṛṣi*
a_3: *vyadyaukṣam*
a_4: *atatanam*

An irregularity here is that P is *hi hi yā au.*

§27. i = 2 a_1: *prathe*
a_2: *pratyaṣṭhām*

This concludes our notes on these ritual chants. They call for two concluding remarks. The first relates to the psychology of the chanters. All these chants are transmitted orally and learned by heart, together with their order, distribution, interrelationships, and ritual applications and uses. Such an astonishing feat of memorization can only be accounted for by assuming that such abstract structures as we have postulated and expressed by symbolic formulas are actually represented, in some form or other, in the minds or brains of the chanters. This reflects the obvious fact that it is possible to remember such vast amounts of material only because of implicit, underlying regularities.

My second concluding remark relates to the significance of these chants. We have witnessed, even in this relatively small sample, many strange forms, strange from a linguistic point of view, and also strange for anyone who is looking for meaning, especially "religious meaning." It should be obvious that language or religion are not proper categories within which to evaluate the significance of these ritual chants. Rather, their significance lies in the structure and composition of the resulting edifice, and the abstract structural qualities that we have represented by formulas. If there are anywhere structures similar to these ritual features, it is in the realm of music. This is not so merely because the Sāmaveda may be described as "mantras set to music." What is more significant is that the structure of these chants, both internally and in relation to each other, corresponds to musical structure. Close parallels to these structures are found, for example, in the complex expressions of polyphonic music in Europe during the eighteenth century. The ritual chants of the Agnicayana resemble in this respect the arias of Bach's oratorios, and are similar in character: Their language is uninteresting, their poetry mediocre, and their meaning trite; but the sounds, with their themes and variations, inversions, interpolations, and counterpoint, and the particular distributions of their elements is what makes them remarkable. To those who have grown up in such a tradition, and who have learned to perceive and appreciate it in its traditional perspective, it is the structure of these chants that reveals to a large extent what is felt to be their beauty.

CHAPTER 3

The Mantra in Vedic and Tantric Ritual*

Wade T. Wheelock

IN ALL RELIGIOUS TRADITIONS, THE words spoken in ritual are regarded as a special subclass of the entire corpus of possible utterances, in terms of their author, content, form, mode or context of delivery, and so on. The explicit, self-conscious delineation of the extraordinary nature of the liturgical utterance, along with an emphasis in both theory and practice on its essential role in the performance of ritual, has not been developed any more elaborately than in Hinduism. The mantra, as a concept and as a recognized element of liturgical performances, has been one of the most important components of the Hindu religious tradition through the entire course of its long history, from the elaborate priestly sacrifices of the early Vedic *śrauta* system to the more personal worship services (*pūjā*) of the manifold forms of medieval Tantra.

Over this span of more than a millenium, there has been a remarkable constancy in the implications of the term *mantra,* as Gonda has thoroughly demonstrated (1963b). The emphasis in both Vedic and Tantric usages is on the mantra as an *effective* word, a word of action, not just of thought. And the action with which the mantra is preeminently connected is that of ritual. (Later in this volume, Alper will re-emphasize this point.) Thus, the orthodox tradition commonly identifies mantra with the *saṃhitā* portion of the Veda, the collection of utterances (hymns, formulas, chants, spells) actually spoken during the *śrauta* rites (Jha [1911] 1978, 110). The Tantric practitioner, *sādhakā,* utilizes mantras in *sādhanā,* a program of spiritual exercises one of whose essential components is the ritual worship of the deity, *pūjā.*

I would like to acknowledge a grant from James Madison University in partial support of the research for this paper.

The striking parallels between the Vedic and Tantric concern for ritual language and the indubitable historical continuity represented by the term *mantra* invite comparative study. This paper will examine the ways mantras are used in the Vedic *śrauta* system and in Tantric *pūjā*, with the view that cross referencing the analysis of one tradition to the other will illuminate not just genetic relationships but also the essential characteristics of the liturgical process specific to each tradition.

Even if Vedic and Tantric ritual belonged to completely unrelated cultural families, if they were separated by continents as well as centuries, it would still be a legitimate temptation to place them side by side to see how each deals with the universal problem of using language to transform a ritual setting into an idealized situation of interaction with the gods. What kinds of things does one say during a ritual? How do they correlate with the things being done? What are the differences in kinds of things said between one ritual tradition and another? And, how do these differences relate to the overall goals of each ritual? Is there an explicit theory of ritual language, or one implicit from usage, that distinguishes one tradition from another? Much of this paper's analysis will be concerned with just this set of questions. Ritual language—that component of the ritual process whose intelligibility makes it the most accessible (though the Tantric examples will severely test this assumption)—merits study in its own right.

SOURCES

The full range of Vedic and Tantric ritual simply cannot be surveyed adequately in this study. The Vedic tradition will be represented by the very complete description of ritual procedures (including mantras) contained in the *śrauta* sūtras. And, here, I will limit myself to a representative sampling, focusing on the New- and Full-Moon sacrifice (*darśa-pūrṇa-māsa-iṣṭi*), a medium-sized, important sacrifice that serves as the paradigm (*prakṛti*) for other rites. The texts used are the *śrauta* sūtras of Baudhāyana (BaudhŚū), Āpastamba (ĀpŚū), and Āśvalāyana (ĀsvŚū).[1]

To represent the Tantric ritual tradition, I have chosen the obligatory daily worship (*nitya pūjā*) for a deity. Since *Tantric* defines a much broader range of variants than does *Vedic*, the task of delimiting a representative selection of texts was more difficult, compounded by the limited availability of editions and translations. The most complete presentation of the ritual, providing the bulk of the Tantric mantras for this study, was the Mahānirvāna Tantra (MNT), an eighteenth century *śākta* text. Additional material was taken from the Kālikāpurāṇa (KP), a text dating from perhaps the eleventh century A.D. that contains considerable Tantric and *śākta* influence. A final source was the description of the *Pāñcarātra*-based temple cult of the Śri Vaiṣṇavas (ŚriV) provided by Rangachari. Other materials were consulted to buttress conclusions on mantra usage or the general structure of a Tantric *pūjā*, even though their presentations of the ritual were incomplete and often sparse in details on the mantras involved. But, I was able to examine at least one work in each of the major traditions—*Śākta, Vaiṣṇava,* and *Śaivite.*[2]

Despite significant variations in detail, there was something of a consensus on the key elements and structure of the Tantric *pūjā*. Although the exact order and degree of elaboration of each of the elements often differed to a considerable degree, their presence in a wide range of textual traditions is remarkable and argues for the distinctiveness of Tantra as a definable pan-Hindu category, at least as far as ritual practice is concerned. As van Kooij has observed, there appeared to be an established form of "common worship" (*sāmānyapūjā*) among all mainline theistic groups in India from at least the eleventh century A.D. (1972, 6).

The ritual structure of the New- and Full-Moon sacrifice (hereafter, NFM) is mirrored in the other Vedic rituals: The *Agnihotra* (and even the standard *gṛhya homa*) are truncated versions; the Soma sacrifice is an enormously expanded and elaborated form, in which the NFM is a basic building block (or, as described by Staal, a fundamental unit of the Vedic ritual "grammar," 1979b; 15–22). The NFM appears immediately more complex than Tantric *pūjā* because it involves several participants: the patron (*yajamāna*), on whose behalf the ritual is staged; his wife; the *adhvaryu* priest, in charge of most of the handiwork, plus his assistant, the *āgnīdhra*; the *hotṛ*, whose principal duty is the reciting of hymns of praise during the offering of the oblations; and the *brahman*, who, for the most part silently, sits supervising the entire operation. The Tantric *pūjā*, on the other hand, is basically a personal worship service of a single individual, often performed in the privacy of one's home. Even when a priest assisted by several attendants performs the *pūjā* in a temple, the rite retains much of the same character, only now, personal devotion has become public duty.

In the most general terms, both the Vedic and Tantric ritual involve a preliminary series of transformations aimed at making the concrete elements involved—the site, utensils, offering substances, and human participants—fit for divine service. This is followed by the worship of the god or gods following a basic pattern of invocation, praise, offering of food and other pleasing substances, and petition. The closing activities of the ritual mirror its beginning but in a reverse order, as the ritual situation is in some fashion dissolved, allowing the participants to return to a condition of normalcy.

The goal of this study is to examine and compare how language—or more broadly, humanly produced sound (since the category "mantra" will sometimes push us to or beyond the boundaries of "language")—functions to bring about the various elements of the ritual situations just outlined. This will require saying something about the ways one can analyze language functions, generally, before proceeding to the specific types of language use in Vedic and Tantric ritual.

CATEGORIZING RITUAL UTTERANCES

The most general and comprehensive way to understand the functions language can perform has certainly come in the burgeoning discussion in recent years concerning *speech acts.* (The principal works here are Austin 1962 and Searle 1969; for other relevant studies, see Wheelock 1982.) This view stresses that making an utterance does not merely express some idea but, invariably, involves accomplishing some purposeful act. To speak is to intend to produce some effect by means of your utterance, usually upon the hearer. For example, the purpose of a simple declarative statement is to convince the hearer of your commitment to the truth of a particular proposition. To utter a command is to intend to affect the behavior of the hearer. Or, to utter the declaration "I now pronounce you husband and wife" is to accomplish the act of transforming the status of two people from single individuals to married couple.

For the purposes of this study, what would prove most useful would be a comprehensive inventory of the types of such acts that can be accomplished through speech. Philosophers of language and linguists have proposed taxonomies of that sort (the one I find most useful is Searle 1979b). But, the problem arises that those taxonomies are designed to characterize *ordinary* language. As I have tried to point out elsewhere (Wheelock 1982), the language of ritual is decidely *extraordinary,* most particularly in that, as a fixed text of constantly repeated propositions, its intended effect can hardly be the communication of information. Instead, it is better understood as serving to *create and allow participation in a known and repeatable situation.* Ritual language effects this general purpose by means of four basic utterance types, each associated with creating some aspect of the ritual situation:

1. Presentation of Characteristics—indicative utterances that define the identities and qualities of the components of the situation;
2. Presentation of Attitudes—statements of personal feeling about the situation, such as optative expressions that define a participant's wishes;
3. Presentation of Intentions—first-person future statements of commitment to action;
4. Presentation of Requests—commands by which the speaker establishes a petitionary relationship with a second person and defines its nature.

These types represent a comprehensive categorization of the things that can be done with speech in a ritual setting. They are the basic building blocks for the linguistic creation of the ritual situation. A few examples will help clarify the workings of these categories.

The characterizing of the components of a ritual is not a simple matter of spontaneously expressing one's recognition of their identity. Instead, the fixed text of the liturgy *presents* the speaker with the characteristics of each object he confronts. The indicative phrases, in effect, *confer* a particular identify upon an object. The mantra is a good case of this general point about liturgical utterances. In the words of Alper (in Chapter Ten of this work), a mantra is "a machine for thinking." That is, the mantra is not a set of words you create to *express* a thought. Rather, it is something passed down to you from a privileged source of authority that you recite in order to *generate* a thought. And, in the ritual setting, not just a thought but a concrete component of the ritual situation is generated. The ritual performer, for instance, will often use a first-person indicative utterance to characterize himself or his activity. Thus, when the Vedic *adhvaryu* priest says, "I carry you [bundle of grass] with Bṛhaspati's head" (BaudhŚū), this mantra, coupled with the fact that he is presently carrying the grass bundle on his head, serves to establish his divine status in the ritual situation.

The entities with which the worshippers interact are often identified by the second-person indicative utterances used in directly addressing them. The gods, for example, take on manifest form in the mantras spoken to them, their intangible natures being incarnated in speech. When the Tantric worshipper says, "O auspicious one, in everything auspicious, o Śivā, who givest success in every cause, who yieldest protection . . . honor to thee" (KP), he is using a second-person statement in a downgraded-predication (a relative or dependent clause) to give a personality to the deity he is revering.

While establishing the characteristics of the ritual situation is largely accomplished with indicative phrases, the presentation of attitudes is primarily associated with optative verb forms. Expressing the performers' attitudes of desiring or wishing for some state of affairs to come about is a key component of any liturgy. The first-person optative may serve to establish that the performer has the appropriate attitude of desire to properly accomplish his ritual duties. Or, as is prevalent in the Vedic liturgy, one may express the desire of prospering by means of the ritual: "By means of it [sacrifice] may we win the sun-filled realms" (ĀpŚū). Similarly, the third-person optative may be used to wish that something go right in the ritual: "O you [wine], may the curse of Śukra be removed from you" (MNT). Or, it may express the hope for some beneficial condition beyond the ritual. (Remarkable is the fact that neither Vedic nor Tantric liturgy has any significant number of second-person optatives.)

The presentation of intentions is a small category, represented by first-person future statements, such as "I will worship the Lord by this lordly action known as the prayer of the morning twilight." Said by a *Śri Vaiṣṇava brāhman* at the start of the morning *sandhyā*, it establishes his commitment to accomplish his ritual duties, a common function in the Vedic tradition as well.

Finally, by means of the category of presentation of requests, one establishes the petitionary relationship basic to the functioning of the ritual. Taking the form of second-person imperatives, in most cases, such utterances supply the dynamic element of purpose, interaction, and intended response in the ritual situation. Many of these utterances are concerned with obtaining the cooperation of the other ritual participants (including people, utensils, and gods) in the production of the liturgical performance. A major component of the Vedic ritual will be the further request for some kind of blessing, directed not just to the gods but to the ritual objects as well. For example, the *hotṛ* asks the bundle of grass to "sweep me together with progeny and cattle" (ĀśvŚū), and also utters the request, "Indra-Agni, slayers of Vṛtra . . . prosper us with new gifts" (ĀśvŚū).

The four utterance categories just demonstrated represent, then, the basic atomic components of a liturgical structure. While analysis could precede by examining the range of utterances in the Vedic and Tantric rites that fall under each heading, I have decided that a more interesting approach will be to show how certain types of mantras from each category combine to fulfill a broader ritual function. That is, the analysis of the ritual texts will focus on the level of the "molecular" rather than the "atomic," although with the advantage of this rudimentary model of the underlying atomic process. The broader ritual functions that will be focused on are (1) the transformations of the concrete components of the ritual from mundane objects to resonances of sacred forces and their subsequent interaction to accomplish the goals of the ritual; (2) the service or worship of the gods, from invocation and praise to offering and petition. These two functions are clearly discernible in both Vedic and Tantric rituals, determining a rough two-stage structure of preparatory transformations followed by the climactic acts of worship. The concern of this paper will be to show what types of mantras are associated with each function and, by using the categories developed to show the ways ritual utterances create situations, to discuss *how* the mantras accomplish the tasks of transformation and worship.

RITUAL TRANSFORMATIONS

The ritual function of transforming the objects involved in the performance is central to both Vedic and Tantric rituals. The Vedic NFM begins with the lengthy procedure of the *adhvaryu's* assemblage and arrangement of the objects to be used in the sacrifice, as well as preparation of the site itself. His activities are accompanied throughout by muttered ($\sqrt{}$*jap*) formulas (*yajus*) that identify the manipulated objects—and his own self—with various sacred forces. From the perspective of the *adhvaryu*, the Vedic sacrifice is an array of powerful forces, controlled by his manual actions, directed by his utterances that, almost independent of the gods involved, fulfills the patron's desires for prosperity. The Tantric ritual in an even more systematic fashion transforms a mundane setting into a precisely and minutely conceived replica of a sacred cosmos. The purification and cosmicization of ritual components covers everything from the individual worshipper (*sādhaka*), whose body becomes an image of the deity in both transcendent and manifest form, to the altar on which the offerings are made, which is changed into a *maṇḍala* housing the entire retinue of divine beings, the manifold body of the supreme deity (see, e.g., Eliade 1969, 219–27). In both traditions, the process of transformation precedes and is viewed as a prerequisite of the service of worship.

The utterance type that predominates in this process is the presentation of characteristics, expressed by sentences in indicative form. The ritual performers will use first-person indicatives to characterize their ritually transformed identities and to describe the sacred actions they can now accomplish in the ritual arena. First-person optative utterances will be added to present those attitudes required of a pious participant in the liturgy. The ritual objects most often will be characterized by directly addressing them with a second-person indicative. Once their transmundane identity is thus established, they can be requested to work for the success of the ritual and directly for the benefit of the worshipper.

THE RITUAL PERFORMERS

To begin with, the ritual performers must undergo a process of metamorphosis. In Tantric *pūjā* this involves a twofold procedure of purification in which the defilements of the mundane body are removed, followed by the recreation of the worshipper in the divine image. The purification of the worshipper begins with the obligatory morning rites (e.g., bathing, *sandhyā*) that always precede the *pūjā* proper. Within the ritual itself, the process becomes more explicit and detailed, being concentrated in the rites of *bhūtaśuddhi* and *nyāsa*. *Bhūtaśuddhi*, as the name implies (purification of the elements), involves visualizing the refining of the worshipper's own body by a process of inwardly re-enacting the destruction of the cosmos and the reabsorption of the basic elements into primal, undifferentiated matter (discussed by Gupta, in Gupta, Hoens, & Goudriaan 1979, 136; van Kooij 1972, 14–16). Some Tantric texts will use first-person indicative mantras to describe what the worshipper sees happening: "I dry up the body both internally and externally, in the order of tatvas [sic] by which it is constituted, by the wind situated in the navel. . . . I burn the body with the several tatvas, all sins, all ignorance . . . by the fire in the abdomen . . ." (ŚriV). With some variation in different texts, the worshipper proceeds to visualize the cosmic fire being extinguished with earth and the resulting ashes finally being washed away with water, completing the process of purification.

While these utterances vividly characterize the changes being wrought, the actual transformation is felt to be accomplished by the multiple repetitions of a series of nonsentence, *bīja* mantras. These monosyllabic vocables, in theory, are sonic manifestations of basic cosmic powers (*śaktis*); literally, seeds of the fundamental constituents of the universe. The *bījas* used for *bhūtaśuddhi* are formed from the series of four semivowels in the Sanskrit alphabet, each standing for one of the four basic cosmic elements. Thus, one repeats (or mediates) on *yaṃ*, the *bīja* of wind, and visualizes the dessication of the body, followed by multiple repetition of *raṃ*, standing for fire, then (in some cases) *laṃ*, the earth-*bīja*, and finally repetition of *vaṃ*, bringing forth the refreshing cosmic waters. (This correlation is discussed by Woodroffe 1963, 43; Padoux [1963] 1975, 271.)

As we will continue to see throughout the discussion of Tantric mantras, these *bīja* mantras are not felt to be mere symbols of the elements, they *are* the cosmic elements in essential form. Such a conception of language will be one of the most distinctive marks of Tantra and that which most significantly differentiates it from the Vedic conception of mantra. The perceived ability of mantras to independently effect a basic transformation in the nature of one of the ritual's components stands in contrast to the Vedic practice, where the mantra will actualize or make explicit a transmundane reality already suggested by the physical symbolism of action or appearance.

But, how are these *bīja* mantras to be understood in terms of the utterance categories? I would suggest that the clue be taken from those mantras cited earlier that describe the visualization process: The *bījas* of *bhūtaśuddhi* are the deep-structure of first-person indicative statements. That is, when repeating the syllable *raṃ*, for example, the worshipper is implicitly making the statement "I am (or have become) fire." Such *bījas*, then, emphatically assert—and, in the theory of the Tantra, actually constitute—the consecrated nature of the ritual performer. (Thus, they are nonsentences only in terms of their surface structure. See Coward's discussion in Chapter Six of this volume on single-word mantras standing for complete sentence meanings.)

Bhūtaśuddhi is followed by the re-creation of the worshipper's body, now as an image of the cosmos. This is accomplished through the process of *nyāsa* (placing). Like *bhūtaśuddhi*, *nyāsa* involves the use of nonsentence mantras but with an accompanying physical act, touching various parts of the body. The mantras, in effect, are applied to the body manually. Two basic types of mantras are used. First, the letters of the Sanskrit alphabet are placed in order on different parts of the body (*mātṛkā-nyāsa*), providing the worshipper's body with the fifty basic elements of the Tantric cosmogony. In effect, one is making a series of indicative statements, "This part of my body that I touch is now the letter (or element) *ka*," etc. (Examples can be found at KP 59.37–40, and MNT 5.106–108.)

Second, a series of essentially reverential mantras are offered to the parts of the body (*aṅga-nyāsa*) to consecrate them as implicitly identical to those of the supreme deity. A typical version is the following from the MNT:

hrāṃ	To the heart, namaḥ.
hrīṃ	To the head, svāhā.
hrūṃ	To the crown-lock, vaṣaṭ.
hraiṃ	To the upper arms, huṃ.
hrauṃ	To the three eyes, vauṣaṭ.
hraḥ	To the two palms, phaṭ.

Disregarding for the moment the *bīja* that begins each of these mantras, a familiarity with Vedic mantras makes it clear that the basic intent is to offer homage. The part of the body occurs in the dative case followed by exclamations frequently occuring in the Vedic liturgy: *namaḥ,* (reference); *svāhā,* an exclamation (of dubious meaning) uttered while the *adhvaryu* offers a libation into the fire from a seated position; *vaṣaṭ* and its variant *vauṣaṭ* (again of uncertain meaning, but perhaps "may he carry") uttered by the *adhvaryu* when offering the more elaborately orchestrated standing oblations; *huṃ,* chanted by the *udgatṛ* to connect portions of *Sāman Veda* used in the Soma sacrifices; and *phaṭ,* an exclamation found in the *Yajur* and *Atharva Vedas* to drive away demons. The *bījas* at the beginning of each mantra are formed from the first letters of the goddess' own *bīja, hrīṃ,* adding the series of long vowels as endings. Most likely, these stand for the respective parts of the body of the goddess, to which the rest of the mantra then offers reverence. A paraphrase of the first mantra, then, might be, "To you, who are the heart of the deity, I offer homage." The mantras of the *āṅga-nyāsa,* then, transmute the purified body of the worshipper into the fully manifest form of the supreme deity and express an appropriate sense of reverence by means of exclamations drawn from the Vedic vocabulary for worship of the gods.

A culminating statement of the Tantric worshipper's identity with the supreme deity comes in the utterance of the *Haṃsa-mantra*: "The swan [*haṃsa*], he am I [*soham*]" (MNT). This mantra, associated with the rites of *bhūtaśuddhi* and *nyāsa,* identifies the *sadhaka* with the symbol of the transcendent form of the deity. All the Tantric literature is clear on the point that "the quintessence of ritual is the priest's acting as a god" (Diehl 156). This is expressed even more explicitly in a Śaivite text, where the priest says, "He who is Śiva, in reality I am he" (*Somaśambhupaddhati* 3.98).

The transformations of the worshipper, so that he conforms with his true but obscured identity, are a necessary precondition of the service of worship to follow. "When the body has been purified by these means, one is always entitled to worship; not otherwise" (KP55.51). The ritual itself, then, is viewed as god offering worship to god, as is well expressed by this repeated formula (called *sātvikatyagām*) in Śri Vaiṣṇava rites: "The divine lord . . . causes this act to be done [insert name of rite, e.g., *saṃdhyā, pūjā*] . . . by himself, for his own sake and for his own gratification"; and at the completion of that rite, "the divine Lord . . . has done this act" (ŚriV). These third-person statements of god's performance of the ritual, uttered by the worshipper in the context of his own enactment of the *pūjā,* assert the identity of ritual performer and deity.

Turning now to the Vedic liturgy, one finds some similar concerns for transforming the ritual performers into divinities and by similar methods. But, first, one needs to recognize that the Vedic ritual works on the assumption of a divison of labor among the various participants, with the speaking role of each expressing a significantly different view of his ritual identity and function. The three major and distinctive parts are those of the *adhvaryu* priest, the *hotṛ* priest, and the *yajamāna* (patron).

The mantras uttered by the *adhvaryu* while preparing the material and arena for the sacrifice express a conception of his transmundane identity. One often-repeated paradigm is a first-person indicative with a modifying instrumental adjunct that defines the priest's actions as actually being accomplished by a god. For example, there is the frequent formula "Under the impulse of the Impeller God, with the hands of Pūṣan, with the arms of the Aśvins, I do [some ritual action] to you [some ritual object]" (BaudhŚū and ĀpŚū). Other examples, "With the arms of Indra, I pick you up"; "I look at you with the eye of Mitra"; "With the eye of Sūrya, I look toward you"; "With Agni's mouth I eat you" (BaudhŚū and ĀpŚū).

One noteworthy difference from the Tantric ritual is that the Vedic priest (usually the *adhvaryu,* but occasionally another priest, such as the *brahman* in the last two examples) identifies parts of his body with parts of a variety of different gods. There is no unified nor even consistent parallel of worshipper and god. As seen earlier, the same priest will use "the arms of the Aśvins" for one action and then "the arms of Indra" shortly thereafter. As will become more obvious soon, the transformations of objects in the Vedic ritual arena does not generate a precisely ordered *maṇḍala* that replicates divine powers in a one-to-one fashion. Rather, one finds a more variegated and constantly changing amalgam of divine resonances.

The parallels to the Tantric ritual, then, are striking and obvious. For both, the ritual is a divine activity—done for and *by* the gods. The significant difference is that, in the Vedic *śrauta* system, this view is largely confined to the *adhvaryu* priest and his manipulations of the physical components of the ritual. It is paralleled in the liturgy of the *hotṛ* by an almost independent view of the sacrifice as a purely human homage to the gods as distinct beings and is prominently displayed in the set of central offerings. The *hotṛ* does not even enter the ritual arena until the *adhvaryu's* preparations are complete. At that point, he declares Agni to be the divine *hotṛ* and then says of himself, "I am [the] human [*hotṛ*]" (ĀśvŚū), thus using a first-person indicative to give a much different characterization of his identity than is found in the mantras of the *adhvaryu*. The *hotṛ* continues the tradition of Rig Veda poetry, which, as aptly characterized by Findly in Chapter One of this volume, emphasized mortal man's difference from the immortal gods. The *adhvaryu* expresses the view of the later Yajur Veda, which exalted the priest to divine status.

The case of the patron (*yajamāna*) of the Vedic sacrifice provides us with yet another way of characterizing a ritual performer. The effect of the sacrifice upon the *yajamāna* is seen as causing him to ascend to heaven so that, momentarily, he becomes godlike. The *yajamāna* enacts this ascent himself at the very conclusion of the rite by striding the "Viṣṇu-steps" from his seat to the *Āhavanīya* fire in the east, while he utters the following mantras: "You are Viṣṇu's step, slaying the enemy. With the Gāyatrī meter, I step across the earth. . . . You are Viṣṇu's step. . . . I step across the atmosphere . . . across the sky . . . across the regions" (BaudhŚū and ĀpŚū). He follows this immediately by worshipping the fire as he says, "We have gone to heaven. To heaven we have gone" (BaudhŚū and ĀpŚū). I would like to draw attention to the role of the mantras in explicitly conferring upon the *yajamāna* the identity implicit in his actions. The first-person indicatives served to characterize his movement toward the *Āhavanīya* fire as ascending the regions, culminating with the past-tense statements of arrival in heaven. The second-person statements identified his steps with those of Viṣṇu, the god who reaches heaven in three strides.

In both Vedic and Tantric ritual, a much more minor role is played by the optative statements of the appropriate attitude needed by the performers of the ritual. The only example in the Tantric material is the special sectarian variation of the Vedic *Gāyatrī* verse (Rig Veda 3.62.10). The general form is "Upon so-and-so may we think (*vidmahe*). Upon so-and-so may we meditate (*dhīmahi*)" where one inserts the name of one's chosen deity. All of the Śakta and Vaiṣnava sources consulted utilized some such Tantric *Gāyatrī* at one or more points in their rites. The general point seems to be to have the worshipper express the desire of turning his thoughts to and then concentrating them upon the central deity. This attitude of wanting the god to be the focus of one's mind is a sine qua non of the *pūjā*. The Vedic liturgy requires a different set of proper attitudes. Most express the wish of successfully performing one's ritual duties. Thus, the patron says of his vow, a series of abstentions to be observed for the course of the ritual, "May I be capable of this which I now undertake" (ĀpŚū). Similarly, the *adhvaryu* begins with the general hope, "May I be capable for the gods" (BaudhŚū), but also expresses such specific desires as "Let me not hurt you," while he cuts the offering cake (BaudhŚū). These examples show, then, that the Tantric performer is more concerned about proper *thinking* and the Vedic performer proper *doing*.

Generally, then, the Vedic liturgy, in comparison to the Tantric, includes a greater variety of mantra forms for the process of transforming the ritual performers into their proper identities and expressing their proper attitudes. As a last note of comparison, the Vedic mantras used to characterize the performers show more dependence on some physical symbolism of trait or action. The Tantric mantras are capable of creating new realities all by themselves, without need of building upon homologies of outward appearance. Thus, unlike the Vedic ritual arena, which is an assemblage of objects (including people) and actions whose discrete forms are suggestive of divine correspondence, the Tantric stage is more of a blank slate, an abstract *yantra* that the worshipper fills with his own imagination. The mantra, however, in both cases is the catalyst that allows the sacred potential of the ritual setting to become a reality.

THE RITUAL OBJECTS

Besides the human participants, the ritual site and the various component objects must also be transformed in order to be fit for the service of the gods. The process begins with expelling the demonic forces from the site itself. Actions and physical objects play a large role in this process for both ritual traditions. The Vedic priest uses a wooden "sword" to draw in the ground the protective boundaries of the altar; utensils are sprinkled with water and singed with fire to expell the demons, and so on. Similarly, the Tantric worshipper prepares the site by sprinkling water, using the "divine gaze" (*divya-dṛṣṭi*), striking the ground with his heel, and burning incense. But, mantras play a key role as well. Thus, the *adhvaryu*, after digging up the ground for the altar, says, "The demon Araru is beaten away from the earth"; or after passing the utensils over the fire, "Burned away is harm; burned away are the enemies" (BaudhŚū and ĀpŚū). The numerous mantras of this type in the Vedic liturgy have some form of evil as the subject in the third person followed by a past participle that defines the just completed act of the *adhvaryu* as doing away with that demonic force. The act itself may be graphic in its symbolic import, but the accompanying mantra is required to make explicit that the action has indeed been effective against the invisible malevolent agencies.

Throughout the Tantric liturgies, on the other hand, one does not *elucidate* the demon-expelling procedure with an articulate statement of accomplished effect but, rather, uses a nonsentence *bīja* mantra to directly augment the process. Most common are the "armor" mantra, *huṃ*, and the "weapon" mantra, *phaṭ*. As their names imply, these forceful sounding vocables are used frequently throughout the ritual in contexts where a place or object is purified of evil influence and protected against further attack. One might interpret these *bījas* as second-person imperatives commanding the evil spirits to depart; or, perhaps, as first-person indicatives that state that the worshipper has indeed destroyed the unwanted spirits and protected the ritual space.

The positive transformation of the ritual objects into sacred entities is one of the major concerns of each liturgy, dominating the preparatory proceedings. Each tradition has elaborated a clear theory of what is involved. For the Vedic ritual, the controlling conception is that of the *bandhu*, the esoteric "linkage" between cosmic force and ritual component, so that the ritual setting is not just a symbolic simulacrum of the cosmos but a point of control over those forces (see the discussion in Wheelock 1980, 357–58). The Tantric ritual, too, emphasizes the homoligization of the ritual to a divine reality. But, this reality is single, not multiple as in the Vedic case. As Gonda says, "The final goal of all cult is, according to the Tantric view, the transformation, in the consciousness of the adept, of his own person, of the cult objects, and of the rite, into that which they respectively really are, and consequently into transcendent unity" (1960–63, II.33). And, of course, the transcendent unity to which everything in the ritual becomes identical is the supreme deity. Thus the Lakṣmī Tantra says, "The (adept should) think about arghya, etc. [the objects to be offered] (as follows); 'The blissful śakti of mine (i.e., Laksmī) . . . *is indeed* the arghya, ācamanīya, and so on" (36.80–86, my emphasis). Therefore, not only the worshipper is made identical to the central deity, as we saw earlier, but all of the components of the ritual as well.

The ultimate goal of each liturgy, then, will be the characterization of a ritual object's bandhu with some sacred power or its identity with the supreme deity. The conferral of a transmundane identity is usually expressed in the liturgy by means of an indicative utterance with the ritual object as subject and its nonliteral identity in the predicative nominative or predicate adjective. (This may often be in a down-graded predication—a subordinate clause or qualifying adjunct.) Such articulate statements are relatively rare in the Tantric liturgy, but one finds, for example, the following mantras addressed to the knife for killing the animal victim in a Śākta *pūjā*: "Thou art Caṇḍikā's tongue" (KP); "To the sacrificial knife, infused with Brahmā, Viṣṇu, Śiva, and Śakti, [let there be] reverence" (MNT). The mundane knife has become a divine appendage. What is particularly significant is that the inanimate ritual object is addressed in the second person, as if it were animate.

That is a particularly prominent characteristic of the Vedic liturgy. A very sizeable proportion of the entire mantra corpus is composed of direct second-person characterizations of the ritual objects. Most typical are indicative statements that use a predicate nominative to metaphorically identify the object with some divine possession. Examples are numerous, "You [wooden sword] are the right arm of Indra, with a thousand spikes, a hundred edges"; "You [*prastara*] are Viṣṇu's top-knot"; "You [butter pot] are Agni's tongue"; "You [antelope skin] are Aditi's skin"; "You [ball of dough] are Makha's head" (BaudhŚū and ĀpŚū).

Since one can address the ritual objects in the second person to characterize them, it is not surprising to see that they are treated as animate entities in other ways as well. For example, many of the objects in Tantric ritual are worshipped (√*pūj*) by uttering the formula, "To X let there be reverence (*namaḥ*)." In this fashion, the MNT has one worship one's seat, the tripod for the offering cup, the offering cup, one's wife, the sacrificial animal, the sacrificial knife, and so on. Implicit in such mantras is the identification of ritual object and deity. One might paraphrase them, "To you ritual object, who are an aspect of the Supreme, let there be reverence."

The personalized treatment of the ritual objects is much more extensive in the Vedic liturgy. The willing cooperation of the sundry physical components of the sacrifice is sought for nearly every activity. For example, the *adhvaryu* addresses the utensijs, "Become pure for the divine act, for the sacrifice to the gods"; he asks the ladles, "Come juhū; come upabhṛt"; and he requests of the purifying waters, "O divine waters, who purify first, who go first, lead this sacrificer in front; place the lord of the sacrifice in front" (BaudhŚū and ĀpŚū). The total volume of such second-person imperative mantras directed to ritual objects shows the Vedic sacrifice to be a dense set of interactions with animately conceived entities that require a careful etiquette of action and speech.

One way of characterizing the ritual setting is unique to the Vedic liturgy. This is the reification of the whole by means of third-person statements about "the sacrifice." At the conclusion of the rite, the patron says:

> The sacrifice became. It originated. It was born. It grew. It became the overlord of the gods. . . . O Agni, the sacrifice is possessed of cows, possessed of sheep, possessed of horses, having manly companions, and, always, indeed imperishable (BaudhŚū and ĀpSū).

At an earlier point, the patron expresses the wish, "May the sacrifice ascend to heaven. May the sacrifice go to heaven. May the sacrifice go along that path which leads to the gods" (BaudhŚū and ĀpŚū). Viewing the sacrifice as an independent reality, over against the various component parts, and even over against and superior to the gods themselves, becomes a hallmark of the developed *brāhmaṇic* theorizing. Such an abstract conception is difficult to represent concretely, so it finds its most adequate expression in such third-person utteances as these.

A final topic of concern regarding the ritual components is the belief in their ability to actually produce benefits for the performers—*independent* of the god(s) in whose honor they are assembled and manipulated. This theme of the causal efficacy of the properly arranged ritual objects is prominent in the Vedic liturgy, but starkly absent in the Tantric. At first, one might attribute this to a greater fidelity in the exclusive power and grace of the deity on the part of the Tantric worshipper. However, in the next section, we shall see that even the service of worship to the deity by and large is not viewed as a vehicle for obtaining one's desires.

Such, however, is not the case in the Vedic ritual. The handiwork of the *adhvaryu*, in particular, is seen as arraying a potent set of forces that can be directed to bring about by themselves various forms of prosperity. This is seen most clearly in the second-person imperative utterances addressed to the ritual objects, asking for some kind of blessing. For example, the *adhvaryu* addresses in turn each one of the set of firmly interlocking potsherds on which the offering cake is baked:

> You are firm. Make the earth firm. Make life firm. Make the offspring firm. Shove his relatives around this sacrificer. You are a prop. Make the atmosphere firm. Make the out-breath firm. Make the in-breath firm. Shove his relatives around this sacrificer. You are a bearer. Make heaven firm. Make the eye firm. Make the ear firm. Shove his relatives around this sacrificer. You are a supporter. Make the quarters firm. Make the womb firm. Make offspring firm. Shove his relatives around this sacrificer. (BaudhŚS and ĀpŚS)

Similarly, the patron says to the grass strewn on the altar, "Make refreshment and vigor swell for me . . . brāhmanhood and splendor . . . warrior-hood and power . . . the commoners and growth . . . life and nourishment . . . progeny and cattle" (ĀpŚū).

One final set of utterances expresses the view of the sacrifice as a direct means for fulfilling one's desires. These are the first-person optative mantras spoken by the patron, indicating his hopeful attitude that the ritual will bring about some specific goal. Uttered immediately after each of the oblations, they include such wishes as

> By the sacrifice to the gods for Agni, may I be food-eating.
> By the sacrifice to the gods for Agni-Soma, may I be Vṛtra-killing.
> By the sacrifice to the gods for Indra, may I be powerful.
> By the sacrifice to the gods for Indra-Agni, may I be powerful and food-eating.
> By the sacrifice to the gods for Mahendra, may I attain to victoriousness and greatness (BaudhŚū and ĀpŚū).

It seems that the hopes of the *yajamāna* are placed not so much on the gods to whom the offering is directed but on the performance of the ritual itself. His expression of the hoped-for direct connection between type of ritual and specific goal becomes the most succinct formulation of the theory of the Vedic sacrifice.

THE SERVICE OF WORSHIP

At the most fundamental and overt level, both Vedic and Tantric rituals are banquets in honor of the gods. As we have just seen, however, the rituals also contain many other levels of identity. But the service of worship is clearly the most prominent theme in each tradition when one examines its place in the ritual structure. In each case, it forms the climactic and culminating phase of the entire ritual sequence, relegating the theme of ritual transformations to a peripheral and largely preparatory status.

Within the worship service proper, there is a fairly well-defined, logical structure. One begins, quite understandably, by invoking the gods, usually with imperative utterance forms that request their presence. This is followed by showing reverence for the deities, with verbal expressions of praise for the god's attributes playing a major part. Here, indicative statements of the gods' praiseworthy characteristics will predominate. Next will come the climactic acts of offering food and other pleasing substances to the honored, divine guests. The complex formal etiquette at this point will invariably involve statements to convey the appropriate obsequiousness and solicitousness on the part of the performers. One will find, for example, indicative utterances that define the worshippers' acts as those of offering or impertative statements requesting and optative statements hoping that the gods will be pleased by the gifts. Finally, one comes to the enunciation of the desires one hopes to attain from the satisfied gods. These are most often couched in the direct address of second-person imperative phrases.

The process of showing homage to the gods, as might be readily inferred, is a very articulate activity, largely accomplished by speech acts. This was less necessarily the case in the transformations of the physical components of the ritual, where the symbolism of appearance and function could carry much of the weight of meaning and where verbal requests could be augmented by physical manipulations to bring about a desired effect. In dealing with the gods, on the other hand, their intangible beings and personalities, their interactions with the participants, become manifest almost exclusively through language; and the performers' relationship to them cannot be one of simple manipulation but must be the epitome of courtesy, which means cushioning every act with words of explanation and concern.

INVOCATION

The participation of the gods in the ritual can only commence upon their arrival at the scene. A very well developed part of Vedic and Tantric liturgies is the invocation of the gods. As might be expected, the simplest means to accomplish this is a second-person imperative asking the god to come. For example, the Vedic *hotṛ* begins the service of offering to the gods by having the *Āhavanīya* fire stoked as he calls upon

Agni: "O Agni, being praised, come to the feast that gives oblations" (ĀśvŚū). But, in accordance with the division of labor characteristic of the Vedic ritual, the invocation of the rest of the gods then formally is turned over to Agni, himself, the divine messenger: "Bring [*ā3vaha*] the gods for the sacrificer. O Agni, bring Agni. Bring Soma. Bring Agni. Bring Prajāpati. . . . Bring Indra-Agni. . . . Bring the gods who drink the clarified butter."

The invocation (*āvāhanam*) of the supreme deity into the ritual setting is also a clearly delineated aspect of the Tantric *pūjā*. However, the deity is not descending from the distant heaven of the Vedic cosmology but is drawn out of the very heart of the worshipper and asked to become manifest in some concrete object in the ritual (Nowotny 1957, 110). For example, Śiva is invoked into a temple's *liṅgam*: "O, Lord, who protects the world, graciously be present in this Liṅga till the end of the worship. . . . O god of gods . . . come for Apiṣēkam, for the protection of the soul" (cited in Diehl 1956, 118). Or, as in this example from Śākta ritual, where the goddess is asked to enter a flower placed on the main *yantra*: "Krīṃ O Ādyā-Kālikā Devī, along with all of your following, come here, come here" (MNT).

A unique concern of the Tantric liturgy is that the gods remain for the entire course of the ritual. Thus, after the goddess is invoked into the flower on the *yantra*, the worshipper addresses her, "O Queen of the Devas, you who are easy to obtain through devotion, accompanied by your followers, be very firm [in remaining here] as long as I will be worshipping you. . . . Remain here, remain here. Settle yourself down here; settle yourself down here. Restrain your feet" (MNT).

As to why the Tantric ritual adds this concern, I can only speculate that the atmosphere of *bhakti* makes the *Sādhaka* more humble about his ability to influence the behavior of the deity, including this very basic issue of whether the deity will deign to come and stay at his ritual. Plus, the Tantric emphasis on experiencing the divine presence as a vivid visualization, which comes only through the lengthy practice of meditation, might tend to produce a sense of uncertainty about the deity's willingness to appear and remain before the worshipper's consciousness. Thus, recall that the only wish expressed in the Tantric liturgy was the optative statement of their *Gāyatrī*, "Upon the deity may we think. Upon the deity may we meditate."

Another unique feature of the Tantric liturgy is that it proceeds from invocation to providing the deity with a detailed manifest form. The deity does not remain just a subtle abstraction of the transcendent source of the cosmos but, through the liturgy, develops into a complex embodiment of the entire created universe. This process begins with the establishment of the life breaths in the image (*yantra*, statue) that the invoked deity has just entered (the rite of *prāṇa pratiṣṭhā*). In a reflex of the mantras used for invocation, a third-person optative is used to express the hope that the life breaths will come into the image and remain there: "Let the five life breaths of the Goddess Tripurā and her spouse be here in the *yantra;* let her soul be here with that of her spouse; let all her sense-organs be here; and let her speech, mind, sight, faculty of hearing and smelling, her life breath, etc. be here" (cited in Gupta, Hoens, & Goudriaan 1979, 150).

A further expression of the deity's acquisition of a manifest form comes with the worship of the limbs of the divine body, using a set of mantras seen before in the Tantric worshipper's rite of *nyāsa.* In the Śākta service, one does homage to the corners of the hexagon within the central *maṇḍala,* saying, "Hrāṃ To the heart, namaḥ. Hrīṃ To the head, svāhā," etc. (MNT). As with the rite of *nyāsa,* the point of these mantras seems to be twofold: to identify parts of the *maṇḍala* with parts of the deity's body; and to express reverence with the set of traditional Vedic exclamations.

PRAISE

The next stage in the service of the gods involves the offering of praise. The most prevalent way of doing this is to recite their worshipful characteristics. In the Vedic sacrifice, this task falls almost exclusively upon the *hotṛ,* whose principal duty is the recitation of selections from the Rig Veda to accompany the major oblations. Most of these are second-person indicative utterances that proclaim the exalted status and function of the god, as in these examples: "Along with them who are the divine priests, you, o Agni, are the best invoker among the *hotṛs*"; "You, O Soma, are a mighty ruler and a Vṛtra-slaying king"; "You [Indra] are the lord of the wealthy rivers" (ĀsvŚū). Or, one mentions the great mythic deeds of the gods, with the implied hope that they will again perform effective acts on behalf of the worshippers: "You two, Agni-Soma, freed the rivers that had been seized from insult and shame"; "You [Indra], who have been invoked many times, you conquered the enemies" (ĀsvŚū).

The Tantric liturgy also may use second-person statements to directly praise the deity, but practically all of these are downgraded predications imbedded in other utterance forms. And, for the most part, they are confined to a single hymn of praise (*stuti*) near the very end of the *pūjā.* As an example, one finds in the KP: "O auspicious one, in everything auspicious, o Śivā, who givest success in every cause, who yieldest protection, Tryambakā, Gaurī, Nārāyaṇī, honor to thee."

Such a relative lack, or at least confinement, of articulate statements of praise seems to be balanced by other forms for expressing the deity's praiseworthy traits elsewhere in the *pūjā.* Much attention is given at the start of the rite to an inner or mental worship (*āntaryāga*), where the *iṣṭadevatā* is supposed to be visualized in minute and precise iconographic detail. The emphasis is on the radiant loveliness of the deity's physical form and dazzling apparel. Frequently, the text's third-person indicative descriptions of the visualization become verbalized mantras, as here, in a set of utterances that Rangachari says are used to praise god at the conclusion of the mental worship: "He [Viṣṇu] is one . . . possessing a body of the color of clouds full of water vapor; one having eyes like the petal of a lotus flower . . .; one having a face like that of a brilliant full-moon; one having a very pleasing and smiling attitude; one having red lips" (ŚriV).[3] Worth noting, then, in conclusion, is that an important part of the homage expressed in the Tantric *pūjā* concerns the physical traits of the deity. This is certainly not the case in the Vedic ritual, where one mentions the deeds and functions of the god with almost no mention of his physical appearance.

A final form used by the Tantric to express the reverable qualities of the deity is sonic in medium but inarticulate. It is the use of a connected series of *bīja* mantras that together form the *mūla-* or root-mantra of the deity. For example, the *mūla*-mantra of the Devī given in the MNT is "*hrīṃ śrīṃ krīṃ Parameśvarī svāhā.*" This mantra (and the case is the same for the *mūla*-mantra of whatever may be the *iṣṭa-devatā* of the particular *pūjā*) is repeated with great frequency and great pervasiveness throughout the course of the ritual. But, the climax certainly comes near the end of the *pūjā* with the rite of *japa.* This mantra is then muttered in a state of rapt concentration for 108 or even 1008 times, as carefully counted by a rosary. (Details on the method can be found in Woodroffe, 1959, 535–36 and Gupta, Hoens, & Goudriaan 1979, 153–54.) In the theory of Tantra, "the mantra of a *devatā* is the *devatā*" (Woodroffe 1963, 235). So, the multiple repetitions of the *mūla*-mantra, in effect, are a means of producing a concrete, sonic manifestation of the deity. The element *svāhā,* like the more frequent *namo* (as in the other sectarian *mūla*-mantras, *namo śivāya* or *oṃ namo vaiṣṇave*), is an expression of reverence directed to the manifest god. And, surely, it is a form of praise to use the mantra to bring the deity to mind and fix one's thoughts on her or him. (Coward will present the grammarians' view that such chanting enables the worshipper to clearly "see" the meaning contained in the words of the mantra.)

The most tangible way in which praise is demonstrated comes with the actual offering of gifts to the gods. The centerpiece of both ritual traditions, the act of offering, is necessarily accompanied by mantras that explicitly define the nature of the act. That is, the rite of offering not only requires the presentation of material objects to the gods but demands a verbal etiquette to express both concern for the gods' feelings and the appropriate intention by the worshippers. This may involve simply stating the verb of action, along with a declaration of the object offered, in the formula used for each of the *upacāras* (sixteen pleasing substances, from water for washing the feet to savory food to incense and lamps) of a Tantric *pūjā*: "I offer water for bathing, clothing, and jewels. Svāhā" (MNT). Or, ore typically, the verb is left understood but the recipient is named and an exclamation is appended to highlight the centrality and finality of the act. For example, the *adhvaryu* offers a butter libation with "To Prājapati, svāhā" (BaudhŚū and ĀpŚū); the Tantric worship presents water to the goddess with "To the devatā, svāhā" (MNT), in each case signalling that the intent of the behavior is to transfer ownership of the item proferred.

Important in Vedic and Tantric ritual is to beseech the invited deities to accept and be pleased by the proffered gifts. Most usually, this is a direct second-person imperative, as in these Vedic examples: "You food eaters and you who are worthy of sacrifice . . . delight in my office of *hotṛ*"; "O you [Agni] who are wealth bestowing . . . enjoy the bestowing of wealth" (ĀsvŚū). Similarly, one finds in Tantric *pūjās* such forms as

> O you who have caused the end of tens of millions of kalpas accept this excellent wine, along with the śuddhi (MNT).
>
> Enjoy this oblation, o Śivā (MNT).
>
> OṂ . . . accept this [name of each particular offering] . . . svāhā (LT).
>
> [O Lakṣmi] accept the mental worship that has been properly conceived (LT).
>
> O Bhagavan, accept this (ŚriV).
>
> What has been given with complete devotion, viz., the leaf, the flower, the fruit, the water, and the eatables presented, do accept these out of compassion (with me) (KP).

A form not found in the Tantric liturgy is the Vedic expression of the gods' having indeed enjoyed themselves at the sacrifice. As part of the *hotṛ's* "well-recited speech" (*sūktavāka*) after the principal oblations have been offered, he says "Agni has enjoyed this oblation, has exhilirated himself, has made (for himself) a superior greatness. Soma has enjoyed" etc., for each of the gods to whom offering was made (ĀśvŚū). This points up a major difference in tone between the Vedic and Tantric rituals. The Tantric *pūjā* exudes the air of *bhakti* humility before the awesomeness of a supreme deity. In a ritual that concludes with such gestures of subservience as prostration (*praṇamam*) and respectful circumambulation (*pradakṣiṇā*), one asks that the god or goddess "accept" [√*grah*] one's offering. The Vedic priest, on the other hand, seems much more a diplomat among superior but manipulable beings. He is more concerned that the gods enjoy [√*juṣ*] the offerings, apparently assuming that acceptance at least is guaranteed. But, a much greater certainty of the results, as well, is seen in the past-tense declarations of the gods' enjoyment. Again, the Vedic sacrifice is seen less as a way of prompting the divine grace than as a seal of a dependable, almost contractual bond between the gods and people.

PETITION

Finally, we come to those utterances that express the desires underlying the motivation for the service to the gods. In the Vedic ritual, these are quite clearly wishes for earthly prosperity and most take the form of direct second-person imperatives addressed to the gods. Many of these are spoken by the *hotṛ* during the major oblations on behalf of the patron. For example,

> Indra-Agni, slayers of Vṛtra with the beautiful thunderbolt, prosper us with new gifts.
> O Indra, bring treaures with your right (hand).
> O Agni grant the enjoyments of a good household; divide among us honors.
> O Agni-Soma, to him, who today dedicates this speech to you two, give manly vigor, wealth in cattle, and possession of good horses. (ĀśvŚū)

The *yajamāna,* particularly at the close of the NFM where he worships the fires and the sun, will direct requests to the gods himself: "O Agni, doing good work, purify yourself for us, giving me splendor, heroism, prosperity and wealth"; "[O Āditya] Give me life. . . . Place splendor in me" (BaudhŚū and ĀpŚū); "He who hates me . . . and he whom I hate . . . all of them, o Agni, burn up completely—he whom I hate and who me" (ĀpŚū).

Noteworthy is the fact that, by comparison, the Tantric liturgy has very few such direct requests. The few instances there are show little concern for forms of earthly prosperity. Thus, in the MNT, one has the request, "Give me [o Devī] endless liberation," when the food and wine is offered; and one says "Let there be success [*siddhi*] for me, o goddess, because of your grace" at the end of the *japa.* The general conclusion seems clear. The reason for performing the Tantric *pūjā* does not lie in some external goal but is the experience of oneness with the deity to be obtained within the ritual itself. It is a form of *sādhana* whose final result should be the consciousness of god doing homage to god.

However, this has not prevented the *pūjā* from becoming a vehicle for obtaining mundane desires. This is done largely by tacking on a set of wishes to the *pūjā* proper. For example, after the *japa* and *stuti* near the end of the rite, the MNT says one is to insert a protective mantra (*kavaca*) that expresses the hopes, "Hrīṃ May Ādyā protect my head. Śrīṃ May Kālī protect my face," etc. for a total of twenty-six parts of the body. The mantra itself is listed in a chapter separate from the rest of the *pūjā.* The MNT also mentions that a special set of oblations may be added after the usual *homa* (fire sacrifice) "for the attainment of one's desires" (6.160). Gupta discusses an entire category of *kāmya-pūjā,* specially designed forms of the basic rite used to achieve particular ends—such as curing disease, ensuring one's safety, or injuring an enemy (Gupta, Hoens, & Goudriaan 1979, 159–61).[4] So, while, in theory, the ritual is an end in itself, the practice tends to be otherwise, though with some recognition that such mundane motives do not belong in the heart of the *pūjā*.

CONCLUSIONS

After surveying the variety of liturgical functions performed by Vedic and Tantric mantras, what can be said about the theories of ritual and language that undergird each tradition? It is clear that both place a premium on ritual as *the* religious practice—creating and entering into the formalized and repeatable ritual situation is the essential means for enhancing one's religious worth. And, we have seen that the general outline of Vedic and Tantric ritual practice is the same—a reverential attendance upon the gods as honored guests, preceded by the transformation of the ritual arena into a microcosm of sacred forces. Yet, despite these broad similarities, the analysis of mantra usage has shown some very distinctive differences.

THE THEORIES OF RITUAL

First of all, the Vedic sacrifice, while also aiming to overcome the separation between man and god, assumes the ultimate reality of that distinction. The priest acts like a god, the patron is translated into heaven, but only temporarily, for the course of the ritual. The great variety of beings that are addressed in the second person—from human participants, to ritual utensils, to the various gods—indicates the basic worldview of the Vedic ritualist. There exist a multitude of powers in the universe, each requiring representation and courteous, diplomatic handling at the sacrifice. On the human side, the Vedic ritual is a complex social institution, involving the verbally orchestrated cooperation of several priests who act as intermediaries for the *yajamāna*, who himself is the representative of his entire family. The Vedic mantras, then, serve not just to link worshipper and deity but to define a whole, complex network of relationships.

The Tantric *pūjā*, on the other hand, postulates the ultimate unreality of all distinctions and seeks to affirm the eternal truth of the worshipper's identity with the deity. The mantras reflect this simplified world view, recognizing fewer distinct beings, focusing on the one relation of man to god, and attempting to express sonically the collapse of the manifest universe into a single category. Therefore, while the Vedic liturgy is using many mantras to state the various bandhus between ritual object and cosmic force, the Tantric liturgy is working to realize the *one*, all-encompassing bandhu: god = ritual = worshipper.

In contrast to this Tantric view, where the deity becomes the ritual, in the Vedic tradition, the ritual becomes a *reification*, "the sacrifice" as an independent force becoming an important topic of the liturgy. And, rather than seeing the ritual as an end in itself, as does the Tantric worshipper for the most part, the sacrifice is seen as the great vehicle for procurring the sundry forms of prosperity, which are what the Vedic life is all about. Thus, much of the mantra corpus in the Vedic sacrifice serves the purpose of expressing the patron's wishes and directing, cajoling, or asking the assembled forces to work toward their fulfillment outside the ritual setting. The Tantric goal of *siddhi* or *mokṣa* will be realized within the ritual itself.

THE THEORIES OF LANGUAGE

The differing worldviews and ritual goals of the Vedic and Tantric traditions, then, are reflected in differing forms of mantra usage. These, in turn, are supported by distinct theories of language and mantra. Throughout the Vedic tradition, the mantra stands as a *means* to the ends of the sacrifice. The Tantric mantra, on the other hand, as the essence of the ritual procedure, is an object of value *in itself,* being in theory the most subtle manifest form of the deity. The Vedic mantra truthfully *describes* and thereby actualizes a bandhu between ritual object and cosmic entity; the Tantric mantra *is itself* the ritual terminus of the bandhu with the divine realm. Such basic differences in evaluation of the mantra lead to significantly different theories of language. The Tantra will focus most of its theoretical energy on analyzing the nature of mantras and language, even being frequently termed the *Mantraśāstra.* The deity becomes manifest as the world first by taking on sonic form, the concrete objects or referents (*artha*) of those primordial words following afterwards in the course of cosmic evolution. (Detailed presentations of this theory can be found in Padoux [1963] 1975, 68–73; Woodroffe 1959, 462–90.)

In contrast, the orthodox formulation of the Vedic tradition, the *Pūrva-mīmāṃsā,* virtually ignores mantras. Its key task is to determine a valid means (*pramāṇa*) for ascertaining dharma. The conclusion is that the Veda provides the sole foundation for reliable knowledge of one's duty, but not in the collection of mantras. Only the set of explicit injunctions to action (*vidhi*) found in the *brāhmaṇa* portion of *śruti* are to be counted as relevant to defining dharma. The exegetical apparatus proceeds to channel most of its efforts into analyzing those passages, relegating a comparatively few pages to discussing the Vedic mantras. (The essential points are summarized in Jha, [1942] 1964, 159; [1911] 1978, 110–11, and 125–26.)

The Vedic mantras, then, form a component of the proper action needed for an effective performance of the sacrifice. While the orthodox tradition will push to an extreme this view of the mantra as an act—or even as a sound substance—needing only to be precisely enacted (i.e., pronounced) not necessarily understood, the original conception seems to be of the mantra as a statement of truth whose mere utterance in the ritual context is an effective act. It concretizes a bandhu that can then be actively manipulated to produce one of the various ends sought through sacrifice. The complex array of forces that must be dealt with to obtain the great variety of goals in the repetoire of the Vedic sacrifice means having a wide assortment of tools at one's disposal. Therefore, the Vedic priest must memorize hundreds—if not thousands—of mantras to serve his purpose.

This leads to a precise individuation of the task of each mantra, so that, for example, in the entire course of the Vedic NFM, there are perhaps less than two dozen repetitions in a total of approximately fifteen hundred utterances. The contrast with the Tantric liturgy is emphatic. Instead of repeating many different mantras, the Tantric worshipper reaches the climax of the performance by repeating one mantra many times. The Tantric mantras take on many forms and perform many ritual functions, as we have seen in detail earlier. However, the end to which they all point is one and the same—realization of identity with the deity. At this point, the mantra is no longer a means to an end, it is a manifestation of the goal itself. And, the repetition of the deity's mantra is not just an act to be mechanically performed but must be accompanied by proper thought, the goal of the ritual being realized when the consciousness of the worshipper blends with the thought-power represented by the mantra. While the Vedic liturgy uses language as a tool of proper action, the Tantric ritual makes action a subordinate of language in producing proper thought (an assessment that will be seconded by Alper's discussion of Śaivite mantras in Chapter Ten).

CONTINUITY AND CHANGE

To be able to understand the factors that produced the continuities and differences between Vedic and Tantric ritual practices and conceptions of mantra, in particular, is a desideratum for historians of Hunduism. (Some remarks on this topic can be found in Nowotny 1957, 114–22.) I have neither the time nor the data to enter into this difficult discussion at this point, but I would like to suggest a developmental structure implicit in each liturgy. One begins with the most overt dimension of the Vedic sacrifice, the service of worship to the gods. It is most overt, quite literally, in that it is the portion of the liturgy that is spoken aloud, by the *hotṛ*, so as to be audible to all present. The utterances of the *adhvaryu* (and *yajamāna*), on the other hand, which are used to transform the sacrifice into an assemblage of potent forces having an independent efficacy, are muttered (√*jap*) under his breath. The *hotṛ* represents the tradition of the Rig Veda, in which insightful thought and the eloquence of the artist are to inspire priestly speech. The language of the *adhvaryu* shows the ascendancy of the Yajur Veda, where the essence of priestly accomplishment has become the workmanlike skill of the technician in performing proper action.

As the theory of the sacrifice develops in the *brāhmaṇa* literature and the place of the gods continues to give way to the action of the sacrifice itself, the further idea is introduced finally that one does not even have to speak to produce an effect in the ritual but may simply *think* about the true identity of some sacrificial component. The *brāhmaṇas* stress the power of "he who *knows* thus" (*yo evam veda*). The conception of the nature of the sacrifice, its correlations or bandhus with the realm of sacred forces, moves from the loudly articulate worship of the gods, to the muttered directing of a multitude of powers, to the silent rehearsal of the most precious truths of homology between micro- and macrocosms. That these layers of sound in the liturgy really represent stages of historical development is difficult to assert with complete certainty. However, the move from sound to silence, from external action to internalized thought, from bewildering complexity to the few most basic bandhus, seems aptly to characterize the tendency of the speculative texts—the *brāhmaṇas, āraṇyakas,* and *upaniṣads.*

Despite the great separation in time, the Tantric conception of ritual and mantra seems to take up the developmental process where the Vedic tradition left off. For the Tantra *begins* with the assumption that the most effective ritual is silent, internalized, and recognizes only one bandhu, namely, the identity of worshipper and deity. Thus, Tantric literature says that external worship of an image of the deity is designed for the lowest human personality type, someone incapable of understanding the higher truth without concrete props. (Woodroffe, 1959, 514; Padoux [1963] 1975, 48). The most effective mantra, as well, is not externalized speech. Rather, "prayer without sound is recommended as the most excellent of all" (KP 57.88). Or, as stated more systematically in the LT:

> The vācika (voiced) [type of japa] is [desirable] for minor rituals, the upaṃsu (silent) [type] is for rituals leading to the achievement of success, the manasā (mental) [type] for rituals yielding the wealth of liberation, [while] the dhyana (meditated) [type of japa] is for achieving success in every [endeavor]. (39.35)

Even when the Tantric liturgy is uttered aloud, the predominance of the monosyllabic *bīja* mantras, which have no exoteric but only esoteric meaning, tends to carry one beyond the boundaries of language. As Padoux (quoting Renou) puts it: "After all, to exalt the *bīja*-mantra, as does Tantrism, isn't that to place at the highest level a form of speech 'situated beyond language and eventually right to the zone of silence'?" ([1963] 1975, 363). The *bīja* mantras do not point outward to some referent in the objective world and thus, are "meaningless" in any ordinary sense of that term. Instead, they point backwards to the source of language, which is the source of all creation itself. (A point made by Padoux [1963] 1975, 294–96 and restated by Eliade 1969, 214.) Thus, nearly every *bīja* ends with the nasalization (*anusvāra*) that draws out the vowel and slowly fades away—representing the final sound of the cosmos before it becomes completely reabsorbed into unity and silence.

But the *bīja* mantras, in another sense, also represent the first manifestations of a new creation. The movement toward internalization, silence, and unity begun in the Vedic ritual tradition, culminates in the Tantric liturgy, but it also begins to reverse itself. After dissolving the universe with *bīja* mantras in the rite of *bhūtaśuddhi* and experiencing the unity of worshipper and deity as one performs the inner *pūja*, the Tantric ritual proceeds to the externalized worship, where the universe becomes re-created in its complex, manifest form. At this point the liturgy is not overwhelmed by the *bīja* mantras but, as was shown earlier, contains a sizable number of utterances that are quite intelligible. As in the Vedic ritual, the utterances then articulate the ideal situation in which the performer arranges the assembly of sacred forces and interacts graciously with the divine guests.

Overtly, the Vedic and Tantric liturgies showed many similarities in the kinds of intelligible mantras in sentence form that they contained. This was a reflection of their common manifest function—to pay homage to the gods. But, just as this outer form is supplanted by a more basic, esoteric understanding of the ritual as a direct manipulation of cosmic forces or a worship of oneself as identical with the deity, so, too, do the external similarities of Vedic and Tantric mantras finally give way to an underlying difference in the conception of language. The language of the Vedic liturgy is eternal, emanating from that fount of all speech and knowledge, the Veda. The complex structure of the world articulated in the Vedic mantras is a primordial truth to be continually reenacted in the sacrifice. The liturgical language of the Tantra, on the other hand, is a creation in time. Even though the Tantric mantras stand for the first manifest forms of creation, they still point back beyond themselves to their ultimate source—silence.

NOTES

1. BaudhŚū included the parts of the *adhvaryu* priest (1.1–1.21), *yajamāna* (3.15–3.22), and *brahman* (3.23–3.26); similarly for the ĀpŚū, adhvaryu (1.1.1–3.14.4), yajamāna (4.1.1–4.16.17), and brahman (3.18.1–3.20.10). ĀśvŚū provided the part of the *hotṛ* (1.1.1–1.11.16). In what follows, all translations from these sūtras are my own.

2. Scholars of Indian religions find it difficult to define Tantra with any precision. However, there is a concensus that the schools whose works will be utilized in this paper, viz. the *Pāñcarātra*, *Śaiva Siddhānta*, and *Śākta*, share a set of "Tantric" characteristics (see Goudriaan, in Gupta, Hoens, & Goudriaan 1979, 6–9).

The material on *pūjā* in the MNT is found from 5.1–7.64. All translations from this text are my own, though greatly aided by Woodroffe (1972). Translations of those portions of the KP relevant to the ritual were taken from van Kooij (1972, 39–90, Chapters 54–59).

Some confirming and supplementary details on *Śākta pūjā* came from A.

Bharati (1965); S. Gupta (in Gupta, Hoens, & Goudriaan 1979); and Nowotony (1957). Another *Pāñcarātra* text consulted was the Lakṣmī Tantra (LT), translated by S. Gupta (1972). Two additional sources on Śaivite practice were the fine study of Diehl (1956) and the ritual manual, *Somaśambhu Paddhati,* edited and translated by Brunner-Lachaux (1963–77, I).

3. Cited in Rangachari (1931, 143). In the MNT, the statements about the visualizations for inner worship much more clearly are instructions rather than liturgical utterances: "In the morning meditate upon her in her Brahmī form as a maiden of ruddy hue, with a pure smile" and so on (5.56).

4. Farquar cites an authority on medieval liturgy that distinguished between "pure" tantras, those that only discuss the path to liberation, and "mixed" tantras, those that also include instructions on worshipping the goddess for earthly blessings (1967, 268). In Chapter Ten, Alper says one could even make a distinction between mantras whose use is "quotidien" (i.e., oriented to pragmatic or magical ends) and those that are "redemptive" (*mokṣa* oriented).

CHAPTER 4

Mantra in *Āyurveda*: A Study of the Use of Magico-Religious Speech in Ancient Indian Medicine

Kenneth G. Zysk

ALMOST EVERY ANCIENT CULTURE HAS witnessed a fundamental union between science and religion at some time in its development. This especially is the case with the science of medicine in Vedic India, for diseases, like blessings, were considered to have been sent by supernatural beings. So in the *Atharvaveda* (and to a certain extent in the *Ṛgveda*), we are presented with an entire pantheon of demons who bring about bodily distress. From the contents of the mantras used to remove the demonically caused maladies, a threefold classification of disease emerges. (1) Internal diseases: these may be divided further into internal diseases related to *yákṣma* (consumption, tuberculosis) or *takmán* (fever syndrome, malaria) and internal diseases not closely related to *yákṣma* or *takmán*. The first includes *yákṣma, takmán* and all diseases and symptoms related to them, while the second encompasses *ámīvā, víṣkandha-sáṃskandha* (tetanus), ascites (Varuṇas's disease), insanity, worms, and urine (and feces) retention. (2) External diseases: these, for the most part, are injuries resulting from war or from accidents and include fractures, wounds, and loss of blood; but skin disorders, e.g., *kilā́sa* (leukoderma), *apacít* (rash with pustules), and loss of hair, also fall into this category. (3) Poisons: these are toxins, whose effects are conceived to be caused by various demonic elements stalking their prey day and night. They include insects, snakes, and vegetable matter.[1]

The cure for these diseases required an elaborate religious ritual in which remedies, used both therapeutically and magically, were consecrated and demons expelled. The actions were performed to the accompaniment of mantras, which in large part came from the *Atharvaveda*. They have a corresponding section (*Bhaiṣajya*) in the ritual text, *Kauśika Sūtra,* which outlines the prescribed rituals in which the charms are to be employed. Unfortunately, the text derives from a later period, so that many of the original rites have been lost. Bloomfield has observed that many of the procedures in the *Kauśika Sūtra* are purely secondary, formulated to fit the context of the particular hymns.[2] Therefore, we cannot completely depend on them to provide accurate information concerning the magico-religious practices of the early Indians. A discernible picture of Vedic medicine, however, can be painted from the contents of the mantras themselves.

The Vedic Indian's attitude toward internal disease was dominated by the superstition that evil spirits and demons invaded the body and caused their victims to exhibit a state of dis-ease. The impetus for the attack may have come from a breach of a certain taboo, from a sin committed against the gods, or from witchcraft and sorcery.

The idea of health in a positive sense is wanting in early Vedic medicine. Any notion of the concept is to be found in the negative sense, as the opposite of what was understood to be disease, or more specifically, in the absence of any particular disease-causing demons, of injuries and damages, and of toxins.

In order to restore the patient to a sound state of mind and body, the healer or medicine man (*bhiṣáj*) would perform various magio-religious rites. He is called one who shakes (*vípra*) and one who chants (*kaví*), suggesting that his actions involved a sacred dance and the recitations of mantras. He possessed a special knowledge of the preparations and uses of medicines, including medicinal herbs or simples and often water, formulas for the consecration of which form a good part of his magico-religious utterance. There is the indication that the healer waved or stroked certain plants over the patient in the course of his ritual performance. He is also noted for his ability to repair bone fractures.

In the medical hymns, we may isolate both "magico-religious" and "empirico-rational" elements of healing. The latter are rarely encountered in isolation, tending to be part of the overall magical rite. The magico-religious techniques occur in the treatment of both internal and external diseases and of poisons. In cases of internal diseases and poisons, the methods are almost exclusively magical. The most commonly employed examples of apotropaic concepts included the use of sympathetic magic, of the rhetorical question, of onomatopoeic sounds, of the identifying name, and of the esoteric word or phrase that, when properly uttered, transferred the power from the demon to the healer. The demons commonly were dispelled into the ground or carried away by birds to places where they could no longer harm the community. Amulets or talismans, usually of a vegetal origin, were ritually bound to drive off the demons and as prophylactic measures to prevent further attacks. Likewise, fragrant plant substances were burnt to protect the victim and to make his environment more favorable for healing.

Mythology also played a significant role in the rituals. Surrounding the auspicious medicinal herbs, mythological stories about plant divinities had the effect of divinizing the particular herbs and plants to be employed in the rite and, therefore, of making them even more efficacious. The reverence for these plants was an integral part of the Vedic Indian's medical tradition, giving rise to an elaborate pharmacopoeia, which is evident in all phases of Indian medicine. The great pains taken to collect, describe, and classify the different types of plants further indicate the origins of Indian scientific thought.

In addition to the evidence of a systematic mode of thinking, the Vedic healers showed that they were familiar with more empirical techniques. Understandably, these are encountered most frequently in the treatment of external diseases: a form of surgery, utilizing a reed as a catheter, was performed to relieve urine retention; lancing and salt were used in the treatment of certain pustules; wounds were cauterized with caustic medicines and perhaps fire; sand and perhaps also reeds were applied to stop the flow of blood from a wound and perhaps from the uterus; a resinous exudation was applied to wounds to prevent bleeding and to aid in the healing process; ointments and dyes were applied to the skin; a special plant was used that evidently promoted the growth of hair; and certain plants may have been utilized in a salve or poultice. Perhaps the most important empirical method of healing was the use of water in a type of hydrotherapy. It was employed for numerous ailments, both internal and external, suggesting that it was a significant therapeutic agent.

The mantra, or magico-religious utterance, was the key component of the healing rite. When properly executed at the designated auspicious time and place, the healer was able to unlock the door to the realm of the spirits and obtain the power necessary to ward off or destroy disease and to make medicines efficacious. Only the healer controlled the mantra, so that he alone governed the power to heal. Armed with his arsenal of mantras and other weapons of magic he set about his task of removing disease.

By the time of the early classical medical treatises, dating from around the Christian era, magico-religious medicine had given way to a medical system dominated by ideas more empirically and rationally based. A reverence for the older medical tradition of the *Atharvaveda*, nevertheless, was still advocated, as expressed in the following passage from the *Caraka Saṃhitā* (*Sūtrasthāra* 30.21):[3]

> Therefore, by the physician who has inquired about [which Veda an āyurvedic practitioner should follow, verse 20], devotion to the *Atharvaveda* is ordered from among the four [Vedas]: *Ṛgveda*, *Sāmaveda*, *Yajurveda*, and *Atharvaveda*. For it is stated that the sacred knowledge [*veda*] of the fire priests (*atharvaṇs*) is medical science because [it] encompasses the giving of gifts (*dāna*), invoking blessings (*svasti*), sacrifice to deities (*ayana*), the offering of oblations (*bali*), auspicious observances (*maṅgala*), the giving of burnt offerings (*homa*), restraint of the mind

(*niyama*), atonement (*prayaścitta*), fasting (*upavāsa*), and the recitation of magico-religious utterances (*mantra*), etc.;[4] and medical science is taught for the benefit of long life.

The focus of this study, therefore, will be on the element of Atharvavedic medicine that functioned as the fundamental key component in the ritual, the mantra, and the ways it was used in *āyurveda*. The sources we shall use are among the oldest of the āyurvedic treatises: *Bhela Saṃhitā*,[5] *Caraka Saṃhitā* (Ca),[6] and *Suśruta Saṃhitā* (Su).[7] The āyurvedic employment of mantras can be grouped into the following general categories: (1) the treatment of swellings or tumors and of wounds and sores (*śotha, vraṇa*); (2) the treatment of poison (*viṣa*); (3) the treatment of mental disorders (*unmatta, apasmāra*); (4) the treatment of fever (*jvara*), and (5) the collection and preparation of certain medicines.

TREATMENT OF SWELLINGS OR TUMORS AND OF WOUNDS AND SORES (*ŚOTHA, VRAṆA*)

The specific swellings or tumors requiring the use of mantras are the external (*āgantu*) types, which have symptoms opposite to the innate (*nija*) swellings. They begin by being painful and then are associated with the wind element. They are treated, according to the *Caraka Saṃhitā* (Sū 18.5), with bandages, mantras, antidotes, plasters, and hot-cold compresses. Similarly, external wounds or sores, being opposite to the innate ones, are distinguished by treatments beginning with mantras, antidotes, plasters, and by their causes and localization of symptoms (CaCi 25.8). It is clear that swellings (*śotha*) and wounds (*vraṇa*) were known to have the same characteristics and, therefore, required very similar treatments, implying that they were considered to be almost synonymous. Both terms, *śotha* and *vraṇa*, are missing from the *Atharvaveda* (and *Ṛgveda*), but parallel expressions such as *vidradhá* (abscess), *visálpaka* (*visálpa*, cutaneous swelling),[8] *apacít* (rash with pustules), and *baláśa* (swelling) are mentioned in the earlier texts. The afflictions *apacít*[9] and *baláśa*[10] have charms devoted to their removal, giving rise, perhaps, to the use of mantras in the cure of swellings or tumors and wounds or sores in early āyurvedic medicine.

TREATMENT OF POISON (*VIṢA*)

The most significant use of mantras in *āyurveda* is found in the branch of medical science that involves toxicology, commonly known as *agadatantra*. The beginning of the science can be traced to the *Atharvaveda* and to the *Ṛgveda*, which contain no less that ten hymns devoted to the eradication of poison deriving from various sources.[11] This is the part of India's medical science that Alexander of Macedonia found to be the most advanced, as Arrian informs us (*Indica*, 15.11–12):

> But as many [as were] Greek physicians, no cure at all had been found by then [for one] who had been bitten by an Indian snake; but in fact Indians themselves cured the ones who were smitten. And in this connection, Nearchus says [that] Alexander kept collected about himself as many of [the] Indians as were very skilled in the healing [art], and had made proclamation throughout his camp that whoever was bitten should have recourse to the king's tent. But these same [people] are physicians also for other diseases and misfortunes.[12]

The knowledge of poisons, then, was one of the earliest medical sciences over which the Indian physicians gained mastery. Both in war and in their general practice, they were confronted with cases of poisoning, which provided ample opportunities to test various remedies. Conceiving that such dreadful effects were caused by different demonically inspired creatures or practices, they devised mantras against each type. Having classified the various types of poisons on the basis of their vectors, they would proceed to recite the appropriate magical utterance, while performing a rite that often included a more therapeutic approach. This early tradition of toxicology was incorporated into *āyurveda*, where we find the same approach employed to the treatment of those afflicted by poison.

In the *Caraka Saṃhitā* (Ci 23.34–37), mantras are mentioned in the list of twenty-four remedies against the poisons deemed to be curable. Caraka also teaches a typical procedure involving the use of mantras in the cure of poison (Ci. 23.61):

> With [the recitation of] mantras, the binding of the [blood] vessels [is to be performed], the rubbing down [of the patient][13] is to be carried out and a self-protection [is to be executed].[14] One must first conquer that "humor" [*doṣa*][15] in whose domain the poison is [situated].

Suśruta explains the acquisition, efficacy and use of mantras in the cure of poisoning from snakebite (Ka 5.8–13):

> 8. And also the one accomplished in the mantra should tie the bandage [i.e., tourniquet] to the accompaniment of the mantra; indeed that [tourniquet] bound by cords, etc., is considered to be an effective remedy against the [spread of] poison.
> 9. The mantras,[16] previously mentioned by gods, *brāhmaṇas*, and sages [and thus] consisting of truth and ascetic heat (*tapas*),[17] are not otherwise; they quickly destroy the poison which is difficult [to cure].
> 10. The poison is checked quickly by the efficacious mantras consisting of truth, holy speech (*brahman*) and ascetic heat, not, therefore, by the medicines employed.
> 11. The acquisition of the mantras is to be made by one who abstains

from women, meat, and honey,[18] who is abstemious in food, who is purified [and] who reclines on a bed of *kuśa*-grass.

12. For the purpose of the success of the mantras, one should diligently worship the divinities by [giving] offerings of perfumes and garlands, by oblations, by muttering [sacred verses] and by [giving] burnt offerings.[19]
13. But since mantras pronounced without observing the proper rules or [recited] with the proper accents and syllables missing, do not attain success, the technique of antidotes is, therefore, useful.[20]

In these verses, a clearly magico-religious attitude, very much Atharvavedic in character, is advocated toward the healing of snake poison by the recitation of mantras. It looks back to a time when only the most primitive techniques of a tourniquet and mantras were employed and a priest rather than a physician performed the healing. Verse 9 refers to "previously mentioned" mantras. In an Atharvavedic hymn (6.12) against the poison from snakes, Verse 2 speaks of a similar *mantra*:

> By that [mantra] which was known by the *brāhmaṇas*, by the sages and by the gods [and] which was in the past, will be in the future and is now in the mouth, I cover your poison.

The last verse (13) is significant because it presents a more rational approach, quite likely of āyurvedic inspiration: Should the charms fail, the best resort is to an antidote.

In the case of hydrophobia (*jalatrāsa*) caused by the bite of a mad dog (*alarkviṣa*; commentary: *unmattakukkura*), *Suśruta* (Ka 7.59cd–62ab) prescribes that the patient should be bathed with cold water containing ingredients consecrated with mantras at a river bank or a crossroad and that an offering should be made while reciting the following mantra:

> O Yakṣa, lord of mad-dogs, lord of the race of dogs, quickly make
> for me him, afflicted by mad-dogs, without pain.

This ritual recalls magico-religious rites prescribed in the *Kauśika Sūtra*. In *Kauśika Sūtra* 26.29–32, in a rite for one possessed by demons, a patient is anointed with fragrant powders and ghee at a crossroad and sprinkled with water containing the fragrant powders while standing in a river against the current; and in *Kauśika Sūtra* 28.1–4, in a rite against poison, obeisance is first made to Takṣaka, a serpent-god, and a patient is sprinkled with and made to drink fresh water and water containing a vegetal medicine. Water also is an effective cure against poison in *Atharvaveda* 6.100.2.[21] Although generally considered inauspicious, crossroads are suitable places to undertake healings because demons frequently congregate there.

An interesting chapter in the *Suśruta Saṃhitā* (Sū 34) teaches that a king who is about to go into battle must be protected from various kinds of poison both by a physican (*vaidya*) skilled in the essences of medicines and by a domestic priest (*purohita*) versed in magico-religious speech. And since Brahmā (Prajāpati) declared *āyurveda* to be a limb of the Veda (*vedāṅga*), the prudent physician must conduct himself in accordance with the judgements of the priest.

The priest in this healing rite is held in greater authority than the doctor, pointing to the antiquity of the practice. Although religion was strongly favored over "science," both were required to secure the protection of the king.

Mantras were also used in the preparations of antidotes. In CaCi 23.223, water, used to treat one suffering from a false fear of poisoning, is purified by means of magico-religious utterances. The preparation of the antidote, *mahāgandhihastī* (the elephant with a great scent), is to be carried out according to the following prescription (CaCi 23.90–94). And while crushing [the medicine], one should utter this effective mantra:

> My mother is conquering (*jayā*), by name; my father is conquering (*jaya*),[22]
> by name. I, the son of conquering [masc.] and conquering [fem.] am victory
> (*vijaya*) and now I conquer. Obeisance to Puruṣasiṃha, to Viṣṇu, to
> Viśvakarman, to Sanātana, to Kṛṣṇa, to Bhava and to Vibhava. [I am][23]
> the radiance of Vṛṣākapi [the Sun], in person [i.e. in life], the radiance of
> Brahmā and Indra, in death. As I do not know the defeat of Vāsudeva
> (Kṛṣṇa), the marriage of a mother and the desiccation of an ocean,
> therefore, let this antidote be successful by this true speech.
> When the best of all medicines is ground together [, say]: "O Hilinili, protect, *svāhā*!"[24]

This antidote, when properly consecrated, was so powerful that the place where it was stored was unaffected by Atharvan mantras (of black magic), by various demons, by sorcery, or by specters (CaCi 23.88).

The religious nature of this mantra is apparent from the reference to various deities whose powers the charmer desires transferred to the antidote. The recitation of the nonsense word *Hilinili* reflects the esoteric nature of the mantra. Speaking this word, the significance of which was known only to the initiated, imbued the medicine with the power to protect and to heal. The first part of the mantra is Atharvavedic in character. Variants of the mother-father-son analogy can be found in a hymn against poison (AV 6.16.2), in a hymn for the consecration of the medicine (*śilācī*; lac?) (AV 5.5.1,8), in a hymn for the consecration of simples (RV 10.97.9), and in a hymn for the consecration of the plant *kúṣṭha* (AV 5.4.8; 19.39.3).

Powerful antidotes were also used to ward off black magic. In CaCi 23.59, the antidote *mṛtasaṃjīvana* is said to be effective, among other things, against evil mantras and mantras of sorcery.

TREATMENT OF MENTAL DISORDERS (*UNMĀDA, UNMATTA, APASMĀRA*)

The recitation of magico-religious speech was both a characteristic and a treatment of insanity (*unmāda, unmatta*). Caraka (Ci 9.20) describes a patient suffering from insanity caused by the demons *brahmarakṣas* as "one, in whom guffaws and dancing predominate, [who is characterized] by [his] hatred of and contempt for gods, inspired men, and physicians, by [his] recitation of eulogies, of mantras to the gods and of law books, and by the self-infliction [of pain] with wooden sticks, etc." Because these actions may characterize any holy man or ascetic, one must presume that the reference is to individuals who imitated the activities and practices of these religious men.

On the other hand, patients sufferings from insanity arising from lust (*rati*) and the desire for worship (*abhyarcana*) are treated by a purely magical rite, utilizing mantras, simples, amulets and various sacrifical, religious, ascetic, and propitiatory observances (CaNi 7.15–16 and Ci 9.23). A similar cure is prescribed for one suffering from insanity from external causes (*āgantu*) (CaCi 9.16,23,93–94) and insanity caused by gods, sages, fathers (i.e., dead ancestors) and Gandharvas (CaCi 9.88–90). Likewise, in the case of *apasmāra* (epilepsy) arising from external causes, mantras, etc., are said to be benficial (CaNi 8.10).

In the *Atharvaveda* (6.111), two types of insanity are implied: the demented state brought on by the patient, as a result of his infringement of certain divine mores or taboos (*únmadita*); and the abnormal mental state caused by demonic possession (*únmatta*). In the same hymn, the insane person is described as having an agitated mind and talking nonsense. He is cured by propitiating Agni, the Apsarases, Indra, and Bhaga through the recitation of the mantra and by the use of medicines consecrated with the mantra. The term *apasmāra* does not occur in the *Atharvarveda* or in the *Ṛgveda*.

TREATMENT OF FEVER (*JVARA*)

The āyurvedic use of mantras in the treatment of fever is especially significant as it appears to be found only in the *Bheḷasaṃhitā*, a text that may contain material earlier than that found in either of the two "classical" āyurvedic treatises, the *Caraka-* and *Suśruta-Saṃhitās*. This unique explanation occurs in Ci 1.46–51 and is said to be "healing by divine intervention" (*jvare daivavyapāśrayacikitsā*):

> 46. Fever, arising from the anger of the Great Lord (Śiva), has been previously mentioned by the great sages. Therefore, for the sake of liberation from fever, one should worship Ṛṣabhadhvaja (Śiva).
> 47. Ritual ablutions, appeasements, burnt offerings, solemn vows, penance, restraint, vegetal oblations, [proper] intentions and the destroyers of fever (*jvaranāśana*) mentioned in the Veda [all] kill [fever].
> 48. Overlord of disease, extremely powerful, the fever [is] the origin of disease; fatal to all beings, sublime, the fever is declared [to be] characteristic of fire.
> 49. Occasional, arising from evil, [it] should be difficult to cure by physicians; therefore, one should check [it] by mantras proclaimed in the Veda and by burnt offerings.
> 50. Fever, therefore, does not enter the man [when the prescribed method of] warding off fever, which [involves] violent action occurring in [the rites of] demonology, is properly executed by a witch doctor (*bhūtavaidya*).
> 51. Moreover, the ancient cure of fever is to be employed by the physician who worships Rudra, who is pure, who practices asceticism and who is prudent [in his duties].

Statements contained in these verses suggest very strongly that the fever (*jvara*) treated is the Atharvavedic *takmán*. In Verse 46, the fever is associated with Śiva, the later Hindu name of the Vedic god Rudra, who in the *Atharvaveda* is inextricably connected with the demon *takmán*.[25] Likewise, Verse 51 speaks of an ancient cure for fever used by the physician who worships Rudra and Verse 50 mentions the use of the magico-religious practices of demonology in the treatment. Verse 47 contains the expression *jvaranāśana* (destroyers of fever), which are said to be of Vedic origin. This calls to mind the phrase *takmanāśanagaṇa* (the group [of Atharvavedic hymns] destructive of *takman*), mentioned at *Atharvaveda Pariśiṣṭa* 34.7.[26] Similarly, "the mantras proclaimed in the Veda," in Verse 49, most likely refer to the list of *Atharvaveda Pariśiṣṭa* 34.7. The āyurvedic explanation of the cause and treatment of fever (*jvara*) found in the *Bheḷasaṃhitā*, therefore, demonstrates a close connection with and even reliance on the more ancient, religiously inspired healing practices of the *Atharvaveda* and points to an antique doctrine retained in a "classical" medical treatise.

COLLECTION AND PREPARATION OF MEDICINES

Mantras also were used during the collection of medicines and in the preparation of certain remedies. The collection of the herbs used in an elixir relating to the removal of physical distress (*nivṛttasantāpīyaṃ rasāyanam*) is undertaken according to a prescribed method (SuCi 30.26–27). Indeed the simples, which have the appearance of a snake, are said to be among the first seven.[27] The uprooting of them is always to be performed with this mantra:

> Certainly for the sake of auspicious [results], [you simples] be appeased by the asceticism and by the radiant energy of Mahendra, of Rāma, of Kṛṣṇa, of *brāhmaṇas* and of cows.

They are then consecrated accordingly (SuCi 30.28–30ab).

> The intelligent [one] should consecrated precisely all [those simples] with this *mantra*:
>
> > The Somas and those equal to Soma cannot ever be obtained by people
> > who are unbelieving, indolent, ungrateful and evil doers. The nectar
> > drunk but for a small remnant by the gods headed by Brahmā, was placed in [these simples], having Soma as their energy, and also in Soma,[28] the Lord of the Simples.[29]

The first *mantra* is recited in order to appease the plants that were uprooted, suggesting an attitude of "nonviolence" (*ahiṃsa*) toward vegetal matter. The collection of medicinal plants by uprooting occurs in the *Atharvaveda* and the propitiation of them for any harm done is found in *Ṛgveda* 10.97.20 and *Vājasaneyi Saṃhitā* 12.98 and 100.[30] The mention of the Vedic plant par excellence, Soma, in the rite of consecration reflects an archaic attitude, similar to that found in the *Atharvaveda*. The plant *kúṣṭha*, the principal medicine against *takmán*, is made efficacious by being closely associated with Soma at *Atharvaveda* 19.39.5–8.

Likewise, a cupful of a certain emetic drug is consecrated with the following mantra (CaKa 1.14; slight variant SuSū 43.3):

> May Brahmā, Dakṣā, the Aśvin-twins, Rudra, Indra,
> Earth, Moon, Wind, Fire, the Ṛṣis, together with the multitude
> of healing plants and host of beings, protect you. May this
> medicine be for you like the elixer of the Ṛṣis, like
> the ambrosia of the gods, and like the nectar of the
> best of the serpents.

In this mantra, the names of both Vedic and later Brāhmaṇic divinities, as well as other sacred elements found in the Veda, are invoked in order to make the emetic especially powerful.

Elsewhere, mantras, especially those in *gāyatrī* meter, are recited while preparing the elixir that promotes sexual desire in old age (*āyuṣkāmarasāyana*) (SuCi 28.9 and 25); and, as we have noticed, they are used in the preparation of certain antidotes.

The use of magico-religious utterances played a dominant role in the collection, consecration, and application of the pharmacopoeia in Vedic medicine. Every cure required a mantra to be recited in connection with its prescribed remedy. Two rather long hymns (RV 10.97 and AV 8.7) are devoted to medicinal plants. In these hymns, the process of collection of the herbs is mentioned, their consecration detailed, and their uses prescribed. The comprehensive knowledge of plants, which the better āyurvedic physicians still possess, derives directly from the early Atharvavedic medical tradition.

CONCLUSIONS

A dependence on the use of magico-religious speech is characteristic of the Atharvavedic medical tradition. In the Vedic medical rituals, it was the key component, upon which the success or failure of a particular treatment hinged. The Vedic physician (*bhiṣáj*) recited mantras during a prescribed rite in order to solicit the healing powers necessary to effect a cure. The mantras were uttered primarily to destroy or to drive away the demonic diseases, to ward off further attacks from them, and to consecrate various medicines.

With the development of *āyurveda* around the Christian era, a quite different approach to medicine began to emerge in India. A more rational or "scientific" attitude had all but replaced the magico-religious medical doctrines of the *Atharvaveda*; and with these revolutionary ideas, mantras assumed a subordinate, if not anomalous, place in the medical treatments prescribed in the early āyurvedic literature. The examples mentioned here are characteristically Atharvavedic and may be considered as representing the final vestiges of that archaic tradition in the newer medicine of *āyurveda*. The diseases treated by mantras are those that have either exact or very similar parallels in the *Atharvaveda*. Although the cures using mantras were magico-religious, one finds that more therapeutic or empirical procedures also were often used or advocated. The duty of reciting the mantras does not always seem to have been given to the physician (*vaidya*) but to a priest (*purohita*) who, in certain cases requiring magico-religious treatment, commanded authority over the doctor. He and the physician worked together to effect a cure. The combining of medical expertise in this way points to the more ancient doctrine, in which religion and medicine were inseparable.

It is important to note that āyurvedic mantras often included both Vedic and later Brāhmaṇic or Hindu names of divinities and sacred elements. This points to a conscious effort to incorporate early religious matter into a late compilation; thereby sanctifying the tradition of medicine.

At all times and in almost every culture, a connection between medicine and religion is demonstrable. The belief that by soliciting divine intervention through prayer and ritual no disease is incurable cuts across cultural boundaries. Cases of miraculous cures abound in Christianity, especially in Catholicism and in Greek Orthodoxy. Inspired by these stories and accounts of supernatural healing documented in religious literature of the tradition, even today, patients suffering from seemingly incurable diseases, for whom the best of modern technological medicine has failed to effect a cure, will seek divine intervention. Prayer vigils, often lasting several days, will be undertaken by friends and relatives at the patient's bedside and special services will be offered. The hope is that, through their prayers, the beneficent beings of the heavenly realm or God will be motivated to heal the patient, to bring him from a state of near death to a healthy, sound condition.

It seems very possible that, in certain cases, the use of mantras in āyurvedic medicine served a similar purpose. More often, however, it appears that mantras and the accompanying magico-religious healing ritual were employed because they reflected the earlier sacred tradition of Vedic medicine. The mantras of Vedic medicine served as models for the mantras of the āyurvedic tradition. The earlier usage of mantras corresponded to their later medical employment. The medical authors merely recast the Vedic mantras according to the newly emerging tradition of Hinduism.

The āyurvedic movement away from magical medicine clearly is illustrated in a passage from the *Suśruta Saṃhitā,* found in connection with the treatment of wounds and sores (*vraṇa*) (Ci 1.75b–77a):

> 75b–76a. Because of [its] establishment in the traditional precepts (*āgama*) and likewise because [it] shows results,[31] this [procedure of cleaning (by evacuation) and treatment] is to be used as if it were a mantra; in no way is it to be called into question.
>
> 76b–77a. And also, by his own resolution, [the physician] must distribute as a remedy the treatments [which are] among the seven beginning with the astringents,[32] which have been previously mentioned by me [in Verses 62–75a].

The author's use of "as if it were a mantra" (*mantravat*) is quite deliberate. It reflects a knowledge of the Atharvavedic use of mantras in the treatment of wounds and sores, which we noticed earlier in the case of swellings and wounds (*śotha, vraṇa*). However, he does not advocate their use in this instance; rather, he emphatically states that the procedure of cleaning [by evacuation] (*śodhaṇa*) and treatment (*ropaṇa*), outlined in the previous verses, must be employed. As a mantra, previously, this healing technique, now, is not to be questioned.

In support of the general thesis of this paper, these verses illustrate well the early āyurvedic doctrinal shift from a magico-religious approach to medicine and to a more empirico-rational one. Later medical evidence demonstrates that magical medicine did not completely vanish vis-à-vis the developing *āyurveda*. It was, however, never to gain the status in āyurvedic medicine that it enjoyed in Atharvavedic medicine.

This examination of the use of *mantras* in *āyurveda* has allowed us to look into the part of medicine that is not purely scientific. It has shown us the role played by magico-religious medicine in a traditional medical system that was becoming dominated by an empirico-rational approach to disease and cure. Being a product of a culture whose peoples' lives are governed by a deeply religious sentiment, it is uniquely Indian, but the underlying belief in the efficacy of magico-religious speech for healing transcends the barriers of both time and culture.

APPENDIX

In the section on children's diseases (*kumāratantra*) of the *Suśruta Saṃhitā*, several chapters are devoted to warding off nine disease-causing demons (Utt 27–36). Concluding each of the chapters are verses to be recited in the course of the overall magical rite. In no instance are these metrical passages called mantras in the text; but the commentator, Ḍalhaṇa, refers to them as "mantras of protection" (*rakṣāmantra*, or *rakṣā* in abbreviated form). The contents of the verses draw largely on classical Indian mythology, derived principally from the *Mahābhārata* and the *Purāṇas* rather than from the Vedic *Saṃhitās*. Parallels cannot be found in the Atharvavedic material, suggesting that their source is from a later tradition. Similarly, not being called *mantra* by the author, it is likely that these verses were not considered to have originated in the sacred Vedic texts. No less efficacious, they have become an important part of the rites for healing children who required protection and favors from demonic forces. Their employment here further demonstrates that specific traditions of magico-religious medicine were incorporated into *āyurveda*. In the case of children's diseases, however, the use of mantras cannot be traced back to Atharvavedic medicine.

The following is a translation of the verses, addressed to the nine deities, all but three of which are female. The sequence begins with soliciting favors from the nine seizers as a group and then proceeds to address each of the nine deities individually.

THE NINE SEIZERS (*NAVAGRAHA*) (SUUTT 27)

18–20. While offerings are thrown into the fire, [the following *mantra* should be recited:]

20b–21. To Agni (fire) and to Kṛttikā,[33] continually say, "*svāhā, svāhā*." Obeisance to the god Skanda,[34] obeisance to the Lord of the seizers. Obediently, I salute you. Will you accept my oblation. May you cause my child to be healthy and without disease.

SKANDAGRAHA (SUUTT 28)

9. One should wash the child with water consecrated with the *gāyatrī*-verse (RV 3.62.10), and light the sacrifical fire with libations.
10. Hence I, the protector, the destroyer of the children's evil shall proclaim [these verses] which are to be made every day by the indefatigable physician (*bhiṣaj*):
11. Let that eternal god Skanda, who is the receptacle of the ascetic heats (*tapas*), of the radiant heats (*tejas*), of honors and of wonderful forms, be gracious to you.
12. Let the god, The Lord of the Army of Seizers, The Mighty One (*vibhu*), The Lord of the Army of Gods, the Lord Guha, destroyer of the foes of the gods' army, protect you.
13. Let the one who is the offspring of all gods [Rudra, commentary], of the Great One, of the Shining One [Agni] and of the Gangā [Ganges], of Umā [Parvatī] and of Kṛttikā, grant you peace.
14. Let the lord wearing a red garland and clothes, embellished with red-sandal [paste], the god Krauñcasūdana (Enemy of Krauñca),[35] whose divine form is red, protect you.

SKANDĀPASMĀRA (SUUTT 29)

7–8. After making the necessary offering to Skandāpasmāra, the child should be bathed at a crossroad [and the following mantra of protection should be recited:]

9. He who is called Skandāpasmāra, the cherished friend of Skanda, is also called Viśākha (branchless, limbless), the one with a deformed face. Let there be the child's welfare.

ŚAKUNĪ (SUUTT 30)

9. One should make various worships (*pūjas*) to Śakunī [and should recite these verses of protection:]
10. Let the Sáakunī [-bird], the goddess who wanders in the mid-space, who is embellished with all adornments, who has a mouth of iron and a sharp beak, be gracious to you.
11. Let the Śakunī [-bird], who has an awful appearance, a great body, a large belly, reddish-brown eyes, pointed ears and a terrifying voice, be gracious to you.

REVATĪ (SUUTT 31)[36]

8–9. After performing the proper rites, the physician (*bhiṣaj*) should, at the confluence [of two rivers], bathe both the female supporter [nurse] and the child [and should recite the following mantra of protection:]

10. Let the dark-coloured goddess Revatī, anointed with unguents, wearing various garments, [donning] different garlands and [sporting] quivering earrings, be gracious to you.
11. Let the goddess Revatī, Śuṣkanāmā (Dry [or Vain], by name),[37] whom the goddess with manifold embellishments constantly esteems, who is large, dreadful, and bent over, and who has many children, be gracious to you.

PŪTANĀ (SUUTT 32)[38]

9. The bathing of the child with water remaining after religious ablutions is prescribed; the goddess Pūtanā is to be worshipped with oblations together with gifts [and the following mantra of protection would be recited:]
10. Let the filthy [impure] goddess Pūtanā, clothed in filthy [impure] garments, who has dishevelled hair and recourse to empty houses [var., empty gardens], protect the child.
11. Let the goddess Pūtanā, who has an awful appearance and a very bad smell, who is dreadful and black like a rain-cloud, and who dwells in dilapidated[39] houses, protect the child.

ANDHAPŪTANĀ (SUUTT 33)

7–8. After making offerings of raw and cooked meat and of blood at a crossroad or inside a house, the child should be bathed with sacred and efficacious water [and the following verse of protection should be recited:]

9. Let the dreadful, tawny, bald goddess, clad in red garments, Andhapūtanā, being pleased, watch over this child.

ŚĪTAPŪTANĀ (SUUTT 34)

7b–8. After making the proper oblations, which include food made of *mudga*,[40] *vāruṇī*-liquor,[41] and blood (*rudhira*), to Śītapūtanā, the child should be bathed at the bank of a lake (literally, receptacle of water)[42] [and the following verse of protection should be recited:]

9. Let the goddess, who has *mudga*-pap as food and who drinks liquor and blood, the goddess Śītapūtanā, whose abode is a lake, protect you.

MUKHAMAṆḌIKĀ (SUUTT 35)

6–8. After having made the appropriate oblations in the middle of a cow pen (*goṣṭhamadhya*), the bathing [of the child] with water purified with the [*gāyatrī*-] mantra[43] is prescribed [and the following verse of protection should be recited:]

9. Let the decorated, beautiful, auspicious Mukhamaṇḍikā, who assumes any shape at will and who is fond of dwelling in the middle of a cow pen, protect you.

NAIGAMEṢA (SUUTT 36)[44]

10. A bathing [of the child] [with water consecrated with the *gāyatrī*-verse, commentary] is commanded [to take place] beneath a Banyan tree; one should offer oblations at a Banyan tree on the sixth lunar day (*tithi*); [and the following verse of protection should be recited:]
11. Let the greatly celebrated, ram-faced, god Naigameṣa, Bālapitṛ [Children's Father], who has quivering eyes and brows, and who assumes any shape at will, protect the child.

ABBREVIATIONS USED IN THIS CHAPTER

AV	*Atharvaveda Saṃhitā* (Śaunakīya recension)
Ca	*Caraka Saṃhitā*
Ci	*Cikitsāsthāna*
HK	Luise Hilgenberg and Willibald Kirfel, trans., *Vāgbhaṭa's Aṣṭāṅgahṛdaya-saṃhitā*, Leiden: E. J. Brill, 1941.
Ka	*Kalpasthāna*
MS	*Maitrāyaṇī Saṃhitā*
Ni	*Nidānasthāna*
P	*Atharvaveda Saṃhitā* (Paippalāda recension)
RV	*Ṛgveda Saṃhitā*
Śā	*Śārīrasthāna*
Su	*Suśruta Saṃhitā*
Sū	*Sūtrasthāna*
TS	*Taittirīya Saṃhitā*
Utt	*Uttarasthāna*
VS	*Vājasaneyi Saṃhitā*

NOTES

1. The introductory material and other discussions of Vedic medicine in this essay derive from K. G. Zysk, *Religious Healing in the Veda* (Philadelphia: American Philosophical Society, 1985), 1–11a. This book includes translations and annotations of medical hymns from the *Ṛgveda* and the *Atharvaveda* and renderings from the corresponding ritual texts.

2. Maurice Bloomfield, trans., *Hymns of the Atharva Veda* (1897, reprinted Delhi: Motilal Banarsidass, 1964), 518–19; Cf. M. Bloomfield, "Contributions to

the Interpretation of the Veda. Fourth Series," *American Journal of Philology*, 12 (1891), 427 n.l; see also K. G. Zysk, *Religious Healing in the Veda*, 12–102, *passim*.

3. Compare CaSū 11. 54, where spiritual or magico-religious modes of healing were considered to be one of three types of medical treatment:

> Cure is threefold: that having recourse to the gods (*daiva*), that having recourse to reasoning (*yukti*), and that which conquers the spirit (*sattva*). In that case, that having recourse to the gods [includes] the recitation of mantras, the use of simples, the wearing of amulets, auspicious observances, offering of oblations, presenting of gifts, giving of burnt offerings, restraint of mind, atonement, fasting, invoking blessings, sacrifice to deities, prostration to gods, and pilgrimages, etc. Moreover, that having recourse to reasoning [involves] the application of the intake of food [diet], herbs and drugs. And, furthermore, the conquering of the spirit [consists of] restraining the mind from hostile objects.

4. The commentator, Cakrapāṇidatta, states, "By means of this, a certain part of the *Atharvaveda* is thus *āyurveda* because of [its] single purpose."

5. *Bhela Saṃhitā*, edited by V. S. Venkatasubramania Sastri and C. Raja Rajeswara Sarma (New Delhi: Central Council for Research in Indian Medicine and Homoeopathy, 1977).

6. *The Caraka Saṃhitā by Agniveśa*, revised by Caraka and Dṛḍhabala, with the *Āyurvedadīpikā* commentary of Cakrapāṇidatta; edited by Jādavaji Trikamji Ācārya (Bombay: Nirṇaya Sāgar Press, 1941). References to the commentary or to the commentator of this text are to Cakrapāṇidatta.

7. *Suśruta Saṃhitā of Suśruta*, with the *Nibandhasaṃgraha* commentary of Ḍalhaṇācārya and the *Nyāyacandrikā Pañjikā* of Gayadāsācārya on Nidānasthāna; edited by Jādavji Trikamji Ācārya and Nārāyaṇa Rāma Ācārya "Kāvyatīrtha" (Varanasi: Chaukhambha Orientalia, 1980 [Jaikrishnadas Ayurveda Series, 34]). References to the commentary or to the commentator of this text are to Ḍalhaṇa.

8. See AV 9.127.1,3; 9.8.2,20; cf. VS 12.97.

9. See AV 6.25,83; 7.74(78).1,2; 7.76(80).1,2.

10. AV 6.14,127.

11. RV 10.191; AV 4.6,7; 5.13; 6.12,16,100; 7.56(57), 88(93) and 107(112).

12. My translation; cf. R. C. Majumdar, ed., *The Classical Accounts of India* (Calcutta: Firma KLM, 1981), 229; and E. I. Robson, trans., *Arrian*, vol. 2 (Cambridge, Mass.: Harvard University Press, 1958), 350–53 (Loeb edition).

13. Commentary: "The wiping away of poison in reverse direction is to be undertaken with mantras."

14. Commentary: "[The self-protection is] for the purpose of preventing demonic possession."

15. The *doṣas* are threefold: wind (*vāta, vāyu*), bile (*pitta*), and phlegm (*kapha, śleṣman*). On analogy with the Hippocratic and Galenic systems, they are vitiating forces in the body.

16. Commentary: "The mantras, beginning with *kurukullā* and *bheruṇḍā* and named in the best treatises, are here not mentioned." The word *kurukullā* is obscure. It could be from *kurukulyā*, "belonging to the Kuru race"; or, more likely, it is the name of a deity in Buddhism. The term *bheruṇḍā* is the name of a goddess, either Kālī or Yaksiṇī. For both words, see Monier-Williams, *A Sanskrit-English Dictionary* (1899; reprinted Delhi: Motilal Banarsidass, 1974).

17. "[They are] consisting of truth by being prescribed by the gods and sages, [and] consisting of ascetic heat by being prescribed by *brāhmaṇas* and sages.

18. Commentary: "Both an intoxicating drink and *kṣaudra*-honey are to be avoided."

19. The commentator adds: "'by meditation' which is unexpressed."

20. Commentary: "The technique of antidotes is proper in the case of the failure of the mantra due to not following the correct procedures or due to defective recitations [i.e., reciting without proper accents, etc.]." Similarly, evil spirits (*bhūta*), not able to be conquered by the offering of oblations (*bali*) or by the recitation of mantras presented in the science of the spirits (i.e., demonology) (*bhūtavidyā*), should be treated with medical prescriptions (*yoga*) (SuUtt 60.36b–37a).

21. Water is often used in the healing rites of the early Veda and is usually consecrated with the following formulaic verse (RV 10.137.6; AV 3.7.5; 6.91.3; P 3.2.7; 5.18.9; and 19.18.9): "The waters [are] indeed medicinal; the waters [are] *ámīvā*-dispellers; [and] the waters [are] medicine for every [disease]. [Therefore,] let them [be] medicine for you."

22. Variant reading: "my father is victory (*vijaya*), by name."

23. The names Puruṣasiṃha, Sanātana, Bhava and Vibhava are uncertain. Puruṣasiṃha (literally, man-lion) could be the name of a hero, or it could refer to the name of the fifth of the black Vāsudevas in Jainism. Sanātana (meaning eternal) may refer to "the mind-born son of Brahmā." Bhava and Vibhava could be "existence" and "evolution," deified. Bhava is often equated with Śiva-Rudra; Vibhava in Vaiṣṇavism is "the evolution of the Supreme Being into secondary forms." See Monier-Williams, *A Sanskrit-English Dictionary*. It is clear from the context that all the appellations in this passage refer to names, most likely, of divinities.

24. A variant to these verses occurs at *Aṣṭāṅgahṛdaya Saṃhitā*, Utt 35.26cd–30, where the antidote is called, Candrodaya, "Ascent of the moon": While a purified virgin (*kanyā*) prepares the best antidote, Candrodaya, the physician (*vaidya*), himself ritually pure, should then recite this mantra:

> Obeisance to Puruṣasiṃha and obeisance to Nārāyaṇa. Just as one does not know the defeat of Kṛṣṇa in battle (variant: Just as that Kṛṣṇa does not know defeat in battle; cf. HK, 686–87), just so, let the antidote succeed for me by this true speech. Obeisance! O Vaiḍūryamātā, O Huluhulu, protect me from all poisons. O Gauri, O Gāndhāri, O Cāṇḍāli, O Mātaṅgi, svāhā!

And when it is ground, a second mantra (is recited):

O Harimāyi, svāhā! (variants: O Hari; O Haritamāyi, svāhā!). Certain names mentioned in this variant are difficult. Unlike in CaCi 23.90–94, these appellations are for the most part feminine: Vaiḍūryamātā is obscure; Huluhulu, like Hilihili, appears to be a nonsense word; Gaurī could refer to Pārvatī, or, perhaps more likely, it is a variant of Gauḍī, the name of a woman from Gaur in central Bengal; Gāndhārī refers to a Gāndhāra woman, Cāṇḍālī a Caṇḍāla woman, and Mātaṅgī a Caṇḍāla or Kirāta woman. Harimāyi is obscure; but, based on the variant Hari, it may refer to Viṣṇu-Kṛṣṇa.

25. See in particular AV 6.20.2; 11.2.3(P 5.12.7= 13.1.14), 22,26. A similar association is only implied at CaCi 3.14 and Ni 1.18ff.

26. See M. Bloomfield, ed., *The Kauśika Sūtra of the Atharvaveda* (1884; rpt. Delhi: Motilal Banarsidass, 1972), 71 n. 1.

27. These seven should include: *ajagarī, śvetakāpotī, gonasī, kṛṣṇakāpotī, vārāhī* (*Dioscorea bulbifera*, Linn), *chatrā*(=*droṇapuṣpī; Leucas cephalotes*, Spreng) and *aticchatrakā*(?= *aticchatrikā*=*droṇapuṣpī*=*chatrā*). I have been able to identify, with the help of the *nighaṇṭus*, only three plants; the other four are obscure. Although *gonasī* is reckoned among the first seven, its inclusion is doubtful because the text (verse 12) states that it has rather the shape of a cow's nose (*gonasākṛti*). The last in the list of a total of eighteen plants mentioned in verses 9-25, however, is *vegavatī*, which is said to resemble a snake's shed skin (*sarpanirmokasannibhā*).

28. Commentary: "in the moon" (*candramasi*).

29. The commentator introduces this passage by saying that it speaks of the views of the ancient, sacred texts; i.e., the Veda (*śruti*).

30. See also *Ṛgvidhāna* 3.42.8–4.1.3. The earliest reference to *ahiṃsā* as applied to plants occurs at MS 3.9.3 and TS 6.3.3.2. Cf. Hanns-Peter Schmidt, "The Origin of *Ahiṃsā*," *Mélanges d' Indianisme: À la Mémoire de Louis Renou* (Paris: Editions E. de Boccard, 1968), 626–55.

31. Commentary: "because it shows a state of nondisease [i.e., health]."

32. The seven, beginning with the astringen.s, constitute the procedure of cleaning and treatment. Following the commentary, they are as follows: the use of astringents, of bandgages, of pastes, of clarified butter, of oils, of semi-solid extracts (*rasakriyā*, cf. CaCi 14.185–192; 26.195), and of powders.

33. The commentator to SuUtt 28.13 explains that this deity is the wife of the seven Ṛṣis, enumerated as six. John Dowson says that they are the Pleiades, the

six nurses of the war-god Kārttikeya and that "they were daughters of a king according to one legend, wives of Ṛṣis according to another" (*A Classical Dictionary of Hindu Mythology and Religion, Geography, History and Literature*. London: Routledge & Kegan Paul, Ltd., 1972, 169).

34. This deity is the god of war and the planet Mars, also called Kārttikeya. In the epics, he is the son of Śiva (Rudra) and is said to have been produced when Śiva cast his seed into fire (Agni), afterwards being received by Gangā (the Ganges River). He was raised by Kṛttikā, has six heads and the name Kārttikeya. His father is sometimes said to be Agni (fire); and Gangā and Pārvatī are called his mothers. He was produced to destroy the evil warrior Tāraka, whose austerities made him an important foe of the gods. He is represented as riding on a peacock, carrying a bow in one hand and an arrow in the other. His wife is Kaumārī (maiden) or Senā (army). He has numerous epithets, including Mahāsena (whose army is great), Senāpati (lord of the army), Kumāra (child), and Guha, (the mysterious one) (*Ibid.*, 152).

35. Krauñca is said to be a pass situated somewhere in the Himālayas, which, according to the *Vāyu Purāṇa*, was created by Kārttikeya's splitting open Mount Krauñca. It also refers to a confederate of Tāraka, against whom Kārttikeya triumphantly led the gods (*Ibid.*, 159). Accordingly, the enemy of Krauñca is Kārttikeya (so also commentary).

36. She was the beautiful daughter of King Raivata and the wife of Balarāma. She was known to be very tall. Balarāma reduced her size with the end of a ploughshare and she became his wife. She is said to have two sons and to have partaken in drinking bouts with her husband (Dowson, *A Classical Dictionary*, 266).

37. Commentary glosses as Śuṣkarevatī.

38. She is a female demon and daughter of Bali, a just, demonic warrior king. She attempted to kill the baby Kṛṣṇa by suckling him, but was sucked to death by the infant (Dowson, *A Classical Dictionary*, 251).

39. Reading: *bhinnāgārāśaya*.

40. The word *mudga* is generally considered to be the name of the plant *Phaseolus mungo* Linn or green gram. Its seeds are often made into a soup and given as the first article of a diet to someone recovering from an acute illness. See G. J. Meulenbeld, *The Mādhavanidāna and Its Chief Commentary*, chapters 1–10. (Leiden: E. J. Brill, 1974) 590; U. C. Dutt, *The Materia Medica of the Hindus* (Calcutta: Madan Gopal Dass, 1922) 150–51; and A. K. Nadkarni and K. M. Nadkarni, *Dr. K. M. Nadkarni's Indian Materia Medica*, vol. 1 (1908, reprinted Bombay: Popular Prakashan, 1954) 939–40.

41. On the one hand *vāruṇī* is a synonym for alcoholic beverages (*surā*), on the other it is a type of liquor made from ground *punarnavā* and *śāli* rice (see Meulenbeld, *The Mādhavanidāna*, 515).

42. Commentary: "near a river."

43. Following the commentary; cf. also SuUtt 28.9.

44. In the *Mahābhārata,* Naigameṣa is the "goat-faced form of Agni." Margaret and James Stutley also cite Coomaraswamy who describes him as antelope-headed and claims that he is connected with procreation in both Hindu and Jaina mythology (*A Dictionary of Hinduism,* London: Routledge & Kegan Paul, 1977, 200).

CHAPTER 5

Are Mantras Speech Acts? The Mīmāṃsā Point of View

John Taber

yad gṛhītam avijñātaṃ nigadenaiva śabdyate,
anagnāv iva śuṣkaidho na taj jvalati karhicit;
(What is merely vocalized without being understood,
like dry wood without fire, never ignites.)

Nirukta 1.18

The Mīmāṃsā is interested in language from the point of view of performance, not of competence.

J. F. Staal

RECENTLY, SEVERAL ATTEMPTS HAVE BEEN made to analyze mantras as speech acts (McDermott 1975; Wheelock 1980, 1982; also the contributions by Alper and Wheelock in this volume). While these studies promise eventually to make more sense out of mantras in terms of our own linguistic theory, it still remains to be seen, for the most part, how those who employ mantras understand them. With this essay, I hope to remedy the situation somewhat. I shall examine the treatment of Vedic mantras in the Mīmāṃsā school of Indian philosophy, which indeed at first sight appears to be comparable to a speech act analysis. I shall then go on to evaluate the range and suitability of applying the concept of a speech act to Mīmāṃsā philosophy of language in general. This discussion, in turn, will have implications for the relevance of that notion for other classical Indian schools of linguistic thought.

WHAT IS A SPEECH ACT?

It should be kept firmly in mind that to designate a certain linguistic item a speech act, in the technical sense developed especially by Searle, involves subscribing to a general way of viewing language. Speech act theory claims that the most fruitful way to approach linguistic phenomena is to see them as actions; that is, rule-governed behavior of intelligent agents for the achievement of certain ends. All utterances are to be viewed in this way insofar as they are instances of linguistic communication. From the standpoint of speech act theory it is not the case that some instances of linguistic communication are speech acts (say, what J. L. Austin 1961 singled out as "performative utterances") while others (say, simple assertions) are not.[1]

To ask, therefore, whether a particular linguistic event is a speech act is tantamount to asking whether anyone means anything by it; that is, whether it was produced with an intention to bring about some reaction or response in a reader or hearer, to establish awareness of some state of affairs, or even to bring a state of affairs into existence—as one does when, in the context of a marriage ceremony, one utters the words *I do*—and so on. Searle makes this point with contrasting reference to noises and marks produced accidentally. Etchings in stone or noises caused by eroison or the wind may appear to be hieroglyphs or voices, but because they are not caused by persons with certain intentions, they are not instances of linguistic communication; they are not speech acts (1969, 16–17).

With this understanding in hand, it appears immediately significant that the concern of the Mīmāṃsā philosopher regarding mantras—here and in what follows, I take Śabara as my principal source—is whether they convey something meant or intended (*vivakṣitavacana*, MīSūBh 1.2.31, I.143). This is not, stricly, a concern about whether mantras are meaningful.[2] For as Kumārilabhaṭṭa explains, in commenting on Śabara (TV, I.143–44), a capacity of words to express meanings is always ascertained. Even in the case of mantras, their meaning is usually evident as soon as they are pronounced. They are grammatical; they make sense of themselves. But, still, when a mantra is presented in the Veda as a formula to be uttered in the context of a ritual, one may take it actually to express what it means, or one may not. One may simply take it as a noise, a mere utterance (*uccāraṇamātra*). And so it is appropriately asked, *kiṃ vivakṣitavacanā mantrā utāvivakṣitavacanāḥ*—that is, not Are mantras meaningful? but, roughly, Are the meanings of mantras intended? Are mantras *meant*? And, this would seem to be none other than the question Are mantras instances of linguistic communication? From the standpoint of speech act theory the question is Are mantras speech acts? (Searle 1971a, 44–45).

THE CONTEXT OF THE DISCUSSION

While it is not well known that pragmatics figures in the Mīmāṃsā treatment of mantras, some features of the discussion have been widely noticed, above all the suggestion that mantras are absurd (Strauss 1927a,

121–25; Renou 1960a, 72–75; Staal 1967, 45–46). In the debate of whether mantras are intended utterances, the Mīmāṃsaka allows his opponent to support the contention that they are not, by indicating that, as far as their literal meaning goes, some mantras are not the sort of sentences that possibly could be intended. They speak of things that do not exist (RV 4.58.3 mentions a being with four horns, three feet, two heads, and seven hands); they attribute purposes to unconscious objects ("O plant, protect this one!" TS 1.2.1); they are self-contradictory ("Aditi is heaven, Aditi is the atmosphere," RV 1.89.10); some of them are simply incomprehensible ("O Indra, your spear sat firm [? *amyak*] for us," RV 1.169.3). Moreover, there are indications that even those mantras that make coherent sense are employed in such a way as to make that sense irrelevant: One is often directed to utter a mantra in circumstances to which its meaning would seem to have already assigned it. (I shall give an example of this problem later.) These objections were not considered for the first time by the Mīmāṃsakas; most of those I have mentioned were aired previously by Yāska, in his etymological treatise the *Nirukta* (1.15), who attributes them to a certain Kautsa.[3]

Although such objections are rightly termed *skeptical*, it would be wrong to suggest that the follower of Kautsa, as presented in the Mīmāṃsā discussion, is a real philosophical skeptic or even an unorthodox thinker.[4] Although he denies the truth of some Vedic sentences, he hardly means to challenge the authority of the Veda in the sense that matters most to the ritualist; namely, as a manual for the performance of the sacrifice. His doubts about the literal meaning of mantras ultimately concern only *how* mantras are supposed to be employed in a sacrificial context. He does not deny *that* they are to be employed in some way, nor indeed that the sacrifice really delivers the benefits promised for it.[5] For the ritualist—that is to say, for the Mīmāṃsaka as well as the Kautsan—the validity of the Veda as a theoretical document is basically beside the point.[6]

Let us, however, step back to gain a wider perspective on the context in which the debate of the issues raised by Kautsa takes place in Mīmāṃsā. The Mīmāṃsā, seen in its most general aspect, is a system of rules for interpreting the directives for carrying out religious ritual presented by the *Brāhmaṇas* in conjunction with the *Saṃhitās,* that is, the Veda proper. (The Śrauta-, Gṛhya-, and Dharmasūtras, as *smṛti* texts, are viewed as secondary in authority to the *Bráhmaṇas.*) The Mīmāṃsā probably evolved at a time when the traditional sacrificial lore was becoming less known. Because it was no longer possible to rely on a continuing succession of specialists who knew the meaning of the ancient texts—who knew such things as which mantras go with which procedures, the sequence of ritual performances, and so on—guidelines had to be fixed for making sense out of them. By the time of the formulation of a sūtra text for Mīmāṃsā (400–200 B.C., attributed to Jaimini [Kane 1930–62, V.1197]) however, the old ritual, especially the public rites, had fallen largely into disuse and the considerations raised begin to take on a rather theoretical tone. A new, more philosophical—or, more precisely, apologetic—concern shows itself. The Mīmāṃsā is now announced as "the investigation into dharma" (*dharmajijñāsā*) in general. Śabarasvāmin (200–400 A.D. [Kane 1930–62, V.1197]), one of the first commentators on the MīSū, especially emphasizes the soteriologic importance of dharma as conducive to the "highest beatitude" (*niḥśreyasa,* interpreted not as *mokṣa* but as *svarga,* "heaven" or "happiness"). Later commentators, such as Kumārilabhaṭṭa (seventh century) follow suit. Just as the development of Vedānta philosophy can be seen, in part, as a response to the emergence of heterodox schools of systematic philosophical thought, so the Mīmāṃsā of Śabara and his successors was probably partly motivated by the need to depict Hindu orthopraxis, the intense concern with ritual still evident in India today that had always served as an object of ridicule for opposed traditions, as a comprehensive worldview.

Now *dharma* is defined in the Mīmāṃsā as *codanālakṣaṇo 'rtha,* something useful that is "characterized," or made known, according to Śabara, by a directive (MīSū 1.1.2). The Veda directs one to carry out religious acts by means of such injunctions as "One who desires heaven should perform the new- and full-moon sacrifice" (ĀŚS 3.14.8);[7] "The daily reading of the Veda should be recited" (ŚB 11.5.6.3); and so on. So, the Veda, specifically Vedic injunction (*vidhi*), is the proper means of knowledge (*pramāṇa*) as far as dharma is concerned. The latter, being of the nature of a ritual performance (dharma is equivalent to *yāga* for Śabara, MīSūBh 1.1.2, I.17–18), does not exist in a form already established, for the senses to perceive. In that way, it is removed from the sphere of the other chief means of knowledge—perception, inference, and so on—discussed in Indian philosophy. Because of the exclusiveness of the authority of injunction with regard to dharma, vigorously argued for by Śabara and others in extensive epistemological debate with representatives of other schools, all portions of the Veda that are to be considered authoritative or "useful" (*arthavat*) in conveying knowledge of dharma must be shown to relate in one way or another to what is exhorted to be done in a ritual context. This stipulation immediately poses a problem for mantras as well as other sentences of the Vedic corpus known as *arthavādas* (MīSū 1.2.1–18).[8]

An *arthavāda* (literally, the statement of a meaning, or of a thing, or of a state of affairs) is essentially a eulogy. In TaitSam 2.1.1, for example, following the declaration that one who desires prosperity should offer to Vāyu a white animal in the *agniṣomīya* ritual, one finds the phrase "Vāyu is the swiftest deity; he approaches [the sacrificer] with his own share; he leads him to prosperity." Now, it is not clear just how this statement contributes to knowledge of the rite in question. On the face of it, it has nothing to do with the result to be effected (*sādhya*), nor with the material means to achieve it (*sādhana*), nor with the procedure (*itikartavyatā*)—

the three standard factors of any productive activity (*bhāvanā*) according to the Mīmāṃsā school—all of these being otherwise specified. This doubt regarding the purpose of an *arthavāda* is resolved (MīSūBh 1.2.7) when it is seen that, even though an *arthavāda* does not indicate any of the principal factors of an injoined rite, it gives a certain force to the injunction. It eulogizes a particular ritual as an effective way of obtaining a desired result, not the result itself, which is always intrinsically desirable and therefore requires no eulogy, but this particular way of achieving it). Thus, it motivates one to proceed with the ritual.[9] For the case at hand, the phrase "Vayu is the swiftest deity," etc., implies that if one carries out the rite in question prosperity will arrive without delay. Insofar as an *arthavāda* helps the effectiveness of an injunction, then, it contributes to knowledge of dharma.

The problem for mantras is roughly parallel: How do the sentences collected in the Saṃhitās, which are assigned to be uttered simultaneously with the performance of sacrificial procedures—hymns (*ṛc*), songs (*sāman*), muttered formulas (*yajus*)—provide knowledge of dharma? How are they *pramāṇa*? These, too, appear for the most part simply to express states of affairs without instructing one how to carry out anything. In TS 1.1.8, for example, various formulas are given to be uttered while preparing rice cakes to be offered in the new- and full-moon sacrifice: "I pour together," the priest is to say as he pours water into a dish containing freshly gound meal; "For generation I unite you," he should proclaim as he mixes the water and meal together. How do such formulas teach the officiant what needs to be done?

But the question immediately arises—and here Kautsa's view is relevant—Do not mantras in fact contribute to the sacrifice as subsidiary sacrificial acts in themselves?[10] If so, then only the utterance of the syllables is important; that by itself would be sufficient to produce a beneficial sacrificial result (*apūrva*; MīSūBh, I.150). In fact, some mantras do not seem to have any meaning—they cannot possibly serve to teach anything—while some of those that do seem not to be intended to convey their meaning.

The former include nonsensical and self-contradictory mantras; the latter, those that are assigned in *Brāhmaṇa* passages to circumstances apparently implicit in their meanings. Thus, TB 3.2.8.4 instructs the *adhvaryu* priest of the new- and full-moon sacrifice to utter the mantra "Expanding one, may you spread wide!" as he spreads out the rice mixture on a dishlike arrangement of heated potsherds. But, the very meaning of the mantra (given independently at TaitSam 1.1.8) insofar as it refers to spreading, already suggests that use. More generally, the fact that when one learns the Veda one concentrates solely on the pronunciation of it suggests that the meaning of mantras is not important, as does the fixed order of words in mantras (in the latter regard, see Staal 1967, 45–47). In light of these objections, the crucial consideration for whether mantras constitute a *pramāṇa* is whether their meanings are *meant;* that is, whether they *convey* information.

MANTRAS ARE INDICATORS

The resolution of the question of the authority of mantras comes down to seeing that "mantras serve to bring to light the subsidiary parts of the sacrifice as it is being performed. . . . For if the sacrifice and its auxiliaries are not made known, the sacrifice cannot be carried out" (MīSūBh 1.2.32, I.150).[11] Neither Śabara nor Kumārila elaborates this idea, but the point seems obvious enough: Mantras indicate, in various ways, the procedures of the sacrifice and the things employed in them.[12] Some do this directly and plainly, in the form of indicative statements ("I cut the grass, the seat of the gods," MS 1.1.2); others do so obliquely, in the form of petitions, directives, expressions of hope, and so forth ("May I extend for long the life of the sacrificer," TaitSam 1.1.6, pronounced by the priest as he gazes at his arms; "Let the wind separate you," TaitSam 1.1.5, muttered as the grain is winnowed); others indicate sacrificial details still more symbolically, identifying the elements of the sacrifice with gods and their accessories ("On the impulse of the god Savitṛ, with the arms of the Aśvins, with the hands of Pūṣan, I pour thee out," TaitSam 1.1.6, uttered as the grain is poured onto a millstone).[13] Regardless of their form, in almost every case, mantras allude to what is going on in the sacrifice as the priest executes it. Thus, recited in the proper sequence, they help the priest see what he is doing and remind him of what has yet to be done.[14] They provide a running narrative of the rite. And so, insofar as they pertain to the factor of *itikartavyatā* (procedure), they are *pramāṇa* with regard to dharma.[15] Just as the texts that lay out the various acts and the order in which they are to be performed are *pramāṇa,* so are the mantras that, during the actual performance of those acts, highlight what is being done and signal what comes next.

But, how do we know that mantras in fact are indicative (*abhidhāna-samartha,* MīSūBh 1.2.31, I.145), that they are intended to refer to things and are not, rather, qua mere sequences of sounds, ritual performances in themselves? We know this, Śabara claims, because "the meaning of words as they occur in the Veda and as they are ordinarily employed is the same. As it is *meant* in ordinary usage, so should it be in the Veda" (MīSūBh 1.2.32, I.150).[16] As sentences do not just have meaning in ordinary language but also are used to *convey* meaning (we mean things by them), so for the Veda. In short, Vedic sentences are instances of linguistic communication.

This claim is introduced without explanation in Śabara's argument. It may be meant merely as a paraphrase of AiB 1.4.9, cited by Yāska at the head of his reply to Kautsa: "This indeed is the perfection of the sacrifice, that it is fully formed (*rūpasamṛddham*), i.e., that while the action is being done the formula (*yajus*) addresses (*abhivadati*) it." A more complete justification for Śabara's claim will emerge, however, as we proceed to consider the Mīmāṃsā's general orientation toward language in what follows. For now, in dealing with the issues raised by Kautsa, it has only to be noted that the various matters brought up which suggest that some mantras are meaningless or that their meaning is irrelevant to their employment, are mistaken according to the Mīmāṃsā analysis. Apparently nonsensical mantras can be seen to be coherent, when appreciated in light of their figurative meaning, or as eulogies (MīSū 1.2.38, 39); the problematic assignment of mantras in certain *Brāhmaṇa* passages can be seen to have injunctive import after all, or else those passages, too, are eulogies (MīSū 1.2.33–35); in studying the Veda one concentrates on the pronunciation because that is more difficult, and so on (Renou 1960a, 70–75).

That mantras serve as indicators (*abhidhāna*) of ritual states of affairs does not mean, however, that they fall only in the speech act category of assertions. The Mīmāṃsā, rather, recognizes many types of mantra besides outright descriptions (*ākhyāna*) and phrases distinguished by the use of the verb *to be* (typically of the form, "Thou art X [the altar, the strew, the hair-knot of Viṣṇu, etc., as at TS 1.1.11]"). There are dedications (ending in *tvā,* e.g., TaitSam 1.1.1.1), benedictions, eulogies, lamentations, directives and questions as well.[17] Indeed, the Mīmāṃsā, in its formal definition of mantra, MīSū 2.1.32, is careful to specify that a mantra is what *expresses* (literally, activates) an indication of a ritual element (*abhidhānasya codaka*); it is not the indication itself. That is to say, mantras imply references to ritual details. As such, they may have a variety of shapes; the references can be packaged in different ways. This approach parallels the insight of speech act theory that a proposition (more properly, a "propositional act") can be expressed in speech acts of different illocutionary force. The proposition "Sam smokes habitually" can be expressed in the simple assertion given, or in a question, "Does Sam smoke habitually?" or in a command, "Sam, smoke habitually!" and so on (Searle 1969, 22–24). All of these speech acts bring to mind the same state of affairs. Mantras, then, are indicators not strictly as assertions but in the most general sense; not only can they take on various syntactic forms, they often depend on mythologic and symbolic associations.

Later, I shall show that the notion that mantras have illocutionary force may have arisen originally from certain considerations regarding injunctions.

MĪMĀṂSĀ AND PHILOSOPHY

Several observations to be made about the solution of the problem of mantras presented by the Mīmāṃsā will bring out more fully its significance and originality. First, this solution turns on an old doctrine, that of the identity of the language of the Veda and ordinary discourse. This idea was put forward by Yāska in his original refutation of Kautsa: "Mantras have meaning, since the words [of the Veda and ordinary speech] are the same" (Nir. 1.16, p. 39).[18] It appears in *prātiśākhya* and grammatical literature in the form of the assumption that accent, morphology, and grammar pertain to Vedic as well as ordinary discourse.[19] Now the Mīmāṃsā goes somewhat beyond Yāska when it says (MīSū 1.3.30) that the words of the Veda and ordinary usage have the *same meanings*. Yāska appears prepared to say only that both are *meaningful*. But Śabara would appear to alter Yaska's doctrine still further when he asserts that the words of the Veda and ordinary language have the same meanings, not just insofar as they denote the same things but also insofar as their meanings are expressed or intended.[20]

This emphasis on the expressiveness of language must be understood in the context of the fact that, in the case of mantras, the question of meaningfulness is subordinated to the question of use. At the head of the discussion of *arthavādas* and mantras, the doubt concerning their uselessness, *ānarthakya*, is raised (MīSū 1.2.1; also 1.2.31). This emphasis, too, appears to be an innovation. In the *Nirukta*, the skeptic's thesis, "Mantras are meaningless (*anarthakāḥ*)," along with Yāska's reply, "Mantras have meaning (*arthavantaḥ*)," does not seem to concern anything other than the established meaning of words. But the Mīmāṃsā sees clearly that mantras must have meaning *to be conveyed*, so as to be able to teach about dharma in the form of expressed assertions. Again, the Mīmāṃsā has, as it were, an appreciation of the Searlean distinction between the illocutionary force and propositional content of a speech act: A proposition is meaningful by itself but only if, in addition, it has illocutionary force can it convey information.

This point about the function of mantras as indicators or assertions, however, is in turn subsidiary to a larger concern to which I have already drawn attention: whether mantras are *pramāṇa*. One would be mistaken to believe that the Mīmāṃsaka is solely concerned with a point about language in his discussion of mantras. Rather, he is also, indeed ultimately, concerned to show that all the sentences of the Veda, the mysterious formulas contained in the Saṃhitās as well as the eulogies and injunctions of the *Brāhmaṇas*, convey *knowledge*, knowledge of dharma.[21]

This interest is the most revolutionary aspect of the Mīmāṃsā treatment of the mantra issue, for it represents an effort to demystify the Veda and convert it into a source of truth. Throughout his MīSūBh, not just in his discussion of mantras, Śabara appears sensitive to a charge of irrationalism leveled against Vedic sacrificial science. In the *tarkapāda*, the opening epistemological discussion of his commentary, an opponent is allowed to assert that the Veda patently contradicts experience, as when it says, "The sacrificer possessed of offering utensils immediately proceeds to heaven [when he dies].'' Manifestly, he goes nowhere; he is completely burned up on the funeral pyre! (MīSūBh 1.1.5, I.41). At 1.1.32, it is wondered whether the Veda is not complete nonsense ''like the speech of children and madmen;'' for it says such things as ''Trees sat at the sacrificial session,'' ''The old bullock sang intoxicating songs'' (p. 103). And, in the many discussions of the figurative sense of Vedic passages, the *pūrvapakṣin* is always ready to suggest that the Veda states what is false or incoherent.[22]

No doubt motivated by an apologetic concern to deal with such attacks Śabara feels compelled to show that, not just some, not even most, but generally all Vedic sentences have real epistemic status.[23] In doing so, however, he takes a step away from the more ancient ritualistic attitude, the one expressed in the Veda itself, which views mantras uttered in ritual circumstances as having a sui generis efficacy; i.e., magical power (*brahman*) (Gonda, 1960–63, I.32–33). Thus, while the Mīmāṃsaka is usually seen as a defender of ritualism, he in fact shows himself to be decidedly innovative. It is the Kautsan, rather, for whom the meaning of mantras is irrelevant because their mere utterance counts as a magical ritual act, who stands closer to the ancient point of view.

The Mīmāṃsā knew that the claim of epistemic status for the directives (*codanā*) of the Veda was highly controversial. Śabara defends this claim with much ingenuity in the *tarkapāda*, appealing to a strictly formal notion of *pramāṇa* yielding knowledge which is definite in content (*niścita*), independent of other sources (*svayaṃpratyaya*), and which does not deviate (*avyatireka*) or later turn out to be false (*na viparyeti*). But even if Śabara's defense of *codanā* is to be judged successful and the Veda thus seen as partly rationalized, the latter still does not attain the status of metaphysical knowledge.[24] It may tell us the truth about what to do, but it does not tell us about the nature of things. Certainly, this shortcoming must have been in part at the basis of the reluctance of other schools to accept *śabda* into the ranks of *pramāṇa*.[25]

In any case, the Vedānta—the other school of Indian philosophy that like the Mīmāṃsā, developed its doctrines strictly in connection with the interpretation of Vedic texts—felt the need to go further and suggest that the Veda indeed provides reliable information about matters of fact. Śaṅkara gives brilliant expression to this idea in the early sections of his *Brahmasūtrabhāsya*, where he presents the principles of an exegesis quite different from that of the Mīmāṃsā. At BrSūBh 1.1.4, he argues that the Upaniṣads have authority insofar as they *describe brahman*, an accomplished entity, a thing; they are not to be seen as concerned in any way with what to do. But *arthavādas* and mantras also have the capacity to convey information about states of affairs (namely, the nature of deities connected with the sacrifice), although, of course, they ultimately subserve injunctions (BrSūBh 1.3.33, pp. 134–35). With this step, the rationalization of the Veda is complete. It now exists as a body of dogma to be set beside other scientific and theological systems. Such a view of the

Veda is the logical outcome of the apologetic process initiated by the Mīmāṃsā.[26]

There is a final observation to be made here about the Mīmāṃsā discussion of mantras. While it reflects a fairly sophisticated understanding of the functioning of language, as a theory of mantric utterance, it is woefully inadequate. The complexity and variety of mantric forms is hardly explained by saying that they serve as reminders. As mere reminders, they would do better with a simpler structure and thinner content. In Sanskrit literature, a certain class of texts are clearly designed to serve a mnemonic function, sūtras, but mantras hardly have that character. Why should there be references to gods in mantras? And, why to particular gods in some mantras, to other ones in others? The Mīmāṃsā makes only the lamest effort to account for such things, invariably taking references to deities to be mere *arthavādas*—and it does that only when forced to. Indeed, it would seem that the Mīmāṃsā is not really interested in explaining mantras at all but only in eliminating them as a potential source of doubt about the rationality of the Veda. In light of this extreme reductionism, it is not surprising that later commentators on the mantra discussion (e.g., Sāyaṇa) sought to restore a measure of the primacy of their literal/figurative content.

MĪMĀṂSĀ AND SPEECH ACT THEORY

We have seen that the observation that language involves the expression of intended meanings (that is, communication) is central to the Mīmāṃsā analysis of mantras. Yet, by itself, that fact hardly warrants the conclusion that the Mīmāṃsā adopts a speech act theory of language similar to that of modern linguistics. In order to be able to draw such a conclusion, it must be seen, at least in addition, that according to the Mīmāṃsā speaking a language involves *doing* certain things. I shall show that this idea indeed plays a significant role in Mīmāṃsā exegesis. The full relevance of this matter to understanding mantras will become clear as we proceed.

Before turning to the Mīmāṃsā exegetic method, it would be well to review the aspect of speech act theory in question here. Speech act theory, of course, does not focus so much on the idea that language is produced by speakers with certain intentions as on the notion that language involves carrying out actions. The former idea actually is entailed by the latter; for according to the general philosophical orientation of speech act analysis, it is in the carrying out of actions that intentions are expressed and realized. The heart of speech act theory is the demonstration of how this happens in linguistic contexts. For Searle, this demonstration comes down to showing that linguistic communication consists in following what he calls constitutive rules (1969, 33–42).

A constitutive rule defines what constitutes a certain activity. It implies that, by proceeding as the rule specifies, one will realize the activity it defines. Thus, a constitutive rule creates the possibility of a specific intention. The definition of a *touchdown* in American football, for example, as "having possession of the ball in the opponents' end zone while a play is in progress" is a constitutive rule. It defines what counts as a touchdown at the same time that it explains what one has to do in order to score a touchdown. The crucial point about a constitutive rule is that, if one wants to achieve the objective it defines, one must follow the rule. If one does not proceed as specified, one will fail. To say that speaking a language consists in following constitutive rules means in particular that the requirements stipulated by the rules must be satisfied for communication to take place.

The way linguistic rules work can be seen readily in the case of promising. According to Searle's analysis of this speech act (pp. 57–71), one of the principal things one must do in order to promise is, of course, to utter a sentence of the form, "I promise that I shall. . ." But this is not sufficient for a promise to have been made. Certain extralinguistic conditions must hold as well. It must be the case, for example, that someone has not already done—or that the person who is promising is not automatically going to do—what is being promised.[27] It also must be the case that the hearer of the promise desires that what is proposed should happen.[28] These sorts of conditions are what Searle refers to as *preparatory conditions* of speech acts.[29] For any type of speech act other conditions, besides these, must be satisfied if the speech act is to "come off." The crucial difference between this way of viewing language and most other theories is that, by speech act analysis, an utterance is evaluated not just from the standpoint of whether it is meaningful or meaningless but also according to whether it is *successful* or *unsuccessful*. This added perspective proves advantageous in dealing with a variety of linguistic and philosophical problems. I shall show that the notion of language as consisting in the performance of acts according to constitutive rules appears to underlay Mīmāṃsā exegesis.

We may begin by observing a feature of several of the objections raised by the Kautsan opponent against the meaningfulness of mantras. Namely, they suggest that if the meaning of mantras were expressed then various injunctions—some of them occurring in the *Brāhmaṇas*, others mantras themselves—would be without effect. I have already mentioned the case of the *Brāhmaṇa* passage that directs the priest to utter a mantra in a context to which the meaning of the mantra manifestly assigns it. Other mantras, having the form of directives (called *praiṣa* mantras), are to be addressed to one or another of the participants in a sacrifice while it is going on. These appear to be quite purposeless when they instruct the participant to do what he already knows he is supposed to do. For example, the mantra "O *agnīdh*, bring out the fires!" (TaitSam 6.3.1) appears purposeless when addressed to the *agnīdh* priest of the *agniṣṭoma* sacrifice, who is fully aware that this (viz., carrying fire from the *āgnīdhrīya* hearth to the other altars after the performance of the *bahiṣpavamāna stotra*) is his job. Therefore, this mantra cannot possibly be employed as expressing what it means (MīSūBh 1.2.32, I.147).

Now, this sort of argument would appear to rest on an insight into the pragmatic nature of language: An utterance has to be more than merely meaningful in order to communicate information; it also has to *work*. That is to say, various extralinguistic conditions have to be met. These conditions will vary for different types of utterance. For commands, they include a preparatory condition parallel to that noted for promises, that the commandee has not already done and is not automatically going to do what he is directed to do.[30] A command that does not meet this and other contextual conditions may well have inherent meaning, but it fails at what one usually wants to accomplish in uttering a command. Its function is frustrated; it is, as the Mīmāṃsā says, "purposeless" (*anarthaka*).

Thus, a sensitivity to contextual factors in the working of language, the very essence of speech act theory, is in part what leads to the question about mantras in the first place. It is at the heart of many other matters as well; for example, the interpretation of *arthavāda* passages. In considering in what manner these can be regarded as *pramāṇa* with respect to dharma the *pūrvapakṣin* is willing to entertain the possibility that some might be interpreted as injunctions. Thus the sentence, "He wept (*arodīt*); Rudra's Rudra-ness is due to his having wept" (TaitSam 1.5.1) could be taken to mean that because Rudra wept others should weep, too (MīSūBh 1.2.1, I.102–103); or, "When the gods sat down at the sacrifice they did not know the directions" (TaitSam 6.1.5) could be construed as an instruction that, at the time of the sacrifice, others should not know the difference between north, south, east, and west. The *pūrvapakṣin,* however, quickly points out that these sentences are useless as injunctions because they recommend actions not within one's voluntary power. No one sheds tears without cause, without separation from what one wants, or without some affliction; no one could *decide* to be confused about the directions when at the sacrificial session. The general point would seem to be that something is to be regarded an injunction only when all the contextual requirements for the *performance* of injunctions are met.[31]

The Mīmāṃsā remains within this framework in posing its solution to the problem of *arthavādas*. As we have seen, *arthavādas* are regarded in the final analysis as commending injoined actions. They encourage the adoption of specific ritual procedures by declaring them especially effective in bringing about desired goals. Now, Śabara suggests that one of the requirements for successful injoining dictates this interpretation of *arthavādas,* that there be some advantage in proceeding as injoined. For, according to the view Śabara works out, injunctions are less commands than requests. In order to work, they must persuade; the person injoined must be convinced that he will gain some advantage if he complies. An *arthavāda* accompanying an injunction serves this persuasive function (MīSūBh 1.2.7, I.117–19). Thus, in effect, *arthavādas* signal the presence of a more or less necessary extralinguistic condition for successful injunctions.[32]

The notion of contextual requirements or "needs" (*ākāṅkṣā*) of injunctions figures in the Mīmāṃsā exegesis in other ways.[33] According to Mīmāṃsā, the bringing into existence (*bhāvanā*) expressed by an injunctive verb always requires three factors: something to be effected (*sādhya*), a means (*sāhana*), and a procedure (*itikartavyatā*) (AS, p. 3; MīSūBh 2.1.1, I.375). The Mīmāṃsā views each of these as supplying the answer to one of three specific expectations to which every injunction gives rise: What ought one bring about? (*kiṃ bhāvayet*) By what (*kena*) ought one bring it about? and How (*katham*) ought one bring it about? Thus, for the injunction, "One who desires heaven ought to offer the new- and full-moon sacrifice" (ĀŚS 3.14.8), the *sādhya*-requirement and the *sādhana*-requirement are satisfied by the references to heaven and the *darśapūrṇamāsa* sacrifice, respectively, and the sentence is to be construed as "One ought to *bring about* heaven by means of the new- and full-moon sacrifice." The procedure-requirement, however, is not immediately supplied; but, one gets it from the other injunctions, "He offers to the kindling sticks" and so forth, in TaitSam 2.6.1. These refer to preliminary offerings of ghee, known as *prayājas*, made in the course of the new- and full-moon sacrifice (Hillebrandt [1879, 94–97] 1880). And so, the complete sense of the injunction "One who desires heaven ought to offer the new- and full-moon sacrifice" becomes "One ought to bring about heaven by means of the new- and full-moon sacrifice by carrying out the *prayājas*."

Now, this scheme can be used to determine the relation of different sacrificial acts mentioned in the *Brāhmaṇas*; that is, it can serve as a guideline for figuring out which of various acts referred to in a text belong together as one continuous rite. This is one of the chief exegetic problems the Mīmāṃsā is designed to solve. In fact, one knows that the *prayājas* mentioned at TaitSam 2.6.1 (a Brāhmaṇa section inserted in the Saṃhitā), go with the new- and full-moon sacrifice, for example, because they stand in need of clarification with regard to a certain factor supplied by the injunction of the new- and full-moon sacrifice. Specifically, the original injunction "One who desires heaven ought to offer the new- and full-moon sacrifice" indicates the what that one effects by offering to the kindling sticks, and so forth, not specified in the injunctions of the *prayājas*. Because both injunctions—or, more precisely, both sets of injunctions—need the clarification of a certain factor, and each supplies it for the other, one knows that they go together, that one action is primary and the others subsidiary (the *prayājas* are subsidiary to the new- and full-moon rite) (AS, p. 8).[34]

Thus, we see that the Mīmāṃā organizes a text, assigning different roles to the sentences in it, by asking essentially what contextual conditions have to be fulfilled for injunctions to *work*.[35] I mention here one final aspect of this way of viewing injunctions. We have seen that the Mīmāṃsā beleves that the meanings of words in the Veda and in ordinary usage must be the same. Somewhat surprisingly, this belief is based on a purely pragmatic consideration: If the meanings of the words were not the same, then Vedic sentences could not be understood by men and Vedic injunctions could not be followed (MīSūBh 1.3.30, I.291). We have here part of what Searle considers the first condition of any speech act, that "normal input and output conditions obtain" (p. 57). That means, among other things, "that the speaker and hearer both know how to speak," and therefore understand, "the same language."

INJUNCTIONS AND THE ETERNALITY OF THE VEDA

If injunctions are acts carried out according to certain rules, who carries them out? When we consider this question we become immediately aware of an interesting conflict at the heart of Mīmāṃsā linguistics.

One of the most well known theses of Mīmāṃsā philosophy concerns the eternality of the Veda: The Veda is not of human origin (*apauruṣeya*). This idea rests on the doctrine of the eternality of language in general, another notion that the Mīmāṃsā holds in common with other early schools of linguistic thought. That is to say, words, meanings, and the associations of words and meanings do not have human authors; rather, they are "original" (*autpattika,* MīSū 1.1.5), prior to any human employment. The absence of a human origin for the Veda ensures its perfect validity in the eyes of the Mīmāṃsā, hence the crucialness of this doctrine. The Veda, simply of itself, causes dharma to be known definitely and irrevocably. Since it does not depend on any such precarious source as human judgement, how could it be unreliable, how could what it says turn out to be false? (MīSūBh 1.1.5, pp. 41–43).

But granted that the Veda is meaningful by itself, by virtue of the eternal connection between words and their meanings, it still remains to be seen how it conveys its meaning. For we have seen that the Mīmāṃsā is sensitive to the fact that communication involves not just the production of sentences that possess meaning (i.e., make sense) but also the intending of them. To be sure, as we also saw, it is declared in the discussion of mantras that the words of the Veda are *meant,* just as in ordinary discourse. But how does the Mīmāṃsā account for this? It would seem that the intentionality essential for communication conflicts with the idea of an absence of a human origin for the Veda, for it would seem that only human beings can have intentions.

The Mīmāṃsā solution of this problem, worked out for the case of Vedic injunctions, is one of the most unique aspects of its theory of language—and one of the most dubious. We have observed that Mīmāṃsā views an injunction as indicating an effective process, a bringing into existence (*bhāvanā*). The pronouncement "One who desires heaven should sacrifice" means essentially that one should *bring about heaven* by means of the sacrifice. But this is only half of the story. The Mīmāṃsā actually distinguishes two types of *bhāvanā* expressed by injunctive verbs (that is, typically, optatives): One, the "objective *bhāvanā*" (*ārthī bhāvanā*), is "an effort with regard to a certain action motivated by a particular purpose"; for example, the effort of the sacrificer to realize heaven by the performance of rites (AS, p. 3). This is the sort of *bhāvanā* we have considered so far. It is said to be expressed by the "verbalness" (*ākhyātatva*) of the verbal suffix.[36] But there is another, "verbal *bhāvanā*" (*śabdī bhāvanā*), which is defined as "a particular activity (or effort) of that which incites one to act [i.e., of *the injunction*] which leads a person to undertake something" (AS, p. 2). The *śābdī bhāvanā* is said to be expressed by the "optativeness" (*liṅtva*) of the verbal suffix. The *ārthī bhāvanā* is carried out by a person, the *śābdī bhāvanā* by the verb itself. Just as an objective *bhāvanā* entails a certain thing to be effected, the *sādhya*, which is heaven in the example I have been discussing, so too the verbal *bhāvanā* has a *sādhya*, namely the objective *bhāvanā* (Edgerton 1928, 176).

Whatever the validity of this theory, the gist of it is that, for the Veda, the act of getting someone to do something usually attributed to the *utterer* of injunctions instead belongs to the injunctions. In other words, Vedic language manifests intentions without anyone ever having spoken them; Vedic injunctions are speech acts without anyone ever having enacted them; Vedic language has *inherent* illocutionary force![37] It did not go unnoticed in Mīmāṃsā that this constitutes a certain difference between Vedic and ordinary language; in common discourse the effort to get someone to do something by uttering an injunction resides in the utterer, a person (AS, p. 2). Still, the basic similarity between Vedic and ordinary language is preserved: Both are intentional and so can serve in communication.

The notion of *bhāvanā* applies to Vedic injunctions. But how do things stand with mantras, which Mīmāṃsā emphasizes are not injunctive (MīSūBh 2.1.31)? Do they, too, have inherent illocutionary force? There is, to my knowledge, no suggestion that they do. And, as they are actually to be uttered by persons while rituals are going on, the need for intrinsic intentionality is less clear in their case. But, it should be noted that the claim that mantras express intended meanings (*vivakṣitavacana*) is based on the general observation that all language, Vedic as well as ordinary, is communicative. Now, since Mīmāṃsā regards injunctions as Vedic language par excellence (i.e., takes them as paradigmatic), the idea boils down to this: Mantras must express intended meanings because injunctions do. And so, while mantras may not have *inherent* illocutionary force, as injunctions do, the view that they are intended utterances seems to reflect a general conviction that language consists in the performance of speech acts, for that is brought home always when, in exegetical discussions, injunctions are analyzed.

CONCLUSION

In this paper I have tried to show that the Mīmāṃsā analysis of mantras reflects an appreciation of language as an intentional activity executed either by people or, by virtue of an expressive force inherent in its verbs, by the Veda itself. In any case, language consists in performances according to the Mīmāṃsā; that is, not just strings of symbols or sentences, but the appropriate production or issuance thereof. To be sure, Mīmāṃsā does not explicitly work out a theory of speech acts. But the basic elements of such a theory serve as a framework for many of its discussions.

Of interest to the modern linguist is that Mīmāṃsā regards intentionality as a feature of *all* language. Indeed, most schools of Indian philosophy consider speaker's meaning (*tātparya*) an essential factor of the meaning of sentences (Kunjunni Raja 1969, 176–87). The particularly intriguing aspect of the Mīmāṃsā view on this matter is that speaker's meaning does not overshadow the given meaning of words; as we saw, while the meanings of words are *vivakṣita,* "intended," their connection with the signs referring to them is still thought to be eternal. This way of viewing the issue contrasts with that of the Nyāya school, which believed that a word can mean anything the speaker wants it to (Kunjunni Raja 1969, 177). On this point, also, the balanced Mīmāṃsā approach parallels modern speech act theory. In *Speech Acts,* Searle argues in opposition to Grice that meaning what one says depends on what that which one says actually means in the language one is speaking (1969, 42–45). "Meaning is more than a matter of conviction, it is also at least sometimes a matter of convention" (p. 45). It may well be that further investigation into Mīmāṃsā philosophy of language will throw new light on this issue of modern linguistics, as well as others.

While the Mīmāṃsaka employs the thesis that all language is expressive to argue that mantras are meaningful, we should have no illusions about where he is going with this argument. He is not hoping to restore the literal or symbolic significance of the Veda. Indeed, he is doing nearly the opposite, reducing the text to a series of mere references. Most of the content of the text thereby becomes immaterial. Again, the Mīmāṃsā attitude here is best understood in contrast to that of the *Nirukta,* from which it borrows so extensively. For Yāska, mantras are meaningful not just as reminders, but, as the *Brāhmaṇas* indicate, as mythical/metaphysical statements, the correct understanding of which is essential for the effectiveness of the sacrifice (Strauss 1927, 113–14). Yāska thus hopes to make real sense out of the Veda by giving the etymology of Vedic words. The Mīmāṃsaka has given up on this; or else, carried away by a rationalist impulse, he sees little philosophical gain in trying to interpret mantras. But, he can still maintain that they are employed for an immediate, nonmystical purpose, that they are, therefore, in a more important sense *arthavat.*

NOTES

1. But Wheelock and McDermott have viewed mantras as speech acts chiefly as performatives. Here, we shall consider other ways in which they might be speech acts.

The following abbreviations have been used in this article:

AS	*Arthasaṃgraha*
ĀŚS	*Āpastambhaśrautasūtra*
BSūBh	*Brahmasūtrabhāṣya*
MS	*Maitrāyaṇī Saṃhitā*
MīNP	*Mīmāṃsānyāyaprakāśa*
MīSū	*Mīmāṃsāsūtra*
MīSūBh	*Mīmāṃsāsūtrabhāṣya*
Nir.	*Nirukta*
RV	*Ṛg Veda*
ŚB	*Śatapatha Brāhmaṇa*
TB	*Taittirīya Brāhmaṇa*
TaitSam	*Taittirīya Saṃhitā*
TV	*Tantravārttika*

2. This is so, even though the question Do mantras express an intended [meaning] or not? (*kiṃ vivakṣitavacanā mantrā utāvivakṣitavacanāḥ*) is meant to elucidate the issue raised in the *pūrvapakṣa* (MīSū 1.2.31) by the expression *mantrānarthakyam*. Kumārila indicates a divergence of opinion about the correct interpretation of this sūtra: Those who would see it as raising a doubt about whether mantras are possessed of meaning at all (*kim arthavanto mantrā utānarthakāḥ*) are wrong, he says.

3. The concern regarding this issue in the *Nirukta* is as follows: If the Veda is without meaning then a science of etymology is unnecessary.

4. Renou (1960a) notes that a *prātiśākhya* of the Atharva Veda school is ascribed to a certain Kautsa (p. 68). See Strauss 1927a, 120.

5. Elsewhere in the MīSūBh the latter doubt is indeed entertained (e.g., 1.1.5, pp. 39–40) but not here in the context of the discussion of mantras.

6. Thus, the mention of "the four-horned, three-headed . . . being" presents a problem for Śabara and Kumārila, it appears, only because no such thing exists *in relation to the sacrifice*: "[A mantra] should make known an object which is a factor in the sacrifice. But there are no such things as [some mantras] name. . . . There is no factor of the sacrifice that has four horns, three feet, two heads, and seven hands" (*yajñe sādhanabhūtaḥ prakāśitavyaḥ. na ca tādṛśo 'rtho 'sti yādṛśam abhidadhati. . . . na hi catuḥśṛṅgaṃ tripadaṃ dviśiraskaṃ saptahastaṃ kiṃcid yajñasādhanam asti*) (MīSūBh 1.2.31, I.147). Although the Mīmāṃsā puts forward important philosophical theses, they typically are required only in order to make

sense out of the Veda as sacrificial science. It argues, for example, for the existence of a self but, ostensibly, only because some continuity of personal identity is required for the meaningful prescription of ritual action; for the same person who enacts a rite must be able to receive the future benefit produced by it. I will explore further the Mīmāṃsā attitude toward theoretical philosophical issues later.

7. Śabara sometimes cites the Śrautasūtras as if they were *śruti*, ignoring the principle, mentioned earlier, that they have only secondary authority (Garge 1952, 46). This is the case particularly for ĀŚS, which next to TaitSam is the text most cited by Śabara (216 TaitSam passages are referred to in the *Śābarabhāṣya* compared to 85 ĀŚS passages). Moreover, Śabara often quotes inexactly; ĀŚS 3.14.8 is the passage in the work that corresponds most *closely* to *darśapūrṇamāsābhyāṃ svargakāmo yajeta*. Śabara evidently relied primarily on his memory in delivering quotations; sometimes, he deliberately rephrased passages to fit his context; in some cases, he may have had a version of a text in front of him that is no longer in existence (Garge 1952, 73–74). The paradigm of a Vedic injunction for Śabara, *svargakāmo yajeta*, is probably not a citation at all but a purely artificial model.

8. I shall not discuss here the difficulties attached to names (*nāmadheya*), treated at MīSū 1.4.

9. "Words of eulogy which, praising the action, make it pleasing [to people], will assist the performers of the action [hence, indirectly the action itself]," (*stutiśabdāh stuvantaḥ kriyāṃ prarocayamānā anuṣṭhātṝṇām upakariṣyanti kriyāyāḥ*) (MīSūBh 1.2.7, I.119).

10. This question is not stated explicitly as such, but it clearly underlies the *pūrvapakṣa*. See AS, p. 17, as well as MīNP, sec. 239, where the matter is more clear.

11. (*Yajñe yajñāṅgaprakāśanam eva prayojanam. . . . na hy aprakāśite yajñe yajñāṅge ca yāgaḥ śakyo 'bhinirvartayitum.*) The Anandāśrama Sanskrit text I have used includes the whole *pūrvapakṣa* in Sūtra 1.2.31, with the *siddhānta* beginning at 1.2.32. I have followed this numbering rather than that of Jha's translation, which has the *pūrvapakṣa* extending from Sūtras 1.2.31–39. The revised Ānandāśrama edition (by K. V. Abhyanakar and G. S. Joshī, 1970–74) also artificially breaks up the *pūrvapakṣa* into nine sections.

12. Thus, often by means of the distinctive content (or "mark," *liṅga*) of the mantra itself one can determine its assignment. See AS, pp. 6–7. Reference to a single sacrificial procedure distinguishes, along with syntactic coherence, a particular mantra as a sentence unit (MīSū 2.1.46).

13. For an account of the procedures that these mantras accompany, see Hillebrandt ([1879, 36–37] 1880).

14. The mnemonic function of mantras is viewed as essential in the later treatise, the *Arthasaṃgraha: prayogasamavetārthasmārakā mantrāḥ. teṣāṃ ca tād-*

ṛśārthasmārakatvenaiva arthavattvam (Mantras recall to memory things connected with some performance. Their usefulness lies in serving to remind one of such things) (p. 17). Cf. TV 2.1.31, p. 433; also MīSūBh 6.3.18 and MīNP, sec. 239.

15. "The knowledge of the meaning of the [mantra] sentence . . . by giving rise to a memory of something to be done in the context of a ritual action [has the character of] procedure" (*vākyārthapratyayaḥ . . . karmasamavetānuṣṭhāsyamānārthasmṛtiphalatvenetikartavyatā bhavati*) (TV, I.150).

16. *Aviśiṣṭas tu loke prayujyamānānāṃ vede ca padānām arthaḥ. sa yathaiva loke vivakṣitas tathaiva vede 'pi bhavitum arhati.*

17. Cf. Yāska's discussion of *ṛg*-mantras, Nir. 7.3. The Mīmāṃsā is content with a rather homogeneous taxonomy. It is interesting to compare the Mīmāṃsā scheme with the one recently worked out by Wheelock (1980). The latter categorizes mantras according to the different sorts of things they present as appropriate to occur at different times in the course of a rite: attitudes (e.g., the wish, "By the sacrifice to the gods for Agni may I be food-eating"), intentions, requests, and ideal states of affairs (e.g., "I pick you [bundle of grass] up with the arms of Indra"). Wheelock's taxonomy, of course, is based on an entirely different interpretation of mantric utterance than that given by the Mīmāṃsā. The unique feature of mantras, according to Wheelock, is that, employed repeatedly in the same situations, they cannot be used for conveying information, which is precisely what is insisted by the Mīmāṃsaka, who believes in the unity of Vedic and ordinary (informative) language. Rather, mantras are "situating speech acts" for Wheelock, by means of which certain situations are created (and recreated) and participated in (1982). The mantra "I pick you up with the arms of Indra" is not a simple assertion but an assertion cum declaration, which for the officiant simultaneously depicts an ideal state of affairs and realizes it.

18. *Arthavantaḥ [mantrāḥ] śabdasāmānyāt.*

19. See the seminal discussion by Thieme (1931). This idea is pronounced as a general thesis, MīSū 1.3.30. On Śabara's relation to the grammarians, see Garge (1952, 236–42). Kane (1930–62, V.1156–57) notes that Patañjali refers to many Mīmāṃsā matters in his *Mahābhāṣya*. Therefore, it is difficult to determine any relation of priority between the two schools; it seems that they developed at around the same time.

20. This, of course, also constitutes a certain interpretation of Jaimini's sūtra (2.1.32).

21. In Sāyaṇa's treatment of mantras, in the introduction to his commentary on the *Ṛg Veda*, the expressiveness of mantras and their *pramāṇatva* are handled as quite separate issues (Oertel 1930, 2).

22. See MīSūBh 1.2.2, p. 108, where this complaint is raised about *arthavādas*.

23. Śabara concedes, at MīSūBh 2.1.32, that some mantras, in fact, are not assertive, but he may well have felt that that did not jeapordize his general

point. (See also 12.4.1, where it is admitted that the mere *japa* of mantras is sometimes called for; cf. AS, p. 18, lines 12–14.)

24. The sacrificial science is rationalized in other ways. Thus, Mīmāṃsā develops the notion of *apūrva*, the unseen force that is the causal link between the sacrificial performance and its fruition at a later time (see the discussion by Halbfass 1980). It is well known that most Mīmāṃsā authors did not postulate the existence of god (*īśvara*); for no such entity is required for the efficacy of the sacrifice. Somewhat more surprising is that Śabara considers references to the deities (*devatās*) of the sacrifice as mere *arthavādas* (Kane 1930–62, V.1208).

25. Of course, it was the Mīmāṃsā doctrine of the intrinsic validity (*svataḥ prāmāṇya*) of cognition, the main pillar of its defense of *śabda*, that drew the most fire.

26. Sāyaṇa works out an interesting intermediate position between Mīmāṃsā and Vedānta. While accepting the Mīmāṃsā arguments in favor of the expressiveness of mantras, he sees mantras as making statements about the divinities involved in the sacrifice, hence as having theoretical import. Their function as reminders is not mentioned. In general, for Sāyaṇa, "Mantras have an intended meaning and are to be employed precisely to convey what they mean" (*vivakṣitārthā mantrāḥ svārthaprakāśanāyaiva prayoktavyāḥ*) (Oertel 1930, 68); while Śabara maintains "The purpose [of mantras] is simply to make known the elements of the sacrifice" (*yajñāṅgaprakāśanam eva prayojanam*).

27. To give a homey example, the sort Searle loves, it would be nonsense for me to promise that I will take out the garbage if you have just done so. This specific condition for promises is a slightly broader version of Searle's condition No. 5.

28. The sentence "I promise that I shall burn your house down" is puzzling as a promise for this reason, although it could make sense as a threat. This is Searle's condition No. 4 (1969, 58).

29. Searle says of preparatory conditions: "This [type of] condition is . . . a general condition on many different kinds of illocutionary acts to the effect that the act must have a point" (p. 59).

30. See the preceding note.

31. Searle, too, stipulates as a preparatory condition for requests that the requested act must be within the hearer's power (p. 66).

32. Here, *more or less* refers to the fact that Śabara admits that an injunction, even the one under consideration, can work without an *arthavāda*. But, when an *arthavāda* is present, it takes over the persuading function. Kumārila and Prabhākara disputed whether injunctions are requests or commands (Kunjunni Raja 1969, 160–61).

33. *Ākāṅkṣā* is another concept employed by the grammarians. For them, it

refers primarily to the relation of dependence between words that form a single sentence (Kunjunni Raja 1969, 151–63).

34. This is the *pramāṇa* of *prakaraṇa* (context), one of six ways of determining the assignment (*viniyoga*) of sacrificial auxiliaries (Jha [1942] 1964, 247–54). Other *pramāṇas*, such as direct assertion (*śruti*), may take precedence over context when they are present but, as they frequently are not, context is relatively important.

35. An injunction, interpreted as a request, will be "felicitous"—to use Austin's expression—only if the person subject to it knows, among other things, *why* and *how* to follow it. Thus, a request to someone to turn up the heat might fail if one asks too specifically, "Please turn that little knob on the wall to the right"—in which case, the requestee may not know why and so may not be *inclined* to comply—or if one asks too generally, "Please make the house warmer"—in which case the requestee may simply not know how to proceed. If these sorts of conditions are not satisfied, the injunction/request will not "come off," even if as a sentence it is perfectly coherent.

36. Cf. Nir. 1.1: *bhāvapradhānam ākhyātam.*

37. Cf. D'Sa 1980, 177–79.

TRANSLATIONS CITED IN THIS CHAPTER

Arthasaṃgraha of Laugākṣī Bhāskara. Ed. and trans. by G. Thibaut. Benares Sanskrit Series, no. 4. Benares, 1882.

Brahmasūtrabhāṣya of Śaṅkara. Ed. by Nārāyan Rām Āchārya. Bombay: Nirnaya Sagar Press, 1948.

Mīmāṃsānyāyaprakāśa of Āpadevī. Ed. and trans. by Franklin Edgerton. New Haven: Yale University Press, 1929.

Mīmāṃsāsūtrabhāṣya of Śabara, with the *Mīmāṃsāsūtra* and Kumārilabhaṭṭa's *Tantravārttika.* 6 vols. Ed. by V. G. Āpaṭe. Ānandāśrama Sanskrit Series, no. 97. Poona, 1929–34.

Mīmāṃsāsūtrabhāṣya of Śabara. Trans. by Ganganatha Jha. 3 vols. 1933. Reprint. Baroda: University of Baroda, 1973.

Nirukta of Yāska with the *Nighaṇṭu.* Ed. and trans. by Lakshman Sarup. Lahore: University of the Panjab, 1927.

Taittirīya Saṃhitā: The Veda of the Black Yajur School. Trans. by A. B. Keith. 2 vols. 1914. Reprint. Delhi: Motilal Banarsidass, 1967.

Tantravārttika of Kumārilabhaṭṭa. See *Mīmāṃsāsūtrabhāṣya* of Śabara.

CHAPTER 6

The Meaning and Power of Mantras in Bhartṛhari's *Vākyapadīya**

Harold Coward

IN HIS BOOK, *The Vision of the Vedic Poets,* Gonda (1963a) suggests that the Vedic *ṛṣi,* in his approach to the real, is thought of as having been emptied of himself and filled with the god (p. 64). Aurobindo puts it even more vividly, "The language of the Veda itself is *śruti,* a rhythm not composed by the intellect but heard, a divine Word that came vibrating out of the Infinite to the inner audience of the man who had previously made himself fit for the impersonal knowledge" (Aurobindo Ghose 1956, 6). Therefore, the words (mantras) the *ṛsi* spoke were not his own, but the words of the god. This suprahuman origin lent his words a healing power and even made them into a deed of salvation. It is this understanding of mantra as being at once inherently powerful and teleological that is so difficult for modern minds to comprehend. Yet, these are the very characteristics that underlie Indian cultic ritual and chant.

In his classic article, "The Indian Mantra," Gonda points out that *mantras* are not thought of as products of discursive thought, human wisdom or poetic phantasy, "but flash-lights of the eternal truth, seen by those eminent men who have come into supersensuous contact with the Unseen" (1963b, 247). By concentrating one's mind on such a mantra, the devotee invokes the power inherent in the divine intuition and so purifies his consciousness.

Because the mantra is understood as putting one in direct touch with divine power (Gonda 1963b, 255), it is not surprising that mantra chanting is controlled with strict rules. McDermott (1975) has emphasized that attention must be given not only to the content of the mantra but also to its context. The reciter of the mantra must have met certain prerequi-

**This paper was presented in the Hinduism section of the annual meeting of the American Academy of Religion in San Francisco on December 19–22, 1981.*

sites: (1) purgation; (2) proper moral basis; (3) requisite practical skills; (4) adequate intellectual grounding; and (5) the status of an initiate in an esoteric tradition. Conventional procedure requires "that the mantra be imparted to the disciple by one who is duly certified to do so and who pays meticulous attention to the minutiae of its proper transmission" (p. 287). The correct procedures for the actual reciting of the mantra (e.g., sincerity of the utterer, loudness of voice, proper breathing, etc.) are also carefully controlled (pp. 288–90).

Recently, Frits Staal argued that there is a direct relationship between ritual actions and mantras. He suggested that *mantras* began as sentences attached to ritual actions, and that these mantra/ritual action units were the raw data from which language arose. In India, said Staal, language is not something with which you *name* something; it is something with which you *do* something (1979c, 9). The Vedic mantra orally handed down is at least as long as a sentence or line of verse that corresponds to one ritual act. Even if the rites are modified or abandoned, the action of mantra recitation is retained (p. 10). Gonda points out that, in post-Vedic India, activities such as bringing the goddess Kali into a stone image, bathing to wash away sins, sowing seeds in the fields, guarding the sown seeds, driving away evil spirits, and meditating to achieve release all had to be accompanied by the action of chanting mantras in order to achieve success (1963b, 261–68).

The question as to whether mantras are meaningful has produced much debate. On the one extreme, Vasubandu maintains that the true meaning of mantras is to be found in their absence of meaning (1969 [1958, 216]). Staal draws our attention to the teaching of Kautsa, who viewed Vedic mantras as effective but meaningless (1969, 508). This understanding of mantras as meaningless appears to dominate much Tantric thinking.[1] The opposite position is taken by the Mīmāṁsakas, who argue that mantras are not meaningless but expressive of meaning. Śabara following Jaimini asserts that mantras express the meaning of dharma. "In cases where the meaning is not intelligible, it is not that there is no meaning; it is there always, only people are ignorant of it" (Jha [1942] 1964, 162). Much of the modern confusion over mantras results from this controversy as to their inherent meaningfulness or meaninglessness. The root of the problem is the modern view of language, as commonly adopted. Whereas, in the Indian tradition, language is thought to be truly and most fully experienced in its oral form, the modern view tends to restrict language to the printed word and then analyze it for a one-to-one correspondence with objective reality.[2] As Klostermaier has observed, contemporary linguistic philosophy sees the word only as a carrier of information and basically studies those aspects of language that a computer can store and retrieve (in Coward & Sivaraman 1977, 88). Emphasizing the computerlike function of language, modern man tends to consign all other dimensions of the word to the unreality of a mystic's silence; either the word is factual and scientific in its referent or it is mystical and has no real function in life.[3] Indian speculations on the nature of language have made room for both the discursive and the intuitive experience of the word. Bhartṛhari, the fifth-century systematizer of the Grammarian School, presents a philosophy of language that proves helpful in understanding both the factual and the intuitive levels of language. Bhartṛhari's *Vākyapadīya* offers a metaphysical, philosophical, and psychological analysis of language, which spans the period from the Vedic through to the Tantric experience of mantra. All the views of mantra summarized earlier (including mantra as "meaningful" and mantra as "meaningless") are encompassed by Bhartṛhari within one understanding in which language is seen to function at various levels.

THE MEANING OF MANTRAS

Bhartṛhari begins the *Vākyapadīya* by stating that the essence of *Brahman* is of the nature of the word (*śabda*) and the word is understood by Bhartṛhari to be synonymous with meaning. Although unitary in nature, this divine word-consciousness manifests itself in the diversity of words that make up speech.[4] The mantra AUM (the *Praṇava*) is identified as the root mantra out of which all other mantras arise (Vāk., I.9). This sacred syllable is held to have flashed forth into the heart of Brahman, while absorbed in deep meditation, and to have given birth to the Vedas, which contain all knowledge. The *Praṇava* and the Vedic mantras are described as being at once a means of knowledge and a way of release (mokṣa) (Vāk., I.5). Fundamental to all of of this is the notion that language and consciousness are inextricably intertwined. *Vākyapadīya* (I.123) puts it this way, "There is no cognition in the world in which the word does not figure. All knowledge is, as it were, intertwined with the word." Bhartṛhari goes on to make clear that the word-meaning, as the essence of consciousness, urges all beings toward purposeful activity. If the word were absent, everything would be insentient, like a piece of wood (Vāk., I.126). Thus, Bhartṛhari's describes the Absolute as *Śabdabrahman* (word consciousness).

The *Vṛtti,* on I.123, goes on to say that when everything is merged into *Śabdabrahman* no verbal usage takes place, no meaning is available through mantras. But, when the absolute is awakened and meanings are manifested through words, then the knowledge and power that is intertwined with consciousness can be clearly perceived and known. Because consciousness is of the nature of word-meaning, the consciousness of any sentient being cannot go beyond or lack word-meaning (Vāk., I.126). When no meaning is understood, it is not due to a lack of word-meaning in consciousness but rather to ignorance or absent mindedness obscuring the meaning inherently present (Vāk., II.332). For Bhartṛhari, words, meanings, and consciousness are eternally connected and, therefore, necessarily synonymous. If this eternal identity were to disappear, knowledge and communication would cease to exist (Vāk., I.124). T. R. V. Murti concisely sums up Bhartṛhari's position, when he says it is not that we have a thought and then look for a word with which to express it or that we have a lonely word that we seek to connect with a thought, "Word and thought develop together, or rather they are expressions of one deep spiritual impulse to know and to communicate" (1974, 322).

All this has important implications for the debate as to whether mantras are meaningful. A meaningless mantra would imply a piece of consciousness without a word-meaning attached and, according to the *Vākyapadīya*, that is impossible. It is possible, however, for a person to be obstructed by his own ignorance and so not understand the meaning of a mantra—even thogh the word or words of the mantra are inherently meaningful. That such an understanding of word-meaning and consciousness was not unique to Bhartṛhari is evidenced by I.24–29 of Patañjali's *Yoga Sutras*.[5] Īśvara, like *Śabdabrahman*, is described as an eternal unity of meaning and consciousness from which all speech evolves. Mantra, as the scriptural truth of the *ṛṣis*, is taken to be the authoritative verbalization of Īśvara's word-consciousness. All this is expressed in the sacred mantra, AUM, which, when spoken, connotes Īśvara and his omniscient consciousness. As was the case for Bhartṛhari, it is the obscuring power of *avidyā* (consciousness afflicted by ignorance) that robs mantras of their inherent meaning and power (*Y.S.*, I.5).

The reason for the speaking of mantras is also traced to the nature of word-consciousness by Bhartṛhari. *Vākyapadīya*, I.51, states that word-consciousness itself contains an inner energy (*kratu*), which seeks to burst forth into expression. "The energy (*kratu*) called the word, existing within, as the yolk in the peahen's egg, has an actionlike function and assumes the sequence of its parts" (*Vāk.*, I.51). In the experience of the *ṛṣis*, this inner *kratu* is the cause of the one Veda being manifested by many mantras (*Vāk.*, I.5). The *ṛṣis* see the Veda as a unitary truth but, for the purpose of manifesting that truth to others, allow the word to assume the forms of the various mantras. On a simple level, this *kratu* is experienced when, at the moment of having an insight, we feel ourselves impelled to express it, to share it by putting it into words. Indeed, the whole activity of scholarship and teaching (which puts bread on our tables) is dependent upon this characteristic of consciousness.

Unlike thinkers who conceive of speech in conventional or utilitarian terms,[6] Bhartṛhari finds speech to contain and reveal its own *telos*. And, that seems to fit exactly the Hindu experience of mantra. In the Vedic experience, mantras not only reveal meaning but also give direction as to how one can participate in this meaning through ritual. This latter aspect has been given careful analysis by Wade Wheelock. In the New- and Full-Moon Vedic ritual, the role of mantra is to identify (*bandhu*) the human participant with a deity and so actualize divine meaning in human form (Wheelock 1980, 357–58). The Mīmāṁsā school agrees that through the teaching of Vedic words participation in the divine dharma (via the ritual sacrifice) is delineated (Jha [1942] 1964, 156). But, for the Mīmāṁsakas, mantra is given a narrow technical definition of being an "assertion" and not an "injunction."[7] For Bhartṛhari both assertion and injunction are taken as meaningful, thus the meaningfulness of all mantras.

In a recent series of publications (1969; 1975a; 1975b; 1979a; 1979c), Frits Staal argued that most mantras are meaningless. With regard to mantras in Vedic ritual, Staal seems to be following the lead of the Mīmāṁsakas and restricting the term *mantra* to assertions occurring within the ritual itself. Since, in Staal's view, ritual activities are self-contained, self-absorbed, and do not refer to other realities, the ritual (and its mantra) is meaningless (1979a, 3). Meaning, for Staal, is obviously conceived quite differently from meaning for Bhartṛhari. It would seem to be the modern positivist notion of meaning as one-to-one correspondence that Staal is applying here. Indeed, if meaning can only be in terms of something other and at the same time consciousness is self-enclosed, as Bhartṛhari maintains, then, of course, the logical result will be to conclude, as Staal does, that ritual, mantra, and life itself may be meaningless (1979a, 22). Perhaps, from a modern perspective on Vedic ritual and mantra, that is not an unexpected result. The essence of Staal's position seems to be that there was originally a separation between the realm of sound and the realm of meaning. Mere sound existed as nonsense mantras (e.g., lullabies, wordless songs, etc.); "Language originated when the domain of meaning, which was hidden, was recognized and attached to the domain of sound, which was already publicly available" (in Coward & Sivaraman 1977, 10). Staal suggests that, through the performance of Vedic ritual, the connection between the two realms was made and language was born.

Although, at first glance, Staal's view seems radically opposed to Bhartṛhari, closer analysis suggests some points of contact. Staal's hidden meaning is rather like Bhratṛahari's unmanifested meaning-consciousness. The sounds Staal describes may be those referred to by Bhartṛhari as the sound patterns remembered from word usage in previous lives (*saṁskāras*). For Bhartṛhari, language involves identifying these remembered sound patterns with the meanings inherent in consciousness. And, for Bhartṛhari, it is the Veda and the natural fitness of a sound to convey a meaning, made known to us through the use of words by elders (*saṅketa*), that makes the learning of language possible.[8] Perhaps, Bhartṛhari's thinking has influenced Staal's notion of the origin of language. Both seem constructed on some kind of superimposition (*adhyāsā*) notion. But, the key question Bhartṛhari would put to Staal would be From whence comes the impulse to connect sound and meaning? For Bhartṛhari, the answer is clear. It is *kratu,* or the expressive energy inherent in meaning consciousness. Staal's answer does not yet seem clear.

The *Vākyapadīya* does not remain at the level of philosophic principles. Bhartṛhari offers a detailed analysis of how the uttered sounds of the mantra reveal meaning. *Vākyapadīya*, I.52–53, describes three stages in the speaking and hearing of mantras on the analogy of a painter:

> When a painter wishes to paint a figure having parts like that of a man, he first sees it gradually in a sequence, then as the object of a single cognition and then paints it on a cloth or on a wall in a sequence. In the same way, the word in verbal usage is first perceived in a sequence, then cognized as a unity with the sequence suppressed. This partless and sequenceless mental form is superimposed, i.e. identified with the previous appearance having sequence and seeming to be separate. It again enters into verbal usage by displaying the characteristics of the sounds, namely, differentiation and sequence, produced by the movements of the articulatory organs. In the same way, the word goes again and again through three stages and does not fail to become both illuminator and the illuminated. (*Vāk.*, I.52, Vṛtti)

Just as a painting is perceived as a whole, over and above its different parts and colors, so our cognition of the mantra is of a meaning whole, over and above the sequence of uttered sounds. *Sphoṭa* (that from which meaning bursts or shines forth)[9] is Bhartṛhari's technical term, designating mantra as a gestalt or meaning whole, which can be perceived by the mind (*pratibhā*, immediate supersensuous intuition). Let us return to the example of the *ṛsi.* At the first moment of its revelation, the *ṛsi* is completely caught up into this unitary idea, gestalt or *sphoṭa.* But when, under the expressive impulse (*kratu*), he starts to examine the idea (*sphoṭa*) with an eye to its communication, he has withdrawn himself from the first intimate unity with the idea or inspiration itself and now experiences it in a twofold fashion. On the one hand, there is the objective meaning (*artha*), which he is seeking to communicate, and on the other, there are the words and phrases (*dhvanis*) he will utter. For Bhartṛhari, these two aspects of word sound (*dhvani*) and word meaning (*artha*), differentiated in the mind and yet integrated like two sides of the same coin, constitute the *sphoṭa.* Bhartṛhari emphasizes the meaning bearing on revelatory function of this twosided gestalt, the *sphoṭa*, which he maintains is eternal and inherent in consciousness (*Vāk.*, I.23–26, 122–23).

From the perspective of a speaker or hearer of the uttered mantra, the process functions in reverse. Each letter-sound of the mantra reveals the whole *sphoṭa*, at first only vaguely. Each additional letter sound of the mantra brings further illumination until, with the uttering of the last letter sound, the *sphoṭa* (the complete utterance as a unity) of the mantra stands clearly perceived[10]—perhaps, something like "the light bulb coming on" image we find in cartoons. As the *Vākyapadīya* puts it, "The sounds, while they manifest the word, leave impression-seeds (*saṁskāra-bhvanā-bīja*) progressively clearer and conducive to the clear perception of the word" (*Vāk.*, I.84, Vṛtti).

The logic of Bhartṛhari's philosophy of language is that the whole is prior to its parts. This results in an ascending hierarchy of mantra levels. Individual words are subsumed by the sentence or poetic phrase, the phrase by the Vedic poem, and so on, until all speech is identified with *Brahman.* But Bhartṛhari focuses upon the *Vākya-Sphoṭa* or sentence meaning as the true form of meaning. Although he sometimes speaks about letter sounds (*varṇa*) or individual words (*pada*) as meaning-bearing units (*sphoṭa*), it is clear that for Bhartṛhari the true form of the *sphoṭa* is the sentence.[11] This has interesting implications for single-word mantras. Since the fundamental unit of meaning is a complete thought (*vākya-sphoṭa*), single words must be single-word sentences with the missing words being understood. For example, when the young child says "mama," it is clear that whole ideas are being expressed; e.g., "I want mama!" Even when a word is used merely in the form of a substantive noun (e.g., tree), the verb to be is always understood so that what is indicated is really a complete thought (e.g., This is a tree) (*Vāk.*, I.24–26, Vṛtti). In this fashion, Bhartṛhari suggests a way to understand single-word mantras as meaningful. A devotee chanting "Siva" may well be evoking the meaning "Come Siva" or "Siva possess me" with each repetition (*Vāk.*, II.326). Thus, such single-word mantras are far from being meaningless.

Both Wheelock (1980, 358) and Gonda (1963b, 272ff.) have pointed out that, in Vedic ritual, mantra is experienced on various levels, from the loud chanting of the *hotṛ* to silently rehearsed knowledge of the most esoteric bandhus. Probably, a good amount of the argument over the meaningfulness of mantras arises from a lack of awareness of the different levels of language. On one level, there is *pratibhā* or the intuitive flashlike understanding of the sentence meaning of the mantra as a whole. At this level, the fullness of intuited meaning is experienced in the "seen" unity of *artha* and *dhvani* in *sphoṭa.* This is the direct supersenuous perception of the truth of the mantra that occurs at the mystical level of language—when *mystical* is understood in its classical sense as a special kind of perception marked by greater clarity than ordinary sense perception.[12] Bhartṛhari calls this level of mantra experience *paśyantī* (the seeing one);[13] the full meaning of the mantra, the reality it has evoked, stands revealed. This is the *ṛṣi*'s direct "seeing" of truth, and the Tantric devotee's visionary experience of the deity. Yet, for the uninitiated, for the one who has not yet had the experience, it is precisely this level of mantra that will appear to be nonexistent and meaningless. If, due to one's ignorance, the *paśyantī* level is obscured from "sight" then the uttering of the mantra will indeed seem to be an empty exercise. Bhartṛhari calls the level of the uttered words of the sentence *vaikharī vāk*. At the *vaikharī* level, every sound is inherently meaningful in that each sound attempts to reveal the *sphoṭa*.

Repetition of the uttered sounds of the mantra, especially if spoken clearly and correctly, will evoke afresh the *sphoṭa* each time, until finally the obscuring ignorance is purged and the meaning whole of the mantra is seen (*pratibhā*). Between these two levels of uttering (*vaikharī*) and supersensuous seeing (*paśyantī*), there is a middle or *madhyamā vāk* corresponding to the *vākya-sphoṭa* in its mental separation into sentence meaning and a sequence of manifesting sounds, none of which have yet been uttered (*Vāk.*, I.142). For Bhartṛhari, the silent practice of mantra is accounted for by *madhyamā* and, of course, is both real and meaningful.

When all three levels of language are taken into account, as they are by Bhartṛhari, it would seem that all Vedic and Tantric types of mantra practice can be analyzed and shown to be meaningful. In cases where the *avidyā* of the speaker or the hearer obstructs the evocative power of the mantra, it may indeed be experienced as meaningless. But even then, the mantra is still inherently meaningful, as is shown when, through repeated practice, the *sphoṭa* is finally revealed and by the fact that the cultured person, not afflicted by *avidyā*, hears and understands the meaning even though the person uttering the mantra does not (*Vāk.*, I.152–54). The argument, of course, is circular and, if it were merely a theoretical argument, Bhartṛhari's explanation would have no power and would have been discarded long ago. The *Vākyapadīya* appeals not to argument but to empirical evidence, the direct perception of the meaning whole (*sphoṭa*) of the mantra. As long as such direct perception is reflected in the experience of people, Bhartṛhari's explanation of the meaningfulness of mantras will remain viable.

THE POWER OF MANTRAS

The meaningfulness of mantras is not merely intellectual, this meaning has power (śakti). Mantras have the power to remove ignorance (*avidyā*), reveal truth (dharma), and realize release (mokṣa). *Vākyapadīya* states it clearly, "Just as making gifts, performing austerities and practising continence are means of attaining heaven. It has been said: When, by practising the Vedas, the vast darkness is removed, that supreme, bright, imperishable light comes into being in this very birth" (I.5, 14, Vṛtti).

It is not only this lofty goal of final release, which is claimed for the power of words, but also the very availability of human reasoning. Without the fixed power of words to convey meaning, inference based on words could not take place (*Vāk.*, I.137). Because of the power inherent in mantras for both human inference and divine truth, great care must be given to the correct use of words. In Vedic practice, the importance of this mantra śakti is recognized in the careful attention given to the correct speaking of the Vedic verses, so as to avoid distortions and corruptions (Gonda 1963b, 270). And, as McDermott observes, in the view of the Tantric, perception of mantra as "the sonic reverberation of divine power, it is hardly surprising that quality control of its components cannot be left to the caprices of the individual reciter" (1975, 290).

From Bhartṛhari's perspective, the special role of grammar (*Vyākaraṇa*) is to control and purify the use of mantra so that its powers will not be wasted or misused (*Vāk.*, I.11–12). Proper grammatical usage, correct pronunciation, etc. are crucial, not only for the success of the Vedic rituals, but also for all other branches of knowledge (*Vāk.*, I.14). Whether it be the communication of meaning within the human sciences or the identification of ritual action with the divine, it is mantra śakti that enables it all to happen. As Wheelock notes in his most recent paper, in both Vedic and Tantric ritual, mantra is the catalyst that allows the sacred potential of the ritual setting to become a reality.[14] Especially important in this regard is the contention of *Vākapadīya*, I.62, "It is with the meanings conveyed by words that actions are connected." Were it not for the power of word meanings, no connection would be made between the ritual action and the divine, then both the Veda and the Tantra would be powerless.

In the Indian experience, the repeated chanting of mantras is an instrument of power (Gonda 1963b, 271). The more difficulties to be overcome, the more repetitions are needed. *Vākyapadīya*, I.14, makes clear that repeated use of correct mantras removes all impurities, purifies all knowledge, and leads to release. The psychological mechanism involved is described by Bhartṛhari as holding the *sphoṭa* in place by continued chanting. Just as from a distance or in semidarkness, it takes repeated cognitions of an object to see it correctly, so also concentrated attention on the *sphoṭa*, by repeated chanting of the mantra, results in *sphoṭa* finally being perceived in all its fullness (*Vāk.*, I.89). Maṇḍana Miśra describes it as a series of progressively clearer impressions, until a clear and correct apprehension takes place in the end.[15] A similar psychological explanation is offered by Patañjali in *Yoga Sūtra* II.44: As a result of concentrated study (*svādhyāyā*) of mantras (including *bija* syllables like AUM) the desired deity becomes visible. Through the practice of fixed concentration (*samādhi*) upon an object, in this case an uttered mantra, consciousness is purified of karmic obstructions and the deity "seen." Since, for Patañjali, AUM is the mantra for Īśvara, the devotee is advised that the *japa*, or chanting of AUM, will result in the clear understanding of its meaning. Vyāsa puts it in more psychological terms:

> The Yogi who has come to know well the relation between word and meaning must constantly repeat it and habituate the mind to the manifestation therein of its meaning. The constant repetition is to be of the Pranava and the habitual mental manifestation is to be that of what it signifies, Īśvara. The mind of the Yogi who constantly repeats the

> Praṇava and habituates the mind to the constant manifestation of the idea it carries, becomes one-pointed.[16]

The power of such mantra *samādhi* to induce a perfectly clear identity with the deity is given detailed psychological analysis in *Yoga Sūtras* I.42. At first, the experience of identity with Īśvara is mixed up with lingering traces of the uttered mantra (AUM) and its conceptual meaning (*artha*). With continued mantra *samādhi*, all traces of uttered sounds and conceptual meaning are purged, until only the direct perception of Īśvara remains. Patañjali's analysis supports Bhartṛhari's claim that such mantra *samādhi* has the power to remove ignorance and reveal truth.[17] This conclusion confirms both the Vedic and the Tantric mantra experience.

CONCLUSION

Against the background of the long debate over the meaningfulness or meaninglessness of mantras, Bhartṛhari's philosophy of language was employed to analyze the nature of such ritual utterances. The *Vākyapadīya* was found to provide a systematic explanation of the inherent meaningfulness of all mantras, with the apparent meaninglessness resulting from the obscuring function of ignorance. When the *Vākyapadīya* notion of the three levels of language was applied, objections against the meaningfulness of mantras by the Mīmāṁsakas and, more recently, by Frits Staal were shown to be overcome—once Bhartṛhari's assumptions were granted. Support was offered for the *Vākyapadīya* interpretation by adducing a parallel analysis of mantra in Patañjali's *Yoga Sūtras*. For Bhartṛhari, mantras are inherently meaningful, powerful in purging ignorance and revealing truth, and effective instruments for the realization of release (mokṣa). Bhartṛhari's *Vākyapadīya* provides a theory of language that helps modern minds understand how mantras can be experienced as meaningful, powerful, and teleological in Vedic and Tantric ritual.

NOTES

1. Bharati acknowledges that this is the view of many European and Indian scholars, but argues that this is erroneous ([1965] 1970, 102).

2. Of course, there are exceptions to this dominant modern view of language. Witness, for example, Michael Polanyi's defense of "tacit knowing" as meaningful. From Polanyi's perspective all knowing involves two things: (1) a deep indwelling or personal participation of the knower in the known; (2) a hierarchy of levels of knowing all directed by a controlling purpose. See M. Polanyi, *Knowing and Being* (Chicago: University of Chicago Press, 1969), pp. 152ff.

3. See, for example, Russell Fraser, *The Language of Adam* (New York: Colum-

bia University Press, 1977), especially Chapter 4, "Mysticism and Scientific Doom."

4. The *Vākyapadīya of Bhartṛhari,* translated by K. A. Subramania Iyer (Poona: Deccan College, 1965), I.1; hereafter cited *Vāk.* See also K. Kunjunni Raja (1969, 142) for a clear demonstration of how far Bhartṛhari's *śabda* is synonomous with meaning.

5. *The Yoga of Patañjali,* translated by J. H. Woods (Delhi: Motilal Banarsidass, 1966); hereafter cited *Y. S.*

6. For example, the early Buddhists, the Cārvākas, or in modern thought, the positivists.

7. The reason given for this is that "the Mantra can be expressive of mere *assertion,* as it functions only *during* the performance of an act . . . if it enjoined the act, its functioning would come before the commencement of the performance." *Śabara Bhasya* as quoted in Jha ([1942] 1964, 160).

8. *Vāk.,* III.1.6. For Bhartṛhari, the usage of words by elders, and one's learning of that usage, is not a human creation but only a making present to ourselves of the existing natural capacity of words to convey meaning. This is what is meant by the "natural fitness" (*yogyatā,* which is eternal and not the work of man, *apauruṣeya*) in the relation between the word meaning and the sounds.

9. For a complete presentation see Harold Coward *Sphoṭa Theory of Language* (Delhi: Motilal Banarsidass, 1980), Chapter 5.

10. *Sphoṭasiddhi of Maṇḍana Miśra,* translated by K. A. Subramania Iyer (Poona: Deccan College, 1966), commentary on *Kārikā* 18. See also *Vāk.,* I.82–84.

11. See, especially, the *Second Kāṇḍa* of the *Vākyapadīya,* in which he establishes the *vākya-sphoṭa* over against the view of the Mīmāṁsakas.

12. See W. T. Stace, *Mysticism and Philosophy* (London: Macmillan, 1961), p. 15. This, of course, is exactly the opposite of the common, modern interpretations given to the term *mystical*: e.g., vague, mysterious, foggy, etc.

13. *Vāk.,* I.142. Note that in *Vṛtti,* sounds of cart-ale, drum, and flute are all forms of *Vaikharī Vāk* and, therefore, potentially meaningful.

14. Wade Wheelock, "The Mantra in Vedic and Tantric Ritual," unpublished paper, p. 19.

15. *Sphoṭasiddhi of Maṇḍana Miśra,* translated by K. A. Subramania lyer, *Kārikās* 19–20.

16. *Bhāsya* on *Y.S.* I.28 as rendered by Rama Prasada (Delhi: Oriental Reprint, 1978), p. 51.

17. In using the *Yoga Sūtra* as a parallel and supporting analysis, it must be remembered that ultimately significant differences exist: The *Vākyapadīya* offers

an absolutism of word consciousness or *Sabdabrahman* while the Yoga system is ultimately a duality between pure consciousness (*puruṣa*) and nonintelligent matter (*prakṛti*). Consequently, Vacaspati points out that Īśvara's *sattva* does not possess the power of consciousness, since *sattva* is nonintelligent in its own nature (Y.S., I.24, *ṭīkā*). Since the concern in this essay is not with the ultimate nature of the metaphysics involved, the discussion has proceeded as if the *sattva* aspect of *prakṛti* indeed were real consciousness. This is in accord with the Yoga view of the nature of psychological processes. The *sattva* aspect of *citta,* insofar as it is clear, takes on or reflects the intelligence (*cāitanva*) of *puruṣa.* For practical purposes, therefore, no duality appears, and *prakṛti* may be treated as self-illuminating (see *ṭīkā* on Y.S., I.17).

CHAPTER 7

Mantras in the *Śivapurāṇa*

Ludo Rocher

EVEN THOUGH THE *ŚIVAPURĀṆA* HAD to compete with the *Vāyupurāṇa* for a place in the list of eighteen *mahāpurāṇas*, and even though it, therefore, was often relegated to the rank of an upapurāṇa,[1] it is nevertheless one of the more extensive, and least uniform, Purānic texts. According to a number of passages in the *Purāṇa* itself, the *Śivapurāṇa* originally consisted of twelve *saṃhitās*. The printed editions, however, contain far fewer than that. One set of editions,[2] is composed of six *saṃhitās*: *Jñāna-*, *Vidyeśvara-*, *Kailāsa-*, *Sanatkumāra-*, *Vāyu-* or *Vāyavīya-*, and *Dharma-*. This article is based on a second, very different set of editions,[3] with seven *saṃhitās*. The text of the *Śivapurāṇa* in these editions is composed as follows:

1. *Vidyeśvarasmaṃhitā* (or *Vighneśasaṃhitā*) (25 chapters)
2. *Rudrasaṃhitā*
   - 2.1 *Sṛṣṭikhaṇḍa* (20 chapters)
   - 2.2 *Satīkhaṇḍa* (43 chapters)
   - 2.3 *Pārvatīkhaṇḍa* (55 chapters)
   - 2.4 *Kumārakhaṇḍa* (20 chapters)
   - 2.5 *Yuddhakhaṇḍa* (59 chapters)
3. *Śatarudrasaṃhitā* (42 chapters)
4. *Koṭirudrasaṃhitā* (43 chapters)
5. *Umāsaṃhitā* (or *Aumasaṃhitā*) (51 chapters)
6. *Kailāsasaṃhitā* (23 chapters)
7. *Vāyusaṃhitā* (or *Vāyavīyasaṃhitā*)
   - 7.1 *Pūrvabhāga* (35 chapters)
   - 7.2 *Uttarabhāha* (51 chapters)

This text of the *Śivapurāṇa*, therefore, is composed of 467 chapters. References in this article will consist of three or four figures: *saṃhitā*, occasionally its subdivision (*khaṇḍa* or *bhāga*), chapter (*adhyāya*), and verse.

Mantras[4]—both in general: the mantra or the mantras, and specifically defined—are omnipresent in the *Śivapurāṇa*. The text itself[5] says that it contains "streams of mantras." It claims to put order in the mantras, for "as long as the *Śivapurāṇa* will not make its appearance on earth, mantras will be in discord."[6] In the metaphorical description of the chariot that Viśvakarman prepared for Indra in view of the destruction of the Tripuras, the mantras are said to be the tinkling bells.[7] On the occasion of the *māhātmya* of the *Mahākāla jyotirliṅga* (4, ch. 17), the *Śivapurāṇa* tells the story of a young boy, the son of a cowherd—and the ancestor of Nanda (4.17.68)—who became a devotee of Śiva and who succeeded in performing *śivapūjā* "even without mantras" (4.17.66: *amantreṇa API*). This was, however, the exception: Under normal circumstances "worshiping Hara is not possible without the use of mantras."[8] "For Śiva worship fully to yield the desired result it shall be accompanied by mantras."[9]

The *Śivapurāṇa* occasionally refers to mantras for gods other than Śiva. It recognizes worship of different gods "each with their own, respective mantras" (1.14.23: *tattanmantreṇa*) and mentions "reciting mantras and performing other forms of worship to one's *iṣṭadeva* (1.14.27: *japādyam iṣṭadevasya*). When Dambha, the son of Vipracitti, did penance in *Puṣkara* to have a son, he firmly recited the Kṛṣṇamantia (2.5.27.12: *kṛṣṇamantraṃ jajāpa dṛḍham*). Elsewhere, the text announces a mantra to the Sun (6.6.38: *mantraṃ sāvitraṃ sarvasiddham . . . bhuktimuktipradam*) and devotes two *upajāti* stanzas to it (6.6.39–40):

> sindhūravarṇāya sumaṇḍalāya namo 'stu vajrābharaṇāya tubhyam /
> padmābhanetrāya supaṅkajāya brahmendranārāyaṇakāraṇāya //
> saraktacūrṇaṃ sasuvarṇatoyaṃ srakkuṅkumāḍhyaṃ sakuśaṃ sapuṣpam /
> pradattam ādāya sahemapātraṃ praśastam arghyaṃ bhagavan prasīda //

In general, however, the *Śivapurāṇa* is, for obvious reasons, concerned with mantras for Śiva. Quite often the mantra is not further specified. For instance, Andhaka, the son of Hiraṇyākṣa, daily offers a part of his body in the fire *samantrakam* (2.5.44.6). Anasūyā fashions a clay image of Śiva *mantreṇa* (4.3.17). When Rāma praises Śiva he is said to be *mantradhyānaparāyaṇa* (4.31.31). Occasionally, the text refers to *rudrajapa* without indicating the mantra that is the object of the recitation.[10] There are good reasons to presume that, when a mantra for Śiva remains unspecified, the *Śivapurāṇa* means to refer to the *praṇava*.[11] The *praṇava*, indeed, is the mantra that is most prominent throughout the text; it is mentioned more often than any other mantra, and it is the mantra that has been discussed in the greatest detail.[12]

The Śivapurāṇa engages in several etymologies of the term *praṇava*, which are of interest insofar as they throw light on the composers' views on the nature and purpose of the mantra. For instance, *praṇava* is the best of boats (*nava*) to cross the ocean; i.e. the *saṃsāra* evolved out of *prakṛti* (*pra*).[13] Or, *praṇava* means that there is no (*na*) diffusiveness (*pra*) for you (*va*).[14] Or, *praṇava* is so called because it is the ideal (*pra*) guide (*na*) to mokṣa for you (*va*).[15] Or, *praṇava* is the ideal way (*pra*) to eliminate all karma of those who recite and worship it, deliver them from *māyā*, and provide them with new (*nava*) divine wisdom, i.e. make them into new (*nava*) purified personalities.[16] Elsewhere, it is said to be the *prāṇa* of all living beings, all the way from Brahmā down to immobile objects.[17]

The Śivapurāṇa distinguishes two forms of *praṇava*: the subtle (*sūkṣma*) and the gross (*sthūla*). The former is monosyllabic (*ekākṣara*), the latter consists of five syllables (*pañcākṣara*).[18] In reality, they both contain five syllables (*arṇa*), but in the latter these are "apparent, manifested" (*vyakta*), in the former they are not (*avyakta*).[19] The subtle *praṇava* is again subdivided into two. The long (*dīrgha*) subtle *praṇava* consisting of *a* + *u* + *m* + *bindu* + *nāda*, resides in the heart of yogins. The short (*hrasva*) subtle *praṇava* consists only of the sound *m*, which represents three things: Śiva, his Śakti, and their union. It should be recited by those who desire to expiate all their sins.[20] The gross *praṇava*, in five syllables, is composed of Śiva's name, in the dative case, preceded by the word *namaḥ*; i.e., *namaḥ śivāya*.[21] Another passage (1.11.42–43) makes a further distinction in connection with this formula: *namaḥ* should precede only in the case of *brahmans*—or *dvijas* generally (?)—whereas it should follow after *śivāya* in all other cases; this also includes women with the exception, according to some, of *brahman* women.

Given its twofold, or threefold, subdivision, it is not always clear to which form of *praṇava* the text refers when it uses the term.[22] Only rarely does it make a clear distinction, as it does when it prescribes OṂ to erect a *liṅga* on a *pīṭha*, but the *pañcākṣaramantra* to prepare a Śiva image (*vera*) for a festival (1.11.16, 18). However, even though the *pañcākṣaramantra* is referred to as the *mantrarāṭ* (6.3.8) and occasionally is praised as the ne plus ultra[23] and even though the Purāṇa devotes three chapters (7.2. Ch. 12–14) to *pañcākṣaramāhātmya*, there are numerous indications in the text that the *praṇava* par excellence is OṂ.[24]

The components of OṂ are referred to in the Purāṇa in a variety of contexts and for a variety of reasons. For instance, each of the three lines of the *tripuṇḍra* mark is presided over by nine deities. They are (1.24.89–94):

—for the first line: the sound *a* (*akāra*), the *gārhapatya* fire, the earth (*bhū*), dharma (Kālāgnirudropaniṣad: *svātmā*), *rajas*, Ṛgveda, *kriyāśakti*, *prātaḥ savana*, and Mahādeva;

—for the second line: the sound *u* (*ukāra*), the *dakṣiṇa* fire, *nabhas*, *antarātmā, sattva,* Yajurveda, *icchāśakti, madhyandinasavana,* and Maheśvara;

—for the third line: the sound *m* (*makāra*), the *āhavanīya* fire, *dyaus, paramātmā, tamas,* Sāmaveda, *jñānaśakti, tṛtīyaṃ savanam,* and Śiva.

In the discussion of various types of *liṅgas,* the first, subtle *liṅga* is identified with the *sūkṣma praṇava;* i.e., OṂ.[25] In addition to this, there are many gross *liṅgas,* of which the *sūta* proposes to deal only with those made of clay. These are five in number: *svayambhū, bindu, pratiṣṭhita, cara,* and *guru* (1.18.31). The text identifies these with *nāda, bindu, makāra, ukāra,* and *akāra* of OṂ, respectively.[26]

The Śivapurāṇa also provides special rules on how to recite OṂ. According to one passage, OṂ is to be recited mentally (*mānasa*) in case of *samādhi,* in a low voice (*upāṃśu*) at all other times.[27] Elsewhere, it is said that, according to the experts on the Āgamas, mental *japa* is the highest form of recitation, *upāṃśu japa* the middlemost form, and verbal (*vācika*) *japa* the lowest (7.2.14.24). In fact, *upāṃśu japa* is one hundred times as efficient as *vācika japa, mānasa japa* one thousand times, and *sagarbha japa,* i.e., *japa* accompanied by *prāṇāyāma* (7.2.14.30), again one hundred times more (7.2.14.29); finally, *sadhyāna japa* is one thousand times better than *sagarbha japa* (7.2.14.33).[28]

As we saw earlier, the *sthūla praṇava* consists of five syllables: Śiva's name in the dative preceded, and occasionally followed, by *namaḥ.* It is most commonly referred to as the *pañcākṣaramantra,* rarely, more shortly, as *pañcākṣara* or, with a variant, *pañcavarṇa.*[29] Occasionally, the Śivapurāṇa speaks of *ṣaḍakṣaramantra* rather than *pañcākṣaramantra.*[30] This is described as "the *pañcākṣaravidyā* to which the *praṇava* is added,"[31] or, more detailed, as "the mantra with Śiva's name in the dative case, preceded by OṂ and followed by *namaḥ.*"[32] Even though it is not given a specific name, the *ṣaḍakṣaramantra* occasionally is further expanded into seven syllables. Pārvatī's adopted son Sundarśana performed the *saṃkalpapūjā* sixteen times with the mantra *oṃ namaḥ śrīśivāya.*[33] On one occasion, Viṣṇu advises the gods and the sages to recite an even longer *śivamantra,*[34] as follows: *oṃ namah śivāya śubhaṃ śubhaṃ kuru kuru śivāya namaḥ om.*[35] Except for the simple *śivanāmamantras,* which will be discussed later, variants on the *pañcākṣara-* or *ṣaḍakṣaramantra* with other names than Śiva are rare. One such exception is the advice by Vasiṣṭha to Saṃdhyā to recite the mantra: *oṃ namaḥ śaṅkarāya oṃ.*[36]

Several passages in the Śivapurāṇa place the recitation of mantras (i.e., *śivamantras*) in a broader context and evaluate their merit in comparison with other forms of worship. To be sure, in those sections devoted to *mantramāhātmya,* the recitation of mantras in general and of the *pañcākṣaramantra* or *ṣaḍakṣaramantra* in particular is extolled as superior to any other form of Śiva worship. Even a single utterance of the five-syllable mantra is ten million (*koṭi,* see later) times better than any form of *tapas,* ritual, or *vrata.*[37] Or, the *pañcākṣaramantra* is compared to a sūtra—"it is a *vidhi*, not an *arthavāda*" (7.2.12.21)—on which all other mantras and every other means of knowing Śiva are mere commentaries.[38] It is like the seed of a banyan tree; however small in itself, it has an enormous potential and is the source of every form of wisdom.[39]

In other contexts, however, we are presented with different and more balanced views. According to one passage (1.15.57), the recitation of mantras and *stotras* constitutes "verbal ritual" (*vācikaṃ yajanam*), as against "physical ritual" (*kāyikaṃ yajanam*), which is characteristic of pilgrimages, *vratas*, etc. Other texts, aimed more directly at Śiva worship, list mantras as one element of it, together with wearing sacred ashes and *liṅga* worship.[40] As to the relative value of these and other elements of Śiva worship, the Śivapurāṇa informs us that, the ultimate goal being mokṣa, wearing *rudrākṣas* realizes one quarter of it, wearing ashes one half, reciting mantras three quarters; only worshiping the *liṅga* and Śiva's devotees realizes everything.[41] In a chapter on *tapas*, in which *tapas* is proclaimed to be the sole way to reach one's goals (5.20.9), *japa* is said to be a part of *sāttvikatapas* (5.20.11,15);[42] it is the domain of the gods and *yatīnām ūrdhvaretasām*, and brings about all desired results (*aśeṣaphalasādhana*).

On one occasion, the recitation of mantras (*mantroccāraṇa*), together with *dhyāna* and *aṣṭāṅgabhūsparśana*, is a form of *vandana*, one of the nine *aṅgas* of *bhakti*.[43] An even more subordinate role is assigned to the recitation of mantras in the story of the *vaiśya* Supriya who, while in prison, taught (4.29.45) his fellow-prisoners the Śiva mantra and idol worship. The leader himself worshiped the idol,[44] some engaged in *dhyāna* or *mānasī pūjā*;[45] only those who did not know better recited the mantra *namaḥ śivāya*.[46]

One passage insists that wearing the *rudrākṣas* without reciting mantras is not only usless but leads to residence in a terrible hell for the duration of fourteen Indras.[47] On the other hand, he who wears the *tripuṇḍra* automatically possesses all the mantras.[48] Reciting mantras is one of the things, together with *dhyāna*, etc., that is useless without the *tripuṇḍra*.[49] Yet, mantras have to be used when one is unable to smear (*uddhūlana*) on the entire body; he shall then apply the *tripuṇḍra* on the head with *namaḥ śivāya*, on the sides with *īśābhyāṃ namaḥ*, on the forearms with *bījābhyāṃ namaḥ*, on the lower part of the body with *pitṛbhyāṃ namaḥ*, on the upper part with *umeśābhyāṃ namaḥ*, and on the back and the back of the head with *bhīmāya namaḥ* (1.24.113–116).

One important aspect of mantra recitation, which is stressed again and again in the Śivapurāṇa, is the benefit of multiple repetition (*āvṛtti*). During his penance, Arjuna stands on one foot, concentrates his gaze on the sun, and "continuously repeats" (*āvartayan sthitaḥ*)[50] the five-syllable mantra (3.39.2).

The benefit to be derived from a mantra increases in direct proportion to the number of times it is recited. One passage enumerates the increasing benefits of the *mṛtyuṃjayamantra*, from one *lakh* of repetitions up to one million.[51] Similarly, when a mantra is recited by way of expiation, the number of its repetitions required is proportionate to the seriousness of the sin one has committed: for omitting a *saṃdhyā* for one day the text prescribes one hundred *gāyatrīs,* one hundred thousand for omitting it for up to ten days; if one neglects it for one month even the *gāyatrī* is insufficient, and one has to undergo a new *upanayana* (1.13.30–31).

A figure mentioned quite often for the repetition of mantras is one or more *koṭis* "one crore, ten million." After repeating one *koṭi* times the mantra *oṃ namaḥ śivāya śubhaṃ śubhaṃ kuru kuru śivāya namaḥ om,* Śiva is supposed to do what he is requested to do (2.5.7.26: *śivaḥ kāryaṃ kariṣyati*).[52] By repeating the *pañcākṣaramantra* one, two, three, or four *koṭi* times one reaches "the worlds of Brahmā, etc.," but five *koṭis* render the devotee equal to Śiva.[53]

Another figure presecribed for the repetition of mantras is 108.[54] More specifically, during the *śivarātri* the mantra shall be repeated 108 times during its first three-hour period (*yāma*); this number shall be doubled during the second *yāma,* quadrupled during the third, and eight times 108 mantras shall be recited in the fourth.[55] Occasionally, the number 108 is replaced by its variant, 1008. When the sūta sits down with the sages he recites the five-syllable mantra 1008 times.[56]

The text also indicates the way in which the number of mantras ought to be counted, using different kinds of objects to keep track of the units, tens, hundreds, etc., up to *koṭis.*[57]

The Śivapurāṇa follows the general pattern that "the mantras relating to gods represent their essence—they are in a sense identifiable with them."[58] Throughout the text the Śivapurāṇa expresses in a variety of ways the idea that Śiva IS the *praṇava* or that the *praṇava* IS Śiva.

Viṣṇu addresses Śiva: *oṃkāras tvam* (2.2.41.14); Brahmā pays homage to Śiva: *oṃkārāya namas tubhyam* (2.5.11.14). In a long eulogy to show that Śiva is superior in every category, the gods list the fact that among the *bījamantras* he is the *praṇava* (2.5.2.43: *praṇavo bījamantrāṇām*). Any devotee should realize that Śiva is identical with the *praṇava* (6.6.29: *praṇavaṃ ca śivaṃ vadet*). Śiva himself declares the *praṇava* to be *madrūpam* (6.3.3), and Arjuna takes on unequaled splendor *mantreṇa madrūpeṇa* (3.38.1). Śiva is *oṃkāramayam . . . pañcākṣaramayaṃ devaṃ ṣaḍakṣaramayaṃ tathā* (6.7.62–63); he is *praṇavātamā* (6.12.20) or *praṇavātmaka* (6.9.23); he is *śabdabrahmatanu* (2.1.8.13.41); etc.

The *praṇava* is, however, not always *identical* to Śiva. Occasionally, Śiva is said to be *praṇavārtha* "the significandum of the *praṇava.*"[59] The same idea can also be expressed in different forms: Śiva is said to be *vācya,* the *praṇava* being *vācaka;*[60] or the *praṇava* is *abhidhāna,* Śiva being *abhidheya.*[61]

According to one passage *om issued* from Śiva: "*Om* was born from Śiva's mouths. The sound *a* first came out of his northern mouth, *u* from his western mouth, *m* from his southern mouth; the *bindu* next came from his eastern mouth, and the *nāda* from his central mouth. The result of this fivefold 'gaping' (*vijṛmbhita*) was then made into one in the form of the single syllable *om*" (1.10.16–19).

The Śivamantra is secret; Śiva alone knows it.[62] Therefore, it is only natural that, as announced by the *sūta* early in the Purāṇa,[63] Śiva himself revealed it to the Devī in the Kailāsasaṃhitā (6.3.1 sqq.). Śiva also taught the mantra to Brahmā and Viṣṇu (1.10.25–26) and advised them to recite it "to acquire knowledge of him."[64]

More generally, Śiva reveals the *praṇavārtha* to those with whom he is pleased.[65] One of those who enjoyed this privilege was the *sūta*; when the sages inquire with him about *praṇavasya māhātmyam*, he responds that he indeed knowns it *śivasya kṛpayaiva*.[66] The reason why the *sūta* happens to be a "fortunate devotee" (*dhanyaḥ śivabhaktaḥ*) is explained elsewhere in the text: Śiva is the *praṇavārtha*; the Vedas were issued from the *praṇava*; the Purāṇas expound the meaning of the Vedas; and the *sūta* is the supreme *paurāṇika*.[67]

Śivamantras have to be learned through the intermediary of a guru (2.1.13.73–74: *gurūpadiṣṭamārgeṇa*); the mantra is *gurudatta*.[68] As a result, a disciple is his guru's *mantraputra*. The mantra is the semen springing from the guru's tongue (the penis) and deposited in the disciple's ear (the yoni). The natural father brings his son into the *saṃsāra*; the *bodhakaḥ pitā* helps him out of it (*saṃtārayati saṃsārāt*).[69] The acqusition of a mantra involves an initiation, *mantradīkṣā*.[70] One passage (7.2.14.1–23), in which the initiation is referred to as *puraścaraṇa* (v. 16; cf. v. 18: *pauraścaraṇika*), describes in great detail the entire procedure, from the time one approaches a teacher up to the acquisition and recitation of the mantra.

The Śivapurāṇa, however, also provides for the eventuality that no mantra was "given" by a teacher: in that case the *gurudattamantra* may be replaced by *nāmamantras*.[71] Śiva's name, rather names, is very prominent in the Śivapurāṇa. The text contains a chapter (4, Chapter 35) enumerating a little over one thousand names of Śiva (*śivasahasranāmavarṇanam*), followed by another chapter (Chapter 36) enumerating the benefits of its recitation, including one hundred times over by kings in distress (4.36.22). On some occasions, the Purāṇa rather vaguely prescribes the recitation of "multiple *nāmamantras*" (4.13.46: *nāmamantrān anekāṃś ca*). The *nāmamantra* to be recited as a substitute for the *gurudattamantra*, however, also can be more precise; it consists in the recitation of eight names of Śiva, in the dative case, preceded by *śrī*: *śrībhavāya śrīśarvāya śrīrudrāya śrīpaśupataye śryugrāya śrīmahate śrībhīmāya śrīśānāya* (4.38.53–55).

The Śivapurāṇa also composes its own *Śivamantras*. On several occasions, the text introduces passages saving that one should "invite" or "pray to" Śiva "with the following mantra(s)."[72] Eventually, these "mantras" contain nothing more than the formula *oṃ namas te* followed by a series of names or attributes of Śiva, in the dative case.[73] It is clear that, in these instances, the dividing line between a *Śivamantra* and a *Śivastotra*—many passages are so introduced in the Purāṇa—has become vague, if not inexistent. In one case, the text explicitly says, "Let the wise pray to Śiva, praising him with the following mantra."[74]

Yet, whatever other *Śivamantras,* and mantras to other gods, there may be, as I indicated earlier, the Śivapurāṇa leaves no doubt that the *praṇava* reigns supreme.[75] In the passage quoted earlier, in which mantras generally are described as the bells of Śiva's chariot, only the *praṇava* is singled out for a different and special function: It serves Brahmā, who is the charioteer, as his whip.[76] In fact, it is so important that even Śiva's residence on the summit of Mount Kailāsa is *praṇavākāra* "in the form of the *praṇava*" (1.6.23).[77]

It goes without saying that the recitation of *Śivamantras* is beneficial. He who recites Śiva's name is considered to be versed in the Vedas, virtuous, wealthy, and wise (1.23.25), is able to see Śiva and obtains a son equal in strength to himself.[78] His face becones a purifying *tīrtha* that erases all sins; even one who looks at him gains the same benefit as if he were to visit a *tīrtha.*[79] More specifically, since Śiva is identical with the mantra, the recitation of *Śivamantras* results in bringing Śiva into one's body.[80] Śiva being the *praṇavārtha,* too, the same result obtains by listening to the explanation of the *Śivamantra.*[81]

A most interesting result of reciting *Śivamantras* pertains to *brahman* women, *kṣatriyas, vaiśyas,* and even *śūdras. Śivamantras* are apt to drastically change their status—presumably in a future existence, even though the text does not say so explicitly. If a *brahman* woman learns the *pañcākṣaramantra* from a guru and recites it 500,000 times, she obtains longevity; by reciting it another 500,000 times she becomes a man and, eventually, attains liberation. By reciting the mantra 500,000 times, the *kṣatriya* sheds off his *kṣatriya*-hood, and another 500,000 recitations make him into a *brahman,* thereby opening the possibility of liberation. If a *vaiśya* recites twice 500,000 mantras he becomes a *mantrakṣatriya,* and, via the same amount of recitations made once more, a *mantrabrāhmaṇa.* In the same way the *śūdra* attains *mantravipratva* and becomes a *śuddho dvijaḥ* by reciting the mantra 2,500,000 times.[82] Elsewhere in the text, we are told that even an outcaste, if he becomes a Śiva devotee, will be liberated by reciting the five-syllable mantra.[83]

I now turn to another important, omnipresent feature of the Śivapurāṇa: its relation to the Vedas generally and to Vedic mantras in particular. I mentioned earlier that the Vedas "arose from the *praṇava*" (6.1.17).[84] Hence, they also arose from Śiva himself; both he and the mantra are described as *vedādi.*[85] Similarly, the *praṇava* is *vedasāra, vedāntasārasarvasva,* etc.[86] It is also described as *atharvaśirasa,*[87] and even as any other Vedic mantra, it has an *ṛṣi,* Brahmā; a *chandas, gāyatra;* and a *devatā,* Śiva.[88]

Vedic mantras in general are referred to repeatedly in the Śivapurāṇa.[89] Śiva himself chants *sāmans* (2.5.46.21). The gods bring Gaṇeśa back to life by sprinkling water on him while reciting *vedamantras* (2.4.17.54–55). The *jātakarma* of Gṛhapati, an incarnation of Śiva, is performed by Brahmā "reciting the smṛti and hailing him with blessings from the four Vedas" (3.14.25–26). After Śiva's penis fell off in the Devadāruvana, a pot had to be addressed "with Vedic mantras."[90] *Tat tvam asi* is said to be Śiva's own *mahāvākya* (2.1.8.49).

One text is mentioned specifically and by title. The *tripuṇḍra* mark has to be put on the forehead *Jābālakoktamantreṇa* (1.13.21).[91] More explicitly, members of all varṇas and āśramas shall apply the *tripuṇḍra* "with seven mantras from the Jābālopaniṣad, starting with 'Agni.'"[92] The seven mantras referred to here appear in the first chapter of the Bhasmajābālopaniṣad: *agnir iti bhasma vāyur iti bhasma jalam iti bhasma sthalam iti bhasma vyometi bhasma devā bhasma ṛṣayo bhasma*. The Purāṇa again refers to the same Upaniṣad on the subject of the *śivavratas*: They are numerous, but ten of them are particularly important, "as taught by the experts on the Jābālaśruti."[93]

One mantra, *ā vo rājānam*, is explicitly identified as an *ṛc*.[94] It corresponds to ṚV 4.3.1:

> ā vo rājānam adhvarasya rudraṃ hotāraṃ satyayajaṃ rodasyoḥ /
> agniṃ purā tanayitnor acittād dhiraṇyarūpam avase kṛṇudhvam.

We, therefore, may assume[95] that the other two mantras quoted in the same context also are considered to be *ṛc*s. They are, to invoke Viṣṇu, *pra tad viṣṇuḥ*; i.e., ṚV 1.154.2:[96]

> pra tad viṣṇuḥ stavate vīryeṇa mṛgo na bhīmaḥ kucaro giriṣṭhāḥ /
> yasyoruṣu triṣu vikrameṣv adhikṣiyanti bhuvanāni viśvā,

and, to call on Brahmā, *hiraṇyagarbhaḥ samavartata*; i.e. ṚV 10.121.1:[97]

> hiraṇyagarbhaḥ samavartatāgre bhūtasya jātaḥ patir eka āsīt /
> sa dadhāra pṛthivīṃ dyām utemāṃ kasmai devāya haviṣā vidhema.

It should, however, be noted that the Śivapurāṇa also claims as *ṛc*s mantras that do not occur in the Ṛgveda;[98] in this case the term *ṛc* seems to alternate freely with *mantra*.

At one point, in the description of *śradddha*, the text indicates that the ritual, and hence the mantras to be recited in the course of it, may be performed "according to the individual's own gṛhyasūtra."[99]

Some of the more important "Vedic" mantras quoted in the Śivapurāṇa without reference to a source or without a generic term can best be treated and identified individually, in alphabetical order.

AGHORAMANTRA[100]

Referred to in connection with the application of the *tripuṇḍra*[101] and waring the *rudrākṣa.*[102]

Sole[103] occurrences: MS 2.9.10; TĀ 10.45.; MahāU 17.3 (##282–283):

aghorebhyo 'tha ghorebhyo aghoraghoratarebhyaḥ /
sarvataḥ śarvaḥ sarvebhyo namas te rudra rūpebhyaḥ.

The text also refers to ashes as *aghorāstrābhimantrita,* which Upamanyu uses in an effort to kill Indra; at Śiva's request, Nandi intercepts the *aghorāstra* in flight (3.32.40–43).

ÍŚĀNAḤ[104] SARVAVIDYĀNĀM

Śiva claims that "the mantras *īśānaḥ sarvavidyānām,* etc." issued from him.[105] The mantra establishes Śiva as the "maker" and "lord" of the Vedas.[106] It is also referred to in connection with the *tripuṇḍra*[107] and the *rudrākṣa.*[108]

Sole occurrences: TĀ 10.47.1; MahāU 17.5 (##285–286); NpU 1.6: *īśānaḥ sarvavidyānām īśvaraḥ sarvabhūtānāṃ brahmādhipatir brahmaṇo 'dhipatir brahmā śivo me astu sa eva sadāśiva om.*

GAṆĀNĀṂ TVĀ

This *pratīka,* quoted to invite Gaṇeśa,[109] may refer to the well-known invocation of Gaṇeśa, which appears for the first time in the Ṛgveda (ṚV 2.23.1), addressed there to Bṛhaspati, and has been repeated throughout Vedic literature:

gaṇānāṃ tvā gaṇapatiṃ havāmahe kaviṃ kavīnām
upamaśravastamam /
jyeṣṭharājaṃ brahmaṇāṃ brahmaṇaspata ā naḥ śṛṇvann
ūtibhiḥ sīda sādanam.

However, in view of the fact that this stanza is absent from TĀ and MahāU, the *pratīka gaṇānāṃ tvā* in the Śivapurāṇa may refer, rather, to a mantra that appears in VtU 1.5:

gaṇānāṃ tvā gaṇanāthaṃ surendraṃ kaviṃ kavīnām
atimedhavigraham /
jyeṣṭharājaṃ vṛṣabhaṃ ketum ekam ā naḥ śṛṇvann ūtibhiḥ
sīda śaśvat.

GĀYATRĪ

When the text alludes to "reciting the *gāyatrī*"[110] (1.24.43: *gāyatrījapena . . . muktir bhavet;* cf. 1.13.26,30), it is not always clear whether the reference is to the ṛgvedic *gāyatrī* (ṚV 3.62.10) or to the *śivagāyatrī*, to which there are also explicit references (1.20.19: *rudragāyatrī;* 3.1.19: *gāyatrīṃ śāṅkarīm*). The latter is known from TĀ 10.1 onward:

tat puruṣāya vidmahe mahādevāya dhīmahi /
tan no rudraḥ pracodayāt.

A "sixteen-syllable" *gāyatrī*[111] presumably refers to an abbreviated form of this. At least once, the Śivapurāṇa has Skanda invoked with a *skandagāyatrī*,[112] which is known solely from the MahāU (3.5 is #75):

tat puruṣāya vidmahe mahāsenāya dhīmahi /
tan naḥ ṣaṣṭhaḥ [or ṣaṇmukhaḥ] pracodayāt.

GAURĪR MIMĀYA

Quoted to invite the Devī,[113] this is a well-known mantra, from ṚV 1.164.41 onward:

gaurī(r) mimāya salilāni takṣatī ekapadī dvipadī sā catuṣpadī /
aṣṭāpadī navapadī babhūvuṣī sahasrākṣarā parame vyoman.

CAMAKASŪKTA

This is one of the *sūktas* to be recited during *śrādha*. A *camakasūkta* appears in the Saṃhitās of most *śākhās* of the Yajurveda (VS 18.1–26; TaitSam 4.7.1–11; MS 2.11.2–5; KS 18.7–12; etc.): *vājaś ca me prasavaś ca me prayatiś ca me prasitiś ca me dhītiś ca me kratuś ca me svaraś ca me ślokaś ca me śravaś ca me śrutiś ca me jyotiś ca me svaś ca me yajñena kalpantām.* Etc., etc.

TAT PURUṢA°

This is to be recited while putting *rudrākṣas* on the ear (1.25.40); equivalent to the *rudragāyatrī* (see earlier).

TRYAMBAKA

This mantra is prescribed, for a *vaiśya* and a *brahmacārin*, while applying the *tripuṇḍra*.[114] It is a well-attested mantra, from ṚV 7.59.12 onward:

tryambakaṃ yajāmahe sugandhiṃ puṣṭivardhanam /
urvārukam iva bandhanān mṛtyor mukṣīya māmṛtāt.

(Cf. under *mṛtyuṃjaya*.)

TRYĀYUṢA

This is referred to not explicitly as a mantra but in connection with putting on the ashes.[115] It is a well-attested verse, from AV 5.28.7 onward:

> tryāyuṣaṃ jamadagneḥ kaśyapasya tryāyuṣam /
> yad deveṣu tryāyuṣam tan no astu tryāyuṣam.

PAÑCABRAHMA

This mantra is quoted in the chapters on the *tripuṇḍra*[116] and *rudrākṣa.*[117] (see under sub *sadyojāta*).

PURUṢASŪKTA

This is listed among the mantras to be recited during *jaladhārā* (or *dhārāpūjā*): *sūktena pauruṣeṇa vā* (2.1.14.69; cf. 6.12.68: *pauruṣaṃ sūktam*). In one passage (2.5.56.27), the *asura* Bāṇa praises Śiva with a *śloka* reminiscent of ṚV 10.90.12:

> brāhmaṇaṃ te mukhaṃ prāhur bāhuṃ kṣatriyam eva ca /
> ūrujaṃ vaiśyam āhus te pādajaṃ śūdram eva ca.

BHAVE BHAVE NĀTIBHAVE

The sequence starting with this mantra, as part of the *praṇavaprokṣaṇa,* makes use, in detail,[118] of sections of a longer sequence, for which see listing under *sadyojāta.* It corresponds to TĀ 10.43–44, MahāU 17.1–2 (##278–280).

MĀ NAS TOKE

This mantra is cited in connection with the *tripuṇḍra,* for *brahmans* and *kṣatriyas.*[119] It is a mantra often quoted from ṚV 1.114.8 onward:

> mā nas toke tanaye mā na āyau (or āyuṣi) mā no goṣu mā no aśveṣu rīrisaḥ /
> vīrām mā no rudra bhāmito vadhīr haviṣmanto sadam it tvā havāmahe (or namasā vidhema te).

MṚTYUṂJAYA

The *mṛtyuṃjayamantra* (2.2.38.21; 2.5.49.42), also called *mṛtasaṃjīvanīmantra* (2.2.38.30), *mṛtyuṃjayavidyā* (2.2.38.20), *mṛtajīvanī vidyā* (2.5.15.47), or *mṛtasaṃjīvanī vidyā* (2.5.50.41), is quoted several times in the Śivapurāṇa. In addition to general references,[120] the mantra is said to have been composed by Śiva himself,[121] who handed it over to Śukra, the preceptor of the Daityas.[122] Śukra, therefore, became the *mṛtyuṃ-*

jayavidyāpravartaka (2.2.38.20); he used it to revive the Asuras (2.5.15.47) and the Daityas and Dānavas (2.5.47.33–34). Śukra also revealed to Dadhīca *mahāmṛtyuṃjayaṃ mantram* (2.2.38.22–29):

> tryambakaṃ yajāmahe[123] ca trailokyapitaraṃ prabhum /
> trimaṇḍalasya pitaraṃ triguṇasya maheśvaram //
> tritattvasya trivahneś ca tridhābhūtasya sarvataḥ /
> tridivasya tribāhoś ca tridhābhūtasya sarvataḥ //
> tridevasya mahādevaḥ sugandhiṃ puṣṭivardhanam /
> sarvabhūteṣu sarvatra triguṇeṣu kṛtau yathā //
> indriyeṣu tathānyeṣu deveṣu ca gaṇeṣu ca /
> puṣpe sugandhivat sūraḥ sugandhiramaheśvaraḥ //
> puṣṭiś ca prakṛter yasmāt puruṣād vai dvijottama /
> mahadādiviśeṣāntavikalpaś cāpi suvrata //
> viṣṇoḥ pitāmahasyāpi munīnāṃ ca mahāmune /
> indriyaś caiva devānāṃ tasmād vai puṣṭivardhanaḥ //
> taṃ devam amṛtaṃ rudraṃ karmaṇā tapasāpi vā /
> svādhyāyena ca yogena dhyāyena ca prajāpate //
> satyenānyena sūkṣmāgran mṛtyupāśād bhava svayam /
> bandhamokṣakaro yasmād urvārukam iva prabhuḥ.

YO DEVĀNĀM

In the course of the *pañcāvaraṇapūjā*, the Śivapurāṇa[124] prescribes, in one breath, the recitation of a series of mantras, from *yo devānām* up to *yo vedādau*. None of these mantras is referred to separately in the Purāṇa, except for the last one.

The entire sequence appears, identically, in TĀ 10.10.3 and MahāU 10.3–8 (##223–234):

> yo devānāṃ prathamaṃ purastād viśvā dhiyo rudro maharṣiḥ /
> hiraṇyagarbhaṃ paśyata jāyamānaṃ sa no devaḥ śubhāya smṛtyā saṃyunaktu //
> yasmāt paraṃ nāparam asti kiṃcid yasmān nāṇīyo na jyāyo 'sti kaścit / vṛkṣa iva stabdho divi tiṣṭhaty ekas tenedaṃ pūrṇaṃ puruṣeṇa sarvam //
> na karmaṇā na prajayā dhanena tyāgenaike amṛtatvam ānaśuḥ /
> pareṇa nākaṃ nihitaṃ guhāyāṃ vibhrājad etad yatayo viśanti //
> vedāntavijñānasuniścitārthāḥ saṃnyāsayogād yatayaḥ śuddhasattvāḥ / te brahmaloke tu parāntakāle parāmṛtāḥ parimucyanti sarve.
> dahraṃ vipāpaṃ paraveśmabhūtaṃ yat puṇḍarīkaṃ puramadhyasaṃstham / tatrāpi dahraṃ gahanaṃ viśokaṃ tasmin yad antas tad upāsitavyam //
> yo vedādau svaraḥ prokto vedānte ca pariṣṭhitaḥ /
> tasya prakṛtilīnasya yaḥ paraḥ sa maheśvaraḥ //

YO VEDĀDAU SVARAḤ

Śiva is invoked with this mantra in the course of the fourth *āvaraṇa* (6.8.13). It is the last in a sequence of mantras beginning with *yo devānām* (see previous listing).

VĀMADEVĀYA

Fifteen *rudrākṣas* shall be worn on the stomach with this mantra (1.25.41). It corresponds to TĀ 10.44.1 and MahāU 17.2 (##279–281). For the text, see listing under *sadyojāta*.

ŚATARUDRIYA

The *śatarudriya*[125] is referred to repeatedly in the Śivapurāṇa.[126] The Vedic way (*vaidiko vidhiḥ*) of installing a clay *liṅga* (1, Chapter 20) uses several *śatarudriya* mantras, apparently according to the Vājasaneyisaṃhitā (VS Chapter 16) rather than any other text.[127] The following lists these mantras in the order in which they appear in the VS (with the verses in the Śivapurāṇa 1, Chapter 20 in parentheses):

1. *namas te rudra* (v. 12)
2. *yā te rudra* (v. 16)
3. *yām iṣum* (v. 17)
5. *adhyavocat* (v. 17)
7. *asau yo* (v. 18)
8. *namo 'stu nīlagrīvāya* (vv. 14, 19, 28)
11–14. *yā te hetiḥ* (v. 24)
15. *mā no mahāntam* (vv. 16, 33)
15–16. id. (v. 30)
16. *mā nas toke* (vv. 23, 30, 33)
26. *namaḥ senābhyaḥ* (v. 35)
27. *namaḥ takṣabhyaḥ* (v. 25)
28. *namaḥ śvabhyah* (v. 25)
29. *namaḥ kapardine* (v. 27)
31. *nama āśave* (vv. 27, 32)
32. *namo jyeṣṭhāya* (v. 28)
36. *namo dhṛṣṇave* (v. 23)
41. *namaḥ śambhavāya*[128] (v. 13)
42. *namaḥ pāryāya* (v. 26)
44. *namo vrajyāya*[129] (v. 29)
46. *namaḥ parṇāya* (v. 26)
48. *imā rudrāya*[130] (v. 29)
48–50. id. (v. 32)

In the same chapter, these *śatarudriya* mantras, however, are interspersed with a variety of other mantras. In addition to the more common *namaḥ śivāya* (v. 11) and *tryambaka* (vv. 19, 28, 34), on the one hand,

and *asau jīva* (v. 18), which is attested only in the Pāraskaragṛhyasūtra (1.18.3), and *namo gobhyaḥ* (v. 35), which seems not to be attested elsewhere, on the other, all these mantras are typically *yajurvedic*. Some of them appear in the Ṛgveda—and, indeed, are introduced as *tryṛc* (vv. 21, 31)—all appear in the Vājasaneyisaṃhitā, most of them also in the Taittirīyasaṃhitā and the other *saṃhitās* of the Kṛṣṇayajurveda:

v. 11. *bhūr asi* (VS, TaitSam, etc.)
v. 12 *āpo 'smān* (ṚV, AV, VS, TaitSam, etc.)
v. 15 *etat te rudrāya* (VS and ŚB only, rudrāvasam)
v. 20 *payaḥ pṛthivyām* (VS, TaitSam, etc.)
dadhikrāvṇena (ṚV, VS, TaitSam, etc.)
v. 21 *ghṛtaṃ ghṛtayāva* (VS, TaitSam, etc.)
madhuvātā, madhunaktam, madhumān no (*tryṛc*: ṚV, VS, TaitSam, etc.; also TA, MahāU)
v. 31 *hiraṇyagarbhaḥ* (*tryṛc*: ṚV, VS, TaitSam, etc.; also TĀ, MahāU)
v. 34 *yato yat* (VS only)
v. 37 *devā gātu* (AV, VS, TaitSam, etc.)

SADYOJĀTA[131]

This mantra is referred to repeatedly in the Śivapurāṇa, most often as *sadyādi*,[132] but occasionally as *pañcabrahma*.

A sequence beginning with *sadya* and ending in OṂ (6.7.41: *omantam*) appears only in TĀ 10.43–47 and MahāU 17.1–5 (##277–286):

sadyojātaṃ prapadyāmi sadyojātāya vai [namo] namaḥ /
bhave bhave nātibhave bhavasva māṃ bhavodbhavāya namaḥ // 1
vāmadevāya namo jyeṣṭhāya namaḥ śreṣṭāya namo rudrāya namaḥ kālāya namaḥ kalavikaraṇāya namo balāya namo balavikaraṇāya namo balaprathanāya namaḥ sarvabhūtadamanāya namo manonmanāya namaḥ // 2
aghorebhyo 'tha ghorebhyo aghoraghoratarebhyaḥ /
sarvataḥ śarvaḥ sarvebhyo namas te rudra rūpebhyaḥ // 3
tat puruṣāya vidmahe mahādevāya dhīmahi /
tan no rudraḥ pracodayāt // 4
īśānaḥ sarvavidyānām īśvaraḥ sarvabhūtānāṃ brahmādhipatir brahmaṇo 'dhipatir / brahmā śivo me astu sa eva sadāśiva om // 5

This sequence of mantras is prescribed as the second "Vedic" way—for the first, see the listing under *śatarudriya*—to install a clay *liṅga* (1.20.39–41). Cf. the same sequence, with one inversion (1, 2, 4, 3, 5): 2.1.11.49–51. On one occasion, while the *saṃnyāsi* applies ashes to various parts of his body, the entire sequence is referred to in reverse order.[133] The Śivapurāṇa also establishes a connection between these five mantras and the constituent parts of OṂ: *a, u, m, bindu,* and *nāda,*[134] and, in reverse order, with the five syllables of *namaḥ śivāya.*[135]

The Bhasmajābālopaniṣad, quoted earlier in this chapter, refers to *sadyojāta* as the first of the *pañcabrahmamantras* (Chapter 1: *sadyojātam ityādipañcabrahmamantrair bhasma saṃgṛhya . . .*); cf. also the Kālāgnirudropaniṣad. In the Śivapurāṇa, Śiva himself is referred to as *pañcamantratanu* (6.12.15) and *pañcabrahmatanu* (7.2.12.9).

HAṂSAMANTRA

The text occasionally refers to *haṃsamantra* (6.6.52: *haṃsamantram anusmaran*) and prescribes, without further specification, the *haṃsanyāsa* (6.6.77).

The *haṃsamantra,* which is known from the Ṛgveda (ṚV 4.40.5) onward, appears in numerous later texts:

> haṃsaḥ śuciṣad vasur antarikṣasad dhotā vediṣad atithir duroṇasad /
> nṛṣad varasad ṛtasad vyomasad abjā gojā ṛtajā adrijā ṛtam [bṛhat].

In contrast to the preeminence of and constant recourse to "Vedic" mantras, one cannot fail being struck, in this *śaiva* Purāṇa, by the very subordinate role played by Tantra generally and Tantric *bījamantras* in particular.

To be sure, the text refers a number of times to the *astramantra,*[136] once to *astramantravinyāsa* as well.[137] Elsewhere, the mantra is described as *astrāya phaṭ* (6.6.50) or *om astrāya phaṭ* (6.6.49).[138]

Again, in the same chapter of the Kailāsasaṃhitā, entitled *saṃnyāsapaddhatau nyāsavidhiḥ,* there are occasional references to Tantric mantras. The *nyāsa* shall be performed, reciting "*hrām,* etc."[139] At another stage of the *nyāsa,* the ascetic "recites the *praṇava* first, followed by *hrīm, hrām, sa.*"[140] A mantra "ending in *hrām, hrīm, hrūm*" is mentioned in connection with the *nyāsa* of the limbs.[141] However, the principal mantras involved in the *nyāsa* are OṂ and the five mantras, mentioned earlier, starting with *sadya* (6.6.63–75).

The single instance in which Tantric *bījamantras* have been quoted more extensively concerns the *rudrākṣas.* Different mantras have to be recited, depending on the number of "faces" (*vaktra, mukha*) of the *rudrākṣas,* from one to fourteen (after 1.25.81):

1. *oṃ hrīṃ namaḥ*
2. *oṃ namaḥ*
3. *klīṃ namaḥ*
4. *oṃ hrīṃ namaḥ*
5. *oṃ hrīṃ namaḥ*
6. *oṃ hrīṃ huṃ namaḥ*
7. *oṃ huṃ namaḥ*
8. *oṃ huṃ namaḥ*

9. *oṃ hrīṃ huṃ namaḥ*
10. *oṃ hrīṃ namaḥ*
11. *oṃ hrīṃ huṃ namaḥ*
12. *oṃ krauṃ kṣauṃ rauṃ namaḥ*
13. *oṃ hrīṃ namaḥ*
14. *oṃ namaḥ.*

Efforts to account for the source, or sources, of the many mantras quoted in the Śivapurāṇa, at this stage, can yield only tentative and partial results. As I indicated earlier, one important restriction derives from the unavoidably limited scope of Bloomfield's (1906). *Concordance.* Even though nearly all "Vedic" mantras found in the Purāṇa are listed in it, it remains possible that the immediate source on which the composers of this version of the Śivapurāṇa relied was not available to Bloomfield. A second restriction, of a very different nature, derives from the fact that a number of *pratīkas* used in the Purāṇa are too short to allow us to identify with absolute certainty the mantras for which they stand. Such Pratīkas include *agnir vai* (6.12.89), *atra pitaraḥ* (6.12.74), *eṣa te* (1.20.34), *devasya tvā* (1.20.31), etc.

Keeping these restrictions in mind, it is clear that there is no single source for the mantras in the Śivapurāṇa. I indicated earlier that a number of mantras are explicitly, yet not always correctly, introduced as *ṛcs* and that for some of these, such as *ā vo rājānam,* the Ṛgveda may indeed have been the direct source. This conclusion, however, is not justified in a majority of cases including such mantras as *āpo hi ṣṭhā* or *yasya kṣayāya* (1.13.22) and other mantras quoted earlier; even though, ultimately, they are indeed Ṛgvedic mantras, they also appear in many other potential sources.

Far more important than the Ṛgveda is the Yajurveda. The *śatarudriya* mantras as quoted in the Śivapurāṇa proved to conform to their readings in the Vājasaneyisaṃhitā. On the other hand, many mantras, including some of the more prominent ones throughout the text, are unique to the Taittirīyaśākhā generally and its Āraṇyaka in particular. This is the case for *om āpo jyotiḥ* and *āpo vai* (6.4.21), as well as for the *yo devānām, sadyojāta,* etc. mentioned earlier. I pointed out that, as far as the *Vedic Concordance* allows us to judge, besides the Taittirīyāraṇyaka, several of these mantras appear only in the corresponding passages of the Mahānārāyaṇa Upaniṣad; for some of them, such as the *skandagāyatrī,* the Mahānārāyaṇopaniṣad, indeed, is the single known source. This fact, combined with the explicit references in the text to the Jābālopaniṣad and the possibility that the Varadatāpanīyopaniṣad may have been a source for the mantra *gaṇānāṃ tvā,* seems to suggest that some of the later Upaniṣads may have been among the principal sources that the composers of the Śivapurāṇa drew upon for their knowledge of "Vedic" mantras.

NOTES

1. These problems are discussed in Ludo Rocher, *The Purāṇas* in *A History of Indian Literature*, J. Gonda, general editor. Wiesbaden: Harrassowitz, 1986, p. 33.

2. Bombay: Gaṇapatikṛṣṇājī's Press, 1884; Bombay: Veṅkaṭeśvara Press, 1895–96; Calcutta: Vaṅgavāsī Press, 1908.

3. Bombay: Veṅkaṭeśvara Press, 1906 and 1965; Kāśī: Paṇḍitapustakālaya, 1962–63. The translation in *Ancient Indian Tradition and Mythology*, vols. 1–4 (Delhi: Motilal Banarsidass, 1969–70 and variously reprinted) also follows these editions.

4. Occasionally, not always for metrical reasons, the term *mantra* is replaced by *manu*. E.g., 1.24.35: *pañcabrahmādimanubhiḥ, tryambakena manunā*; 1.24.36: *aghoreṇātha manunā*; 3.32.17,28: *japan pañcākṣaraṃ manum*; 6.12.15: *praṇavādīn manūn*. Another term used occasionally instead of *mantra* is *vidyā*. E.g., 2.5.15.47: *vidyayā mṛtajīvinyā*; 4.20.45 and 7.2.13.4: *pañcākṣarīṃ vidyām*; 6.10.13: *śrīmatpañcākṣarī vidyā*. More examples of both *manu* and *vidyā* will be found in other quotations later in this article.

5. 1.2.66: °*satsaṃkḷptamantraugha*° . . . °*yuktam*.

6. 1.2.12: *tāvat sarve mantrā vivadante mahītale / yāvac chivapurāṇaṃ hi nodeṣyati mahītale*.

7. 2.5.8.17: *balāśayā varāś caiva sarvalakṣaṇasaṃyuktāḥ / mantrā ghaṇṭāḥ smṛtās teṣāṃ varṇapadās tadāśramāḥ*. The sole exception to this is the *praṇava* (see below, and note 76).

8. 4.38.34: *amantrakaṃ na kartavyaṃ pūjanaṃ tu harasya ca*. Later in the description of the śivarātri, it is said that every object offered to Śiva should be accompanied by its own, specific mantra (4.33.48: *tasya tasya ca mantreṇa pṛthag dravyaṃ samarpayet*). These mantras are not identified.

9. 2.1.11.59: *mantrapūrvaṃ prakartavyā pūjā sarvaphalapradā*. At one point (1.14.41), the text seems to restrict worship with mantras to *brahmans: tasmād vai devayajanaṃ śaivābhīṣṭaphalapradam / samantrakaṃ brāhmaṇānām anyeṣāṃ caiva tāntrikam*.

10. 4.38.18: *śivārcanaṃ rudrajapa upavāsaḥ śivālaye / vārāṇasyāṃ ca mantraṇaṃ muktir eṣā sanātanī*.

11. Terms such as *mūlamantra* (1.25.42; 2.1.13.41), *rudramantra* (2.5.6.7), *rudrajāpya* (3.7.8), etc., most probably refer to it as well.

12. On one occasion the *praṇava* is anthropomorphized (3.8.33: *amūrto mūrtimān . . . uvāca*) and made to sing the praise of Śiva (vv. 34–35).

13. 1.17.4: *pro hi prakṛtijātasya saṃsārasya mahodadheḥ / navaṃ nāvāṃ varam iti praṇavaṃ vai vidur budhāḥ*.

14. 1.17.5ab: *praḥ prapañco na nāsti vo yuṣmākaṃ praṇavaṃ viduḥ.*

15. 1.17.5cd: *prakarṣeṇa nayed yasmān mokṣaṃ vaḥ praṇavaṃ viduḥ.*

16. 1.17.6–8: *svajāpakānāṃ yogināṃ svamantrapūjakasya ca / sarvakarmakṣayaṃ kṛtvā divyajñānaṃ tu nūtanam // tam eva māyārahitaṃ nūtanaṃ paricakṣate / prakarṣeṇa mahātmānaṃ navaṃ śuddhasvarūpakam // nūtanaṃ vai karotīti praṇavaṃ taṃ vidur budhāḥ.*

17. 6.3.14: *brahmādisthāvarāntānāṃ sarveṣāṃ prāṇināṃ khalu / prāṇaḥ praṇava evāyaṃ tasmāt praṇava īritaḥ.*

18. 1.17.8–9: *praṇavaṃ dvividhaṃ proktaṃ sūkṣmasthūlavibhedataḥ // sūkṣmam ekākṣaraṃ vidyāt sthūlaṃ pañcākṣaraṃ viduḥ.*

19. 1.17.9: *sūkṣmam avyaktapañcārṇaṃ suvyaktārṇaṃ tathetarat.*

20. 1.17.12–15: *sūksmaṃ ca dvividhaṃ jñeyaṃ hrasvadīrghavibhedataḥ // akāraś ca ukāraś ca makāraś ca tataḥ param / bindunādayutaṃ tad dhi śabdakālakalānvitam // dīrghapraṇavam evaṃ hi yoginām eva hṛdgatam / makāraṃ taṃ tritattvaṃ hi hrasvapraṇava ucyate // śivaḥ śaktiś tayor aikyaṃ makāraṃ tu trikātmakam / hrasvam evaṃ hi jāpyaḥ syāt sarvapāpakṣayaiṣiṇām.*

21. 1.17.33: *śivanāma namaḥpūrvaṃ caturthyāṃ pañcatattvakam / sthūlapraṇavarūpaṃ hi śivapañcāksaraṃ dvijāḥ.*

22. For instance, when it says about Gṛtsamada: *hṛdaye saṃsmaran bhaktyā praṇavena yutaṃ śivam* (5.3.63).

23. 3.39.3: *pañcākṣaraṃ manuṃ śambhor japan sarvottamottamam.*

24. 1.11.16: *udīrya ca mahāmantram oṃkāraṃ nādaghoṣitam*; 3.42.21: *praṇave caiva oṃkāranāmāsīl liṅgam uttamam*; 4.18.22: *praṇave caiva oṃkāranāmāsīt sa sadāśivaḥ*. Several other passages to be quoted later in this article point in the same direction.

25. 1.18.27: *tad eva liṅgaṃ prathamaṃ praṇavaṃ sārvakāmikam.*

26. 1.16.113–114: *praṇavaṃ dhvaniliṅgaṃ tu nādaliṅgaṃ svayambhuvaḥ / binduliṅgaṃ tu yantraṃ syān makāraṃ tu pratiṣṭhitam // ukāraṃ caraliṅgaṃ syād akāraṃ guruvigraham / ṣaḍliṅgapūjayā nityaṃ jīvanmukto na saṃśayaḥ.*

27. 1.11.38: *samādhau mānasaṃ proktam upāṃśu sārvakālikam.*

28. For definitions of the first three types of *japa*, see 7.2.14.26–28: *yad uccanīcasvaritaiḥ spaṣṭāspaṣṭapadākṣaraiḥ / mantram uccārayed vācā vāciko 'yaṃ japaḥ smṛtaḥ // jihvāmātraparispandād īṣad uccārito 'pi vā / aparair aśrutaḥ kiṃcic chruto vopāṃśur ucyate // dhiyā yad akṣaraśreṇyā varṇād varṇaṃ padāt padam / śabdārthacintanaṃ bhūyaḥ kathyate mānaso japaḥ.*

29. E.g., 3.32.16: *tatrāvāhya śivaṃ sāmbaṃ bhaktyā pañcākṣareṇa ha*; 4.38.57: *anyathā pañcavarṇena toṣayet tena śaṅkaram.*

30. E.g., 1.20.50: *ṣaḍakṣareṇa mantreṇa tato dhyānaṃ samācaret*; 1.24.27: *japyo mantraḥ ṣaḍakṣaraḥ*; 2.1.4.65: *sarvaśrutiśrutaṃ śaivaṃ mantraṃ japa ṣaḍakṣaram*.

31. 4.20.45: *pañcākṣaramayīṃ vidyāṃ jajāpa praṇavānvitām*.

32. 6.7.38: *oṃkārādi caturthyantaṃ nāmamantraṃ namo'ntakam*.

33. 4.13.44: *tadoṃ namaḥ śivāyeti śrīśabdapūrvakāya ca / vārān ṣoḍaśa saṃkalpapūjāṃ kuryād ayaṃ vaṭuḥ*.

34. There is also a reference to a ten-syllable mantra (1.11.48: *daśārṇamantra*).

35. 2.5.7.25–26: *praṇavaṃ pūrvam uccārya namaḥ paścād udāharet / śivāyeti tataḥ paścāc chubhadvayam ataḥ param // kurudvayaṃ tataḥ proktaṃ śivāya ca tataḥ param / namaś ca praṇavaś caiva* . . . For the benefits of this mantra, see vv. 40–42.

36. 2.2.5.62–63: *mantreṇānena deveśaṃ śambhuṃ bhaja śubhānane / tena te sakalāvāptir bhaviṣyati na saṃśayaḥ // oṃ namaś śaṅkarāyeti om ity antena santatam / maunatapasyāprārambhaṃ tan me nigadataḥ śṛṇu*.

37. 7.2.13.11–13: *abhakṣā vāyubhakṣāś ca ye cānye vratakarśitāḥ / teṣām etair vratair nāsti mama lokasamāgamaḥ // bhaktyā pañcākṣareṇaiva yo hi māṃ sakṛd arcayet / so 'pi gacchen mama sthānaṃ mantrasyāsyaiva gauravāt // tasmāt tapāṃsi yajñāś ca vratāni niyamās tathā / pañcākṣarārcanasyaite koṭyaṃśenāpi no samaḥ*.

38. 7.2.12.32–33: *saptakoṭimahāmantrair upamantrair anekadhā / mantraḥ ṣaḍakṣaro bhinnaḥ sūtraṃ vṛttyātmanā yathā // śivajñānāni yāvanti vidyāsthānāni yāni ca / ṣaḍakṣarasya sūtrasya tāni bhāṣyaṃ samāsataḥ*.

39. 7.2.12.7: *tad bījaṃ sarvavidyānāṃ mantram ādyaṃ ṣaḍakṣaram / atisūkṣmaṃ mahārthaṃ ca jñeyaṃ tad vaṭabījavat*.

40. 1.24.27: *bahunātra kim uktena dhāryaṃ bhasma sadā budhaiḥ / liṅgārcanaṃ sadā kāryaṃ japyo mantraḥ ṣaḍakṣaraḥ*.

41. 1.16.115–16: *śivasya bhaktyā pūjā hi janmamuktikarī nṛṇām / rudrākṣadhāraṇāt pādam ardhaṃ vai bhūtidhāraṇāt // tripādaṃ mantrajāpyāc ca pūjayā pūrṇabhaktimān / śivaliṅgaṃ ca bhaktaṃ ca pūjya mokṣaṃ labhen naraḥ*.

42. The text here distinguishes three kinds of *tapas: sāttvika, rājasa*, and *tāmasa* (5.20.9).

43. 2.2.23.31. The nine *aṅgas* are *śravaṇa, kīrtana, smaraṇa, sevana, dāsya, arcana, vandana, sakhya*, and *ātmārpaṇa* (2.2.23.22–23). On sixteen kinds of *pūjā*, see 1.11.26–29.

44. 4.29.48: *tadādhīśena tatraiva pratyakṣaṃ śivapūjanam / kṛtaṃ ca pārthivasyaiva vidhānena munīśvaraḥ*.

45. 4.29.47: *kecit tatra sthitā dhyāne baddhvāsanam anuttamam / mānasīṃ śivapūjāṃ ca kecic cakrur mudānvitāḥ*.

46. 4.29.49: *anyac ca ye na jānanti vidhānaṃ smaraṇaṃ param / namaḥ śivāya mantreṇa dhyāyantaḥ śaṅkaraṃ sthitāḥ*.

47. 1.25.83: *vinā mantreṇa yo dhatte rudrākṣaṃ bhuvi mānavaḥ / sa yāti narakaṃ ghoraṃ yāvad indrāś caturdaśa.*

48. 1.24.64–65: *saptakoṭi mahāmantrāḥ pañcākṣarapuraḥsarāḥ / tathānye koṭiśo mantrāḥ śaivakaivalyahetavaḥ // anye mantrāś ca devānāṃ sarvasaukhyakarā mune / te sarve tasya vaśyāḥ syur yo bibharti tripuṇḍrakam.*

49. 1.24.79. Cf. 1.24.22: *akṛtvā bhasmanā snānaṃ na japed vai ṣaḍakṣaram / tripuṇḍraṃ ca racitvā tu vidhinā bhasmanā japet.*

50. For this construction as a typical expression of "continuance," see W. D. Whitney: *Sanskrit Grammar*, Leipzig: Breitkopf & Härtel, 1889 (often reprinted), par. 1075c.

51. 2.1.14.23–24: *lakṣeṇa bhajate kaścid dvitīye jātisambhavaḥ / tṛtīye kāmanālābhaś caturthe taṃ prayacchati // pañcamaṃ ca yadā lakṣaṃ phalaṃ yacchaty asaṃśayam / anenaiva tu mantreṇa daśalakṣe phalaṃ bhavet.* See later, for the number of recitations for a *brahman woman*, a *kṣatriya*, *vaiśya*, and *śūdra*, to improve their status.

52. Cf. 2.5.6.7–8: *jajāpa rudramantram . . . sārdhakoṭipramitam*; 1.25.58: *rudrākṣeṇa japan mantraṃ puṇyaṃ koṭiguṇaṃ bhavet*; 4.14.40: (*mṛtyuṃjayaṃ*) *daśakoṭimitam . . . samāvṛtya.*

53. 1.11.43–44: *pañcakoṭijapaṃ kṛtvā sadāśivasamo bhavet // ekadvitricatuḥkoṭyā brahmādīnāṃ padaṃ vrajet.*

54. 2.1.14.44: *śatam aṣṭottaraṃ tatra mantre vidhir udāhṛtaḥ*; 6.8.32: *dhyātvā devaṃ ca devīṃ ca manum aṣṭottaraṃ japet.*

55. 4.38.50: *śatam aṣṭottaraṃ mantraṃ paṭhitvā jaladhārayā / pūjayec ca śivaṃ tatra nirguṇaṃ guṇarūpiṇam.* For the successive multiples of 108, see vv. 63, 67, 73.

56. 1.11.46: *japed . . . aṣṭottarasahasraṃ vai gāyatrīṃ prātar eva hi*; 6.10.13: *śrīmatpañcākṣarīvidyām aṣṭottarasahasrakaṃ saṃjapya*; again, 6.10.23.

57. 7.2.14.34–36: *aṅgulyā japasaṃkhyānam ekam evam udāhṛtam / rekhayāṣṭaguṇaṃ vidyāt putrajīvair daśādhikam // śataṃ syāc chaṅkhamaṇibhiḥ pravālais tu sahasrakam / sphāṭikair daśasāhasraṃ mauktikair lakṣam ucyate // padmākṣair daśalakṣaṃ tu sauvarṇaiḥ koṭir ucyate / kuśagranthyā ca rudrākṣair anantaguṇitaṃ bhavet.*

58. J. Gonda 1963b, 274.

59. 6.1.17: *praṇavārtho maheśvaraḥ*; 6.12.6: *praṇvārthaś śivaḥ sākṣāt prādhānyena prakīrtitaḥ / śrutiṣu smṛtiśāstreṣu purāṇeṣv āgameṣu ca.*

60. E.g., 1.10.17: *vācako 'yam ahaṃ vācyo mantro 'yaṃ hi madātmakaḥ / tadanusmaraṇaṃ nityaṃ mamānusmaraṇaṃ bhavet*; 6.3.20: *praṇavo mama vācakaḥ*; 6.11.47–48: *praṇavo hi paraḥ sākṣāt parameśvaravācakaḥ / vācyaḥ paśupatir devaḥ paśūnāṃ pāśamocakaḥ // vācakena samāhūtaḥ paśūn mokṣayate kṣaṇāt / tasmād vācakatāsiddhiḥ praṇavena śivaṃ prati.*

61. 7.2.12.19: *tasyābhidhānamantro 'yam abhidheyaś ca sa smṛtaḥ / abhidhānābhidheyatvān mantraḥ siddhaḥ paraḥ śivaḥ.*

62. 1.18.158: *rahasyaṃ śivamantrasya śivo jānāti nāparaḥ.*

63. 1.2.37: *kailāsasaṃhitā tatra tato 'pi paramā smṛtā / brahmasvarūpiṇī sākṣāt praṇavārthaprakāśikā.* On one occasion, in the chapter on *saṃnyāsamaṇḍalavidhiḥ* (6, chapter 5) the function of "illuminating, manifesting" the *praṇavārtha* is transferred to the *yantra* in the pericarp of the *maṇḍala: karṇikāyāṃ likhed yantraṃ praṇavārthaprakāśakam* (6.5.9).

64. 1.10.15: *tasmān majjñānasiddhyarthaṃ mantram oṃkāranāmakam / itaḥ paraṃ prajapataṃ māmakaṃ mānabhañjanam.*

65. 6.2.1–2: *durlabhaṃ hi śivajñānaṃ praṇavārthaprakāśakam // yeṣāṃ prasanno bhagavān sākṣāc chūlavarāyudhaḥ / teṣām eva śivajñānaṃ praṇavārthaprakāśakam.*

66. 1.7.2: *asyottaraṃ mahādevo jānāti sma na cāparaḥ / athāpi vakṣye tam ahaṃ śivasya kṛpayaiva hi.*

67. 6.1.16–17: *tasmāt paurāṇikī vidyā bhavato hṛdi saṃsthitā / purāṇāni ca sarvāṇi vedārthaṃ pravadanti hi // vedāḥ praṇavasambhūtāḥ praṇavārtho maheśvaraḥ / ato maheśvarasthānaṃ tvayi dhiṣṇyaṃ pratiṣṭhitam.*

68. 1.20.53: *japet pañcākṣaraṃ mantraṃ gurudattaṃ yathāvidhi.*

69. 1.18.90–92: *śiṣyaḥ putra iti proktaḥ sadā śiṣyatvayogataḥ / jihvāliṅgān mantraśukraṃ karṇayonau niṣicya vai // jātaḥ putro mantraputraḥ pitaraṃ pūjayed gurum / nimajjayati putraṃ vai saṃsāre janakaḥ pitā // saṃtārayati saṃsārād gurur vai bodhakaḥ pitā / ubhayor antaraṃ jñātvā pitaraṃ gurum arcayet.*

70. 1.11.40: *dīkṣāyuktaṃ guror grāhyaṃ mantraṃ hy atha phalāptaye.* Pārvatī requests Śiva: *kṛpayā parameśāna mantradīkṣāvidhānataḥ / māṃ viśuddhātmatattvasthāṃ kuru nityaṃ maheśvara* (6.2.12). Śiva, in response: *jagau dīkṣāvidhānena praṇavādīn manūn kramāt* (6.2.15).

71. 4.38.51: *gurudattena mantreṇa pūjayed vṛṣabhadhvajam / anyathā nāmamantreṇa pūjayed vai sadāśivam.*

72. 1.20.55: *prārthayec chaṅkaraṃ bhaktyā mantrair ebhiḥ subhaktitaḥ* (mantra: vv. 56–60); 2.1.13.47: *paścād āvāhayed devaṃ mantreṇānena vai naraḥ* (mantra: vv. 47–53); 2.1.13.67: *arghaṃ dadyāt punas tasmai mantreṇānena bhaktitaḥ* (mantra: vv. 68–69); 2.1.13.76: *tataḥ puṣpāñjalir deyo mantreṇānena bhaktitaḥ* (mantra: vv. 77–80).

73. For instance, the mantra Śukra recites to find a way of escape after having been swallowed by Śiva: *śāmbhavenātha yogena śukrarūpeṇa bhārgavaḥ / imaṃ mantravaraṃ japtvā Śambhor jaṭharapañjarāt // niṣkrānto liṅgamārgeṇa . . .* (2.5.48.40–41). The—long—mantra is quoted before the first verse of Chapter 49. Shorter, 6.6.42: *namaḥ śivāya sāmbāya sagaṇāyādihetave / rudrāya viṣṇave tubhyaṃ brahmaṇe ca trimūrtaye.*

74. 4.38.77: *prārthayet sustutiṃ kṛtvā mantrair etair vicakṣaṇaḥ* (mantras: vv. 78–

81). For the use of the gerund merely as a modifier of the main verb, see Ludo Rocher, "A Note on the Sanskrit Gerund," *Recherches de linguistique. Hommages à Maurice Leroy* (Brussels: Université Libre, 1980), pp. 181–88.

75. 1.19.11: *yathā sarveṣu mantreṣu praṇavo hi mahān smṛtaḥ*; 7.2.12.30: *bahutve 'pi hi mantrāṇāṃ sarvajñena śivena yaḥ / praṇīto vimalo mantro na tena sadṛśaḥ kvacit*; 7.2.12.35: *tenādhītaṃ śrutaṃ tena kṛtaṃ sarvam anuṣṭitam / yenoṃ namaḥ śivāyeti mantrābhyāsaḥ sthirīkṛtaḥ.*

76. 2.5.8.24: *pratodo brahmaṇas tasya praṇavo brahmadaivatam.*

77. There are two exceptions, though, to Śiva's total—and unique—identification with the *praṇava*. First, an adoration to Skanda begins: *oṃ namaḥ praṇavārthāya praṇavārthavidhāyine / praṇavākṣarabījāya praṇavāya namo namaḥ* (6.11.22). Second, one should honor Gaṇeśa: *caturthyantair nāmapadais namo'ntaiḥ praṇavādibhiḥ* (2.1.13.29).

78. 5.3.7: *tena japaprabhāvena satyaṃ drakṣyasi śaṅkaram / ātmatulyabalaṃ putraṃ labhiṣyasi maheśvarāt.*

79. 1.23.7–8: *śrīśivāya namas tubhyaṃ mukhaṃ vyāharate yadā / tanmukhaṃ pāvanaṃ tīrthaṃ sarvapāpavināśinam // tanmukhaṃ ca tathā yo vai paśyati prītimān naraḥ / tīrthajanyaphalaṃ tasya bhavatīti suniścitam.*

80. 1.17.132: *śivasvarūpamantrasya dhāraṇāc chiva eva hi / śivabhaktaśarīre hi śive tatparamo bhavet*; 1.17.133–134: *yāvad yāvac chivamantraṃ yena japtaṃ bhavet kramāt // tāvad vai śivasāṃnidhyaṃ tasmin dehe na saṃśayaḥ.*

81. 6.3.1–2: *tasya śravaṇamātreṇa jīvaḥ sākṣāc chivo bhavet // praṇavārthaparijñānam eva jñānaṃ madātmakam / bījaṃ tat sarvavidyānāṃ mantraṃ praṇavanātmakam.*

82. 1.17.122–128. Within the system of shedding off a previous status first and then acquiring a higher status, each time with 500,000 mantras, the *śūdra* should attain *mantravipratva* after 3,000,000 rather than 2,500,000 mantras.

83. 7.2.13.7: *mayaivam asakṛd devi pratijñātaṃ dharātale / patito 'pi vimucyeta madbhakto vidyayānayā.* 7.3.13.10 adds that the mantra has to be the *pañcākṣaramantra*; any other mantra is useless.

84. Cf. 1.10.23: *vedaḥ sarvas tato jajñe tato vai mantrakoṭayaḥ / tattanmantreṇa tatsiddhiḥ sarvasiddhir ito bhavet.*

85. 6.3.19–20: *īśānaḥ sarvavidyānām ityādyāḥ śrutayaḥ priye / matta eva bhavantīti vedāḥ satyaṃ vadanti hi // tasmād vedādir evāhaṃ praṇavo mama vācakaḥ / vācakatvān mamaiṣo 'pi vedādir iti kathyate.*

86. 6.3.3: (*mantraṃ praṇavanāmakaṃ*) *vedādi vedasāraṃ ca*; 1.5.16: *vedāntasārasaṃsiddhaṃ praṇavārthe prakāśanāt*; 6.1.45: *vedāntasārasarvasvaṃ praṇavaṃ parameśvaram.*

87. 5.3.10: *mantram adhyāpitaṃ śārvam atharvaśirasaṃ mahat.*

88. 6.6.61: *praṇavasya ṛṣir brahmā devi gāyatram īritam / chando 'tra devatāhaṃ vai paramātmā sadāśivaḥ.*

89. E.g., 2.1.11.60–65: *mantrāṃś ca tubhyaṃ tāṃs tāta sarvakāmārthasiddhaye / pravakṣyāmi samāsena sāvadhānatayā śṛṇu // pāṭhyamānena mantreṇa tathā vāṅmayakena ca / rudreṇa nīlarudreṇa suśuklena śubhena ca // hotāreṇa tathā śīrṣṇā śubhenātharvaṇena ca / śāntyā vātha punaḥ śāntyā māruṇenāruṇena ca // arthābhīṣṭena sāmnā ca tathā devavratena ca // rathāntareṇa puṣpeṇa sūktena ca yuktena ca / mṛtyuṃjayena mantreṇa tathā pañcākṣareṇa ca // jaladhārāḥ sahasreṇa śatenaikottareṇa vā / kartavyā vedamārgeṇa nāmabhir vātha vā punaḥ.*

90. 4.12.35: *vedamantrais tatas taṃ vai kumbhaṃ caivābhimantrayet / śrutyuktavidhinā tasya pūjāṃ kṛtvā śivaṃ param.* Cf. v. 37; *tatra liṅgaṃ ca tat sthāpya punaś caivābhimantrayet.*

91. Cf. 1.4.49: *tatraite bahavo lokā bṛhajjābālacoditaiḥ / te vicāryāḥ prayatnena tato bhasmarato bhavet.*

92. 1.24.8: *agnir ityādibhir mantrair jābālopaniṣadgataiḥ / saptabhir dhūlanaṃ kāryaṃ bhasmanā sajalena ca*; 6.3.60: *agnir ityādibhir mantrais tripuṇḍraṃ dhārayet tataḥ.*

93. 4.38.9–10: *bhūri vratāni ma santi bhuktimuktipradāni ca / mukhyāni tatra jñeyāni daśasaṃkhyāni tāni vai // daśa śaivavratāny āhur jābālaśrutipāragāḥ.*

94. 6.8.15: *dakṣiṇe tu yajed rudram ā vo rājānam ity ṛcā.*

95. Even though, different from ṚV 4.3.1, these also occur in other possible sources.

96. 9.8.17: *uttare viṣṇum āvāhya gandhapuṣpādhibhir yajet / pra tad viṣṇur iti procya karṇikāyāṃ daleṣu ca.*

97. 6.8.19: *brahmāṇaṃ paścime padme samāvāhya samarcayet / hiraṇyagarbhaḥ samavartata iti mantreṇa mantravit.*

98. E.g., 1.20.24: *ṛkcatuṣkena*; 27, 29; *ṛcā*; 32: *tryṛcā.*

99. 6.12.76: *svagṛhyoktena mārgeṇa dadyāt piṇḍān pṛthak pṛthak.*

100. On Śiva's birth as Aghora, see 3.1.26.

101. 1.18.62: *aghoreṇātmamantreṇa*; 1.24.36: *aghoreṇātha manunā vipinasthavidhiḥ smṛtaḥ.*

102. 1.25.40: *aghoreṇa gale dhāryam.* 1.25.41 refers to *aghorabījamantreṇa*, unspecified.

103. I.e., as far as they are listed in Bloomfield (1906).

104. On Śiva's manifestation as Īśāna, see 3.1.33.

105. 6.3.19: *īśānaḥ sarvavidyānām ity ādyāḥ śrutayaḥ priye / matta eva bhavantīti vedāḥ satyaṃ vadanti hi.*

106. Cf. 4.42.23: *īśānaḥ sarvavidyānāṃ śrutir eṣā sanātanī / vedakartā vedapatis tasmāc chambhur udāhṛtaḥ.*

107. 1.24.37: *śivayogī ca niyatam īśānenāpi dhārayet.*

108. 1.25.40: *śirasīśānamantreṇa . . . dhāryam.*

109. 6.7.15: *mūrtiṃ prakalpya tatraiva gaṇānāṃ tveti mantrataḥ / samāvāhya tato devaṃ dhyāyed ekāgramānasaḥ.*

110. Cf. the etymology of *gāyatrī: gāyakaṃ trāyate pātād gāyatrīty ucyate hi sā* (1.15.15).

111. 4.13.43: *śivagāyatrīṃ ṣoḍaśākṣarasaṃyutām.*

112. 6.7.19–20: *padmasya vāyudikpadme saṃkalpya skāndam āsanam / skandamūrtiṃ prakalpyātha skandam āvāhayed budhaḥ // uccārya skandagāyatrīṃ dhyāyed atha kumārakam.*

113. 6.7.64–65: *gaurīrmimāyamantreṇa praṇavādyena bhaktitaḥ / āvāhya . . .*

114. 1.24.34: *vaiśyas tryambakenaiva;* 35: *triyambakena manunā vidhir vai brahmacāriṇaḥ.*

115. 1.24.19: *śivāgnikāryaṃ yaḥ kṛtvā kuryāt triyāyuṣātmavit / mucyate sarvapāpais tu spṛṣṭena bhasmanā naraḥ.*

116. 1.24.35: *pañcabrahmādimanubhir gṛhasthasya vidhīyate;* 1.25.42: *pañcabrahmabhir aṅgaiś ca.*

117. 6.12.68: *citte sadāśivaṃ dhyātvā japed brahmāṇi pañca ca.*

118. 6.7.72–76: *bhavebhavenātibhava iti pādyaṃ prakalpayet / vāmāya nama ity uktvā dadyād ācamanīyakam // jyeṣṭhāya nama ity uktvā śubhravastraṃ prakalpayet / śreṣṭhāya nama ity uktvā dadyād yajñopavītakam // rudrāya nama ity uktvā punar ācamanīyakam / kālāya nama ity uktvā gandhaṃ dadyāt susaṃskṛtam // kalavikaraṇāya namo 'kṣataṃ ca parikalpayet / balavikaraṇāya iti puṣpāni dāpayet // balāya nama ity uktvā dhūpaṃ dadyāt prayatnataḥ / balapramathanāyeti sudīpaṃ caiva dāpayet.*

119. 1.24.33: *mānastokena mantreṇa mantritaṃ bhasma dhārayet / brāhmaṇaḥ kṣatriyaś caiva prokteṣv aṅgeṣu bhaktimān.*

120. 1.25.60: *tripuṇḍreṇa ca saṃyuktaṃ rudrākṣāvilasāṃgakam / mṛtyuṃjayaṃ japantaṃ ca dṛṣṭvā rudraphalaṃ labhet;* 2.1.14.22: repetition of *mṛtyuṃjayamantra;* 4.14.39–40: *candreṇa ca tapas taptaṃ mṛtyuṃjayena mantreṇa pūjito vṛṣabhadhvajaḥ // daśakoṭimitaṃ mantraṃ samāvṛtya śaśī ca tam / dhyātvā mṛtyuṃjayaṃ mantraṃ tasthau niścalamānasaḥ.*

121. 2.5.50.41: *tapobalena mahatā mayaiva parinirmitā.*

122. 2.5.50.42: *tvāṃ tāṃ tu prāpayāmy adya mantrarūpāṃ mahāśuce / yogyatā te 'sti vidyāyās tasyāḥ śucitaponidhe.*

123. For several terms in this mantra, see under *tryambaka.*

124. 6.8.33–34: *japed dhyātvā mahādevaṃ yo devānān iti kramāt / yo vedādau svaraḥ prokta ityantaṃ parameśvari.*

125. The term *śrutirudrasūkta* (1.24.47) may also refer to it; it sets free (*mucyeta*) one who insulted Śiva or the wearer of the *tripuṇḍra.*

126. 1.20.36: *śatarudriyamantreṇa japed vedavicakṣaṇaḥ;* 1.20.54: *paṭhed vai śatarudriyam;* 1.21.51: *tataḥ pañcākṣaraṃ japtvā śatarudriyam eva ca;* cf. also 2.1.14.68; 3.8.54–55; 4.12.36; 6.1.7; etc.

127. See the following three notes.

128. TaitSam, KS, MS: *śambhave.*

129. VS only.

130. Absent from TaitSam.

131. Sadyojāta is Śiva's first *avatāra* in the nineteenth (*śvetalohita*) *kalpa* (3.1.4). Cf. 3.41.36: *sadyojātāya vai namaḥ.*

132. 1.11.13: *sampūjya liṅgaṃ sadyādyaiḥ;* 16: *sadyādibrahma coccārya;* cf. also 1.18.26; 6.7.8,41; 6.10.8; etc.

133. 6.4.23: *īśānādi samārabhya sadyāntaṃ pañcabhiḥ kramāt.*

134. 6.3.26–29: *sadyādīśānaparyantāny akārādiṣu pañcasu / sthitāni pañca brahmāṇi tāni manmūrtayaḥ kramāt // aṣṭau kalāḥ samākhyātā akāre sadyajāḥ śive / ukāre vāmarūpiṇyas trayodaśa samīritāḥ // aṣṭāv aghorarūpiṇyo makāre saṃsthitāḥ kalāḥ / bindau catasraḥ sambhūtāḥ kalāḥ puruṣagocarāḥ // nāde pañca samākhyātāḥ kalā īśānasambhavāḥ / ṣaḍvidhaikyānusaṃdhānāt prapañcātmakatocyate.*

135. 7.2.12.9: *īśānādyāni sūkṣmāṇi brahmāṇy ekākṣarāṇi tu / mantre namaḥ śivāyeti saṃsthitāni yathākramam / mantre ṣaḍakṣare sūkṣme pañcabrahmatanuḥ śivaḥ.*

136. 6.6.7: *abhimantrya tatas tasmin dhenumudrāṃ pradarśayet / śaṅkhamudrāṃ ca tenaiva prokṣayed astramantrataḥ;* 6.7.9: *avaguṇṭhyāstramantreṇa saṃrakṣārthaṃ pradarśayet / dhenumudrāṃ ca tenaiva prokṣayed astramantrataḥ.*

137. 2.5.58.26, on the Daitya Dundubhinirhrāda, who was unable to attack a *brahman* meditating on Śiva: *kṛtāstramantravinyāsaṃ taṃ krāntum aśakan na saḥ.* There are other references to weapons used "with mantras"; e.g., Kālī, in her fight with Śaṅkhacūḍa: *brahmāstram atha sā devī cikṣepa mantrapūrvakam* (2.5.38.9). In turn, Śaṅkhacūḍa: *cikṣepa divyāny astrāṇi devyai vai mantrapūrvakam* (11). Again, Kālī: *jagrāha mantrapūtaṃ ca śaraṃ pāśupataṃ ruṣā* (16).

138. Cf. VtU 2.2 and NpU 2.2, respectively.

139. 6.6.10: *ṣaḍaṅgāni hrāṃ ityādīni vinyaset.*

140. 6.6.24: *praṇavaṃ pūrvam uddhṛtya hrāṃhrīṃsas tadanantaram.*

141. 6.6.26: *vinyasyāṅgāni hrāṃhrīṃhrūmantena manunā tataḥ.*

ABBREVIATIONS USED IN THIS CHAPTER

AV	Atharvaveda
KS	Kāṭhaka Saṃhitā
MahāU	Mahānārāyaṇa Upaniṣad (numbers refer to Varenne 1960)
MS	Maitrāyaṇīya Saṃhitā
NpU	Nṛsiṃhapūrvatāpanīya Upaniṣad
ṚV	Ṛgveda
ŚB	Śatapatha Brāhmaṇa
TĀ	Taittirīya Āraṇyaka
TaitSam	Taittirīya Saṃhitā
VS	Vājasaneyi Ṣaṃhitā
VtU	Varadapūrvatāpanīya Upaniṣad

CHAPTER 8

The Use of Mantra in Yogic Meditation: The Testimony of the *Pāśupata*

Gerhard Oberhammer

THE POINT OF DEPARTURE FOR the investigation of the meaning and function of mantra in the meditation of the Pāśupatas is the observation that, in the religious traditions of India, we find the use of mantra in yogic meditation primarily in theistic meditation while, on the other hand, one cannot say that every theistic Yoga meditation demands the use of a mantra. For example, Bhāsarvajña, who, I believe I have demonstrated (Oberhammer 1984, Teil II "Transzendenz, das zu Verehrende"), was a convinced theist of the Pāśupata type, does not mention the use of mantra in his exposition of meditation (NBhū, pp. 588, 15-590, 12), although he was strongly influenced by Patañjali and the Pāśupatas certainly knew of the practice of muttering mantras (*japaḥ*) in meditation. This inconsistency in the phenomenon suggests how to clarify the full complexity of the question raised and, possibly, the way to answer it.

In my studies of the spirituality of Yoga (Oberhammer 1977, 162ff.), I have shown that Patañjali, in his presentation of the Nirodha-Yoga that is attained through *īśvarapraṇidhānaṃ,* after all, discusses the basic structures of what was originally a purely theistic meditation and that he brings to the service of his nontheistic spirituality. We have then in the *Yoga-sūtras,* perhaps the oldest statement of the basic structure of an authentic theistic meditation. It is noteworthy that the use of a mantra in the meditation is attested even here in the context of classical yogic meditation, where the single aim is to attain a vision of one's own transcendental Puruṣa, where a mantra is not necessary, where, indeed, strictly speaking there is no meaningful use for a mantra.

Patañjali explains the realization of theistic *samādhi* in YS 1.27 and 28, "The one, denoting him (*īśvaraḥ*) is the *praṇava,*" and in YS 1.28, "muttering it (*praṇavaḥ*) and its realization of its object." Despite the extremely terse diction, the whole mantra problem and its meaning for the act of meditation is brought into focus: For, when Patañjali says "the one denoting Him is the *praṇava*," he is veiling the deeper dimension of this problem, at least for the Yogi outside the theistic tradition. While interpreting the *praṇava* in terms of a trivial linguistic denotation, the specific function of the mantra, although not negated, cannot be grasped in its full complexity under the horizon of the understanding of *puruṣa* in Sāṃkhyā. One even gets the impression that Patañjali, in his reception of theistic meditation, consciously did not make use of the particular function of the mantra for the process of meditation. Its original presence, however, can be proven by a peculiar inconsistency of Patañjali's thought: If the *praṇava* in the context of meditation were nothing more than a word expressing god, then it should be a word for god like the word "*īśvaraḥ*" or the name Viṣṇu or Śiva. This, however, is not the case. The word *OṂ* is not a term for god. YS 1.27, however, says that "the one denoting god (*īśvaraḥ*) is the *praṇava*".

When Vyāsa, in his commentary on this sūtra, expressly discusses the problem of the *praṇava* as a linguistic phenomenon, he is obligated to specify its nonlinguistic dimension. Then the original function of mantra in meditation comes more distinctly into view,[1] even though nothing more is said about it:

> The one denoting him is the *praṇava*. The denoted one (*vācyaḥ*) [related] to the *praṇava* is god (*īśvaraḥ*). Has [now] the relation between the denoted and the denoter (*vācyavācakatvaṃ*) of the *praṇava* come about through convention (*saṃketakṛtaṃ*) or is it like the shining of a lamp existent [beforehand] (*avasthitaṃ*)?
>
> [Answer:] The relation between the denoted and the denoter exists [beforehand]. The conventional usage (*saṃketaḥ*), however, mediates (*abhinayati*) the object of god (*īśvarasya*) that exists beforehand [correlated to the *praṇava*] as indeed the existing relation between father and son is expressed through the conventional usage of language [when one says] "he is that one's father, this one is his son." (Ybh, 77, 2–6)[2]

It becomes evident here that the relationship between the mantra and god, who is to be realized in the meditation (though expressed by Patañjali in terms of denoter and denoted), cannot be identical with the linguistic relation between word and its object in human language and has to be prior to any linguistic convention. As Śaṃkara says in his commentary on Vyāsa[3] cited earlier, "This is because if the relation spoken of here is not [independent of any convention of language] it is not true that through the form of the *praṇava* god is met face to face." What is the original relation between the *praṇava* and god spoken of here by Vyāsa, and, like the relation between father and son, independent of linguistic conventions? Why, in meditation, is the *praṇava*, rather than the designations of god mentioned previously, "the one denoting god"? The texts of Pātañjala Yoga are silent about this.

The investigation of a meditation of a purely theistic tradition, namely, that of the Pāśupata, leads further; all the more so because this meditation seems to correspond to the type of meditation incorporated by Patañjali and, perhaps, even is historically identical to it. Like the theistic meditation found in Patañjali, it is practiced by muttering mantras. This meditation is described in a rather long passage in the *Ratnaṭīkā*, which was written around 900 A.D. I would like to quote it in extenso:

> What then is the means [for thinking of] god constatly (*devanityatve*)? [On this] he says: Muttering [of mantras] and meditation (*japadhyānaṃ*). The muttering [of mantras] and meditation (*japaḥ*) consists in repeating the third (*aghora-*) and fourth (*tatpuruṣa* = *gāyatrī*) mantra. This is twofold, namely [muttering of mantras] which results in the withdrawal of the senses (*pratyāhāraphalaḥ*) and that which results in *samādhi* (*samādhiphalaḥ*).
>
> [Objection:] Muttering [a mantra], which is performed while one is attached to anything else (*anyāsaktatve*), does not, even in a hundred years, bring about the withdrawal of the senses (*pratyāhāram*), but brings to him [who practices it] only harm (*doṣam*).
>
> [Answer:] Right, so it is. But here, because of the distinguishing between a lower and a higher, a twofold withdrawal of the senses (*pratyāhāradvaividhyam*) is admitted; of these it is the lower [withdrawal of the senses] which presupposes the psychic apparatus (*antaḥkāraṇapūrvakaḥ*). If the mind (*cittam*) is free of stains due to the muttering [of mantras] connected with this [withdrawal of the senses] and stands firm in Brahma(-mantra)—like a fire-brand [swing in] a circle—without depending on any effort, then this is the higher withdrawal of the senses. It is said that it presupposes the muttering [of mantras] (*japapūrvakaḥ*). For it makes the mind (*cittam*) steady (*niścalīkaroti*) with regard to the reality to be meditated upon (*dhyeyatattve*), after the karma acquired in numerous births has already been burnt up (*dagdhvā*) even in its slightest indication (*lakṣaṇamātreṇa*).
>
> Meditation (*dhyānam*) is the continuous flow of reflection (*sadṛśaś cintāpravāhaḥ*) with respect to the reality of Rudra (*rudratattve*). This [meditation] is twofold, i.e., one which presupposes the muttering [of mantras] and one which presupposes the fixing [of thinking] (*dhāraṇāpūrvakam*). The [meditation] then, which presupposes the muttering [of mantras], has [already] been expounded implicitly before, the [meditation] which presupposes the fixing [of thinking], will be expounded [now]. The "fixing" is the mind (*cittam*) of one whose consciousness is in no way affected (*amūḍhasya*), [his mind being] deprived of external objects (*nirālambanam*). Insofar as the mind of one, who is in an unconscious or stupified state, is likewise without objects, because an act [of thinking] is not taking place, it has been said in order to exclude it "one, whose consciousness is in no way affected (*amūḍ-*

> *hasya*)." One, who by means of his mind (*buddhyā*), which is supported by knowledge (*vidyā*), causes his mind to be without objects, is one whose consciousness is in no way affected. The mind which has been freed from stains (*nirmalīkṛtaṃ*) and has attained steadiness in the reality of Rudra by means of fixing (*dhāraṇayā*), does not deviate [from this] for a long time. On account of this the venerable author of the *Bhāṣya*[4] calls this meditation in comparison with the meditation previously [mentioned] higher. (RṬ 19, 27–20, 12)

Such is the description of the *Ratnaṭīkā*. If one attempts to interpret it with the help of the commentary to the *Pāśupatasūtras* (cited by the *Ratnaṭīkā* itself) then, it turns out, that in this text, corresponding to its type, at least two different forms of meditation (*dhyānaṃ*) are discussed, of which both are carried out with the help of mantras, even if this is not immediately obvious.

The basic character of Pāśupata meditation is fundamentally different from Patañjali's yogic meditation: Meditation for the Pāśupatas is nothing more than the meditative accomplishment of what the Pāśupata ascetic aims at during the whole path of salvation; i.e., the union (*yogaḥ*) of the ātma with Maheśvara, which for the Pāśupatas is basically a spiritual disposition in life and a state of meditative experience. Thus, the so-called yoga of the Pāśupatas is not about the individual, systematically arranged exercises through which a specific psychic state should be reached, but it is actually concerned with the spiritual disposition consequently aimed at in Śaiva mysticism. The contemplation (*dhyānam*) expounded in the *Ratnaṭīkā* is the meditative actualization of this mysticism, which is realized differently on different stages of the mystical path of salvation, even when its basic character remains the same. The two forms of meditation differ in the degree of immediacy and in the intensity of the experience of union with Maheśvara that they facilitate. The degree of immediacy and intensity of this experience, in turn, seems to be based on the use of mantras, which are differently structured and therefore functionally different.

In accordance with the Pāśupata understanding of yoga as the union of the soul with god, both types of meditation, the lower as well as the higher contemplation dealt with in the *Ratnaṭīkā*, presuppose that the ascetic has purified his mind and character from the "impurity" (*kaluṣam*) of moral deficiency and emotional turmoil by means of his conduct and by ritual practices. According to Kauṇḍinya, the term *impurity* refers to hatred, desire, and wrath, which arise, for example, on the first stage of the path of salvation from emotionally uncontrolled dealings with women and *Śūdras* and from looking at excrements, etc. (cf. Kauṇḍinya 40, 5ff); that is to say, from all psychic motions that prevent the mystical union and the orientation of his existence towards Maheśvara.

From what has been said so far, it is clear that Pāśupata meditation, in its lower form, can be practiced even by the beginner from *dīkṣā* onwards. But, in the proper sense, it can be fully realized as meditative mediation of and absorption in the mystical union only in the third stage of the path of salvation; that is, when the ascetic has become habitually free from every impurity and, therefore, has achieved the competence authorizing (*adhikāraḥ*) mystical experience in meditation for him.[5] Nevertheless, already in the contemplation anticipated on the first stage of the path of salvation, one circumstance of great importance for the question of the function of mantra in meditation becomes obvious.

It is noteworthy that this meditation of the type of lower contemplation (*dhyānam*), when it is anticipated on the first stage of the path of salvation, is not, in its actual function, meditation in the sense of contemplation proper to the third stage. It is primarily a spiritual exercise, a psychic ritual (*mānasī kriyā*)[6] aiming at the removal of mental impurity[7] in which the purifying practice—touching the ashes (*upasparśanam*) and breath-control (*prāṇāyāmaḥ*)[8]—is reinforced by the muttering of mantras (*japaḥ*).[9] But it does not obviate the necessity of *vidhi*[10] and asceticism. This spiritual exercise, mantra-muttering, when performed, naturally induces a sort of meditative communion with Maheśvara, which can be called a first anticipation of the contemplation (*dhyānam*) to be fully realized later. This is because, after the purity of the mind has been achieved (cf. PS 1.20)—this has to be understood in the sense of a relative gradation—the union (*yogaḥ*) of the soul with Maheśvara arises due to it. In accordance with that, Kauṇḍinya answers the question of the purpose of muttering mantras (*japyam*) in the following way: "[The muttering of mantras] is done for the purpose of removing Adharma (*vyucchityartham*), for the purpose of turning away from [all] evil (*akuśalebhyo vyāvartanārtham*) and of fixing [the mind] (*upanibandhanārtham*) upon the continuous series of words [of that] Brahma[-mantra]" (52).

This statement of Kauṇḍinya, at first glance, is a statement about mantra muttering as such and not necessarily a statement about the function of mantra muttering (*japaḥ*) in meditation. Nevertheless, one can postulate that this statement about the effect of mantra is valid for mantra in general and, therefore, for mantra in the context of meditation. Insofar as it concerns the kind of effect and not whether that effect appears, the mantra is a reality whose effect is attained out of itself and not on account of certain circumstances. Moreover, the third of the effects described by Kauṇḍinya leads into the process of meditation. If this is correct, then we can say on the basis of Kauṇḍinya's conception of the purpose and effect of mantra muttering that the effects mentioned can also be attributed to the mantra in meditation, especially on the first stage of the path of salvation, where the ascetic is still occupied with the purification of his mind.

Accordingly, one can, indeed one must, speak of a power of the mantra to purify the mind and character of the meditating subject from any impurity. In spite of the effect mentioned earlier (i.e., the concentration of the mind on the respective Brahma mantra, an effect that under certain circumstances, may also be understood as psychological), this power has a clearly "sacramental" character. We will return to this sacramental character in order to understand it in its complexity. For now, it is sufficient to say that the word *sacramental* in the faith of the Pāśupata ascetic implies only that the mantra has an objectively operating power, which up to now could be ascertained as a power purifying the mind and character of the ascetic.

This is corroborated by the *Ratnaṭīkā's* characterization of the five Brahma mantras used by the Pāśupata ascetic as the "five purifiers" (*pañca pavitrāṇi*) (cf. RṬ 17, 2; 18, 14, and 19, 2). In this regard, it is interesting that Vyāsa also defines the *svādhyāya* of *kriyāyoga* or *niyama* as "muttering of the 'purifiers' such as, for instance, the Praṇava" (Ybh. 128, 3). He thus testifies to the purifying effect of the mantra. This testimony gains significance, if one remembers that, according to Patañjali, the mantra is used not only as a "purifier" among the acts preparatory to meditation but also as a mediating factor in meditation, just as among the Pāśupatas (cf. YS 1.27f.).

I turn now to the use of mantra in the Pāśupata meditation that the *Ratnaṭīkā* calls "lower contemplation" (*aparaṃ dhyānam*) and that is discussed in Section 5.21–23 of the *Pāśupatasūtras*. This meditation begins with the intentional withdrawal (*pratyāhāraḥ*) from the objects of the senses and with the deliberate concentration upon the act of meditation. This "lower *pratyāhāra*," as it is called by the *Ratnaṭīkā*, is intensified by the muttering of the so-called Brahma mantras[11] in such a way that the worshipful attentiveness of the meditating subject is transformed into contemplation of the "lower" type, for which reason the *Ratnaṭīkā* calls this *pratyāhāra* "higher."

This intensification of the *pratyāhāra* reveals the third effect of mantra muttering mentioned by Kauṇḍinya; namely, the concentration on the Brahma mantra, which must now be discussed briefly. If the concentration necessary for the contemplation is already achieved by means of the lower *pratyāhāra*, one has to ask whether the effect of the mantra mentioned earlier, in fact, is only of a psychological nature, as previously had been considered a possibility.

This question is actually raised in the *Ratnaṭīkā*, albeit in another way: "Muttering [a mantra] which is performed while one is attached to anything else (*anyāsaktatve*) does not bring about the withdrawal of the senses (*pratyāhāram*) even in a hundred years, but brings to him [who practices it] only harm (*doṣam*)." In the answer this, characteristically, is not denied. It remains thus that the mantra brings only harm to someone who practices it without having turned away from objects. This seems to mean that the mantra possesses an objective power that cannot be explained psychologically.

In light of this, the characterization of the higher *pratyāhāra*, which at the same time indicates the definition of the lower contemplation (cf. RṬ 20, 7) gains an entirely different significance. The *Ratnaṭīkā* says, "if as a result of this [mantra] muttering, which is connected with this [lower withdrawal], the mind is free from any impurity and without depending on exertion . . . , stands firm in Brahman (i.e., the Brahma mantra)[12] then that is the higher *pratyāhāra*" (RṬ 20, 3f.). It accordingly defines the meditation thus initiated as "the continuous flow of reflection (*cintā*) with respect to the reality of Rudra" (RṬ 20, 6); that is to say, as the perpetuation of the state of mind thus initiated.

To summarize, one must say, first, that the purifying power of the mantra already mentioned retains its significance in meditation; second, that the mantra, if used without deliberate detachment from sense objects, as it were in a frivolous and unworthy manner, far from helping the meditating subject, does him harm. Thereby, it has to be kept in mind that the *Ratnaṭīkā* says this explicitly in connection with meditation. And, third, it has to be kept in mind that the mantra is what makes the mind of the meditating subject stand firm in Brahma; that is to say, in the Brahma mantra itself and in the reality of Rudra mediated by it. In the following pages, I will discuss this further.

The mantra, and only the mantra, endows the concentration that has been evoked intentionally by means of the lower *pratyāhāra* with its true inalienable content. Why, and in what way? Both questions imply an inquiry about which mantras have to be used by the Pāśupata ascetic in meditation. Strangely enough, the *Pāśupatasūtras* (PS 1.17; 5.21 and 22) enjoin only the third and fourth Brahma mantras, which, at the very same time, are identical with the third and fourth invocations of Śiva in TĀ 10.43–47, respectively. There can be no doubt that these two mantras are not to be understood here as examples but to be considered as enjoined for contemplation. Naturally, it must be left undecided whether the Pāśupata ascetic could not and did not also utilize the other Brahma mantras, as it were from a personal urge—all the more so since, in precisely the same way, a particular mantra, *oṃkāra,* was designated for the "higher contemplation."

The two Brahma-mantras enjoined for the lower contemplation are the so-called *bahurūpī* (add *ṛc*), which is the mantra of Śiva as Aghora (see Kauṇḍinya 39, 16f.), and the *raudrī gāyatrī,* which is the mantra of Śiva as Tatpuruṣa (39, 9). Why are these two, in particular, enjoined for meditation? Most probably, the reason is to be found in the historical form and in the particular contents of the Śaiva tradition of meditation,[13] a tradition to which the linguistic form and the theological content of these two mantras seem particularly to conform.

I will analyze these two briefly with regard to their function in meditation. The mantra corresponding to the Aghora form of Śiva is "To the nonterrifying, to the terrifying, and to the more terrifying, oh terrifying, to all, oh Śarva, to all forms of Rudra, to thee be homage!"[14] The ductus of the invocations is unmistakable. The datives rise gradually from the enumeration of the three groups of the forms of Śiva—namely the nonterrifying, exceedingly peaceful, grace granting[15] forms; the terrifying ones that are not benevolent and are unappeased;[16] and the third that delude the souls[17]—to the mention of "all forms of Rudra" and on to the dative of the personal pronoun of the second person that, Kauṇḍinya says, evokes Śiva as the unique god who is the ground and cause of everything (Kauṇḍinya 91,7).

The true dynamic of the Aghora mantra, which is decisive for meditation, reveals itself in the formula of worship, *namas te*: Kauṇḍinya (53, 16f.) says that *namas* means offering one's self (*ātmapradāne*) and worship (*pūjāyāṃ ca*). He comments upon the use of this word in the mantra in the following manner: "As one who is impelled to [that] in his own self (*ātmaprayuktaḥ*), [he says] 'namas'" (Kauṇḍinya 91, 7). By expressing worship, the Aghora mantra meditates the meditative subject in the attitude of self-offering in worship; that is, according to the Pāśupata understanding of yoga, in the union of the soul with god. By mentioning the totality of the many forms of god, which are included in the intentional relation by the use of the dative, this self-offering in worship solidifies itself as an unconditional commitment to god in the full complexity of his reality that reveals itself in the superior abundance of his manifestations or, as it is designated by Kauṇḍinya through a technical term, in his *vibhūti* (91, 4f.).

Furthermore, the linguistic value of the Aghora mantra deserves attention. Its meaning is not conveyed by a proposition articulated and based on rational reflection but by "indications" of god. For it is not that these manifestations of Śiva, mentioned in the mantra, are predicated as being "his" manifestations, rather they are juxtaposed as his "indications" against the decisive dative "to thee," so that, as evocations juxtaposed against that very reality, they merge in the concrete identity of Śiva. They are nothing but he himself. In these evocations he himself, in the manifoldness of his *vibhūti*, is encountered as the real object of devotion (*bhaktiḥ*) and worship (*pūjā*).

In the Tatpuruṣa mantra (i.e., the *raudrī gāyatrī*), however, we come across an inverted mediation of god, "We make the Puruṣa [of these manifold forms] the aim of our knowledge. We contemplate Mahādeva. May Rudra impel us to that!"[18] This is the wording of the mantra that is an imitation of the Vedic Gāyatrī and that also is meant to substitute for it, in its emotive valuation.[19] It no longer mediates god in the abundance of the different manifestations constituting his *vibhūti* but in his uniqueness as substratum of these forms (cf. Kauṇḍinya 107, 8ff.). "In so far as he [sustains and] directs all the effects, e.g., knowledge; etc., while pervading them (*vyāptādhiṣṭhātṛtvam*), fulfilling (*pūraṇam*) characterizes him; insofar as he has the power to create an infinite number of bodies etc. by will, the nature of being Puruṣa (*pauruṣyam*) characterizes him" (RṬ 11, 18f.). Such is the *Ratnaṭīkā*'s theological interpretation of the word *puruṣaḥ* as a characteristic of Śiva. Kauṇḍinya expounds in accordance with *Nirukta* 2.3 and TĀ 10.3 "because of the nature of being a Puruṣa and because of fulfilling, he is [called] Puruṣa. The nature of being a Puruṣa characterizes him, because he abides in many forms. The nonterrifying forms have him as their [supporting] being" (Kauṇḍinya 107, 12f.).

The decisive elements of this mantra, which mediates the content of meditation in the sense of the higher *pratyāhāra,* are the representations of Śiva as Tatpuruṣa and Mahādeva. It is not possible here to develop, even approximately, the complete horizon of the Pāśupata theology implied by these two names of Śiva. The theological dimension of the word *Tatpuruṣa* has already been explained briefly. The representation of Śiva as Mahādeva, however, must be indicated at least. Like *Tatpuruṣa,* it has to be understood in a strictly theological sense. Kauṇḍinya comments on the name *Mahādeva* as follows:

> Here *'mahān'* is [used] in the sense of "more excellent than" (*abhyadhikatve*). He is more excellent than all souls, he is supreme and surpasses [them]. He is *ṛṣi,* i. e., the one ruling over every effect,[20] he is *vipra,* i. e., having *jñānaśakti,*[21] he is *adhipati,* i. e., being the overlord.[22] We will explain his being-Sadāśiva and his being-more-excellent-than [later on].[23] [When it is said] *deva* [it refers to] the root *div* in the sense of playing. . . . Playing indeed, the Exalted One, produces the threefold effect, that is knowledge, the elements of worldy existence and souls, helps them and makes them perish again.[24] (Kauṇḍinya 14, 18–23)

In the horizon of the theological belief implied by these names, these two representations of Śiva (that is, Tatpuruṣa and Mahādeva) serve as the central element in the mediating structure of the Tatpuruṣa mantra. They mediate god, who abides as inner controller (*adhiṣṭhātā*) in all manifestations of Śiva and who is to be encountered, not in the sense that they would literally contain assertions about this god, but in the sense that they contribute to an horizon of expectations to be fulfilled by the reality of the object to be encountered. The meditating subject knows of this reality from his faith and he knows himself to be on the way in order to encounter this reality in his experience. Kauṇḍinya, in the introduction to his commentary on the Tatpuruṣa mantra, says, "After the practicing subject has recognized the unity and oneness of the Exalted One, who is taught to be the cause etc., he undertakes to realize it [in his own experience] (*tatsādhanam*)" (107, 8f.).

The mantra expresses the wish to contemplate and experience Śiva. Because of this, when recited with existential sincerity, the mantra creates an intentionality in the meditating subject that opens him radically for encountering the reality of Śiva. This openness in fact, is deepened and intensified when the mantra to be recited induces the meditating subject to surrender himself irrevocably to the power and might of Śiva, while invoking him with the words "May Rudra impel us to that." Kauṇḍinya says, "To impel (*codanam*) means the association of the power of knowledge and the power of doing in the sense of 'drive me on'," and he quotes an old gloss on it, "That association of the power to know and the power to do, which presupposes the wish of Rudra, i.e., its occurrence in the souls etc., is called by the teachers, 'impelling' (*codanam*)" (108, 16–19).

Let me summarize these brief indications of the linguistic content of the two mantras; i.e., the *bahurūpī ṛc* and the *raudrī gāyatrī*, which are used in the lower contemplation. According to their linguistic meaning, the two mantras form a complementary unit in that god is mediated in his *vibhūti* or one transcends his *vibhūti* in the direction of the inner controller (*adhiṣṭhātā*). In the two cases, taken together or individually, the one god is mediated in experience as correlated to the manifoldness of the phenomenal world. Thus, both mantras, together or individually, might have been used in meditation. Because "both [mantras] are equally Brahma, both realize the same purpose (*tulyārthasādhakatvam*) and both are accepted by Maheśvara (*maheśvaraparigṛhīte*), one should mutter the mantra pertaining to the one (*ekām* = *raudrī*), i. e. Tatpuruṣa, or the other, pertaining to the multiform (*anekām* = *bahurūpī*) god, after having taken ashes (*upaspṛśya*)" (Kauṇḍinya 39, 20f.).

Having briefly considered the description of the contents of both mantras as mediation structures of lower contemplation, I will return to the text of the *Ratnaṭīkā* and inquire as to the nature of the other kind of contemplation, which the *Ratnaṭīkā*, following Kauṇḍinya, calls "higher." From the remark of the Ṭīkakāra, that lower contemplation (*dhyānam*) is practiced by means of mantra muttering while higher contemplation is practiced by way of *dhāraṇā*, one could suppose that this is the difference between these two kinds of meditation and that, therefore, mantra has no function at all in higher contemplation. If one consults Kauṇḍinya's text, to which the author of the *Ratnaṭīkā* himself refers in this context, it becomes clear that this is not the case (RṬ 20, 12f.). Kauṇḍinya introduces the discussion of the higher contemplation with the following question: "Should he, who recited the *ṛc* (mantra) while meditating (*adhīyatā*), stand still (*stheyam*) with his mind concentrated (*yuktena*) on Brahma, which consists of a sequence of words and sounds, or is another more subtle [form of] worship (*upāsanā*) in sight (*dṛṣṭā*)?" (124, 12f.). Kauṇḍinya answers this question affirmatively by reference to *Pāśupatasūtra* 5.24: "He (the meditating subject) may turn his attention [reverently] to the *oṃkāra* (*oṃkāram abhidhyāyīta*)." The contemplation itself, which is precisely that higher form of *dhyāna* of which the *Ratnaṭīkā* speaks,[25] also is similarly practiced by means of *dhāraṇā*, according to Sūtra 5.25 for it says: "he should perform the fixing in his heart (*hṛdi kurvīta dhāraṇām*)."

Here one sees clearly that the distinction between the two forms of contemplation cannot be found in the fact that the lower contemplation is brought about by means of mantra muttering and the higher one by means of *dhāraṇā*. For, as the *Pāśupatasūtras* show, the higher contemplation also is brought about by means of a mantra: namely, the *praṇava* or the *oṃkāra*. What then is meant by *dhāraṇā* in PS 5.25, if it does not replace mantra muttering in contemplation?

The twofold injunction of the *Pāśupatasūtras*—first, that the meditating subject should turn his attention reverently to the *oṃkāra* and, second, that he should perform the fixing in his heart—serves as point of departure for answering this question. Both injunctions, in fact, appear to be two aspects of a single act. Kauṇḍinya in his commentary of PS 5.24 says, "The *oṃkāra*, is determined [by the Sūtra] to be the object of contemplation (*dhyeyatvena*), but this is not true of [other mantras] such as the Gāyatrī" (125, 1). He continues, "One should meditate (*bhavitavyam*) while the mind is in contact with the *oṃkāra* (*oṃkārasannikṛṣṭacittena*). . . . Only the Oṃkāra is to be contemplated (*dhyeyaḥ*) and no other [mantra]." Further, in the introduction to his commentary on PS 5.25 he asks, "What is the place of contemplation (*dhyānadeśaḥ*)? In what place is the 'fixing' to be done? What is to be done by the one who contemplates?" He answers, "This is said [in PS 5.25]: 'he should do the fixing in his heart' " (125, 10–13). Thus, Kauṇḍinya takes PS 5.24 as determining the object of the higher contemplation and 5.25 as indicating the way of turning attention to the *oṃkāra* (cf. *abhidhyāyīta*), namely by fixing in one's heart.

If this is correct, then the word *dhāraṇā* must have a different meaning than in the *saṃyama* meditation of Patañjali, where *dhāraṇā* is defined as "the fixing of the mind on a specific place."[26] According to the *Pāśupatasūtras*, it is not that the mind should be fixed in the heart in order to mediate a particular content of meditation or in order to attain a particular *siddhi* related to the *dhāraṇā* on the heart. Kauṇḍinya leaves no doubt about this in his commentary on PS 5.25. He writes,

> Here the *oṃkāra* is that which has to be fixed; not the *ātmā*, but the reality of the *ātmā* in the *ātmā* is that which has to be fixed; [that is to say] when somebody has been turned away from objects by means of *oṃkāra* and is simply in a state of pure [objectless mental][27] activity (*vṛttivikāramātreṇa*), then this turning away is the *pratyāhāra*. After having turned away [from the objects], he should perform the fixing in the heart; and that which he should fix is the recollection of the *oṃkāra* (*oṃkārānucintanam*). It is only then that the focusing of attention [on the Oṃkāra] (*adhyayanaṃ*) becomes a [state] which endures for a long time. Thus, the contemplation by means of *dhāraṇā* is the highest. (126, 9–13)

In order to understand this text, one must know that Kauṇḍinya takes the word *heart*, occurring in PS 5.25, as a synonym for the word *ātmā* (see Kauṇḍinga 125, 14ff.). The object of fixing is not the mind nor is the mind to be fixed in the heart. Rather, it is the *oṃkāra*, in so far as it is a reality of the *ātmā* in the *ātmā*, that is to be fixed. Therefore, the fixing of the *oṃkāra* in the *ātmā* turns out to be, in the terms of a spiritual psychology, the fixing of the recollection of the *oṃkāra* (*oṃkārānucin-

tanam) (cf. Kauṇḍinya 126, 12). This "recollection" (*anucintanam*) is not only a rational "thinking about." It implies a volitional /emotional opening of oneself to the reality that, in the very act of this opening of the subject, determines the subject in his existential authenticity. If one considers this, then it becomes clear that the practice of the spiritual life in which the *bhakti* of the devout Pāśupata ascetic is brought into meditation, has to be located in the "act of *oṃkāra* recollection." This fixing of "*oṃkāra* recollection" in the heart could be understood as the longing for the presence of the *oṃkāra* in the *ātmā* and as the affirmation of the *oṃkāra*'s presence, an affirmation that becomes concrete in radical devotion (*bhakti*) (also compare page 217).

What meaning, however, can be assigned to the *oṃkāra* in this higher contemplation (*dhyānam*)? How can one conceive of this existential openness of the meditating subject actualized in *oṃkāra*-recollection? Why does the mind stand firm in the reality of Rudra as a result of such a fixing (*dhāraṇā*) of the Oṃkāra in the *ātmā*, that is, as a result of the recollection of the *oṃkāra*? Finally, all these questions are implied by the primary question of the nature and reality of *oṃkāra*.

At first, *oṃkāra* is not like the *bahurūpī ṛc* or the *raudrī gāyatrī* in the lower form of contemplation, "a brahma consisting of a sequence of words and sounds" (see Kauṇḍinya 124, 12f.). It is rather, as Kauṇḍinya says, "another word for that which is to be muttered, for example, Vāmadeva, etc."[28] The comparison with Vāmadeva shows that the *oṃkāra* first of all is a linguistic representation of god and not a proposition about him. This function of the *oṃkāra* in theistic meditation is already attested in Patañjali. The *oṃkāra* is that which "denotes" (*vācakam*) god.

The *Ratnaṭīkā* deepens this preliminary understanding of the Oṃkāra when it speaks about the Oṃkāra as a *guṇadharma* of god, by which the one transcendent god and primary cause of the world (*kāraṇam*) can be thought of and expressed in the manifold terms of language (cf. page 217). But the exact meaning of the term *guṇadharma* is not all that clear. I have not come across this term outside the Pāśupata tradition, and the few clues there are all too meager. In any case, the world *guṇadharma* must be understood to have a technical meaning; a meaning that is clearly circumscribed by the ontology specific to this system. Therefore, I do not think that these *guṇadharmas* are divine *Qualitätsattribute* as was F. A. Schultz's opinion (1958, 79). According to its actual usage, the notion *guṇadharma* designates specific representations of god that are traced out linguistically and structured conceptually. In addition, in so far as they are based ontologically on the divine reality, these *guṇadharmas* also account for the fact that the one transcendent god, as such, can be named by various linguistic expressions and that it is certainly god himself who is named, called upon, and not simply described as possessing such characteristics. Therefore, I do not think it justified to understand the *guṇadharmas* as qualities of god.

For these reasons, I would prefer to see the conception of *guṇadharma* as a specific linguistic representation of god, a representation, to be sure, that is based in the reality of god, but one that, as it is structured in language, must not be understood as an ontological differentiating determination of his reality. Therefore, in these *guṇadharmas,* god comes quite properly into view in all his manifold reality. This is not to say, however, that his infinite reality is limited, for example, by an ontological qualification such that he would be manifold in an objective sense. *Guṇadharma,* therefore, is that "quality" of god whose ontological character is that of a dharma; that is, a mental and linguistic attribution, whose ontological content, however, is nothing but the one undivided reality of god expressible by various attributions. To put it in another way, the *guṇadharma* is an expression in language that declares the one undivided reality of god in its different relations to the world and that is objective because it is based upon the reality of god.

One of these *guṇadharmas* is Śiva's being *oṃkāra.* The *Ratnaṭīkā* defines this in the following manner: "[Śiva's] being-*oṃkāra* is his only way of being an object for comtemplation, which is the cause of the end of suffering"[29] (RṬ 11, 21). This can only mean that the *oṃkāra* is Maheśvara himself in so far as he is present as the OṂ mantra in the act of contemplation (however one might conceive of this presence) and, thus, out of his grace, effects the end of suffering; i. e., emancipation.

I return to the lower contemplation practiced by means of the Aghora or Tatpuruṣa mantra. What is the difference between that contemplation and this higher contemplation, in which *oṃkāra* is the object of meditation? Whatever the difference is, it does not lie in the use or nonuse of mantras, because mantras are used in both cases. A remark of Kauṇḍinya may help answer this question, at least in a preliminary manner. He says that the contemplation (*dhyānam*) of the *oṃkāra* represents a "more subtle form of meditative worship" (*sūkṣmatarā upāsanā*) (Kauṇḍinya 124, 13). But, why is meditation that uses *oṃkāra* a more subtle form of meditative worship?

Kauṇḍinya does not tell us explicitly, so we are left with conjecture. In any case, one has to say that mantras of the lower contemplation (*dhyānam*) differ from the *oṃkāra* in their linguistic structure. In contradistinction to the *oṃkāra,* these mantras are propositions, linguistic formulations of an intentional relationship of the meditating subject to Śiva. They thus linguistically mediate the reality of god only in an indirect way. *Oṃkāra,* in contrast, is a linguistically undifferentiated sound that thus can effect Śiva's salvific presence immediately; i. e., without a prior propositional mediation. If this is correct, then I have to inquire again and more deeply into the function and meaning of *dhāraṇā* for the act of higher contemplation. The necessity of *dhāraṇā* in contemplation that is realized by means of the syllable OṂ is theological. This is because the syllable OṂ is the "being-an-object for contemplation" of god himself without requiring any mediation by sentence meaning. As such, contemplation on it is the only sort of contemplation that can effect the end of suffering.[30] Such a presence of god, which is no longer conveyed by means of sentence meaning,[31] can only be retained in the heart; that is, in the *ātmā* by means of a radical "recollection of the *oṃkāra*," which becomes concrete in surrender (*bhaktiḥ, ātmāpradānaṃ*) and worship (*pūjā*) (see page 215).

The following seems to be basic for the evaluation of the contemplation of the *oṃkāra* as "higher" and as a "more subtle form of meditative worship" (*sūkṣmatarā upāsanā*): While the presence of god is mediated by mantras in all cases, the various forms of mantra meditation successively mediate the experience of increasingly subtle, less objective forms of Śiva's presence. The contemplation begins with the experience of god in his manifoldness (*bahurūpaḥ*) or of god guiding and, sustaining this manifoldness (*tatpuruṣaḥ*), rises to the experience of god who transcends the multiplicity of the world as well as his relation to this multiplicity. Therefore, one must say that the lower and the higher contemplation can be classified hierarchically according to the relative intensity of union with the saving god (*īśvarasaṃyogaḥ*). Actually, Kauṇḍinya, too, associates the reality of Śiva "as he is in himself" with the *oṃkāra*. In spite of this, according to the belief of the Pāśupatas, god in his pure transcendent reality (i. e., without mediation by the mantra) seems to remain inaccessible to human experience. Consequently, the final, radical union with Śiva (*śivasāyujyam*) occurs only in the fifth stage of the path of salvation; that is, at death.

As to the object of higher contemplation Kauṇḍinya, refering to PS 5.24, 26, and 27 and in terms of the mediation structure of *oṃkāra*, says the following:

> [When] *oṃkāra* [is said], then the object of contemplation (*dhyeyam*) is [thereby] pointed out. [When] '*ṛṣiḥ, vipraḥ, mahān*, and *eṣai* [are said], then it is expressed, that [these *guṇadharmas*] are made into qualities of the object of meditation (*dhyeyaguṇīkaraṇam*). [And when] '*vāgviśuddhaḥ*' [and] '*niṣkalaḥ*' [are said], then it is expressed that the object of meditation is determined (*dhyeyāvadhāraṇam*) [in this way, i. e., as free from any linguistic attribution (*vāgviśuddhaḥ*) and as transcendent to any form of being (*niṣkalaḥ*)]. (128, 13f.)

It is worth noting that all of the denotations of god named by Kauṇḍinya in this passage are *guṇadharmas* in the sense of the *Ratnaṭīkā*, *guṇadharmas* that are consciously related to the object of meditation, Śiva as *oṃakāra*. Therefore, they can be understood as a dynamic conception of experience of the higher contemplation.

It would lead us too far afield to document textually the theological meaning of each and every one of these designations. *Ṛṣi* is Śiva as *kriyāśakti*, (RṬ 11, 21; cf. Kauṇḍinya 126, 21ff.), he is *vipra* as *jñānakśrti* (RṬ 11, 22; cf. Kauṇḍinya 127, 1ff.), he is *mahat* as the substratum of them (RṬ 11, 22f.; cf. Kauṇḍinya 121, 4–7), but he is *eṣay* as the one who always and everywhere (RṬ 11, 23f.; somewhat different Kauṇḍinya 127, 7–9) has an unchanging nature, he is *vāgviśuddha* as the one who transcends all propositions made possible by the *guṇadharmas* (RṬ 11, 24ff.). Kauṇḍinya relates all of these representations of Śiva, manifest as they are in language, to the manifestation of Śiva as *oṃkāra,* which is decisive for meditation and therefore also for human salvation. This means that the model of experience of the higher contemplation proceeds from the *oṃkāra* as single object of contemplation, to the four representations understood as "qualifications" of god, which are mediated by the Oṃkāra, and finally to the reality, namely *vāgviśuddha* and *niṣkala,* that is the *oṃkāra* itself in so far as it transcends its own reality as a *guṇadharma*.

I turn now from the concrete process of Pāśupata meditation to the more philosophical question of the function of mantra. If one is impartial, one must admit that in terms of content the mantra brings nothing more to meditation than what the believing Pāśupata would already bring along as a conviction of faith. If he wanted simply to meditate on a certain content of faith, he could do so with any number of mental and linguistic constructs.

This observation is important because it shows that the meditation in which mantras are used has nothing to do with the appropriation of truths of faith and, moreover, nothing to do with the deepening of theological insights through some meditative experience. For all that, one needs no mantra. If one recalls that, according to Kauṇḍinya, mantra muttering has the purpose of removing *adharma* and of bringing about the purity of mind and character (see page 208), and if one further recalls that Kauṇḍinya designated the contemplation of the *oṃkāra* in contradistinction to the lower contemplation as "the more subtle form of meditative worship" (*sūkṣmatarā upāsanā*), then one clearly can see the actual purpose and the actual nature of the contemplation practiced by means of mantras: It is basically worship that is realized as contemplation. That is why the meditating subject must be pure in thought before he is competent for contemplation in the true sense of the term.[32] In regard to the contents, a mantra does not introduce anything new into contemplation, but it transforms the possibility of transcendental experience into the actuality of an event. Though he is ever known and affirmed in faith, the meditation of the mantras effects an actual encounter with god.

The contemplation realized by means of mantras is basically an existential act in which one reverently disposes oneself to transcendence, but it does not concern pious sentiments and spiritual experiences. To be sure, it also concerns them, but this is not the essential character of the contemplation that requires the use of mantras. And, in so far as the mantra actually makes god present as an event, the sacramental character mentioned at the beginning of this essay characterizes mantras and the meditative worship practiced with their help. Whether this sacramental character arises from "wishful thinking" or whether it involves an objective reality, is a question that can be left aside here. We must say only that to make possible an experience of transcendence requires not only the transcending of the human spirit and the a priori model of experience structured in language but, at the same time, a mediation that is a real event. Only by means of such a mediation can transcendence become the horizon for an encounter in which the person actually and responsibly behaves in the face of the absolute meaning of his existence (*Dasein*).

Such a mediation of transcendence arising in an actual event, one that goes beyond the mythic mediation that can be accomplished by every linguistic expression of transcendence, belongs to the mantra and only to the mantra. In contemplation, the mantra is the only reality that is clearly delimited and set in a certain point of time. Therefore, it alone is capable of transforming the mythic mediation of transcendence immanent to it into an event. This is true, provided, that what is mediated has a transsubjective nature. This inherent transsubjectivity of what is mediated (i. e., its mediation as something actually encountered, a transsubjectivity that occurs in every genuine mediation) is proper to the mantra only on the basis of the conviction that the mantra not only has the capability of mediating an insight but also the power to make the transcendent present to the subject in a fully effective manner.[33]

Now I come to the last section of this essay, where I will attempt to authenticate the notion of the effective power of mantra according to the self-conscious articulation of Pāśupata belief and to make it theologically explicable. Because of the lack of textual evidence, I can prove this only by way of suggestion. It is certain that, according to the Pāśupata doctrine, mantra not only has a sense and meaning but also an effective power. How else could the *Ratnaṭīkā* say that the mantra brings only harm (*doṣaḥ*) to him who uses it without the appropriate attitude. Moreover, how could the mantra effect the purification of the mind and the removal of *adharma*, which indeed the Pāśupatas believe to be the case? Kauṇḍinya also accords the mantra an effective power when he says, for example, that the third and fourth Brahma mantras bring about the same fruit (*tulyaphalasādhanatvam*).

According to Pāśupata theology, such effective power is not inherent in the mantra due to its own nature, nor can one treat it as a śakti of Śiva. On the contrary, it seems to get its effective power only by a positive act of Maheśvara. It is in this sense that Kauṇḍinya, in order to establish why both Brahma mantras have the same effectiveness, says that they are *maheśvaraparigṛhīta,* "accepted by Maheśvara and made his own" (39, 21). He expresses the same idea with respect to the many forms of Śiva named in the Aghora mantra. They, too, are manifestations accepted by Śiva and made his own.[34] Therefore, one can assume that these mantras, just like Śiva's many manifestations, are sustained in their effectiveness by his power and that they produce their effect owing to his sovereign saving intention. One would like to believe that Bhāsarvajña (about 900 A.D.) advocates Pāśupata doctrine in this respect when he rebuts the Mīmāṃsā conception in the following way:

> The acquisition of the fruit does not result from the power of the word (*śabdaśaktiteḥ*), because it would then follow that mantras, if used inaudibly or mentally, would have to be without fruit or that the alternative [of the choice] of time would have to be absent and that they would not be dependent on a specific injunction and intention. [But if the acquisition of the fruit] results from the power of [their] author (*puruṣaśaktitaḥ*), then this flaw does not occur. However and in whatever way [the author] establishes the convention, in that way, because of the observance of the convention, does the fruit [of the mantra] arise, on account of the effectiveness which his decree ascribes (*tatsamabhivyāhāra*); or, like a king, this particular deity [itself] supports the [convention], while the convention protects it. (Nbhū 404, 2–6)

Not every being has the power of establishing such a convention, but only those who have the capability of realizing wishes spontaneously (*satyasaṃkalpatā*); that is, as Bhāsarvajña says, only god himself on account of the sovereignity appropriate to his nature (*svābhāvikaiśvarya-prabhāvāt*) and the *Mahārṣis* on account of their constancy in discipline (*ahiṃsābrahmacaryasatyādisthairyaprabhāvāt tapaḥprabhṛtiprabhāvād vā*) (Nbhū 403, 16–17).

On the basis of the structure of the mantras and their function in meditation, there can be no doubt that these mantras can be traced back to nothing but the decree of Śiva himself. Therefore, one can say further that, in using these mantras in meditation, Śiva communicates himself for the salvation of men. This is because, and in so far as, he alone enables these mantras to mediate himself as the means of salvation in an actual encounter. It is only in *this* encounter that the meditating subject opens himself up in actual worship to the god who is mediated through the mantra. Thus, he can become the recipient of salvation. The mantra magnifies the "mythic presence" of transcendence in meditation in the sense of a sacramental event in that the mantra gives the experience of transcendence the dimension of encounter and allows the positive salvific intention of the sovereign god to become an individual event.

NOTES

1. The reason for this can be found in the religious development and history of ideas of India at that time. Around the middle of the first millenium A.D., the Sāṃkhyā system loses its importance as a path of salvation, while the theistic traditions with their theistic meditation are emphasized more and more, so that

the use of mantra in meditation had to be understood in a new way even in Sāmkhyistic Yoga.

2. Regarding the phenomenon of language compare also Ybh. 266, 7-272, 5.

3. Ybh. (Vivaraṇam) 79, 13: *vācyavācakayor asthitasaṃbandhatve tu praṇavarūpeṇābhimukhībhavatīśvara iti nāvakalpater.*

4. Kauṇḍinya 126, 13.

5. Cf. RṬ 6, 20 and the objection 19, 30ff.

6. See Kauṇḍinya 39, 21f. Its realization is described by the *Ratnaṭīkā* in the following way: *grame vā yadi vetyādi/*

> *upasparśanenākṣapitakaluṣakṣāpaṇārthaṃ prāṇāyāmaḥ/ koṣṭhyasya vāyor gatinirodhaḥ prāṇāyāmaḥ/ tatropaspṛśya kāraṇatīrthakaragurūn anupraṇamya prāṅmukha udaṅmukho vā padmakasvastikādīnām anyatamaṃ yathāsukham āsanaṃ baddhvā kṛtam unnataṃ ca kṛtvā śanaiḥ saṃyatāntāḥkaraṇena recakādīn kuryāt/ kaluṣbhāve 'pi cittasyātinirmalatvāpādanārtham abhyāsārthaṃ nityaṃ kuryāt/ uktaṃ hi—*
>
> *prāṇāyāmair dahed doṣān dhāraṇābhiś ca kilbiṣam/*
> *pratyāhāreṇa viṣayān dhyānenānīśvarān guṇān//*
> *prāṇāyāmena yuktasya viprasya niyatātmanaḥ/*
> *sarve doṣāḥ praṇaśyanti sattvasthaś caiva jāyate//*
> *jalabindukuśāgreṇa māse māse ca yaḥ pibet/*
> *saṃvatsaraśataṃ sāgraṃ prāṇāyāmaikatatsamam//*
> *prāṇāyāmaviśuddhātmā yasmāt paśyati tatparam/*
> *tasmāt kiñcit paraṃ na asti prāṇāyāmād iti śrutiḥ/*
>
> *tad akṣapitakaluṣakṣapaṇārthaṃ japaḥ kartavyaḥ/ tritīyacaturthayor anyatarasmin brahmaṇi prayatnaniruddhaṃ cittaṃ saṃpūrṇākṣarānubodhena tadarthānubodhena vā punaḥ punaḥ sañcārayed iti./* (RṬ 12, 23-13, 8)

7. Cf. PS 1.15–20, where the *akaluṣamati* is the precondition for the state of yoga caused by meditation.

8. Cf. Manu 6.72.

9. Cf. Kauṇḍinya 38, 1f. and 39, 5ff.

10. RṬ 12, 9–13: *dharmārthaḥ sādhakavyāpāro vidhiḥ/ sa dvividhaḥ pradhānabhūto guṇabhūtaśceti/ tatrāvyavadhānena dharmahetuyor vidhiḥ sa pradhānabhūtaś caryeti vekṣyate/ yastu caryānugrāhakaḥ sa guṇabhūto 'nusnānādiḥ./*

11. Except for a few minor variant readings, these Brahma mantras are the invocations of Śiva in TĀ 10.43–47.

12. See Kauṇḍinya 52, 9.

13. In the *Mṛgendratantra* (*Yogapāda* 1.51ff.), for example, we find a type of meditation whose content seems to correspond in its structure to the content of

the Pāśupata meditation that is realized by means of these two mantras, even though the character and realization of the meditation differs from that.

14. PS 3.21–26: *aghorebhyaḥ, atha ghorebhyaḥ, ghora ghoratarebhyaś ca, sarvebhyaḥ śarva sarvebhyaḥ, namas te astu rudra rūpebhyaḥ.* Compare MS 2.9, 10; TĀ 10.45.

15. *atiśāntāni;* Kauṇḍinya 89, 12.

16. Kauṇḍinya 89, 16f.

17. *saṃmohakarāṇi;* Kauṇḍinya 90, 4.

18. PS 14.22–24: *tatpuruṣāya vidmahe, mahādevāya dhīmahi, tan no rudraḥ pracodayāt.* Compare MS 2.9,1; KS 17.11; TĀ 10.46 and 10.1,5.

19. Cf. Kauṇḍinya 39, 15: *atra raudrīgrahaṇād vaidikyādigāyatrīpratiṣedhaḥ.*

20. Kauṇḍinya 127, 1.

21. Kauṇḍinya 127, 1ff.

22. Kauṇḍinya 145, 16f.

23. See Kauṇḍinya 146, 11: *atra sadā nityaṃ santatam avyucchinnam ity arthaḥ.* Kauṇḍinya 146, 14–16: *atra śiva ity etad api bhagavato nāma. śivaḥ kasmāt? paripūrṇaparitṛptatvāc chivaḥ. tasmāt sadāśivopadeśān nityo duḥkhāntaḥ, kāraṇādhikāranivṛttiḥ.*

24. For the designations of god as *ṛṣi, vipra,* and *adhipati,* see Kauṇḍinya 126, 21-127,3: *atra ṛṣiḥ ity etad bhagavato nāṃadheyam. ṛṣiḥ kasmāt? ṛṣiḥ kriyāyām. ṛṣitvaṃ nāma kriyāśaṃsanād ṛṣiḥ. tathā kṛtsnaṃ kāryaṃ vidyādyam īśata ity ataḥ ṛṣiḥ. tathā vipra ity etad api bhagavato nāma. vipraḥ kasmāt? vida jñāne. vipratvaṃ nāma jñānaśaktiḥ. vyāptamanena bhagavatā jñānaśaktyā kṛtsnaṃ jñeyam ity ato vipra iti;* and Kauṇḍinya 145, 16–18: *patyuḥ patiḥ adhipatiḥ rājarājavat. patiḥ pālane, patir darśane bhoge ca. pālayate yasmād brahmādīn īśvaraḥ. pāti brahmādikāryam. adhipatiḥ brahmā. adhipatir īśvaraḥ.*

25. This equation is based on the reference of the *Ratnaṭīkā* to the discussion of the higher contemplation by Kauṇḍinya (RṬ 20, 12) and the fact that the higher contemplation of the *Ratnaṭīkā,* as well as that of Kauṇḍinya, is realized by means of *dhāraṇā,* whatever the meaning of this term is in this context. Finally, the concept of *dhāraṇā* in the *Ratnaṭīkā* corresponds to the signification of *dhāraṇā* in Kauṇḍinya.

26. *deśabandhaś cittasya dhāraṇā* (YS 3.1). Compare also G. Oberhammer 1977, 216ff.

27. Here the term *objectless* corresponds to the turning away from worldly objects but does not indicate that the acts of consciousness are devoid of contents.

28. Kauṇḍinya 124,16: *om ity eṣa japyaparyāyo vāmadevādivat.*

29. It also seems to correspond, finally, to the reality of Śiva as Sadāśiva, when one recalls the explanation of this name of Śiva in Kauṇḍinya (146, 14ff.).

30. Cf. duḥkhāntanimittam dhyānaikaviṣayatvam oṃkāratvam (RṬ 11, 21. Cf. also Kauṇḍinya 126, 12.).

31. Cf. *nirālambanaṃ cittam amūḍhasya dhāraṇam. . . . yo vidyānugṛhītayā buddhyā svaṃ cittaṃ nirālambanaṃ karoti, so 'mūḍha ity ucyate. tayā dhāraṇayā nirmalīkṛtaṃ cittaṃ rudratattve sthāpitaṃ sudīrghakālaṃ na cyavate . . .* (RṬ 20, 8–11. For the translation, see page 206).

32. Cf. RṬ 20, 13f., as well as PS 1.15–20 and PS 5.20–28, respectively.

33. There is also a theistic meditation, in which mantras are not used as mediating factors of the meditative experience of god, as shown by the example of Bhāsavajña, mentioned earlier on page 204. Such meditation seems to evolve basically from a spirituality that is structured differently and that is determined substantially by the conceptual reflections of reality. In this meditation, the presence of god is not mediated as an event by means of the sacramental dynamics of the mantra but by means of the true knowledge of the nature and existence of god (Bhāsarvajña speaks about the highest *ātmā* as "place" of *dhāraṇā;* see Nbhū 589, 12ff.) and by means of the experience of his reality arising out of the conception of god who is known to be present (cf. Oberhammer 1984, 202 ff.).

34. Cf. Kauṇḍinya 39, 17: bahurūpasyoktaparigraheṣv ākāreṣu vartata iti bahurūpī.

ABBREVIATIONS USED IN THIS CHAPTER

Kauṇḍinya	Pañcārthabhāṣya of Kauṇḍinya
KS	Kaṭha Saṃhitā
MS	Maitrāyaṇī Saṃhitā
Nbhū.	Nyāyabhūṣaṇa of Bhāsarvajña
PS	Pāsupatasūtra
RṬ	Ratnaṭīkā
TĀ	Taittirīya Āraṇyaka
Ybh.	Yogabhāṣya of Vyāsa
YS	Yogasūtra

CHAPTER 9

The Pāñcarātra Attitude to Mantra

Sanjukta Gupta

PĀÑCARĀTRA IS ONE OF THE oldest Vaiṣṇava sects. It is named and its main doctrines are expounded in *Mahābhārata* XII, the *Śāntiparvan* (MBH 12.321–22). The extant literature of the sect is vast and spans a period of more than a thousand years. Even its primary scriptures spread over half a millennium, from approximately 500–1000 A.D. They are mostly called *saṃhitā*, occasionally *tantra* (Schrader 1916, 2–22; Gonda 1977a, 38–57; Smith 1975–80, vol. 1 passim).

Pāñcarātra has a great deal in common with other tantric sects, and this holds also for its attitude to mantra. Like the other sects, Pāñcarātra refers to its own scriptures as *mantraśāstra* (virtually, "the Bible of mantra") and regards them as teaching mantras, meditation on those mantras, and the ritual accompanying that meditation; the whole constituting the means (*sādhanā*) to salvation (*mukti*). Pāñcarātra has certain distinctive doctrines, especially in cosmology, which require exposition if one is to understand its view of mantra in detail. What is most distinctive, however, about this view is that for Pāñcarātra the power of mantra (*mantraśakti*) is the expression or embodiment of god's saving grace (*anugrahamūrti*). This emphasis on God's mercy, not just his power and majesty, is consonant with the general tenor of sectarian Vaiṣṇavism as against the Śiva/Śākta sects.

INTRODUCTORY REMARKS ON THEOLOGY AND COSMOGONY

The sect believes in one all-inclusive god, who is a person (*puruṣa*), the highest person (*mahā Puruṣa*). He is creator, lord, and ruler of all. He is transcendent and also immanent, permeating all beings as their essence and inner controller (*antaryāmin*). He is the supreme soul (*parama ātman*) and the totality (*śeṣin*) in which all souls are contained. He is called Nārāyaṇa.

Although he is one and unique, god manifests himself in various forms to engage in certain divine activities. Most of these activities fall under five categories: self-concealment (*tirodhāna,* also called punishment, *nigraha*), creation, sustenance, resorption, granting grace (*anugraha*) (LT 12.12; also Gupta 1972, xxvi). These five, in turn, can be grouped as cosmogonic (the first four) or salvific (the fifth).

God is self-existent, pure bliss and consciousness. He is chiefly referred to in Pāñcarātra as *Bhagavat,* and the term is interpreted to mean that he possesses (six) divine glories (*bhaga*), his divine attributes.[1] These are knowledge/omniscience (*jñāna*); sovereignty (*aiśvarya*); potency (śakti); indefatigable energy (*bala*); the ability to remain unaffected by any change, even the evolution of the universe out of him (*vīrya*); brilliant and self-sufficient conquering power (*tejas*). The first of these attributes, omniscience, is primary: It is god's essence (SS 2.33). The other five attributes are its effects, contained in it in dormant state before they evolve.[2]

Another way of expressing the same idea is that these six attributes of god, taken together, constitute his Śakti, which may be translated as his power, potency, and potentiality rolled into one. Obviously, this Śakti, which is also called *Kalā,* is not the same as the śakti which is the third attribute. I shall distinguish the superordinate Śakti, which is of supreme importance in the sect's theology, by spelling it with a capital letter. Śakti is god's essential nature, his personality or "I-ness" (*ahaṃtā*) (LT 2.12). So, just as god's primary attribute is omniscience, Śakti is said to be primarily intelligence or thought (*saṃvid*), and the other five attributes emanate from this *saṃvid.* Śakti is thus a hypostatization, a concretization of god's personality and activity. This concretization of an abstraction is taken a step further when she is personified. In Pāñcarātra, her personified form is called *Lakṣmī* and she is said in mythology to be god's wife.[3]

Indian philosophy posits that any phenomenon has three kinds of cause: the efficient, the material, and the instrumental. In Pāñcarātra, god relates to the universe as all three. He is the efficient cause, the agent, because his essence is consciousness and free will—the basic definition of any agent. He is the material cause, because he is the sole reality and the source of all. He is the instrumental cause, because creation proceeds through the instrumentality of his power, his Śakti. From this, it will readily appear that Pāñcarātra accepts the theory of causation according to which effects preexist in their cause, albeit in a dormant or unmanifest condition (*satkāryavāda*).

God's causal relation to the universe is regularly expressed in terms of his Śakti. All creation is considered to be a special *state* of his being (*bhūti*) and a result of the *action* of his sovereign will, acting in the light of his omniscience. Thus god's Śakti is said to manifest herself in two aspects. Dynamically viewed, she is god's omnipotent creative activity, *kriyāśakti*. More statically viewed, she is god manifest as the creation, *bhūtiśakti*.[4]

The creation, or *bhūtiśakti*, comprises all objects both sentient and insentient. Sentient objects (or, more strictly, sentiences) are souls (*jīva*). It is here that we understand why God's self-concealment is a cosmogonic activity. The sentient world is created by encompassing little bits (*aṃśa*) of god's own self with Śakti's veiling, deluding power, māyā. Thus, māyā, in this system, is another expression for *tirodhāna*.[5] It refers to the concealment of god's totality from the parts, so that they imagine themselves to be limited (*aṇu*) in space and time. It is also through māyā that the insentient world evolves; its primary level, undifferentiated matter, is *prakṛti*. From *prakṛti*, evolves the phenomenal world accessible to our senses. As in all Indian cosmologies from Sāṃkhya on, the final product, the world of everyday appearances, is termed *gross* (*sthūla*); just above this in the cosmic hierarchy, accessible to the senses of the advanced yogin, is the penultimate stage in evolution, the subtle (*sūkṣma*). At the resorption of the universe, "gross" effects merge back into their "subtle" causes, and so, back by stages, until matter reverts to its undifferentiated state as *prakṛti* (LT 3.24–31 and 7 passim).

There are three levels of creation (*sarga*): the pure (*śuddha*), the mixed (*miśra*), and the impure (*aśuddha*). The impure is the creation of the insentient world, from undifferentiated *prakṛti* down to the gross level accessible to our normal senses; it is reversed by resorption. The mixed is the creation of individual souls by god's self-concealment; it is reversed, as we shall see, by his grace. The two creations are preceded, both logically and chronologically, by the pure creation. While everything said so far about creation applies to all tantric sects (except for some details of terminology), the elaborate scheme of the pure creation I am about to describe is peculiar to Pāñcarātra (see Schrader 1916, 29–59; Gonda 1977, 60–65).

The pure creation is the creation of gods. Gods embody specific aspects and attributes of god. (Thus, like Śakti, they could be said to represent hypostatizations and then personifications of theological abstractions.) As contrasted with *bhūti*, god's self-contraction (*ātmasaṃkoca*) into phenomena, the deities are called *vibhūti*, because they "diversely" or "especially" (*vi-*) manifest god's omniscient might/being (*bhūti*). They fall into two categories: *vyūha* and *vibhava* (SS 1.25–27). Some late texts add a third category: images (*arcā*).[6]

The *vyūha* gods relate to the cosmogony. The transcendent, immutable, and unique Nārāyaṇa manifests himself just before creation displaying all six of his attributes in their full glory. This manifestation transcends the creation and is called the supreme (*para*) Vāsudeva. The four *vyūhas* head the pure creation; they are the primal differentiated manifestations of *para* Vāsudeva. When his creative dynamism, his *kriyāśakti*, comes into operation, it is said to vibrate. At this vibration, the six divine attributes contract, becoming dormant within the *kriyāśakti*, and *para* Vāsudeva is no longer manifest. When his six attributes thus are in temporary eclipse (*śāntodita*), Vāsudeva is called *differentiated* (*vyūha*), in contradistinction to *para* Vāsudeva, whose attributes are always manifest (*nityodita*) (SS 2.70). The three other *vyūha* deities are Saṃkarṣaṇa, Pradyumna, and Aniruddha. Each displays just two of the six glorious attributes: Saṃkarṣaṇa displays *jñāna* and *bala*; Pradyumna *aiśvarya* and *vīrya*; Aniruddha śakti and *tejas*. Each of the three represents a stage in the creation of the cosmos and an aspect of the activities of the *kriyāśakti*. Thus, like the dual aspect of Śakti as *bhūtiśakti* and *kriyāśakti*, they have static and dynamic aspects. They represent Vāsudeva's gradual transition from transcendence to appearing as the phenomenal world. This will be elaborated later, when I have introduced *mantra*. For the moment, suffice it to say that the fourth *vyūha*, Aniruddha, creates, sustains, and in a sense also *is* our world of experience, gross phenomena.

The *vibhava* deities are all the other aspects of Vāsudeva, such as his discus, Sudarśana, and also the gods of mythology. Thus all gods and aspects of gods are considered partial manifestations of His omniscient and omnipotent majesty. Both categories of gods, *vyūha* and *vibhava*, are described as sparks of light shooting out of the central reality (SS 5, 8), which is seen by successful yogins in trance. This central mass of light, the sum total of all the gods, is called the *Viśākhayūpa*.

Before introducing mantra into this scheme, I must conclude these preliminary remarks with a few more words about bondage and liberation, as seen from the human point of view, or seen from the divine end, about god's activities of punishment and grace. Why does god conceal himself? Because he is the supreme ruler and guardian of moral law, and so punishes the sinner.[7] Man sins, basically, through his feelings of inadequatcy and desires for something not within himself, through a lack of self-sufficiency. This is due to a wrong idea of his real nature, the delusion of māyā. Thus, māyā, which we have already seen to be but another term for *tirodhāna* and an aspect of Śakti, puts man in a transient material world and makes him feel limited and subject to change. Aniruddha, who is Vāsudeva at this level of phenomena, deploys his power (śakti as one of the six glorious attributes) to maintain moral law and order (*karman*).

But Vāsudeva is also the benevolent saviour; his *anugraha*, his saving grace, is always present. So, whereas *tirodhāna/nigraha* brings about the mixed and impure creations, māyā, his *anugraha* is manifest in the pure creation, the deities. The deities, all being aspects of god, save man. And, we shall see that as saviours they are primarily mantras. Mantras are the pure creation, and at the same time they are the means and the path to salvation. This salvation is the same as release from the influence of māyā and of the desire which is its consequence. The simultaneous result of such release is to attain Vāsudeva's highest abode (*paramaṃ padam*), which is the same as his great presence (*dhāman*), the supreme paradise of omniscience and bliss (Gonda 1967, 80–85 and passim).

How, in practical terms, is one to attain this salvific gnosis, this freedom from desire, this experience of god? For the Pāñcarātrin, the answer is total surrender to god, *prapatti*. But, *prapatti* is not passive. It requires unwavering faith in God's boundless mercy; but also the renunciation of everything but his service (*upāsanā*). This *upāsanā* consists of uttering mantras, performing the rites which accompany them, and finally of meditating with one-pointed concentration on the mantras and the divinities of which they are the primary form. This last statement leads us into the heart of our subject.

LANGUAGE IN COSMOGONY

The theory that the supreme reality (*brahman*) is sound (*śabda*) or word (*vāc*), the idealized essence of language, was developed by philosophers of language and *mīmāṃsaka* thinkers. Their concept of *śabdabrahman* greatly influenced all tantric cosmogonies. As monotheists believing in a personal (*puruṣa*) supreme god, Pāñcarātrins did not accept the theory that the sole ultimate reality was the impersonal *śabdabrahman*. But they gave it second place in their cosmogony and cosmology, equating it with Śakti in their scheme. (This equation no doubt was made easier by referring to *śabdabrahman* by its synonym, *vāc*, a feminine abstraction which can be hypostatized and even personified *pari passu* with Śakti.) More precisely, *vāc* is equated with God's *jñānaśakti* or *saṃvid-śakti,* which we saw to be his first and most essential attribute. Earlier, I referred only to two aspects of Śakti: *bhūtiśakti* and *kriyāśakti*. But Śakti, being but god in action, can be infinitely subdivided. What concerns us here is that *kriyāśakti,* god's efficacy, has two integral aspects: god's omniscience, hypostatized as *jñānaśakti* or *samvid*-śakti; and his free will, hypostatized as *iccha*-śakti. As soon as Nārāyaṇa wills to create, the quiescence of his *jnana*-śakti is disturbed. This is the first polarization between god and his thought. At this stage, the polarization does not affect the essential oneness of god and his nature, Śakti, and God is still known as *para* Vāsudeva. At this moment, just before Śakti acts to create, the whole of creation (pure, mixed, and impure) appears simultaneously, perfect in every detail, like a flash of lightning, "/as God's thought/Śakti" (AS 5.3–5). Thus, the first polarization is a change of state in god's *jñāna* from the potential to the actual, to omniscience. Seen in terms of *vāc,* it is a change from *parā vāc,* the unmanifest form (also called *nāda*), to *paśyantī vāc,* the "seeing." Pāñcarātrins also call it *bindu* (drop, the first crystallization) and *sudarśana* (perfect sight). Though at this stage *śabda*/*vāc* is still a single integrated phenomenon, it contains the designations (*nāma*) of every referent (*artha*), every object in the universe. This ideal speech is imprinted on god's thought like a craftsman's blueprint of the ensuing creation. It is god's idea of what he is going to create; the way he "sees" it, as a modern creative artist might say.[8]

In the yogic tradition, there were four levels of awareness, moving from the gross through subtler awareness to transcendent unity: waking (*jāgrat*), dreaming sleep (*svapna*), dreamless sleep (*suṣupti*), and the fourth (*turīya*). Later, when discussing Pāñcarātra meditation, I shall show how these are made to correspond to the levels of reality in the *vyūha* theory. The *śabdabrahman* theory, too, posits four levels of increasing subtlety of speech/language/word: from the bottom, they are called *vaikharī, madhyamā, paśyantī,* and *parā.* Since there are four *vyūhas,* one might have expected that these four would simply correspond, and at one point the *Lakṣmī Tantra* (LT 24.8–11), which is not always consistent, indeed makes them correspond: *nāda* (which is another name for *parā vāc*) is Vāsudeva; *bindu* (=*paśyantī vāc*) is Saṃkarṣaṇa, *madhyamā* is Pradyumna, and *vaikharī* is Aniruddha. But this is not the usual Pāñcarātrin theory. The usual theory accepts the correspondence on the lower two levels, but higher up, things are more complicated because of the theology of the two forms of Vāsudeva. *Paśyantī vāc,* in fact, corresponds to everything from the first polarization between god (*para* Vāsudeva) and his *jñānaśakti* to Saṃkarṣaṇa.

How is this transition envisaged? Vāsudeva temporarily loses sight, as it were, of his Śakti, so that he wants to create; in a plenum there is no lack and can therefore be no desire. Thus god's *icchāśakti* is activated, and sets his *kriyāśakti* in motion. The temporary eclipse of his omniscience, as we have seen, is what brings about the first differentiation (*vyūha*), namely *vyūha* Vāsudeva. The resultant release of effective power, the prime movement of creation, has several names besides *kriyāśakti*: it is called *vibration* (*spanda*), *swinging* (*āndolana*), and *breathing* (*prāṇa*). These names highlight various figurative aspects of creation.[9]

As god recovers his omniscience and begins to create, he is known as Saṃkarṣaṇa. Saṃkarṣaṇa is the first state of diversity, the potential state of the diverse universe. At this stage, the causal unity of the creation is still held together, but traces of the diverse effects are there in a dormant condition. On the other hand, Saṃkarṣaṇa is the definitive manifestation of *paśyantī vāc.*

Vāc is figuratively represented by the fifty letters of the Sanskrit alphabet. The vowels are more essential than the consonants, because in utterance the consonants need vowels to stand on, so the vowels are created first. This group of fifty letters is termed *mātṛkā,* the matrix or source. It is a source in the sense that words cannot be formed without knowing it, but, as we have seen, it is also the cosmic matrix. In sum, *śabdabrahman* or *vāc* is in Pāñcarātra identical with god's Śakti, the divine personality hypostatized as the creatrix and indeed personified as Lakṣmī, Vāsudeva's wife.[10]

THE ONTOLOGY OF MANTRA

So far, I have not used the term *mantra* in my cosmogonic account; but its relation to *vāc,* etc., is about to appear. On the doctrinal basis that ideal speech appeared before the world of experience, creation is divided into two categories: the designating (*vācaka*) and the designated (*vācya*). Without knowing the former, one cannot experience the latter. This idea is not new to Pāñcarātra or to the other tantric sects which share it. Already, in the early *Upaniṣads,* the world is said to consist of names (*nāma*) and forms (*rūpa*). In systematic philosophy, this same relation becomes that between word (*śabda*) and referent (*artha*). In Pāñcarātra theology, as in all tantric theology, this relation is applied to mantras and their deities: a mantra designates a deity.

Deities have three forms (*mūrti*): as personifications (*devatāmūrti*); as symbolic diagrams (*yantramūrti*); and as sound (*mantramūrti*). The sonic form of a deity is a mantra. Empirically, a mantra is a formulaic utterance. As should by now be clear, it is the sonic form of the god which is primary, since the designating epistemologically and ontically precedes the designated. The power (*bala*) of the deity inheres in the first instance in the mantra form and attaches itself to the other two forms by derivation. The mantras are *vācaka,* the other two forms *vācya* (SS Introduction, p. 31). And Lakṣmī is the matrix of all mantras and, hence, of all gods.

The relation between language and its referent, as normally is understood, applies only on the grossest level, that of *vaikharī vāc.* In this final stage of its manifestation, speech/language is discerned as divided into syllables, words, and sentences, and its separation from its referents is complete. One level higher, *madhyamā vāc* possesses *saṃgati,* denotation, but in an ideal form; the language is not produced but is an impression on the mind (*saṃskāra*). Higher still, *bindu* conveys denotation, though the denoting and the denoted are not yet separated. At the highest level, *nāda, vāc* does not yet carry any denotation (*vācyatā*); there is no differentiation between the designator and the designated (LT 18.16ff.). This takes us back to the fact that the primal *vāc* is equated with God's primal thought, *saṃvid,* the single entity that evolves into both knowledge and the contents of knowledge. This is also Śakti as Lakṣmī, who thus again is the matrix of all words and all referents.[11]

We have now seen that the designated, *vācya,* corresponds to *bhūtiśakti* and the designating, *vācaka,* to *kriyāśakti.* In fact, Pāñcarātra schematizes the creation of the cosmos in six ways, called *adhvan.* These ways are grouped into three designating and three corresponding designated ways. *Śabda,* sound, designates the *adhvan* of *kalā,* the six glorious divine attributes. Mantra designates the *adhvan* of *tattva,* which normally means "cosmic categories" but in this context refers to the *vyūha*s. Pada, which here refers to the four states of consciousness of the meditator, from waking upwards, designates the *adhvan bhuvana,* the "worlds" of (the meditator's) experience. Lakṣmī declares that of these six, *śabda* and mantra are the most important (LT 22.13–19). Mantra is the salvific aspect of *śabda*.

THE GENERAL PLACE OF MANTRA IN PĀÑCARĀTRIN GNOSIS

In Pāñcarātra, salvation has two aspects. Though they are inextricably intertwined in the system, they can be analytically distinguished. On the one hand, salvation is gnosis, realization of one's unity with god. Historically, this is the older aspect. It is associated with yogic tradition. On this view, salvation is *achieved* by *meditation*. In explaining salvation, it is therefore natural to begin at the bottom, as the practitioner (*sādhaka*) must. On the other view, salvation is a state of blissful communion with god, an emotional experience. Historically, this view is associated with monotheism and, especially, with Vaiṣṇavism. Salvation is *granted* by god's grace, and the essential requirement is total emotional *surrender* (*prapatti*). In explaining salvation from this angle, it is necessary to begin at the top with theology, as I have been doing in this article.[12]

As I have briefly mentioned earlier, the combination of these two very disparate views of salvation means that, for the Pāñcarātrin, *prapatti* is not just passive; it must make itself effective by service to god, *upāsanā*. Though *upāsanā* is sometimes translated as meditation, it is much more than that, both because it has an emotional or, better, devotional aspect and because it is necessarily associated with ritual action. I shall return later to the ritual practice associated with mantra *upāsanā*. But, first, I must finish clearing the way to a theoretical understanding of what is going on.

First, let me briefly take the worm's eye view of the meditator. He is to take four steps (*pada*) of increasing awareness, moving up from gross diversity to transcendental unity. As in all schools of yoga, the four steps are termed *waking, dreaming, deep sleep,* and *"the fourth."* In Pāñcarātra, these correspond to the four *vyūhas*. Thus, "the fourth" corresponds to *vyūha* Vāsudeva. To *para,* Vāsudeva corresponds a further stage called *beyond the fourth* (*turyātīta*); this stage is fusion in *para* Vāsudeva. The *sādhaka* meditates on god in his sonic, mantra form. He begins with the mantra of Aniruddha. As Aniruddha is the world on the gross level, he represents the totality of the contents of one's awareness of the diverse universe. The meditator merges himself in that mantra until he has realized his identity with it, in other words with god at the lowest level, that of mundane phenomena. The process is then to be repeated at successively higher levels. Thus, the *sādhaka* moves towards the primal unity of the content of his awareness and the awareness itself.[13] This move from diversity to unity is also understood in terms of *vāc/śabda,* for awareness is identified with the designating (*vācaka*) sound and, thus, relates to its contents as the designated (*vācya*).

The *sādhaka*, thus, aims step by step to reverse the process of creation and return to the primal unity. When Saṃkarṣaṇa, Pradyumna, and Aniruddha stand for these mystical stages of yogic experience, they are known respectively as Acyuta, Satya, and Puruṣa.[14] In Pāñcarātra doctrine, these names designate the three *vyūha* gods as merely potential effects dormant in their source and locus, Vāsudeva. The *sādhaka*'s progress thus reabsorbs effects into their causes. The mantras, the sonic forms of the gods, give the *sādhaka* the mental support (*mānasālambana*) that he needs to achieve this: They are what he has to concentrate on (LT 22.16–20). The pure creation, taken as a whole, is god's embodied grace, his *anugrahamūrti*. Since effects are reabsorbed into their causes, it is equated with Vāsudeva, both in his *para* and *vyūha* forms; he comprises Acyuta, Satya, and Puruṣa. Vāsudeva is signified by his "single-formed" (*ekamūrti*) mantra (SS 2.71–72; 5.68). Of course, this is no different from Śakti/Lakṣmī; she too is god's *anugrahamūrti*. With talk of God as the saviour, I return once more to the bird's eye view of salvation.

GOD'S SAVING GRACE IN HIS FOUR EMANATIONS

A Pāñcarātrin sees god as the almighty lord who, with the aid of his intrinsic energy, has fashioned individuals (*jīva*) from his own self, but he has made them limited in every sense. While god is omnipresent, the *jīva* is of limited dimensions (*aṇu*); while he is omnipotent, the *jīva* is limited in action by the predetermined cosmic law of *karman* (*niyati*); while he is omniscient, the *jīva* has only very limited knowledge. These limitations involve the individual in a perpetually transient and changing existence, *saṃsāra*. The one aim of a Pāñcarātrin is to get free of this involvement. Freedom is achieved when he attains a clear understanding of his own essential nature, of god's nature, and of the nature of the world of experience, an understanding that amounts to grasping that the three are essentially identical. But, he can achieve this understanding only through divine intervention.[15] The sovereign God may interrupt the operation of his cosmic laws and suspend *tirodhāna*/*māyā* for his devotee. This divine grace is available only to the devotee who has totally surrendered himself to god's mercy (*prapanna*) and proved his devotion by incessantly and ardently performing god's service (*upāsanā*), following the path of monotheism (*aikāntika mārga*).

God is so merciful that he takes measures for the salvation of souls even as he effects the creation. The three primal divine emanations (Saṃkarṣaṇa, Pradyumna, and Aniruddha) are endowed with salvific functions. The late commentary on the *Sāttvata Saṃhitā* by Alasiṃha Bhaṭṭa gives a coherent account of these three *vyūha* gods in the Pāñcarātra scheme of salvation (see the commentary on the SS, Chapter 5).

Saṃkarṣaṇa, as the divine knowledge and indomitable energy (*jñāna* and *bala*), is the embodiment of the Pāñcarātra scriptures (mantra-*śāstra*) and its religious discipline; in other words, of *śāstra* and *sādhanā*. Pradyumna, the divine sovereignty and heroic power, incorporates the knowledge and wisdom derived from the *śāstra*. He is the intelligence (*buddhi*) of Saṃkarṣaṇa (LT 6.9). He illuminates the significance of the *śāstra* and, in particular, reveals to the *sādhaka* the underlying meaning of a mantra (AS 5.21; LT 23.2). To make a mantra work its effect, a *sādhaka* must realize its meaning; Pradyumna through his infinite grace provides this essential insight (AS 5.22–23).

The last *vyūha*, Aniruddha, is in a sense the most important, for he makes the *sādhaka*'s goal (*sādhya*) available to him. In Pāñcarātra, *bhakti* is a two-way emotional transaction, a sharing of feeling with god. God, the object of adoration, has to be in direct contact with his devotee. In his transcendent form as Vāsudeva, god is beyond the empirical world of the senses. Aniruddha embodies the divine energy and resplendence (*śakti* and *tejas*) and is said to be the divine ego (*ahaṃkāra*) within the world of the senses. His is the form in which the devotee envisages his god. In other words, Aniruddha represents all the forms (such as images) in which the devotee finds god accessible (*sulabha*) to his senses. Thus, it is through Aniruddha, that god grants his devotee attainment of the goal of his *sādhanā*, direct experience of his presence (AS 5.23–25; LT 3.58–60; 6.6–12).

PĀÑCARĀTRIN PRACTICE AND ITS GOALS

Practice (*sādhanā*) consists in service (*upāsanā*) of god, aiming to please him. This, in turn, has two compnents: meditation and ritual. In Pāñcarātra, as in other tantric sects, these two are never dissociated but always are practiced together. In this sect, meditation is called *the internal sacrifice* (*antaryāga*) and ritual *the external sacrifice* (*bahiryāga*). The early scriptures say that the internal sacrifice is the more important; in this they reflect the yogic tradition. Over the centuries, however, this tradition faded and the emphasis on meditation was gradually lost.

So far, I have spoken of liberation as the one goal of the Pāñcarātra *sādhaka*. This is not untrue to the spirit of the early texts. All tantric practice is said to have the two goals of *mukti* and *bhukti*, liberation and enjoyment (won by the use of power). However, the Pāñcarātrin scriptures appear uneasy with *bhukti*; they admit it into the scheme of things but piously interpret it as instrumental to bringing about release. It does this by making the *sādhaka* satiated with material prosperity; his disgust with the pleasures of the senses leads to detachment and, by this route, to a profound and lasting surrender to god. Thus Pāñcarātra groups the mantras and their gods under two heads. The higher class leads to *mukti*; the lower ones have more limited aims and effects, leading variously to prosperity, to physical safety, and to a spiritual purification which makes their practitioner worthy of the higher kind (LT 22.3; SS 1.26–27).

CLASSIFICATION OF MANTRAS

The alert reader may have noticed that, so far, I have referred specifically only to the mantras of *vyūha* gods and said nothing of the mantras of *vibhava* gods. Though there are exceptions, one can broadly say that the higher class of mantras mentioned in the previous paragraph are those of the *vyūha* gods, the lower class those of the *vibhava* gods. In other words, it is usually the *vyūha* gods who are meditated on for *mukti*, the *vibhava* gods for *bhukti* or as a preliminary stage before entering on the practice which aims at full realization.

As the *Lakṣmī Tantra* says, all mantras are addressed to Śakti, but only those who understand Śakti as the cosmic creative force, *kriyāśakti*, realize this fact. Those less understanding receive from their gurus mantras to suit their level of ability, mantras ostensibly addressed to other deities. Only the advanced are straightaway given Śakti mantras (LT 18.46).

Mantras are classified as higher or lower according to their place in the pure creation. We have seen that there are three categories hierarchically ordered: *para, vyūha,* and *vibhava. Vyūha* and *vibhava* can be subdivided. Each *vyūha* deity represents a comprehensiveness (*vyāpakatā*), which becomes fragmented into various aspects. Each aspect is represented by a sub-*vyūha* deity (*vyūhāntara-devatā*); there are twelve of these, three to each *vyūha*. The *vibhava* deities, who are grosser and more limited, are divided into such groups as the ten *avatāra*s of Viṣṇu. As a *vyūha* deity can stand for all his *vyūhāntaras,* the *viśākha-yūpa* can stand for the mantras of all the *vibhava* deities.

Mantras can also be classified by their power, as explained earlier. The *vibhava* mantras bestow *bhukti.* The *vyūha* and *vyūhāntara* mantras are primarily for *mukti,* though they also give *bhukti* as a by product. Vāsudeva's mantra, the *para* mantra, leads to *mukti* alone (SS 19.179; see also the commentary).

A third way of classing the mantras is by the stage of sonic manifestation to which they belong. This classification, however, applies only to seed mantras (see next section). Thus OṂ is a *prakṛti* mantra; in this context *prakṛti* means "source." Other seed mantras are said, at the same time, to be the evolving source and the evolved effect (*prakṛti-vikṛti*). The third and lowest category consists of mantras belonging to the gross world (*vikṛti*) (LT 18.47–51; 24.48; 41.33).

It will be readily apparent that these three modes of classification are merely alternative ways of articulating the same hierarchy. The *sādhaka* graduates from grosser to subtler and more powerful mantras as he progresses intellectually and spiritually, until his guru initiates him into the highest, the *para,* mantra.

ANALYSIS OF THE MANTRA

Any mantra which a *sādhaka* receives from his guru can be analyzed into two or into four parts.

Its two parts are the seed mantra (*bīja mantra*) and the *pada mantra*. The seed is said to be its soul and the rest its body. Unlike the souls of individuals, the souls of mantras are neither influenced by māyā nor limited by time and space (SS 9.20–30).

Its four parts are *bīja, pinda, saṃjñā,* and *pada*. These are said to correspond to the four steps (*pada*) of the soul (waking, etc.) (LT 21.11). A *bīja* is a monosyllabic sound. It may contain one vowel or more (as in a diphthong) or one or more consonants plus a vowel and always ends with the pure nasal sound, called *bindu* (SS 9.20–21; LT 21.12). A *piṇḍa* (mass) is a cluster of consonants, often connected with vowels, inserted between the *bīja* and the body of the mantra (cf. the Śaiva/Śākta *kūṭa*-mantra). The *saṃjñā*-mantra is the reverent address to the diety, who is in the dative, with some such word as *namas*; it is preceded by OṂ. A *pada*-mantra is a complete sentence expressing a prayer and praise of its deity (LT 21.13–14). It seems that the last two parts can overlap.

A complete mantra, which a guru imparts to a *sādhaka* with solemn ceremony, must have all four parts. It is called the *sādhaka*'s *mūla*-mantra or *iṣṭa*-mantra while it is the focus of his practice. He conjures up a visual image of the mantra's deity by analyzing his mantra and applying its parts to the parts of the visualized deity. This leads us, at last, to practice.[16]

THE GURU

Practice begins, at every stage, with initiation by a guru. The guru is the point where the bird's eye view and the worm's eye view of salvation meet, for he is the living incarnation of god's grace and the point where any devotee first makes direct contact with the divine. The guru is god incarnate. The *Lakṣmī Tantra* (13.34) asserts that a guru, irrespective of his sect or creed, is a manifestation of Śakti's aspect as savior. He is like a doctor who knows the exact treatment for his disciple's ailment, the bondage of *saṃsāra*. He holds the key to the mysteries of the scriptures; he is the repository of the secret lore of the mantras and their applications in ritual and meditation. For he is in the pupillary tradition of the sect and, as such, knows the esoteric tradition which is only orally transmitted. The aspirant, therefore, must be initiated into the sect before he can be entrusted with this secret knowledge. The guru is a successful *sādhaka*, a *siddha*, who has attained union with god's loving personality by identifying himself with Śakti by means of his mantra and its power. Since Śakti is the essence of all mantras, he can now handle any mantra.

IDENTIFICATION WITH ONE'S MANTRA

Pāñcarātra *sādhanā* is the path of mantra (mantra-*mārga*); the *Lakṣmī Tantra* says that a person who desires salvation must always practice *upāsanā* of Śakti's mantra-body (*mantramayī tanu*). He must regard his mantra as personified, with a body (*kṣetra*) and a soul (*kṣetrajña*). All the theology, philosophy, and liturgy he learns from his guru, he is to apply to his mantra and its relation to his goal, salvation (LT 17.50; 18.2–8). He can only follow the prescribed *upāsanā* of his mantra when he has ritually and intellectually identified himself with it; as Pāñcarātra scriptures put it, he must identify his ego with the mantra's ego (JS 11.41–42; SS 17.36); that is to say, its body and soul. He must understand all the different aspects of his mantra and how it relates to god and himself. Though he may glean some idea of these matters from texts, friends, or general gossip, only direct instruction by a guru can provide even the most erudite aspirant with understanding and experience of the mantra's palpable divine personality.

The guru teaches his pupil the ideology by concretizing the concepts in ritual and even by making him act them out. Thus, abstractions become real for him. To enable the novice to understand how god is personally present in the mantra and how to identify with it, the guru analyzes its component parts in terms of the human anatomy.

CULLING THE MANTRA

At the very beginning of his *sādhanā,* the *sādhaka* participates in two ritual acts, called *mantroddhāra* and *nyāsa*. The character of mantra as god is made explicit in the rite of *mantroddhāra;* its character as the means to salvation is dramatized in the rite of *nyāsa*. The *sādhaka* must master the techniques of both, for every *upāsanā* begins with them.

The word *uddhāra* means extraction, culling. Before being used in the rites, each mantra must be ritually made manifest from its sonic source, the *mātṛkā*. When the aspirant is initiated and first receives his mantra, the rite of culling it is performed by his guru. On all subsequent occasions, he performs it himself (cf. LT 23.5–12; 24.48; 41.33).

On a clean and ritually purified platform, the *sādhaka* draws a *maṇḍala,* a cosmogram of lotus or wheel design, with its petals or spokes pointing in the eight directions and its center encircled by a pericarp or hub. If the mantra refers to a female deity, the lotus design is used; otherwise the wheel design (LT 23.I2). "OṂ", the supreme mantra representing sabda-brahman (see later), is inscribed on the center. The sixteen vowels of the Sanskrit alphabets are arranged on the pericarp or hub; the consonants are arranged on the petals or spokes; the last nine letters, *m–h,* are distributed on the inner side of the circumference and the composite-letter *kṣa* is written outside it. The guru worships this diagram and demonstrates how to envisage it as the manifest *śab-*

dabrahman in its seminal state of *nāda*. The *sādhaka* learns to imagine *nāda* as a luminous entity existing inside his heart, which he imagines to be inside two lotuses. The luminosity symbolizes its nature as potential knowledge. This brilliant *nāda* is visualized as constantly pouring out the vibrating *mātṛkā*, the potential *vāc* (SS 2.67–68; LT 20.9).

OṂ represents this *nāda* form of *śabdabrahman* before it is disseminated over the cosmos. Each letter of the *mātṛkā* is in its own right a mantra with a distinct personality. One has to add the pure nasal to it in order to indicate that it is a mantra, because the pure nasal, which is called *bindu*, indicates Śakti in her first crystallized (*paśyantī*) form and is the mantra's soul and its energy (*bala*). Each letter has one or more proper names and a fixed position in the cosmic pattern. Both the name and the position show the specific aspect of Śakti which is revealed in the letter. The guru divulges the secret nature of the letters to his pupil before he starts drawing the diagram of the *mātṛkā*, so that when he comes to teach him how to extract his mantra he knows the designation and significance of its letters and its position in the total scheme of the pure creation (*śuddha sarga*). By extracting his mantra letter by letter from the body of the *mātṛkā* (vāc, visualized as Lakṣmī, whose body is entirely made of the Sanskrit alphabet, LT 23.13–29), the *sādhaka* enacts a birth of the mantra from its source. This strengthens his conviction that his mantra is a part of the totality of the sonic emanation of Śakti, namely *nāda*.

As an example, one can take the mantra OṂ. It is made of the letters *a* + *u* + *m* + *bindu*. The *sādhaka* first extracts *a*, designated Aniruddha, the pervasive one, the primal one within the realm of the world of senses, etc. Next, he extracts and adds to *a* the letter *u*, designated Pradyumna, the irresistible, etc. Then, he extracts *m* and adds it to the former two. *M* stands for Saṃkarṣaṇa, the time that exists just before and after the advent of the differentiated world. To this sound cluster OM is added *bindu*, the pure nasal, which is the seminal Śakti immanent in all created entities. But, the mantra OṂ also contains the pure sound vibration or resonace (*nāda*) symbolized by the sign of the half-moon (*ardhacandra*). Thus, the mantra OṂ contains all the cosmic stages of creation from the undifferentiated to the differentiated but here the movement is reversed. It shows that state of the emanating Śakti in which all the differentiated world exists in a potential state; namely, *śabdabrahman*.

OṂ is the supreme mantra because it represents the supreme emanation of the divine Śakti. Through it, the *sādhaka* identifies himself with Śakti as the undifferentiated manifest sound, *nāda*, which represents god still at the differentiated pole of his transcendent being. But the meditation on OṂ should lead the *sādhaka* to a state of consciousness in which his mind is merged in the mantra until it stops being aware of the sound of resonance; it reaches "the end of the resonance" (*nādānta*). This indicates the state of primal unity and ineffability. In this state, all dichotomy of the divine and his essential nature, Śakti, is totally submerged in a single luminous unit, supreme *Brahman* (*jyotis tat param brahma*). This is the supreme presence of Viṣṇu (*vaiṣṇavaṃ dhāman*), the goal of the *sādhaka*'s *sādhanā* (LT 24.11–12).

Every initiate is to perform these and the following spiritual exercises in imagination. But to imagine something still is not to realize it fully. The difference between the *sādhaka* and the *siddha* consists just in this: The *sādhaka* is still rehearsing what it would be like to realize these identifications; while, for the *siddha,* they are real.

OṂ is seen here as a combination of 3 + 1, the totality, and is used in a series of equations. Its three letters are equated with all basic groups of three: the three basic vowels (*a, i, u,* the first Śiva-sūtra of Pāṇini's grammar); the three Vedas; the three varṇas (*brāhmaṇa,* etc.); the three constituents (*guṇa*) of primal matter (*sattva, rajas,* and *tamas*); the three luminaries (fire, sun, and moon); the three cosmic gods (Brahmā, Viṣṇu, Rudra); the three worlds. All these series are equated to the three manifest *vyūha* gods. These, then, are added to the fourth, the all combining entity signified by the pure nasal and resonance, the two states of Vāsudeva. Vāsudeva, as we have seen, is Sáakti in her two states; namely, the transcendent and the immanent (LT 24.19–20). The idea of considering the world of diversity as a multiplication of the basic three is not peculiar to Pāñcarātra; like many of its other concepts, it comes from the Upaniṣads (cf. ChU 6.4–6).

The *sādhaka* visualizes himself as extracting the mantra from the mātṛkā diagram before him, concentrating on it as the sonic form of Śakti. This process of visualization applies to the acquisition of all mantras, from OṂ down to the mantras of most limited power, like the common spells. For even they are conducive to the final goal of *mukti,* because they are used as the lower rungs of a spiritual ladder to the transcendent realm of OṂ, which together with its four *pada* mantras forms the last five rungs of that ladder (LT 28.74). The choice of this mantra as the basic as well as the most comprehensive one (LT 28.72) shows the Pāñcarātra leaning to Vedic orthodoxy. The Upaniṣads already regarded OṂ as the essence of the Vedas, the mantra par excellence (ChU 1.1.1ff.; for details, see Padoux 1978a).

PHYSICAL APPLICATION OF THE MANTRA

The next step in Pāñcarātra *upāsanā* is *nyāsa,* again a universal tantric rite. After extracting his mantra from the diagram of *mātṛkā,* the *sādhaka* proceeds to place or deposit (*nyāsa*) it on his psychophysical person. As mentioned earlier, the mantra has a form similar to human anatomy. It is divided into six main limbs (*aṅga*) and six secondary limbs (*upāṅga*). The first group consists of the heart, head, top-knot (*śikhā*), armour/trunk (*kavaca*), eyes, and the weapon/power (*astra*). The second group corresponds to the navel, back, arms, thighs, knees, and feet. For instance, the six angas of OṂ are *ā, ī, ū, ṝ, ai,* and *au;* and the *upāṅgas* are *jñāna, aiśvarya, śakti, bala, vīrya,* and *tejas,* the six divine attributes (*kalā*). Step by step, the *sādhaka* deposits the *aṅgas* and *upāṅgas* of his mantra on his own corresponding physical parts by touching them while saying what he is doing. First, he names the mantra, then the appropriate seed mantra, then the relevant *aṅga* in the dative and the word of salute such as *namas* or *svāhā.* The terms of salutation are called *jāti mantras.* He thus acknowledges the deification of that part of his own anatomy. In this way, in vivid concentration, he replaces his mundane body with the body of his mantra. In his imagination, he becomes consubstantial with his god (Padoux 1980).

A corollary and necessary coda to this mental and ritual act of *nyāsa* is the rite of purifying one's soul (*ātma-śuddhi*). The mantra is divided into its constituent sounds; each of these is then identified with Śakti's consecutive steps in the cosmic process of creation. Thereafter, the *sādhaka* identifies his own soul (*ātman*) with the grossest manifestation of the cosmic hierarchy. He, then, sets about dissolving effect back into cause. We continue to take OṂ as our example. He identifies himself with Aniruddha (*a*), Śakti's grossest *vyūha* form. This, he then dissolves into Pradyumna (*u*) and rises from the gross to the subtle state. This, he then imagines to merge in Saṃkarṣaṇa (*m*), and he rises to a subtler and more seminal state in the process of creation. Finally, this state, too, he imagines to be dissolved into *bindu* (*ṃ*). At this stage, the *sādhaka*'s journey in imagination towards his soul's source and essence comes to a point at which he automatically passes from *bindu* to *nāda* and becomes merged in the essential and primal unity of god and his Śakti. As said earlier, the first four steps correspond to the older theory of the four states or steps (*pada*) of the individual soul's spiritual flight to its original unity with the supreme soul, the only reality, *Brahman.* To these four steps is then added in Pāñcarātra (and in other tantric sects) a fifth step, which brings the *sādhaka*'s soul to the divine presence. Having thus reached his ultimate source, the *sādhaka* then starts retracing these steps, thereby, in imagination regenerating himself, now divine in body and soul and identical with OṂ, the divine sonic emanation. In this way, the *sādhaka* conforms to the general tantric rule that, before starting to worship a deity, one must oneself become deified (*nādevo bhūtvā devaṃ yajet*).

REALIZATION

At the time of initiation, the guru performs these two rites first on himself and then on the disciple, teaching him the steps as he goes along.[17] After his initiation, the novice has learned the nature and function of his mantra and the rites connected with it. He retires to some holy and quiet place and starts his daily religious practice, the *upāsanā* of his mantra, which always culminates in a long meditation on the mantra. He withdraws his senses from external phenomena and contemplates the mantra by mentally repeating it (*japa*) a great many times. He determines the number of repetitions in advance. With acts of worship and with meditation, he fulfils the two basic requirements of a Pāñcarātrin. He intensifies his passionate devotion for and trust in god with his worship (*pūjā/yāga*); he sharpens his awareness to a razor's edge and finally achieves gnosis. When that happens his experience of his mantra's true nature becomes real and the identity with it which he imagined during the practice is realized. He becomes the possessor of the power (śakti) of his mantra. All his religious practice prior to this is technically known as *puraścaraṇa* (acts performed previously), i.e., before acquiring the mantra's power. The goal which was in front of the practitioner is now an accomplished fact (*siddha*) and he is henceforth designated a *siddha*.

In keeping with the spirit of passionate devotion and total self-surrender, the Pāñcarātrin equates the power he has derived from his mantra with god's grace. By acknowledging Śakti as divine grace, he professes his humility and dependence on god.

PĀÑCARĀTRA AND VEDIC ORTHODOXY

How does a Pāñcarātrin locate his mantra-*śāstra* in the religious tradition? The Pāñcarātra literature as a whole reveals a pronounced leaning to Vedic orthodoxy,[17] which provided mediaeval Indian literature with a comic motif.

Pāñcarātrins considered their scriptures a continuation of the Vedas. The scriptural corpus mainly consists of mantras and exegesis of the ritual in which mantras are used. For the grammarians and the Mīmāṃsakas, who evolved the theory of *Śabdabrahman,* the Vedic corpus was the *Śabda* par excellence. The Pāñcarātrins took over not only the concept of *Śabdabrahman* but also the view that the supreme authority, the mantra-*śāstra* par excellence, was the Vedic scriptures. They considered the Vedas the primary manifestation of god's *śabda-śakti,* which is the same as *Śabdabrahman* (SS 2.67). This manifestation is coordinate to Saṃkarṣaṇa, the emanation of Vāsudeva's absolute knowledge (*jñāna*) and unimpeded power to act (*bala*) (LT 2.29). Thus, Pāñcarātrin agree with the general Hindu tradition that the Vedas are a spontaneous revelation of the creator's omniscience and that the creation ensued according to their instructions. Hence, to legitimize their own scriptures, Pāñcarātrins claim that they have evolved directly from the Vedas and are equally valid as revealed knowledge (SS 2.5; VS 8.6). Vāsudeva revealed this mantra-*śāstra* to Saṃkarṣaṇa to supply sinning creatures with a means of salvation. But, these scriptures can be taught effectively only to an initiated Pāñcarātrin. Just as one has to undergo Vedic initiation to perform Vedic rituals, so also one must undergo Pāñcarātra initiation to perform Pāñcarātra *upāsanā* (SpS 16.20). The main purpose of such statements is to align Pāñcarātra *mantra-śastra* with the Vedas. We see a series of equations and analogies.

1. Para Vāsudeva is Para Brahman;
2. Parā Śakti is *Śabdabrahman;*
3. Pāñcarātra initiation is analogous to Vedic initiation;
4. Pāñcarātra *mantra-śastra* is analogous to the Vedas;
5. Pāñcarātra *upāsanā* is analogous to Vedic sacrifice.

The term *upāsanā* is replaced by the traditional term for sacrifice, *yāga*. For actual sacrifice Pāñcarātra retains the word *homa*.

Moreover, besides adopting a great many other Vedic mantras for their rituals, often taken out of their Vedic context, Pāñcarātra took over two Vedic hymns, the *Puruṣa sūkta* (ṚV 10.90) and the *Śrī sūkta* (ṚgVKh 5.87), as well as the Vedic OṂ (*praṇava*). The LT asserts that the most important mantra for worshipping Nārāyaṇa is the *Puruṣa sūkta*. God is offered eighteen items in the worship; each item is offered while uttering one stanza from that hymn. We have already seen how OṂ is taken to be the supreme seed mantra of Vāsudeva. It is interesting to see that the LT mentions the four most important Vaiṣṇava mantras (*"Oṃ namo Nārāyaṇāya"*; *"Oṃ namo Viṣṇave"*; *"Oṃ namo bhagavate Vāsudevāya"*; and the long mantra *"Oṃ jitaṃ te puṇḍarīkākṣa namas te Viśvabhāvane namas te 'stu Hṛṣīkeśa mahāpuruṣa pūrvaja"*) as *pada* mantras; that is, subordinate to OṂ. This tendency to synthesis is also evident when the same text adopts the *Śrī sūkta* for the worship of Lakṣmī, the highest Śakti. It is better to quote the text in translation. Keeping in mind the Vedic stanza *"tad viṣṇor paramaṃ padam, sadā paśyanti sūrayaḥ divīva cakṣusātamam"* (ṚV 1.22.20) Lakṣmī states

> both of us [Lakṣmī and Nārāyaṇa] are seated in the supreme expanse of the void (*parame vyomni*) for the purpose of bringing happiness to all souls; the two of us masters served by the sages. Once there arose in our heart the intention to find some means for the deliverance of living beings. The great ocean śabdabrahman is the energy which arose from us. Then two nectarlike hymns emerged from churning that [ocean]; the hymn of Hari, the Person, and similarly the hymn of myself [the *Śrī sūkta*]. Each of them are related to the śakti of the other, being furnished with each other's sound. The hymn of unmanifested Person [i.e., para Vāsudeva, cf. SS 1.25] has Nārāyaṇa as its seer. The other, which is called *Śrī sūkta*, has me as the seer. The five [other] mantras starting with the *praṇava*, have been already revealed to you. (LT 36.69–75)

These clear statements that Pāñcarātra mantras are subordinate to the Vedic mantras explain how Pāñcarātra views its relation to Vedic orthodoxy.[18]

Moreover, for its philosophy, Pāñcaratra mainly depends on the Upaniṣads. Again the texts clearly say so. The SS calls Pāñcarātra *mantraśastra* the *Brahmopaniṣad* (SS 2.5) and its followers the worshippers of "sadbrahman who is called Vāsudeva" (SS 2.4). The Upaniṣadic doctrine makes *puruṣa Brahman,* which is unique and exclusive, and places it above matter in the scheme of creative process. Theistic Pāñcarātra identifies *Brahman* with their supreme Nārāyaṇa but reconciles their concept of him as a personal god with the immutability and exclusiveness of Brahman by grafting on to the Brahman doctrine the concept of divine energy, Śakti.[19] We have already noticed how, in other points, too, Pāñcarātra syncretizes with Vedic concepts.

The same motivation leads the SS to place the yogin, the practitioner of Pātañjala Yoga, above the non-yogin; i.e. a nonrenouncer Pāñcarātrin. Again, driven by *Brahmanical* othodoxy, the SS allows only the *brāhmaṇa* initiate to worship the *vyūha* gods with their mantras. Others (the *kṣatriya, vaisya* and *sūdra*) are not initiated in the *vyūha* mantras. But, if they are totally self-surrendering devotees, they may worship the *vyūha* gods without their mantras.

It was this orthodoxy which earned them a lot of ridicule. Jayanta Bhatta in his play, the Āgamaḍambara or Sanmatanāṭaka, makes a Vedic sacrificer complain that the Pāñcarātrins have adopted the social behavior of *brahmanas.* They even, complains the Vedic priest, recite their Pāñcarātra texts exactly as the Vedic texts are recited. Moreover, from the moment they are born they claim that they are *brahmanas* and belong to the most orthodox segment of society (Raghavan & Thakur 1964).

The most beneficial effect of this tendency was the sect's decision to reform itself by appointing very learned and prestigious orthodox *brahmana* scholars as their supreme religious teachers. The first of them was Nāthamuṇi, the second Yāmuna, and the third and most renowned, Rāmānuja. All three came from outside the Pāñcarātra sect; but they provided what Pāñcarātrins wanted very much to attain, a generally recognized system of orthodox philosophy to support their theology. This system is called the *Viśiṣṭādvaitavāda,* the doctrine of qualified monism.

CONCLUSION

The Pāñcarātrin view of the nature and functions of mantra is rooted in the common tantric heritage; its use of mantra at first sight seems almost the same as that in the practice of other tantric sects. In the ideology of all Hindu tantrics, mantra embodied god's sovereign power and wisdom; and this view was preserved with little change in the Śaiva and Śākta systems. In Vaiṣṇava tantra, however, an early difference in emphasis led in time to a very different religious orientation.

We may not know all the factors that made Vaiṣṇavism acquire its distinctive character, but that character had two main resultant features: social conservatism and extreme devotionalism.

The social conservatism is closely connected to the Vaiṣṇava vision of god. For them, god, as the creator and sustainer of the cosmos, is by the same token the creator and maintainer of universal law and order, which includes the caste system. It is already clear in the *Mahābhārata* that the Vaiṣṇava God is no detached, indifferent yogin but deeply involved in human affairs.[20] The theory of the *avatāra* is a natural outcome of this ideal: God is so involved with the fate of men that he descends among them to restore balance and harmony to the world. This vision of god made Vaiṣṇavas tend to accept Vedic orthodoxy and to respect its moral and social rules. They adapted the esoteric doctrines of the Upaniṣads, with their emphasis on world renunciation in pursuit of perfect gnosis, to lives lived in the world in conformity to social norms. Renunciation became a matter of inner attitude rather than external forms. At the same time, yogins were treated with reverence.

Vaiṣṇava devotionalism, too, is connected with the theory of the *avatāra*. A corollary of passionate love for god and trust in his protecting care is that there should be personal contact between god and devotee. This view of salvation through emotion is, as we have seen, very different from early tantric soteriology. To reconcile their emotional *bhakti* with the doctrine of the power of mantras, the Pāñcarātrins radically changed the concept of that power: It is just god's grace. All mantras are manifestations of god in his pristine glory as saviour. God decides to make himself available to his devotee in a form he can understand and approach. God's thus presenting himself in forms suited to the needs of each individual represents His accessibility (*saulabhya*) (Carman 1974, 173–75). Mantras are god's forms assumed out of grace, embodiments of that grace (*anugraha-mūrti*). The *sādhaka* identifies himself with his mantra in love and trust, as he knows it to be a form of god's presence.

The Pāñcarātrin scriptural corpus was composed over several centuries, spanning the second half of the first millennium A.D., or even somewhat longer. In that period, the concept of *bhakti* developed considerably. In the earlier texts, we find the synthesis between the tantric gnostic soteriology, Vedic orthopraxy, and Vaiṣṇava *bhakti,* which I outlined in these pages. But, later, the encounter with the more intensely emotional *bhakti* of the South led Vaiṣṇavas, including Pāñcarātrins, to adopt a neo-*bhakti,* which they called *prapatti-bhakti.* To the earlier threefold path to salvation, *karman* (praxis), *jñāna* (gnosis) and *bhakti, prapatti* is added as a fourth, distinct path. In this path of total self-surrender, two mantras together assumed paramount importance. Known as *the pair* (*dvayam*), they express total reliance on Nārāyaṇa and his consort Śrī, another name for Lakṣmī. With this formulation, the Pāñcarātra attitude to mantra reaches its devotional culmination.[21]

We do not know the date of this final development, but it is probably later than the *Lakṣmī Tantra,* a text (itself of uncertain date) which seems to stand at about the point when the earlier synthesis of *bhakti* and gnosis were being tilted towards extreme devotionalism. The *Lakṣmī Tantra* defines mantra as follows:

> māṃ trāyate 'yam ity evaṃ yogeṇa svīkṛto dhvaniḥ
> guptāśayaḥ sadā yaś ca mantrajñaṃ trāyate bhayāt
> sa mantraḥ saṃsmṛto 'haṃtāvikāśaḥ śabdajaiḥ kramaiḥ
> pūrṇāhaṃtāsamudbhūtaiḥ śuddhabodhānvayo yataḥ.

> (A mantra is known as the sonic phenomenon which always saves an adept of mantra, who through yogic practice has totally understood its secret purport and so is convinced "It will save me." It is a sonic manifestation of the divine personality/essence, emanating from the complete divine personality, and thus is identified with pure consciousness/knowledge.) (LT 18.44–45)

The first part of this definition puts the mantra on a par with the saviour god. The second part reveals its efficacy to bring about pure knowledge or consciousness, for it is a link between the *sādhaka,* an individual with limited knowledge, and the divine, pure gnosis. What one misses here is any mention of the power which when acquired, puts the *sādhaka* on a par with his god. That idea is indeed conspicuous by its absence. The *sādhaka* seeks not for power but for god's favor in acknowledging the *sādhaka*'s yearning for him and granting the final union.

Śakti is the mediator,[22] whether in her form as a mantra or as god's wife. Her mediating role is illustrated in a charming myth current among the Śrī Vaiṣṇavas, the sect which developed out of Pāñcarātra and was systematized by Rāmānuja. It narrates the sins and atrocities committed by a demon called *Kāka* (crow), who lusted after Lakṣmī, wife of the supreme god Vāsudeva, and harassed her. Vāsudeva's anger fell on him in the form of a discus, the divine weapon and symbol of indomitable power. To flee this terrible weapon, the demon sped through the three worlds, but it followed him, ever in hot pursuit. Finally, the wretched sinner fled back to Lakṣmī, who was seated at the side of Vāsudeva, and took refuge at her feet. In compassion, the goddess looked at Vāsudeva, imploring him with her lovely eyes. Moved, the god at the last moment checked his weapon and saved the sinner from destruction.[23]

Whether it reveals god's true nature or secures his mercy (as was increasingly emphasized), for Pāñcarātrins, mantra is the link between the devotee and his god. God created his sonic manifestations to save his creatures.[24]

NOTES

1. LT 2.26–34; for an explanation of the term *bhaga* see Viṣṇu Purāṇa 6.5.74. Although the number of the divine attributes is usually six, the name of an attribute may vary in different texts; also c.f. Ahirbudhnya Saṃhitā (AS) 2.28, "He is praised as bhagavān because he possesses six attributes. He is called Vāsudeva because he is the locus of all creation."

2. AS 2.56–61; LT 2.26, *"śeṣam aiśvaryavīryādi jñāna dharmasanātanaḥ"* (the rest [of the divine attributes like] *aiśvarya, vīrya* etc. are the eternal attributes of *jñāna*).

3. LT 3.1, *"ahaṃ nārāyaṇī nāma sā sattā vaiṣṇavī parā"* (I am indeed Nārāyaṇī [i.e. Lakṣmī] the supreme essence of Viṣṇu).

4. LT 29.6–9; AS 3.27–33 and 39. These two śaktis are also called *soma* and *sūrya* śaktis, respectively.

5. LT 12.13–20; here *avidyā* and *māyā* are used synonymously. The act of *tirodhāna* produces a sheath of nonknowledge encapsulating the beings. This sheath is called *māyā koṣa* (the sheath of *māyā*).

6. LT 2.59–60 *"arcā'pi laukikī yā sā bhagavadbhāvitātmanām// mantramantreś-varanyāsāt sāpi ṣāḍguṇyavigrahą /* (also the images [worshipped by] those whose minds have been [purified being full with the]/ thought of God [belong to the group of *vibhava* gods who emanate from Aniruddha]. Through the influence of mantras and their gods deposited on [these images], they too embody the six attributes).

7. LT 3.13–35 "Nārāyaṇa is the supreme Lord of all and I [Lakṣmī] am His lord-hood (*īśatā*). O Purandara, that which is subordinate (*īśitavya*) is known as [either] conscious [or] unconscious. Absolute consciousness determines the state of the [conscious] enjoyer (*bhoktṛ*). . . . That conscious [subordinate], influenced by beginningless nescience which is introduced by me, becomes the enjoyer and, on account of its own egoism, identifies itself with nonconscious objects in terms of the relationship 'I' and 'mine.' When through the influence of knowledge that nescience is eliminated, a conscious entity, having dropped its ego-concept, recaptures my essential nature. That knowledge present in the pure creation is introduced by me as the supreme *vyuha* [in its mantra form], out of compassion I reveal [this] knowledge [to the adept of the *vyuha* mantras]. The relationship between the two creations [pure and impure] is that of protector and protected. . . . [Although in the created world the individuals experience the distinction between the Lord and the subordinate, īśa and īśitavya] this [distinction] cannot be related to my [Lakṣmī's] own or Nārāyaṇa's essential nature. . . . I create a mixed creation [of subordinates], because I take into account the cumulative results of acts (*karman*) committed by the beings who are under the influence of beginningless nescience. This *karman* is regarded as my instrument in fulfilling my creative function."

8. Cf. AS 5.7 "*prekṣaṇātmā sa saṃkalpas tad sudarśanam ucyate*" (that divine decision (*saṃkalpa*) is the same as [his] seeing [omniscience], and it is called sudarśana); LT 18.16 and 21.5 "*mayi prakāśate viśvam darpaṇodaraśailavat*" (on me [as the locus] the universe becomes visible, in the same way as a mountain [is reflected] in a mirror).

9. LT 5.33: "*guṇaḥ prāṇasya tu spando*" (the attribute of *prāṇa* is vibration).

10. Sātvata Saṃhitā (SS) 19.128 "*tac chabdabrahmabhāvena svaśaktyā svayameva hi / muktaye 'khilajīvānām udeti parameśvaraḥ//*" (In order to liberate individuals, supreme God Himself becomes manifest as *śabdabrahman* by means of His own Śakti); cf. LT 20.7, which is a copy of SS 19.128.

11. LT 18. 51. 27–28 "*vācakātmānamasya tvam samāhitamanāḥ śṛṇu / śuddhasaṃvinmayī pūrvaṃ vivarte prāṇarūpataḥ // tattat sthānaprasaṅgena vivarte śabdatas tathā / sāntā sūkṣmā tathā madhyā vaikharīti vivekinī //* (Now listen attentively [I define] its [i.e., Sakti's] nature as the designator (*vācaka*). Consisting of pure knowledge, I first evolve into *prāṇa*. Then through specific stages I evolve into [subsequent states] known as *śāntā, sūkṣmā, madhyā* and *vaikharī*".

12. The former view I have designated the "worm's eye view" and the latter the "bird's eye view."

13. LT 14.4–10; in fact, the form of the deity of a mantra greatly helps the mediator. For instance, Saṃkarṣaṇa represents *śabda-brahman*'s *paśyantī* state, manifest but not yet differentiated. He also represents the third step of the meditator's awareness; i.e., the state of deep sleep (*suṣupti*). LT 4.14 describes Saṃkarṣaṇa's image as the divine form that carries the diverse phenomena of the universe as if painted on it (*tilakālakavat*). When a yogin meditates on the Saṃkarṣaṇa mantra and in his awareness becomes identified with its deity he perceives that the universe is not differentiated from his self.

14. SS 2.72; the SS says that Para Vāsudeva is always accompanied by the three deities Acyuta, etc.; sometimes, these are iconographically represented together with Vāsudeva, while at other times, they are just imagined.

15. LT 23.1–4: "*ahaṃtā paramā tasya Śaktir nārāyaṇī hyaham // anugrahāya lokānām aham ācāryatām gatā / saṃkarṣaṇa svarūpeṇa śāstram pradyotayāmyaham // punaśca gurumūrtisthā samyagvijñānaśālinī/ śaktimayyā svayā dṛṣtyā karuṇāmantrapurṇayā // pālayāmi gurubhūtvā śiṣyānātmopasarpiṇaḥ / tasmād jñeyaḥ sadā śiṣyair ācāryo 'sau madātmakaḥ//* (I am the supreme Śakti of Nārāyaṇa, His "I-hood." In order to help people I become the preceptor and in the form of Saṃkarṣaṇa, I radiate the sacred scriptures. Dwelling in the frame of the guru and equipped with true knowledge I, through my glance full of śakti and by means of compassionate mantras, protect the disciples who approach me [i.e., guru]. Hence disciples should always regard their preceptor as identical with myself).

16. For another comparable system of classification of the mantra, see Hélène Brunner(-Lachaux) 1963–77, 1.xxxvi.

17. One important item to learn is the hand gesture that accompanies a mantra. Such a gesture is called a *seal* (*mudrā*); it proclaims the divine sovereignty and power invested in the mantra (SS 10.52 and the commentary thereof; see also Brunner-Lachaux 1963–77, 1.xxxvi.

18. The LT categorically declares the superiority of Vedic religious practices to all other forms of religiosity.

> The wise should not violate the Vedic religion even in thought. Just as even a king's favorite, who defiles a river which is useful to that monarch, a source of pleasure and beneficial to the community for raising the crop, incurs the [death penalty] on the stake, even though he be indifferent to [the river], so also a mortal who disregards the norm laid down in the Vedas and thereby disobeys my [Lakṣmī's] command forfeits my favor, although he be a favorite of mine. (LT 17.96–98)

19. Of course, this is true for all theistic tantric sects who believe in qualified monism (*viśiṣṭādvaitavāda*) in one form or another.

20. Cf. the legend of King Māndhātā, a devotee of Viṣṇu who wanted to hold the god's feet; Viṣṇu in his grace fulfilled his desire (MBH 12.64.10–13).

21. These two mantras are (1) "*śrīmān nārāyaṇacaraṇau śaraṇam prapadye*" and (2) "*śrīmate nārāyaṇāya namaḥ.*" K. K. A. Venkatachari briefly explains their meaning and importance in Śrīvaiṣṇava theology (Venkatachari 1978).

22. For an excellent explanation of Lakṣmī's role as the divine mediator, see Narayanan 1982.

23. Venkatachari narrated this story when teaching Piḷḷai Lokācārya's Śrīvachanabhuṣaṇam. This story is current among the Śrīvaiṣṇava theologians as the mythology of *puruṣakāra*, meaning the mediator. See also Carman 1974, 240–44.

24. For the transmission of mantraśāstra, see my article, "The Changing Pattern of Pāñcarātra Initiation: A Case Study in the Reinterpretation of Ritual." In *D. J. Hoens Felicitation Volume*, Utrecht 1983.

ABBREVIATIONS USED IN THIS CHAPTER

Ahirbudhyna Saṃhitā (AS)	Ed. (2) V. Krishnamacharya, 2 volumes, Adyar Library, Madras 1966. (Ed. (1) M. D. Ramanujacharya.)
Jayākhya Saṃhitā (JS)	Ed. Embar Krishnacharya, Gaekwad's Oriental Series vol. 54, Baroda 1931.

Chāndogya Upaniṣad (ChU)	Ed. V. P. Limaye and R. D. Vadekar, Poona 1958.
Lakṣmī Tantra (LT)	Ed. V. Krishnamacharya, Adyar Library Series 87, Madras 1959.
Mahābhārata (MBH)	Ed. S. K. Belvalkar, Poona 1954.
Ṛgveda Saṃhitā (ṚV)	Ed. N. S. Sonatakke and C. G. Kasikar, vol. IV, Poona 1946.
Ṛgveda Khila (ṚgVKH)	Ed. N. S. Sonatakke and C. G. Kasikar, vol. IV, Poona 1946.
Sātvata Saṃhitā (SS)	Ed. V. V. Dviveda, The Yoga Tantra Department of S. Sankrit University, Varanasi 1982.
Śrīpraśna Saṃhitā (ŚpS)	Seetha Padmanabhan, Kendriya Sanskrit Vidyapeetha, Tirupati 1969.
Viṣvaksena Saṃhitā (VS)	Ed. Lakshmi Narasimha Bhatta, Kendriya Sanskrit Vidyapeetha, Tirupati 1972.

CHAPTER 10

The Cosmos as Śiva's Language-Game: "Mantra" According to Kṣemarāja's *Śivasūtravimarśinī*

Harvey P. Alper

writing always means hiding something in such a way that it then is discovered.

—Italo Calvino

without mantra there would be neither words nor meanings nor the evolution of consciousness.

—An Āgama

if one doesn't understand the hidden sense of a mantra, one will have to surrender to an authentic master.

—ŚSūV 2.3

INTRODUCTION

PROGRAM

THE PRIMARY PURPOSE OF THIS essay is to describe the function and understanding of mantras in that complex of interlocking soteriological traditions that, for convenience, are collectively referred to as Kaśmiri Śaivism. I focus upon Kṣemarāja's *Śivasūtravimarśinī* (ŚSūV), a representative text that offers something like a normative account of Mantraśāstra, the "science" of mantra, as employed and understood in the mature, central tradition of Kaśmiri Śaivism.[1]

Secondarily, this essay is an exercise in the study of religious language. My point of departure is problematic, developed in that sort of philosophy of religion that has been responsive to the work of Ludwig Wittgenstein. I attempt to describe Kaśmiri Śaiva mantric utterance in terms of the categories Wittgenstein devised in his later work, especially the *Philosophical Investigations* [PI]. My application of these Wittgensteinian concepts to the study of mantras, in part, will test their applicability to non-Western religious traditions. It is my hope that this will contribute to the growing internationalization of the philosophical study of religion, which is coming routinely to take cognizance of ways of speaking religiously not found among the three Semitic theisms.[2] This study is accordingly addressed to both Indologists and philosophers of religion.

INDOLOGICAL BACKGROUND

During the first millenium of its evolution (roughly between 600 B.C. and 400 A.D.) the current of Hindu religious life that was focused on the god Śiva developed preeminently as a family of myths associated with a particular view of the world (a prototheology), as well as with certain social, ritual, and iconic traditions. During this period, Śaivism emerged as a popular, pan-Indian form of "Hinduism," drawing selectively upon the Veda as well as upon the uncodified ritual practices of "village India." The mythological consensus of this generic Śaivism received its definitive literary expression in a group of "anthologies" known as *Purāṇas* ("Histories"). By the third quarter of the first millenium A.D., a comparable ritual consensus had emerged and received expression in a group of specifically Śaivite scriptures, usually dubbed *Śaivāgamas* because they were accepted as having "come" (*āgama*) from Śiva himself. Eventually, these authoritative texts became the canonical basis of several more or less regional forms of Śaivism, each exhibiting its own practical and theological interpretation of the common Puranic mythology and Āgamic ritualism that they presupposed. Among these regional Āgamic "Śaivisms" were the Śaiva traditions of Kaśmir, which, in spite of their "name," were by no means limited to Kaśmir but were connected in important ways with the Sanskrit Āgamic traditions of the South.[3]

The *Āgamas* are characteristically concerned with Śaivite ritual in general:

> They give instruction in the "symbolical meaning," execution and application of those gestures, words, and visible forms, through which man while being in this world can enter into contact with the world of Śiva. . . . [Hence they] served as the doctrinal basis of Śivaite monasticism and as fundamental manuals for liturgies and religious practices. (Gonda 1977a, 166, 173)

Central to the ritualism of the *Śaivāgamas* was an implicitly theological preoccupation with "the power of Speech . . . the power of the energy concealed in the Divine Word" (Gonda 1977a, 167). One ritual presupposition of this concern was mantric utterance. The Śaivāgamic traditions inherited and developed the conviction that mantras were soteriologically central. They were believed to be potent instruments enabling one to attain that perfection which was tantamount to recognizing oneself as Śiva (cf., Gonda 1977a, 170).

The earliest specifically Kaśmiri Śaiva work is usually considered to be the *Śivasūtras* (ŚSū), in Gonda's words (1977a, 209) a "small, obscure, and utterly concise" text of seventy-seven "verses," which had probably been edited in its present form by the early ninth century.[4] Although attributed to Vasugupta, the quasilegendary paterfamilias of Kaśmiri Śaiva "non-dualism," the sūtras may be characterized as anonymous like the *Āgamas* whose authority they assume. Cryptic as they are, they are clearly meant as a soteric guide to selected Śaivāgamas. The ŚSū distill from the Śaivāgamas those themes the understanding of which was taken to be crucial for the expeditious attainment of liberation. They focus on the techniques that were believed to yield a progressive (re)integration into, an achievement of "equality" with, Śiva.[5] As such they necessarily deal with mantric utterance.

Along with its sibling (still essentially anonymous) work, the *Spandakārikās* (SpK), the ŚSū provided points of departure for the central theological and soteriological tradition of Kaśmiri Śaivism. This tradition is defined by the work of four writers: Somānanda (fl. c. mid-ninth century), Utpaladeva (fl. c. early tenth), Abhinavagupta (fl. c. 1000) and Kṣemarāja (fl. c. early eleventh).[6] Since the publication of J. C. Chatterji's *Kashmir Shaivism* in 1914, it has become conventional to distinguish the literature of these writers from that of their predecessors by genre or school (*śāstras*). This division, however, is misleading. The three terms used for this purpose—*āgama*, *spanda* (pulsation) and *pratyabhijñā* (recognition)—are not strictly parallel: the first is literary, the second ontological, the third soteriological. Rather than a movement from one sort of literature to a second and then a third, one finds in the central tradition of Kaśmiri Śaivism a linear development, the emergence of sophisticated theological reflection upon certain experiential traditions that had been given canonical, scriptural formulation in the *Śaivāgamas*.

Broadly speaking, the *Śaivāgamas* along with the ŚSū and SpK may be characterized as Tantric (on the meaning of this problematic term, see Padoux 1981). The theology that Somānanda and his successors devised in response to this literature thus may be classified as a Tantric theology, a theology that sought to elucidate the sort of religious experience assumed to be the summum bonum in Śaiva Tantra. In other words, these figures created a theology that was meant to give rational account of those ritual and meditative techniques that were believed to make possible the experience that was the primary raison d'être for Kaśmiri Śaivism's existence, coherence, and survival.

Kṣemarāja, disciple of the intrepid Abhinavagupta, was more or less the last major Kaśmiri Śaiva author. Unlike his distinguished predecessor, he was more the sober theological exegete, the loyal scholiast than the innovator. His commentary on the ŚSū is a secondary work, a treatise *about* liberation. In effect, Kṣemarāja gives mantric utterance nonmantric exposition. In his work of theological exegesis, Kṣemarāja has the advantage of being both a philosopher and an adept who must himself have employed mantric utterance for the achievement of his own spiritual goals. The ŚSūV thus provides something of a privileged vantage point from which to explore mantric utterance as one form of Hindu religious language. Understanding how Kṣemarāja understood mantric utterance may then facilitate our proposing an interpretation of mantric utterance in nonmantric terms accessible to the twentieth century scientific mind.[7]

PHILOSOPHICAL BACKGROUND

In the past century, academic philosophy increasingly has come to focus on the analysis of language and the context of its use. Several movements growing out of this "linguistic turn" thus potentially provide tools with which the systematic problems in the study of mantra may be addressed. I draw upon the Wittgensteinian tradition because I believe that it provides a useful point of departure for the description of mantra. Wittgenstein's late works—the posthumously published *Philosophic Investigations* (1953), *On Certainty* (1972), and *Zettel* (1967b)—may be read as sketching out the grounds for a typology of linguistic uses.[8] They suggest a strategy for discriminating among the different ways in which words are used that can help establish whether a peculiar sort of utterance, such as a mantra, makes sense or is merely gobbledygook. In other words, Wittgensteinian categories may provide a philosophical vocabulary in whose terms one can establish whether a given mantric utterance should count as linguistic; whether it has meaning, reference, and point; and, if so, what are the meaning, reference, and point.[9]

This essay responds to the challenge to deal with mantra systematically and rigorously. It is a complement to the works of McDermott (1975) and Wheelock (1980, 1982), like whom I presuppose that mantric utterance counts grossly as both linguistic and "religious." I propose to employ a certain set of tools borrowed from Wittgensteinian thought broadly conceived in order to contextualize as precisely as possible the phenomenon of mantric utterance, as Kṣemarāja reports it, within the broader universe of Hindu religiosity.

Students of Wittgenstein who have dealt with his "critique of language" are by no means in agreement about its implications. At least three currents have arisen in response to this strand of Wittgenstein's thought. One, typified by Peter Winch's (1976) *The Idea of a Social Science* is sociological; a second, typified by the work of D. Z. Phillips (1970), is theological (i. e., Christian); a third is that of the philosophy of religion. I shall draw upon this third sort of response to delimit the problem to which this essay speaks. For orientation to Wittensteinian philosophy of religion, I utilize a recent study, Patrick Sherry's (1977) *Religion, Truth and Language-Games.*[10]

Relying in part on Sherry's analysis, in the next section of this essay, I discuss the problem in whose terms this inquiry is framed. The body of the essay is an exegetical study of the "doctrine" of mantras in the ŚSūV. In the first portion of my exegesis, I describe the sociological dimension of mantric utterance. In the second portion, I describe the epistemological dimension of mantric utterance and discuss its theological implications. In a very brief conclusion, I suggest how this Wittgensteinian approach to Kaśmiri Śaiva mantra might cast light on the nature and variety of religious language as such.

THE PROBLEM

WITTGENSTEIN ON LANGUAGE

In his early work, especially in the *Tractatus* (T), Wittgenstein understands language to be a means of representing the necessary form of the world. He relegates the religious—indeed, the entirety of human value—to the realm of the "unsayable" or "mystical."[11] While formally allowing for a positive evaluation of the religious, this view does not invite the philosophical exegesis of religious language. In PI, in contrast, Wittgenstein begins from the observation that representation is only one among the many functions of language. To help in the parsing of the variety of linguistic functions, Wittgenstein coins two enigmatic technical terms, language-game and form of life.[12] Attempts to develop a Wittgensteinian philosophy of language, to a great extent, have been stimulated by the desire to fathom the meaning and extend the application of these terms. In philosophy of religion, this has helped focus attention on the nature and coherence of religious language.

Wittgenstein asks, in Toulmin's words, "by what procedures do men *establish* links between language and the real world?" (1969, 67). To answer this question, he directs attention to the different ways in which people use words. "*Any* linguistic expression . . . [he observes] acquires a linguistic significance by being *given a use* in human life" (1969, 67). Meaning follows use; use grounds utterance in its immediate context, human behavior.[13] The countless different ways in which language is used (die unzählige verschiedene Arten der Verwendung) (PI 23) convey meaning because they are constituted in activity; "*all* language is meaningful, on account of being *ein Bestandteil der Handlung*" (70).

The question is How does language work? Wittgenstein's answer is threefold. The explication of language-games leads one to consider forms of life; their explication leads one to the context of life *überhaupt*. Language-games are "units of sense" (Finch 1977, 69) that acquire their meaning from forms of life. The latter are "units of meaningful action that are carried out together by members of a social group and that have a common meaning for the members of the group" (90).

By *form of life,* Wittgenstein does not refer to a finite number of *particular* cultural, no less psychological or biological, facts. Rather, the term directs attention to "all social or cultural behavior *in so far as it is meaningful*" (90). "Forms of life" are the "interpretive conventions" (cf. *Blue Book,* 24) of a particular social group. Since speaking is an interpretive activity "embedded in acting" (Finch 1977, 93), one cannot hope to understand what someone says unless one grasps it contextually as a "speech act."[14] Wittgenstein observes that there is no one-to-one correspondence between a particular language-game and a particular form of life. What, then, makes the countless combinations possible? Finch is probably correct in suggesting that Wittgenstein recognized a "still wider context presupposed by both [language-games and forms of life], the context of everyday life and everyday certainties" (1977, 100). Finch calls these simple and indubitable convictions "framework facts" (1977, 222).

Another way of articulating this "third level" is suggested by Wittgenstein's use of the term *Umgebung* (also *Umstände*)—surroundings, circumstances, context—to which Strawson (1966, 55, 62) first drew attention. Thus, PI 583:

> Could someone have a feeling of ardent love or hope for the space of one second—*no matter what* preceded or followed this second?—What is happening now has significance—in these surroundings. The surroundings give it its importance.[15]

Wittgenstein seems to conclude that the coordination of speaking and doing depends upon the world of human experience as a whole, to use a phenomenological term, upon the *Lebenswelt.*[16] He recognizes that the context that makes speaking meaningful transcends the individual speaker. As a social phenomenon, language has a twofold character. It is fabricated by people, but once having been fabricated, it assumes a kind of "objectivity" over against the individual. As Wittgenstein says, "Es steht da—wie unser Leben" (OC 559).

The concepts language-games, forms of life, and the *Umgebung* of speaking are heuristic. They do not oblige us to go on a treasure hunt for forms of life hidden in medieval Sanskrit texts. They do call for a particular style of reflection. By attending to the social facts and the interpretive conventions that a language-game assumes and by attending to the wider circumstances that those conventions assume, one ought to be able to map the various ways in which human beings live verbally in the world. Wittgenstein did not develop a typology of usage. To do so was not part of his task as a therapeutic philosopher, it is part of the task of philosophers of religion and others interested in probing the integrity of religious discourse. To understand mantric utterance one must explore the interpretive conventions and the circumstances taken for granted among mantra users.

WITTGENSTEIN AND THE PHILOSOPHY OF RELIGION

Sherry on Religious Language-Games

In *Religion, Truth and Language-Games* (1977), Patrick Sherry proposes a method to facilitate the study of discrete sorts of religious language. He calls for the explication of the "logic" of individual religious concepts and for the delineation of how they refer to life and experience (1977, 189). According to his account, the exegete of religious language faces three tasks. These he labels, somewhat eccentrically, *locating, relating,* and *validating.*[17]

By the term *locating,* Sherry designates the identification of the smallest constituent sorts of religious utterance in terms of those circumstances that lend them meaning. Locating is essentially sociological. It means delimiting those "situations and facts" that are invariably concomitant with (the "necessary conditions" for) the occurrence of a particular form of religious utterance (1977, 84; cf. 50, 68). Locating is preliminary. It prepares the ground for further reflection by making the social ground of a religious language-game, its irreducible specificity, explicit.

By *relating,* Sherry means determining the critical differentiae between one language-game and another, while discriminating the forms of life with which they are necessarily associated (cf. 1977, 49, 56). Relating focuses on the linguistic action involved in an utterance. Locating asks *When* does one say something? Relating asks *What* does one do in saying it? Relating, for Sherry, is transitional, a specialized form of locating that invariably leads to the question of validating. It is important because it makes clear that in delimiting the social dimensions of a religious language-game one begins to uncover the sort of cognitive claims made, implicitly or explicitly, by that manner of speaking and the sort of evidence needed to verify or falsify these claims. In other words, relating compels one to face the fact that complete and honest description of meaning, in and of itself, raises the question of truth.

Validating is Sherry's term for the process of evaluating the truth of religious assertions (1977, 49f.). One might well question whether this can be part of a Wittgensteinian program for the analysis of language. Wittgenstein had been concerned primarily to discover how utterances make sense (Sherry 1977, 2f.). He concluded that meaning is dependent upon function, "Only in the stream of thought and life do words have meaning" (Z 173). As a consequence "there are many kinds of so-called descriptive or fact-stating language, and these relate to the world in different ways" depending on their subject matter, their "methods of projection," and their "grammar" (17). To Sherry, this conclusion is easily misconstrued. He argues, persuasively, that acknowledging the variety of language-games underscores rather than obviates the need for ajudicating competing claims. Since "areas of discourse overlap, then it follows that there must be some connection between their criteria of evidence, rationality and truth" (Sherry 1977, 161). Since language-games and forms of life depend upon "framework facts," the multiplicity of ways of speaking is not in itself evidence for a multiplicity of unrelatable sorts of truth. If the ontological implications of different language-games conflict, then a decision is called for. One is not compelled to speak in contradictions. Even "believers" cannot be wholly "oblivious of the facts" (Sherry 1977, 84).

Language-Games and Christian Fideism

Most Christian theologians who have been attracted to Wittgenstein employ his thought in order to emancipate Christian "truth" from the criteria of scientific or secular truth. They typically argue that religious language is "noncognitive," and they use Wittgenstein's thought as a tool to deflect the positivist demand for "verification." A religious assertion, they tell us, is sui generis; it need only "be itself" for it to be "in order."[18]

Sherry rejects the attempt to finesse the question of validation and argues that the use of Wittgensteinian thought to defend Christian fideism distorts Wittgenstein.[19] His position may be clarified in contrast to that of Winch (1976). Proceeding from Wittgenstein's observation that meaning varies according to usage, Winch argues that different "modes of social life" engender different sorts of rationality.

> Criteria of logic . . . are not a direct gift of God, but arise out of, and are only intelligible in the context of, ways of living or modes of social life . . . science is one such mode and religion is another; and each has criteria of intelligibility peculiar to itself. (p. 100)

Sherry, in contrast, emphasizes the fact that all language-games and forms of life are responses to an experienced world, the implicit unity of which underlies and makes possible the diversity of human culture. Sherry thus avoids an ultimate bifurcation between scientific and non-scientific language-games, just as he avoids the solipsistic relativism of cultural "worlds" that a Winchian perspective would seem to imply.

From Sherry's point of view, in principle, there are ways of resolving conflicts between the cognitive claims of various sorts of human utterance (1977, 39, 167). A particular religious language-game can claim a particular kind of truth only if it refers to a particular state of affairs (1977, 185). A particular claim may be verified or refuted because every language-game and every form of life actually speaks to some human state (172).

Mantraśāstra and Hindu Fideism

Sherry justly observes that many attempts to apply Wittgensteinian thought to religious issues have been "disappointing." Wittgenstein's philosophy, he notes, "has tended to be used in an attempt to provide over-simple, evasive, and question-begging solutions to very fundamental problems" (1977, 193). Whittaker (1978, 193) has similarly observed that the facile use of Wittgensteinian jargon, like the "facile reading of Wittgenstein as an unswerving" noncognitivist, is played out. The misuse of Wittgensteinian thought as an apology for Christian fideism might seem irrelevant to a study of an eleventh century Sanskrit text. However, any number of people—Neo-Hindu thinkers, devotees of one or another "new religious movement," professional mystics—today facilely exempt the Hindu tradition from the rigorous epistemological standards of scientific, or even traditional Indian, thought. In effect, they are arguing for a Hindu fideism. The apparent inscrutability of Mantraśāstra would seem to support such a position, but I believe that it does not. One purpose of this essay is to show that mantric utterance is a complex and subtle manner of speaking that does not provide evidence for an unequivocally fideistic reading of the Hindu tradition. Hence, the utility of Sherry's formulation of Wittgensteinian philosophy of religion: It directs attention to an aspect of religious language consideration of which is too easily evaded, the conformity of various religious claims to the facts.

Limiting myself to the evidence of the ŚSūV, and thus essentially in mantras used in a redemptive context, in this essay I propose (1) to attend to the social context of mantric utterance, (s) to delineate what distinguishes it as a tool of cognition, and (3) to attempt to decipher the implicit claims about the universe that it makes. There is a general correlation between the two succeeding sections of my exegesis and Sherry's three moves. In the next section of this essay, I venture a delineation of the social dimension of mantric utterance according to the ŚSūV. This corresponds broadly to locating. In the subsequent section, I describe the epistemological dimension of mantric utterance and assess its theological implications. In doing this, I attempt to determine what cognitive claims are implicit in mantric speech and to suggest how they may be evaluated. This accordingly corresponds to both relating and validating.

Apologists for theism have dismissed mantras as magical; enthusiasts for the mystical East have accepted them uncritically. In spite of their paradigmatic character, few have attempted to examine the theological claims implicit in their use carefully. The utility of my approach will be corroborated if it enables me so to describe the circumstances *when* certain pivotal Kaśmiri Śaiva mantras are uttered and the *character* of their utterance so that one will be prompted subsequently to assess the truth of the claims about the cosmos that—in part metaphorically, in part metaphysically—they make.

THE SOCIAL DIMENSION OF MANTRIC UTTERANCE

ORIENTATION

In the Hindu tradition, to a far greater extent than in most other, ostensibly more self-conscious religious traditions, there is an explicit awareness that achieving religious consummation involves the mastery of specifiable techniques.[20] Ironically, this situation obscures the fact that the mastery of specifiable techniques itself presupposes a prior mastery of skills that resist specification. The successful use of an "instrument" such as mantric utterance presupposes that one has already acquired the proper attitudes, demeanor, and expectations—that is, the proper frame of mind—by having been successfully socialized in the society that recognizes mantric utterance as an "authorized" technique that makes possible one of the kinds of transcendence it is deemed acceptable to experience.

The confident, routine use of mantras surely presupposes a specific, identifiable set of convictions concerning the human condition, the ideal social order, and the purpose of existence. Acceptance of these convictions is the tacit ground without which Mantraśāstra would neither have been invented nor have remained vital. Whatever reasons might be adduced to defend these convictions, their acceptance is not itself discursive, it is social. As lived, they are part of the forms of life, "the formal conditions, the patterns in the weave of our lives" (Gier, 32), that give meaning to the language-game of uttering mantras.

In this portion of my essay, I attempt to delineate, on the basis of Kṣmarāja's ŚSūV, the social grounding of mantric utterance, what constitutes it as an intentional social act. Obviously, no such delineation can be complete, for any social act is embedded in a complex of customs and institutions (PI 337); "what belongs to a language-game is a whole culture" (*Lecture on Aesthetics,* 26).[21] Self-evidently, the language-game of uttering mantras is situated within a social cosmos organized according to the principles of caste hierarchy, culminating in and yet transcended by institutionalized renunciation (*saṃnyāsa*), which, as such, recognizes the authority of an elite of "perfect spiritual masters" (gurus) and which experiences the cosmos as a fabric interwoven of various "powers," as *śaktic.* These are, in general, the "situations and facts" that are invariably concomitant with mantric utterance. They are the preconditions that make it possible and lend it meaning. Keeping this social cosmos in mind, one may discern the most prominent formal characteristics of the speech act of uttering mantras: (1) that uttering a mantra is a thing done, and hence, a learned activity; (2) that uttering a mantra is both a context- and a rule-dependent activity; (3) that the activity of uttering a mantra may be compared profitably to a move in a game.

I do not here attempt a comprehensive social scientific portrayal of Kaśmiri Śaiva mantric utterance. I merely attempt to demonstrate that conceptualizing mantric utterance as a social activity is plausible. This will, I trust, indicate possible directions for future study; for example, the examination of the social skills drawn upon in Mantraśāstra from the perspective of developmental psychology or the sociology of knowledge.

MANTRIC UTTERANCE AS ACTIVITY

Mantra as Cause and Effect

The discussion of mokṣa in the ŚSū begins with Sūtra 1.5: "Bhairava is the efflorescence [of Śiva] (*Udyamo bhairavaḥ*)" (18).[22] In his exposition of this sūtra, Kṣemarāja cites an Āgamic fragment which he attributes to the *Svacchanda Tantra* (SvT):

> [Only] the mantras of a man who is united with the eternal, that is, one who has realized that he is Bhairava, are successful, oh Goddess.[23]

The use of the verb *pra-siddh*, typical in such a context, is noteworthy. It means "be efficacious," "work," "be successful," and logically implies that mantras may be uttered unsuccessfully.[24] To borrow a term from J. L. Austin's discussion of speech acts, locutions such as this suggest that the articulation of a mantra may be "unhappy."[25] If one asks Under what circumstances do mantras work? one is immediately presented with a dialectical contradiction. In spite of the fact that mantric utterance, at least within the milieu of the ŚSūV, is the premier instrument for attaining the goal of the religious quest, it looks as if a mantra cannot be successfully brought into play until and unless one has already attained the goal in question. (It is as if one couldn't successfuly drop-kick a football in order to make a conversion unless one had already been awarded an extra point.) Kṣemarāja acknowledges this in the introductory sentence of his commentary to ŚSū I.5:

> Sūtra 1.5 points out the method (*upāya*) [for attaining] the pacification of that bondage [which has just been discussed]; it is that reality [where one is already] reposing in the object to be attained (*upeya*).[26]

Numerous passages—and not only in the literature drawn upon by the *Pratyabhijñā*—reinforce this anomaly: Mantras work only for those who would appear no longer to need them. Commenting on ŚSū I.19 Kṣemarāja cites another Āgamic fragment:

> Unless one has been reunited [with *śakti*] one can neither be initiated, attain perfections, [use] mantras, apply mantras, nor even [make use of] yogic attraction.[27]

Mantric utterance appears at once as magical and methodical: on the one hand, as a formulaic power that one may wield as a *result* of one's inner perfection; on the other hand, as the *cause* of that inner perfection.

Which view is correct? Commenting on the passage attributed to the SvT cited earlier, Kṣemarāja observes, "the verb *bhū* [to become, to realize] refers to that cognition (*vimarśa*) which is the overwhelming inner emergence [of Bhairava]."[28] The use of the technical term *vimarśa* (transcendental judgment, the capacity of Śiva-who-is-consciousness to make himself the object of the cognition "I")[29] suggests how Kṣemarāja understands mantras: not fundamentally as magic formulae that allow one to impose one's inner will upon the world but as tools for engendering (recognizing) a certain state of affairs. To put this in our terms, for Kṣemarāja a mantra works, is redemptive, when and only when it engenders the proper sort of "cosmic" consciousness; otherwise, it is empty. For someone who doesn't understand this, it appears to be magical. For someone who does understand it, it appears to be a comprehensive personal activity, something one does.

For Kṣemarāja, a redemptive mantra must be understood as a linguistic act that, in and of itself, effects a state of mind—if and only if it is properly uttered. *Preparing* to utter a mantra redemptively is never presumed to be easy; on the contrary, for the novice, it is a supremely arduous social achievement. Uttering it, however, turns out in the end to be effortless. One achieves freedom merely by saying one is free. Kṣemarāja's use of *udyantṛtā* to echo the sūtra's *udyama* cannot be unintentional. Both words, derived from the verb *ud-yam*, conceal a double meaning. On the one hand, they are technical terms that refer directly to a state of yogic excitement, of "elevated" consciousness, a spiritual "high." At the same time, they never wholly lose their ordinary meaning of "effort." They remind the aspirant that freedom is won as a result of intense, heroic exertion. Put in this context, we can begin to apprehend the view implicit in Kṣemarāja's position: The utterance of a mantra must be understood as an act—a social act—that yet turns out to be no action at all. Mantraśāstra must be understood in terms of the dialectic between *upāya* (method) and *anupāya* (methodless method), which is a leitmotif of the *pratyabhijñā*'s utilization of the *Śaivāgamas* in general.

Mantra as Ritual

Even clearer evidence that Kṣemarāja implicitly understands the utterance of a mantra to be an activity is found in his comment on ŚSū 2.2. The sūtra reads: "[In the case of mantric utterance] an effort is effective [in achieving a goal] (*prayatnaḥ sādhakaḥ*)" (48). Kṣemarāja elaborates:

> It is an unfeigned effort—namely the effort that [already] has been established in the first chapter [of the ŚSū] as being the desire to be merged (*anusaṃdhitsā*) with a mantra whose form has been specified—which imparts identification of the utterer of the mantra (*mantrayitur*) with the god [i. e., the object] of the mantra.[30]

The use of the denominative agent noun *Mantrayitṛ* (one who mantras a mantra) suggests that Kṣemarāja understands uttering a mantra as an integral personal action. But does Kṣemarāja really envision the "efforting," upon which successfully putting a mantra into play depends, as an activity involving intense personal exertion? A passage attributed to the *Tantrasadbhāva* (TSB) that Kṣemarāja cites suggests he does:

> Just as a hawk, hovering in the sky, notices his prey, my dear,
> And quickly, naturally, with a lunge, plucks it to himself (*akarṣayet*)
> A master yogi, in this very way, should send out (*vikarṣayet*) his mind to the foundation point (*bindu*);
> Just as an arrow placed on a bow flies [to its target] when it has been carefully shot (*yatnena ātāḍya*)
> So, Goddess, the foundation point flies [to the yogi] by means of his enunciation (*uccāra*) [of the mantra].[31]

Kṣemarāja explains:

> The master yogi, by means of an unfeigned and natural exertion should send out his mind to the foundation point; he will then attain the supreme illumination (*paraprakāśa*); that is, by means of one's enunciation [of a mantra], which is to say, by means of unfeigned, overwhelming elevation (*akṛtakodyantṛtā-*), the foundation point flies [to one], that is, it flows forth (*prasarati*).[32]

The dialectical tact of these lines and their interpretation is remarkable. The images of the hawk and its prey and of the arrow and its target are used to illumine the relationship between the enunciator of a mantra and that reality (here *bindu* equated with *paraprakāśa*) at which he aims, without suggesting either that the utterer does nothing (like a hawk, he sends out his mind) or that his action is soterically self-sufficient (like the arrow, the *bindu* flies to him). On the contrary, the passage suggests awareness that successful mantric utterance is an activity demanding skill, dedication, and presence of mind; an activity designed to elicit a response from a reality toward which the action is directed.

As such an action, mantric utterance, when used redemptively, does not stand alone. It is part of an involved "tantric" *sādhanā*. That "discipline," in turn, makes use of a sequence of ritual gestures and presupposes the sometimes tacit, but always vital support of the complex, fissiparous, highly segmented hierarchical social world we call Hindu. Staal surely is correct in situating the use of mantras in the broad context of Indian ritual life.[33] Its place in the Hindu ritual cosmos merits reflection. As Dumont has observed, the Hindu social order seems to require institutionalized renunciation (*saṃnyāsa*) for its "completion." The renouncer completes the map of Hindu society and provides transcendental justification for it. Similarly, one might add, institutionalized renunciation seems to require the guru, the most successful of renouncers to complete and justify *saṃnyāsa*. There is substantial ritual continuity between the *sādhanā* of the guru and the "older" traditions of *yajña* and *pūjā*. Indeed, the guru may be understood to manifest the efficacy of ritual as such, thus affirming the wholeness of the Hindu world.

The uttering of mantras may well be the most characteristic Hindu ritual gesture. It accompanies and supplements various ritual acts at once in Vedic, popular, and Tantric settings. An analogy suggests itself. Just as the guru completes society by "transcending" it; so, too, mantric utterance may be understood to complete ordinary language-games by "transcending" them. If this is so, far from being mystical instruments of individual isolation, mantras may help define and facilitate the performance of the public rituals of *pūjā* and *yajña*.[34] Mantras are highly refined, dialectically complex instruments of personal inner transformation. For this very reason, they are able to function at the intersection of the "public" and "private" realms of the Hindu cosmos. Hence, a preliminary conclusion: As a learned action, mantric utterance depends upon and affirms the order and values of the very society that it is designed to transcend.

MANTRIC UTTERANCE AS RULE-DEPENDENT

There can be no doubt that, as an activity, successfully putting a mantra into play is context- and rule-dependent; for the meaningfulness of any utterance depends upon its being uttered in an appropriate context and its conforming to a web of partially explicit, partially tacit regulations. (This is the conclusion of both speech-act analysis and Wittgenstein's exploration of language-games.) The rule-conforming character of mantric utterance is further evidence of its intrinsically social nature: "One person alone cannot follow a rule" (PI 199). Hence, if one grants that mantric utterance is linguistic, then one will be compelled to conclude that even the lone adept uttering a monosyllabic mantra repetitiously and in silence will be able to do so only because, in fact, he presupposes and conforms to the norms of the linguistic community of which he is a member.[35]

Can one understand the rules to which mantric utterance is subject? To a certain extent, one can easily, for they are public. The texts dealing with *sādhanā* include many handbooks of Mantraśāstra that provide detailed "instructions" for using mantras, often with bewildering and minute specificity.[36] The impression that these manuals give is that little is left to chance. The deity himself has revealed everything that his devotees have to know to use his mantras. All that the Mantravādin has to do is carry out directions properly; individual imagination or taste could hardly be relevant.

In spite of their prolixity and abundance, the apodictic regulations governing mantric utterance are deceiving. To a great extent the use of mantras is optional rather than mandatory, and all the more so in a redemptive context. Hence, the majority of mantric utterances invariably presuppose at least a certain number of individual judgments. Applying a rule, moreover, is never mechanical; application is interpretation. Even more significantly, in a Tantric setting, use of a mantra is almost never "free lance"; it depends upon accepting the guidance of one's spiritual master.

On this dependence upon the guru, ŚSū 2.6, with Kṣemarāja's introductory phrase, could not be clearer: "in the matter of getting mantras to work (*manrtravīryasādane*) 'it is the guru who is the path' (*gurur vpāyaḥ*)" (59). Kṣemarāja's commentary on this sūtra emphasizes at once the indispensability of the guru in using mantras successfully and that it is the guru's mantric utterance that accounts for his power:

> The guru is he who proclaims (*gṛṇati*) . . . the truly real (*tāttvikam artham*); he is the path in that he is the one who indicates how mantras work.[37]

In his interpretation, Kṣemarāja draws upon the widespread Hindu conviction that the guru is the supreme mediator between the ordinary and the real and that, as such, his words count intrinsically as mantra. This consensus—if it is that—is artfully expressed in the *Guru Gītā*, a Purāṇic text popular today among the followers of Siddha Yoga, a new religious movement inspired in part by the traditions of Kaśmiri Śaivism. Verse 174 of this text aptly characterizes the *guru*'s role as psychopomp:

> It is the guru who is the supreme passageway (*tīrtha*), [in comparison to him] any other passageway is of no use;
> And it is the big toe of [the guru's] foot, Goddess, upon which all [lesser] passageways depend.[38]

Verse 76 of this same text elaborates the guru's paradigmatic role:

> The guru's form (*mūrti*) is the source of trance (*dhyāna*), the guru's foot is the source of ritual action (*pūjā*);
> The guru's utterance (*vākya*) is the source of mantra, the guru's compassion (*kṛpā*) is the source of freedom (*mokṣa*).[39]

Thus, it is not surprising that Kṣemarāja cites passages from several authoritative texts to reinforce the point that the guru holds the key to the efficacy of mantras because of the unique quality of his speech. He quotes Śiva himself as saying in the *Mālinīvijaya Tantra* (MVT): "He who illumines [i. e., manifests (*prakāśaka*)] the efficacy of mantras is said to be a guru equal to me (*matsamaḥ*)."[40] So, too, he cites the SpK, where one is told to do obeisance to the "eloquence of the guru" (*gurubhāratī*), which is a vehicle equipped to carry one across the bottomless ocean of doubt.[41] Finally, he cites two passages, one attributed to the MVT, the other to the *Mantriśirobhairava,* that assess a guru's utterance (*guru-vaktra*). The guru's utterance, we are told, is the "wheel of power" (*śakticakra*); the guru being the divine power that grants release.[42] Accordingly, Kṣemarāja is able to conclude: "'The power [of the guru] which proceeds from his utterance is greater than the guru himself,' that power, which provides a favorable opportunity [to attain freedom] is the path."[43]

These quotations suffice to illustrate the social role of the spiritual master in Mantraśāstra, as understood in the ŚSūVim. The guru, like the mantra itself, is liminal. Both stand on the threshold between the public and the private, the threshold between "inner" and "outer" experience. As such, the guru and his intrisically mantric discourse, by his very existence in the Hindu social world, helps make belief in the complex efficacy of mantras plausible for a myriad of individuals who have, as a practical matter, little hope of using mantras successfully themselves, at least in a redemptive context.

MANTRIC UTTERANCE AS A MOVE IN A GAME

Further insight into the social character of mantric utterance, as Kṣemarāja implicitly understands it, may be found in his commentaries on Sūtras 1.22 and 2.3, where both the efficacy of mantras (*mantravīrya*) and their "selection" (*mantroddhāra*) are discussed. ŚSū 2.3 says: "The secret of mantra is the body of wisdom (*vidyāśarīrasattā mantrarahasyam*)" (50). In explicating this sūtra, Kṣemarāja quotes a long, complex, important passage from the TSB (cf. Goudriaan & Gupta 1981, 39; Padoux 1963, 112ff.). The secret ("*rahasyam*" is glossed "*upaniṣad*") of mantras is unfolded, Kṣemarāja tells us, in the TSB:

> All mantras consist of Transcendental Phonemes (*varṇas*) and [thus], my dear, they are really śakti
> Śakti, however, should be known as the Mother [of the cosmos] (*Mātṛkā*) and she should be known as really Śiva.[44]

Continuing, the passage, in effect, explains why mantric utterance seems so obscure in comparison with other language-games:

> [Those who have] abandoned action [in conformity with *dharma*], who have [only] mundane goals [and values], who are satisfied with deceit and fraud
> Don't even know that the guru is god and that this is in agreement with the scriptures (*śāstra*)
> For just this reason, goddess, I have concealed (*pragopitam*) the efficacy [of mantras]
> Because of this concealment (*guptena*) they are hidden (*gupta*);

> only the Transcendental Phonemes [which the uninitiated do not know how to use] remain[45]

These lines, the beginning of a detailed, exceedingly beautiful Tantric cosmology, attempt to explain the dialectical duality of mantric utterance: Mantras are at once "open" and "closed," clear and obscure; speaking socially, they are both public and private. In the preface to this passage, Kṣemarāja homes in on this duality as the clue to understanding the efficacy that alone allows mantras to be used successfully: "In this passage from the TSB, the efficacy of mantras [*ayam artham* = *mantravīryam*], having been [appropriately] ordered (*vitatya*), has been clarified (*sphuṭīkṛtah*) in spite of the fact that it is exceedingly secret (*atirahasyo 'pi*)."[46]

These lines—indeed, these two sections of the ŚSūV as a whole—make it clear that, on the one hand, mantras are simply something there, something "given"; after all, they are Śiva-who-becomes-the-cosmos. On the other hand, it is equally plain, they are something one must go out and "get." They need to be the object of a special intuition (*anubhava*, 1.22 [44]), the object of a ritual of "extraction" (*mantroddhāra*, 1.22 [45]); they have to be "entered into" (*anu-pra-viś-*, 1.22 [45]) or "accomplished" (*sādh-*, 2.3 [50]). Without doubt, the ŚSūV portrays mantric utterance as both accessible and inaccessible, both simple to use and tricky to use. This suggests the utility of understanding mantric utterance as a species of ritual play: Uttering a mantra is making a particular move in a particular game. Like many of the moves in a game, it requires peculiar expertise. Yet, it is exceedingly simple once one has learned how to do it.

In proposing this, I draw upon the work of a number of historians and social scientists who, following Johan Huizinga's *Homo Ludens* (1955), have explored the role of play in human culture. My classification of mantric utterance as "ludic" is not meant to be disparaging. On the contrary, with Huizinga (1955, 6), I assess play as potentially a deadly serious business, a form of expression so serious that it often "wholly [runs] away with the players" (1955, 8). Ritual play is often of this sort. As Huizinga had the wit to recognize, every ritual system presupposes a metaphor, more exactly a set of metaphors:

> Behind every abstract expression there [lies] the boldest of metaphors, and every metaphor is a play on words. Thus in giving expression to life man creates a second, poetic world alongside the world of nature. (1955, 4)

This means, Huzinga goes on, that ritual play,

> creates order, *is* order. Into an imperfect world and into the confusion of life it brings a temporary, a limited perfection. (1955, 10)

From this perspective, mantric utterance would surely have to be characterized as "make believe." Can one, in that case, still take seriously its claim to be a method for attaining a real religious transformation, a fundamental reorientation of one's way of being in the world? I believe one can—provided one takes care to exegete its playful character. Understanding mantric utterance as a move in a game helps one understand its character as a particular sort of social action. It is a manner of speaking indirectly that is dependent upon a precise set of metaphors. At the same time, it intends to be referential. This description of mantric utterance as a move in a game prepares the ground for assessing the truth of a mantra's referential claim precisely because it allows one to decipher the poetic vision in whose terms a mantra's reference is cast.

Kṣemarāja's comments on ŚSū 1.22 may be understood in this light. The sūtra reads: "[Only] through immersion (*anusaṃdhāna*) in the great lake (*mahāhrada*) [which is śakti] may one directly intuit (*anubhava*) the efficacy of mantras."[47] Kṣemarāja elaborates:

> Mantric efficacy . . . is the judgment (*vimarṣa*) of the transcendental "I" (*parāhantā*) who expands into the [transcendental] verbal-mass (*śabdarāśisphārātmaka-*) [from which the ordinary verbal world evolves];
>
> Its direct intuition (*anubhava*) is due to immersion in the great lake, which is to say, it is due to the internal, uninterrupted judgment of being united with it (*antarmukhtayā anāratam tattādātmyavimarśana*);
>
> This direct intuition explodes [into view] as oneself (*svātmarūpatayā sphuraṇam bhavati*);
>
> [This is explained] in the MVT in the passage which begins "The śakti of the creator of the cosmos (*jagaddhātṛ*) . . ."
>
> [Since it has been] shown [in that passage] that śakti consists of the entire world which is formed from the mother [of the cosmos] (*mātṛkā*) and the sequence [of transcendental phonemes] (*mālinī*) which [in turn] take form as the fifty different . . . powers beginning with volition, the extraction of mantras has been made clear;
>
> Supreme śakti alone is the great lake, for this reason it has been correctly said that the direct intuition of the efficacy of mantras which is really the efficacy of *mātṛkā* and *mālinī* is due to immersion in her.[48]

In this passage the "extraction" of mantras—a particular, specifiable social act—is correlated, first, with an epistemological event, a specific cognition (*vimarśa*) of the Mantravādin. It is correlated, second, with an ontological fact, that the world is nothing but the fabric of śaktic sounds and vibrations that in the end, are the body of Śiva. Hence, for a mantric utterance to be successful one (and one's guru) must know both the rules (a social reality) and that to which a mantra refers (its ontological referent). Kṣemarāja summarizes:

> —It has been shown that the secret of mantras, which are the embodied amalgam of transcendental phonemes (*varṇasaṃghaṭṭanāśarīrāṇām*), is, as has already been explained, none other than Bhagavatī [i. e., Śakti], whose being is the 'body of wisdom.' This is why (*ayam eva āśayaḥ*) the discussion of the "extraction" of mantras is preceded, in every scripture (*pratyāgama*), by the "deploying" (*prastāra*)[49] of the Mother [of the cosmos] (*mātṛkā*) or the [transcendental] sequence of phonemes (*mālinī*).[50]

Mantraśāstra can be understood to make sense if it is understood as a ritual gesture predicated on the assumption that the Hindu may experience a śaktic universe. Padoux summarizes this presupposition clearly:

> Two powers are associated with every Mantra: one power (*vācakaśakti*), which "expresses" or "signifies", is the Mantra itself. [The other] (*vācyaśakti*), which is "to be expressed" or "signified," is the *devatā* [the god or "object" of the mantra]. Here as elsewhere the second aspect follows from the first, for it is the Word which is primal, the fecundator who precedes her object. (1963, 298)

It follows, too, that the right mantra used in the proper way by the qualified person is believed to be a key that unlocks the śaktic structure of the cosmos. Under those, and only under those, socially determined circumstances, it becomes a "signifier" that leads the one who wields it to that which it "signifies." So it is that mantric utterance at once designates that for which one ought to strive and asserts that one may attain it in the very act of designation. As a key move in the very complex game of "being Hindu," it has the effect of socially fabricating the reality to which it claims to refer. It is accepted as a form of speaking that effects one of those ultimate transformations that Hindu society optimally demands, because it is understood to lead one "back" to the very roots of ordinary discourse. Just as the practice of playing chess turns a piece of wood into a chessman, the practice of a Tantric discipline in a cosmos believed to be śaktic turns the syllables of a mantra into a subtle, linguistic tool for apprehending that the cosmos is nothing but Śiva's game-encompassing language-game.[51]

THE EPISTEMOLOGICAL DIMENSION OF MANTRIC UTTERANCE AND ITS THEOLOGICAL IMPLICATIONS

ORIENTATION

In order to appraise not only the social ground of mantric utterance but its intended and actual social function as well, one must assess its epistemological character. Mantric utterance, being a religious language-game, functions as a theodicy, providing reassurance that "it's an OK world."[52] What differentiates mantric utterance from other Indian religious language-games is the precise manner in which it provides this reassurance: It is taken to be a tool of cognition that, under the right circumstances, leads the person who utters it to cognize the world in such a way that he "realizes" that the world "really is all right."

That mantric utterance, as described by the ŚSūV, is more an intellectual than a magical way of speaking is not surprising. As early as the *Upaniṣads*, there has been a Hindu religious elite who conceptualized "bondage" and "freedom" in fundamentally epistemological terms. From their point of view, everyday life (*vyavāhara*) was understood to exhibit a double nature. It inhibited apprehension of the deep structure of the cosmos, but by this very obscuration, it provided the means that made it possible for religious virtuosi to perform certain axiomatically perceptive acts of cognition that were tantamount to knowing reality as such.

Keeping this historical context in mind, one may understand mantric utterance as a "mechanism" for thinking a certain privileged class of thoughts. From Kṣemarāja's viewpoint, reaching the right conclusions about Śiva-who-becomes-the-world is that which "saves." Such saving acts of cognition cannot be appropriated cheaply. (Saying them without meaning them doesn't count!) One cannot get the point without playing the game; one can only get the point if one plays the game properly.

Both the real and the traditional etymology of the word *mantra* focuses attention on its intellectual nature. According to the former, a mantra is an instrument (*-tra*) of reflection (*man-*); according to the latter a mantra is a thought (*manana*) that saves (*trā-*). In both cases, allusion is made to the extraordinary intellectual objectivity attributed to mantras. They appear as "machines" in the "tool-box" of the Tantric adept, machines whose raison d'être is to serve as the means for attaining the cognition that can be reclaimed only because, ultimately, it has never been lost. In this context, the chief epistemological characteristics of mantric utterance may be discerned: (1) mantras are tools of cognition; (2) mantras are elements in a system of discourse that depends upon certain root metaphors; (3) mantric utterance is experienced as disclosive.

In a redemptive context, mantric utterance does not appear to be either empty or ineffable. It has a "message:" It is understood to be a cognitive instrument that provides ultimate consolation because, in its very articulation, it dispels the cognitive darkness of nescience.

MANTRIC UTTERANCE AS A TOOL OF COGNITION

Kṣemarāja clarifies his epistemological understanding of mantric utterance in ŚSūV 2.1. The sūtra says: "A mantra is [an act of] consciousness (*cittam mantraḥ*)" (47). Kṣemarāja takes this to be an explication of the fundamental character of mantric utterance (*mantrasvarūpa*). His interpretation emphasizes that the utterance of a redemptive mantra is a specific act of cognition:

> "*citta*" is [that act of consciousness] by which ultimate reality (*paraṃ tattvam*) is cognized (*cetyate*), that is to say, [that act of consciousness by which] one becomes aware (*vimṛśyate*) [of it]; it is that [self]-awareness (*saṃvedana*) which is formed by the realization (*vimarśa*) of [mantras] such as the *Praṇava* and *Prāsāda* which are really the flowering of the fullness [of Śiva-who-becomes-the-cosmos] (*pūrṇasphurattā-*).
>
> It is solely that act of consciousness which is mantrically cognized in secret (*tad eva mantryate guptam*); by this [mantric cognition] that act of consciousness is judged (*vimṛśyate*) to take form as god (*parameśvara*) who is internally non-dual; this is the "derivation" [of the word] Mantra.
>
> In other words, mantra is explained as having the character of that cognition (*manana*) which is the primal vibration [in the cosmos] and [thus] as having the character of rescuing one from [*trāṇa*]—that is pacifying [*praśamana*]—*saṃsāra* which is [the realm] of dualities.[53]

Any doubt that Kṣemarāja takes the epistemic character of mantric utterance seriously ought be dispelled by the summation of his commentary on this sūtra. Kṣemarāja understands a mantra, in the proper sense of the term, to be a tool of redemptive thought. This, he contrasts with ununderstood "mantras," which may be caricatured as useless strings of nonesense syllables:

> A mantra is not merely an amalgam of different syllables; it is [in contrast] precisely the act of consciousness of a patient devotee (*ārādhakacittam*) who, because [his very utterance of the mantra] is a cognition of that to which the mantra refers (*mantradevatāvimarśaparatvena*), attains fusion with that reality.[54]

The citations with which Kṣemarāja concludes this section of his commentary reinforce his assertion that mantric utterance is grounded in and hence able to lead one back to Śiva-who-is-consciousness. One quotation is attributed to the *Śrīkaṇṭhīsaṃhitā*:

> So long as the person uttering a mantra (*mantrī*) is separate from the mantra itself, [his utterance] will never be successful (*siddhyati*);
>
> This whole cosmos (*idam sarvam*) is founded on consciousness (*jñanamūla*), unless that were the case [the uttering of a mantra] could never succeed (*siddhyati*).[55]

A second is attributed to the *Sarvajñānottara [Tantra]*:

> Mantras which are merely enunciated [verbally] are known not really to be mantras; the haughty *devās* and *gandharvās* have been deluded (*mohitā*) by the erroneous conclusion (*mithyājñāna*) [that an ununderstood mantra counts as a mantra].[56]

One may easily imagine an objection to the interpretation of mantras as epistemological instruments. Mantras, a sceptic might argue, are tools of meditation (or of ritual) that, far from being intellectual, are expressly designed to extirpate discursive, objective cognition and to evade its consequences. This objection carries considerable weight, yet there is a rejoinder. The central tradition of the *Pratyabhijñā,* as befits a theological response to Tantric *sādhanā,* shares the widespread Indian conviction that the root problem in human existence is ignorance, "miscognition." The antidote to this erroneous judgment is knowledge, as would have to be the case. The antidote does not demand an absence of cognition, it calls for correct cognition. Mantric utterance can be consistent with this conviction only if it is understood as the "mother" of correct cognition. This makes practical sense, too. The adept does not disappear in trance. Realization does not mean the dissolution of the thinking mind. If they really are redemptive, mantras have to be taken just as they are taken, as tools that lead the adept to a comprehensive, but ultimately discursive, vision of a coherent śaktic world, a world ultimately to be experienced as itself mantric, as Śiva's playful verbal self-expression.

MANTRIC UTTERANCE AS METAPHORIC

Root Metaphors of Mantra

Among the passages cited in the *Vimarśinā*'s discussion of Sūtra 2.1 is a verse attributed to the TSB. It places one immediately within the system of metaphorical discourse that Kṣemarāja's Mantraśāstra presupposes:

> It is imperishable (*avyayā*) śakti which is recollected to be that which animates mantras (*mantrānāṃ jīvabhūtā*); save for her, goddess, they would be fruitless like autumn clouds [from which no rains fall].[57]

Here, as often, the word *śakti* has a double sense. On the one hand, it refers directly to one or more deities who may be identified by name and objectified in ritual or meditation. On the other hand, it refers indirectly to one or more "capacities," of which the goddess or goddesses in question are in some sense "personifications." The phrase "*mantrānāṃ jīvabhūtā*" (literally, that which is the life of mantras) refers to that without which mantras would be "dead"; that is, would not work. To describe this animating factor as śakti is to draw upon a set of symbolic conventions that provide a vocabulary in whose terms the Mantravādin may account for, and affirm the ultimate value of, a particular experience of the world. As employed in accordance with the oral instruction of one's preceptor and as exegeted theologically in the ŚSūV, mantras assume meaning solely as elements within this mythic system of discourse.

That mantric utterance presupposes a set of metaphoric conceits does not mean that it is poetic, in the ordinary sense of the word. A metaphor is a trope or figure of speech; that is, an epistemological tool designed to describe and assess the human situation indirectly. Mythic discourse is, in turn, a body of religious narratives that make use of a particular set of metaphors. As a narrative elaboration of metaphor, mythic discourse assembles a complex of indirect comments concerning especially salient aspects, or the totality, of the experienced world.

Mantric utterance as "something done" is grounded in the Hindu social world. So, too, as a tool of cognition, it takes for granted certain Tantric variants of Śavite myth and cosmology. Historically, neither Śaivite spiritual discipline nor Śaivite thought has ever been wholly divorced from the mythic discourse of Śaivism. By teaching it how to view the world, the mythic tradition unconsciously shaped the religious expectations of the "community" of Śaivas. It, thus, set the stage on which discipline was followed and theological explanations debated.[58]

Given the widespread assumption of the Hindu religious elite that nescience is the root cause of human suffering, it makes sense that the Tantric version of Śaivite myth focuses in large measure on exposing both the limits and the potential of human cognition. Therefore, one must decipher the system of mythic discourse that the ŚSūV assumes and the root metaphors upon which that mythic discourse is built before one will be able to understand its epistemological portrayal of mantric utterance. One can "translate" a mantra (that is, explicate its meaning in direct, nonmetaphorical language) only if one sees the point of the metaphors it takes for granted. Only to the extent one has proposed a plausible nonmetaphoric translation can one assess the truth of the existential assertions implicit in a mantra.[59]

By and large, the ŚSūV offers a nonmantric exposition of mantric utterance; its exposition is not nonmythic, however. Its mythic discourse is built on a root metaphor that is at once organic and personalistic: The universe in which and in whom human beings live is understood to be Śiva, who transforms himself into the cosmos. As the cosmos, he is understood to be a constant, complex interaction of potencies, of personalized forces, of *śaktis.* Two especially significant secondary metaphors are drawn upon to fill out this essentially animistic vision. First, Śiva is understood as "sprouting," unfolding, exploding; as that primal pulsation (*spanda,* etc.) that becomes the living-moving (*calana*) world. The other secondary metaphor brought into play is verbal: Śiva is the Word.

In terms of these entirely plausible metaphors, the human world is pictured and, one may assume, experienced at once as a world in constant process and as an organic unity, a coherent set of complementary tendencies. Under the spell of the metaphor of "World as Word" both the organic unity and the diversity of the world are understood as the articulation, the expression (*vācya*), of Śiva-who-is-Transcendental-Speech (*parāvāc*) (cf. Padoux 1963, 141ff.). In his capacity to speak transcendentally Śiva is the one who articulates, expresses (*vācaka*), the world. As Kṣemarāja innocently assumes, in a world so constituted, it is natural to take mantras as peculiarly apt tools for "tricking" the utterer into a unique and uniquely valuable sort of cognition. Mantric utterance gets singled out as the one form of discourse that enables a human being to assert (to re-cognize) his freedom within the cosmic process. To put this metaphorically, it allows the adept so to identify himself with Śiva, who is at once Transcendental Speech and its mundane expression, that he, too, places himself verbally at once at the center and at the peripheries of the cosmic process. He, thereby, identifies wholly with the God-who-becomes-the-world, who both is and isn't limited by his limitation.

Myths of Mantra

The fundamentally mythic context of Kṣemarāja's understanding of mantras reveals itself most dramatically in his comments concerning ŚSū 1.4, 2.3, 2.7, and 3.19. In each of these sections, Kṣemarāja draws upon the well-developed Śaivāgamic myth of Mātṛkā, the cosmic mother of miscognition. The basic cosmology is laid out in ŚSūV 1.4. In 2.3 and 3.19, Kṣemarāja supplements his account by citing two cosmogonies. The first, a portion of which was quoted earlier, is from the TSB. The second is from the *Mālinīvijaya Tantra* (MVT). In his comment on 2.7, Kṣemarāja draws upon a version of the myth of Mātṛkā, which he attributes to the *Parātrīśikā* (PT), a text fragment largely devoted to the mytheme of "God as the Word that becomes the World."[60]

The use of the mythic discourse of the *Śaivāgamas* to make a fundamentally epistemological point is well illustrated by ŚSūV 1.4., where Kṣemarāja weaves together metaphorical and literal statements. The sūtra reads "Mātṛkā is the foundation of cognition (*jñānādhiṣṭhānāṃ mātṛkā*)" (16). The reader already knows from Sūtra 1.2 that limited "cognition" (*jñāna*)—in contrast to "consciousness" (*caitanya*)—may be equated with the root problem in human existence, "bondage" (*bandha*). Kṣemarāja's introductory sentence, using vocabulary introduced in the previous sūtras, thus indicates that the sūtra identifies the cause of bondage: "The fourth sūtra answers the question:

> '[How] is the threefold "blemish" (*mala*), that is, "cognition which is miscognition" (*ajñānātmakajñāna*), the *yonivarga*, and the *kalāśarīra*, bondage?',"[61]

Kṣemarāja begins his answer in a straightforward manner:

> The threefold blemish [which plagues human existence] is said to be essentially the diversity of cognitions (*vividham jñānarūpaṃ*). This amounts to pure and impure [karmic] impressions (*vāsana*), the extension of differentiated objects of thought (*bhinnavedyaprathā*), and the feeling of incompleteness (*apūrṃam manyatā*) [i. e., finitude].[62]

After this perfectly direct epistemic reading of the human condition, Kṣemarāja picks up the sūtra's mythical reference to Mātṛkā:

> The uncognized mother (*ajñātā mātā*), of this [threefold blemish] is Mātṛkā, [the "matrix"] who begets the world (*viśvajananī*) and whose form [is the verbal cosmos extending] from "a" to "kṣa" [the first and last letters of the Sanskrit alphabet].[63]

This mythic statement is interpreted as attributing human imperfection to the fact that we are linguistic animals. Its explication, once again, is direct and literal:

> [She is the matrix] who imparts (*ādadhānā*) forms such as sorrow, astonishment, joy, and passion to cognitions that involve the appearance of various limited (*saṃkucita*) objects of cognition. [These cognitions] amount to the judgment (*parāmarśa*) that there has been an appearance, [i. e., that something is the case], irrespective of whether [that appearance] is "predicative" or not (*avikalpakasavikalpaka*). [Examples of such judgments are] "I am a performer of the *agniṣṭoma* sacrifice," "I am skinny" or "I am fat," [and] "I am finite." [She, thus, transforms cognitions] by infusing them with various expressive words (*vācakaśabdānuvedhadvāreṇa*).[64]

Any suspicion that Kṣemarāja takes his direct, epistemic statements seriously and his mythic ones lightly is dispelled by the remainder of the commentary, beginning with a verse attributed to the *Timirodghāṭa*:

> The Mahāghorās are the deities of the *pīṭhas;*
> They wield (?) the noose of Brahman,
> They abide in the *Karandhra*-consciousness;
> They delude (*mohayanti*) [people] again and again.[65]

Stimulated by this verse and seemingly undeterred, as those of a different psychic temperment would be, by her portrayal here as the mother of that which is most baneful about the human world, Kṣemarāja offers what is in effect a brief prose paean to Mātṛkā:

> She shimmers with that sequence of śaktis beginning with Brāhmī who are the inner controllers (*adhiṣṭhātṛ*) of [the constituent elements of the cosmos] such as the *vargas* and the *kalās*. She incites the assembling of

> the sequence of letters which is well known from the *Sarvavīra* and other *āgamas*. She is graced (*-cumbitā*) with the circle of powers (*śakticakra*) whose names are Ambā, Jyeṣṭhā, Raudrī, and Vāmā. She is Śakti the inner controller.[66]

From this Śaivāgamic perspective, the entire cosmos may be experienced through ritual and in meditation exactly as it is envisioned metaphorically, as animated by circles upon circles of goddesses. Seen in this light Kṣemarāja's theory of nescience reads like a demonology. No matter that, in the final analysis, the śaktic world is sublated in that single complex cognition who is Śiva. In the meantime, *śakti,* in her countless guises, is Kṣemarāja's real object of religious fascination. His utilization of this mythic material is astute: He neither loses himself in the metaphoric forest of the Śaivāgamas nor repudiates it. Like his predecessors in the *Pratyabhijñā* tradition, he wirtes to provide a direct, public, philosophically responsible articulation of what we can today recognize as an essentially mythic view of the universe. Hence, he can conclude his commentary of Sūtra 1.4 with a direct epistemological assertion supplemented by two quotations from the SpK that allow him to return to a mythic vocabulary:

> Because [Mātṛkā] alone is the foundation of [ordinary cognition] (*tad* = *jñāna*) and because, as a consequence, [ordinary cognitions] in no way attend to [their own] inner nonduality (*antara 'bhedānusaṃdhivandhyatvāt*), ordinary cognitions are always externally oriented, not even for a moment do they attain repose (*alabdhaviśrāntīni*).[67]

It seems as if Kṣemarāja takes as his point of departure the fact that "mātṛkā" refers at once to a mythic "figure," the mother of the constellation of potencies (*śaktis*) that are understood to be the hidden controllers of the cosmos, and to the linguisticality of the experienced cosmos as such. He, thus, makes the simple epistemological point that human existence is bondage because it is linguistic. The verses he cites from the SpK make the point metaphorically:

> The individual self (*sa*), his [intrinsic] grandeur having been stolen by activity (*kalā*), having become the plaything (*bhogyatām*) of the array of powers (*śaktivarga*) that arise from the [transcendental] verbal-mass (*śabdarāśi*) is known as a bound (*paśuḥ*) [creature]. Save for the infusion of [cognitions] by words (*śabdānuvedhena . . . vinā*) ideas (*pratyaya*) could not arise; for this reason [i.e., because ideas do arise, we know that] the śaktis are constantly alert (*utthita*) to obscure the true nature of the individual self.[68]

Space precludes a detailed exegesis of any other passages that might exhibit the mythical substratum of Kṣemarāja's theology of mantras. I trust, however, that a sufficient number of passages have been cited to convey the flavor of Kṣemarāja's utilization of Śaivāgamic myth. I trust, too, that the main point is established: Kṣemarāja accepted mantric utterance as a privileged, specialized linguistic instrument that could be used to attain ultimate freedom. He was persuaded that mantras were effective because he was convinced that their very utterance, in the proper circumstances, was a redemptive cognition. Kṣemarāja may be understood as having an essentially mythic worldview. The system of mythic discourse he took for granted taught him that each human being is fundamentally deluded because he is a linguistic creature. It is reasonable to assume that this mythic viewpoint predisposed Kṣemarāja to understand mantric utterance as the one form of speaking that allowed a human being to overcome the evils of linguisticality, because in its very utterance, it disclosed the roots of language itself. It remains to explore how he understood this disclosive power.

MANTRA AS DISCLOSIVE UTTERANCE

Duality

Our exploration of the epistemological dimension of mantric utterance as understood in the ŚSūV began with the exegesis of Kṣemarāja's commentary on Sūtra 2.1 (*"cittaṃ mantraḥ"*). At the end of that commentary, Kṣemarāja cites a number of authoritative verses to substantiate his thesis that a mantra is something more than an inert conjunction of sounds. His final citation is SpK 2.2. Now that the mythic, and thus metaphoric, element in Kṣemarāja's understanding of mantra has been indicated, we are able to return to the citiation in which it is taken for granted that mantras, on the appropriate level of reality, are animate beings.

It is necessary to read SpK 2.1 and 2 together, as Kṣemarāja does in the *Spand Nirṇaya* [SpN]:

> Mantras, possessing the power of omniscience, resorting to the power [of the primal vibration, *spanda*], exercise authority just as the senses do for embodied selves; untainted and at peace, they, along with the consciousness of their patient utterers, melt into that very [reality]; [as such] they possess the characteristic of being Śiva (*śivadharmin*).[69]

In his commentary on ŚSū 2.1, Kṣemarāja expresses his conviction that when a person utters a mantra properly, he attains fusion (*sāmarasya*) with the object of that mantra (the *Mantradevatā*). He cites SpK. 2.2 in order to make the point that, from an ultimate perspective, a mantra and its utterer "become" Śiva because they already "are" Śiva. This is the apparent force of the *kārikā*'s "have the characteristic of being Śiva."

What can this mean? The *kārikā* suggests that "being Śiva" involves an intrinsic doubling of role: On the one hand, there is the "exercising of appropriate authority" (*pravartante 'adhikārā*); on the other hand, there is "being at peace" (*śāntarūpa*). This is an antithesis but, probably, not an alternative: Ultimately the *Pratyabhijñā* authors agree that any being is able to act "externally," that is, to exercise the authority appropriate to his place on a particular level of cosmic "evolution," solely because, in some ultimate sense, he remains "internally" at peace. This intimation that "being Śiva" involves two complementary sorts or modes of existing is confirmed by ŚSūV 3.15, where Kṣemarāja discusses the character of the adept who has achieved perfection.

ŚSū 3.12–14 speaks of an adept who, by means of a certain sort of yoga, has attained (*siddh-*) a realization of his own intrinsic "self-dependence" (*svatantrabhāva*). Sūtra 15 implicitly addresses the question, "How should such a perfected one behave?"

> Such a yogi should certainly not be indifferent (*udāsīna*). On the contrary;
>
> "He [should] attend to the 'seed' (*bījāvadhānam*)" (15). The "seed" is supreme śakti, the primal pulsation, the cause of the world, as is said in the reknowned *Mṛtyujit* [*Tantra*],
>
> "She is the womb of all the gods and of their countless (*anekadhā*) powers too
>
> She is the [union] of Agni and Soma, therefore the entire cosmos comes forth [from her].
>
> Continuously [the yogi] should be attentive to, which is to say, direct his mind into, the "seed" that is supreme śakti.[70]

The contrast between *udāsīna* (indifference, sitting on the side) and *avadhāna* (attention, placing oneself within) is instructive. One suggests passivity, the other, attention, which at least leaves open the possibility of active involvement. I think, it is characteristic of the central soteriological tradition of the Pratyabhijñā that ultimate realization is not portrayed merely as an absolute abstraction from the chaos of the world but as absolute attention to that chaos. Realization amounts to meditative attention to that chaos that is the world as it proceeds from and is śakti (this is the *double entendre* of *pra-vṛt-*).

ŚSū 3.15 directs the accomplished yogi to be attentive to the *bīja*,[71] presumably to the Mṛtyujit or Netra mantra OṂ JUṂ SAḤ. In other words, one is to direct attention to the "alphabetic" form of śakti, her mantric form conceived of as the womb of cosmic multiplicity. Mantra is a path of return through the maze of the śaktic world. Kṣemarāja and the tradition he follows take mantric utterance as fundamentally transformative, creating a special way of being in the world. When used well, a redemptive mantra is accepted by this tradition as disclosing a "new" reality, one to which the utterer of the mantra was previously unable to direct his attention.

What does such a mantric utterance disclose? In ŚSū 3.15, the *bīja* is portrayed as the womb of the multiplicity (*anekadhā*) of the śaktic universe. This is critical, for it seems to be a distinctive trait of mantric utterance as understood as an *upāya* in the ŚSūV that it is intrinsically and appropriately twofold. Just as "being Śiva" must, in the final analysis be thought of as intrinsically double,[72] so, too, the disclosive force of mantric utterance must be thought of as intrisically double. For Śiva, as for mantras, this intrinsic duality is the fruit and the "proof" of their intrinsic unity.

From one point of view, a mantra discloses an apparently "external" object, the "*devatā*." This point of view is "lower" but entirely legitimate. Indeed, assuming that it is Śiva's "nature" to express himself as the śaktic world, this point of view is necessary. The complementary point of view is, however, "higher" precisely because it puts the "lower" point of view in the proper perspective. From this perspective no distinction may be drawn between the mantra, the object of the mantra, and the utterer of the mantra. The utterance is directly disclosive. It is self-disclosive. One might say that it "saves" in that, for every properly prepared adept, it is believed to disclose Śiva to himself.

Epistemology

A contemporary philosopher of the social sciences, Karl Otto Apel, has observed that "all linguistic utterances and, moreover, all meaningful human actions and physical expressions (in so far as they can be verbalized) involve claims . . . and hence can be regarded as potential arguments" (1973, 259). In reaching this conclusion Apel has appropriately drawn upon Wittgenstein whose *Sprachkritik* has significantly influenced his own work. From this perspective even metaphoric statements whose contexts are mythic must be understood implicitly to be making assertions, variously about some aspect of the human world or about reality as such. Ricoeur's exploration of metaphor also supports the conclsuion that nonliteral language is implicitly "fact-stating." If Apel and Ricoeur are correct, as I am persuaded they are, it follows that an assertion implicit in a metaphoric (or mythical) utterance earns no exemption from the ordinary standards of epistemology. Its truth or falsity may, in principle, be evaluated in a straightforward, conventional manner.

The instinct of most students of mantra has been to stress its "symbolic" character, while discounting the possibility that mantras make cognitively judicable claims about matters of fact. If my reconstruction of the epistemological dimension of mantric utterance, as it is portrayed in the ŚSūV, is in some measure correct, this position must be reconsidered. If the utterance of a mantra is intended as a privileged act of cognition and if its coherence presupposes a complex of metaphors and myths, the truth or falsity of its indirect claims about matters of fact may be evaluated, provided—and this is a crucial proviso—their implicit claims can be translated into the language of ordinary, direct discourse.

Furthermore, if mantric utterance, in a redemptive context, intends itself as disclosive, then appraising the truth of its claims about reality cannot be incidental. It is central. The point of the utterance, what gives it significance in its own terms, is the disclosure. Properly described, in the context of the ŚSūV, the utterance of a mantra seems to present itself as a social act, presupposing a family of Śaivite metaphors and myths, promising to be that unique cognition that discloses an individual's real identity as Śiva. If this is the case, the theological implications cannot responsibly be evaded. It makes a difference whether Śiva is "really there," whether the world really is the way mantric utterance seeks to show the person who uses it that it is.

Self-Disclosivity

The self-disclosivity of the well-uttered mantra and the claims it makes find clear expression in ŚSūV 2.7, which contains one of the mythic cosmogonies mentioned earlier. The preceding sūtra (*"gurur upāya"*) having asserted the indispensibility of the guru, 2.7 describes what one obtains through him: "from a guru who is favorably disposed (*prasanna*) '[a disciple gains] perfect understanding of the circle [of powers that emerge from] Mātṛkā (*mātṛkacakrasambodhaḥ*)'."

In the first portion of his commentary (60, line 9; 63, line 3), Kṣemarāja summarizes, apparently in his own words but on the authority of the PT and other *āgamas,* the emergence of the world of complexity envisioned as linguistically structured. He pictures the complexity of the world analogically with the complexity of language. Just as the limited number of elements, phonemes (*varṇas*), in (the Sanskrit) language may be combined in an infinite number of sentences, so too the cognitive subjects and objects of the world have the capacity to form an infinite number of combinations. In both language and cognitive interaction, the chaos of infinite possibility is seen as structured and contained within a finite number of categories. Both are taken to be vehicles that one may follow back to god, their common ground. God is their common substratum because he is accepted as being—we would have to say, metaphorically—both Consciousness and the Word.

In the second portion of his commentary (63, line 3; 67, line 8), Kṣemarāja expounds the soteriological significance of this Tantric cosmology. In doing so, he naturally focuses on the self-disclosive power of mantric utterance, the utterance that leads one to cognize oneself as Śiva-who-is-the-Word. He begins with the simple observation that one should cause oneself to recollect, more precisely to re-cognize, the entirety of the very complex verbal cosmogony that has just been summarized (*iti pratyabhijñāpitum*).[73] The remainder of the commentary, in effect, is an explanation of how mantric utterance facilitates this saving re-cognition.

Kṣemarāja begins with the statement of his thesis: *AHAM* ("I"), the great mantra, encapsulates the cosmos. He supports this thesis by a quotation from Utpaladeva's *Ajaḍapramātṛsiddhi*:

> Therefore the reality (*tattvam*) of the judgment "I" (*ahaṃvimarśa*), which accounts for the efficacy of the great mantra (*mahāmantravīryātmano*), is this: The cosmos (*viśvam*) is simply that which is cocooned (*garbhīkṛtam etad ātmakam eva*) by means of *pratyāhara*, between Śiva and śakti, that is to say, between "that beyond which there is nothing higher" (*anuttara*) and "the unstruck sound," [i. e., between *a* (*akāra*), the first letter of the Sanskrit alphabet, and *ha* (*hakāra*), the last, respectively]. As has been said by our illustrious master (*parameṣṭhi*) Utpaladeva:
>
> > For it is well known that the state of being an "I" (*ahaṃbhāva*) is the self-subsistence of illumination (*prakāśasyātmaviśrāntir*); moreover, this state is known as stasis (*viśrānti*) because, in it, dependence on anything else [external to itself] is suppressed (*sarvāpekṣānirodhataḥ*); similarly [it is known] as self-dependence (*svātantryam*), agency (*kartṛtvam*), and primal lordship (*mukhyam īśvaratā*).[74]

In this sort of Śaivite Tantra there is a tendency toward duplication. It is Śiva who becomes the world, but he does so in his feminine mode, as Śakti. Accordingly Kṣemarāja, having explained that Śiva, the cosmic "I," becomes the verbal world, turns to Śakti, to Mātṛkā, to identify her with Śiva, the "I," and to portray her as the womb of the verbal cosmos:

> The reality (*tattvam*) of Mātṛkā that has thus been delimited is precisely that which has finally been revealed by the *Kūtabīja*, [that is, the letter *kṣa*, (*kṣa-kāra*)], which [is formed] by the essential conjunction of "that beyond which there is nothing further," [the letter *a* understood to pervade the consonants represented by *ka*], and *visarga*, [the sign for aspiration which comes at the very end of the Sanskrit alphabet, understood to represent the sibilants including *sa*], which is to say, by the *pratyāhara* of *ka-kāra* and *sa-kāra*; this is a sufficient clarification of that which is secret.[75]

Having asserted the parallelism between "*aham*" and Mātṛkā, Kṣemarāja is ready to explain that understanding of the circle of powers that emanate from Mātṛkā, which one gains from a well-disposed guru:

> [The word *sambodha* in this sūtra means] understanding (*bodha*) that is precisely (*samyak*) attaining (*samāveśa*) one's own self, which is a mass of consciousness and bliss, [that is, understanding] the collection of powers beginning with *anuttara*, *ānanda*, and *icchā*, which have already been mentioned, [powers that make up] the circle that is connected to

> Mātṛkā, whose glory [*prabhāva*) has been specified in scriptural verses of this sort: "There is no science (*vidyā*) higher than Mātṛkā."[76]

After reference to Abhinavagupta's *PTVivaraṇa* and *Tantrāloka*, Kṣemarāja concludes his commentary on ŚSū 2.7 with a long quotation attributed to the *Siddhāmṛta* and a verse from the SpK. These passages reassert the dialectical reciprocity of Śiva and Śakti, or god and world, understood analogously to the reciprocity of *a-kāra* and *visarga*, that is to say the vowel *a* and the circle of consonents.[77]

The last lines from the *Siddhāmṛta* and the verse from the SpK underscore the soteric value of the *mahāmantra* AHAM, which encompasses the universe, and of the guru without whom one could not utilize it properly:

> Mantras that did not begin with *a* and end with *m* would be [as useless] as autumn clouds; the defining characteristic of a guru is, accordingly, that he can reveal [a mantra] beginning with *a* and ending with *m*.
>
> Such a knowledgeable master (*jñānin*), being, in effect, the god Bhairava, merits worship (*pūjyaḥ*) just as I, [Śiva, merit worship].
>
> Because he knows that any [utterance], for example, a *śloka* or a *gātha*, is endowed with *a* as its beginning and *m* as its ending, [the guru] sees the cosmos (*sarva*) as being wholly mantric (*mantratvenaiva*).[78]

For Kṣemarāja, then, the great mantra is a vital, effective tool of redemption, the skeleton key to the cosmos. It liberates because it recapitulates in its inner structure the inner structure of bondage that is believed to be at once linguistic and cognitive. So SpK 3.16:

> It is Śiva's śakti, that is, his power to act, who, dwelling
> within limited creatures, causes bondage;
> When she is known as herself the path, she is the one who
> makes perfection (*siddhi*) possible.[79]

CONCLUSION

How should we understand the great mantra AHAM? How may we translate it? Keeping our exegesis of Kṣemarāja's understanding in mind, I propose that it be read as a sentence consisting of a single word. "I" is the subject of the sentence; its predicate has to be supplied. There would seem to be two possibilities. If one concludes that the implied referent is personal, then the great mantra may be translated as "I [am Śiva]!" If one concludes that the implied referent is impersonal, then it may be translated as "I [am That]!" In the first case, we would have to classify the sentence as mythological. In the second instance, we can admit that it is meant literally. If the two sentences are taken, as must surely be the case, to have the same referent, then the word *That* in the second sentence must refer to that to which the word *Śiva* refers metaphorically. What can that be but the cosmos understood comprehensively as the redeeming object of religious fascination. The mantra AHAM taken to mean "I am Śiva!" is thus revealed to be a metaphorical utterance whose indirect reference is precisely conveyed through the literal statement "I am That!"

If one were a contemporary Śaivite theologian, such a nonmythological translation of the mantra AHAM could be of considerable interest. Without doubt, it is the Hindu tradition's metaphorical density that gives it emotive appeal. If, however, one wants to defend its claims about matters of fact as internally coherent and true, as having both meaning (*Sinn*) and Reference (*Bedeutung*), one has to know what it is really talking about. Otherwise, one has no way of determining whether it is epistemologically responsible to credit that tradition's claims. (Of course, it may be psychologically and socially responsible, and for many people, that will be more than sufficient.)

To be sure, neither Kṣemarāja nor the Śaivāgamic texts for which he attempts to provide a rational theology have the vocabulary to speak of religious language in terms of the modern, Western categories of "myth" and "metaphor." I suspect, however, that Śaiva Tantra, as systematized in the ŚSūV, makes something like the same point in its own terms. We have just seen that the mantra AHAM, for the ŚSūV the *Mahāvākya* of Śaiva Tantra, may be taken literally. It is interesting that it is paired with another mantra, which phonemically mirrors it while being constructed in the same way and making the same point. If the mantra AHAM means "I am That!" it may be put into Sanskrit as "*so 'ham,*" and this, in fact, is frequently done. The mirror image of "*so 'ham*" is the mantra HAṂSAḤ. Since the word *haṃsa* refers to the mythological gander long taken to symbolize the Self, this mantra may be translated, "[I am] the Cosmic Bird." Kṣemarāja deals with it in ŚSūV 3.27, with which we may conclude the exploration of mantric utterance as intentionally disclosive.

The sūtra, speaking of someone who has become "equivalent to Śiva" (*Śivatulya,* 3.25 [110]), says: "[All of his] discourse is the repetition [of the Name of God] (*kathā japaḥ*)" (113). Kṣemarāja exegetes this in a familiar manner:

> [The discourse of a master is *japa*] because he truly has constant inner realization (*bhāvanā*) of being the supreme "I" (*parāham*). This is in accordance with the maxim of the SvT: 'I myself am the supreme *Haṃsa,* Śiva, the primal cause'."[80]

As the *haṃsa* is Śiva, so, too, the knowledge attained throught the HAṂSA and AHAM mantras is one:

> Without exception, the conversation of [an adept who] has acquired the unfabricated cognition "I" (*akṛtakāhamvimarśārūḍhasya*), [the cognition] that is really the great mantra [AHAM,] becomes *japa*, which is to say, the incessant repetition of the cognition (*vimarśa*) of oneself as god (*svātmadevatā*).[81]

We have come full circle, it would appear. In this passage, the ŚSūV offers as the sign of the highest spiritual attainment nothing more than *japa*, the endless muttering of scared syllables, one of the most common social and ritual practices of India. While an examination of *japa* is beyond the scope of this paper, a strategy may be suggested, in keeping with the dialectical subtlety of Kasmiri Śaivite Tantra.

Just as an intrinsic duality is believed to be running through Śiva and the cosmos he becomes; just as language is believed to express itself in both a supreme form as the Word (*Parāvāc*) and in penulitmate forms; just as mantric utterance can be socially distinguished into quotidian and redemptive categories according to context; so, too, *japa* reveals itself as a complex phenomenon varying with context. From the perspective I have adopted in this paper, this is exactly what one would expect. A single sentence can be used to convey different meanings depending on circumstances and intention. For example, if I were to utter the mantra AHAM eighteen thousand times, the first utterance in the sequence ought to be significantly different from the last. The point of the endless repetition, after all, would not be for me to lose myself in trance, but for me as *sādhaka* to get it right. Close as I might eventually come, the utterance would be "unhappy" unless and until it became redemptive; that is, unless and until I really, at each stage, had gotten the "final" point.

This is, I think, what Kṣemarāja has in mind when he concludes the commentary on ŚSū 3.27 by pointing out that getting the utterance of the great mantra correct is at once the easiest and the most difficult of tasks. He cites two verses from the VBT that summarize what he has to say about the dialectical self-disclosity of mantric utterance:

> *Japa* is the progressive realization of the supreme state (*pare bhāve*);
> It is precisely this—one's own primeval sound (*svayaṃ nādo*) which is a mantra—that is to be repeated (*jap-*);
>
> With the letter *sa* [the breath] is expelled, with the letter *ha* it reenters;
> The individual being (*jīva*) constantly repeats the mantra, "*haṃsa, haṃsa*"
>
> Day and night, 21,600 [times] this repetition [of the mantra] of the goddess is enjoined;
> It is simple to achieve this, but difficult for dullards.[82]

In the modern West, we have often assumed that religion is a fundamentally alinguistic phenomenon. The very term *religion* is commonly taken to refer, as Rilke put it, to that "experience" (*Erlebnis*) for which "the domains of the sayable did not really seem to suffice" (1938, 227). In this regard, the tradition of radical monotheism and certain strands of Western philosophy agree. Wittgenstein, too, in both the T and PI was inclined by training and temperament to see that which could not be spoken as more valuable than that which could. Many mystical traditions beyond the West further support this picture of the ultimate as ineffable.

There is another story, however. The Wittgensteinian method does not necessitate this faith in the inarticulate. Read the way I have suggested and used the way I have attempted to use it, it might lead to the opposite conclusion: Anything significant can be articulated, albeit imperfectly or in an eccentric manner. This paper attempted to explore one strand of thought that dissents from the widespread adulation of mystic silence. The central tradition of Kaśmir Śaivism figures the ultimate mythically as Transcendental Discourse (*Parāvāc*), as the goddess Śakti. Ontologically, it asserts that the ultimate is transcendentally linguistic, for it is that which makes possible the mundane conversation of men. Soteriologically, it teaches that uttering the great mantra is the tool that puts one in touch with her (or it). In the end, it holds out the hope that, for those who know, ordinary discourse as a whole will be redemptive. Wittgenstein's *Sprachkritik* is meant to be therapeutic. So, too mutatis mutandis, the utterance of mantras is meant to be therapeutic. If, for a time, we are able to put aside some of our assumptions and prejudices, the study of mantra might be similarly salutory. Perhaps, it can help us overcome the linguistic poverty of Western monotheism. Perhaps, it can teach us to understand the world through a radically different verbal frame.

NOTES

1. The phrase *Kaśmiri Śaivism* is a recent Western invention and does not correspond to any term in the indigenous vocabulary. While it would be best if the term fell into disuse, it is conventional and convenient. For bibliographical orientation see Alper (1979, 386; 387 n. 1, 403–407 n. 7). An introductory handbook, *Approaching the Śaivism of Kaśmir,* is currently being prepared. It is scheduled to appear in the State University of New York Press Series on the Śaiva Traditions of Kaśmir; it will contain a comprehensive annotated bibliography.

On the problem of defining mantra, see the introduction to this volume. There I propose a rough distinction between the "quotidian" and the "redemptive" use of mantras. While the various Śaivāgamic preceptorial traditions surely knew of and accepted the quotidian use of mantras, the ŚSūV focuses on the redemptive. In this essay, I thus limit myself to those mantric utterances believed to effect (or to express) freedom as such.

The first epigraph is taken from *If on a Winter's Night a Traveler* (New York: Harcourt Brace Jovanovitch, 1981), p. 193. The second, *na tair* [=mantrair] *vinā bhavec chabdo nārtho nāpi citer gatiḥ*, is quoted by Abhinavagupta in the IPKV 1.5.14 (KSTS 22:212). The third is *yadi rahasyārtho na buddhyate, tasmāt sadgurusaparyā kārya* (55). I would like to acknowledge valuable contributions made during my work on this essay by my colleagues Lonnie D. Kliever and Charles M. Wood, by John Taber (Case Western Reserve University, Cleveland), and by Osbourne P. Wiggins (the New School for Social Research, New York). I am particularly indebted to André Padoux (Centre national de recherche scientifique, Paris), who kindly read the manuscript and suggested a number of improvements. Needless to say, none of these individuals is responsible for any errors that remain in my account. I also wish to acknowledge the encouragement of my friends Marie Pardue and Jocko DiGiacomo.

2. By now, the literature on Wittgenstein is enormous. A brief orientation may be found in Toulmin (1969) or Cavell (1962); for a more extensive survey, one might consult the two volumes of Finch (1971, 1977); and a thoughtful guide to reading Wittgenstein for oneself is Coope and associates (1970). I cite Wittgenstein in the standard English translations while providing the German original as appropriate. I follow the usual conventions in citing paragraph rather than page whenever possible.

3. It would be accurate to say that there was a single pan-Indian Āgamic tradition, which, in the course of history, became regionally refracted. No one has yet definitively catalogued the *āgamas* recognized by the various "regional" Śaivisms, no less the different intersecting Kaśmiri perceptorial-soteriological traditions. The ŚSūV cites a number of unpublished or problematic *Āgamas*. Tracing and collating quotations from these sources is a desideratum. I use a certain number of Śaivāgamic technical terms in this essay. In most cases, one may find reasonably clear English equivalents, but such terms defy simple, precise translation: *uccāra, prakāśa* (see Alper 1979), *bindu, bīja, mantroddhāra* (see Padoux 1978a), *mālinī, varṇa, śakticakra, śabdarāśi*, and *spanda*. See, in general, Padoux (1963) and the works of Lilian Silburn (1961; 1980; 1983).

4. All translations from the ŚSū and ŚSūV are my own unless otherwise noted. They are based on the text in KSTS 1 [=J. C. Chatterji 1911] and cited by chapter (*unmeṣa*) and sūtra as well as page and, as needed, line. The ŚSū and the V have been translated several times: twice into English (Shrinivas Iyengar 1912; Jaideva Singh 1979), once into French (Silburn 1980); there are also Italian (Torella 1979) and Hindi translations, but I had not yet seen them at the time this essay was written. The most reliable of these translations are by Silburn and Torella; Jaidev Singh's should be read as an—interesting—English *bhāṣya*. On the several accounts of the "revelation" of the ŚSū to Vasugupta see Chatterji (1916 [1914] 26ff.). Surviving commentaries on the ŚSū include, in addition to the ŚSūV, an anonymous *Vṛtti*, a *Vārttika* by Bhāskara (fl. mid-tenth century) [both =KSTS 4], and a *Vārttika* by Varadarāja (fl. fifteenth century) [=KSTS 43]. The exact relationships among these commentaries are not entirely clear. Chat-

terji (1916 [1914], 29f., 34) is inclined to credit Bhāskara (this is not the commentator of Abhinava's IPKV) with preserving the most authentic interpretation of the *Sūtras*. The original meaning of the ŚSū is beyond the scope of this essay. Cf., n. 22 of this essay.

5. In addition to *śivatulya* (3.25), for example, the sūtras speak of a "getting together" (*saṃghāna, saṃghatta*), a "becoming connected" (*sambandha*), a "being immersed in" (*ni-majj*), an "entering into" (*pra-viś*) Śiva; Kṣemaraja speaks of "penetration" (*samāveāa*) and "fusion" (*sāmarasya*), for example. A detailed study of this vocabulary is a desideratum.

6. In his commentary, Kṣemarāja effectively treats the SpK as an elucidative appendix to the ŚSū. In general, one may see Jaideva Singh's (1980) translation of the SpK with Kṣemarāja's commentary, the *Nirṇaya* (SpN). In dating the major Kaśmiri Śaiva figures, I generally cite Rastogi's (1979) revision of Pandey's (1954) calculations.

7. Staal is certainly correct in cautioning us not to assume that a "Hindu" scholastic interpretation of Mantraśāstra is necessarily accurate merely because it is indigenous. In the broadest sense, however, scholarly interpretations of Mantraśāstra cumulatively become one with the phenomenon they purport to elucidate; hence, they merit elucidation in their own right. Even if one wished to deny this to "unfriendly" Western interpretations, it surely holds for traditional ones.

8. Wittgenstein himself did not set out to construct such a typology. To do so is *not* following in Wittgenstein's footsteps; it is *not* practicing philosophy the way he did. It is proposing a disciplinary amendment to his philosophical program.

9. As I discussed in the Introduction to this volume, whether a mantric utterance is linguistic is disputed. I believe that one could frame an argument to demonstrate the linguistic nature of mantra, but I do not attempt to do so here. Another possibility might be to argue that ostensibly nonlinguistic mantras must be understood analogically with those that are linguistic, rather than vice versa. Or, one might argue that the utterance of a mantra is a linguistic act in that it functions linguistically.

10. On the sociological adaptation of Wittgensteinian thought, see Dallmayr and McCarthy (1977), part III ("The Wittgensteinian Reformulation"). The theological use of the Wittgensteinian tradition can best be grasped by reviewing the work of D. Z. Phillips in light of Kai Nielsen's critiques of what he has labeled *Wittgensteinian fideism* (e. g., 1967, 1973). On Wittgenstein and the philosophy of religion, besides Sherry, there are the works and collections of High (1967, 1969), Hudson (1968, 1975), Trigg (1973), and Keightley (1976); see also the review article of Whittaker (1978).

11. The status of the aesthetic, the ethical, the logical, and the mystical in the *Tractatus* are incisively surveyed in Zemach (1964–65); cf. Lucier (1973).

12. The term *language-game* is used throughout PI; see in particular 1–38. It is

important to keep in mind that initially *language-game* is used analogically, Wittgenstein *compares* ways of speaking (languages) to games; only secondarily does he come to speak of speaking as, in fact, a "game"; see Specht (1969), Chapter II ("The language-game as model concept in Wittgenstein's theory of language"), and Baker and Hacker (1980) 1.6 (language-games). On the tension between the "transcendental" and "realistic" interpretations of language in Wittgenstein, see Harries (1968). *Form of life* is used only fives times in PI, paragraphs 19, 23, 41, and Pt. II, pp. 174 and 226. On some of the options in interpreting *form of life,* see Hunter (1971).

13. Hence, the famous aphorism (PI 43); "For a *large* class of cases—though not for all—in which we employ the word *meaning* it can be defined thus: the meaning of a word is its use in the language" (*Man kann für eine* grosse *Klasse von Fällen der Benützung des Wortes "Bedeutung"—wenn auch nicht für alle Fälle seiner Benützung—dieses Wort so eklären: Die Bedeutung eines Wortes ist sein Gebrauch in der Sprache*). An exploration of this thesis may be found in Hallett (1967).

14. Although *speech act* is a technical term used especially by John Searle in his elaboration of Austin's analysis of language, it seems equally appropriate in a Wittgensteinian setting.

15. *Könnte Einer eine Sekunde lang innige Liebe oder Hofnung empfinden,*—was immer *dieser Sekunde voranging, oder ihr folgt?—Was jetzt geschieht, hat Bedeutung—in dieser Umgebung. Die Umgebung gibt ihm die Wichtigkeit.*

16. A phenomeonological reading of Wittgenstein is ventured by Gier (1981); see especially Chapter 6, "The Life-world".

17. Sherry's analysis of the method implicit in Wittgensteinian thought provides a convenient summary of the main methodological issues. This should not obscure its artificiality. The questions it separates for the purpose of analysis must in actuality often be addressed to the material one is interrogating in an untidy melange.

18. For orientation to the fideism controversy in recent Protestant theology, see Diamond and Litzenberg (1975); on traditional Western fideism, one might read Montaigne, in the context of Popkin (1979).

19. The argument is scattered through Sherry (1977), relevant passages can befound on 21, 40, 48, 59, 172ff., 180ff., 211.

20. The most astute portrayal of "popular" Hinduism from this perspective remains Carl Gustave Diehl's (1956) *Instrument and Purpose*. For a complementary portrait of "folk" Hinduism, see Abbott (1933), *The Keys of Power*.

21. This theme is explored in PI 240, and Part II, p. 223; and at greater length in the later works, for example, Z 114–17, OC 167, 204.

22. For the purposes of this inquiry, one may treat the three sections into which both Kṣemarāja and Bhāskara divide the ŚSū together, for no significant difference is apparent in their understanding of mantra. A discussion of the

treatment of *upāya* in the ŚSū as a whole cannot be offered here. One should keep in mind, however, that the sūtras were probably subject to diverse preceptorial interpretation from the start. Kṣemarāja, whose text has seventy-seven sūtras, dubs the three chapters (*unmeṣas*) of his commentary the *Śāmbhavopāya-*, the *Śaktopāya-*, and the *Aṇavopāya-*, respectively. Bhāskara, whose text has seventy-nine sūtras, titles the corresponding three chapters (*prakaśas*) of his commentary the *Sāmānyacit-*, the *Sahajavidyodaya-*, and the *Vibhutispanda-*.

Most studies of Kaśiri Śaivism take Kṣemarāja's analysis at face value and assume that "Kaśmir Śaivism" teaches three or, if one considers *anupāya* a path, four "paths." This is misleading. Even a cursory reading of the relevant, published Śaivāgamic sources reveals that no single scheme for codifying and classifying techniques was recognized to aid in attaining liberation. Minimally, the tradition of three (or four) *upāyas* must be differentiated from that of the six *adhavans*.

The theory of three *upāyas* quite properly strikes one as a scholastic construction, attempting to impose order on a disorderly body of traditional techniques; it has benefited from its tidiness and from the prestige of Abhinavagupta, who utilizes it in the TĀ and who presumably invented it. Critical examination suggests that the ŚSūV itself attempts to reconcile a myriad of soteriologically distinct, but overlapping, techniques. Thus, it is prudent to take Kṣemarāja's classificatory scheme with caution. Note especially that the *Śāmbhavopāya* is so called, *not* (as is sometimes said) because it is a "path of Śiva" *as opposed to* Śakti, but because according to it the culminating experience of human life is mergence with Śakti, with *Śiva's* capability; it is called *Śābhavopāya* because it focuses on becoming Bhairava. Even as "orthodox" an interpreter as Jaideva Singh recognizes that Kṣemarāja's scheme cannot be applied mechanically, cf. his discussion of the "dis-cordant" references to *Śaktopāya* and *Śāmbhavopāya* in the third *unmeṣa* (1979, xliff.). In any case, a definitive sorting out of all this awaits an elucidation of the sources of the TĀ of the sort being assayed by Alexis Sanderson (1986).

23. Ātmano bhairavaṃ rūpam bhāvayed yas tu puruṣaḥ / tasya mantrāḥ prasiddhyanti nityayuktasya sundari//(20). This verse does not seem to be found in the published text of the SvT; the editor of the KSTS text, J. C. Chatterji (1911, 270) indicates that the quotation is a variant of SvT 2.142 (1.80) (not 2.137!) to which verse Silburn (1980, 42) also refers.

24. It is explicitly recognized, of course, that there can be "defects" in the attempted use of a mantra. Elaborate classifications of possible defects and methods to rectify them are contained in treatises on Mantraśāstra. In allowing for errors and their rectification, Mantraśāstra is showing that self-protective cunning that usually characterizes expert systems.

25. Cf. the discussion of "Infelicities" in Austin (1962, 14ff.). In a paper read at the American Oriental Society in 1982, I sketched a preliminary defense of the application of speech-act theory to mantric utterance. In that paper, which I hope to revise for publication, I argued that "the uttering of a mantra is perlocu-

tionary in its intention, but illocutionary in its actuality"; i. e., its effect. To put this in terms of Searle's revision of Austin's categories, the sort of redemptive mantras with which I am here concerned might be considered "declarations" that "overlap" with the class of "assertives" (cf. Searle 1979a, 19f.).

26. *Etad bandhapraśamopāyam upeyaviśrāntisatattvam ādiśati* (18).

27. *Na saṃdhānaṃ vinā dīkṣā na siddhīnāṃ na sādhanam/ na mantro mantrayuktiś ca na yogākarṣaṇaṃ tathā//* (39). Kṣemarāja attributes this to a *Lakṣmīkaulārṇava*; I have been unable to ascertain whether a text of that name is extant; the exact force of "mantrayukti" is unclear to me.

28. Bhāvanaṃ hi atra antarmukhodyantṛtāpadavimarśanam eva (20). Silburn recognizes the dialectical tension when she treats *udyantṛta,* and related terms, as indicative of a "*ferveur intense,*" an "*élan purement intérieur au moment du retour à l'indifférencié, mais toujours élan intérieur* propre au premier moment du Désir (*prathamatuṭi*) qui contient virtuellement tout ce qui se développa par la suite" [emphasis mine] (12 and see glossary).

29. My translation of the term *vimarśa* reflects my convictions about the sort of technical term it is. It is often interpreted as if it were part of a system of ego psychology. In contrast, I am persuaded that it is part of a system of transcendental metaphysics. If I am correct, it refers to the transcendental capacity of Śiva that allows him to objectify himself as the subject, to make the judgment "I am Śiva." I have argued for this understanding, not with as much clarity and accuracy as I would like, in a paper to appear in 1987. I expect to return to the issue.

30. The context is established by Sūtra 2.1 (*cittam mantraḥ*), which I shall discuss later; *yathoktarūpasya mantrasya anusaṃdhitsāprathamonmeṣāvaṣṭambhaprayatanātmā akṛtako yaḥ prayatnaḥ sa eva sādhako, mantrayitur mantradevatātādātmyapradaḥ* (49).

31. *āmiṣaṃ tu yathā khasthaḥ saṃpaśyañ śakuniḥ priye*
kṣipram ākarṣayed yadvad vegena sahajena tu//
tadvad eva hi yogīndro mano binduṃ vikarṣayet
yathā śaro dhanuḥsaṃstho yatnenātāḍya dhāvati
tathā bindur varārohe uccāreṇaiva dhāvati (49).

32. —*akṛtakanijodyogabalena yogīndro manaḥ karma, binduṃ vikarṣayet*
paraprakāśātmatāṃ prāpayet iti/ tathā binduḥ paraprakāśaḥ
akṛtakodyantṛtātmanā uccāreṇa dhāvati, prasarati ity arthaḥ/ (49f.)
Kṣemarāja quite appropriately interprets "*mano binduṃ*" as a double accusative, "*manas*" indicating the direct object, "*bindu*" indicating the indirect object.

33. See Chapter 2, Staal's contribution to this volume. Obviously, because I am persuaded that the utilization of mantras can count as an instance of linguistic activity, I cannot follow Staal in seeing mantra as ritual gesture *simpliciter.*

34. I use the term *public* as the opposite of private in the sense of individual,

as in the phrase *private language*. In these terms, the rituals of the "householder" are public while the practices of a hermit are not.

35. Cf. Apel (1973, 258f.) who, drawing upon Wittgenstein, speaks of a "*Gemeinschaft von Denkern*" and an "*Argumentationsgemeinschaft.*"

36. See the relevant sections of the Bibliography.

37. Gṛṇati upadiśati tāttvikam artham iti guruḥ; so 'tra vyāptipradarśakatvena upāyaḥ (59). The exact meaning of *vyāpti* in this sentence is unclear to me. My translation follows J. C. Chatterji (59, n. 33) who glosses: *vyāptir atra mudrāvīrya-mantravīryasvarūpā.*

38. *Gurubhāvaḥ paraṃ tīrtham anyatīrthaṃ nirarthakam*
Sarvātīrthāśrayaṃ devī pādāṅguṣṭhaṃ ca vartate (54).

39. *Dhyānamūlaṃ guror mūrtiḥ pūjāmūlaṃ guroḥ padam*
Mantramūlaṃ guror vākyaṃ mokṣamūlaṃ guroḥ kṛpā (28).

40. *Sa gurur matsamaḥ prokto mantravīryaprakāśakaḥ* (59). This passage is taken from MVT 2.10.

41. *Agādhasaṃśayāmbhodhisamuttaraṇatāriṇīm/ vande . . . gurubhāratīm* (59). This passage is taken from SpK 3.20 [=4.1].

42. *Gurur vā pārameśvarī anugrāhikā śaktiḥ/ Yathoktaṃ śrīmālinīvijaye "śakticakraṃ tad evoktaṃ guruvaktraṃ tad ucyate"* (60).

43. *Śrīmantriśirobhairave 'pi "guror gurutarā śaktir guruvaktragatā bhavet" iti. Saiva avakāśāṃ dadatī upāyaḥ* (60).

44. *Sarve varṇātmakā mantrās te ca śaktyātmakāḥ priye*
śaktis tu mātṛkā jñeyā sā ca jñeyā śivātmikā (51).

This verse and the verses from the same passage cited later presuppose a number of technical terms whose *sitz im leben* is the Tantric, meditative cosmology that envisions the evolution of the world within god as sonic. No translation can capture all of the connotations of the original: Succintly, *varṇa* is "transcendental phoneme"; *mātṛkā,* "[sonic] mother [of the cosmos]"; *śabdaraśi,* "[transcendental] mass of words/sounds [from which the cosmos evolves]"; *mālinī,* "[transcendental] sequence of phonemes [which structures the cosmic evolution]"; the verbs *sphṛ-, sphar-, sphur-* (to pulsate) allude to the theory of *spanda,* the evolution of the cosmos structured by pulsating sonic energies.

45. *Na jānanti guruṃ devaṃ śāstroktān samayāṃs tathā*
dambhakauṭilyaniratā laukyārthāḥ kriyayojjhitāḥ
asmāt tu kāraṇād devi mayā vīryaṃ pragopitam
tena guptena te guptāḥ śeṣā varṇās tu kevalāḥ (51).

46. *Tatraiva ca ayam arthaḥ atirahasyo 'pi vitatya sphuṭīkṛtaḥ* (51). I translate *vitatya* on the assumption that, consciously or not, it is an allusion to the derivation of the word *tantra* from *tan* (to extend).

47. Mahāhradānusaṃdhānān mantravīryānubhavaḥ (44). The term *hrada,* which I translate as lake, in order to reinforce the imagery of soteric immersion also means "[primal] sound." The following passage uses technical concepts that cannot be explicated here.

48. —*tasyānusaṃdhānāt, antarmukhatayā anāratam tattādātmyavimarśanāt; vakṣyamāṇasya śabdarāśisphārātmakaparāhantāvimarśamayasya mantravīryasyānubhavaḥ, svātmarūpatayā sphuraṇaṃ bhavati/ ata eva śrīmālinīvijaye 'yā sā śaktir jagaddhātuḥ . . . /' ity upakramya icchādipramukhapañcāśadbhedarūpatayā mātṛkā-mālinīrūpatām aśeṣaviśvamayīṃ śakteḥ pradarśya, tata eva mantroddhāro darśitaḥ; iti paraiva śaktir mahāhradaḥ; tataḥ tadanusaṃdhānāt mātṛkā-mālinīsatattvamantravīryānubhava iti yuktam uktam/* (44–45).

49. That is, the decoding of the elements of the mantra precedes its construction. I wish to thank André Padoux, who some time ago pointed out the relevance of Schoterman's discussion of *prastāra* to this passage.

50. —*varṇasaṃghaṭṭanāśarīrāṇāṃ mantrāṇāṃ saiva bhagavatī vyākhyātarūpā vidyāśarīrasattā rahasyam iti pradarśitaṃ/ pratyāgamaṃ ca mātṛkāmālinīprastārapūrvakaṃ mantroddhārakathanasya ayam eva āśayaḥ/* (2.3, 55).

51. This analogy was suggested by Canfield (1981, 26), whose exact words I have borrowed, in part.

52. I use the term *theodicy* in the extended sociological sense associated with Weber. The phrase "OK world" is borrowed from Peter Berger (1968).

53. *Cetyate vimṛsyate anena paraṃ tattvam iti cittaṃ, pūrṇasphurattāsatattvaprāsādapraṇavādivimarśarūpaṃ saṃvedana; tad eva mantryate guptam, antar abhedena vimṛśyate parameśvararūpam anena, iti kṛtvā mantraḥ/ ata eva ca parasphurattātmakamananadharmātmatā, bhedamayasaṃsārapraśamanātmakatrāṇadharmatā ca asya nirucyate/* (47); the *praṇava* mantra is OṂ; the identity of the *prāsāda* mantra seems to vary from tradition to tradition, here it is SAUḤ.

54. *Atha ca mantradevatāvimarśaparatvena prāptatatsāmarasyam ārādhakacittam eva mantraḥ, na tu vicitravarṇasaṃghaṭṭanāmātrakam/* (47f.).

55. *Pṛthaṅmantraḥ pṛthaṅmantrī na siddhyati kadācana*
jñānamūlam idaṃ sarvam anyathā naiva siddhyati (48).

56. *Uccāryamāṇā ye mantrā na mantrāṃś cāpi tān viduḥ*
mohitā devagandharvā mithyājñānena garvitāḥ (48).

57. *mantrāṇāṃ jīvabhūtā tu yā smṛtā śaktir avyayā*
tayā hīnā varārohe niṣphalāḥ śaradabhravat (48).

58. I have in mind especially the mytheme of Śiva as the God-who-is-the-world, a root mytheme that enabled the Śaiva traditions to make creative use, first, of the Sāṃkhyan scheme of psychocosmic evolution and, second, of the Tantric scheme of the sonic evolution of Śakti. The source of this mythic-theological complex might well be the Vedic cycle of Prajāpati; for an intriguing

exploration of this, see Deppert (1977). I recognize that my insistence on the mythic background of Śaiva *sādhanā* requires substantiation that I cannot attempt to provide in this essay.

59. My understanding of metaphor is generally indebted to Paul Ricoeur. I have borrowed the notion of "root metaphor" from Stephen Pepper, *World Hypotheses* (1942). My understanding of myth is dependent on Rudolph Bultmann's discussion of "demythologization." I am not, however, following these three authors systematically.

60. Speaking of the "myth" of Mātṛkā and treating *Mātṛkā* as a name as well as a term is speculative, but I think justified by context. It serves the secondary purpose of indicating that tantric "verbal cosmogonies" merit study in their own right.

61. Atha katham asyājñānātmakajñānayonivargakalāśarīrarūpasya trividhasya malasya bandhakatvam ity āha (16). Neither a discussion of the technical terms used in this statement nor a general evaluation of Kṣemarāja's "doctrine of evil" is possible here. In ŚSūV 1.1–2, Kṣemarāja interprets *(a)jñāna* as *āṇavamala* (the blemish of individuality); *yonivarga* (literally, the class of root causes) as *māyīyamala* (the blemish of *māyā*), and *kalāśarīra* (literally, the body of activities) as *kārmamala* (the blemish of *karma*).

62. *Yad etat trividhamalasvarūpam apūrṇam manyatābhinnavedyaprathā-śubhāśubhavāsanātmakaṃ vividhaṃ jñānarūpam uktam* (16).

63. *Tasya ādikṣāntarūpā ajnātā mātā mātṛkā viśvajananī* (16).

64. *Tattatsaṃkucitavedyābhāsātmano jñānasya "apūrṇo 'smi," "kṣāmaḥ sthūlo vāsmi," "agniṣṭoma yājyasmi," ityāditattadavikalpakasavikalpakāvabhāsaparāmarśamayasya tattadvācakaśabdānuvedhadvāreṇa śokasmayaharṣarāgādirūpatām ādadhānā* (16f.). Note that three paradigmatic cognitions illustrate the threefold blemish, *āṇava-*, *māyīya-*, and *kārmamala*, respectively. Note, too, that, in striking contrast with the usage of the Buddhist logicians, according to this scheme both *savikalpaka* and *nirvikalpaka* cognitions are understood, from an ultimate perspective, to be verbal.

65. *Karandhracitimadhyasthā brahmapāśāvalambikāḥ*
pīṭheśvaryo mahāghorā mohayanti muhurmuhuḥ (17).
The technical terms in this verse refer to yogic physiognomy. For explication, see the various translations.

66. *Vargakalādyadhiṣṭhātṛbrāhmyādiśaktiśreṇīśobhinī śrīsarvavīrādyāgamaprasiddhalipikramasaṃniveśotthāpikā ambājyeṣṭhāraudrīvāmākhyaśakticakracumbitā śaktir adhiṣṭhātrī* (17).

67. *Tadadhiṣṭhānād eva hi antara 'bhedānusaṃdhivandhyatvāt kṣanam api alabdhaviśrāntīni bahirmukhāny eva jñānāni, ity yuktaiva eṣāṃ bandhakatvoktiḥ* (17).

68. *etac ca*
śabdarāśisamutthasya [śaktivargasya bhogyatām

kalāviluptavibhavo gataḥ san sa paśuḥ smṛtaḥ]
ity kārikayā,
savrūpāvaraṇe cāsya śaktayaḥ satatotthitāḥ
[yataḥ śabdānuvedhena na vinā pratyayodbhavaḥ]
iti ca kārikāyā saṃgrhītam (17f.).

The first quotation is SpK 3.13 (KSTS 42:65), the second is SpK 3.15 (KSTS 42:70).

69. *tadākramya balaṃ mantrāḥ sarvajñābalaśālinaḥ*
pravartante 'dhikārāya karaṇānīva dehinām
tatraiva saṃpralīyante śāntarūpā nirañjanāḥ
sahārādhakacittena tenaite śivadharmiṇaḥ (KSTS 42.45).

My translation of *a-kram-* as resort to was suggested by that of Jaidev Singh (1980, 110). In this passage, mantras are taken to "exist" on several levels of reality: on the mundane level, they are utterances; on higher levels, they are deities. In the SpN on these verses, Kṣemarāja describes mantras as "illustrious beings who for the sake of the embodied perform [the five great cosmic acts] including the emission and withdrawal [of the world] and the obscuring and unveiling [of ultimate reality], exuberantly, expansively, by virtue of their characteristic powers such as omniscience" (*bhagavanto . . . mantrāḥ sarvajñabalena sarvajñatvādisāmarthyena ślāghamānā jṛmbhamāṇā adhikārāya dehināṃ pravartante sṛṣṭisaṃhāratirodhānānugrahādi kurvantīty arthaḥ* (KSTS 42.45). A final assessment of Kṣemarāja's understanding of mantra will have to take into account the SpN as well as the Śaivāgamic commentaries.

70. *Na caivam api udāsīnena anena bhāvyam api tu—bījāvadhānam* (15)
kartavyam iti śeṣaḥ/ bījaṃ viśvakāraṇam sphurattātmā parā śaktiḥ/ yad uktaṃ śrīmṛtyujidbhaṭṭārake
sā yoniḥ sarvadevānāṃ śaktīnāṃ cāpy anekdhā
agnīṣomātmikā yonis tataḥ sarvaṃ pravartate
ityādi/ tatra paraśaktyātmani bīje, avadhānaṃ bhūyo bhūyaś cittaniveśanaṃ kāryam (94).

Mṛtyujit is another name for the *Netra Tantra.* This passage is found at 7.40 (KSTS 46.170). The *dvandva "agnīṣoma"* is a common figure of speeh in this literature for "fundamental oppositions." J. C. Chatterji (94, n. 62) glosses *saṃhārasṛṣṭi-pramāṇaprameya-prāṇāpāna-sūryasomādiśabdābhidheyā.*

71. *Bīja* has both a singular and a plural reference, to the womb of the cosmos and to the constituent elements out of which mantras are constructed, respectively.

72. If one were writing a contemporary, "liberal Hindu" defense of Mantraśāstra, this could, I think, provide a theological rationale for endorsing, or at least tolerating, quotidian mantras, as well as a way to account for their reputed success.

73. The object of this recollection is *viśvam.* It is presumably a sui generis act of cognition rather than a mere meditative recapitulation of the cosmic order. An

exact delineation of the meaning of *pratyabhijñā* for Kṣemaraja and the other writers in his tradition remains a significant desideratum.

74. *Ata eva pratyāhārayuktyā anuttarānāhatābhyām eva śivaśaktibhyāṃ garbhīkṛtam etad ātmakam eva viśvam; iti mahāmantravīryātmano 'haṃvimarśasya tattvam/ yathoktam asmatparameṣṭhi śrīmadutpaladevapādaiḥ*
prakāśasyātmaviśrāntir ahaṃbhāvo hi kīrtitaḥ
uktā saiva ca viśrāntiḥ sarvāpekṣānirodhataḥ
svātantryam atha kartṛtvaṃ mukhyam īśvaratāpi ca/
iti (63).

The quotation is AJPS 22cd-23 (KSTS 34.9f). My translation of *anahāta* as unstruck was suggested by the comments of Jaidev Singh (1979, 113, n. 17). There is a double meaning; *anahāta* may also mean unslain; Silburn (68) translates it effectively as *"le son non-issu de percussion." Pratyahara* is a grammatical term and may be understood in this context as referring to the elision of two sets of *varṇas* by reference to the beginning of the first set and the end of the second.

75. *Tadiyat paryantaṃ yan mātṛkāyās tattvam tad eva kakāra-sakāra-pratyahāreṇa anuttaravisargasaṃghaṭṭasāreṇa kūṭabījena pradarśitam ante; ity alaṃ rahasyaprakaṭanena/* (63). On *kṣa-kāra* and the *kuṭabīja* see Padoux (1963, 242).

76. *Evaṃ vidhāyāḥ '. . . na vidyā mātṛkāparā' ity āmnāyasūcitaprabhāvāyā mātṛkāyāḥ saṃbandhinaś cakrasya proktānuttarānandecchādiśaktisamūhasya cidānandaghanasvasvarūpasamāveśamayaḥ samyak bodho bhavati* (63f.).

77. In this passage *akāra* seems to be equated with *bindu* and *visarga* with *hakāra*, thus portraying *aham* as a double of Śiva and Śakti.

78. *Ādimāntyavihīnās tu mantrāh syuḥ śaradabhravat*
guror lakṣaṇam etāvad ādimāntyaṃ ca vedayet
pūjyaḥ so 'ham iva jñānī bhairavo devatātmakaḥ
ślokagāthādi yat kiñcid ādimāntyayutaṃ yataḥ
tasmād vidaṃs tathā sarvaṃ mantratvenaiva paśyati (66f.).

79. *Seyaṃ kriyātmikā śaktiḥ śivasya paśuvartinī*
bandhayitrī svamārgasthā jñātā siddhyupapādikā (67) [=SpK 3.16].

80. *'Aham eva paro haṃsaḥ śivaḥ paramakāraṇam' iti śrīsvacchandanirūpitanītyā nītyam eva parāhaṃbhāvanāmayatvāt* (113).

81. *Mahāmantrātmakākṛtakāhaṃvimarśārūḍhasya yad yad ālāpādi tat tad asya svātmadevatāvimarśānavaratāvartanātmā japo jāyate/* (113). My translation of the phrase *svātmadevatāvimarśānavaratāvartanātmā* is intentionally polemical. One might translate, for example, "the unceasing awareness of the deity who is your Self." To me, such a translation obscures the point, which, I think, is as radical as it sounds.

82. *Bhūyo bhūyaḥ pare bhāve bhāvanā bhāvyate hi yā*
japaḥ so 'tra svayaṃ nādo mantrātmā japya īdṛśaḥ

sakāreṇa bahiryāti hakāreṇa viśet punaḥ
haṃsa-haṃsety amuṃ mantraṃ jīvo japati nityaśaḥ

ṣaṭśatāni divārātrau sahasrāṇy ekaviṃśatiḥ
japo devyā vinirdiṣṭaḥ sulabho durlabho jaḍaiḥ (113f.) [= VB 145, and 155f.].

Cf. Silburn (1961, 164, 170) for a discussion of Kṣemarāja's citation of these verses.

CONCLUSION

Mantras—What Are They?

André Padoux*

"When *I* use a word," Humpty-Dumpty said in a rather scornful tone, "it means just what I choose it to mean—neither more nor less."

AS HE NEARS THE END of this book, the reader may believe he knows all there is to know about mantras. But, this would be a great mistake: The subject of mantras is so vast that much more still could be usefully written on it—though with the risk of making matters more rather than less obscure. Much could still be said, for instance, about Indian theories on the nature of mantras, as they were developed in the Tantric period, in Kashmir or elsewhere. Or else on certain practices, (ranging from the recitation of Vedic mantras and their uses as described in the *Brāhmaṇas* to later phenomena such as the peculiar and sometimes bizarre practices of Tantric Mantraśāstra, with all its sectarian variants), to which, for lack of space, the preceding essays make only brief allusion. Not to mention the fact that mantric practices and speculations are not just things of the past, and that contemporary practitioners and theoreticians of mantra might also be studied.[1] This volume, finally, is concerned with the Brahmanic-Hindu tradition and leaves aside both Jainism and Buddhism. Jain Mantraśāstra, in fact, does not differ in its essentials from the Hindu version and is not very developed. But, Buddhism, whether from Ceylon, India, Tibet, China, or Japan, etc., is a vast area containing many and various theories and practices concerning mantra. And, though this area is far from unknown, it has never, I think, been assessed as a whole and so constitutes a possible field for further research.

I am grateful to Harvey Alper and to Frits Staal for their comments and criticisms on the draft of this essay. A special thank is due to Barbara Bray, friend and neighbor, who kindly read it and corrected the English.

To say that a number of questions relating to mantras might still be studied implies no criticism of the contents of this book nor of its authors, far from it. Neither does it mean that I intend to fill the gaps to which I have drawn attention; I would not presume to do so, even if I were able, which I am not. What I should like to attempt here, since this can be useful without being impertinent, is simply to develop some of the ideas or data put forward in the preceding set of essays and, also, in conclusion, to mention briefly some relevant fields of research that either have recently been the object of study or, in my opinion, might well be.

There can surely be no doubt about the "centrality of mantric utterance" not only to Śaivāgamic (Tantric) soteriology, as Alper well points out in this book, but more generally to Tantric Hinduism of all sectarian tendencies. This is true in spite of the fact that, as a religious instrument or procedure, mantra may be considered as somehow subordinate to ritual action or yogic practice, if only because it is normally used within the larger frame of ritual or yoga. (Yoga is taken here to include all the corporeal-mental and spiritual practices of *dhyāna* and *bhāvanā,* or those making use of the control of *prāṇa* in its general sense of cosmic energy.)

Admittedly, a rite or a spiritual practice may consist only of the utterance of a mantra. But such an utterance, in any context, has a meaning, an efficiency, a usefulness, only with a view to the end ascribed to that ritual or practice and only insofar as it takes place within this ritual practice or action. There is no doubt that the role of mantras is fundamental to Hinduism (not to Vedism, except in a different way). The oft-quoted words from *Principles of Tantra,* "From the mother's womb to the funeral pyre, a Hindu literally lives and dies in mantra" sound very pompous nowadays. Nevertheless, they express a truth that, for Tantric Hinduism—(and for a thousand years, most Hinduism has been either Tantric or Tantricized)—is underlined by the fact that Mantraśāstra is often taken as a name for *tantraśāstra*: The doctrine of the Tantras is that of the mantras.

The fundamental role of mantras, their great variety, the powers ascribed to them, and the fact that belief in their efficacy has survived in India from the Vedas down to our own day does indeed confront us with a problem: How is one to explain the mantric phenomenon? Some of the authors here (Staal, Wheelock, Alper) try to solve it or to tackle some of its aspects, with great penetration. One must indeed try to find out why mantras exist and why they have survived even into our own "enlightened" age. What can explain the persistent use of a type of utterance that, at first sight, looks like nothing but abracadabra, "meaningless jabber" as some Indologists used to say? There is a widespread tendency now to believe that the existence of mantras can be explained rationally, even if the phenomenon as such is irrational.

If this is to be done, however, I, for one, have no doubt that mantras as they exist in actual fact (that is, in the area of Indian civilization) can be properly explained and understood only within the Indian tradition, with its metaphysical and mythical notions about speech.[2] This is a culture where speech—*vāc,* which may perhaps be rendered as "the Word"[3]—has always been considered as essential, as of divine origin, as playing a fundamental role in creation. The *bràhman,* a term which became the name for the absolute, in the Vedas, is the sacred word or speech. The name (*nāman*) is the essence of a thing. Speech is creative, "for by speech everything here is done" (Śatapatha-Bráhmaṇa 8.1.2.9). But, also, "mind (*mati*) doubtless is speech, for by means of speech one thinks everything here" (ibid. 8.1.2.8).

From the earliest period of Indian culture, speech has remained at its very center. Certain notions concerning the nature and the powers of speech, especially those of the mantras, have always been present, even if only in the background, forming the basis and directing the course of the whole of Indian thought on that subject. In this context, it is worth noting that, from the outset, the sort of speech or word considered all-powerful was spoken not written: All speculations and practices always concerned, and still concern, the oral field only. Mantra is sound (*śabda*) or word (*vāc*); it is never, at least in its nature, written.[4]

To this, one should add that, since the Vedic period, in spite of the superiority of the spoken word, the highest and most efficacious form of that word was not the loudest or the most intense but, on the contrary, the most silent and subtle—the inner utterance, the purely mental one. This is a fundamental trait of speech "à l'indienne." Indian civilization, which, it seems, has more than any other cultural area given to speech or word (*vāc*) a central, basic role and endlessly reflected upon it, studied it, and considered it all powerful, the divine energy itself; this civilization, in fact, has placed at the acme of speech, at the heart of every utterance, not sound but silence.

It is enough in this connection to remind the reader that the whispered utterance (*upāṃśu*) of a mantra was always considered higher than the audible one, and highest of all was the silent (*tūṣṇīm*), that is to say the mental (*mānasa*), utterance. Wheelock quotes in this respect from the Lakṣmī Tantra. One could easily cite earlier references, such as the Laws of Manu (2.85). Earlier still, in the *Brāhmaṇas,* silence or indistinct or undefined (*anirukta*) speech represent the innumerable, the unlimited, "undefined meaning unlimited, he thereby lays complete, unlimited, vigor into him: therefore he answers here undefinedly" (Śatapatha-Brāhmaṇa 5.4.4.13, Eggeling's 1882–1900 translation). Silence, for the *Brāhmaṇa,* is creative: One speaks in a low voice "since seed (*retas*) is cast silently" (ibid. 6.2.2.22). Wheelock, here, while stressing the continuity of this point from Vedism to Tantrism, also underscores the importance of the "silent rehearsal of the most precious truths of homology between microcosm and macrocosm." It is not impossible, in this respect, that the layers of sound from articulate to inarticulate may reflect, or correspond to, a historical development. But it surely appears that, from the

Vedic to the Tantric period, the mantras tend to become more and more repetitive (Wheelock page 119), to have an increasingly poorer linguistic content and an ever reduced phonetic variety, thus in some way tending toward silence. An evolution that may well be due, as Wheelock believes (page 119), to the fact that (to quote him) "while the Vedic liturgy uses language as a tool of proper action, the Tantric ritual makes action a subordinate of language in producing proper thought." However, this should not lead us to believe that the Vedic rites are purely action, without any corresponding ideology or doctrine, as Staal seems (to me) somehow to believe. Wheelock's comments in the last page of his essay strike me as particularly illuminating.

I should like to stress, however, that, although there certainly was an evolution from the Vedic to the Tantric attitude concerning the role of mantras in ritual, as tools of action or as thought-producing or thought-sustaining devices, nevertheless, the admission of thought or consciousness as identical to the highest and silent level of speech is an ancient conception.

The quotation from the Śatapatha Brāhmaṇa shows that the idea of the inseparability of speech or word and thought appeared very early. The notion is mentioned here by Coward in his examination of the ideas of Bhartṛhari. For Bhartṛhari, however, cognition, idea (*pratyaya*), is inextricably intertwined with word (*śabda*); that is, language, not exactly speech (*vāc*) and consciousness: It is more a philosophical notion than a metaphysical one, though it is linked to the metaphysical ideas and cosmological conceptions that are more specifically those to which mantric theory refers.

For mantras, the idea that the highest level of speech is pure consciousness is surely one of the reasons for the superiority, in mantric practice, of silence over actual speech, of the unsaid over the said. The *brahmàn* also, in Vedic times, was the silent but necessary witness of the ritual.[5] The ideology of retention, which is present at all levels in so many domains and particularly in the field of ascetic practice, may have contributed, accessorily, to the supremacy of silence. This unity on the highest level of *vāc* and consciousness explains why the Śivasūtra describe the mantra as consciousness (*cittaṃ mantraḥ,* ŚSu. 2.1; cf. Alper page 268). It also accounts for the way in which the efficacy of mantra is construed and how it works from the Indian point of view and explains why the working of the mantra is considered inseparable from the mind of the user. Indeed, when one looks at how a mantra is put into practice by an adept, one may well ask oneself whether the real nature of mantra is not consciousness rather than speech, the answer perhaps being that mantra is speech, but that speech, for India, is ultimately consciousness.

Similarly, some important features of the mantric theory of later times can be properly explained only with reference to the ancient Vedic conception of speech as efficient sacrificial speech and, especially, as setting up those explanatory identifications and micro-macrocosmic correlations, which the *Brāhmaṇas* first called *nidāna* or *bandhu*, and later *upaniṣad*, an enunciation whose verbal content and internal organization were more important than its discursive meaning. These mantras also sometimes were made of, or mixed with, syllables without any apparent meaning. They also could be uttered altering the order of syllables or words, so that whatever empirical meaning they may have had disappeared but without diminishing their supposed efficacy in the least. All these are features one finds in Tantric mantras. Hence, the value of such essays as those of Staal or Wheelock, which survey all these ancient traits and show how they survived into the later periods. For, we must not forget that the old Vedic-Brahmanic rites never entirely disappeared.[6] More to the point, a number of "Vedic" mantras have either been kept or, more often probably, been reincorporated into the *āgamas* or Tantras in the course of time by Tantric groups, who included them in their ritual. So much so, that most of what concerns Vedic mantras, their forms, their structure, or the way in which they function, is not only of historical interest but still apposite down to the present. The Vedic tradition survives, thus, by coexisting with the Tantric one, or combined with it, or by forming a sort of substratum inasmuch as Tantrism either inherited the more ancient ideas and practices or adapted them to suit its own purpose.

In brief, I would say that all that India has said on mantras is to be explained or justified much less by what language or speech actually is than by what Indians, or some of them, have considered it to be—by their notions, that is, as to the nature of speech and language and the way these are supposed to function. I believe this should always be borne in mind when studying mantras, to avoid being enticed into apparently brilliant but ultimately arbitrary theories.

To be sure, these Indian notions, concerning as they do linguistic or phonetic facts, form a part of linguistic theory. They often include precise phonetic observations and sometimes penetrating insights into the nature and working of language. Though they may not be what we should call scientific, they can certainly be explained in terms of real, factual, features of language and their possible uses. This aspect of research into mantra has been touched upon here by all those (for instance, Staal, Taber, Coward, Oberhammer, and Alper) who have taken up the question of the nature (as speech acts or otherwise) of mantras and of their efficacy. Research in this field is certainly to be pursued further, provided one does not confuse or mix two different approaches or yield to the seduction of Indian metaphysical or mystical theoreticians and take their speculation for fact. One should never lose sight, I feel, of the fact that mantras are a form of speech (or sound) within an Indian context; that is, that they are a part of a certain type of practice, functioning within a definite ideology, that of Hinduism, where mythic elements play an essential role, and within a particular anthropological (social, psychological) framework. Theirs is not a case of speech or language in general (if there is such a thing), still less of language as we conceive or use it. Mantras function and have a "meaning" within a certain universe of discourse, within an articulated and systematized whole, that imposed by a particular use of language in the Indian context, outside of which they can no more exist than a fish out of water, if only because of the great difficulty of defining what a mantra is outside that context. Mantras are culturally defined and, therefore, necessarily would differ very widely in their aspects and functioning from one culture to another. It would be unwise, I fear, to neglect these facts when writing about mantras and either try to remain simultaneously in two different universes of discourse or allow the two to intermingle. However, it is obvious that while keeping to one of them, our own, one can contribute effectively to an understanding of the other. This book is proof of the usefulness of pursuing the study of Indian theories and practices from the standpoint of our own scientific approach to language. We also (cf. Alper and Oberhammer) can look at mantras from our own philosophical standpoints, though in such case the danger of syncretism, or the risk of being seduced by Indian theories, is certainly greater.[7]

Little has been done in this book to define mantras. The word is not printed in italics like other Sanskrit words; it is a word in common use.[8] We know, or believe we know, what a mantra is. In fact, the term is both impossible to translate and very difficult to define properly. One may refer in this connection to Gonda's pioneering study (Gonda 1963b), "The Indian Mantra," which still makes interesting and useful reading and where a number of definitions and explanations of the term are brought together. Also, more than twenty years ago, I (Padoux 1963) put forward a longish definition[9] that has been criticized for not being theoretical enough. Though I never considered that attempt at a definition entirely satisfactory, I would probably use the same words again now, with only minor alterations, because that earlier attempt, being purely descriptive, seems to me, all things considered, both serviceable and not too misleading.

But should one try to define mantras at all? I am not sure. Perhaps, we could just as well avoid doing so (even if it entails sacrificing some pet theories) and remain content with what is done in this volume; i.e., with noting the uses and forms of mantras, the varieties of mantric practices and utterances (or some of them), as well as some of the Indian theories on the subject. Functional (and, thus, perhaps, unfashionable) as such an approach may be, it still seems to me to be the safest, and probably the most useful one, giving an overall and generally fair idea of what mantras may be in theory as well as in practice. The wide variety of mantras and of their uses, from Vedic times to the present day, is one more reason for following such a course. Even, if we do not draw a distinction between Vedic and Tantric mantras, as Renou did twenty-five years ago (1960a) and as I did more recently (for which Staal here takes me to task, pages 59–60), the great diversity of mantras in the

Hindu and Tantric fields, together with their different forms and uses, are surely enough to make any general definition very difficult and probably rather useless.

Another aspect of mantras is more important and, in fact, much more than the question of definition, has engaged the attention of the authors of these essays, that of their meaning. Are mantras meaningful? Or, what sort of meaning have they?

The difficulty here is a double one: First, what is one to understand by "meaning" in the present case? Second, how can we find, on the question of the (problematic) meaning of mantras, an answer that applies equally well to all possible cases? Can one apply the same reasoning, on the one hand, to a mantra that appears, when one reads or hears it, to have some more or less obvious meaning and, on the other hand, to a series of Vedic *stobha* or to a Tantric mantra made up of a syllable, or group of syllables, forming neither a sentence nor a word?

If, however, one refers to what some have written here and to what I said earlier on the Indian conception of speech, one notices (this is underlined by Staal) that from the Vedic period onward mantras appear to possess characteristics that differ from those of ordinary language. Mantras do not abide entirely by its rules: sometimes as to their form, always as to their use. Of course, since mantras have something to do with language in that they are uttered (or that they are, theoretically, utterable), using a mantra, like speaking, is "engaging in a rule-governed form of behavior" (to use Searle's words). But the rules of mantric performance and use are of a very particular sort. The inner organization of mantras and, especially, their phonetic structure are more important than their obvious meaning, if any. They do not always "say," or mean, what they seem to be saying. This comes, among other reasons, from the fact, as Findly and Wheelock point out, that they are part of a ritual performance outside of which they cannot really be understood. The "rule-governed form of behavior" of which they are a part is a ritual one, and they have a "meaning" (by which I mean a use, a usefulness, or a role), significance, and value only within that ritual activity.

Staal once said that, in India, "language is not something with which you *name* something, but in general something with which you do something" (1979c), a remark that probably refers to the active conception of language in Indian civilization, where speech (*vāc*) is energy (*śakti*), which especially is true where mantras are concerned, their case being precisely one where you "do things with words" (insofar, naturally, as mantras are words). In fact, there are cases where mantras may seem to "name" something, usually a deity. But, in such cases, they are the deity's *vācaka* (its sound-form and efficient essence, or *svarūpa*), so that uttering the deity's mantra, which may be its name but more often is not, is not naming the deity but evoking or conjuring its power or, perhaps, as a means to open oneself to it (cf. Oberhammer, page 218); in any case, *doing* something.

Considering the phonetic aspect of Vedic mantras and the role played in them by *stobhas* devoid of all proper "meaning," considering also the particular way in which they are sometimes recited and the importance attached to their exact pronunciation, Staal remarks (page 65) that these mantras have a musical character and that they cannot be understood unless this quality is taken into account. This explains, he says, "why mantras cannot be explained wholly or perhaps even partly in terms of language." This musical or, more generally, phonetic or acoustic aspect of mantras is undoubtedly important and should be considered seriously (cf. infra pages 73–74).

This and all that has been said in the ten essays that make up the book underscores, I believe, two fundamental points: First, that mantras, whether in the form of sentences, words, or sounds, have a "meaning" (by which I mean that they help to do something), which very well may not appear in their verbal or phonetic sequence. Second, that their function is not one of the usual ones of language (namely, informative, constative, communicative) but is a direct action, generally a ritual one, or a psychological or mystical[10] one (see here Oberhammer's or Gupta's point of view, to which I shall return later on). This being so, the efficacy mantras are supposed to have in all these cases, as constitutive parts of a ritual or of a mental or spiritual practice, is not linked to a situation of interpersonal communication nor, usually (but here one must tread carefully), of inner deliberation or thought, all of which are the "normal" uses of language.[11]

Perhaps, one could say that mantras have no meaning in the usual sense of the word, which is not to say that they do not make sense for those who use them, but they do have efficiency. They bring about an effect or, to be more precise, they are deemed, within their own cultural context, to bring one about. This is the main difference between a mantra and a word in a language, even if you believe the meaning of a word to be what you do with it[12] or to result from the use given it in human life. Evidently, the case with a mantra is not that of a "normal" speech situation. Mantra has to do with humanly uttered sound, it is even a linguistic phenomenon since it is uttered in speech or mentally. But, it is a linguistic phenomenon of a very particular, not to say peculiar, sort.

A mantra has a use rather than a meaning—a use in context. Findly underlined the fact that, in Vedism, a mantra cannot be understood outside of its use in the ritual (pages 15–16). This applies equally, in later times, to all mantric utterances in a ritual context. As Wheelock writes (page 99): "the language of ritual is decidedly extraordinary"; it does not communicate information, but serves "to create and allow participation in a known and repeatable situation." This is true. But, though the terms *known* and *repeatable* are very important here, I would add that, as a ritual enunciation, a mantra not only brings about a particular situation but may also, at least in some cases, produce a change (sometimes an irreversible one) in the mental state of the person who utters it (cf. Oberhammer). This change results from its utterance in association with the concentration of the utterer's attention upon it. Though these effects may respond to some inherent possibilities of language, or rather of humanly produced sound, it is quite foreign to the usual communicative or informative uses of language.

One might be tempted simply to consider mantras as examples of the magical use of language. But, the explanation by magic alone, though useful, seems inadequate. First, because the uses of mantras are not restricted to what may legitimately be called magic, which, even in Tantrism, is only a limited part of a vast amount of practice and speculation on the holy or sacred, of which magic is but a profane or profanatory handling. Second, and even more important, because the distinction between magic and religion, always a difficult one, is practically impossible in the case of Tantrism, where one can seldom know where the domain of the holy ends or what exactly is profane. "Magical" acts performed with mantras, such as the *ṣaṭkarmāṇi* for instance, the aims of which are usually purely worldly, are undoubtedly within the realm of religion. (But, then, what exactly is "religion" in India? Can we use this Western notion to describe such a system of practices and beliefs as Hinduism or Buddhism?)

We should try to go deeper: If the use of mantras is of a magical (or of some other) nature, we must ask ourselves what, in speech or language itself, makes such a use possible. For, obviously, this peculiar mantric use of the constituent elements of speech can exist only insofar as, in the phonic substance of speech or in language, there are some factors, some possibilities, that permit such use. Undoubtedly, language fulfills more than only the purposes of ordinary communication, which is the transfer of information from an emitter to a receiver, or that of inner reflection or introspection. Up to a point, it may also be an end in itself; the medium can be the message. In such cases, the attention of the user (and/or receiver) is focussed on the words or sounds emitted or on the syntactical aspect of the message not on some referent of the phonic or verbal sequence. In the case of mantras, from this focussing on the verbal or phonic form, the attention of the user may pass on to another plane, be it a postulated inner nature or essence of the mantra or some higher, transcendent reality of which the mantra is the expression (*vācaka*) and which would be intuited nondiscursively by the user through an intense and concentrated mental effort (*dhāraṇa* or *bhāvanā*).

Such use of the linguistic or acoustic resources of language or of sounds may be called *magical*, especially if we consider that sounds or words used in this way are deemed to have an innate efficiency. However, this is nothing but a particular application of the symbolizing capacity of language: that is, its capacity to represent something other than itself; to point towards something, to make one grasp something; to turn and focus the attention on something, whether an external referent or some inner meaning supposed inherent or to be identical with its phonic substance or to be some higher reality into which this substance eventually is supposed to dissolve.

Language, being a symbolical system, can symbolize in different ways, including the use of sounds to which conventional values are attributed and in which the efficient energy of speech, as well as in words, is thought to reside. This is true generally, not only within the Indian theory of speech. The total number of possible sounds is greatly in excess of those actually in use in any language. Such sounds have been used always and everywhere. Anthropology and psycholinguistics (not to mention personal experience) show us that among such sounds none is entirely "innocent" or meaningless; not only words or interjections but mere sounds emitted by man are felt to have meaning, an aura of meaning, or a connotation, be this a product of nature or of culture. There is, we know, a a pulsional basis of phonation.[13] Therefore, we consider that mantras in some of their forms, the *bījas* mostly, answer the deeply ingrained urge to emit sounds that are both arbitrary (i.e., not part of language or of ordinary linguistic use) and not innocent (i.e., having a "meaning" or evoking something).[14]

In his essay, Staal underlines this primitive, archaic aspect of mantras and refers to mental patients, to the babbling presleep monologues of babies, and to glossolalia (pages 75–80). He is certainly right also in underlining the fact that this archaic level of speech is present in all human beings: "man, he says, cannot become an animal; he always is one." He quotes me, in this connection, as saying that this archaic level is "the source of creation itself," which I wrote when attempting to set forth the Kashmir Śaiva conception of mantras, a conception one may take as a metaphysical, mythical expression of the intuition that such an archaic level exists.

In the Tantrāloka, Abhinavagupta mentions another form of this deep level. He describes the panting, the "ha-ha" sound, which he calls *kāmatattva*, or the *sītkāra*, the "sss" sound, uttered by a woman during coition or at the moment of orgasm. "This imperishable, spontaneous vibration appearing involuntarily in the throat of the beloved one, is pure sound *(dhvani)* produced neither by meditation nor by mental concentration. If one applies one's mind to it wholly, one suddenly becomes master of the universe" (TĀ 3.147–48). In this context, such a sound, since it issues spontaneously from the depths of the self, goes beyond the bounds of ordinary human existence. It is felt as going back to the source of life, hence, the powers acquired by the yogin who immerses himself in it. True, such sounds as *ha-ha* or *sīt* are not exactly mantras, if only because they do not have the formal, socially sanctioned traits of mantras. But, since, for Abhinavagupta (following Śivasūtra 2.1) all speech on a transcendent plane is mantra (cf. Alper) we still have here an instance of what a mantra may be—or of what it may "mean"—in the Kashmir Śaiva context. This nature and "meaning" is very near to that generally ascribed to *bījas* by Wheelock as "sonic manifestations of basic cosmic powers: they *are* the cosmic elements in essential form".

True, mantras also have ordinary linguistic forms, notably, but not only, in Vedism. Here, another use of language may be mentioned, poetic language. In fact, in cases where mantras appear to possess a "normal" linguistic form, they still do not "function" as ordinary language. "Even if a Vedic mantra seems to be a verse", says Staal (page 60), "in its ritual use it is not treated like a verse at all." Such mantras, as we see in this book, were the products of the vision of Vedic poets, of their "insight touching upon the riddles of the world" (Findly, page 20): "The poetic word, says the Ṛgveda (2.35.2), comes from the heart of the poet."

Poetry, in language, is what is, or may be, nearest to the ineffable, that which best attempts to express the inexpressible, to bestow through words but somehow beyond them the direct awareness of physical and spiritual reality that gives man the feeling that he oversteps his limits. The mantra used in the course of a spiritual exercise, in its own way, can help the *sādhaka* to obtain a similar sort of experience.

In poetry, as in mantras, the verbal sequence cannot be altered; like mantras, poetry rests on contiguities. Moreover, a poem, like a mantra, cannot be expressed in other words; it means what it says as it says it or else it ceases to be. Poetry and mantra both act on the user through and by their own verbal and phonic form. If we add that many Western poets since the Romantics have tended to believe, rather like Vedic bards, that poetry may be a path if not to eternal truths at least to a reality that usually escapes us, it is clear that there are analogies between poetry and mantra. Or rather—and this is more important for us—that mantra, like poetry, legitimately calls upon the expressive and revealing powers of language, powers that exist even if not used in current interpersonal communication. Naturally, we must be careful not to carry the analogy too far, if only because Vedic poetry, when it is mantra, is used in a ritual context, unlike a poem, and because a Tantric *bījamantra* is not a poem nor is it psychologically felt and used as one. Still, in all poetic texts, a catalyzing power is always at work, analogous in many respects to that which Wheelock notes (page 108) when he says that, in Vedism as in Tantrism, the mantra is the catalyst "that allows the sacred potential of the ritual setting to become a reality."

But, whatever role we ascribe to the mantra as such, we must never forget that all spiritual and mystical experiences obtained with the help of mantras are experiences of the human mind. They are states of consciousness, for which mantra or ritual are merely instrumental; different means could bring about the same result. This is only to underline the fact that the mantric use of the phonetic material and the symbolizing powers of language, though peculiar, are a perfectly legitimate variant of the uses generally made of human speech and of the powers usually, if not always officially, attributed to it.

As regards the nature of mantra, are we to see them as speech acts (as Searle understands speech acts) or as illocutionary acts? Staal and Findly take opposite stands on the subject. I prefer not to adopt a definite position, if only because the variety of mantric forms and uses makes it difficult to bring them together under one explanatory or classifying principle.

However, I should like to remark in passing that the efficiency (if any) of mantras is not something they actually possess but something traditionaly ascribed to them, which they are believed to possess. Mantras, as I have said, exist only within this traditional context and survive only through this belief. The so-called illocutionary power of some speech acts amounts to nothing other than this. Except in the subjective and psychological fields (and perhaps that of aesthetics), the alleged power of speech is nothing but that of the speaker, who has no other power than that bestowed upon him by his social group, which also decides the conditions in which this power may be used. This holds true for legal pronouncements as well as for the formulas of everyday speech, all of which have no other effects than those assigned to them by social consent when they are used "felicitously," that is, at the proper time and in the proper circumstances, as they are socially determined.

In much the same fashion, mantras, the uses of which are strictly codified, have, mutatis mutandis, no other efficacy than that ascribed to them by the Hindu, Jain, or Buddhist traditions to which they belong and within the ritual prescribed by these traditions. Or, at least in *yoga, bhāvanā,* and the like, they are effective elements of a practice, the rules of which are traditionally established and believed to be efficacious. Should mantras be represented as part of a language-game, I would point out that in no game are the rules not fixed by the group among whom it is played. We therefore may ascribe the so-called efficacy of mantras to culture—that is, to the ideological aspect of society—inasmuch as it conditions individual beliefs and mental attitudes.

That being so, the best approach to this cultural and psychological phenomenon is probably to make use of the concept of symbolic efficacy.[15] This concept, in my opinion, probably best explains how the varied ensemble of mantric conducts work with a recognized "efficacy" within the mythical Brahmanic-Hindu (or Buddhist) world. Mantras have an efficacy because the people concerned, the users of mantras and the rest of their group, believe them to be efficacious: Symbolic efficacy has a subjective social basis. It also has an objective cultural one, since among these symbolic actions, which are fixed by tradition and are rule-governed, some are more objectively effective than others. Such an explanation has the advantage of applying equally well to poetic metaphors and to ritual or "magical" practices, to formulas suited to particular social circumstances, to any psychical or physiological effects that may appear, and to those practices of meditation or mental creation (*bhāvanā*) by which the reality "expressed" by a mantra may be realized mystically. A realization made possible, within this symbolic framework, because the practitioner brings the mantra into play by concentrating upon it all the forces of his psyche. This psychological, or consciousness, aspect of mantras, I feel, is fundamental. Hence, also, the usefulness of the notion of intentionality, which borders upon that of belief in the understanding of how they are approached by the practitioner.

The intention or wish to express (*vivakṣ*) is for the Mīmāmsā (Taber, page 159) a feature of all language. But, whatever the Mīmāmsaka's views, we may take the notion of intentionality of speech to mean that any utterance, when one speaks, "wants to say" (as it is put in colloquial French)[16] something: expresses an intention to communicate, to signify, or at least to express something, an intention that (within, of course, the limits of conventional behavior, i.e., of social exchange) often "means" (wishes or is made to convey) more than is actually said; hence, a greater richness and larger efficacy of the message. This intentionality I believe to be a fact one can admit without necessarily belonging to the phenomenological school of philosophy.

Should we not ascribe similar intention to mantric utterances? Staal thinks not (page 66 ff.). He may be right where Vedic ritual is concerned.[17] But, I cannot bring myself to follow him where later, and especially Tantric, ritual is concerned. First, I cannot see how a mantra can be used without some reason. It is not uttered as an involuntary noise but for a purpose: An intention surely is always there. More specifically, Tantric texts on Mantraśāstra always assign a use (*viniyoga*), and thus a purpose, to mantras.[18] Clearly, such an intentionality is not that of the mantra but of its user. It can be attributed only metaphorically to the mantra itself. An ambiguity as to where the intentionality lies, however, is kept up in such systems as the Śaiva nondualist ones, which treat consciousness and mantra as identical at their highest levels: This appears clearly in Kṣemarāja's Vimarśinī on Śivasūtra 2.1 (cf. Alper page 262).

For Oberhammer (page 212), the mantra "by means of the wish to contemplate, or experience . . . effects in the meditating subject . . . an intentionality that opens him radically for encountering the reality of Śiva." The mantra thus appears as strengthening this intentionality, as allowing it to become actual inasmuch as the mantra, according to Oberhammer, is a means for the contemplation of the godhead. To quote him again, this is done by the mantra "because in contemplation only the mantra is a reality which is clearly delimited and set in a certain point of time and is therefore capable of making this mythic mediation of transcendence which is immanent to it, an event."

This formulation of the problem would be worth exploring further. It refers to a particular approach to religious experience that owes much to the philosophy of Husserl or Heidegger. It is very illuminating. Oberhammer's remarks, which refer to the Pāśupatas, are all the more interesting as the same approach also, I feel, could be usefully adopted in relation to the conception of the Śaiva nondualists, such as the Kula, Pratyabhijñā, or Krama, concerning the nature, uses, and soteric efficacy of mantras.

But, interesting, fundamental even, as the redemptive aspect of mantras may be, we should not forget that only a minority of mantras are redemptive. Mantras first and foremost are words and sounds of power for ritual use and only secondarily, if centrally, soteric devices.

Perhaps I went too far earlier when I juxtaposed mantra and poetry (pages 305–306). A mantra is a word of power, considered self-efficacious and thus something very different from poetry, whatever conception one may have of the latter.

With the possible exception of at least some of the Vedic mantras, which originally were poetic texts later adapted for ritual purposes, mantras and poetry are things apart; their only common feature is they are both forms of speech (or uses of phonetic material of language), which are regarded as more efficient and powerful than ordinary forms of speech or language.

Whatever its merits and in spite of Rimbaud and a few others, poetry cannot do much to free mankind from the snares of everyday life. At most, it may avoid involving him deeper in such toils, unlike ordinary language (especially that of commerce, politics or ideology). Could mantra do more and set man free from deception? Certain observers believe it does, at least sometimes (cf. Alper page 263). Hence, the idea that there might be mantras for the West, which would help us to free ourselves not only from Western but also from human bondage.

Such mantras are certainly conceivable, and some even actually exist. Should we wish, however, to import them to the West for our own use, we should never forget the following two fundamental points: (1) Mantras are efficient forms of speech within a particular tradition, where speech is conceived of within a particular mythico-religious framework. If we pluck them from this cultural milieu, which is their nourishing soil, is "the luminous bud of mantra," as A. Avalon used to say, likely to survive? One may well doubt it. (2) We must remember that mantras, even in their higher, supposedly redemptive forms, are always part of a precise and compulsory ritual context, outside which they are useless and powerless. A mantra may be a liberating word but only in accordance to precise and binding rules.

I stress these two points because of the parallel I allowed myself earlier between mantra and poetry; because of the notions sometimes entertained about poetry and its "power"; because, also, of the conception of mantras as the deepest or highest level of speech, expressive of the core of reality, among other things, near to the source of language as well as to that of our energies or drives. Mantra could then be considered as spontaneous speech. But, in point of fact, in the Indian context, mantra is never free or liberated speech. It has nothing in common, say, with surrealist poetry. Neither is mantra babbling or glossolalia, even if it may be compared with them, with reference to the origins of language, and of the mantric form of speech (Staal pages 75 ff.). Nor is a mantra a spontaneous cry of joy, ecstasy, or trance, whose utterance may make the ego may feel liberated. Mantra is not nature; it is culture. That the nature of mantra as a part of ritual (i.e., socially organized behavior) is abundantly underscored in this book.

Though Sanskrit texts describe mantras as *sahaja,* this is not to say that they are spontaneous utterances but that they are forms of *vāc,* the divine word, innate in man, born of itself without external help, the word that reveals the highly organized, sophisticated form of poetic utterance, the Veda. All the letters of the Sanskrit alphabet, supposedly born in the godhead, may be regarded as mantras. Born of themselves as spontaneous movements of the divine energy, they appear "freely" but according to the traditional and very rational order of the *varṇasamāmnāya.* Even when a mantra is regarded as a form of the deeper inner level of speech, which one can perceive in oneself, it is nevertheless a word transmitted and organized by tradition not something one freely discovers by introspection or otherwise. No one finds out or coins a mantra; he receives it ritually from a master who has it from tradition. (Not to mention, of course, the larger mass of mantras used in rituals, which are routinely employed.) Admittedly, there are such cases as those of the *sītkāra,* previously mentioned, or of the *hamsa,* or the *ajapājapa,* but these also are declared by tradition to be mantras and they are used according to ritual and magisterial prescriptions. These "natural" sounds are taken up, organized, codified by culture, and never left at the disposal of people to use them as they wish.

Such a use of mantras, taken from their Indian context and transferred to our own, is precisely what some Westerners now propose. As I said earlier, I do not believe this to be entirely legitimate, since we cannot (or only very exceptionally) really adopt all the Indian cultural context in which they are grounded together with the mantras. For mantras to work within our own civilization, we must use them within a philosophical framework of our own, drawing to a greater or lesser extent on the fund of Western religious thought and beliefs and on our traditional notions concerning the powers of speech, which differ from Indian ones. This framework, even though adapted to the mantras and probably "orientalized" to some degree, would still inevitably transform our mantras into something other than the Indian ones. They might still prove useful, efficacious as means to mental concentration, spiritual effort, or mystical life or as forms of prayer. Like their Indian models, they would be endowed with the evocative power of sounds or words and would exert the influence that such sounds or sound patterns undoubtedly have on the body and on states of consciousness. But, would they still be mantras properly so-called? Would there even be any point in calling them mantras?

If we try to look at mantras in a perspective wider than the Indian one, as among the particular uses of language or of humanly produced sounds, we also realize that they belong to the vast universal mass of practices and notions that contains not only prayers and religious utterances but also spells and incantations; all the "words of power," all the abracadabras reflecting the ceaseless, irrational wish to act efficaciously through words or sounds; all cases where, through words or sound, wish or will becomes action or produces effects.

Indians have speculated subtly on this archetypal theme and eventually worked it out in their theories on *vāc*, on the efficacy of mantras (*mantravīrya*), and on the consciousness aspect of mantras, aspects very carefully studied here by Alper. Brilliant and ingenious as these theories may be, they nevertheless rest basically, I believe, on the bedrock of the ancient belief in the intrinsically "magical" efficacy of speech, a belief as widespread as it is strong.

With respect to this belief, I should probably refer again here to the question of supernatural powers and of the "magical" effects of mantras. Mantras, in India, are clearly used much more often to gain such powers or to produce such effects than for redemptive purposes. But especially interesting is the fact that mantras may very well have (and are usually held to do so by most Tantric texts on the subject) both redemptive *and* magical effects. With mantras, we are at once in the world of spiritual experience and in that of supernatural powers or of magical action, if we prefer to call it that. Hence, I presume, the appeal of mantras to so many people: A mantra, on the magical plane, gives them what they wish for. On the spiritual (or redemptive) plane, it is an effective tool for concentration and, thus, can bring about the spiritual state a person craves and which, once obtained, either confers supernatural powers upon him or brings him to regard them as despicable, the satisfaction is the same in either case. The problem of the link between mantras and the search for (or obtaining of) supernatural powers is interesting and would be worth investigating systematically from the Indological point of view,[19] as well as that of anthropology or psychology. (Not to mention that of psychoanalysis, which would probably detect in those who believe they have such powers the survival of infantile dreams of omnipotence or traits usually considered typical of mania.)

Many more aspects of mantras or problems relating to them, even if already studied, would still be worth further study. We may note, for instance, that despite their variety, the essays in this book examine only certain types of mantras and mantric practices. According to the Hindu tradition, there are seventy million mantras, though the real figure is certainly much smaller. But nobody, I think, has ever attempted to assess or guess their actual number. The task is probably not worth attempting. But it would be very useful, using modern methods, to gather together a large number of mantras, with information on their uses. However repetitive the mantras themselves and however seemingly stereotyped the ways in which they are used, we are still far from knowing most of them. In addition to Vedic uses (on which not all has been said here for lack of space), the essays in this book are more concerned with the religious and, more specifically, the soteric uses of mantras, whereas in actual fact (as I pointed out before) the majority of mantras used in Hinduism are employed for purely ritual purposes, whether during *pūjās* or during all the ritual acts in the daily life of a Hindu. In all such cases, the action is either accompanied by mantras or consists merely of their utterance. The user feels he is uttering words or sounds that are efficient, though their effect may not be visible, in the sense that, uttered together with the proper rites, they accomplish what they say or what they are supposed to effect: They drive away demons, transform water into nectar, place spiritual entities on the body or on an object, etc.[20] In all such cases, is what is being done (i.e., the mantra plus the act) believed to act *ex opere operato,* by some sort of direct effect, as soon as the prescribed conditions are observed? Or, does the efficacy of the rite depend also on the intellectual attitude or spiritual effort of the actor? The answer is probably twofold: (1) The spiritual factor is a necessity in *mantra-sādhana* and in all spiritual practices aimed at liberation or wordly results (*mukti* or *bhukti*). But, (2) in the case of all obligatory rites, or those of current practices, that is, in the vast majority of cases, the only necessary condition for the mantra to be "efficacious" is to use it while keeping strictly to the prescribed rules.

Concerning the possible effects of mantras upon their users, we may also note, that in all daily acts except those of worship (bath, meals, work, etc.), mantras also have (or at any rate appear to us to have) a psychological function in addition to their ritual role, which is to sanctify, so to speak, the action being done. While the person acts and utters the mantras, they focus attention on the godhead or on the cosmic or religious meaning or bearing of the action. This aspect of the practical function of mantras must not be overlooked. Focussing attention is especially important in one act, which plays an essential part in the daily life of Hindus and of Buddhists, although not dealt with in the essays in the book, I believe: *japa,* the muttering of a mantra. Is *japa* a ritual act? (*Japa,* performed with a rosary, *akṣamālā,* is highly ritualized, see, for instance, Chapter 14 of Jayākhyasaṃhitā.) Is it an act of spiritual quest or a prayer? (And, then, does it act by mere repetition or through the spiritual effort of the devotee?)[21]

The essays in the book concentrate mainly on mantras for redemptive uses but, except in the case of the Pāñcarātra studied by Sanjukta Gupta, they hardly mention the way in which mantras actually are put into practice. This is a field still open for research. There is, for instance, nothing on the Śaiva/Śākta sects or schools comparable to Beyer's (1973) *The Cult of Tara.* This study, together with those of Alex Wayman on Tantric Buddhism, to mention only two, give facts and interpretations of the utmost interest on *mantrayāṇa.* Consider the variety of Śaiva or Śākta schools or sects in Northern India; their geographical extension, which includes notably Nepal; the large number of āgamas and tantras, many still unpublished; and the different traditions, for instance, Kula with its subvarieties Tripurā, Kubjikā, etc., or Krama and so on. We can see that there is a vast field still far from catalogued, where mantric practices are to be found everywhere, all with different mantric patterns. This whole area deserves to be carefully surveyed and studied.[22]

There is scope for research in Vaiṣṇavism, too, even after such important studies as those of S. Gupta and E. C. Dimock. Such works as the Jayākhya and the Śeṣa-Saṃhitā, to name only two well-known texts available in print, would be worth systematic study from the mantric point of view. Of course, so would the actual practices of the Vaiṣṇavas who use such texts: There is scope here for field work. The same sort of study also could be carried out on a wealth of other texts: Purāṇas for instance, or Upaniṣads, etc. If we add that Sanskrit texts are only a part of what has been written on or about mantras (and there are oral traditions), the possible field of research emerges as very wide. Admittedly, Tantric literature is very repetitive, and mantras and mantric practices are very stereotyped. The variety, therefore, is far from infinite. Still, it is certainly very large and well worth studying.

In addition to this study of various texts, as complete and systematic an inventory as possible should be drawn up of mantras and mantric practices. Alphabetic lists of mantras are needed, together with their textual references, the circumstances of their use, and their meanings. An inventory of rites where mantras occur, with all that serves to put them in actual use (*nyāsa, mudrā, yantra, maṇḍala, dhyāna, japa,* etc.) as well as such yogic or spiritual practices as *smaraṇa, uccāra, bhāvanā,* etc. also should be made, together with a study of variant practices, both Hindu and Buddhist.[23] These, to use Alper's words, are "lived situations where mantras are used," which ought to be studied and classified.

Such an inventory of mantras and mantric practices was planned by the Equipe de Recherche N°249 "'Hindouisme: textes, doctrines, pratiques" of the French Centre National de la Recherche Scientifique, which was set up in 1982. It has made little progress however, through lack of funds and facilities. A card-index such as the one the Equipe de Recherche is trying to make is not adequate: Information should be gathered on the scale of an international program and should be stored in computers. Another project of the same Equipe, a glossary of technical terms of Mantraśāstra, has also made very little progress.

There is also the history of Mantraśāstra. As always in India, the difficulty is the lack of precise historical data. Some problems, however, may be tackled at least tentatively. That of the origin, Vedic or otherwise, of Mantraśāstra is probably impossible to solve; so, too, is that of its geographic origin. But origins do not matter very much. More interesting, and perhaps less difficult to solve, is the problem of the transition from Vedic mantras to Hindu Mantraśāstra. To quote Staal (page 65) "The curious fact that monosyllabic mantras of the *stobha* type reemerged in Tantrism after apparently lying dormant for more than a millenium." I am not sure they actually lay dormant so long. But, the question as to how and why Tantric Mantraśāstra appeared and developed is certainly an interesting, and still unsolved, one.

The relationship between Hindu Mantraśāstra and Buddhist Mantrayāna, the history and mutual relationships of the different schools and traditions within Hindu Mantraśāstra, or those of the Buddhist-Tantric sects, with their different mantras; local mantric traditions (in Kashmir-Nepal, or Bengal-Assam, or also Central and Eastern India, or Kerala, not forgetting "Greater India") are all fields that are certainly not unknown but in which further study from a "mantric" point of view would undoubtedly be rewarding.

All these are fields for Indological research, but mantras should also be tackled from another angle than the textual or historical. They are also to be viewed as a living practice, in India and, perhaps, elsewhere. Other methods than those, mainly historical and philological, of Indology therefore should be used as well.

Indeed, such different approaches are not entirely foreign to īndologists. The problem linguists are set by mantras as particular forms of speech or as particular uses of the phonetic resources of speech have been taken up in the essays in this book (Staal, Wheelock, Alper, etc.). But, precisely because they show a particular use of Sanskrit or of humanly produced sound, mantras as such should be studied systematically from the point of view of their phonology, sound pattern (repetitions, alliterations, etc.), and syntax when they consist of sentences. A semantic study perhaps also may be carried out from a properly linguistic, not religious or philosophical, point of view.

A psycholinguistic approach to mantras also would be interesting. Sounds as well as words have intrinsic expressiveness, emotive or intuitive associations, meanings, or connotations; and these certainly exist in the case of mantras. This aspect should be studied in relation to the users of mantras, too. We know there is a phonetical symbolism, certain sounds elicit certain representations or responses. Even though the meanings and connotations of mantras are fixed by tradition, they undoubtedly have emotive associations or connotations, too, and these are probably made use of (albeit unconsciously) by the traditions and contribute to their religious or spiritual efficacy. There is no doubt that the traditionally admitted connotations or symbolic values of mantras are conventional not natural. For instance, the associations or feelings evoked in a Hindu by OṂ do seem to be entirely fixed, organized, and oriented by the Hindu tradition, by culture. But there are still probably areas and a number of cases, where psycholinguistic research should prove rewarding.

Psychological or psychophysiological research methods could be applied to *mantrayoga,* where mantras, visualized as being in the subtle body whose image is superimposed by *bhāvanā* on that of the physical body, are usually considered as acting and moving together with *kuṇḍalinī,* which itself is a very particular internalized mental construction.[24] Such mental and physical practices result in a particular image of the body, fashioned with the help of mantras, which abide in it and animate it. One could try to find, in this respect, how *nyāsas* act on the psychological plane. How, we may ask ourselves, does a yogin experience his body as he "lives" it[25] when it is entirely imbued with mantras, supposedly divinized or cosmicized by them? The experience is sure to be of an unusual sort, which it would be interesting to know.

Mantras are also used in traditional medicine: Zysk tackles the subject here. But, in addition to their "magical" use in the preparation of drugs or in the cure of bodily ills, which are of interest mainly for ethnology, mantras have an important role also in the treatment of mental illnesses by mystics, shamans, or tranditional doctors, a field for psychiatry and psychoanalysis.[26]

Staal (page 65) draws our attention to the fact that one cannot understand mantras without refering to their musical aspect. Mantras, indeed, should be studied from the point of view of acoustics, which implies recordings of mantras and the study of such recordings. To this musical, rhythmic, prosodical, approach should be added a physiological one, which would be linked to the psycholinguistic study I mentioned earlier. Since mantras, among other things, are sounds emitted by human beings, they must certainly have some effect or influence on body and mind or, more exactly, on the psychosomatic human structure, a structure always considered in India as a whole. In *kuṇḍalinī* yoga, phonemes and mantras are associated with the centers (*cakra*) of the subtle body. Such connections between sounds and *cakras* look contrived and arbitrary, but we should not reject such notions immediately as absurd. Even if inaccurate and artificial in their traditional form, they may still hold a measure of truth. Man, indeed, lives in language and sound. He never ceases to emit and receive words and sounds. These act on his body as well as on his mind. Neurophysiology shows this very clearly. Scientific investigation has shown that certain sounds (as well as the complete absence of sound) have effects, and the effect produced when the sound is emitted or received seems to be related to certain parts of the body. Some sounds may cause the body to vibrate, may have physiological effects, or may help to awaken certain states of consciousness. (Some psycho-acousticians, for instance, consider shrill sounds to have an energizing effect.) Traditional music, religious chants, aim precisely at such results: spiritual results foremost, but also probably other effects, therapeutic ones especially. All this is important. It would therefore be interesting to study some mantras scientifically, together with the way in which they are uttered, repeated, or chanted, to find out if they have any real effect on the user and, if so, which ones and how.

There is also the interesting question of the relation between mantric practices and the experience of time. A mantra used for redemptive ends is a means to free oneself from time, to experience the "Great Time" (*mahākāla*), which is the matrix of all temporality. Such, for instance, is one aspect of the "seed of the Heart," the mantra SAUḤ, in northern Śaiva schools. Mantric practices of this sort in Tantric nondualist Śaivism of the Kashmiri brand or in the Buddhist Kālacakra ("Wheel of Time") school would be worth investigating. More generally, we may ask ourselves whether the alteration of the grammatical order of words or of the normal sequence of syllables in a mantra, sometimes resorted to in Vedic and in Tantric practice, is not used (among other reasons) as a means by which to destroy time, since a basic characteristic of the syntagmatic order is precisely its being produced in the process of time: Speech is an aspect of the flow of time, a way to experience it or to live in it. By interfering with the normal sequence of speech, one, thus, also would interfere, symbolically at least, with the usual experience of time.[27]

Mantras rank among the courses of action men have devised to satisfy a deep urge within them to overstep their limits, to be all powerful and all knowing, a dream of omnipotence. There also is the wish to be free from fear, to fill the void men feel surrounds them. Hence, the magical words. Hence, mantras. Hence, the word (words, rather, for they are many) of life and of salvation. Such longings are so ancient and so widespread as to be respectable. The wide variety of conducts devised to satisfy them make a fascinating study. The force of the libido invested in such conduct brings about physiological effects as well as particular states of consciousness. All this deserves the most careful study—and a very rewarding one it is sure to be. While carrying it out, however, we must carefully avoid wishful thinking. We must make sure not to keep "confusing mantras with names, sounds with things, and silence with wisdom," like the people in a "myth" told by Staal.[28] But, we must certainly go on studying, mantras as well as other things, until the vast riddle of the world is solved—if it can ever be.

NOTES

1. In this respect, reference might be made to a number of modern spiritual masters: to Sri Aurobindo, for instance; to the Transcendental Meditation group; to the Radhasoamis, with their *sumiran* practice; to the theories of Swami Pratyagātmānanda Saraswati in his *Japasūtram;* etc.

2. Or, in traditions that have received and adopted elements of the Indian tradition, such as some schools of Chinese and Japanese Buddhism.

3. In French, one would say *la parole,* written with or without a capital *p,* a term that underlines both the spoken, oral, aspect of speech and its possible metaphysical values as the Word. I believe however that *vāc* should not be translated "discourse" since though *vāc* may be speech, its essential nature is nondiscursive. In this, I admittedly differ from Alper, at least in matters of translation.

4. Written mantras and speculations on how to trace them are to be found in Chinese and Japanese *mantrayāṇa,* with the use of a script derived from *brāhmī,* called *siddham.* See van Gulik 1956.

5. See Renou 1949a, 11–18; or H. W. Bodewitz, "The Fourth Priest (the Brahmān) in Vedic Ritual," *Selected Studies in the Indian Religious, Essays to D. J. Hoens* (Leiden: Brill, 1983), 33–68.

6. They survive in the sphere of domestic rites and among a few small very orthodox Brahmin groups. An instance is the *agnicayana,* the Vedic rite of the fire-altar, of the Nambudiris, described by Staal. But, most of the public (as opposed to domestic) Vedic rites performed nowadays in India are quasi-archeological constructions, trying rather artificially to revive a thing of the past.

7. I believe, for instance, that one simply cannot discuss the truth or falsity of mantric utterances, if only because we cannot know "whether or not Siva 'is really here' " (Alper page 277).

8. The Oxford Concise Dictionary, for instance, does not print mantra in italics. It defines it as "Vedic hymn; Hindu or Buddhist devotional incantation."

9. The definition given was

> *Une formule, ou un son, qui est chargé d'efficacité générale ou particulière et qui représente—ou plus exactement qui est—la divinité ou un certain aspect de la divinité, c'est-à-dire qui est la forme sonore et efficacement utilisable par l'adepte de tel ou tel aspect de l'énergie et qui se situe par là même à un certain niveau de la conscience.* (p. 297)

10. Here, I use *mystical* in a rather vague fashion for the uses of mantras in all forms of intuitive realization of some postulated transcendent entity or reality.

11. One might quote, here, Robert A. Paul: "These syllables are without discursive meaning, but they must be so since they are generative elements, not surface structures: a seed does not display the likeness of a stalk of wheat, nor does a drop of semen resemble a man." (*The Tibetan Symbolic World: Psychoanalytic Explorations.* Chicago: University of Chicago Press, 1982, p. 30.)

12. One can, naturally, reduce the meaning of a word to "its use in the language" (cf. Alper page 253 quoting Wittgenstein). Any abracadabra, in fact, can be used so as to have some use in some language. Would that, however, still be language and meaning, in the usual sense? But, this touches upon the problem of the magical uses of language.

13. See Istvan Fónagy, *La Vive Voix* (Paris: Payot, 1983), on "les bases pulsionelles de la phonation."

14. This is a point to be kept in mind when saying (with reference to *bījas* and the like) that mantras make sense: they certainly do—to those who use them. But so do their utterances or babblings, to mental patients and babies.

15. See Claude Lévi-Strauss, *Anthropologie Structurale,* vol. I (Paris: Plon, 1958).

16. The colloquial French for What does this mean? is *Qu'est-ce que cela veut dire*? which, literally translated, is What does this want to say?

17. Staal, in a seminar on ritual held in Paris/Nanterre in May 1984, gave a fascinating description of the Vedic ritual as "a cathedral of sounds and actions" constructed according to preestablished rules, where everything happens as prescribed, outside of any personal intention on the part of the performers, who act simply because it is prescribed that they should. This does not seem to me to apply to Pauranic or Tantric ritual, which is to be performed with more than a general intention (*saṅkalpa*). It is to be done with a will, with faith and devotion (*bhakti*), and therefore the mental attitude, the intention and expectation, of the performer is of fundamental importance.

18. When a text prescribes the use of a mantra to some purpose, it always gives the *ṛṣi* (the name of the sage who has first "seen" the mantra), the meter (*chandas*), the *devatā* "expressed," the phonic seed (*bīja*) that is the quintessential form of the mantra, sometimes also the *śakti, kīlaka,* etc., and finally, always, the use (*viniyoga*) of the mantra in question.

19. See Goudriaan (1978), where the *ṣaṭkarmāṇi* (the six magical acts) are studied, especially. On the more general problem of powers (*siddhi*) in Hinduism, see Pensa (1969).

20. The rule that one cannot separate mantra from ritual is expressed, for instance, in the Śaivāgamaparibhāṣamañjarī (60): *kriyāśarīram ityuktaṃ mantraṃ jīvam iti smṛtam* (The [ritual] action is said to be the body; the mantra is the soul). Or, *mantrahīnā kriyā nahi* (There is, indeed, no [ritual] action without mantra).

21. All these aspects are there in varying degrees. I study them in a third installment of my "Contributions à l'étude du *mantraśāstra*" for a forthcoming issue of the *Bulletin of the École Française d'Extréme-Orient*. See also my paper "Un rituel hindou du rosaire: Jayākhyasaṃhitā, Chapter 14," to be published in the *Journal Asiatique* 275, no. 1 (1987).

22. The edition and translation of the Ṣaṭsāhasrasaṃhitā by J. S. Schoterman (1982) is a very useful contribution to this field. I also should mention here the research presently being carried out by T. Goudriaan, in Utrecht, on the Kubjikāmata and on the Niḥśvāsasārasaṃhitā. There is also my own work on the Yoginīhṛdaya, with Amṛtānanda's Dīpikā, which was recently published. See A. Padoux, ed., *Mantras et diagrammes rituels dans l'hindouisme* (Paris: Editions du

CNRS, 1986). Among the papers is one by T. Goudriaan on "Kubjikā's *Samaya-mantra* and Its Manipulation in the Kubjikāmata."

23. A study of one particular practice is provided by S. Schoterman (1982), in the appendix of his edition of the Ṣaṭsāhasrasaṃhitā on the diagrams, called *prastāra* or *gahvara,* used for the *uddhāra* of mantras.

24. On such *mantrayoga* practices with *kuṇḍalinī,* see for instance my paper "Un japa tantrique: Yoginīhṛdaya, 3.171–190" in *Tantric and Taoist Studies in Honor of R. A. Stein* (Bruxelles, 1981).

25. I refer here to what psychoanalysts of the Daseinsanalyse school, notably Ludwig Binswanger, call *Leib,* as opposed to *Körper. Körper* is the physical body; whereas the *Leib* (*corps vécu,* in French) is the body one experiences or feels psychologically. The limits of such *Leib* do not necessarily coincide with those of the physical body.

26. The subject is studied in Sudhir Kakar (1982). See also a paper read by A. Rosu during the panel on "Mantras et diagrammes rituels dans l'hindouisme," Paris, June 1984, on "*Mantra* et *Yantra* dans la médecine et l'alchimie indiennes," now published in the *Journal Asiatique* (1986); 203–268.

27. Years ago, Mircea Eliade underlined the role abnormal use of language (*sandhābhāṣā,* etc.) in Tantrism may play in introducing the adept to the awareness of a different ontological plane of existence.

28. As an epilogue to his (1975a) study.

NOTES ON THE CONTRIBUTORS

Harvey P. Alper was associate professor of religious studies, Southern Methodist University, where he taught since 1974. In 1976 he received the degree of Ph.D. from the University of Pennsylvania in South Asian studies. His professional interests ranged from the history of religion, with special attention to the religious traditions of South Asia, to religion and culture, with special attention to the spatial arts and to film. He served as editor of the series on the Saiva Traditions of Kashmir for the State University of New York Press and as co-editor of *The Encyclopedia of Indian Philosophy*. He contributed several articles to professional journals and collections. Professor Alper died suddenly on April 4, 1987, after completing the editorial work on the present volume.

Harold Coward is director of the Calgary Institute for the Humanities and professor of religious studies at the University of Calgary. He received his Ph.D. from McMaster University and has been a research scholar at the Center for Advanced Study in Theoretical Psychology, University of Alberta, and the Center for Advanced Study in Indian Philosophy, Banaras Hindu University, India. He is the author of fifteen books as well as numerous articles and chapters.

Ellison Banks Findly is associate professor of religion and Asian studies at Trinity College in Hartford, Connecticut, and director of the Trinity Hunger Action Project Fellowship (THAPF). She received her Ph.D. from Yale University in 1978. Prior to joining the faculty at Trinity College, Dr. Findly taught at Mt. Holyoke College and served as visiting curator of Indian miniature painting at the Worcester Art Museum. She has published widely on Vedic religion, Indian miniature painting (*From the Courts of India*, 1981), and Mughal cultural and religious life. She is the author of *Nūr Jahān: Empress of Mughal India (1611–1627)* (forthcoming).

Sanjukta Gupta was the senior lecturer at the Institute of Oriental Languages and Cultures of Utrecht (Netherlands) University for twenty years, until her retirement in 1986. She now lives in Oxford, England. Before that, she taught Sanskrit and Indian philosophy at Jadavpur University (Calcutta). She received her Ph.D. in Indian philosophy at Visva Bharati University (Santiniketan), and a D.Lett. from Jan Gonda at Utrecht University. Her books include *Studies in the Philosophy of Madhusūdana Sarasvatī, Lakṣmī Tantra, A Pāñcarātra Text, Translation with Introduction and Notes, Hindu Tantrism* (with Hoens and Goudriaan), and *A Survey of Hindu Tantric and Śākta Literature* (with Goudriaan).

Gerhard Oberhammer is head of the department of Indology at the University of Vienna. He received his Ph.D. from the University of Innsbruck, after studying philosophy and comparative linguistics and Indology there and at the Sorbonne. After two years in India, he became a lecturer on Indian philosophy in the Netherlands. Professor Oberhammer's research interests include epistemology and logic of the brahmanic systems of the first millenium A.D.; the philosophy of the Hindu systems, especially the system of Viśiṣṭādvaita; and the contrastive reflection of the religious contents of Hinduism and Christianity. Some of his publications are *Yāmunamunis Interpretattion von Brahmasūtram 2,242–45. Eine Untersuchung zur Pāñcarātra-Tradition der Rāmānuja-Schule* (1971); *Strukturen yogischer Meditation* (1977); *Materialien zur Geschichte der Rāmānuja-Schule: Parāśarabhaṭṭas Tattvaratnākaraḥ* (1979); (with H. Waldenfels) *Oberlieferungsstruktur und Offenbarung. Aufriß des Phänomens im Hinduismus mit theologischen Bemerkungen* (1980); *Wahrheit und Transzendenz. Ein Beitrag zur Spiritualität des Nyāya* (1984); *Versuch einer transzendentalen Hermeneutik religiöser Traditionen* (1987). G. Oberhammer is the editor of the publications of the De Nobili Research Library and of the *Wiener Zeitschrift für die Kunde Südasiens.*

André Padoux, directeur de recherche at the Centre National de la Recherche Scientifique, Paris, and member of the French National Council for Scientific Research, leads a research unit on Hinduism, in particular Tantrism and Mantraśāstra. His published works in French and English are on these subjects. An English translation of a revised version of his doctoral thesis, *Recherches sur la symbolique et l'énergie de la parole dans certains textes tantriques* (1963) is due to be published in the United States.

Ludo Rocher is professor of Sanskrit and W. Norman Brown Professor of South Asian Studies at the University of Pennsylvania. He received his D.Jur. and Ph.D. from the University of Ghent, Belgium. Before coming to Philadelphia, he taught at the University of Brussels. Dr. Rocher's research and publications include classical Indian studies generally, with special emphasis on classical, and colonial, Hindu law. He is the editor and translator of Sanskrit law texts; his most recent book is The *Purāṇas* (1986), a volume in the new "History of Indian Literature."

Frits Staal, professor of philosophy and of South Asian language at the University of California (Berkeley), studied and taught in Europe, Asia, and the United States. His interests range from logic and mathematics to the humanities. His books in English include *Advaita and Neoplatonism* (1961), *Nambudiri Veda Recitation* (1961), *Exploring Mysticism* (1975), *The Science of Ritual* (1982), *AGNI: The*

Vedic Ritual of the Fire Altar (2 vol., 1983), *Universals: Studies in Indian Logic and Linguistics* (1988), and *Kailas: Center of Asia* (1988).

John Taber is assistant professor of religion at Case Western Reserve University. Dr. Taber received his D. Phil. in philosophy from the Universität Hamburg. His publications include articles on Indian philosophy and contemporary philosophy of religion. He is the author of *Transformative Philosophy: A Study of Śaṅkara, Fichte, and Heidegger* (1983). Since 1985, when he was a Fulbright Scholar in Madras, India, Dr. Taber's research has focused on the Pūrva Mīmāṃsā school of Indian philosophy.

Wade T. Wheelock is associate professor of religion and head of the department of philosophy and religion at James Madison University in Harrisonburg, Virginia. He received his Ph.D. in the history of religions from the University of Chicago Divinity School in 1978. Dr. Wheelock has written articles on Vedic ritual as well as theoretical and comparative studies of ritual and language.

Kenneth G. Zysk is in the department of history and philosophy at Eastern Michigan University. He received his M.A. from the University of California at Santa Barbara and his Ph.D. from the Australian National University (Canberra). Dr. Zysk taught at the University of Wisconsin at Madison and the University of Toronto and was research historian at the University of California at Los Angeles. His background includes Indology, religious studies, and ancient medicine (East and West) and articles by him have been published in American and international journals. Dr. Zysk is author of *Religious Healing in the Veda* (1985) and is completing a book on *Early Buddhist Monastic Medicine.* Since 1986, Dr. Zysk has been treasurer and a member of the board of directors of the International Association for the Study of Traditional Asian Medicine (North America).

ABBREVIATIONS USED IN THIS VOLUME

TEXTS

KEY:

Ār = Āaṇyaka;	*B = Brāhman;*	*Bh = Bhāṣya;*	*Gr = Grhya;*
Dh = Dharma;	*P = Purāṇa;*	*Saṃ = Saṃhitā;*	*Śās = Śāstra;*
Śr = Srauta;	*Sū = Sūtra;*	*T = Tantra;*	*U = Upaniṣad;*
Fr. = French;	*Ger. = German;*	*Skr. = Sanskrit;*	*C. = Commentary.*

AiB, Ār	*Aitareya Brāhmana, Āraṇyaka*
Āp	*Āpastamba, Āpastambīya*
AV	*Atharvaveda Saṃhitā*
BhāgP	*Bhāgavata Purāṇa*
BhG	*Bhagavad Gītā*
BṛhU	*Bṛhadāraṇyaka Upaniṣad*
BSū	*Brahmasūtrās*
BVP	*BrahmavaivartaP*
ChU	*Chāndogya Upaniṣad*
GṛSū	*Gṛhyasūtras*
KauṣB	*Kauṣītaki Brāhmaṇa*
KauśSū	*Kauśika Sūtras*
KubjT	*Kubjikāmata Tantra*
KulāT	*Kulārṇava Tantra*
MahāU	*Mahānārāyaṇa Upaniṣad*
MaitU	*Maitrāyaṇi Upaniṣad*
Mhb	*Mahābhārata*
MM	*Mahārthamañjarī*
NṢA	*Nityāsoḍaśikārṇava*
PpSara	*Prapañcasāra (Tantra)*

Rām	*Rāmāyaṇa*
ṚV	*Ṛgveda Saṃhitā*
ṢaṭSam	*Ṣaṭsāhasra Saṃhitā*
ŚarTlk	*Saradatilaka (Tantra)*
ŚB	*Śatapatha Brāhmaṇa*
ŚST	*Śaktisaṃgama Tantra*
SV	*Sāmaveda Saṃhitā*
ŚvetU	*Śvetāśvatara Upaniṣad*
SvT	*Svacchanda Tantra*
TaitU	*Taittirīya Upaniṣad*
TS	*Tantrasāra*
VaikhDhSū	*Vaikhānasa Dharmasūtra*
VP	*Vākyapadīya*
YH	*Yoginīhṛdaya*
YSū	*Yogasūtras*
YV	*Yajurveda Saṃhitā*

JOURNALS, PUBLISHERS, AND SERIES

KEY:

Diss. = *Dissertation;* *KS* = *Kleine Schriften;* *ND* = *New Delhi;*
NY = *New York City;* *Orig.* = *Original;* *Rep.* = *Reprinted;*
Rei = *Reissued;* *UP* = *University Press.*

AA	*American Anthropologist*
AARP	*Art and Archeology Research Papers*
ABORI	*Annals of the Bhandarkar Oriental Research Institute* (Poona)
ActaOr	*Acta Orientalia* (L=Leiden; C=Copenhagen; B=Budapest)
AIOC	*All-India Oriental Conference*
AIIS	American Institute for Indian Studies
AKM	*Abhandlungen für die Kunde des Morgenlandes* (DMG)
ALB	*Adyar Library Bulletin [=Brahmavidyā]* (Madras)
ALP	*Adyar Library Publications*
ALRC	Adyar Library Research Center
ALS	*Adyar Library Series*
ArAs	*Arts Asiatiques* (Paris)
ArchOr	*Archiv Orientálni* (Prague)
ARW	*Archiv für Religionswissenschaft* (Berlin and Leipzig)
ASS	*Ānandāśrama Sanskrit Series* (Poona)
AUS	*Allahabad University Studies*
BDCRI	*Bulletin Deccan College (Post-Graduate and) Research Institute* (Poona)
BÉFEO	*Bulletin de l'École française d'êxtreme-orient* (Hanoi)
BÉHÉ	*Bibliothèque de l'École des hautes études*

BÉPHE	*Bulletin de l'École pratique des hautes études*
BeSS	*Benares Sanskrit Series*
BHU	*Benares Hindu University*
BI	*Bibliotheca Indica* (Calcutta)
BORI	*Bhandarkar Oriental Research Institute* (Poona)
BOS	*Bhandarkar Oriental Series*
BSOAS	*Bulletin of the School of Oriental and African Studies*
BSPS	*Bombay Sanskrit and Prakrit Series*
BVB	Bhartīya Vidyā (Bhavan) (Bombay)
BVB	*Bhartiya Vidya Series*
CA	*Current Anthropology*
CASS	Center for Advanced Study in Sanskrit (Univ. of Poona)
CHI	*Cultural Heritage of India*
ChowSSe	*Chowkhamba Sanskrit Series*
ChowSSt	*Chowkhamba Sanskrit Studies*
CIS	*Contributions to Indian Sociology*
CNRS	Centre national de recherche scientifique (Paris)
ColUP	Columbia University Press (NY)
CSS	*Calcutta Sanskrit Series*
CUP	Cambridge University Press
DAWB	Deutsche Akademie der Wissenschaften zu Berlin
DAWIO	Deutsche Akademie der Wissenschaften zu Berlin, Institut für Orientforschung
DeNRL	*De Nobili Research Library* (Wien)
DMG	Deutschen Morgenländischen Gesellschaft
DRT	*Disputationes Rheno-trajectinae*
ÉFEO	École française d'êxtreme-orient
EIPh	*Encyclopedia of Indian Philosophy*
ÉPHE	École pratique des hautes études
ÉVP	*Études védique et pāṇinéennes*
EW	*East and West* (Rome)
FestRSD	*Festschrift Rajeswar Shastri Dravid*
GOS	*Gaekwad's Oriental Series* (Baroda)
GTU	Graduate Theological Union (Berkeley, Calif.)
HIL	*History of Indian Literature*
HJAS	*Harvard Journal of Asiatic Studies*
HO	*Handbuch der Orientalistik* (Leiden/Köln)
HOS	*Harvard Oriental Series*
HR	*History of Religions* (Chicago)
HUP	Harvard University Press
IA	*Indian Antiquary* (Bombay)
IHQ	*Indian Historical Quarterly* (Calcutta)
IIJ	*Indo-Iranian Journal* (The Hague)
IJHS	*Indian Journal of the History of Science*
IL	*Indian Linguistics [= J. of the Linguistic Society of India]* (Poona)

IS	*Indische Studien* (18 vols., Berlin: 1849–98)
IT	*Indologica Taurinensia* (Torino/Turin)
JA	*Journal Asiatique*
JAAR	*Journal of the American Academy of Religion*
JAAS	*Journal of Asian and African Studies*
JAIH	*Journal of Ancient Indian History* (Calcutta)
JAOS	*Journal of the American Oriental Society* (New Haven)
JBiRS	*Journal of the Bihar Research Society*
JBORS	*Journal of the Bihar and Orissa Research Society* (Patna/Bankipore)
JCyBRAS	*Journal of the Ceylon Branch of the Royal Asiatic Society*
JDLCU	*Journal of the Department of Letters* (Calcutta University)
JGJRI	*Journal of the Ganganatha Jha Research Institute* (Allahabad)
JIPh	*Journal of Indian Philosophy*
JISOA	*Journal of the Indian Society of Oriental Art* (Calcutta)
JOIB	*Journal of the Oriental Institute*, Univ. of Baroda
JOR	*Journal of Oriental Research* (Madras)
JRAI	*Journal of the Royal Anthropological Institute*
JRAS	*Journal of the Royal Asiatic Society*
JRASBe	*Journal of the (Royal) Asiatic Society of Bengal*
JSSR	*Journal for the Scientific Study of Religion*
JUB	*Journal of the University of Bombay*
KPTT	Kegan, Paul, Trench, Trubner and Co.
KSS	*Kashi Sanskrit Series* (Benares)
KSTS	*Kashmir Series of Texts and Studies*
MB	Motilal Banarsidass
MUSS	*Madras University Sanskrit Series*
NIA	*New Indian Antiquary* (Bombay)
Numen	*Numen, International Review for the History of Religions*
OA	*Oriental Art* (London)
OAW	Österreichische Akademie der Wissenschaften
OAZ	*Ostasiatische Zeitschrift* (Berlin)
OH	Otto Harrassowitz
ORT	*Orientalia Rheno-Traiectina*
OUP	Oxford University Press
PAIOC	*Proceedings and Transactions of the All-India Oriental Confrence*
PÉFEO	*Publications de l'École française d'êxtreme-orient* (Hanoi)
PI	Wittgenstein: *Philosophical Investigations*
PICI	*Publications de l'institut de civilisation indienne*, série in-8
PIFI	*Publications de l'institut français d'indologie* (Pondichéry)
POS	*Poona Oriental Series*
PPMGM	*Prajā Pāṭhashālā Maṇḍa la Grantha Mālā*

PUF	Presses Universitaires de France
RevPhil	*Revue Philosophique*
RHR	*Revue de l'histoire des religions*
RKP	Routledge and Kegan Paul
RO	*Rocznik Orientalistyczny* (Krakow/Warsaw)
RSO	*Rivista degli Studi Orinetali* (Rome)
RSR	*Religious Studies Review*
SBE	*Sacred Books of the East*
ŚK	*Śrautakośa*
SOR	*Serie orientale Roma*
SUNYP	State University of New York Press
TT	*Tantrik Texts* (Calcutta, Madras)
UCaP	University of California Press
UChP	University of Chicago Press
VIJ	*Vishveshvaranand Indological Journal* (Hoshiarpur)
VKAWA	*Verhandelingen der koninklijke Akademie van Wetenschapen te Amsterdam*
VKNAW	*Verhandelingen der (koninklijke) Nederlandse Akademie van Wetenschapen*
VKSKS	*Veröffentlichungen der Kommission für Sprachen und Kulturen Südasiens* (OAW)
VPK	*Vaidika Padānukrama Kośa*
VVRI	*Vishveshvaranand Vedic Research Institute* (Hoshiarpur)
WZKM	*Wiener Zeitschrift für die Kunde des Morgenlandes*
WZKSO	*Wiener Zeitschrift für die Kunde Süd- und Ostasiens und Archiv für Indische Philosophie*
YUP	Yale University Press
ZDMG	*Zeitschrift der Deutschen Morgenländischen Gesellschaft* (Leipzig)
ZII	*Zeitschrift fur Indologie und Iranistik* (Leipzig)

A Working Bibliography for the Study of Mantras

PRELIMINARY REMARKS

The purpose of this essay is both bibliographical and methodological: first, to compile, in so far as practical, a list of the most useful sources that deal directly or indirectly with mantras; second, to indicate by the organization of the material some of the methodological options and the research lacunae in mantric studies.

The use of mantras, to be sure, is so general in South Asian culture that nearly any source dealing with religion, especially with ritual, might contain interesting material. For this reason, no bibliography dealing with mantras could be exhaustive; it must be selective. In selecting and organizing materials for this essay, I have been guided by the following considerations.

(1) An effort has been made to include all significant items dealing exclusively with mantra.

(2) Texts and translations are sometimes included for the convenience of the reader but, in general, the emphasis falls on secondary sources. This is simply because specialized studies, often scattered through a wide range of publications, are frequently difficult to identify and locate, while specialists will have direct access to the texts.

(3) Although many items are relevant to several subjects I have, with the exception of certain surveys which may function as standard references, rarely listed a work more than once. I have included numerous items which strike me as potentially throwing light on a subject even if they deal with it only indirectly.

(4) Certain pivotal topics are covered as evenly as feasible, given the library resources, time, and space at my disposal: the Vedic *Saṃhitās,**

**I regularly use the abbreviations explained in the List of Abbreviations.*

the Vedic *Sūtras*, classical Hinduism, Vyākaraṇa and philosophy of language, and Tantra.

(5) I have devoted nearly half of the Bibliography to Tantra because its significance still is often unrecognized and because, unlike the Veda, at this time, few bibliographic resources deal with it.

(6) The majority of items in the Bibliography are in English. I have, however, regularly included items in French and German; and selectively included items in Italian, Dutch, Hindi, and a few other languages. The material in the Indian vernaculars is limited but respresentative, I hope. However, I have not attempted to comb the Indian periodical literature. Unfortunately, I have not included items in either Russian or Japanese, two languages of which I am totally ignorant.

(7) I have endeavored to write the Bibliography in a manner that would maximize its intelligibility to a large variety of readers. In particular, I hope that it will prove useful to scholars in various disciplines—e.g., anthropology, history, linguistics, philosophy, and religious studies—who are concerned with India but who are not trained as classical Indologists. In the end, I would be most gratified if it served not only the scholar and the serious student but also the "common reader" interested in Indian religious life. For this reason, from time to time, I have indicated some of the items I feel would be most appropriate for the general reader.

The essay brings together references hitherto scattered through a number of sources and specialized bibliographies. For further information the reader may go to such standard bibliographies as Renou (1931), Dandekar (1946–73), Potter (1970), and Cardona (1976). I wish to acknowledge my indebtedness to these works, to the multitudinous volumes of Jan Gonda, and to the works of Teun Goudriaan, without which the compilation of this Bibliography would have been exceedingly difficult.

In styling this a "working bibliography," I acknowledge at once its goals and its deficiencies. Although I have sought to weight equitably the various subdivisions of the essay, imbalances undoubtedly remain. Some areas of interest (e.g., the *Arthaśāstra*, *Āyurveda*, the *Dharmasūtras*, the *Purāṇas*, the treatment of language in *Nyāya-Vaiśeṣika*) are overlooked or treated cursorily. I trust that this will not detract from the utility of those sections treated more lavishly, and that the imbalance will not seem inappropriate in a working bibliography.

Selection obviously involves judgment. I have been guided by what strikes me as the likely utility of each item to the potential readers of this volume. Others would doubtless opt for a somewhat different selection. Unfortunately, I have not been able to see all of the items I have listed. I have tried whenever possible to verify dates and page numbers, but assume that some errors remain. For this, I ask the reader's indulgence. Although I do not know today whether I shall eventually revise this essay, I solicit the advice of readers in correcting errors, recasting sections, and filling lacunae. For now, I shall judge the essay to have served its purpose if it stimulates and facilitates fresh reflection and exploration of mantras and other forms of Indian religious language.

Finally, a few technical notes: (1) For logistical reasons, with few exceptions, I have not listed reviews of the works cited. (2) For the convenience of the reader the Bibliography brings together items cited by the essays in this volume even if not discussed here. (3) In most instances items on any single topic are arranged chronologically rather than alphabetically, so the reader may grasp at a glance something of the development of the field. (4) Anyone who has worked with Indian bibliography will understand that absolute consistency in transliterating Indian names is difficult to achieve. To those unfamiliar with the problem, let me offer one suggestion. If one attempts to locate items written by Indian authors, especially through computerized data bases such as the OCLC, remember to try alternative spelling of a name and also to try initials instead of full names.

ON MANTRA AND MANTRAŚĀSTRA IN GENERAL

Although it appeared over twenty years ago, Jan Gonda's essay "The Indian Mantra" ([1963b] 1975b, 4) has no peer. It remains the only well-documented synthetic survey of Indian Mantraśāstra.* It should now be supplemented with Gonda (1980a, 213–29), which focuses on the domestic ritual as portrayed in the sūtra texts. Besides it, and the essays brought together in this volume, I have uncovered only two thoughtful, well-focused articles dealing with mantra in general: Dasgupta (1956) and Wayman (1975). Padoux (1978b) offers some brief, programmatic suggestions for mantric research. For a popular introduction to Mantraśāstra that attempts to tease out the contemporary spiritual potential of mantric utterance, see Alper (1983). For contemporary Hindu apologetics dealing with mantra, see the citations under neo-Hinduism pages 441–43. The reader in need of general background may consult Basham (1954) or, preferably, the standard introductions to Indian religion (Gonda 1960–63) and Indian civilization (Renou et al. 1947–53), in German and French, respectively.

As this volume illustrates, most, but not all, students of mantra assume that it should be approached as a special sort of religious language. There is a large literature concerning religious language written from the perspectives of *Religionswissenschaft* and the philosophy of religion. But, as Gonda ([1963b] 1975b, 4.249) observes, in this literature, the mantra "is conspicuous by its absence." This fact notwithstanding, such literature is important in that it establishes an intellectual context in whose terms mantra can be compared and contrasted with forms of

---

**I use the term* Mantraśāstra *broadly to refer to the theory and use of mantras.*

verbal and ritual discourse found outside of India. Ironically, by and large, it establishes this context by default. It takes as its model (or models) prayer (praise, thanksgiving, petition, and one-on-one dialogue with a transcendent god) as practiced in the paradigmatic religious traditions that originated in the Semitic world. In doing this, it demonstrates well that mantric utterance is not prayer. Perhaps, the more intriguing question runs the other way, might it be that much of what passes for prayer in the West functions more or less the way mantric utterance does in India?

In the past twenty years, considerable work has been done on the problems of religious language and ritual, and I intended originally to devote a major section of this essay to surveying the potentially relevant methodological and theoretical literature, especially dealing with religious language but also on the study of ritual and on mysticism. The extent of the Indological material, however, has rendered that impractical, and the following items will have to suffice.

For the classical approach of the history of religions, Heiler (1923; and 1961, 236–339, "Das heilige Wort") and van der Leeuw (1963, 113–51, "Beautiful Words"; 1967, 403–46) are standard works; cf. also Larock (1930) and Frick (1931). Basic orientation to the vocabulary and bibliography of linguistics and the "sciences of language," broadly conceived, is found in Ducrot and Todorov (1979). The philosophical analysis of religious language has arisen largely out of the Anglo-American tradition of "ordinary language" or "analytic" philosophy. For introductions to this approach, see Alston (1964), Rorty (1967), and Searle (1971b). The point of departure for the analysis of language in this tradition is Austin's classic essay, *How to Do Things with Words* (1962). His ideas have been most systematically explored in Searle (1969; 1971a; 1979b); see, too, Cole and Morgan (1975) and Holdcraft (1978). Among the voluminous literature on Wittgenstein, I believe the following provide especially helpful orientation: Cavell (1962), Coope et al. (1970), Finch (1971; 1977), and Brand (1979). Representative works exploring religious and theological language include High (1967; 1969), Vesey (1969), Trigg (1973), Keightley (1976), and Sherry (1977). In evaluating this literature, one might keep in mind the work done more recently on the nature of metaphor; for example, Ricoeur (1977), Lakoff and Johnson (1980), and Johnson (1981), with its valuable annotated bibliography (329–52).

A number of nineteenth and early twentieth century scholars (e.g., F. Max Müller, James G. Frazer, Lucien Lévy-Bruhl) tended to view language pathologically, as contributing to the religious and magical misapprehension of the world. Tambiah ([1968a] in Goody 1985, 32f.) discusses four more recent figures who speak similarly of the magical power of words, Ogden and Richards (1923), Cassirer (1953), and Izutsu (1956). This material should be considered in light of the discussion on comparative rationality; on which, see Wilson (1970) and Horton and Finnegan (1973).

The literature on mysticism and on the study of ritual is as wide ranging and varied as that on language. That the majority of essays in this volume focus on mantra as linguistic should not mislead. In the end, a coherent theory of mantra will presuppose an understanding not merely of the nature of language but of the nature of ritual and mysticism as well. On mysticism, some idea of the problems and the literature can be gained from Staal (1975b), Bharati (1976b), and Katz (1978; 1983). For mystical traditions concerning the repetition of the name of god and for analogies to mantras in the mystical traditions in the West, see page 442.

In the past, the study of ritual has been carried on predominantly by Christian liturgicists and ethnographers studying preliterate societies. Recently, in an effort to work toward an integrated theory of ritual, the area of ritual studies has emerged within religious studies. Grimes (1985) discusses this in a "programmatic essay" and provides a bibliography of some sixteen hundred items. This bibliography focuses on theory and does not systematically collect ethnographic items. Its treatment of South Asian ritual is cursory. Complementing this is Grimes (1982), which is undoubtedly the best survey so far of ritual studies. It gives special attention to psychosomatic, anthropological, and theatrical perspectives on ritual. I here list only a few works that strike me as either representative or potentially helpful to the student of mantras. I particularly try to provide sufficient references, so that someone unfamiliar with the field can begin to get a theoretical handle on the knotty relationship between language and ritual.

For major anthropological treatments of ritual, see Goody (1961), Turner (1969; 1974), Douglas (1978); for the sociological perspectives on ritual, Nagendra (1971); for a revised Freudian view of ritual, see Gay (1979), and, on violence and ritual, Girard (1977); on the perspective of "performance theory," see Schechner (1977) and Schechner and Schuman (1976). As models for the application of anthropological theories of ritual in the study of texts, there is Burkert (1983) and, more theoretical, (1979). The interpretation of ritual as a language has been popular and, for a theoretical statement, see Lawson (1976). It has been applied to Indian rituals in a number of ways, see, for example, Orenstein (1968) and Ferro-Luzzi (1977). The immense literature dealing with specific kinds of ritual cannot be surveyed here. Two items are, however, of special relevance: Mair (1969), a survey of European and non-European witchcraft provides background for the study of the use of mantras with the intent to cause harm; Turner (1979), an anthropological study of pilgrimage, for the use of mantras in that context.

Deciding whether mantras are in some sense symbolic depends in large measure on how one decides to use the word *symbol*. Among recent approaches to symbolism, see Turner (1967) and R. Firth (1973); Sperber (1975), which attempts to discard a linguistic model of symbolism, is of special interest, as is Jarvie (1976). Grimes (1985, 6) observes that Jarvie's discussion of the "limits of symbolic interpretation" is relevant to the approach to ritual in Staal (1979a); in this regard, see too the interesting debate on ritual sound and percussion by Needham (1967) and Jackson (1968); and on glossolalia, cf. May (1956) and Hutch (1980). For the approach to ritual from the perspective of the biological sciences, see, for example, Huxley (1966), Birdwhistell (1970), and d'Aquili (1979); for the related "ecological" approach, see Rappaport (1979) and Lincoln (1981), a work that will be known already to Indologists. Another relevant work from the sciences is Hesse (1961), which traces the concept of "action at a distance" in the history of physics.

For anthropological perspectives on religious language in general, see Malinowski (1923), J. R. Firth (1957), Baumer and Sherzer (1974), Sanches and Blount (1975), Samarin (1976), Sapir and Crocker (1977), and Tambiah (1981). Anthropological analysis of religious language in the context of various "preliterate," "tribal," or non-European societies include Evans-Pritchard (1929), Pitt-Rivers (1967), Strathern and Strathern (1968), Finnegan (1969), B. Ray (1973), Rosaldo (1975), Ong (1977), Gill (1977), and Tambiah (1977a), which focuses on Thailand. Attempts to apply speech act theory to various sorts of religious language include Tambiah (1968a), Bauman (1973), Ware (1981), and Wheelock (1982). For an analysis of the performative aspects of the Roman Catholic liturgy, see Ladriere (1973); and for a computer-assisted analysis, Wheelock (1984).

The attempt to analyze mantric utterance in a philosophically responsible manner, as linguistic utterance and as ritual act, has barely begun. Besides the essays by Alper, Findly, Staal, Taber, and Wheelock in this volume, see McDermott (1975), Wheelock (1980), and Staal (1982; 1984; 1985).

THE VEDIC WORLD

THE WORLDVIEW AND PRACTICE OF THE VEDA

Mantras are quintessentially Vedic. Their nature, function, and history can only be understood against the background of Vedic civilization. They emerge in a preliterate, pastoral society, among a cattle and horse-loving folk, who considered themselves "noble" (*āryan*), who spoke a family of Indo-European languages we today call Vedic, who saw the world in which they lived as a good, supportive place only because they believed themselves to possess the means without which humanity could not cope with the baleful jokers in the human condition. What, in the first instance, allowed them to cope—and what, in their own judgment, set them apart from all other peoples not so equipped—was the existence among them of inspired poets who apprehended the truth and made it available in words. Many of the compositions of these seers were preserved by a sacerdotal class, who created a complex group of ritual sciences. The oral literature compiled by these priests is the

Veda. Before tackling the subject of Vedic ritual and Mantraśāstra, one would do well to review some general works on the people who produced the Veda. See, for example, on the Āryans in India and Iran, Ghirshman (1977); on the archeological background to the Vedic age, Thapar (1983, with refs.); on Vedic society and polity, Rau (1957).

In approaching the Veda, the general reader is at something of a disadvantage. Most of the scholarly literature and many of the best translations are in French or German. Many works of scholarship that would otherwise be accessible cite Sanskrit sources without providing a translation. Nonetheless, there is such a wealth of material that even someone limited to English, with patience, can enter the Vedic world. Much of the voluminous scholarly literature on the Veda is relevant to the study of mantras, but it can hardly be surveyed here. Accordingly, this portion of the Bibliography focuses on those aspects of Vedic society, ritual, and speculation that seem most likely to shed light on the contribution of the Vedic period to Hindu Mantraśāstra in general. Surprisingly, the considerable understanding of the Veda that has been amassed through a century of scholarship has not yet been presented in any synthetic work. The exemplary survey of Vedic literature, Gonda (1975a), is fortunately in English. For less technical introductions, the general reader might see the individualized surveys of de Nicolas (1976) and Pannikar (1964). For further references, one should consult the standard sources surveyed, for example, in Santucci (1976) and Bechert and von Simson (1979) and the bibliographies mentioned earlier.

The Understanding of Speech and Speaking in the Veda

Mantras became mantras because of their origin as inspired poetic utterances and their use in power-bestowing rituals. To understand this, it is necessary to grasp the Vedic understanding of the power of speech, a subject on which there has been a considerable amount of work. One can best approach the subject through an examination of the technical vocabulary of the Veda, particularly the terminology for the valences of speech and speaking. The most reliable, brief introduction to this subject, albeit limited to the *Ṛgveda Saṃ* (ṚV), may well be Renou (1955). For a general survey of Vedic speculation about language, there is Śivanārāyaṇa Sastri's (1972) survey in Hindi. There is no substitute, however, for Gonda (1963a), an extended study, with a synthetic introduction (pp. 7–67), dealing with the "Vision of the Vedic Poets." Although highly technical, it will repay careful study even by the general reader. For a brief account of the method followed there, see Gonda (1961a), an important essay on the study of ancient Indian religious terminology. Among the technical terms with which Gonda (1963a) deals are *ṛta, ṛṣi, kavi, kratu, cakṣ-, darśana, dṛś-, dṛṣṭi,* , *dhī-, dhīti, dhīra, dhyāna, mati, manas, manīṣā, vāc, vipra,* and *ven-*.* In all cases, he provides references

**Since one of Gonda's central points is that terms such as these resist translation by any single non-Indian equivalent, I refrain from providing translations here.*

to earlier secondary literature, which in general I have not duplicated here. I have grouped the materials on the power and significance of names in both Vedic and post-Vedic India on pages 359–63.

In the Veda, several figures embody the sounds of the sacrifice: Bṛhaspati, Brahmaṇaspati, Vācaspati, and Vāc. In the development of the tradition, Vāc, characterized by W. N. Brown ([1965] 1978, 44) as "the apotheosis of the spell, the final exaltation of the magic sound," is the most important of these personifications, but in the ṚV only a few poems, principally 1.164, 10.71, and 10.125, deal extensively with "her."

A graphic intimation of the emotional centrality of speech in the Brahmanic-Hindu world is Vāc's association with the cow. ṚV 1.164.41 addresses her as the thousand-syllabled buffalo-cow (*gaurī*). In ṚV 8.101.16 (cited by Gonda 1963a, 91f.), the cow, identifying herself as the "navel of immortality," refuses to be slaughtered in sacrifice. She describes herself as coming from the gods, divine (*devīṃ*), the one who has found speech, the one who causes speech to come forth, and the one who approaches with all visionary intuitions (*viśvābhir dhībhir*). Gonda interprets the cow in this passage as "a mediator between the Invisible and the world of men in that she transmits speech and 'vision,' two faculties indispensable to those beings who want to rise above the level of inertia, materiality, or animal existence." With this, one might compare the term *dhiṣaṇā*, variously understood as a goddess of suckling and a personification of poetic inspiration, on which see Renou (1955), Johannson (1917), and other references in Gonda (1963a, 116).

For general accounts of Vāc, see Essers (1952a; 1952b) in Dutch, and Heilmann (c. 1944), W. N. Brown (1965; 1968b), and Miśra (1967). On ṚV 10.71, see Patel (1938), and Staal (1977); on 10.109—where Vāc, the wife of Bṛhaspati is abducted by Soma—see Bhawe (1955). On 1.164, see pages 430–31. As a goddess and personification of speech, Vāc is a cosmogonic figure. In this regard, see, for example, Scharbau (1932). Albrecht Weber (1865) compares the Indian Vāc and the Greek *logos.* On one side, the figure of Vāc in the ṚV has been explored as "the power behind the throne," the power of poetic inspiration and sacrificial utterance. On the other side, Vāc has been discussed as a philosophical category in the system of Bhartṛhari and in Tantra. Very little attention seems to have been devoted to the mythological treatment of Vāc in the interim, in the *Atharvaveda Saṃ* (AV), the *Brāhmaṇas,* and beyond. The narratives discussed in passing in Deppert (1977, 286ff.) and O'Flaherty (1980, 134, 276) suggest that Vāc-as-woman might have been treated mythically with the same ambivalence as was Vāc-as-language. Whereas, mythically, she was the procreator who was potentially a destroyer, epistemologically she was the creator of name and form but thereby seducer. On the significant development of the figure of Vāc in a Tantric context see pages 430–31.

Philosophically speaking the most significant term associated with sacred utterance in the Veda is obviously Brahman. In its pre-Vedāntic guise, it is a complex, multivalent term, on which one may consult the representative essays of Charpentier (1931), Renou and Silburn (1948–49), Gonda (1950), and Thieme (1952), which interprets Brahman as "(dichterische) Formulierung." The treatment of Brahman in the later philosophies is beyond the scope of this Bibliography, but on the concept of *śabdabrahman* and on OṂ see pages 354–55.

Poems and Poetic Inspiration

There may at first glance appear to be little connection between the visionary traditions of the Vedic age and the use of mantras in later periods. The former inspired the composition of a body of original, complex poetry, the latter was repetitive and formulaic. The continuity is, however, far from negligible and understanding the former arguably can throw light on the latter. Gonda (1963a, 64) goes to the heart of the matter when he observes that it is poetic intuition (*dhī*) that "enables the seer or 'poet' to compose 'texts' which conform to the requirements of religious hymns and formulas, that is to say, which may be expected to influence the deities presiding over the powers and phenomena on which man feels himself dependent." What was held to be the case when the mantric tradition arose, is still held to be the case three thousand years later: Mantras are used because of the conviction that they enable one to subdue an unruly cosmos, or enable one to have desirable religious experiences.* Gonda appropriately cites J. W. Hauer who, in 1922, indicated the desideratum of studying the connections between the creation of the Vedic poems, their use in magic and sacrifice, and ecstatic experience. I hope that this section of the Bibliography will stimulate and facilitate such inquiry.

According to Gonda's account, the paradigmatic terms for poetic inspiration are derived from the verb *dhī-*. Gonda adopts (1963a, 68) the English term *vision* as his general translation for *dhī-*, understanding by this "the exceptional and supranormal faculty, proper to 'seers,' of 'seeing,' in the mind, things, causes, connections as they really are, the faculty of acquiring a sudden knowledge of the truth, of the functions and influence of the divine powers, of man's relation to them etc., etc." The largest portion of Gonda's monograph (pp. 68–258) thus is devoted to this family of terms. Derivatives from *man-* seem to live within the same semantic field as *dhī*. Thus, *mantu* (Gonda 1975a, 255, with refs.) may be understood as "intentional and efficient thought," while *mati*, *manman*, and, of course, *mantra* itself are terms denoting the "material" product of the thought/feeling that inspires poetic composition.

The best known technique used to stimulate poetic inspiration was the ingestion of a liquid pressed from the *soma* plant. The discussion of Soma today generally begins from Wasson (1968), which argues that

**Gonda (1963a, 66) goes further, speaking of the "essential identity" of the Vedic and later doctrines of mantras, but this is rather incautious, and it is safer to speak of continuity.*

Soma is the hallucinogenic mushroom, fly agaric (*Amanita muscaria*). The earlier investigations, which were extensive, are summarized by O'Flaherty in a chapter she contributed to Wasson (1968, 95–147). The mythical background is well introduced in O'Flaherty (1981, 119–38, with refs.). For the continuing discussion, see Kuiper (1970), Brough (1971), Ingalls (1971), and Swamy (1976), with responses in Wasson (1970; 1971; 1972; 1979). For translations, see Bhawe (1957–62). There is a large literature on the use of drugs to attain mystical states in various cultures. It cannot be surveyed here, but see Nettl (1953) on meaningless peyote songs.

A few generalizations about the Vedic understanding of intuitive vision may be helpful in unpacking its role in the formation of a society in which Mantraśāstra came to play a central part. (1) The Vedic world saw an unbroken continuity between ordinary seeing, poetic seeing, and the sight of the gods. Thus, "there was in principle no difference between mental and other qualities attributed to divine and human persons" (Gonda 1963a, 45). Indeed, the epistemological kinship between the seers and the gods, just as later the kinship between gurus and gods, seems stronger than that between ordinary men and seers. (2) Just as with initiation later in Tantra, poetic inspiration was less an event in and of itself than the beginning of a process during which the zeal and activity of the poet helped determine the progress he made (cf. Gonda 1963a, 106). (3) As one would expect, from the start, the value and nature of intuition was described not only in its own terms, as a sui generis mental apprehension, but with the aid of metaphors. Three groups of metaphors seem especially significant in both the Vedic and later contexts. First, there is frequent recourse to perception and to the power of sight and the eyes. Second, as Gonda (1975a, 68, n. 31) says, in the Veda, "there is a constant use of terms denoting 'light, shining, bright' etc. with regard to the sacral word and the state of bliss." Third, the dialectic of revelation and concealment is suggested by the image of the heart and the cave; that is, the secret inner places.

Gonda (1963a, 51, 276–88) is a discussion of the heart. The complex of sight-eye-light imagery has been discussed by Gonda in several places: (1963a, 266–75) deals with the notion of a "flash of insight"; (1969) is an important monograph on the "eye and gaze" in the Veda; (1966) deals with the cosmological and soteriological category of *loka* (etymologically, more or less as "place in which the daylight shines"), with which cf. Malamoud (1976); also, Gonda (1963a, 302–17) deals with the image of the eye in Buddhism. Perhaps, the imagery of light was so frequent because it lent itself to use in a great variety of cosmogonic, epistemological, and meditative contexts, as suggested by the use of *jyotir*, *bhā-* and *bhās-* and related terms in Vedānta, or by the Pāli term *obhāsa* (in Sanskrit, *avabhāsa*) (cf. Gonda 1963a, 268f.).

In spite of the extensive shifts involved in the transformation of "Brahmanism" into "Hinduism," a single principle seems to have been presupposed continuously: That which comes from the heart may lead to the heart, that which comes from vision may lead back to vision. Hence, mantra is that instrument of ecstasy that, arising in visionary intuition (*dhī*), enables one to attain meditative vision (*dhyāna*). On derivatives from *dhyā-*, see Gonda (1963a, 289–301) and the shifting understanding of the Gāyatrī discussed on pages 353–54. This dialectic between visionary initiation and meditative vision is far from trivial and is as characteristic of Tantra as of the Veda. In both cases, the initiatory inspiration begins a process in which the active participation of the poet is indispensable. On the one side, it is only through the application of his poetic skill that the raw intuition is shaped—given the significance of *tapas,* I am tempted to say cooked—into an instrument sufficient to influence the gods. On the other side, it is only through the application of meditative skill that the mantra implanted by initiation flourishes and bears fruit in the adept's consciousness. Only one who concentrates, with zeal and steadiness, upon those well-formed visionary instruments, the mantras, may realize the truth they impart (cf. Gonda's summary 1963a, 300, also 229). This suggests further how the various Indian traditions tolerated the continuing creation of "new" mantras even after the canonization of the Śruti: The visionary master, the guru who has used mantras to achieve his own meditative victories, is qualified to create new mantras, or one might say, more in the spirit of the tradition, *see* other mantras.

There is considerable overlap and continuity between the Vedic understanding of vision and various later reflections on imagination. Gonda (1963a, 327, n. 27) singles out Sreekantaiya (1937), which deals with "imagination in Indian poetics," for special praise. See, in general, the discussion of poetics and of *pratibhā* on pages 380–81. The Vedic concept of poetic inspiration is also the proper point of departure for inquiry into later traditions of supernormal perception, yogic cognition (*yogipratyakṣa*), and divine or human omniscience (*sarvajñātva*). The material on this is treated in many general works on Yoga, Vedānta, and Buddhist thought and cannot be summarized here. See, for example, Beyer (1977) on the vision quest in early Mahāyāna, Ramjan Singh (1974) on the Jain concept of omniscience, and Steinkellner (1978a) on the problem of Yogic cognition in Buddhism; and, for comparative background, Pettazoni (1956).

A passion for precision characterized Vedic religious utterance, just as it characterized ritual action and the expression of poetic intuition. This demand for exactness—in matching words, time, and action, in pronunciation, stress and rhythm—is central. Precision alone defines an utterance as ritual and is believed to guarantee its effectiveness. Not surprisingly, the fixation on the right drill provides one of the major continuities between the Vedic, Hindu, and Tantric use of mantras. Bharati (1965, 122) points out that today even *Saṃnyāsis* and "other religious specialists chant verses reminding them about the importance of *śikṣa* (phonetics), in their daily observances." Priests and renouncers have a common fixation on exactitude in form.*

From the point of view of a rationalist, one of the paradoxes of Vedic ritualism—and of Tantra—is that the mantric texts, upon which the ritual depends, are systematically deformed in the very effort to preserve and utilize them. Indeed, it is probably not going too far to say that, from both the Vedic and Tantric points of view, that very deformation underwrites the mantra's numinous efficacy. In the ritual, unnatural form is good form. This characteristic of Mantraśāstra can be seen at work in the well-known Vedic traditions of stylized rearrangements of the text and in the little-studied Tantric traditions of manipulating or ornamenting mantras while they are being repeated in *japa*. One is struck by the concomitance in these traditions of earnestness and playfulness. This is not entirely surprising. Religious life has always been, in part, recreational: playing games is a passionately rule-oriented business. A brief overview of the Vedic traditions of "safeguarding" a text through systematic rearrangement may be found in Gonda (1975a, 17), where he discusses the *kramapāṭha, jaṭāpāṭha*—the "twisted hair arrangement," on which, see Thibaut (1870)—and *ghanapāṭha*. Among contemporary scholars, Frits Staal is virtually alone in drawing attention to these traditions. See his work on the Nambudiri Brahmans (1961; 1983a), as well as his series of studies on ritual published since 1979, especially (1985a); on the musical implications, cf. Howard (1983).

Before mantras are "deconstructed" they exist. In many instances, for example in Mīmāṃsā and various theistic traditions, they are taken at face value. When they have a plain sense, that plain sense should not be overlooked. While it would be very misleading to think of mantras as poetic, in the ordinary sense of the term, it should be kept in mind that, in the first instance, mantras are fragments of poems. In any case, whether they have ordinary meaning or not, the interpretation of mantras presupposes an understanding of Vedic style in general. (To an extent, even post-Vedic mantras reflect certain features of Vedic style.) A few sources may be mentioned for the reader's convenience. Gonda (1975a, 173–267) provides a detailed overview of Vedic style, with copious references. Especially important in this regard is the preponderance of repetition and other formulaic devices in the Veda. In general, see Gonda (1971) and the references in Gonda (1975a, 213, n. 20). On repetition, see Bloomfield (1916), Gonda (1959a; 1959b; 1960), and Mainkar (1956). Related to the Vedic predilection for indirect utterance is the use of brevity, ellipsis, and ambiguity in style; on these, see Renou (1939; 1954a), Gonda (1960), and Velankar (1969). See, too, the items concerning style and enigma on pages 383–90. Given its poetic and ritual context

**Bharati (1965, 159, n. 69) refers to TaitU 1.2, "śīkṣāṃ vyākhyāsyāmaḥ, varṇaḥ svaraḥ, mātrā balam, sāma santānaḥ" (Limaye & Vadekar 1958, 50) understood as meaning "may we learn correct pronunciations of letter and sounds, the exact volume and force of the syllables."*

Hindu Mantraśāstra always presupposed the extensive use of metaphors and cognate figures of speech. As an introduction to the use of metaphor and simile in the Vedic period, see Hirzel (1890), Weller (1927), Gonda (1939), and Leidecker (1954); for further references, see Gonda (1975a, 254, n. 1). On meter, the standard survey remains Arnold (1905). The meters, like the *sāmans,* were understood in Vedic speculation as concrete forms of Vāc, a matter that assumes a central role in some Upaniṣads. In connection with this, see Siddheshwar (1953) and Mylius (1968). On the extensive tradition of classical Sanskrit poetics, see pages 355–58.

The Social and Ritual Context of Vedic Mantraśāstra

The enormous literature on Vedic ritual cannot be surveyed here. Suffice it to note that from the earliest time the Vedic poets were aware of and concerned with ritual, but not with the same elaborate, formal ritual system that eventually developed. Determining to what extent and at what point particular mantras were meant for particular rites, thus, remains a matter of conjecture. Gonda (1979) discusses the mantras used in the *pravargya,* an ancillary Soma ritual in which hot milk is offered to the Aśvins (cf. Staal 1983a, 53ff., and van Buitenen 1968). See the discussion of the ṚV on pages 342–43. In approaching Vedic sacrifice, no introduction in English can be recommended to the general reader. One valuable point of departure, in French, with references to the classical studies is Biardeau and Malamoud (1976), with which one might compare a new synthesis, also in French, by Staal (1985b). For a recent methodological statement see Malamoud (1983). A good idea of the employment of mantras in the fully developed Vedic ritual, as understood in the *Brāhmaṇas* and *Sūtras,* may be obtained from the classic reconstructions, such as Hillebrandt (1880), Schwab (1886), Levi (1898), Caland and Henry (1906), P. E. Dumont (1927; 1939), and Staal (1983a), which is the most accessible to the contemporary, general reader, well illustrated, and with an accompaning film and cassette. For good advice on how to read the secondary literature on and translations of Vedic sacrificial texts, see the remarks of Ikari and Arnold in Staal (1983a, 2.478f.), and for further references, see Gonda (1977b, 492–93, n. 23).

Three specialized subjects merit preliminary comment: On connections between ritual and grammar, an influential if somewhat speculative essay by Renou (1941–42) attempts to situate the origin of the Pāṇinian system, like that of the Mīmāṃsā, in the context of Vedic ritual. On the use of mantras in the initiatory and consecratory rituals of the Vedic age, besides the general works on ritual already mentioned, see the discussion of *dīkṣā* on pages 426–27. One way of focusing on the conceptual difficulties involved in coming to terms with Vedic ritual is to ask in what ways they might be classified as "science," or "magic," or both. In this regard, an interesting exercise might be to compare Oldenberg (1919) on "*vorwissenschaftliche Wissenschaft*" with Staal (1982) on the

"Science of Ritual," and see the discussion of magic in the context of the AV and Tantra on pages 401–402.

The agonic context of poetic utterance, and thus of the magic of articulation and ritual, in the Vedic age should not be overlooked. Attempts at general surveys of the "numinous" and "playful" in Vedic culture have been few; however, see Parab (1952) and von Schroeder (1908). Considerable work has been done on the well-known Vedic—nay, Indian—love affair with riddles and enigmatic verses, what Gonda (1975a, 132) more formally characterizes as "the propensity to elliptic diction and veiled, indirect or paraphrastic expression." On this, see Haug (1875), Renou (1949b; 1949c; and, in English, 1960b), and Bhagvat (1965). The popularity of riddle collections is noted in Sternbach (1974, 73f.), with additional references. On the use of similes and other figures of speech also see Bergaigne (1934–35; 1935–36), Velankar (1938; 1940; 1963; 1965), P. S. Shastri (1948), and Potdar (1953, 248–68).

The best known social locus for this love of the indirect are the so-called Vedic symposia or poetry-contests (*sabhā, samasyāpūraṇa*), the interpretation of which has been widely debated. Of note is the theory, not universally accepted, according to which these contests were related to a New Year's festival; on this, see Kuiper (1960). On the *brahmodya*, perhaps the most significant of the devices for conveying metaphysical enigma and on the speculative traditions of which they seem to have part, see Renou (1953a; 1953c; 1956), Esteller (1962), Heesterman (1968), and W. Johnson (1980), which is one of the few attempts to read ṚVedic poetry in terms of contemporary literary studies. Krick (1982) draws attention to the agonic elements in the ritual for the installation of a sacred fire (*agneyādheya*). For a Tibetan Buddhist parallel to the poetry contests see Sierksma (1964).

The *locus classicus* of Vedic enigma is doubtless the much-discussed ṚV 1.164 (*asya vāmasya*). Relative to it, see, from varying perspectives, Thieme (1949), Kunhan Raja (1956), P. S. Shastri (1957), Lommel (1958), Agrawala (1959; 1963), Brown (1968), Kuiper (1974), W. Johnson (1976), and other references listed by O'Flaherty (1981, 308). In this context, note that Ruegg (1959, 15ff.), while discussing Vedic speculation concerning the divisions (i.e., the levels) of Vāc, draws attention to a possible precedent in the Indian game of dice; on this, see Lüders (1907), Caland (1908b), Keith (1908), Held (1935, 253–77), and de Vreese (1948). One source of ideas for analyzing these traditions is the analysis of play and sport in human culture, on which the classic work remains Huizinga (1955). For surveys of recent trends, see Ehrmann (1971) and Miller (1973). As one might have anticipated, this vein has been well mined by theologians seeking to defend the relevance of religion as "play that really matters." See, for example, Cox (1969), Neale (1969), Rahner (1972), and Novak (1976); the trend is discussed briefly in Kliever (1981, 124–52).

The existence of an elite class, or classes, of people accepted as poets or seers is the social coefficient of the Vedic understanding of the power of poetic speech. The semantic field in which the vocabulary for poetic inspiration falls tends to strike the modern reader as a unity. Perhaps, for this reason, it is difficult to get a handle on the vocabulary for the various sorts of poets and seers: principally, *ṛṣi, kavi, muni,* and *vipra.* It seems intuitively obvious that, at one time, there must have been clear differentiation among types of poets. Many of the sources discussed earlier, at the beginning of the previous section, including Gonda (1963a), deal with the poets and attempt such discrimination. But the many Vedic terms for *poet* resist exact translation, and to the best of my knowledge, no one has convincingly demonstrated the character of the different kinds of poets. For example, Gonda (1963a, 48) summarizes that the term *kavi,* as applied to people, "unmistakably denotes those who mentally or spiritually enter into contact with divine power, the transcendent and the world of the unseen," while a few pages earlier (p. 40), he concludes that a "*ṛṣi* obviously is the functionary who enters into contact with divinity." For a brief attempt to convey the meaning of the relevant terms, which Gonda admits are "to a certain extent used promiscuously," see (Gonda 1975a, 71): *Vipra* is a poet distinguished by the experience of "fervency," "enthusiasm," and "spiritual rapture"; *karu* is a "spokesman," "performer," and "eulogist"; *kavi* is "an inspired sage who possessing esoteric wisdom sees [things hidden from others] with his mental eye" and also sometimes (Gonda [1963b] 1975b, 4.273) "shaper of the poem he discovers" (*mantrakṛt, mantrakartā*).

Perhaps the most intriguing technical term for *poet* is *vipra,* discussed by Gonda (1963a, 36–39). In the first instance, he is described (ṚV 10.97.6) as a physician, slayer of demons, and dispeller of diseases, perhaps by the wielding of mantras. More suggestive is the derivation of the term from *vip-* (to tremble, vibrate, or quiver). Hence Gonda (p. 39) concludes that the *vipra* is "the man who experiences the vibration, energy, rapture of religious and aesthetic inspiration." See also Zysk (1985b, 8–9) on the relation of Kavi and vipra to *bhiṣas,* "healers." This cannot fail to remind anyone familiar with Tantra of the metaphysical notion of *spanda,* the incessant sonic vibration that underlies the cosmos. So Gonda is led to entertain the hypothesis that *vipra* "may originally have denoted a moved, inspired, ecstatic and 'enthusiast' seer as a bearer or pronouncer of the emotional and vibrating, metrical sacred words, a seer who converted his inspirations into powerful 'carmina'."* In this connection one might reflect upon AV 5.20.8 (cited Gonda 1963a, 227), which may be interpreted as speaking of war-drums being constructed with mantras (*dhī*). Gonda quite properly cites ethnographic literature on drums, to which one might now add the essays on percussion cited on page 332.

**According to Ernout and Meillet (1959, 100b),* "Mot ancien, qui désigne une formule rythmée, notamment une formule magique."

On the poets in general, see Regnaud (1905), Patel (1930), and Kunhan Raja (1963); on the *ṛṣi,* Rahurkar (1956–57); on the *kavi* in the AV, Shende (1967); on "female seers," Kumari Devi (c. 1920). For a comparative perspective on the poets and oral traditions of poetry, see Bowra (1952) and Chadwick and Kershaw (1932–40). Accounts of the poets as individuals are speculative rather than historical. One is on far firmer ground in delineating the poet-families or clans for, as Gonda (1975a, 77) puts it, "The weak sense of individuality and the strong sense of family unity and solidarity prevent us from having more than hazy and confused notions of 'authorship.'." On the family traditions, see Oldenberg (1888) and Bhargava (1971). On the Vedic schools—Gonda (1975a, 30) comments that "the assembly of scholars is a cultural institution of great antiquity in India"—and their role in the composition of the Veda, Renou (1947) remains standard. On the evolution of the Vedic schools in the "age" of the *Sūtras,* see Gonda (1977b, 474–88) and Parpola (1968). In connection with this social genealogy of the mantras, see Brough (1953) and the references provided by Gonda (1975a, 31ff.). On the evolving role of priests and "teachers" in the *Brāhmaṇas,* relevant to the emergence of the various sorts of gurus in classical and Tantric Hinduism, see Hopkins (1908), Shende (1963; 1965), and the discussion of the guru on pages 412–14.

Finally, it can be observed that the religious life of the Āryan speakers of Vedic India could hardly have been monolithic. The Vedic tribes also must have had their "folk religion." It is not unlikely that the evolving tradition of Mantraśāstra was influenced by various strata of the population—might one speculate a "silent majority"—beyond the Brahman and Kṣatriya orders, just as the Little and Great Traditions later inform each other. One way of exploring this hypothesis might be to examine the rituals for dealing with relative outsiders, namely the *vrātyastomas.* On this, one may see Konow (1926), Hauer (1927b), Biswas (1955), Heesterman (1962; 1967), C. Sen (1963), and Parpola (1983a). In this context see the exploration of the concept *ārya* in Thieme (1938). It should also be kept in mind that the mantric traditions incorporated in the *Gṛhyasūtras* (GṛSū) are largely independent of, and at most ancillary to, the Śrauta tradition. On this, see page 348.

VEDIC TEXTS

The Ṛgveda

At least as early as *Śatapatha Brāhmaṇa* (ŚB) 1.31.28 (Gonda [1963b] 1975b, 4.260), quotations from the Vedic *Saṃhitās* have been referred to by the term *mantra.* Following this usage, it has become customary to define mantras, in the first instance, as the verses of the Veda in general. The mantras of the Veda, however, were not believed to be efficacious because they *came out* of the Veda. On the contrary, it is because the verses were apprehended as efficacious (that is, as mantras) to start with that certain poems—it is somewhat misleading to call them hymns—were preserved, collected, and recognized as Veda. Moreover, as has often been pointed out (Gonda 1975a, 88 citing Renou), the ṚV "occupies an anomalous position: through chronologically older and the source of most of the formulas contained in the Yajurveda, it was peripheral to what became the main tradition of ritualism into which it was intercalated only at a later date."

Perhaps it is appropriate that the ṚV as the fount of mantras is difficult to approach and comprehend. Unfortunately, there is no complete and adequate English translation. To get something of its flavor, the general reader might turn to O'Flaherty (1981) and Velankar (1972). For greater breadth and to acquire a feel for the Sanskrit, one could turn to annotated, partial translations, in particular, Velankar (1963–68), which covers Books II, III, and VII, and Bhawe (1957–62), which deals with poems to Soma *pavamāna,* IX.1–70. On the place of the ṚV in the sacrificial cult, see Renou (1962); and, for a general survey, but with caution, Potdar (1953). Among the literature ancillary to the ṚV, the *Ṛgvidhāna* merits special attention in any history of Mantraśāstra. It serves as a practical handbook for the uses of mantras in ordinary life and, if one prefers, may be considered magical. As Gonda (1975a, 37f.; cf. 1980a, 223f.) notes, it is a work that illustrates the transformation of Brahmanism into "Hinduism" and "throws light on the adaptation of Vedic subject-matter" (1975a, 38) in the post-Vedic age. It has been translated by Gonda (1951).

The Sāmaveda

Generally speaking, the *Sāmaveda Saṃ* (SV) is the musical digest of the classical Vedic ritual. Among the texts, translations, and introductions to the SV are Benfey (1848), Caland (1907a), Raghu Vira (1938), and Kunhan Raja (1941).* The English translations of the SV are of varying quality and somewhat difficult to use. The general reader might be advised to approach the text from the secondary literature. A summary account of texts and studies may be found in Gonda (1975a, 313–22); a valuable, extended survey is provided by Parpola (1973). See, additionally, Caland (1907b—for an English translation of this, see Nilakantha Sastri 1935—and 1908c), and Faddegon (1951). Renou (1952) discusses the mantras in the SV of non-Ṛgvedic origin.

The character of the SV suggests that, for the Vedic people, certain melodies were apprehended as having magical efficacy independent of the ritual action or verbal formulae with which they became associated at a certain point. Indeed, it is possible that the original meaning of the term *sāman* was "appeasing" or "propitiatory song" (Santucci 1976, 9). Gonda (1975a, 315, n. 18) summarizes:

**Benfey is an editor and German translator of the* KauthumaSaṃ. *Kunhan Raja is an editor of the same with Sanskrit commentaries. Caland is an editor of the* JaiminīyaSaṃ *with a valuable German introduction.*

> Part of the oldest *sāmans* were presumably popular melodies, to which already in prehistoric times religious songs were sung at various celebrations; others—especially those that were interspersed with exclamations . . . may have originated in circles which attributed a decidedly 'magical' power to certain tunes and chants, a practice surviving and systematized in the Sāmavidhāna-Brāhmaṇa, part II.*

The most significant precedent in the SV for later mantric utterance, as Staal emphasizes, is the tradition of *stobhas.* In Gonda's words (1975a, 316), they are "modifications to which a *ṛc* is subjected when it is sung to a melody of the Sāmaveda," namely, the modification of syllables, "repetitions, breaking up of words, [and] insertions of apparently insignificant words or syllables such as *hoyi, hūva, hōi.*" As Gonda stresses, this intentional deformation of the verses was undoubtedly felt to enhance the esoteric force of the chants. He further (1975a, 315, n. 18) cites an interesting passage, *Āpastamba* (Āp) DhSū 1.3.10.19, according to which "the sound of *sāmans* and musical instruments was, like the barking of dogs and the cries of wolves, jackals, and owls, a reason for discontinuing the study of the Veda." The assumption of the text must have been that music and the cries of animals have an inherent and disruptive power. The implication, I think, is that the ritual (that is, the mantras) unleash a competing but similar potency. If so, this tends to corroborate Staal's argument that one of the models for mantras was the songs or sounds of animals. In any case, Mantraśāstra in post-Vedic India built upon *both* the poetic tradition of the ṚV and the musical/magical tradition of the SV. Only to the extent that it takes as its model the cantillation of the SV, rather than the poetic utterance of the ṚV, the SV may be understood to provide evidence for the meaninglessness of mantras.

On the SVedic and other musical traditions, see Howard (1977; 1983); also, van der Hoogt (1930), Bake (1934; and 1935), Rajagopala Aiyar (1949), Iyer (1962–63), Raghavan (1962b), Nejenhuis (1974), and Staal (1968). Staal (1984b) discusses Vedic music in relationship to ritual and mathematics; in connection with this, see Seidenberg (1983, with refs.), R. N. Apte (1926), Bag (1971), and Michaels (1978), as well as the discussion of *yantras* and *maṇḍalas,* relevant to the notion of "sacred geometry" on pages 405–406. H. C. and Anna Earwicker—not to mention Claude Lévi-Strauss—notwithstanding, our culture does not ordinarily think of music as a vehicle for theological and literary embellishment. The works that follow in the wake of the SV show that India does. One of the most instructive among these is the *JaiminīyaB,* the narrative traditions of which have recently been ingeniously presented in O'Flaherty (1985), with appended bibliography of texts, translations, and studies. For a few modern interpretations of the music of mantras, see page 443.

**For the latter text and a German translation, see Konow (1893); also, on "magical kāmya-rites," V. Ch. Bhattacharyya (1959).*

In connection with the SV, it is well to remember that silent recitation, and silence itself, played a significant role in Vedic ritual sequences; on this, see Renou (1949a). There undoubtedly is a direct continuity between the Tantric conviction that, in the end, the highest "pronunciation" of a mantra is a silent, meditative pronunciation and the well-attested Vedic predilection to envision the highest portion of a reality as transcendent and beyond speech. Already, *Maitrāyaṇi Upaniṣad* (MaitU) 6.22–23, a passage dealing with the mantra OṂ, quotes an earlier verse that pictures as necessary the relationship between articulation and silence: "There are two Brahmans to be known, the Brahman that is Sound and one that is higher; those who are immersed in the Brahman that is Sound reach the higher Brahman, too."* On the relevant concept of *anirukta,* see Renou (1954d). Wayman (1974) is a thoughtful contrast of the *muni* tradition of transcendental silence with the *satya* tradition of articulable truth. Note especially the remarks concerning *Manusmṛti* 2.83: "The monosyllable (i.e., OṂ) is the highest Brahman. Suppressions of the breath are the best austerity. But nothing surpasses the Sāvitrī. Truth is superior to silence." This dialectic between articulation and silence, finally, might be seen as paralleling the important dialectic in Vedic ritual and culture between emptiness and fullness; on this, see Malamoud (1975). For a comparative perspective on mystical silence, see Mensching (1926).

Other Saṃhitās *and* Brāhmaṇas

The *Yajurveda Saṃ* (YV) and the various *Brāhmaṇas* are concerned predominantly with ritual action. The secondary literature dealing with these texts is extensive and, by and large, focuses on the utilization of mantras during the Vedic period or among groups of Brahmans who preserve Vedic ritual, more or less, as an anachronism. For orientation on the YV, see Gonda (1975a, 323–37). An essay that focuses on the use of the mantras from the YV is Thite (1972); otherwise, see the references on Vedic ritual on pages 339–40 and on the *Sūtra* literature on pages 347–48.

The *Brāhmaṇas* once again reinforce the impression that the meaning of the mantras was a secondary concern for the evolving Vedic ritual system. As Gonda (1975, 369) says, "the deities to whom they [the mantras] are devoted or who are mentioned in them, the meters and certain numerical conditions were generally regarded as more essential than their contents." For orientation on the *Brāhmaṇas* in general see Gonda (1975a, 339–422); on the ŚB, see Minard (1949–56). Concerning the social and religious world of the *Brāhmaṇas,* see, for example, Schayer (c. 1917; 1925), and dealing with the AV as well, Devasthali (1965) and J. Basu (1969).

---

* dve brahmaṇi veditavye śabdabrahma paraṃ ca yat
śabdabrahmaṇi niṣṇātaḥ paraṃ brahmādhigacchati *(Limaye & Vadekar 1958, 344)*

It is increasingly recognized (cf. Grimes 1985, 8–12) that the distinctions usually made in the West between religion and magic are question-begging and apologetic rather than descriptive. The term is most often used to describe what turns out, upon close examination, to be ritual practices that are at once popular and practical; hence, it is no surprise that the AV has been considered magical in contrast to the Three Vedas. Following this dubious convention, it is convenient to consider items concerning the use of mantras as magical tools in a Vedic context here. The magical use of mantras in a Tantric context will be considered on pages 410–12.

Depending on the ideological convictions of an author, the sacrificial system of the Veda may or may not be classified as "magic." Keeping this in mind, on Vedic magic in general, besides the obvious chapters in the standard surveys, there are the still quite serviceable syntheses of Hillebrandt (1897), Caland (1900; 1908a), and Henry (1909). On the AV itself there are the surveys of Shende (1949; 1952) and, dealing with rituals to avert harm and promote well-being, Mālavīya (1967) in Sanskrit.* One important group of Artharvic mantras, one may call them "charms," is directed against diseases and demons. For a brief description of these medical formulae (*bheṣaja, bhaiṣajya*), see Gonda (1975a, 278ff.) and Zysk (1985b, passim). On particular topics relevant to the magical force of mantras, see, for example, Lommel (1932), Velankar (1954), and Kwella (1973). According to Gonda (1975a, 307ff.), the AV *Pariśiṣṭas* (Par) are an especially rich source for the popular religion of the "late Vedic and early Hindu period," but no secondary work on them seems to be reasonably available. For further references on the use of mantras in healing, see page 391.

MANTRAS IN THE BRAHMANIC TRADITION

Commentaries on the Veda

The composition of commentaries on the Veda and digests of Vedic Mantraśāstra went on well into the post-Vedic age. For example, Gonda (1975a, 39f.; also 1977b, 657f.) discusses the *Brāhmaṇasarvasva* (D. Bhattacharyya 1960), a work of Halāyudha, a writer associated with the court of Lakṣmaṇasena of Bengal towards the end of the twelfth century. It contains an explanation of "all the Vedic *mantras* (not more than four hundred in number) prescribed for recitation in the domestic rites as performed by the followers of the Kāṇva recension of the Vājasaneyī Yajurveda." Gonda notes that Halāyudha adapts the meanings of the mantras "to the requirements of even the minor rites," illustrating the recurring attempt of the Brahmanic tradition to understand the utilization of mantras in ritual as intelligible.

**Goudriaan (1978, 425, n. 3) describes this as a "praiseworthy study . . . which contains more than is suggested by its title, but has, unfortunately for the non-specialist, been written in Sanskrit."*

Such is the explicit stance of Sāyaṇa, the representative Brahmanic commentator. In the introduction to his ṚVBh (1972, 4) he states, "the meaning of [apparently meaningless] mantras such as "*amyak sā ta indra ṛṣṭiḥ*" [1.169.3] has been explained by Yāska in the *Nirukta*. The failure of those unfamiliar with that book to understand them suggests no fault of the mantras."* Sāyaṇa similarly ascribed to the theory that all mantras had a ritual use. If it was not explicit, it was to be inferred from the "context," as Gonda notes (1975a, 83, n. 4), for Sāyaṇa *gato viniyogaḥ* amounts to *laiṅgikaḥ;* i.e., when the use has been lost, it is to be reconstructed from the characteristics (*liṅga*) of the mantra. In other words, Sāyaṇa insisted that mantras were ritually meaningful. In this regard, see Biswas (1959).

The Sūtra Literature

The *Śrauta, Gṛhya,* and *Dharma Sūtras,* very roughly in that order, are transitional. They are continuous with the *Brāhmaṇas,* on the one hand, and the practices of classical Brahmanic society, on the other. In the *Sūtra* literature, one finds a systematic outline of the utilization of "Vedic" mantras in the ritual and social setting that one might style Brahmanic "Hinduism." Thus, Rājaśekhara (ninth–tenth century, cited in Gonda 1977b, 467, n. 8) defines *kalpa* as "[that] *sūtra* [text] which enjoins the employment of the *mantras* that belong to the various 'branches' [traditions: *śākhā*] of the Veda." In spite of the usual tendency to contrast Veda and Tantra, one should by no means assume that the world of the *Sūtras* and that of the *Tantras* are entirely discontinuous. On the contrary, they share at least one fundamental concern. What Gonda (1977b, 470) says of the *Sūtras* could be said equally well of the *Tantras:* "They are also unique as ritual handbooks and mines of information on that which has always fascinated the Indian mind to a high degree, viz. the technique enabling the man who knows to exert influence upon the Unseen."

For a brief introduction, with references to texts and translations, to this literature, see Gonda (1977b). General introductions or orientations, of different sorts, is provided by Hillebrandt (1897), Caland (1903), Sehgal (1960), S. Kashikar (1966), and Rolland (1971; 1975). For additional information, on Dharma in the broadest sense, there is Kane (1930–62), five volumes in eight parts, an exemplary work of synthesis and reference; on the *Śrauta* rituals, there is the *Śrautakośa,* with Sanskrit texts and partial English translations in Kashikar and Dandekar (1958–70), also the critical studies of C. G. Kashikar (1960a; 1960b; 1961; 1972), for example. Discussions of the social condition of late Vedic India, their relevance limited, of course, to those classes that supported Brahmanic ritual, include B. Ghosh (1941–42), V. M. Apte (1954), Choudhary (c.

---

* *amyagādimantrāṇām artho yāskena niruktagranthe 'vabodhitaḥ tatparicayarahitānām anavabodho na mantrāṇām doṣam āvahati*

1953), Gopal (1959), Chattopadhyaya (1967), and, with a broad scope, N. N. Bhattacharyya (1975).

The degree to which the utilization of the mantras in the ritual can serve as evidence for their meaningfulness as ritual statements is debatable. Gonda (1977b, 503) argues strongly for the ritual intelligibility of the mantras:

> the impression that as a rule the bonds between word and action are rather loose, that in many cases there is no perceptible connection at all has proved false. On the contrary, a correspondence between formula and rite, so much appreciated by the ancient authorities, is often clearly discernible, albeit sometimes owing to secondary adaptation.

For an overview of the treatment of the mantras in the *Sūtras,* with references, see Gonda (1977b, 502–508); also V. M. Apte (1939–40; 1940–41; 1946), Renou (c. 1957; 1962), and Krishna Lal (1967 and, in Hindi 1970). The *KauśikaSūtras* (KauśSū), a work belonging to the AV, is a text that illustrates one of the persistent themes running through the history of Mantraśāstra, the impossibility—and I would argue inadvisability—of separating magical and religious strands. Gonda summarizes its significance and provides references (1977b, 611–15); he discusses its mantras in (1980c). The most extensive exploration of the use of mantras according to a particular text is Gonda (1965b), a meticulous translation and exegesis of a section of the KauśSū. In terms of the general inextricability of magic and ritual, see Bloomfield (1890), Caland (1900), Gonda (1965b) and Zysk, (1985b); also Weber (1858) and the items cited for the AV on page 334.

In this connection one should also note the *Nidānasūtras* (Gonda 1977b, 536f., with refs.), traditionally attributed to Patañjali. It assumes a connection between "religious realities and ritual acts" and explains the relationship between sacrificial acts and *sāmans* on the basis of a principle of identification. Allied with the GṛSū is a group of texts, some still unpublished, that might be styled handbooks or compendia of mantra for use in the domestic ritual. Gonda (1977b, 578–81) mentions the *Mantrabrāhmaṇa,* associated with the *GobhilaGṛSū* (for refs. see p. 578, n. 94), the *Mantrapāṭha,* associated with the ĀpGṛSū, translated by Winternitz (1897), and the Vaikhānasa *Mantrasaṃhitā,* on this, see page 368.

Mantras in Daily Life

The ritual traditions of the GṛSū and the literature related to them have not been studied as extensively as the three early *Saṃhitās* or the mythological and theistic traditions of classical Hinduism. Therefore, it is not yet possible to sketch a synthetic social portrait of the use of mantras in the Brahmanic tradition nor to propose a history of the long transitional period between Vedism and Hinduism. Gonda has, however, mapped out the territory for the first time in two recent works (1977b;

1980a). Used in conjunction with Kane's history of *Dharmaśāstra* (1930–62), it is now possible to get an overview of the rituals and the texts in which they are discussed, and this greatly assists the student setting out on detailed study. The latter of Gonda's two volumes, a thematically arranged guide to the rituals and a monument of patient erudition, is especially valuable. It provides a brief but thorough, systematic analysis of the use of mantras in the domestic and other "nonsolemn" ritual. For summary statements, see Gonda (1977b, 565–81; 1980a, 213–29).

This picture Gonda paints of mantric usage in a domestic context is one of great flexibility, practicality, and intelligibility. Thus, one should not be surprised that estimates—there is no exhaustive list—of the number of Vedic mantras cited in the GṛSū vary from a low of 1000 to a high of 2500 (cf. Gonda [1963b] 1975b, 4.270, n. 4; 1977b, 565)! The "Vedic schools," he reports, "did not regard as unalterable the text of formulas which were foreign to their own *Saṃhitā.* [Hence] not infrequently *mantras* have been rearranged or combined, extended or curtailed" (1977b, 565). Indeed, he notes, "many of [the mantras] are liable to variation even to the point of showing almost all possible variants that the words constituting them are capable of," while "even in two editions of the same text the *mantras* may vary considerably" (p. 565). Gonda further (1977b, 568) notes that "contrary to expectation the bonds between the *Gṛhya* contexts and the *mantras* contained in them are on the whole closer, their connections less vague than those between *Śrauta* contexts and their formulas." In the first instance, this literature tends to serve as evidence that for a significant strand of the Brahmanic tradition mantras were expected to make sense, be intelligible and convey meaning. But this generalization must be tempered by the recognition that the texts often stipulate different mantras for identical situations. This variation suggests an ultimately arbitrary element in Mantraśāstra.

On the use of mantras in Hindu *saṃskāras* in general, besides Kane, see V. M. Apte (1954) and R. B. Pandey (1969). On variant configurations of the major *saṃskāras* in the DhSū, see Banerji (1962). On the ritual of marriage, with attention to IE parallels, see Haas (1862), Weber (c. 1855), and Winternitz (1892). Specifically on the *saptapadī,* the "seven steps" that, with its accompanying mantras, might be seen as the heart of the complex marriage ritual, see Jolly (1903), Krishna Lal (c. 1958), and Patyal (1976). On non-ṚVedic mantras, some 425 in number, used in the marriage ceremony, see Narayana Pillai (1958). On the *sīmantonnayana* ("dividing of the hair" during first pregnancy), see Gonda (1956); for a comparative and psychological perspective on the meaning of hair, see Leach (1958), Lincoln (1977b), and Obeyesekere (1981), with a bibliography. On *upanayana* ("thread investiture"), besides the relevant chapters in the general works and materials on *dīkṣā* discussed on pages 426–27, see Gonda (1965a, 284–314), a survey of the concept of *brahmacarya.* On the mantras used in the Vedic funeral ritual, see Caland (1888; 1893; 1896). On the complex rituals for the ancestors, see Sureshcandra (1940) and D. R. Shastri (1963). For a comparative perspective on these rituals, one might consult Knipe (1977) and Nicholas (1982).

In general, one should be cautious in interpreting the *saṃskāras* as predominantly educational and utilitarian. They are protective or, if one prefers, sacramental (cf. Gonda 1980a, 365). All of these rituals presuppose a theory of personal purity and impurity on which there is a summary discussion in Gonda (1980a, 280–85); one may also consult Saraf (1969) or Panse (1968) on rituals of purification, and Scheftelowitz (c. 1914); S. Joshi (1969) deals with gold in the *saṃskāras*. There is a large ethnographic literature on the Indian experience of purity and pollution and on *rites de passage* in particular communities. I cannot survey that here, but see L. Dumont (1980).

Among other specialized studies: Gonda (1980c) deals with the mantras used in two sequences of ritual worship, the *agnyupasthāna* and the *sautrāmaṇī;* on the mantras used in the Vedic rituals of expiation (*prāyaścitta*), see Gampert (1939); on the daily ritual of the twice-born, see Bodewitz (1976); and on the rituals involved in building a house, A. Rai (1960).

The permeation of Hindu daily life with mantric utterance is profusely attested in the classical texts and also in popular manuals and in the reports of some ethnographers. This is as one would expect, for the common acts of daily life always stand in greatest need of ritual validation. A passage from the earliest *Upaniṣad* is emblematic. *Bṛhadāraṇyaka* (BṛhU) 6.4.21 reads: "Then he spreads her thighs apart, saying: 'Spread yourself apart, Heaven and Earth.' After having inserted his member in her and joined mouth with mouth, he strokes her three times as the hair lies." At this point, the text inserts three mantras taken almost literally from ṚV 10.184.1f. beginning, "Let Viṣṇu make the womb prepared. Let Tvaṣṭṛ shape the forms. Let Prajāpati pour in." Presumably these are mantras to be uttered in order to assure successful procreation.*

But the question remains Is the mantric element in these social rituals really central? For one thing, different GṛSū specify different mantras for the same ritual. Second, the interesting fact is that, as Gonda (1977b, 557, n. 16) puts it, "in the case of a girl these ritual acts [i.e., the *jātakarman,* "birth ceremonies"] may, it is true be performed but—as all *saṃskāras* from birth to *cūḍākarma* [i.e., first haircut]—without the accompanying mantras." This could be interpreted to mean that the mantras, after all, were epiphenomenal to the physical ritual itself. Alternatively, it could mean that, from the perspective of the Brahman priests, girls were not entitled to full *saṃskāras* at all. This merits exploration, as does

* athāsyā ūrū vihāpayati—vijihīthāṃ dyāvāpṛthivī iti
tasyām arthaṃ niṣṭhāya mukhena mukhaṃ saṇdhāya trireṇām anulomām
anumārṣṭi—viṣṇur yoniṃ kalpayatu tvaṣṭā rūpāni piṃśatu
ā siñcatu prajāpatir. *(Limaye & Vadekar 1958, 279)*

The translation is taken from Gonda ([1963b] 1975b, 263); cf. Fišer (1966, 116).

the even more important question of whether women used and use "mantralike" verbal formulae in formal or informal rites of passage of their own. On the role of women in these rituals, see Gonda (1980a, 197–205), which includes comments on the "so-called women's rites (*strīkarmāṇi*)."

Mantras and Renunciation

Nothing shows the centrality of Mantraśatra in the Indian religious imagination as clearly as the renunciatory traditions. On the one hand, from a Brahmanic perspective renunciation is above all else a retiring from the performance of the Vedic rites, thus a renunciation of the use of sacrificial mantras. On the other hand, when renunciation is seen as the adoption of a specific style of religious life in its own right, then it, too, emerges as a thoroughly mantricized phenomenon.

Renunciation can be understood to stand at the pivot between the overlapping sets of Vedic-Brahmanic and Hindu-Tantric mantras. This dialectic between them is well brought out in the very ritual through which one formally became a renouncer. Olivelle (1984, 118f.) discusses the account of this rite in the *Baudhāyana* and *Vaikhānasa* (Vaikh) DhSū. The former speaks of a rite of entrance into the Sāvitrī (*sāvitrīpraveśa*). "It consists of reciting each quarter-verse (*pāda*) . . . followed by the words 'I enter Sāvitrī' (*sāvitrīṃ praviśāmi*), and then the whole formula followed by the same words." By this formula, Olivelle continues, the apprentice ascetic "ritually expresses his rejection of all ritual formulae (*mantra*) except the mystic syllable OṂ." Even if OṂ were not granted an exception, what one seems to have here is a mantric ritual of demantrification. According to both traditions and to later authorities, the essential element in the ritual sequence, what really makes one a renouncer, is the recitation of a mantra that came to be called the Praiṣa, namely, "I have renounced" (*saṃnyastaṃ mayā*). The VaikhDhSū inserts a third formula between the *sāvitrīpraveśa* and the Praiṣa: "I enter the mendicant *āśrama*" (*bhikṣāśaramaṃ praviśāmi*). The text then observes, "Thus he enters it" (*iti taṃ praviśati*) which, Olivelle judges, "can only mean that by reciting these words the candidate enters the renouncer's *āśrama* . . . the actual moment of renunciation is when the candidate utters these words." Now, in terms of the use of mantras, the differences between the texts are minor. Any of the three formulae surely count as mantras created *to effect* renunciation. Moreover, one has here as clear an example of a mantra functioning "performatively" as one is likely to find.

The use of mantras in renunciation and by renouncers surely merits further investigation. Gonda ([1963b] 1975b, 4.262) provides a few examples of the daily use of mantras among renouncers; see, too, his discussion (1965a, 377–90) of "The Dīkṣā of Ascetics," which focuses some attention on Buddhist and Jain material. Besides the essay I have already cited, see Olivelle (1974a; 1975; 1978; 1981). Derrett (1974) illustrates the continuing practical significance of the portrayal of renunciation in the texts. On *saṃnyāsa* in the textual tradition, see Sprockhoff (1976), a general survey in German, and Olivelle (1976–77), an English translation of the *Yatidharmaprakāśa* of Vāsudeva, a late seventeenth or eighteenth century treatise on renunciation. For theoretical perspectives on renunciation in Indian society, see, for example, J. M. Masson (1976), Dumont (1960), and Heesterman (1964). For comparative purposes, one might see H. Chakraborti (1973), Olivelle (1974b) on Buddhist, or Deo (1956) and Caillat (1964) on Jain monasticism. The so-called *Saṃnyāsa Upaniṣads* will be discussed on page 359 in the context of Hindu theism. Materials on Yoga, including the *YSū* are discussed on pages 428–30 under Tantra. Consider, too, the evidence of neo-Hinduism on pages 441–43.

The "Act of Truth"

One of the most important traditions of the magical force of mantric utterance, broadly construed, is the Act of Truth, evidence for which is both Hindu and Buddhist. Gonda (1975a, 142–48) outlines the Vedic background, on which see Parab (1949; 1952). See, principally, Burligame (1917), Venkatasubbiah (1940), and W. N. Brown (1963; 1968c; 1972a; 1972b). Note Brown's reference to the discussion of *ṛta* and *satya* in the second volume of *Varuṇa* (Lüders 1959, 486–509). Brown's treatment of this theme should be compared with the interpretation of Wayman ([1968b] 1984, 393f.) who observes, "The verbal form of the Rite of Truth is not a traditional *mantra*. It is rather analogous to the Upaniṣadic expressions called Vidyās, which are really *upāsanā-s* or meditative exercises."

The Act of Truth as a literary motif underscores the fact that mantric utterance was taken for granted not only in religious (sacrificial and ascetic) but also in "secular" contexts. It further draws attention to the fact that it has retained its place in Indian culture in part because of the conviction that words uttered with the proper intensity could not fail to be effective. In this regard, one might draw attention to the tradition of stylized ritual abuse and obscenity. The comparative and ethnographic literature on this cannot be summarized here. Suffice it to mention one of the Vedic precedents, the *Mahāvrata*, on which there is an essay, with attention to IE and Hindu parallels by Gonda (1961b).

The Survival of Exemplary Mantras in the Hindu Period

The passages that assume exemplary status in Brahmanic ritual and then in the various forms of Hindu theism reinforce the impression gained from the earlier literature. One might imagine that mantras are powerful because they are situated within and contain a distillation of texts that are otherwise considered sacred. As an hypothesis, I would suggest the opposite: The mantras, especially single syllables such as OṂ, are sacred because of their poetic origin and/or ritual use. They are auspicious formulas (*maṅgalas*) that lend their sancitity and effectiveness to poems (*sūktas*), chapters (*anuvākas, hṛdayas*), and texts.

From the start, certain *sūktas* and certain mantras were considered exemplary repositories of power. A community-by-community, tradition-by-tradition enumeration and study of such texts would be valuable. For example, Gonda (1980a, 214) provides a list, with textual references, of nearly a dozen quite diverse mantras and formulas that "are so well known that they are indicated by names": Sāvitrī, Vimukha, Ekākṣaryā, Aṃhomucaḥ, Virūpākṣa, Prapada, Prajāvat, Jīvaputra, Mahānāmnis, Śākvarīs. Do we find these, or others comparable to them, so proverbial that they were cited in passing in the *Purāṇas*, in drama, in poetry? The *Sūktas*, which have been similarly singled out for attention, have usually been treated in their Vedic context or in terms of later philosophical exegesis. Little work as been done on their ritual application or their echo or citation in literary works. Among the most significant are the *Puruṣasūkta* (ṚV 10.90), on which see W. N. Brown (1931) and Mus (1962; 1968); Gonda (1980a, 222f.) briefly discusses its ritual use; the *Viṣṇusūkta* (ṚV 1.154), which is regularly used in Vaikhānasa ritual; and the *Śrīsūkta* (*khila* 2.6), on which see Scheftelowitz (1906) and G. Hartmann (1933).

ṚV 3.62.10 is the most famous Vedic mantra: TAT SAVITUR VAREṆYAṂ BHARGO DEVASYA DHĪMAHI/ DHIYO YO NAḤ PRACODAYĀT. It is known either as the Gāyatrī, after its meter, or as the Sāvitrī, after the *deva* to whom it is dedicated, Savitṛ, a god identified with the sun; but it is not merely named, it is personified as a Goddess, "the mother of the Veda" ([Gonda 1963b] 1975b, 4.290).* Gonda (p. 288) notes that the noun *dhī* here means visions; that is, poetic "intuitions which are to be transformed into mantras." The verse should therefore be translated, "may be obtained that desirable (excellent) radiance of god Savitar who is to impel our 'visions'." This is in distinction from the later Hindu interpretations: "may we meditate on the lovely splendor of the god Sāvitṛ so he may inspire our minds."** Gonda (1963a, 291) notes that the mis- or rather reinterpretation of the verb (*dhīmahi*) as if it were a form of *dhyā-* (to reflect, to meditate) rather than *dhī-* (to see, to think) could arise because of "the extremely high importance attached to dhyāna and to the firm belief that the identification with the object of concentration resulted in 'obtaining' that object by way of identification." In any case, it became the "Shema" of Brahmanical religion and instruction and its utterance is central to the *upanayana* ceremony of initiation for "twice-born" men.

The Gāyatrī elicited a lively response in Indian civilization and this is surveyed in Gonda ([1963b] 1975b, 4.288–98, with refs.). For a general discussion, there is Krishna Lal (1970). As one would anticipate, "sectarian" variants of the Gāyatrī are by no means uncommon. Gonda (1970b, 37, with refs.) discusses the *Rudragāyatrī*—TATPURUṢĀYA VID-

---

**Although dedicated to a god, the meter is feminine.*

***I follow Basham (1954, 162) who, like most translators, give a Hindu reading of this mantra.*

MAHE, MAHĀDEVĀYA DHĪMAHE, TAN NO RUDRAḤ PRACODAYĀT— and other mantras based upon it. Similarly, the Gāyatrī was the subject of Tantric speculation, as in the *Gāyatrītantra,* the second chapter of which "discusses the meaning of the Vedic *vyāhṛtis*" (Goudriaan & Gupta 1981, 103). Its prestige was such that it became exemplary among mantras as, let us say, the Ganges is exemplary among rivers: hence, the notion that the HAṂSA mantra is an "unmuttered Gāyatrī" (*ajapagāyatrī*) Gonda (1970b, 280). In other words, more then any other mantra, the Gāyatrī was understood by Indian culture in general to concentrate the power of the Veda. This did not have an ethical dimension and the Gāyatrī was naturally employed in "magical" contexts. For example, AVPar 34 (Gonda 1980a, 221) discusses the inversion of the Sāvitrī for use as a malevolent spell called the *pratilomā sāvitrī.* The so-called *Gāyatrī Upaniṣad* forms a considerable part of the *GopathaB,* the untranslated *Brāhmaṇa* of the AV, on this, see Bloomfield (1899a; 1899b). One final example, various *kāmagāyatrīs* are found among the Vaiṣṇava Sahajiyās of Bengal (Dimock 1966, 228ff.). At least some of these are at once poetic, Tantric, and erotic. Dimock cites one that he describes as a "near, serious, and almost blasphemous parody" of the Vedic Gāyatrī: KĀMADEVĀYA VIDMAHE PUṢPABĀṆĀYA DHĪMAHE TAN NO'NANGAḤ PRACODAYĀT. He translates, "We meditate on the god of love, whose arrows are flowers, so that the bodiless one may compel it," and observes that "*tat*" (it) refers to *rasa,* which refers to semen.

Without doubt, OṂ is the single most significant syllable in the repertory of Indian religious language. Representative of its usage is the *Īśvaragītā* (P.-E. Dumont 1933), which says (8.9) "The lord of all knowledge, the god of [all] creatures, the Illustrious One whose form is OṂ, I am Brahma, [I am] Prajāpati."* Surprisingly, the usage and interpretation of OṂ, to the best of my knowledge, has never been summarized systematically. Perhaps most useful is Boeles (1947); see also Bloomfield (1889), Mehta (1916), C. C. Chatterji (1935), Laksminarasimhia (c. 1943), T. S. Raghavan (c. 1956), Agnihotri (1964), and Parpola (1981); on OṂ in Oriyan folk usage see N. Das (c. 1958).

On OṂ as the Vedic *bīja* (see pages 432–37) par excellence Gonda ([1963b] 1975b, 4.285) cites R. V. Joshi (1959); on the migration of OṂ to Tibet and Southeast Asia, see Boeles (1947); Govinda (1950–51) discusses the significance on OṂ in Tibet and its use as a foundation stone of Mantraśāstra. The treatment of OṂ as a mystical and meditative

---

* īśānaḥ sarvavidyānāṃ, bhūtānāṃ parameśvaraḥ
oṃkāramūrtir bhagavān, ahaṃ brahmā prajāpathiḥ

Cf. 11.56f. where the paramaṃ kośaṃ *(inner treasury ?) of the lotus is described as* oṃkāravācyam *and 11.62 where Śiva would seem to be described as the eternal reality that is understood as OṂ (*oṃkārabodhitaṃ tattvaṃ śāśvataṃ śivam ucyate*).*

cynosure in the Purāṇic and Tantric literature merits study. Gonda (1977a, 206) notes, for example, the analysis of the "twelve stages of the production or pronunciation (*uccāra*) of the *mantra Om*" in the *Svacchanda Tantra* (SvT).

Allied with the notion of OṂ is that of *akṣara*, the designation of the ultimate as the "Imperishable," a designation that was to gain in significance because of the use of the term to refer to the letters or syllable of the Sanskrit language. On *akṣara*, see Modi (1932) and van Buitenen (1959). In this connection, one should note that the explication of OṂ, in Vedāntic circles, has been heavily influenced by the *catuṣpad* doctrine based on the *MāṇḍūkyaU* and the *Gauḍapāda Kārikās*. For an introduction to this material, see Hacker (1972); for further references on Gauḍapāda, see Potter (1981, 607); a study of the four states of consciousness theory in Advaita psychology is forthcoming from Fort. Relevant to the concept of *turīya* (the fourth state) is D. Bhattacharya (1978).

Related to OṂ are the potent syllables known as *vyāhṛtis*, "mystical utterances" (Gonda 1980a, 226). The term and usage is attested at least as early as *Taittirīya Upaniṣad* (TaitU) 1.5.1, which lists the three syllables BHŪR BHUVAḤ SVAḤ, the *Mahāvyāhṛtis*. On these, there is Nazari (1897). The number and list of syllables vary from text to text, naturally. They are sometimes understood as the names of the seven worlds: the *Mahāvyāhṛtis* plus MAHAḤ, JANAḤ, TAPAḤ, and SATYAṂ (Apte 1957–59, 3.1521a). According to *Aitareya Brāhmaṇa* (AiB) 5.32.5 (cited in Gonda 1980a, 226), the *vyāhṛtis* are the internal connections of the Veda and serve paradigmatically as a universal expiation (*sarvaprāyaścitti*), for with them "one unites whatever in the sacrifice has come apart." As the "first-fruits" of OṂ, they might be seen as ritual counterparts of the mantras that are philosophically central to the Vedānta, the *Mahāvākyas*.

POST-VEDIC TRADITIONS OTHER THAN TANTRA

READING, WRITING, AND SPEAKING IN TRADITIONAL INDIA

Mantras distill the authority of the Veda. Mantras are ritual acts. Mantras are meditative instruments. Mantras are articulated. Mantras are muttered. Mantras are thought. In considering these diverse modes of mantric "utterance," one should keep in mind the complex relationship between oral and written composition in traditional India. The authoritative works of the Indian traditions, in the course of time, have been written down, but this is adventitious to their authority. Even after being written down or printed, they remain "oral" in character. As Coburn (1984b, 437) remarks, they have a "profoundly spoken character." Staal (1979b, 122), a brief but suggestive note on "the concept of scripture in the Indian tradition," points out that "Vedic civilization flourished without literacy" and that writing, once it was introduced, has been "held in lower esteem than memory or the sound of recitation." Indeed, even written texts were reproduced orally. The typical manuscript was not copied from another manuscript, it was written down while it was being recited (cf. Schoterman 1982, 18). To a certain extent, the Brahmanic and Buddhist traditions differ in the degree to which they give priority to the oral. The date at which the ṚV was put into writing is not known (Gonda 1975a, 18). The Buddhist tradition, in contrast, tells us that the canon became "scripture" at a council held late in the first century B.C. (Staal 1979b, 123).* On the whole, the low status of writing is illustrated by the statement of AiĀr 5.5.3 (cited Staal 1979b, 122f.) that "a pupil should not recite the Veda after he has eaten meat, seen blood or a dead body, had intercourse or engaged in writing."

Mantraśāstra illustrates the priority of the oral. Coburn (1984b, 449f.) suggests a "subtle and continuous" dialectic between two passions in traditional India: on the one hand, the desire for "literal preservation"; on the other, the desire for "dynamic re-creation." Both are oral. The first is exemplified by the meticulous preservation of the *Vedasaṃhitās*, the second by the Vaiṣṇava "miracle plays," for example, which have been studied by Hein (1972), Schechner and Hess (1977), and Hawley (1981). One may or may not be persuaded by Coburn's suggestion (1984b, 448) that the terms *śruti* and *smṛti* be used to refer to these "two different kinds of relationship that can be had with verbal material in the Hindu tradition." More significant is his observation that a text such as the *Devīmāhātmya* functioned in both ways. Mantra is surely the paradigm for the utterance that functions in both ways.** Mantras are held to be eternal, immutable, transhuman (*apauruṣeya*), and yet infinitely malleable. The culture takes for granted an ability to create new ones at will. There is one qualification. This license is unacknowledged and probably unacknowledgeable: "New" mantras cannot be "made" they must be "discovered."

With the introduction of writing came a tension between the old prestige of the oral and the new prestige of the written. One of the ways in which this worked itself out was in the utilization of writing for magical purposes. In other words, there was competition between the magic of the oral word and the magic of writing. This amounted to a

---

**This difference may well be due to the evolution of Buddhism into a pan-Asian "missionary" tradition, subjecting the originally oral canon to the contingencies of geographical and cultural distance. Indeed, it appears that the canon was first written down in Ceylon, far from the* āryan *homeland in Northwestern India. It probably is not accidental that the first references to writing in India are found in the earliest stratum of the Pāli Canon (c. fifth century* B.C.*), some two centuries before the Aśokan inscriptions, rather than in a Brahmanical text (Losty 1982, 5).*

***As they stand, the fivefold and twofold typologies that Coburn sketches do not really allow for this phenomenon.*

contest between two different sorts of imagined permanence.* On the one hand, mere possession of a Tantric manuscript was considered to be auspicious (Goudriaan & Gupta 1981, 22). On the other hand, book learning was no substitute for the real thing. Thus, the *Kaulāvalīnirṇaya* comments (Goudriaan & Gupta 1981, 12), "The fool who, overpowered by greed, acts after having looked up [the matter] in a written book without having obtained it from the guru's mouth, he also will certainly be destroyed."** Mantras reflect this dialectic between the power of the oral and written word, they are not exceptions to it. One finds a continuum of usages. At one extreme, the mantra is "pronounced" in the heart; that is, without being articulated. This is the exemplary "high" usage of Tantra. At the other extreme, the mantra is written, for example, in an amulet (refs. in Gonda 1975a, 271). This is exemplary "low" usage of folk religion and magic. In light of this dichotomy, it would appear, pace the mystics, that the ordinary pronunciation or muttering of a mantra is normative.

On the character of reading, writing, and speaking in traditional India, see Gaur (1979) and Losty (1982); on the significance of the spoken word, see V. M. Apte (1942–43); on the nature of the scholastic tradition, there is Ghurye (1950), Ingalls (1959), Saraswati (1972), and Pollack (1985), for example. The literature on "Sanskritization" is obviously relevant to an appraisal of the place of speech and writing in Indian society but is beyond the scope of this Bibliography. For a brief summary, see Babb (1975, 23–28). For discussion of the status of the Veda as scripture, see page 384.

Recently, anthropologists have begun to reflect on the relationship between orality and literacy, and their work is quite relevant to the Indian situation. See Goody (1968; 1977) and Tedlock (1983), all three sources with generous bibliographies; in comparison with Goody (1968), see especially Gough (1968a; 1968b), which deal with India, and Tambiah (1968b), which deals with Thailand. On considering writing (and reading) as ritual acts, see Lincoln (1977a) and Stahl (1979). Scholars who work with texts that have been written in largely oral societies can learn

---

**I am not aware of any research on this. Some speculation might be interesting: Was there a difference in the way various classes responded to the introduction of writing? As an hypothesis, one could propose that the religious elite and the intelligentsia, while becoming literate, generally retained their belief in the priority of oral recitation; but the peasantry who remained illiterate were more deeply impressed by the power of writing. To what extent was that true? Was the use of written amulets more common among the illiterate than the elite? Were written aids to meditation more common among Jains and Buddhists than in Brahmanic circles? To the extent this is the case, would it be the obverse of the situation in traditional China? One way of attacking this problem might be to trace the use of metaphors that refer to writing in Sankrit, Pāli, Prakrit, and early vernacular literature.*

***A number of my friends are American followers of contemporary Indian gurus and they believe that the guru's power is conveyed by either* reading *or* having *his books, even if they were printed in the U.S. and distributed through ordinary bookstores. In the tradition, there are numerous accounts of valid initiations taking place in dreams (cf. O'Flaherty 1984, 142). Are there many—or any—accounts of valid initiations while reading a book?*

much from students of oral tradition. On the nature of those traditions, there is Vansina (1965). Kelber (1983, 227–39) provides a bibliography on the interface between oral traditions and text criticism.

RELIGIOUS TRADITIONS

Hinduism: General Remarks

The nomenclature is disputed: Hinduism, classical Hinduism, the Great Tradition, on the one side; popular Hinduism, village Hinduism, folk Hinduism, the Little Tradition, on the other. Taken together, these terms attempt to name the unity and the diversity of the central tradition of Indian religious life. All of these terms are useful but problematic attempts to denote a tradition that did not have a name for itself. It is a categorical mistake to picture that tradition as either a single *organized* religion or as a conglomerate of *identifiable* units. Any attempt to draw fixed external or internal boundaries is bound to fail. For at least the past millenium, all of Hinduism has been Tantricized. Similarly, if to a lesser extent, all of Hinduism is arguably Vedicized. Yet, the bulk of mantras were surely uttered in contexts that were not explicitly Vedic or Tantric; that is, they were uttered without reference to *Dharmaśāstra* or to particular Tantric *guruparaṃparas*.

Ironically, this characteristic use of mantras is the most elusive and difficult to study. In comparison with the wealth of secondary literature that deals with Vedic and even Tantric Mantraśāstra, the bibliography of ordinary or popular Mantraśāstra is relatively scanty. In part, this reflects the lack of attention observers have given to this subject. In part, it reflects the diffusion of possible sources. A careful sifting is needed of all of the works, primary and secondary, dealing with the great traditions of Hindu ritual, mythology, and devotion, of anthropological literature, of works of fiction and folktales, if one is to sort out the place of mantras in Hindu imagination and practice. In the absence of such a survey, this section of the Bibliography merely indicates some possible lines of exploration. It is offered in the hope that it will stimulate further research.

Studied from the point of view of Mantraśāstra, the history of Hinduism is a story of the proliferation of mantras. This growth was a seamless process that went on unconsciously on all levels of the society from the tribal to the Brahmanic. Indeed, the integrity and uniformity of the process well illustrates how various movements (Jainism, Buddhism, Sikhism) cannot be classified as "religions" in the usual Western sense. Indian Muslims have not escaped this net of mantras (see page 437) and one wonders whether Indian Christians really have.

One reason for the expansion of the arsenal of mantras was the restrictions placed on the use of Vedic mantras. They could be employed neither for Śūdras nor in the domestic ceremonies of the twice-born, which were performed for women (cf. Gonda [1963b] 1975b, 4.264). This surely stimulated the creation of new mantras from scratch as well as the acceptance of older religious formulae as really mantras.* This means that the history of Mantraśāstra is potentially one of the main sources that casts light on the fate of the Veda in the post-Vedic age. Much work has already been done on the dissemination of the Veda and the transformation of the ways in which it was understood. The classic summary is the suggestive monograph of Renou (1960a). It should be supplemented with the important evidence now available for the continued survival, if not the vitality, of Vedic textual and sacrificial traditions in various parts of the subcontinent. On this see Renou (1949d), Kashikar (1958; 1964), Staal (1961; 1968), Raghavan (1962a), and Sukul (1964); also Kashikar and Parpola (1983), Somayajipad (1983), Narayanan and Kesavan Veluthat (1983), Raghava Varier (1983), the last four works are all in the second volume of AGNI (Staal 1983a, 199–299). For Vedic texts used in orthodox Hindu ritual, in general, one may still consult Vasu (1909); for the use of Vedic mantras in Tantric ritual, generally, see Chakravati (1952).

One of the continuities between the Vedic and post-Vedic ages is the genre of the *Upaniṣad*, itself not stable. The post-classical *Upaniṣads*, the exact number of which is difficult to determine, are a rich source for studying the evolution of religious practices in the Brahmanic tradition. They contain numerous discussions of OṂ and other mantras. Many of them have been conveniently edited and translated at Adyar. For publication they have been classified somewhat arbitrarily into *Yoga-, Vaiṣṇava, Śākta-, Sāmānya Vedānta-, Śaiva-*, and *Saṃnyāsa Upaniṣads*.** For the texts see F. O. Schrader (1912), Mahadeva Śāstri (1920; 1921; 1923; 1925a; 1925b), and Chintamani Dikshit (1929). For English translations see T. R. Śrīnivāsa Ayyaṅgār (1938; 1941; 1945; 1953), and Krishna Warrier (1967); also Narayanaswami Aiyar (1914). Woodroffe (1922) has compiled a group of "Kaula and other" *Upaniṣads*. For other texts see Ācārya (1948). Many of these texts have been translated into German by Deussen (1921) and the German has now been retranslated into English by Bedekar and Palsule (1980). There are also standard French translations of many of these texts in the series *Les Upaniṣads*. The only sophisticated study of this material of which I am aware is Sprockhoff (1976), which has a valuable bibliography.

The Significance of Names

Although mantras cannot, in general, be taken as the "names" of "powers," the names and epithets of divine beings are among the most

---

**These older "mantras" may be considered of extra-Vedic origin, with Gonda ([1963b] 1975b, 264); that is, not attested in the extant recensions of the* Saṃhitās. *The chance of classifiying them as ultimately* āryan *or* non-āryan, *no less Dravidian, is nil at the present state of knowledge.*

***Narayanasvami Aiyar even speaks of "physiological" Upaniṣads. On the quality of the editions and on the distinction between "principal" and "minor" Upaniṣads, which has been common only since the late nineteenth century, see Sprockhoff (1976, 9–11).*

important elements out of which they are constructed. Moreover, as the multivalent phenomenon of *japa* indicates, the power of names and the power of mantras are cognate. Of course, a considerable ethnographic literature concerns the power of names among preliterate peoples. I cannot attempt to deal with that here, but see the methodological suggestions on page 332. On analogous practices in the Western traditions, see pages 441–43.

The repetition of the names of the gods* is central to mantric utterance, especially in a popular and Bhaktic context. This is not surprising, for in India the mystery of a deity's names has from early on been understood as an index of the deity's reality and power. It is not hyperbole to assert that for many devotees the name, functionally speaking, is the deity. So, Tulsī Dās is able to assert "that the name is greater than God himself who is unknowable until revealed by the Name" (Hill 1952, xxix cited Gonda [1963b] 1975b, 4.257, n. 8). This is not to say that there is anything like identity between mantras and the names of deities; but, there is significant overlap. For example, the *NarasiṃhaP* reports that the name *Kṛṣṇa* is called a "mantra granting all bliss" (Hacker 1960: 159, cited Gonda [1963b] 1975b, 4.279). For the Great Tradition, any deity meriting service, any deity worth worshipping, will be understood to have a host of names.

Consider a Śaivite example (see Gonda 1970b, 38–40). *KauṣītakiB* (KauṣB) 6.1ff. (to which Gonda compares ŚB 6.1.3.7ff., etc.) is an example of early Śaiva theism, wherein Prajāpati is described as the great god of eight names, distributed through the world in eight ways. In spite of the undoubted significance of the number eight in Śaivite cosmology, the central motif is that the names of the deity, however many and however enumerated, are coordinated with powers, characteristics, and mantras. They map the deity's existence in (or as) the world. This Śaiva usage exemplifies a presupposition that may be expressed in a slogan, "the more names, the more powers." As Gonda (1959a, 32, citing van der Leeuw) puts it, "For the Name is no mere specificiation, but rather an actuality expressed in a word."

Once again the standard survey, especially strong on the Vedic background, has been written by Gonda (1970a), with which one should compare (1959a) on the closely related matter, "epithets." The philosophical significance of *nāman* as a classificatory category as been studied most extensively in the compound *nāmarūpa* (ordinary, empirical existence), which, in Gonda's words (1970a, 45f., with refs.), "plays, without a breach of continuity in the development of the idea from the Upaniṣads up to later philosophers, an important part in Buddhist thought, but also in Tantrism." See especially Falk (1943); Śaṃkara's use of the term is discussed in Hacker (1950); see also, from various perspec-

---

**Here, I use the word* gods *generically to refer to male and female deities.*

tives, Renou (1958), Vishva Bandhu (1967), van Buitenen (1968), and Bhise (1969).

Concern with and the manipulation of names is characteristic of traditional civilizations. India is no exception. For example, many traditions, irrespective of their degree of Sanskritization, seek to protect an individual by protecting or obscuring a name. Thus, one of the *saṃskāras* of name giving (*nāmakaraṇa*) is secret "in order to prevent injury through its use by enemies" (Gonda 1977b, 558). Conversely, the use of the names of deities as or in apotropaic formulae, amulets, and the like must be general in Indian "folk medicine" and magic. A typical example, the *Nārada pāñcarātra*, explains that the "various names of Rādhā are believed to protect the parts of the worshipper's body" (Gonda 1977a, 132).

Unfortunately, no one has made this use of names in Hindu texts the subject of a focused study comparable to Gonda's work on names, which focuses on the Veda. Nor has anyone synthesized the evidence of travelers, missionaries, and ethnographers. For the evidence of Indian ethnography on the signigificance of names, however, there is Masani (1932; 1966). In general, one should see the literature on magic, cited on page 330 and on the ritual of *nyāsa* cited on pages 409–10.

The tradition of praising the innumerable, figuratively the 1000 or 1008, names of the gods became especially prominent in the post-Vedic age. In literary terms, this yielded the tradition of the *Nāmastotra;* in ritual terms, the tradition of the *nāmakīrtana* that Gonda (1977a, 267) traces as far back as the *Bhagavad Gītā* (BhG). For a brief discussion of these traditions, see Gonda (1970a, 67–76); for a summary of the available material, Gonda (1977a, 267ff.); for an enumeration of the chief names of Viṣṇu and Śiva, Gonda (1970b, 12–17). The tradition of *kīrtans* and *bhajans* has been extensively studied in the context of contemporary urban Hindu devotionalism. A representative study is Venkateswaran (1968); for a background to this, see Raghavan (1959) and, on Bhakti in general, Zelliot (1976).

No one has yet attempted a detailed comparative survey or proposed a typology of *Nāmastotras,* but cf. Dandekar's remarks concerning the *Anuśāsanaparvan* of the *Mahābhārata* (Mhb), cited by Gonda (1970a, 72). Determining the exact text and delineating the exact social and ritual function of various *Nāṃastotras* are analogically relevant to determining the meaningfulness of mantras, at least in a popular and Bhaktic context. Consider the position, taken by Nīlakaṇṭha in his commentary on Mhb 13.17.30ff. He draws upon the Mīmāṃsāka conception of *apūrva,* according to the tradition, the character of a Vedic ritual act to produce an effect after the act itself has been completed. It is summarized by Gonda (1970a, 72f.):

> Although in an enumeration of God's 1008 names for eulogistic purposes there may, at first sight, be tautology and repetition with regard

> to the form as well as the meaning of the names, this impression proves, on second thought, to be incorrect because the so-called *apūrva,* i.e. the positive force or virtue left or produced by a ritual act by which the desired object is, in a mysterious manner, achieved, is not the same in case one pronounces the words *viśvātman-* and *sarvātman-* [both meaning self of the world] which at first sight might be regarded as synonymous. In a ritual formula directed to Agni one cannot indeed substitute another name of the god, for instance Vahni, if the word Agni expressing a specific meaning is the traditional and prescribed mode of address.

The *Śatarudriya* is one of the sources out of which the tradition of reciting the thousand names of god arose. One of the earliest classical texts of the Śaiva tradition, it is a section of the YV (4.5) meant to accompany a sequence of 425 oblations (described ŚB 9.1.1), and it is understood to avert the wrath of Rudra through the recitation of his hundred names. A translation with comments on variants in the different recensions of the YV is found in Keith (1914, II.353–62); it is also translated, along with the ritual it accompanies, by Eggeling (1882–1900, 5.150–69). Gonda (1980b) is a study of its significance in the context of the history of Śaivism. Certain of the items, he notes (p. 77ff.), are of particular interest: the citation of the Aghoramantra in the *ŚvetāśvataraU* (ŚvetU); the use of the text in a ritual of *nyāsa* found in the *MānavaŚrSū;* the tradition of *rudrajapa,* which Yājñavalkya in the *JābālaU* says enables one to attain immortality. In regard to the influence of the *Śatarudriya,* Gonda (1980b, 81) refers to passages in the *Sāntiparvan* of the Mhb, as well as the *Brahma-, Śiva-, Liṅga-, Kūrma,* and *Vāyu Purāṇas.* He also (1980b, 82–88) analyzes a *Stotra,* the *Rudrārthasārastava* of one Aruṇādri, as an example of the creative expansion of a classic text from a Bhaktic perspective. This text has been published, on the basis of a single manuscript, in the *Stotrasamuccaya* (Aithal 1969, 1.222–39), an important collection of *Stotras* containing a great deal of previously unpublished material. Śivaramamurti (1976), which attempts to elucidate the epithets of Śiva contained in the *Śatarudriya* by coordinating them with Śaiva iconographic motifs, contains a fresh translation and reveals nicely the power that this text can still exercise for a contemporary Śaiva.

For other *Nāmastotras* and related literature, the *Śivasahasranāma* itself is found at Mhb 13.17. On it, see Anantakrishna Sastri (1902). On the *Īsvaragītā* (identified as a section of the *KūrmaP*), see P. E. Dumont (1927). For a *Sahasranāmastotra* directed to Ganeśa, see Anantakrishna Sastri (1927). On the *Viṣṇusahasranāma,* which may be traced back to Mhb 13, see Raghavan (1953), Parathasarathy (1966), Rama Sastry (1960–61), and Ramanujacariyan (n.d.). Among similar important texts are the *Kālikāsahasranāmstotra* and the *Lalitāsahasranāmastotra,* Gonda (1977a, 270) singles it out for special praise; on this, see Anantakrishna Sastri (1970).

Almost all of the published and unpublished *Stotra* literature, including a vast number of vernacular poems, is relevant for establishing the context in which it can be taken for granted that repetition of mantras and of the divine name is fraught with power and danger. This literature cannot be summarized here, but a few items may indicate the range of material available. Ramakrishna Dikshithar and Sarma (1980) is a collection of *Stotras* by the sixteenth century Advaitin Appaya Dīkṣita. Perhaps the most accessible source in English, through which the general reader can get some sense of the traditions concerning the names of deities, is Coburn (1984a), a study and translation of the *Devīmāhātmya,* a collection of poems to Devī, associated with the *MārkaṇḍeyaP*. For theological reflection on the name, see Siauve (1959), a French translation of a portion of Madhva's commentary on the *Brahma Sūtras,* wherein it is argued that the true object of the Veda is the names of Viṣṇu.

Eventually, the ancient tradition of the thousand names of god flowed together with the sonic mysticism of the Tantras. For example, Īśvaradāsa Vārahatta of Jaipur, initiated in the tradition of the Siddhas, a devotee of "the efficacy of using divine names as mystic formulae (*nāmamantra*)," wrote a (Rajasthani) poem to Śakti called the *Deviyāna*. In Sanjukta Gupta's words (GG 1981:210), in it,

> the Goddess is addressed by all possible names in all her aspects. The poem starts with a profusion of the letter *ka* . . . which is the first letter of Kālī's seed-mantra, *krīṃ*. The poet uses this form of alliteration quite often, thereby hinting at the Goddess's mystic form as the *varṇamātṛkā* (the primal alphabet), the wellspring of all *mantras*.

As a precedent for this literature in Sanskrit Gupta cites the *Kakārādikālīsahasranāmastava* of Pūrṇānanda. One might also compare the *Kādistotra* cited in the *Mahānirvāṇa Tantra* (7.8–32); text, Woodroffe (1920, 166–69; Eng. tr., Woodroffe 1971, 164–72). Woodroffe (1913) is a collection of translated devotional poems to various goddessess, including the *Karpūrādistotra* to Kālī.

Finally, many of the items cited in the next section, dealing with Hindu theism, will contain information concerning the "cult of the divine name" in the various *saṃpradāyas*. Special attention should be given to Vaudeville (1968–69), a study of the "cult of the divine name" in the thirteenth century Marathi *bhakta,* Jñāneśvara. To the best of my knowledge, no one has collected and catalogued the innumerable contemporary vernacular pamphlets dealing with the names of God. Gonda (1977a, 104, n. 78) describes one in passing.

Hindu Theism and the Great Saṃpradāyas

There is nothing like an up-to-date survey of the development of Hindu theism, no less of the use of mantras in the various "movements." The most useful orientation is provided by Jan Gonda's (1970b) monograph on Viṣṇuism and Śivaism. The chapter "Ritual" (1970b, 62–86) is especially relevant. The general reader may also consult Bhattacharji (1970). Bhandarkar (1913), Carpenter (1921), and Daniélou (1964) should be treated with some caution. Of special significance are the traditions of the thousand names of Viṣṇu and other deities and the ritual muttering of a divine name, *japa,* which is at once a theistic, Bhaktic, and Tantric phenomenon. On the first of these, see page 360; on the second, page 430. For the sake of convenience I am dividing the material on Hindu theism somewhat arbitrarily into four sections, using literary, chronological, and sociological criteria catch-as-catch-can. First, I shall deal with *generally* earlier material irrespective of "sectarian" inclination, the evidence of the epics, *Purāṇas,* and material contemporary with them. Second, I shall deal with the Vaiṣṇava and cognate traditions and third, with the Śaiva and cognate traditions, mostly as represented by their major surviving regional forms. Finally, I shall consider the evidence of regional ethnography, material largely reflecting the conditions of the nineteenth and twentieth centuries. Obviously this division is imperfect. It is meant to take into account the fact the earlier evidence tends to be "pan-Hindu" while the more recent evidence tends to be communally specific, and the fact that the division of Hinduism into component traditions is somewhat artificial. Śāktism is discussed later on pages 397–401 in connection with Tantra.

With the exception of Rocher's essay in this volume, few, if any, studies deal exclusively with the evolving treatment of mantras in the Mhb, *Rāmāyaṇa* (Rām) and the *Purāṇas.* Nonetheless, this is an important area to cover if one were to understand the evolution of Indian Mantraśāstra from the Vedic to the Tantric ages. In regard to the treatment of mantras in the Epics and *Purāṇas,* a catalogue of which figures (gods, humans, *ṛṣis, asuras,* and so forth) in Hindu narratives resort to mantras and in what circumstances would be most useful, albeit tedious to compile. For example, Scheuer (1982, 61–64) contains a discussion of the mantras that Durvāsas compels Kuntī to use to enable her to become pregnant by Pandu in a time of distress (*āpaddharma*) (Mhb 1.113.32ff; cf. 1.104.1ff.). The exact phraseology of such passages has hardly been scrutinized carefully. Here, the text speaks of an *abhicārasaṃyukta . . . mantrāgama.* Van Buitenen (1973, 254) translates, "a canon of spells accompanied by sorcery." Scheuer speaks of a "faisceau de formules" and remarks that the term *abhicārasaṃyukta* undoubtedly has magical connotations. The Mhb, and the world it reflects, is hardly primitive. The need for further systematic study, I trust, is obvious.

I am here limited to a few references that indicate some lines of inquiry. Hopkins (1901) discusses Yoga in the Mhb; Meinhard (1928) discusses the major Śaiva mantras in the *Purāṇas.* Hazra (1940) discusses Purāṇic evidence for Hindu ritual. P. Kumar (1974) surveys Purāṇic evidence for Śāktism—on which, see page 399. Gonda (1970b, 42) draws attention to the modification of certain Saiva mantras, first cited in the

HiraṇyakeśiGṛSū, in the *LiṅgaP*. Padoux (1978c) discusses mantras and mantric practices in the *AgniP*. Gonda (1980b, 79f.) lists passages in the Mhb that refer to the *Śatarudriya*. For general reference on the *Purāṇas*, see L. Rocher (1986). One of the most interesting sources for the transformation of Hindu Mantraśāstra in the post-Vedic, preclassical period is the *MahānārāyaṇaU* (MahāU) (TaitĀr 10), around fourth–third century B.C., which has been edited and translated by Varenne (1960). Among items of interest in it are a set of mantras to Rudra (MahāU 270–316), which include (vv. 277–286) the earliest occurrence (cf. Gonda 1970b, 42–44) of the *pañca suvaktramantrāḥ*, the mantras of the five faces of Śiva, and also, I believe, the earliest occurrence (v. 274) of the paradigmatic Śaiva mantra, the *pañcākṣara*, ŚIVĀYA NAMAḤ.

A sense of the prestige and centrality of mantras in the Kṛṣṇaite tradition, as it solidified in a Purāṇic milieu, can be gained from certain sections of the *BrahmavaivartaP* (BVP), a North Indian text allied to both the Vallabha and Caitanya traditions and reflecting the religious atmosphere of the fifteenth and sixteenth centuries. It is discussed in C. M. Brown (1974; see esp. 79–112). Certain motifs that appear in this text are probably rather widespread and merit study. Note, in particular, the definition (p. 79) of a devotee in terms of alleigance to a particular mantra, *manmantropāsakas* (worshippers or followers of my *mantra*): "Into whose ear, from the mouth of his *guru*, has entered the mantra of Viṣṇu, He is a Vaiṣṇava, greatly purified, according to the wise"; the assumption that the apparently external act of receiving a mantra signals an inner transformation; the placement of mantra in the midst of a battery of practices including *japa*, the recitation of *Stotras* and *stavas*, and *kīrtana*; the specification (p. 86) that *samaraṇa*, the "rememberance" of god, has four principal objects: god himself, his name, his feet, and his mantra. Finally, it is particularly significant that the BVP (111) frequently refers to the true devotee as a *jīvanmukta*. Even after death in *goloka*, Kṛṣṇa's paradise, divine service including *japa* continues. In this regard, I am convinced that the BVP is representative: The study of Mantraśāstra has deepened my conviction, previously reached on other grounds, that the distinction between *marga* and *mokṣa* is functionally meaningless. Finally, having discussed some evidence from both Śaiva and Vaiṣṇava texts, one might wonder whether the two traditions treat or use mantras in divergent ways. Gonda ([1963b] 1975b, 4.283) stresses that Vaiṣṇava mantras are characteristically eight or twelve syllables in length, while Śaiva mantras are five. It is not clear to me how far one can carry such a generalization. Here, too, discrimination will require further study.

Two facets of the use of mantras in classical Hinduism easily are misunderstood and merit being underscored before we turn to the Śaiva and Vaiṣṇava traditions in their more developed forms. First, the use of mantra is typically in a context at once Tantric and Bhaktic. Second, it is often in a context at once Sanskrit and vernacular. In other words, the use of mantras is representative of "mainstream" Hinduism. Any facile distinction between ritualistic and devotional or between Sanskritic and non-Sanskritic can be misleading. For example, Zvelebil (1978, 181), speaking of the *Kumarātantra,* a Śaiva Siddhānta *Āgama* (see pages 417–420), notes that in spite of the enormous prestige of Sanskrit among Tamil Brahmans:

> The South Indian tradition of the Kaumāra sect is ready to accept Tamil *mantra-s* as almost equally potent. Thus, e.g. the popular formula in Tamil *veluṃ mayiluṃ tuṇṇai,* "the spear and the peacock are (my) protection," is considered "the great *mantra*" which should be constantly repeated by devotees of Subrahmaṇya-Murugan.

This is by no means deviant. Examples could be found in all of the languages of the subcontinent. Goudriaan and Gupta (1981, 83) note that the *KālīvilāsaT* contains a mantra in a form of Bengali and observe (1981, 113) that a mixture of Sanskrit and vernacular mantras is typical of what he calls "magical Tantras." One further example is instructive. S. B. Dasgupta (1962, 17) discusses how the rise of Tantric Buddhism in Bengal involved the creation, or at least the textual recognition, of non-Sanskritic mantras (Prakrit, Apabhraṃśa, and so forth), which supplemented rather than displaced Sanskrit mantras.

In sum, Mantraśāstra is exemplary and this suggests likely strategies for its study. The evolution of Mantraśāstra appears to parallel the evolution of South Asian society, just as synchronically its anatomy mirrors India's social organization. South Asian society has been organized organically. It has been traditionally segmented into "communities," not organized into "religions." One might hypothesize that mantric utterance plays a significant role in maintaining this organization, facilitating both Sanskritization and the comparable adaptation of popular practices among the various elites. Its social role merits study, not least to correct the Western instinct to study mantric utterance as if it were the self-conscious articulation of an identifiable religion or the expression of an individual's consciousness.

As the evidence of regional ethnography suggests, the mantras specific to a particular group define and reinforce the social identity of the group. Gonda (1970b, 67) expresses this strongly, with a vocabulary oddly reminiscent of Biblical theism: "Using strange mantras means following strange gods and dissociating oneself from the traditions of one's group, and this implies a serious infraction of the *dharma.*" This suggests that a comparative study, at once ethnographic and textual, of the use of mantras "on the ground" might yield interesting results. This and the subsequent section of this essay can only begin to suggest some of the material available.

The best documentation for the use of mantras among the various Vaiṣṇava traditions is probably found in the ritual literature of the Pāñcarātra *saṃpradāya* of South India, for as Gonda (1977a, 69) notes, "the interpretation of *mantras* is one of the favourite subjects" of the Pāñcarātra *Saṃhitās*. The term *Pāñcarātra* is itself problematic and has elicited some discussion, see Raghavan (1965), H. D. Smith (1973), and P. P. Apte (1974). For surveys of the literature and general introductions there is F. O. Schrader (1916) and especially, for example, the recent work of H. D. Smith (1963; 1972; 1975–80; 1978). Gonda (1977a, 67ff.) may serve as a brief introduction, including references to lists of Vedic mantras surviving in the Pāñcarātra liturgies. Among mantras central to the Pāñcarātra tradition, Gonda (1977a, 68) cites three: OṂ NAMO NĀRĀYAṆĀYA; OM NAMO BHAGAVATE VĀSUDEVĀYA; and, one of the so-called "sectarian" variants on the Gāyatrī, OṂ NĀRĀYAṆĀYA VIDMAHE, VĀSUDEVĀYA DHĪMAHI, TAN NO VIṢṆUḤ PRACODAYĀT. Representative texts are summarized by Gonda (1977a, 87–107). Among the more accessible of these, see the *LakṣmīT*, edited by Krishnamacharya (1959) and translated by Gupta (1972); for a study see Kalia (1977), in Hindi. Another well-known text is the *AhirbudhnyaSaṃ*, a translation of which is included in F. O. Schrader (1916), and in which Lakṣmī is portrayed as *mantramayī kriyāśakti*, the manifestation of Śrī who is the "verbal activating power in the cosmos who consists of mantras" (Gonda 1977a, 68).

In dealing with the literature of the Pāñcarātra—and the same point holds true for virtually all Indian religious traditions: Vaiṣṇava, Śaiva, Śākta, or even "non-Hindu"—one should not fall into the trap of making hard and fast sectarian distinctions. Distinctions are there, but they are regional, communal, familial, and preceptorial. This is well illustrated by R. V. Joshi (1959), which by and large, is the most accessible introduction to the contemporary Vaiṣṇava ritual. Written in French, it focuses on the Kṛṣṇaite tradition of South India, which is based on the Pāñcarātra *saṃmhitās*. Among items of interest, R. V. Joshi (p. 15ff.) discusses the initiatory use of the Gopālamantra, KLĪṂ KṚṢṆĀYA GOVINDĀYA GOPĪJANAVALLABHĀYA SVĀHĀ, which invokes Kṛṣṇa as protector, the beloved of the Gopīs; and the "explication mystique" of the (p. 22ff.) mantras of Śrī Kṛṣṇa containing eight, twelve, or eighteen *akṣaras;* i.e., the first two mantras cited in the previous paragraph and the Gopāla. The chapters (29–43) dealing with *puraścaraṇa,* on this see page 423, could well serve as an introduction to this ritual tradition, for it contains brief but clear explications of the use of various sorts of rosaries, *japa, maṇḍalas,* and *bījas*. On the use of mantras in Pāñcarātra expiatory rites (*prāyaścitta*), see H. D. Smith (1966). Gonda (1977a, 137ff.) briefly summarizes Pāñcarātra speculation on the names of god. See, finally, Gupta's contribution to this volume.

The Śrī Vaiṣṇavas are an important community of South Indian Brahmans, who are *viśiṣṭādvaita* in thought, essentially Pāñcarātra in ritual, and related to the Smārta tradition sociologically. The use of mantras in their daily domestic and temple worship is discussed in

Rangachari (1931). This is a work of ethnography written by a devotee and conveys well the flavor of Śrī Vaiṣṇava worship. Although it is not as scrupulous and up to date as Joshi or as Brunner's translation of the *Somaśambhupaddhati* (see page 418), both of which, in any case, are in French, it is far more reliable and less misleading than Vidyarnava (1918), which deals with "the daily practice of the Hindu." I especially commend it to the general reader. Unfortunately, Vidyarnava has been reprinted recently and, to the best of my knowledge, Rangachari has not.

The Vaikhānasas are a small, archaizing, historically interesting Tamil and Telugu community of Vaiṣṇavas, whose liturgical traditions parallel those of the Pāñcarātrins. Gonda (1977c; also 1977a, 140–52) can serve as a brief general introduction. The literature is discussed further in Caland (1928; 1929). On Vaikhānasa daily liturgy, see Goudriaan (1970); on the use of Vedic mantras in the Vaikhānasa ritual, see Gonda (1972b). One Vaikhānasa work, the *Vaikhānasamantrapraśna* or *Mantrasaṃhitā*, particularly relevant to the study of the liturgical use of mantras, was edited in 1926 but has not been translated or widely studied. By far the most accessible introduction to the use of mantras among the Vaikhānasas, at least as indicated by the texts, is Goudriaan's (1965) English translation, with copious helpful notes, of the *Kāśyapa-Jñānakāṇḍah*, in spite of its name, a representative ritual handbook probably dating between 800–1000 A.D. It takes as its point of departure (p. 21) the sages' question to Kāśyapa: "Venerable Sir, which deity has man to worship, and in what method, with which formulas (*mantra-*), in order to reach the highest abode?" Note should be made of the alphabetized list (pp. 313–27) of mantra *pratīkas* accompanied by translations and parallel citations in other texts.

Within the family of Vaiṣṇavism, the Bengali tradition that looks to the fifteenth–sixteenth century figure of Śrī Caitanya as its founder was probably the best-known form of Kṛṣṇaite devotionalism in the West, even before the transplantation of the movement, suitably adjusted, by Bhaktivedanta Swami and the organization he founded, ISKCON. On the Caitanya movement, De (1961) provides a respectable survey and introduction. Of particular importance is De's discussion (pp. 448–519) of the ritual practices taught in Gopāla Bhaṭṭa's *Haribhaktivilāsa*. Apparently written during the early sixteenth century, De (p. 137) describes it as "a work of patient and extensive Purāṇic and Tantric erudition." Its special significance for the study of mantras lies in its being a work of scholastic devotionalism, poised as it were between Brahmanic respectability, Bhakti, and Tantra. In De's terms, it is "a complete guide to the Vaidhi Bhakti, in which devotional acts proceed from Vidhis or Śāstric injunctions [i.e., from scriptural imperatives]." Illustrative of the text's synthesis of fervor and ritualism is the treatment of the power of the divine name (p. 486f.). Note especially the concepts of *nāmamāhātmya* (the Magnification of the Name), that is, its inseparability from Kṛṣṇa himself—thus the slogans *nāmanāminor abhedhaḥ* and *bhagavatsvarūpam eva nāma** (cf. p. 289), of *nāmāparādhas* (offences to the Name) (cf. p. 175), and the long list of the powers of taking refuge in the Name. The list of quotations from various Purāṇic and Tantric texts De provides (pp. 519–29) is especially valuable. One of the subjects not discussed in the *Haribhaktivilāsa* is domestic rites of passage. These, however, are treated in a lesser known work, the *Satkriyāsāradīpikā,* also but questionably attributed to Gopāla Bhaṭṭa. De discusses (pp. 529–41) this work that, as one would expect, illustrates the thorough intermingling of Vedic and Tantric mantras in the domestic litury of a late, regional, popular movement such as the Śrī Caitanya Saṃpradāya.

The Tantricizing tendency that gradually becomes more obvious in the Śrī Caitanya Saṃpradāya becomes even more pronounced in the overtly Tantric, not wholly respectable, Vaiṣṇava Sahajiyā tradition of Bengal. This has been discussed by Bose (Basu) (1927; 1930), S. B. Dasgupta (1962), and Dimock (1966); also, for a folk parallel, Chakravati (1930). Dimock's study merits special attention because of its patient attempt to set the Sahajiyā movement in a comparative context. See the discussion of Sahajiyā *sādhanā*** (pp. 222–48), in particular, the use of mantras of the sacred name of Kṛṣṇa and of the *kāmabīja,* KLĪṂ. See also Dimock's discussion (pp. 234–45) of the use of mantras according to the *Nāyikāsādhanaṭīkā,* a mid-nineteenth century Bengali text that deals with the "technique of transmuting kāma [pleasure] to prema [love]." Were one to pursue further the study of mantras in Bengali culture, one would be led to examine not merely Śākta, but also Buddhist and Muslim traditions of ritual and poetic ecstasy. A sense of this material is provided by S. B. Dasgupta (1962), and see the material on regional ethnography, pages 373–75.

The rather complex history, nomenclature, and mutual relationships of the various sorts of Śaivism prominent since the age of the Epic have never been adequately synthesized. A brief survey of some of the material may be found in Lorenzen (1972, 1–12). Pathak (1960) provides a survey of inscriptional evidence (mostly) from Northern India. In the posthumously published and incomplete fifth volume of his history of Indian philosophy, S. N. Dasgupta (1955) surveys some (mostly Southern) Śaivite systems. The most extensive survey I have come across is K. C. Pandey (1954, i–ccvi), which was published as an introduction to an English translation of Abhinavagupta's IPK *Vimarśinī* as understood by its commentator Bhāskara. These works, in part, can help place the following comments in historical and systematic context.

The oldest Śaiva tradition of which we have evidence is the Pāś-

**These slogans assert the "nondistinction of the name and the bearer of the name" and that "the name is the essence of the deity," respectively.*

***The terms* sādhana *and* sādhanā *have the same meaning. In general, I follow the usage of most specialists in using the latter.*

upata. It is clear that in general terms mantric utterance of a certain sort must have been a central element in the extensive repertory of Pāśupata practices. *PāśupataSū* 1.17 speaks of the repetition of a Raudric Gāyatrī, *raudrīṃ gāyatriīṃ bahurūpīṃ vā japet,* while verse 3.17 (*apitadbhāṣet*), as understood by Kauṇḍinya, recommends speaking in an extraordinary, even nonsensical manner. Verse 1.8 lists an array of practices:

> One should approach [Maheśvara] with an offering [of the following acts]: laughing, singing, dancing [presumably, laughing, singing and dancing in imitation of Śiva], making the sound *ḍuṃḍuṃ* [or *huhuṃ* or *huḍuk;* i.e., lowing like a bull], making obeisance and the repeating [of a mantra—according to the commentary, the Sadyojāta mantra].*

The seventh verse of the *Gaṇakārikā,* a later text on which the tenth century Naiyāyika Bhāsarvajña has written a commentary, confirms the centrality of *japa* to the Pāśupatas:

> Impregnating oneself with the doctrine, appropriate conduct, meditatively disciplined repetition [of a mantra] (*japadhyāna*), constant recollection of Rudra and the favor [of Maheśvara] are considered to be the five means of attaining the goal.**

More interesting, then, the injunctions concerning *japa* is the systematically antinomian context in which they are to be carried out. On this, see the well-known essay of Ingalls (1962). It might also be observed that the case of the Pāśupatas suggests the possible antiquity of a *sādhanā* in which simple but meaningful theistic mantras (e.g., SADYOJĀTĀYA VAI NAMAḤ, *PāśupataSū* 1.41) coexist with the other sort of Mantraśāstra, techniques of flamboyant meaninglessness designed to transport the adept beyond the ordinary realm and, not incidentally, scandalize the orthodox.

The *PāśupataSū* have been edited with the commentary of Kauṇḍinya by R. A. Shastri (1940), the *Gaṇakārikā,* probably by Haradattācārya, with Bhāsarvajña's commentary by Dalal (1920). The Sū and their commentaries have been translated into English, rather mechanically, in Chakraborti (1970). For a brief account, see Lorenzen (1972, 173–92, with further refs.). For a survey of Pāśupata thought, one may consult Schulz (1958). Perhaps the most exemplary work on the Pāśupatas is Hara (1958), a careful translation of the Pāśupata chapter of Mādhava's *Sarvadarśanasaṃgraha.* The parallel passages cited in the footnotes are es-

---

*hasita-gīta-nṛtta-ḍuṃḍuṃkāra-namaskāra-japyopahā reṇopatiṣṭhet

**vāsaś carya japadhyānaṃ sadārudrasmṛtis tathā
prasādaś caiva lābhānām upāyaḥ pañca niscitāḥ

I have followed Hara (1958, 15, n. 49) in translating vāsa.

pecially valuable but, unfortunately for the general reader, they are not translated. Note, however, that none of these items deal with Pāśupata practice exclusively. Oberhammer's contribution to this volume is the only systematic discussion of mantric usage among the Pāśupatas; cf. Oberhammer (1984).

Often associated with the Pāśupatas are other, sometimes historically related movements of which the most important are the Kālāmukhas and the Kāpālikas. The evidence for these movements is carefully synthesized in Lorenzen (1972, with refs.), which is particularly helpful in juxtaposing literary and inscriptional evidence. See also C. Chakravati (1932) on the closely related, if not identical, *Sauma, Soma,* or *Somasiddhānta* tradition.

During the second and third quarters of the first millenium A.D., Śaivism in large measure reformulated itself, or at least systematized its ritual, in a set of texts that, paralleling the *Pāñcarātrāgama,* designate themselves *śaivāgama.* The *Śaivāgamas* are significant for the study of daily Śaiva domestic and temple ritual, especially as this has been preserved in South India. They are also one of the major repositories for early Śaiva Tantra and, accordingly, I treat them in the context of Tantric texts on page 417.

Two regional concentrations of Sanskritic Śaivism arose, partially on the basis of the *Śaivāgamas,* in the last quarter of the first millenium. The movements to which they gave rise have received considerable attention. The older, a complex congeries of movements, was centered in Kashmir. It should be noted, however, that none of the movements prominent in Kashmir called themselves, nor should they be called, *Kashmir Śaivism.* Systematic philosophical reflection on the *Śaivāgamas* was highly advanced within the Śaiva traditions associated with Kashmir, and they offer significant evidence for the evolution of Mantraśāstra in a rich environment, compounded of Tantric, Bhaktic, and scholastic elements. Because I am preparing a comprehensive bibliography on these traditions, I exclude them from this essay. The important evidence of the *Parātriṃśikā* is, however, discussed on pages 432–33.

The second regional Śaivagamic tradition flourished in South India, especially in Tamilnad. Styling itself *siddhānta,* "the final established truth," today the Śaiva Siddhānta is the best organized surviving form of regional Śaivism. Indeed, it is one of the forms of Hinduism that has flourished in the West among expatriate Indians, mainly Tamils, and Western converts. Better known for its devotional and philosophical writings than for its ritual and meditative life, it might best be described as the form "orthodox" Āgamic Śaivism has assumed in the devotional and cultural milieu of Dravidian India. Sivaraman (1973, 372–404) provides a clear survey of Śaiva Siddhānta *sādhanā* from a philosophical perspective, with attention to the nature and function of *dīkṣā* and the symbolic significance of the *pañcākṣara* mantra. Piet (1952) provides an annotated translation of Meykaṇṭar's (thirteenth century) Tamil treatise

Śivajñānabodha, the ninth *sūtra* of which (138–143) deals with the *pañcākṣara* mantra. The practical significance of this mantra is underscored by a quotation (143) from the *Tevāram,* the canonical collection of the Tamil Śaiva devotional poets (*nāyanārs*):

> He who utters the Namaḥ-śivāya mantra with the love of a wife for her husband and with a mind that is melted to tears is led to heaven, for this mantra is the essence of all that which is contained in the four Vedas.

After Meykaṇṭar, the most important representative of the Śaiva Siddhānta is probably Umāpati Śivācārya (c. early fourteenth century), a figure associated with the great temple at Cidambaram. His *Śataratnasaṃgraha,* an Āgamic anthology that includes considerable material on *dīkṣā,* has been edited and translated in Thirugnanasambandhan (1973).

The most distinctive Śaiva group in the South are the Vīraśaivas (Liṅgāyats), an organized, "reformist," devotional community concentrated in the Kannada-speaking region around Mysore. Consistent with their simplifying temper, the Vīraśaivas revere only OṂ and the *pañcākṣara* mantra, which they count as one of the eight emblems or "aids to faith" (*aṣṭāvaraṇa*) and which, in the words of Nandimath (1942, 39), they glorify as the "king of mantra" (*mantrarāṭ*). The Vīraśaivas are an antiritualistic community who yet have developed their own ritualism. Therefore, comparing and contrasting their use of the *pañcākṣara* mantra with that of the Tamil Śaiva Siddhāntins might be instructive. The general reader can get a good feel for the ethos of Vīraśaivism in Ramanujan (1973). For a general survey see Nandimath, also McCormack (1957); and, on Vīraśaiva monasticism, see Sadasivaiah (1967).

The diverse traditions known collectively as the Nāthasampradāya illustrate well the impossibility of disentangling Tantric, Bhaktic, and folk elements of Indian religious life. It generally is associated with the Śaiva pole of the Hinduism; however, this is a half-truth. As Gonda (1977a, 221) observes, "Their Śivaite origin is very uncertain . . . [and] in the West of India they are nearer to Viṣṇuism, in Nepal to Buddhism, and their customs and literature evince a tendency to adopt many heterodox elements." Whatever the degree to which this characterization is correct, it can serve as a reminder than any attempt to devise a single classification of Hindus "sects" will wind up imposing a Semitic sense of religious order on India. In any case, Nāthism is an especially important source for that "sonic mysticism" central to the Tantric understanding and use of mantras.

For a summary introduction to some of the texts that claim the authority of Matsyendranāth or Gorakṣanāth, see Gold and Gold (1984, 114, n. 3). The most popular of these works—the *Haṭhayogapradīpikā,* the *Gheraṇḍasaṃhitā,* and the *Gorakṣaśataka*—have been published and translated many times. See, for example, for the *Haṭhayogapradīpikā,* Walter

(1893), T. R. Śrīnivāsa Ayiyangar (1972), and especially Michael (1974); for the *Gheraṇḍasaṃhitā*, R. Schmidt (1908); for the *Gorakṣaśataka*, the translation in Briggs (1938, 284–304), Kuvalayānanada and Shukla (1974), S. J. S. Pandey (1978), and especially, for an edition and German translation, Nowotny (1976). See also, for the *Śivasaṃhitā*, Vasu (1914–15), and on the *Kaulajñānanirṇaya*, Bagchi (1934). Among various histories and collection in Hindi or Bengali, some with English translations, see Mallik (1950; 1954), H. P. Dvivedi (1957; 1966), Barthwal (1971), and N. Upadhyaya (1976). For an introduction, one may consult Briggs (1938), which still provides the best survey for the general reader. Among the older literature, see S. C. Mitra (1927). Recently, a few Western scholars have begun to devote serious attention to the Nātha tradition. The most extensive study of Nāthism to date is Unbescheid (1980, with bibliog.), which is in German and focuses on the Kathmandu valley. Gold and Gold (1984) is a sociological analysis of the creative tension between householder and renouncer in Nāthism. As an indication of the contemporary vitality of Nāthism, one may see A. K. Banerjea (1962).

Closely related to the family of Nātha traditions is the so-called school of the Siddhas. It, too, straddles the historically murky divide between Hindu and Buddhist Tantra and the even murkier divisions between various sorts of Hinduism. Pathak (1960, 26f.), for example, mentions an inscription (Rewah, M. P.) of Malayasiṃha—I suppose the vassal of Vijayasiṃha, the last Kalachuri ruler of Tripurī (twelfth–thirteenth century)—which "begins with an invocation to Mañjughoṣa—an originally Buddhist god of learning," describes the Siddhas as ascetics who "go to high heaven, having performed painful austerities," characterizes Malayasiṃha himself as a *siddhārthayogī*, and "extols the worship of Rāma." On the tradition of the Siddhas, see Sāmkṛtyāyana (1957), T. Schmidt (1958), and, specifically on Tibet, Grünwedel (1916) and especially Robinson (1979); also the information on Indian and Tibetan Buddhism cited on pages 390–91. Finally, in this complex of ascetic, ambiguously Śaiva groups, mention may be made of the Aghorapanth, on which, see Barrow (1893) and Balfour (1897); and cf. Lorenzen (1972).

Besides functioning as instruments through which individuals achieve some goal, mantras also function as indices through which different communities rank themselves comparatively. This is the conclusion of Inden (1976), in an influential anthropological and historical exploration of marriage and rank in pre-modern Bengal. Inden notes that for traditional Bengali culture the "word" was thought of as substance rather than idea: "The par excellence 'substances' of worship . . . consisted of the uttered sounds (*śabda*), the powerful words (*mantra*) of texts such as the Vedas and the Tantras. . . . In fact, it was precisely the combination of these sounds with human bodily substance that defined a *jāti* as *ārya* or Hindu" (p. 16). Presumably, one could map the different regional complexes that make up the Hindu tradition by different mantras and the way they are used by different groups in the population. For example, speaking of Chhattisgarh, Babb (1975) suggests at least three types of mantras and levels of mantric utterance: the (presumably) Vedic mantras of the Brahmans; the predominantly therapeutic and theistic mantras (p. 207) of the *bhaigas* (healers and exorcists); and the mantras of Durgā, which make up the text of the *Devīmāhātmyam* (p. 218). Finally, one might ruefully underscore the fact that the use of mantras by women and in women's rituals is a subject of vast importance about which, to my knowledge, no one has yet devoted any study.

Regional examinations of mantra are few. On the use of mantra in Tamilnad, we have the remarkable study of Carl Gustav Diehl (1956), *Instrument and Purpose, Studies on Rites and Rituals in South India*. Bharati (1965, 110) justly describes this as "the most thoroughgoing enquiry into the import of *mantra*, from a modern anthropological angle," although not all anthropologists would agree. For most regions, one would have to sift through a mass of ethnographic reports. For example, on various aspects of the popular religion of Bengal, Bihar, and Orissa, see the works of Sarat Chandra Mitra listed in Eliade (1969, 464), and for Bengal, also C. Chakravati (1930). This might be collated with the evidence of the various *sahjiyā* movements. Fresh field work would be helpful.

There is a large literature on the cult of the semipersonal powers, gods, and goddesses in village Hinduism and, to a certain extent, on their appearance in iconography and classical Sankrit scriptures. The literature is beyond the scope of this survey, but three representative works may be noted: Peri (1917), on the goddess Hāritī; Coomaraswamy (1928–31), on *yakṣas;* and Meyer (1937), on the powers of fertility. Compare the proposed classification of mantric *devatās* on page 420. It is possible, but far from certain, that the patterns established in their worship has influenced the evolution of Mantraśāstra, at least in its Tantric form. A continuum might be assumed between the Tantric tradition of using Mantraśāstra to effect harm without physical contact or even proximity and folk sorcery and witchcraft; but, to the best of my knowledge, the possible relationship has not been systematically explored. See Roy (1927, 28–31), which marshals evidence for witchcraft from Orissa.

One should not neglect the use of mantras by folk healers. On the occult powers of folk healers in the Panjab for example, see Burne (1910). On the prophylactic use of amulets in Bengal, see Moberly (1906). It would be interesting to collate the evidence of ethnography, medicine, and literature on the use of mantra as written. For example, Bāṇa in the *Kādambarī* (cited Lorenzen 1972, 16f.)—a work that satirizes popular and Tantric practices—speaks of Queen Vilāsavatī of Ujjayinī who, among other ritual actions, "carried about little caskets of mantras filled with birch-leaves written over in yellow letters" in order to ensure the birth of a son. In this regard, a comprehensive study of those mantras deemed protective and designated *kavacas* (coats of mail, amulets) (Gonda 1977a, 80, n. 211; speaking of the Pāñcarātra) might yield interesting results. On the use of "secret messages and symbols" on the folk level see Crooke (1919) and the discussion of codes on pages 416–17.

Is the evidence of folk usage relevant to Mantraśāstra? A classicist might demur: These are not really mantras. To which one could respond, if verbal formulae are called mantras or used like mantras or mixed with textually authentic mantras, well, then they are mantras.

THE PHILOSOPHICAL AND SCIENTIFIC TRADITIONS

The doxographic division of Indian philosophy into six (or more) "schools,"* while undoubtedly reflecting social reality, has distracted attention from the scholastic and conceptual unity of Indian thought: Hindu, Buddhist, and Jain. It is particularly inappropriate in considering Indian theories about language, since much of the discussion of philosophy of language was stimulated by Vyākaraṇa, "Grammar," a tradition propaedeutic to rather than one of the so-called six *darśanas*. This is not to say that problems concerning language were equally significant to all of the Indian philosophical traditions. It received special attention in Mīmāṃsā, Nyāya, Buddhism, and Vedānta, perhaps in that order. This section of the Bibliography is accordingly divided into two sections. First, I provide material on the tradition of the Vaiyākaraṇas in general. It is properly background—indispensable background—to the section in which reflection about language in the Pūrvamīmāṃsā and other traditions is discussed. I have tried to list items that would allow a philosopher not trained in Indology to approach this material. However, I have excluded reference to standard surveys, such as those of Dasgupta, Hiriyana, Radhakrishnan, and Tucci. For guidance on Indian philosophizing in general, Potter (1963) has no peer.

One caution might be helpful. In this area, many items range rather widely over authors and texts. I have attempted to place each item where I expect that it will be most helpful to readers, but I have not resorted to extensive cross referencing. A certain amount of arbitrary classification seemed unavoidable. It might strike some readers that the material in this section is rather far removed from Mantraśāstra. I include it for the following reason: On the popular level, as well as among the intelligentsia, the use and understanding of mantras was colored by convictions about the nature and significance of human language and about the Word as an ultimate metaphysical category. While scholars today are not obligated to accept any of the indigenous views of language, a complete account of the intellectual context in which mantric utterance makes sense must include them.

**Ganganath Jha, for example, observed 45 years ago, "as late as the fourteenth century the name 'Ṣaḍ-darshana', 'Six Systems of Philosophy', had not become stereotyped as standing definitely and specifically for the Six Systems now known" (1942, 2).*

Vyākaraṇa *and Philosophy of Language*

Although focused on the figure of Pāṇini, Cardona (1976), in fact, provides a comprehensive, readily accessible bibliographical survey of Indian grammatical and, to a lesser extent, philosophical reflection on language as such. I have drawn extensively on Cardona's analysis, attempting to select from it works most likely to shed light on the intellectual context in which mantric utterance was given systematic, philosophical explication, as well as works likely to provide guidance for a beginner. It has also enabled me to be more generous in citing contemporary works in Indian languages than in other sections of this Bibliography. I additionally draw attention to some works that have appeared since the mid-1970s.

There are several useful introductions to Indian speculation and reflection concerning language, many of them ranging widely over earlier and later materials. On the history of the grammatical tradition is the exhaustive survey, in Hindi, of Yudhiṣṭhira Mīmāṃsaka (1973); Renou's brief, but rather technical, introduction to his edition of the *Durghaṭavṛtti* (1940); a lively and informative selection of primary sources in Western languages edited by Staal (1972); and survey articles by R. Rocher (1975) and Staal (1976). Among older studies in English, Belvalkar (1915) and P. C. Chakravarti (1930; 1933) are still useful. More recent and more selective are the critical essays of Ruegg (1959), on which see the review of Staal (1960). Philosophically speaking, Biardeau (1964a), which focuses on Bhartṛhari and his predecessors, is doubtless the most valuable introduction to Indian speculation on "*la connaissance et philosophie de la parole.*" Unfortunately, no such intellectually engaged, introductory survey yet exists in English. See, however, the general works on theory of meaning (i.e., semantics) and on Bhartṛhari listed on page 380.

The general reader will probably be best served by approaching this subject through the surveys of R. Rocher and Staal just mentioned. Brough (1951) and Emeneau (1955) provide brief, readable, but not up-to-date summaries. For brief philosophically oriented surveys, see Strauss (1927), de Smet (1960), and Murti (1974), and the more technical essay of Thieme (1956). On more specific topics, but still capable of serving an introductory function, are Subramania Iyer (1948; and, perhaps, also 1942 and 1950–51).

As Cardona (1976, 185) observes, "There has not been published to date in a European language a single work in which Pāṇini's total system is set forth clearly and with insight." Moreover, I fail to see how anyone who has not studied Pāṇini in the original with a qualified teacher can appreciate the foundational role that the Pāṇinian scheme played in Indian intellectual life. Still, attention might be drawn to some items of general utility. The standard translations of Pāṇini's Grammar, the *Aṣṭādhyāyī*, each with its own strengths and weaknesses (see Cardona 1976, 142ff.), are in German (Böhtlingk 1887) and French (Renou 1948–54). The technical terminology is explicated, however darkly, in

Abhyankar and Shukla (1977), Renou (1942), and also K. C. Chatterji (1964a); two indispensable reference works, both in Sanskrit, are the *Mīmāṃsā Kośa* (Kevalanandasarasvati 1952–66) and the *Nyāya Kośa* (Jhalkikar and Abhyankar 1928), which deal with the technical vocabulary of grammar, logic, and ritual as utilized, respectively, in the Mīmāṃsā and Nyāya traditions; on the relationship between Pāṇini and the Veda, see Thieme (1935); among works of reference on ancillary matters, one might mention Sarup (1927) on Yāska's *Nirukta*, on which, also see B. Bhattacharya (1958); and Allen (1953) on phonetics. As introductions for the general reader, one might follow Staal (1972, 432) in recommending three essays of Louis Renou (1940; 1957, both in French, and 1969, in English, which places Pāṇini in the context of the science of linguistics).

The relevance of the Pāṇinian tradition for the investigation of mantric utterance is twofold: In the first instance, it determined to a significant extent the intellectual framework in which all educated Indians thought and spoke about language, including—even especially—"religious" language. In the second instance, unlike most if not all of the grammarians and philosophers of language of the West, the Vaiyākaraṇas understood the study of language to have a transcendental goal and dimension. As Cardona (1976, 242) notes, according to the *Mahābhāṣya* "one of the purposes of grammar is merit (*dharma*) obtained through knowledge and use of correct speech." He continues, "Indeed, Pāṇinīyas consider grammar not only a means whereby correct usage is taught but also a means of attaining ultimate release (*mokṣa*)." To judge that in traditional Indian culture correct usage was instinctively understood as having something like a magical value does not transform the grammarians—no less all educated speakers—into mystics. It does help delineate the mindset in whose terms the soteriological value of mantric utterance will make perfectly good ritual and linguistic sense.

Unfortunately, the issue of the religious purpose of the Pāṇinian tradition has generated more heat than light. Cardona's (1976, 243) call for subtlety should be heeded. In relationship to this issue one might see Thieme (1931), P. C. Chakravarti (1934), Subramania Iyer (1964), and the brief Sanskrit essays (cited by Cardona 1976, 346, n. 334) of Periveṅkateśvara Śāstrī (1971) and Rāmanārāyaṇa Tripathi (1971). Readers of this volume should especially note Staal (1963b)—a review of Scharfe (1961)—where the author with good reason protests against a facile mystical reading of the Indian grammarians. There is more than a little continuity between the "no nonsense" approach he adopts there and his approach to mantra today.

The most famous of the Indian grammarians after Pāṇini was Patajali, author of the *Mahābhāṣya*. There is no standard English translation of this text. Cardona (1976, 245f.) discusses the options. Philosophically speaking, the most important section of the *Mahābhāṣya* is the Introduction (*paspaśā*), of which there is a translation by K. C. Chatterji (1964b) that Cardona (p. 246) commends for copious annotation. See also the Sanskrit essay by Venkatarama Sarma (1966–67). As Staal (1976, 102) points out, the *Mahābhāṣya* is "an important work not only for grammar, but also for logic, methodology and philosophy." Among essays dealing with the philosophical aspects of Patajali's grammar one might note—variously for their quality or influence—Paranjpe (1922), P. C. Chakravarti (1926), Strauss (1927b), B. Bhattacharya (1956), Sreekrishna Sarma (1957), Frauwallner (1960b), and Scharfe (1961), on which, see the previously mentioned review of Staal (1963b). Cf. Cardona (pp. 256–59); he singles out for praise the Sanskrit treatise of Rama Prasada Tripathi (1972), which deals with the treatment of epistemological issues (*pramāṇa*) in Patajali and other Pāṇinians.

Patajali is one of the earliest figures for whom grammatical, exegetical (i.e., Vedic), and philosophical/soteriological concerns intersect. No single work analyzes this, but I know of three interesting essays that explore Patajali's exegesis of Vedic mantras relevant to the evolution of the Indian understanding of the nature and force of speech: Thieme (1967) deals with ṚV 1.164.5, one of the riddles in the *Asya Vāmasya;* Thieme (1964) deals with ṚV 8.69.12 [discounting the Vālakhilya sūktas, 8.58.12], a verse to Varuṇa (in a poem to Indra) understood as referring metaphorically to the origin of speech (?); and Palsule (1969) deals with ṚV 10.71.2, a verse from a poem to Vāc.

From both a conceptual and religious point of view Bhartṛhari (c. fifth century A.D.) is the single most significant figure in the Indian tradition of philosophy of language. His position is especially pivotal in the case of mantric utterance, because his thought marked a conceptual watershed. On the one hand, he looks back towards the apotheosis of speech as ultimate in certain strands of the Veda. On the other hand, he lays the philosophical groundwork for the elaboration of a "science" of mantras in certain of the Tantric traditions. (To be sure, most Tantras are interested only in "significant results." They do not elaborate a philosophical defense of their *sādhanā*. Where, however, as with some of the Śaiva philosophers of Kashmir, philosophical grounding is provided for the soteriological use of mantra, Bhartṛhari is often drawn upon, explicitly or implicitly.)

The date, text, and authorship of the commentaries on Bhartṛhari's principal work, usually called the *Vākyapadīya* (VP), has raised a number of vexing questions. A survey of this material, which is discussed by Cardona (1976, 295–305), is beyond the scope of this essay. Suffice it to note that, in the past few decades, the most serious, sustained work on Bhartṛhari has been done by K. A. Subramania Iyer, Wilhelm Rau, and Ashok Aklujkar. For historiographic and textual orientation, one should see Rau (1971) and Aklujkar (1972). Philosophically speaking, the most obviously appealing section of the VP is the *Brahmakāṇḍa,* the first of its three sections. On this, Biardeau (1964b) and Subramania Iyer (1965a) have written accessible annotated translations. One might also see the edition of Varma (1970), which is provided with commentaries in English, Sanskrit, and Hindi. A competent, comprehensive survey of the Bhartṛharian system is provided by Subramania Iyer (1969); see also the unpublished dissertation of Aklujkar (1970b) and Varma (1971) in Hindi. For the general reader, the best introduction to Bhartṛhari is Coward and Sivaraman (1977), which provides a brief overview stressing Bhartṛhari's "yogic psychology." Coward accepts the identity of Bhartṛhari the grammarian, author of the VP, and Bhartṛhari the poet, author of the *Śatakatraya*. The validity of this traditional identification has been questioned, of course. Curiously this issue is (diplomatically) left undiscussed by Cardona (1976, see 365, n. 514). For Bhartṛhari's treatment of mantra see Coward's essay in this volume. On the discussion of Indian philosophy of language in the Chinese Buddhist pilgrim I Tsing (634–713 A.D.), see Brough (1973). A monograph on the survival and development of Indian philosophy of language in Tibet would be most helpful, in this regard see Nakamura (1955).

For Bhartṛhari, cognition is intrinsically linguistic; to be human is to use language. Therefore, nothing can be more important than using language properly. The soteriological raison d'être and the metaphysical stance of this philosophy is concisely articulated by Cardona (1976, 300) in a passage that merits citation:

> Basic to Bhartṛhari's general philosophy is the concept of Brahman, the ultimate being, whose very essence is speech (*śabda*) and from whom evolves (*vivartate*) all that there is. Grammar (*vyākaraṇa*), as a means of discriminating correct (*sādhu*) from incorrect (*asādhu, apabhraṃśa* . . .) usage, is a means of attaining ultimate release (*apavarga*), what we call salvation. For, through the use of correct forms (*sādhuprayoga*) one achieves merit (*dharma*), and through the knowledge of correct usage one gains the insight that speech in its essence is not differentiated. One thus reaches a stage of speech which is not dispersed (*avyatikīrṇa*), which is the source (*prakṛti*) of evolved speech (*vāg-vikāra*), and which is called *pratibhā* or *paśyantī* ("seeing" . . .). And finally one reaches the ultimate (*parā*) source (*prakṛti*) of all evolutes, namely brahman. . . . Grammar is thus the cure for the stains which affect speech (*vāṅ-malānāṃ cikitsitam*)—that is, incorrect usages—and the door to salvation (*dvāram apavargasya* . . .).

In comparison to thinkers of comparable stature, critical examination of Bhartṛhari is still in its infancy. Nonetheless, by now, a considerable secondary literature has clustered around certain significant issues. I group the references around three themes: semantics in general, *sphoṭa* and *pratibhā*, and the relationship between "word" and "world." One caution is in order: Various students of Bhartṛhari have been tempted to overemphasize the religious components in his thought. It is safer to conclude with Staal (1976, 125, citing Kunjunni Raja) that "Bhartṛhari's philosophy is best understood as a metaphysical superstructure to a semantic theory."

Bhartṛhari's work served as the point of departure for the discussion of meaning, not only for the Vaiyākaraṇas but for the Indian scholastic tradition generally. A brief overview of Indian semantic theory may be found in Aklujkar (1970); an older but still useful account is Brough (1953). Kunjunni Raja (1969), on *Indian Theories of Meaning,* is a model of clear, concise exposition and ably summarizes the main issues. One may also see B. Bhattacharya (1962) and, focusing on Bhartṛhari, Gaurinath Shastri (1959). R. C. S. Pandey (1963) should be used with caution. On Pandey and Kunjunni Raja, see the review essay of Staal (1966). One might also consult the Hindi syntheses of K. D. Dvivedi (1951) and Rama Suresa Tripathi (1972).

The semantic reflection of the scholastic tradition, of Naiyāyikas and Mīmāṃsākas as well as Vaiyākaraṇas, eventually focused on a few concepts and issues, chief among them, on the related concepts of *sphoṭa* and *pratibhā.* (The meaning of these two technical terms cannot be readily conveyed by unexplicated translation: roughly, *sphoṭa* indicates the eternal and divisible entity of verbal reference, especially of a sentence, while *pratibhā* is the spontaneous intuition of verbal meaning.)*

There is a large literature on the concept of *sphoṭa.* Coward (1980) provides a recent overview. Besides the relevant sections of the standard works cited earlier—and keeping in mind that *sphoṭa* is first and foremost a serious, semantic category, not a vague mystical effusion—one might see Liebich (1923), Ramaswami Sastri (1932–33), G. Bhattacharya (1937), Heimann (1941), Subramania Iyer (1947), Herman (1962–63), and, in Sanskrit, Kapil Deva Shastri (1967), Periveṅkateśvara Śāstri (1971) and Viśvanātha Miśra (1971). On variants of or opposition to the classical theory of *sphoṭa,* see Subrahmania Iyer (1937).

Eventually, the discussion of *sphoṭa* became something of a scholastic growth industry. For example, see the *Sphoṭanirṇaya,* a section of Kauṇḍabhaṭṭa's *Vaiyākaraṇabhūṣaṇasāra* (seventeenth century) edited and translated by S. D. Joshi (1967). Among the primary works devoted to the discussion of *sphoṭa,* Cardona (1976, 369, n. 542) singles out two as especially meriting attention. The first is the *Sphoṭasiddhi* of the well-known "academic" philosopher Maṇḍana Miśra (seventh–eighth century), edited by Rāmanātha Śāstrī (1931) and translated into French by Biardeau (1958) and into English by Subramania Iyer (1966). The second is the *Sphoṭavāda* of the Pāṇinian Nāgeśabhaṭṭa, edited by Krishnamacharya (1946). For a technical exposition of these and other post-Bhartṛharians, see Subha Rao (1969). Finally, for an analysis of the treat-

---

**It should be kept in mind that Bhartṛhari does not use the word* pratibhā, *nor the term* dhvani *(for him, the phonic reality of a word), in the sense of the latter tradition of poetics and aesthetics; on Bhartṛhari's use of* dhvani, *see Subramania Iyer (1965b).*

ment of *sphoṭa* in Sāyaṇa/Mādhava's *Sarvadarśanasaṃgraha,* see Abegg (1914).

Many of the works cited so far deal, to one extent or another, with *pratibhā* as well as *sphoṭa.* More especially, Gopinath Kaviraj, a scholar who most often wrote in one or another Indian language, provides a lucid (1924) overview in English. Gonda (1963a, 318–48) provides a valuable discussion of the term as a counterpart of the Vedic *dhī-* and he surveys its use in Nyāya, Yoga, and Alaṃkāra, as well as in Bhartṛhari. He offers the general definition (p. 319): "*Pratibhā* is that function of the mind which, while developing without any special cause, is able to lead on to real knowledge, to an insight into the transcendental truth and reality. It is intuition from within, the divine spark which suddenly illumines darkness into light. It is that which gives the realization of identity." See also Subramania Iyer (1941) and, in Sanskrit, Raghunātha Śarmā (1964c).

In evaluating the metaphysical and religious components in the philosophy of Bhartṛhari and those who followed him or borrowed from him, it is important not to misconstrue or overestimate their spiritual nature. Nonetheless, the Bhartṛharian tradition provided a conceptual impetus, and vocabulary, for the development of more explicitly theological and soteriological traditions, especially those of the various intersecting Vedāntic and Tantric ontologies. For the student of mantra as it has manifested itself since the middle of the first millenium A.D., knowledge of the Vyākaraṇa is vital but its significance is indirect. It illumines the partially explicit, partially implicit preunderstanding of the nature and significance of speech in the communities where mantric utterance was at once taken for granted and cultivated.

The central concept of Bhartṛharian ontology is *Śabdabrahman,* the primal Word/Sound that becomes the world. With this term, Bhartṛhari characteristically looks back to the Veda, for the term is known as early as MaitU 6.22 (Ruegg 1959, 64, n. 1), and looks forward to the developed sonic ontologies and soteriologies of Tantric systems, such as the *spanda* tradition of Kashmir. On *Śabdabrahman,* see Harāṇacandra Sastri (1937), Anjaneya Sarma (1965), and Lienhard (1968); the critique of this concept by the Naiyāyika Jayanta is discussed in Gaurinath Sastri (1939). Cosmogonically and mythologically, the counterpart of the concept of *Śabdabrahman* is *sṛṣṭi,* the evolution of the world of complex "sentences" within the Word that is god. On this, there is a Sanskrit essay by Rāma Prāsada Tripaṭhi (1971). One development of this sense of the world as evolute of the word was the notion of the threefold (among certain Śaivas in Kashmir this will become fourfold) nature of Speech. Justification for this notion was found, among other places, in ṚV 1.164.45, on Bhartṛhari's treatment of this, see Kapila Deva Shastri (1966). Epistemologically, the counterpart of the concept of *Śabdabrahman* is *śabdādvaita,* the position that anything that might appear to exist as "a second over against the primal Word'' is ultimately sublatable. On this, there are Sanskrit essays by Raghunātha Śarmā (1964b) and Haridatta Śhāstrī (1971).

While, at first blush, the theories of *Śabdabrahman, sṛṣṭi,* and *śabdādvaita,* might strike one as simple enough, evaluating their precise force in the Bhartṛharian scheme turns out to be rather tricky. In large measure, this has taken the form of a debate that is partially cast in the vocabulary of Vedāntic polemics, which long postdate Bhartṛhari. The two central questions are In what sense might Bhartṛhari be characterized as a monist and/or also as an illusionist? May Bhartṛhari's position be characterized as either *pariṇāmavāda* or *vivartavāda*? The still classic treatment of these issues, in part because of its lucidity, is Hacker (1953). See also Ramaswami Sastri (1938), Ruegg (1958), and Gaurinath Sastri (1968–69). The precise philosophical delineation of the relation between an ultimate, which in one sense is but in another sense isn't quite the world, obviously invites certain conceptual gymnastics. Relevant to these logical maneuvers is a series of essays by Kapil Deva Shastri (1964a; 1964b; 1964c; 1965) on Bartṛhari's understanding of comparison (*upamāna*) and coreferentiality (*sāmānādhikaraṇya*); see also Motilal (1973) on the Vaiyākaraṇas understanding of substance. The last word has certainly not been said on these issues, and further work shall have to take into account Bhartṛhari's knowledge of traditions other than Vedānta, without reopening the question of Bhartṛhari's Buddhism. In this context see Ramaswami Sastri (1936–37; 1952) and Dave (1966). For an attempt to use Hacker's analysis of *vivarta* to explicate a theme in Abhinavagupta, an author who was in part indebted to the Bhartṛharian ontology, see Alper (1979).

The mytheme of ''the god who becomes the world'' can be seen as one of the root images in the Indian religious traditions (cf. Pensa 1972). The theologies that attempt to articulate and defend this mytheme drew variously upon many of the conceptual resources of Indian scholastic philosophy. Much work remains before Bhartṛhari's contribution to this strand of Indian religious life can be assessed with confidence. However, there has been considerable debate concerning the religious identity of and influences on Bhartṛhari, in particular discussion of the ways in which he might be considered to be a Buddhist or a Vedāntin. Such doxographic placement, however, is of questionable value. It is more fruitful to describe and assess Bhartṛhari's religious practices and convictions as carefully as possible. Many of the works cited so far attempt this in passing; more specifically, one may see Filliozat (1954) and, on Bhartṛhari's concept of mokṣa, Subramania Iyer (1964).

The Bhartṛharian understanding of Speech at once looks back to the ṚVedic concept of Vāc and forward to the elaboration in a Tantric context of Vāc as Śakti. For a general interpretation, see P. S. Shastri (c. 1955); on possible Vedic precedents for this development see Madhava Krishna Sarma (1943), Marulasiddiah (c. 1951), and Sreekrishna Sarma

(1957); for the treatment of Vāc in the Tantric traditions see the survey of Padoux (1963) and the discussion on page 430; for the South Indian Śaiva Siddhānta, see Sivaraman (1973, 220–34), which focuses on the concepts of *nāda, bindu,* and the evolution of the *śabdaprapaca* (the speech-world).

Pūrvamīmāṃsā

Of the so-called systems of philosophy, Mīmāṃsā is arguably the one whose significance has been most underestimated. Its importance lies quite simply in its paradigmatic character. Along with Vyākaraṇa, it sets out positions concerning the efficacy of ritual action and the efficacy of verbal authority that touch the central preoccupations of Indian culture or at least of Indian "high culture." At the risk of overgeneralization, one might observe that India has been fascinated by the ritual and psychological possibilities for "action at a distance" and by the power of speech. Staal (1976, 109) remarks, "Indian culture may be characterized by its emphasis on linguistics in the way Western culture may be characterized by its emphasis on mathematics."* It is the word and not the number that had been central. To put it more carefully, in spite of the numerical systems in Indian ritual and in spite of the penchant of Indian scholasticism for numerical classification—for instance, 273 kinds of *ṛk mantras* (Jha 1942, 166), 1032 distinct sorts of inference (Potter 1963, 91, citing Stasiak, 1929)—it was the rhetorician rather than the mathematician who was a culture hero. Hence, the intellectual priority of Vyākaraṇa and Mīmāṃsā, and hence, too, the social priority of the guru, for the guru is master of the word (see pages 412–14).

The best general introduction to the Mīmāṃsā tradition is probably provided by G. Jha (1942); for briefer but older accounts, see Keith (1921) and Kane (1924), also P. Shastri (1923). The literature is surveyed in a seventy-five-page essay by U. Mishra (1942), published as an appendix in Jha (1942). One must approach the Mīmāṃsā both from the perspective of Vedic exegesis and scholastic philosophy. Śabara cites roughly two thousand passages from the Veda, but none of these are from the *Sāma-* or *Atharvaveda,* and only forty-six are mantras from the ṚV. Most are from the texts of the Taittirīya tradition (i.e., the YV), and some two hundred, "being unidentifiable, may be supposed to have been quoted from texts lost to us" (Gonda 1975a, 50, n. 53, citing Garge; Renou 1960, #40).** On the treatment of the Veda in the Mīmāṃsā the works of Garge (1949; 1952), focusing on the use of the ṚV, are especially valuable. The foundational text of the system is the *ŚabaraBh,* a commentary on Jaimini's *MīmāṃsāSū.* From it, two interpretative traditions have di-

---

**Staal makes this remark while speculating, in reference to Allen (1955), that the "linguistic zero" may well have preceded the "mathematical zero."*

***I cite this work by paragraph so that reference can be made equally to its French and English versions.*

verged. One takes its point of departure from the work of Kumārila Bhaṭṭa (seventh century), author of the *Ślokavārttika, Tantravārttika* and *Ṭupṭīkā,* which together provide a commentary on the *ŚabaraBh,* the other is from the work of Prabhākara Miśra (seventh/eighth centuries),* author of an alternative commentary on Śabara's *Bhāṣya,* the *Bṛhatī.* Available translations (variously reprinted) include, for the *ŚabaraBh,* Jha (1933), with index by U. Mishra published separately (1945), and on *MīmāṃsāSū* 1.1.1–5, see Frauwallner (1968); for the *Ślokavārttika,* Jha (1900–09); for the *Tantravārttika,* Jha (1903–24); also on Prabhākara, see Jha (1911). The *Mīmāṃsā Kośa,* a standard reference work in Sanskrit, was referred to earlier on page 377.

Three late, brief treatises, all reflecting the Kumārila tradition, may also serve as introductions and may well be more accessible to the general reader. Chief among them is the *Mīmāṃsānyāyaprakāśa* of Āpadeva (early seventeenth century), translated by Edgerton (1929); see also the *Arthasaṃgraha* of Laugākṣi Bhāskara (late sixteenth century), translated by Gajendragadkar and Karmarkar (1934), and in German see Oertel (1930); and the *Mānomeyodaya* of Nārāyaṇa Bhaṭṭa (early seventeenth century), translated by Kunhan Raja and Suryanarayana Sastri (1933).

Among the large secondary literature, a few items of interest may be mentioned: Edgerton (1928), Garge (1949) on Śabara and the science of grammar, Zangenburg (1962), G. P. Bhatt (1962) on epistemology, Schmithausen (1965) on Maṇḍana Miśra's *Vibrahmaviveka,* D'Sa (1974) on *śabdapramāṇam;* Moghe (1971) and Halbfass (1983) both dealing with Śaṃkara and Mīmāṃsā; on Maṇḍana's *Sphoṭasiddhi* see pages 380–81. A general survey of Mīmāṃsāka theories of language is found in P. K. Mazumdar (1977). Recently, there have been two ambitious attempts to reconstruct the significance of Mīmāṃsā "hermeneutics." Both works, D'Sa (1980) and Gächter (1983), are directly relevant for an assessment of linguistic speculation in traditional India but should be read with caution; cf. the reviews of Taber (1983; 1985). See also Pannikar (1964).

The Mīmāṃsā as a system of exegesis is predicated on the existence of the Veda. In spite of the extraordinary care with which the Vedic corpus was preserved, far greater care than that bestowed on Jewish or Christian scriptures, variants of some of the 10,000 Vedic mantras do occur. These are listed in Bloomfield and Edgerton (1931). There has been very little systematic work on the nature of the Vedic corpus in comparison to the scriptures and canons of other traditions. Comparative orientation may be found in Lanczkowski (1961), O'Flaherty (1979), W. C. Smith (1980), and Graham (1984). Specifically for Indian "scriptures," Coburn (1984) provides a new point of departure. Among other relevant works see Singer (1961), Biardeau (1968), Gough (1968),

**The dates and relationship of these two figures has occasioned considerable discussion that cannot be surveyed here.*

Lancaster (1979), and Coburn (1980). See, too, the discussion of orality and literacy in traditional India, on pages 355–58.

Recently a few scholars, some associated with what might be called the Vienna School of Hindu Studies, have begun exploring the character of religious authority in the various traditions recognizing the Veda. Unlike most Indological work and unlike most work stemming from *Religionswissenschaft*, the work of these scholars is concerned with theological issues and with the shape and integrity of the Hindu tradition qua tradition. The importance of this work for mantric studies is twofold. Besides exploring another strand in the complex religious context of traditional India, it raises the kind of issues that would have to be explored if contemporary theologians were to engage the question May a mantric utterance be assessed as true or false? Oberhammer's (1980) essay on "*Überlieferungsstruktur und Offenbarung*," in the Hindu tradition, is representative. Oberhammer and Waldenfels (1984) undertake an extended exploration of the themes of truth and transcendence in two authors who represent different sorts of theism: Pakśilasvāmin (Vātsyāyana), the fifth century author of the *Nyāyasūtrabhāṣya*, and Bhāsarvaja, the ninth century Naiyāyika and Pāśupata. See also three valuable collection of essays by Oberhammer (1974, on revelation; 1978, on *Transzendenzerfahrung;* and 1982, on *Heilsgegenwart*). The theme of revlation is explored further by Coward and Sivaraman (1977). On the understanding of Vedic authority in the Nyāya and Vaiśeṣika traditions, see Chemparathy (1982; 1983, with refs.). For a study of nineteenth-century Hindu anti-Christian apologetics, see R. F. Young (1981).

The general purpose of Mīmāṃsā is to provide systematic, rational grounding for Brahmanic "orthodoxy". Therefore it begins by discussing the injunctions (*vidhi*) concerning sacrifice found in the Brāhmaṇas. It turns secondarily to the (ritual) uses to which particular mantras are applied. On the ritual and grammatical context in which the Mīmāṃsāka speculation about language emerged, see Renou (1941–42). The texts of Mīmāṃsā do not, in general, provide stipulative definitions of mantra. In the words of Jha (1942, 159), referring to *MīmāṃsāSū* 2.1.32, "the more logical writers on Mīmāṃsā have contented themselves with explaining *Mantra* as a name applied to 'those Vedic texts that are expressive of mere *Assertion* (as distinguished from *Injunction*)'." Representative discussions of the Mīmāṃsā analysis of mantra may be found in many of the introductions and translations cited earlier. See, for example, Jha (1942, 159–86) and the third section ("Mantravibhāga") of the *Arthasaṃgraha* (Gajendragadkar & Karmarkar (1934, 42–46, with extensive annotation 212–227); and, for a dense but clear summary, Renou (1960, #40–44).

Among the major issues in philosophy of language debated by the Pūrvamīmāṃsā were the relation of the words in a sentence to each other and to the sentence as such; whether words denote universals or particulars; and the relationship between word and meaning. For a digest of the discussions, see Staal (1976, 112–17). Many of the works listed above, for example those focusing on Patajali and Bhartṛhari, also deal with Mīmāṃsā. The Mīmāṃsākas assumed that the Veda is not a document of human composition (it is *apauruṣeya*), therefore, they devoted considerable energy to demonstrating the indivisibility of words and the eternality of the Veda. On the latter doctrine, see Abegg (1923). Frauwallner (1960a; also 1961) has argued that the Mīmāṃsāka acceptance of the eternality of sounds reflects the influence of the Vaiyākaraṇas. In this connection, see U. Mishra (1926) on the "physical theory of sound" in Indian thought.

On the fate of the Veda in the post-Vedic age, there is a dense and marvelous monograph by Renou (1960), which is best read in conjunction with works that explore the cultural continuity between "Brahmanism" and "Hinduism" in general; for example, Gonda (1965) and Pensa (1972). The continuation of the oral tradition of Vedic recitation up to the present is well documented, but it is less clear to what extent—if at all—the meaning of the text is understood. Gonda (1975a, 44) observes, the "neglect of the meaning of the Veda, condemned though it was by various authorities [Gonda cites Yāska, Śaṃkara, Manu], led many orthodox Brahmins to indulge in the thought that the meaning of the sacred corpus cannot be known." The best way to explore this problem is probably through the work of Staal, in which context it is fair to say that the trend of the evidence tends to support the position on the intrinsic meaninglessness of mantras qua mantras that Staal takes in this volume. See Staal (1958; 1961; 1963a; 1983); as well as Raghavan (1957; and, for a general survey, 1962); also Bake (1935), Gray (1959), Mencher (1966), C. G. Kashikar (1958), S. Kashikar (1966), and Renou (1949c).

The main features of the Mīmāṃsā attitude toward mantra is crystallized in the so-called Kautsa controversy, a dispute concerning the alleged meaninglessness (*ānarthakya*) of mantras. The earliest evidence for the discussion is found at *Nirukta* 1.15–16, and it occupies *MīmāṃsāSū* 1.2.31–45. The controversy is discussed again by the Vedic commentator Sāyaṇa (fourteenth century), on this, see Oertel (1930). Kautsa, the advocate of the meaninglessness of Vedic mantras, was no iconoclast. He clearly accepted the *efficacy* of Vedic sacrifice. The dispute turns on the nature of the mantras everyone agrees must be used in it. In Staal's words (1976, 112), Kautsa argued "so often the mantras appear simply absurd; they speak of things that simply do not exist (e.g., [a creature] with four horns, three feet, two heads, and seven hands); they are self-contradictory and often redundant; there is a tradition for them to be learnt by heart," but no comparable effort to learn their meanings. Now, Kautsa is, according to Renou, also considered the author of an Atharvan *Prātiśākhya*. This leads both Renou (1960a, 45) and Staal (1967, 24) to stress that the apparent context for Kautsa's "scepticism" was magical rather than rationalistic. It is not surprising, Staal (1967, 24) tells us, "that those ritualists who treated the mantras as charms, were hardly in a position to regard them at the same time as linguistically meaningful utterances."

This merits reflection. In many respects, Kautsa strikes one as a bedfellow of those Christian theologians who took the absurdity of revelation as a sign of its authenticity. And yet, his views scandalized the Brahmanic establishment. In other words, the Mīmāṃsakas seem to have put themselves in the interesting position of using mantras as if they were meaningless but thinking about them as if they were meaningful. From that social dichotomy flows many of the differences of opinion about mantras today. On Kautsa, there are succinct precis in Staal (1976, 112; 1967, 24f.) and a longer account in Renou (1960a, 45–50), also Garge (1940). For a further discussion of these issues see the essay by Taber in this volume.

Other Philosophical Traditions

Uttaramīmāṃsā or Vedānta is that strand of the Brahmanical tradition that focuses on the *jānakāṇḍa,* the portion of the Veda dealing with liberating knowledge, knowledge of what is ultimate, rather than with sacrificial action. The lion's share of attention has gone to one form of Vedānta, the Advaitism, which reverses without always following the figure of Śaṃkara. The tradition is multifaceted nonetheless. Even within Advaita, the differences between one philosopher and another are hardly negligible. I shall not attempt to sketch out the differences here but instead focus on those aspects of Vedāntic reflection on language common to the tradition as a whole.

As a soteriology, the goal of Vedānta is to facilitate the direct apprehension of Brahman. As a philosophy, its goal is to articulate the principal point of the Veda. Obviously, then, assessing the status and soteriological role of the Vedic utterances that refer to Brahman was a subject of special importance for all forms of Vedānta. But the Vedāntic attitude toward language and, hence, toward the Veda is riddled with ambivalence.

All the forms of the tradition are suspicious of language: It is the premier tool of human bewilderment, however that is technically understood.* On the other hand, all are committed to an apparently verbal document, the Veda, as containing or being the chief means of awakening to the truth. In the final analysis, only two self-consistent positions appear possible. One may assert the ineffability of the ultimate, or conversely, one may assert its essential linguisticality. In its

**The general reader should be alerted to the fact that the different Vedāntins, even the different Advaitins used different vocabulary and strategy to explicate human nescience* (avidyā). *In particular, the followers of Śaṃkara diverge from Śaṃkara. Therefore, it is advisable to avoid the word* illusion *in explicating their thought unless one specifies exactly what is meant. See the references to the work of Paul Hacker.*

pure forms, the first position is paradigmatically Advaita and is taken by Śaṃkara and certain of his followers, notably Sureśvara; the second position is also Advaita but not in the way that term is often understood in the popular literature. It is taken paradigmatically by Bhartṛhari.

In other words, there is an internal debate within Vedānta concerning the status of verbal expressions as instruments of liberation. The different sorts of Vedānta evaluate differently the key mantras of the Veda, and by analogy any other mantra. It is not a question of whether they are effective but of how and why they work. It is important to grasp that the ambivalence towards words was real and deep. This means that, for traditional India, the ineffable nature of mystic experience was by no means self-evident. Bhartṛhari (VP 3.3.20) pins the tail on the donkey with admirable directness, "that which is spoken of as unspeakable, as soon as it is obtained as spoken of by that unspeakability, is spoken of."*

Potter (1981, 54) summarizes this by contrasting the attitudes toward language of Śaṃkara and the Maṇḍana Miśra. The former, he tells us, characterizes language as an instrument of ignorance but "finds the mechanism of liberation ultimately in an act that requires speech." For him, even the most significant pronouncements of the Veda "are ultimately false." Nonetheless, "one can be liberated by a falsehood, just as one can be killed by being frightened by an illusory snake." The latter, in contrast, endorses the *śabdāvaita* thesis that Brahman is language. For him, "Brahman is consciousness, . . . consciousness is the power of speech, . . . Brahman is of the nature of speech; the whole universe is a manifestation (*vivarta*) of speech."

The single most important focus of this discussion are the *mahāvākyas,* four or more "Great Utterances" found in the Upaniṣads.** Now the *mahāvākyas,* at least in some regards, are mantras: They are verses from the Veda; they are objects of repeated meditation; they are instruments of liberation; they are slogans enunciating the truth. It is interesting that the divergence in the Vedāntic attitude toward the *mahāvākyas* exactly parallels the divergence in attitude towards mantras in general that exists in the tradition and in the scholarly debate today. For those who believe they are really linguistic instruments, aligning themselves with Bhartṛhari and Maṇḍana, they work because they lead to understanding, albeit deep, extraordinary understanding. For those who believe they are nonlinguistic, aligning themselves with the tradition of mystic ineffability, they work "magically," by occasioning a

---

* avācyam iti yad vācyaṃ tad avācyatayā yadā
vacyam ity avasīyeta vācyam eva tadā bhavet.

This is cited by Kunnjuni Raja (1969, 254). I cite the translation of Staal (1976, 126).

***The exact number varies. The four sentences most commonly cited are* ahaṃ brahmāsmi *(I am Brahman), BṛhU 1.4.10;* tat tvam asi *(You are that), ChU 6.8.7ff.;* prajānaṃ brahma *(Brahman is wisdom) AiU 3.5.3; and* ayam ātmā brahma *(This self is Brahman),* MāṇḍūkyaU *4.2.*

"leap," an ultimately inexplicable transformation of one's way of being in the world.

Another crux of interpretation is the term *vācārambhaṇa*, which occurs in the *sadvidyā* (ChU 6.1ff.), the teaching of Uddālaka about the "being" or "substance" that underlies phenomenal diversity. It has been translated, for example, as "verbal handle" and "seizing by Speech." Specifically, on this phrase or chapter, see van Buitenen (1955b; 1958), Kuiper (1957; 1958), Hamm (1968–69), and Morgenroth (1970).

The hermeneutical ambivalence of Vedānta led it to adopt a number of strategies, in particular employing the concept of "secondary meanings" and metaphorical interpretaion to explicative Vedic statements about Brahman. A capsule account of this may be found in Staal (1976, 126f.). This opens out towards an extensive primary and secondary literature on Indian poetics, which is obviously central to any apprehension of the place of language in traditional Indian culture. Its relevance to the study of mantras, however, is limited or, at least, as yet unexplored. Suffice it to mention the most accessible general works: De (1960), Kane (1961), Raghavan (1942), and for a survey of the literature, Gerow (1977). On the term *alaṃkāra,* see Gonda (1939b). On possible connections between grammatical and poetic reflection, see Renou (1941) dealing with Mammaṭa, the late eleventh–early twelfth century author of the *Kāvyaprakāśa*.

There is an extensive but not entirely reliable literature on Vedānta. I mention a few items, especially on Śaṃkara, some of which the reader might otherwise overlook. For a summary of the treatment of philosophy of language in early Advaita see Potter (1981, 46–61). In my judgment the most reliable and accessible brief introduction to Śaṃkara in English is Mayeda (1979, 3–97). Still unsurpassed, however, is the extended discussion in de Smet (1953), a dissertation on the theological method of Śaṃkara that, mysteriously, has never been published. For a brief digest, see de Smet (1954). Mostly in German, the writings of Paul Hacker are without peer; see the bibliography in Hacker (1978). For a general survey of the interpretation of the Veda in the Advaita tradition of Vedānta one may see the monograph of K. S. Murty (1959), which gives special attention to the problem of "language and Brahman" (pp. 53–67) and the *Mahāvākyas* (pp. 68–87); see also G. Miśra (1971).

For comparable discussions on Rāmānuja, see van Buitenen (1956, 48–69) and Carman (1974), which also deals (pp. 158–66) with Rāmānuja's understanding of the names of god. As this suggests, several forms of Vedānta were allied with Vaiṣṇava devotionalism. Rāmānuja himself is supposed to have written a work on rites on purification, and Vedāntadeśika "wrote a considerable number of theological works in explanation of the mantras which . . . were considered to be of fundamental significance"; for instance, the *caramaśloka,* BhG 18.66, "Abandoning all duties, come to me alone for protection; I shall release you from all evils, be not grieved" ([Gonda 1963b] 1975b, 4.268). As to the Davita tradition, see Siauve (1959), *Les Noms védiques de Viṣṇu,* a translation of Madhava's commentary on BSū 1.1. *adhikaraṇa* 2–12. See, too, the material on Vaiṣṇava theism on pages 366–69.

Vedānta, like Mīmāṃsā, defines the context in which the use of mantras makes sense, but in a curiously divergent manner. There is a direct continuity between the Vedāntic discussions concerning language and illusion and the popularity of mantras as epistemological tools in Tantra. Vedānta articulates the underside of India's love affair with words: A widespread ontological suspicion that ordinary language is a snare. If verbalization is the most pregnant mark of the common, the *vyavahārika,* if verbalization is the problem, then it is poetically just for a radical form of verbalization, a form that can be considered verbal-yet-more-than-verbal, to serve as an antidote. If one were surprised by the use of mantras both for transcendental and mundane, even malicious, ends, one should remember that the concept of *māyā* was employed with equal enthusiasm in Vedānta and in Indian magical texts. In this regard, see the important essay of Goudriaan (1978), especially Chapter 5, "Under Indra's Net" (211–250).

The systematic reflection of Buddhism forms a broad counterpart to the Hindu intellectual traditions and was probably a stimulus for the systematization of it. Within India, what we call Hinduism and Buddhism were overlapping strands of a single culture. Just as the Brahmanical tradition defined itself in terms of the authority of the Veda, Buddhism defined itself in terms of the authority of its scriptures. The exegetical and philosophical problems that arose from these two enterprises, therefore, were comparable. Since it is hardly feasible to survey this development here, I limit myself to citing a few items that may provide philosophical background for the treatment of language in Buddhist philosophy. For some references on mantras in Indian and Tibetan Buddhism, see pages 439–40.

Whatever they shared, the flavor of Buddhism is distinctive. Staal (1976, 118) goes so far as to say that "the entire early Buddhist approach constitutes the origination of a kind of analysis which reminds us of British 'ordinary language' philosophy. Both proceed in an essentially similar way: specific examples from ordinary language and philosophically interesting cases are discussed, but no general semantic theory is evolved." Of course, between the era of the *Abhidharma* (beginning c. 300 B.C.) and the figure of Dignāga (fifth century), the Buddhist community developed not just a formal semantics but an entire philosophical tradition of great subtlety. The best place to begin examining it is perhaps with Jayatilleke (1963), which set a new standard in the study of early Buddhist thought. The last half of the book deals with problems of authority, reason, logic, meaning, and truth. See especially paragraphs 520–59 on the emergence of Indian linguistic philosophy. On the analysis of words and meanings among the Vaibhāṣikas, one of the early schools, see P. S. Jaini (1959).

Although the application of Western philosophical categories to the Indian context is somewhat problematic, it is possible to characterize Buddhist thought as "nominalistic," over against the "realism," at least, of the Nyāya tradition. This contrast has been explored a number of times from different perspectives. The issues are set out clearly, but with a Naiyāyika bias, by D. N. Shastri (1964). This provides sufficient background to approach the *apoha* theory of the Buddhist logicians: The meaning of a word refers neither to a class (*jāti*) nor to a discrete particular (*svalakṣaṇa*), it merely "excludes" everything else to which it does not refer; on this, see Frauwallner (1930–37). If one traces the development of the different strands of Buddhism, notably Vijñānavāda and Madhyamaka, one finds a tension between the need to affirm and the need to transcend ordinary reality. As in Vedānta, this leads to the development of a "two truths" epistemology and the complex problems of illusionism and idealism. For example, see the essays in Sprung (1973).

Āyurveda *and Other Traditions of Indian Science*

It seems likely that the Indian scientific traditions did not escape the pervasion of Indian culture by mantras. One wonders especially to what extent their use came into conflict with the empirical elements of those traditions. But the study of the use of mantras in the Indian scientific, and especially medical, traditions has hardly begun. Much work will have to be completed before the scientific background, if any, to Mantraśāstra can be sketched. I can do no more here than testify to the need for such exploration.

Healing is a field in which scientific and folk practitioners have surely competed. As indicated earlier, a significant portion of the mantras in the AV can be considered medical. Kakar (1982) in exploring various forms of counseling and psychotherapy in contemporary India discusses the use of mantra in two contexts. For his treatment of mantric healing among tribal shamans see page 436. More interesting is a long, sympathetic exposition (Kakar 1982, 151–90) of Tantric healing, to which, of course, utterance of the right mantra is central. Kakar's account places Tantra in a popular, oral setting of fears and fantasies in whose terms one can begin to see the psychological sense Mantraśāstra makes in India today, something which is by no means self-evident from the texts. His treatment is further noteworthy in avoiding the extremes of credulity typical of "devotees," on the one hand, or the conclusion, on the other, that mantric utterance merely leads, in the words of J. M. Masson (1980, 130), to a "peculiar loss of rational faculties"; for a discussion of Yoga and psychoanalysis, see Masson (1976).

In light of this, one is tempted to classify the often Tantricized traditions of exorcism and demonology as a form of traditional Indian "psychiatry" rather than magic. See the significant study and translation of the *Kumāratantra* by Filliozat (1937), in connection with which, see

Goudriaan (1977). This text, which circulated in Tamil, Arabic, Cambodian, and Chinese, should not be confused with a different text of the same name cited on page 419. The most extended analysis of a healing tradition that involves mantric utterance I have come across is Stablein (1976) and, for a briefer account, (1973), which, however, focuses on "ritual blessings" in the Tantric Buddhism of Tibet. On medicine, besides Zysk's essay in this volume, his larger work (1985b) examines Vedic healing mantras and their religious and ritual significance and incorporates philological analysis of the Vedic verses. Also important is Karambelkar (1961) and, among general works, Filliozat (1943; 1949; 1952). (Jean Filliozat has written numerous essays on the intersecting fields of Indian medicine, yoga, and psychology. See the bibliography in Filliozat 1974, xi–xxv.) The literature on South Asian shamanism is too large to be surveyed here. See, for example, Hitchcock and Jones (1976). For further references on healing traditions, see the section on regional ethnography, pages 373–75.

I assume that the use of mantras or analogous formulas can be found in the Indian alchemical tradition, whether it be classified as chemistry, psychology, or mysticism. Among standard works, one might see, on chemistry, P. C. Ray (1902–09) and P. R. Ray (1956). Specifically on the alchemical (*rasāyana*) tradition, see P. R. Ray (1967). A certain amount of work has been done on the figure of Nāgārjuna the physician and mystic, who is presumably not to be identified with the author of the *Madhyamikakārikās*. See, for example, Filliozat (1940) and Walleser (1923). Some further bibliography may be found in Eliade (1969) with attention to Chinese parallels.

TANTRA

ORIENTATION AND GENERAL STUDIES

For the most part, in all of the contexts in which they have been employed—in the domestic ritual of the householder, the communal ritual of the temple, the discipline of the solitary renouncer, the *sādhanā* of a guru and his disciples—the mantras of the past millenium have been Tantric. Coversely, it is commonly conceded that the use of mantras is, in Bharati's (1965, 101) words, "on the technical side . . . the chief instrument of Tantrism." Thus, to understand Mantraśāstra presupposes reaching at least a preliminary assessment of Tantra as such.

For long, Tantra was a stepchild of Indology, ignored or undervalued by Western scholars and representatives of the so-called Hindu Renaissance. Today, Tantra is in the process of becoming fashionable. Yet, the meaning of the term resists precise definition and its history remains unclear. Moreover, as is now generally acknowledged, there is no strict distinction in usage between the textual terms *tantra*, *āgama*, and *saṃhitā*. A careful semantic history of the term *tantra* remains a desideratum. Ideally, such an account would connect the Tantric meaning of the term with its meaning in the Vedic sacrificial system—loom, thread, framework, "the structure common to sacrifices of a certain sort" (cf. Renou 1954c, 69f.)—as well as its common literary meaning, as in the title of the famous collection of tales, the *Pañcatantra, "The* Five Books." Pending a general semantic mapping, the exact force and connotation of the term must remain somewhat uncertain. Yet, the Vedic and literary meanings seem relevant. The first usage suggests the liturgical precision that characterizes Tantra as a ritual system. The second usage suggests the notoriety, the heady rebelliousness against "establishment" sensibility, that characterizes Tantra as a social phenomenon.

In the past twenty years and especially in the past decade, the foundation has been laid for a sophisticated scholarly examination of Tantra. The "renaissance" in Tantric studies began with the publication of Padoux (1963) and, in the English-speaking world, Bharati (1965). The former, especially central to the student of Mantraśāstra, is to appear soon in a revised English version. The latter is a work that, whatever emendations specialists might today wish to propose (Goudriaan [1981, 2] characterizes it as "not a reliable guide"), remains a model for its clear textual, philosophical, and sociological method. See, however, the extended review of Saraf (1974). More recently, the three landmarks in Tantric studies have been the relevant volumes of the HIL and the HO: Gonda (1977a), Gupta, Hoens, and Goudriaan (1979), and Goudriaan and Gupta (1981).* Before consulting these volumes, one should see the review of the second written by Padoux (1981).

Among other general introductions to Tantra one may consult, but should not rely on uncritically, Bagchi (1939), Chakravarti (1963), Kapali Śāstry (1971), and N. Bhattacharyya (1982). Caution also should be exercised in consulting Evola (1949) and Varenne (1977). For a philosophically engaged introduction to Tantric thought, there is K. Mishra (1981), which focuses on the Tantric Śaivism of Kashmir as understood by the late and revered *paṇḍit*, Rameshwar Jha. For a, more or less, Marxist analysis that attempts to situate the rise of Tantra within the history of popular "materialism," see Chattopadhyay's study (1959) of the *Lokāyatas*. Perhaps the best way to gain a representative contemporary Indian (i.e., neo-Hindu) view on Tantra in English is through the relevant, lively, sympathetic essays in the fouth volume of CHI (H. Bhattacharyya, 1956), namely those of Basu, Bagchi, Pratyagatmananda (Sarasvati), A. B. Ghosh, K. R. Venkataraman, B. Bhattacharyya, Sen, S. B. Dasgupta, V. V. Ramana Sastri, and C. Chakravarti. Alternatively, one might see R. K. Rai (1976), L. P. Singh (1976), and the items concerning neo-Hinduism on page 435. For general introductions to Buddhist Tantra, see pages 438–39.

In spite of the many strictures that can be expressed, it seems to me

**The bulk of the material I cite from this volume comes from part I (1–172); hence, I usually cite it as Goudriaan and Gupta (1981).*

that one should not in general turn up one's nose at the work of Sir John Woodroffe (Arthur Avalon) (d. 1936). To be sure, it is "pioneering," which is to say methodologically unsophisticated, yet its very naivety can charm, and it still has its uses.* His introduction to the *Kādimata* or *TantrarājaT* (rep. 1971), which Goudriaan and Gupta (1981, 64) describe as a "useful, but sometimes whimsical" survey that often fails to discriminate between the Tantra and its commentary, is representative. The varying evaluations of the *MahānirvāṇaT* itself illustrates the swings in attitude: cf. Woodroffe (1959); Bharati (1965, 321), "the most important Hindu Tantra"; Derrett (1977), who classifies the text as a "juridical fabrication"; and Halbfass (1981), who considers the matter in the context of discussing Rammohan Roy's "hermeneutical situation."

Those able to read Indian languages can consult the studies and collected essays of the traditionally trained and renowned Gopinath Kaviraj (1963a), in Bengali, and (1963b; 1963–64), both in Hindi. In evaluating Gopinath's contribution to our understanding of Tantra, one may consult Dviveda (1978). Vraj Vallabha Dviveda, in fact, is the "dean" of contemporary *paṇḍits* specializing in Tantra, and there is no more concise digest of traditional Tantraśāstra than his introduction to the NṢA (1968), an abridged English translation of which, prepared by Teun Goudriaan, is to be published in a handbook on the Śaiva traditions of Kashmir edited by Alper (forthcoming). One might see, too, the "Upodghāta," which Dviveda has contributed to the fourth volume of the GOS edition of the ŚST; the various prefaces in English and Sanskrit he contributed to Gopinath Kaviraj's edition of the YH and the introduction to his edition of the MM (1972). Bharati (1965, 332) cites a *Mantraśāstramātṛkāgranthānām Vivaraṇātmikā Sūcikā* (Descriptive Index of Mantra Texts and of Mātṛkās) (Subramanya Sastri n.d.); he praises it as an "excellent, critical and modern catalogue of Tantric material"; but I have not seen it nor found reference to it in other secondary literature and cannot vouch for its utility. For other contemporary works in the Indian vernaculars, see pages 434–39.

THE IDEOLOGY OF TANTRA

Bharati (1965, 13–40) provides a brief but clear-headed discussion of the "philosophical content of Tantra." He points out that what is common to Tantra is an attitude: "the systematic emphasis on the identity of the absolute (*paramārtha*) and the phenomenal (*vyavahāra*) world when

---

**It seems to me, too, that Woodroffe's influence in setting the agenda for Tantric studies and in disseminating an attitude towards Tantra can easily be underestimated. For example, in his introduction to the* Mahānirvāṇa Tantra *([1913] 1973, 66), Woodroffe cites a potent metaphor but without a clear textual reference: The guru is the root (*mūla*) of initiation; initiation is the root of mantra; mantra is the root of* devatā*; and* devatā *is the root of* siddhi*. In effect, this enters the handbooks as a definitive statement, being cited in Renou et al. (1947–53, 597. #1225) without attribution, and in Gonda (1963a, 37) with attribution.*

filtered through the experience of *sādhanā*" (p. 18). In other words, what defines Tantra is practice (*sādhanā*) rather than thought. There is really no such thing as a single Tantric ideology, no less systematic philosophy. Thus, while Buddhist and Hindu praxis is essentially identical, the vocabulary and conceptual schemes in whose terms they are understood and articulated differ to the extent of being irreconcilable.

The intellectual schemes implicit or explicit in many Hindu Tantras reflect several currents of the common Hindu thought-world of the middle of the first millenium A.D. The one that has received the most attention is probably Advaita. As a current in the common Indian mentality, rather than as an organized philosophical system, it seems to have become gradually more prestigious and influential century by century. It will be discussed on pages 441–43.

Broadly conceived, the Sāṃkhya tradition was arguably more significant in providing an ideology for Tantra, at least in its formative period. From Sāṃkhya, Tantra has borrowed and embroidered large elements of cosmology, including the analysis of reality in terms of three constitutive strands (*guṇas*), the concept of *prakṛti* as a primal and feminine *Urstoff,* and the ostensibly cosmogonic scheme of *tattva* evolution. This Sāṃkhyan component of Tantra has directly influenced Tantric Mantraśāstra, but to the best of my knowledge, it has never been made the subject of focused study. To take an example from the Tantric currents prominent among the Śaiva traditions of Kashmir, the notion of a hierarchy of types of animate *beings,* arrayed in terms of an expanded Sāṃkhyan cosmology, includes *Mantras, Mantreśas,* and *Mantramaheśas.* This is discussed at length in the ninth and tenth *āhnikas* of Abhinavagupta's *Tantrāloka,* which well illustrates the soteriological interests that shaped the use of Sāṃkhyan material in Tantra. The system of *pramātṛs* is currently being examined by Chr. Humbrecht.

Another motif that reflects Sāṃkhyan influence, as well as that of Bhartṛharian thought, and that has received some attention, is that of the so-called six paths (*ṣaḍadhvan*). These are two triads of sequences, each sequence consisting of five elements or "levels", must be understood at once as processes of cosmic emanation and of individual "return." One of the triads corresponds to the realm of the "signifying agent" (*vācaka*) and the other to that of the "signified object" (*vācya*). The sequences belonging to the former, arranged from most to least subtle, are designated *varṇa-, mantra-,* and *padādhvan;* that is, the *adhavans* of *akṣaras* (primordial letters) of mantras that are intermediate and of the prototypes of words and sentences (*padas*). It would be inappropriate to provide more detail here. Suffice it to say that, in this Sāṃkhyan context, mantra has been reified as a cosmological category but only so that it can be presented as the central element in a complex meditative soteriology. This scheme, and the Sāṃkhyaizing of Mantraśāstra in general, certainly merits further study. See the forthcoming revision of Padoux (1963, 261–91), which will devote a chapter, focusing on the eleventh section of the *Tantrāloka* and the fourth section of the *SvacchandaT*, to the *ṣaḍadhvan*. As background, one should see Hacker's study (1961) of the Sāṃkhyization of the emanation doctrine in the *Purāṇas*. In general, in a Tantric context the schemata of emanation became more and more baroque, as did the parallel schemes of meditative stages, deities, and mantras. Meriting special study is the elaboration of the four, five, seven, or however many internal constituents of OṂ (for example, cf. Goudriaan, in Gupta, Hoens, & Goudriaan 1979, 52f.).

As the section of this Bibliography dealing with Śaktism will indicate, the hypothesis that Tantra is a development of village Hinduism and an expression of folk consciousness has proved attractive to a number of researchers. One of the clearest and most outspoken statements of this theory is Chattopadhyay (1959) who, as mentioned earlier, places Tantra within the context of an indigenous Indian materialism. It should be observed that in regard to Mantraśāstra this theory complements those that emphasize its ritual character and especially its magical *Sitz und leben*.

Tantric Deities

In considering the deities of Mantraśāstra or of Tantra more broadly, two motifs and two lines of inquiry emerge. On the one hand, one may consider the deities to whom mantras are addressed or whose existence they presuppose as prima facie, external to both the mantra and the person who utters it. In that case, the task is to catalogue the deities. From another perspective, the mantra, its *devatā*, and the person who utters the mantra are held to be or to become in some sense one, although the difference between them is never *wholly* effaced (or denied). In this case, the task is to understand the nature of the asserted unity and to decipher how mantric ritual is understood to effect or manifest it. Obviously, for a well-rounded comprehension of mantric deities both lines of inquiry must be followed. The first approach will be most significant when considering mantric utterance in a quotidian context, the second will be most significant in a redemptive context, to the extent that redemptive Mantraśāstra became self-reflective. I limit myself here to a few remarks concerning the deities considered as external. For the second line of inquiry, see the sections dealing with Tantra and Advaita, and with *sādhanā* (pages 401–402 and 411, respectively).

Goudriaan (Gupta, Hoens, & Goudriaan 1979, 63–66) gives some sense of the complexity of mantric theism, but care should be taken in recognizing that, in India, we find neither an organized pantheon nor even a group of overlapping organized pantheons. A coherent typology for comparing and contrasting mantric deities has not yet been proposed. A few guidelines may be offered provisionally, however. One way of making a rough distinction among mantric *devatās* would be in terms of a scale paralleling the one I proposed in the Introduction. Setting up a continuum with the quotidian and village contexts at one pole and Tantric *sādhanā* practiced for "redemption" on the other, one might discriminate three sorts of mantric deities.

First are the small-scale deities, usually, but not always, goddesses who control particular powers. These are originally the objects of folk ritual, and to use the vocabulary of *Religionswissenschaft,* they may be construed as *Sondergötter* or *Daseinsmächte;* that is, specialized or location-specific "godlings," "power-substances" (cf. Gonda [1961b] 1975, 15). The use of mantras to compel these forces to behave in an acceptable manner is well illustrated in Diehl's *Instrument and Purpose.*

In the middle is the vast range of pan-Indian or major regional deities possessing (more or less) elaborate mythologies and literatures. Considering the extent of mantra as *the* characteristic form of Indian religious language, considering the numinous aura believed to surround the names of these gods and goddesses, it is probable that in one way or another every deity who has been "worshipped" has been the recipient, the *devatā,* of a mantra. While mantras have never been preeminently instruments of praise, it is probable that every deity has at one time or another been glorified mantrically. To cite an example of a deity whose adoration was once prominent but is no longer, Gonda (1977a, 240f.) cities the *Sūryāryadvādaśaka,* a Stotra to the Sun-god based on ṚV 1.50.11 to which *bījamantras* and the "twelve significant names" of the deity are added. Obviously, the innumerable refractions of Viṣṇu, Śiva, Kālī, their families, and their entourages fall in this group. This second broad category may remind us that the tendency of Westerners to compartmentalize Tantra and Bhakti as if they were opposites is misleading. In fact, there is considerable overlap. For one presentation of the issues, see Bolle (1965a).

Finally, at the other extreme would be those deities who exist solely as meditative hypostatizations, deities who are known solely as objects of meditative *sādhanā* and not as objects of devotion or supplication or subjects of sacred narrative. Such figures are best known in the Buddhist Tantra of Tibet, but their place in the Hindu meditative traditions merits exploration.

A list of the deities discussed in the various Tantras, and even in the secondary literature, is beyond the scope of this bibliography. Two illustrations of different sorts of material will have to suffice. On the deities mentioned in Kṛṣṇānanda's *Tantrasāra,* Goudriaan and Gupta (1981, 1.2) cite Sircar (1972–73). On the "boundary figure" of Tumburu—Gonda (1977a, 207) describes him as "a Gandharva [known in the Mhb and the BhāgP (?)] who in the course of time had become a hypostasis of Śiva"—see Goudriaan (1973).

Tantras "Śākta" and "Śāktic"

Within a Tantric setting, virtually all mantric utterance is śāktic, yet any discussion of "Śāktism" and Mantraśāstra is hindered from the start by the imprecision with which the term *Śāktism* has been used. As André Padoux (1981, 347) has put it, "The difficulty in defining the relationship between Tantrism and Śāktism is in fact due largely to the imprecision of these two notions which we inherited from a time when the Tantric texts were as yet little known, and when we had not yet realized the extent of the Tantric phenomenon."

On one pole are those scholars who interpret Śāktism in terms of the modern, Western myth of the Great Mother, which has been derived from the theories of Johann Jakob Bachofen and Carl G. Jung, for example. Allowing for individual differences, this position is represented by Heinrich Zimmer (1938), Erich Neumann (1963), Mircea Eliade (e.g., 1969, 202ff.), Stella Kramrisch (1975), and Wendell Beane (1977); compare Przyluski (1934; 1938); and on the theme of bipolarity in Indian religion, see Pensa (1974). Whatever its other merits might be, its Indological utility has been questioned, for instance by Kinsley (1975, 131),

> The weakness of this interpretation, especially as articulated by Neumann, is obvious. In an attempt to exegete Hindu mythology, another mythology has been offered as a key, the somewhat parochial, Western, male-chauvinist myth of individual assertiveness as expressive of the redeemed man (or the psychologically healthy man).

On the other pole are all those scholars who focus on *śakti* as a precise technical term in particular—Tantric *and non-Tantric*—texts. These scholars have found that the term refers to a capacity or capability that may or may not be personified as a goddess and that functions variously as epistemological, cosmological, ritual, and meditative (i.e., psychological). Somewhere between these two poles are the large number of scholars who have used the concept of Śāktism as a tool in the reconstruction of Indian religious history. They have tended to focus especially on the interaction between elite and popular or, especially in the past, Āryan and non-Āryan strata in the culture. Their definitions of Śāktism have varied but focus, in the end, on primordial cult of village goddesses. For example, N. Bhattacharyya (1974, xi) speaks of the "cult of the Female Principle." Kumar (1974, 1) speaks of the "worship of *śakti* or the female principle." He adds, apparently without sensing a possible contradiction, that "the term *śakti* represents female divinity in general and stands for the energizing power of some [male] divinity."

To compound the difficulty the terms *Śāktism* and *Tantra* frequently have been used as if they were interchangeable, but this is imprecise and misleading. Taking advantage of the ability to make either a Sanskrit or an English adjective out of the word *śakti,* I shall here adopt a convention I use in my own teaching: by *Śākta* I refer to those works, movements, or rituals in which ultimate reality is identified as some particular goddess; by *śaktic* I refer to those works, movements, or rituals that—however they identify ultimate reality: as a god, a goddess, or impersonally as, e.g., Brahman—presuppose that ultimate reality expresses itself in and as the world through a web of capabilities or potencies known as *śaktis*. This distinction facilitates the following generalization, from which, I believe, there are few if any exceptions: all Tantra is śāktic, but not necessarily Śākta; the worship of goddesses may be both, neither, or one but not the other.

On the various strands of Śāktism (Śākta and śāktic) a number of general works may provide initial orientation: N. Bhattacharyya (1974) provides a readable historical survey; Payne (1933) and Thompson and Spencer (1923) focus on the case of Bengal; von Glasenapp (1936b), in an essay in German, focuses on Śāktism in the Tantric context, on which one may still consult Woodroffe's classic *Shakti and Shakta* (1959); see also P. C. Chakravarti (1940), Sinha (1966), Sircar (1967), a valuable collection of essays; in Bengali, S. B. Dasgupta (1961) and U. K. Das (1966); in Hindi, R. Śarmā (1977), and Poddar and Goswami (1934). Many of these works are now superceded (cf. Coburn 1984a, 3) by the historical survey of Tiwari (1985), which, however, I have not yet seen.

J. N. Banerjea (1938) discusses the folk goddesses of the ancient and medieval periods, while P. Kumar (1974) surveys Purāṇic evidence for Śāktism. Tucci (1929–30) discusses the plausible, but by no means certain, hypothesis that the cults of the village goddesses contributed to the rise of Tantra, with which compare Tucci (1930). For Śāktism within a Buddhist context, see the important essay by Wayman (1962), which, by the way, contains a clear exposition of the sequence of *bījas* OṂ ĀḤ HŪṂ. His remarks on terminology ([1962] 1973, 165f.) should be noted:

> Modern scholars have been somewhat confused on [the subject of female energy and symbolism in Buddhism] by wholesale use of the term *śakti* (power) in reference to Buddhist goddesses. This term, general in Hindu Tantras, seldom occurs in the Buddhist Tantras, which actually employ the following generic words for the goddesses or females: *prajñā* (insight), *yoginī* (female *yogin*), *vidyā* (occult science or know-how—wisdom in its historic meaning including all academic learning), *devī* ("goddess" or queen), *mātṛ* (mother), *mātṛkā* (mother or letters), *ḍākinī* (fairy), *dūtī* (female messenger), *śurī* (heroine), and *mudrā* (seal or gesture).

From a ritual perspective and in a meditative or practical context, the proliferation of *śaktis* is typical of Tantra, but in order to understand the theory of Mantraśāstra, the figure of Vāc, with her refractions, is central. On this, see the discussion of the Tantric alphabet on pages 431–33; for background the discussion of Vāc in the Veda, see pages 334–35.

It is vital to remember that there is no unanimity as to whether there is a figure to be known as *the* Goddess; the goddesses vary in character as much as the gods. This is brought out clearly in a recent collection of essays, Hawley and Wulff (1982), which, however, focuses on Rādhā. There is not as yet any agreed upon typology to assist the general reader in sorting out the various goddesses, all of whose history is complex and some of whom share a number of names and titles. For rapid orientation, see the clear and helpful glossary in Hawley and Wulff (pp. 369–81), for a more detailed introduction see the discussion of epithets in Coburn (1984a, 89–208), which deals with the terms *caṇḍikā, ambikā, kālī, durgā, mahāmāyā, cāmuṇḍā, śakti, gaurī, lakṣmī,* and *śrī,* among others. The large and scattered ethnographic literature on the cult of the various goddesses cannot be surveyed here. For further references, see the selected bibliographies in Beane, Coburn, and Hawley and Wulff.

Among the various goddesses who figure prominently in Tantra, Kālī has probably attracted the most attention. But one should hardly imagine that most, no less all, Tantric goddesses are forms of Kālī. At the very least, in a Tantric context, one should distinguish Tripurasundarī "the most important Tantric form of Śrī/Lakṣmī" (Goudriaan & Gupta 1981, 1.58, 75), styled by Goudriaan patron of the Śrīkula and associated with the Śrīvidyā and Śrīcakra, from Kālī, the horrific patron of the Kālīkula. For a sensitive introduction to Kālī in general, see Kinsley (1975), also C. G. Hartman (1969) and Beane (1977). On the figure of Durgā, see Mazumdar (1906–07). A great deal has been written about the cult of Kālī and Durgā in Bengal; for instance, see Clark (1955), C. Chakravarti (1957), and Lupsa (1967), which deals with the eighteenth-century Bengali *bhakta* Rāmaprasād. Kapera (1966) collects material on the cult of Kālī in contemporary Benares. On the worship of Kālī in Kerala, Menon (1959); on Kāmākhyā, see Kakati (1948), a work that draws especially on the *KālikāP* and the *YoginīT* (Goudriaan & Gupta 1981, 1.84). On Lalitā, a figure apparently homologus to Śrī and Tripurā, see Dikshitar (1942).

The *KālikāP*, major sections of which are concerned with the worship of the Devī of Kāmarūpa (that is, Mahāmāyā and Kāmākhyā), is an important work that illustrates the continuity between Purāṇic and Tantric currents. On it, see van Kooij (1972) and, from a different but interesting perspective, Zimmer (1956). Van Kooij (pp. 4–5) indicates that the *KālikāP* "won a great amount of popularity among several Sanskrit writers on cults and festivals from the fourteenth century onwards," serving especially as a guide for the performance of the Durgāpūjā in Bengal and Assam. It thus might serve as the starting point of a careful examination of the continuum between text and context, as well as between mantric and Bhaktic utterance; that is, between temple ritual and devotional song in a major festival. It is interesting that as van Kooij reports,

> When A. Tarkatīrtha discovered that the actual practice of this festival was not based on any Sanskrit text known to him and "because a practice which is not founded upon the ancient Brahmanical texts has no merit at all, is even harmful" he composed the *Kālikāpurāṇīya-*

> *durgāpūjāpaddhati* in order to bring the ceremonies into harmony with the rules laid down in the KP. The book was published as late as 1920.

Might this indicate that in recent decades—or centuries—popular mantric utterance has been subject to the process of Sanskritization? Has this tempered or reversed the trend toward the gradual accretion of new, if anonymous mantras? The same questions could appropriately be asked concerning any of the major festivals.

Śāktism is one of those areas of scholarship where the unconscious bias of male scholars is especially noticeable. This bias seems to have operated in two directions. On the one hand, the very conceptualization of "*the* Goddess" tends to obscure the diversity of female deities, implicitly dehumanizing the diversity of women. After all, there is no comparable scholarly literature on the mythology of "*the* Great God." On the other hand, although much is sometimes made of Tantra as an expression of "the feminine" strand of Indian religious life, little solid reflection and research has been devoted to exploring the role of women in Tantric Hinduism. In the context of this essay at least two questions merit attention: First, how frequently did women become ritual or meditative authorities in Tantric circles? As an example, Goudriaan and Gupta (1981, 1.156) mentions Prāṇamañjarī, the third wife of the eighteenth-century Tantric writer Premanidhi. Second, in the course of the thousand years from 500 to 1500 A.D., were women's rituals Tantricized in a different fashion than men's rituals? In regard to Mantraśāstra, it would be interesting for a team of anthropologists to compare and contrast the use of mentras by men and women in a single Tantric communal context, but to the best of my knowledge, such a field project has never been undertaken. Indeed, detailed descriptions of goddess rituals by trained anthropologists are rare in any case. See Freed and Freed (1962).

Tantra and Advaita

The identification of all, most, or some Tantra as Advaita has been flawed by a failure to clearly distinguish the different meanings of that term.* If by nondualism one refers to the position that Brahman is the sole unsublatable reality or to the radical fideism of a Śrī Harṣa (see Granoff 1978 and Matilal 1977), then it is likely that few if any Tantras are nondualistic. But much of Hindu Tantra is nondualistic in that it envisions ultimate reality as *the unity of a single set*. In this sense, Tantra articulates a species of qualified Advaita that stresses the śāktic expressiveness of reality. The tension between the śāktic and the Advaitic in Tantra is reflected in the hagiographic account in the life of Śaṃkara (the *Śaṃkaradigvijaya*), according to which the Goddess is supposed to

**For the sake of convenience I use the English expression* nondualism *in a philosophically loose sense as a ready translation of Advaita.*

have appeared to the master of nondualism and revealed the ultimacy of Śakti to him (Bharati 1965, 36, n. 9). On a theoretical level, this tension expresses itself in two ways: The *devatá* of a mantra may be understood as either external to or internal to the person who employs the mantra; second, the *devatā* may be understood as either external to or one with the mantra itself. The underlying consensus of Tantra is that the mantra is in some sense the deity. Thus, the *NetraT* conceives of god as *mantrarāja*, king of mantras, in all of which he is present (Gonda 1977a, 207f.). There is no easy way out: To assert, as is routinely done, that "Mantra is Consciousness" and thus ultimately redemptive but also that different mantras serve different mundane purposes raises the same philosophical puzzle as asserting both that ultimate reality is nondual and that it is the cause of the world.

The "traditional" classification that distinguishes between dualistic and nondualistic Tantras, although emphasized in certain secondary works, can be misleading. While it is true that metaphysical speculation was a bone of contention among competing Tantric groups, the fundamental dividing issues were often ritual or devotional, which is to say, in both cases, social. As examples of the polemical literature Goudriaan and Gupta (1981, 1.171) cite several works of Kāśīnātha Bhaṭṭa Bhaḍa (Śivānandanātha) (seventeenth/eighteenth centuries), for example, the *Kaulagajamardana* (Trampling the Kaula Elephant), a polemic against "left-handed," radical Tantrism; and the *Durjanamukhacapeṭikā* (Slap in the Face of the Wretches), a polemic in favor of devotion to Devī. The latter has been translated into French by Bournouf, in the preface to his translation of the *BhāgP*. The treatise "A Refutation of the Position of Left-handed Path [Tantra]" (*Vāmācāramatakhaṇḍana*) was discussed in the *Journal of the (Royal) Asiatic Society of Bengal* in 1939. As Goudriaan justly recognizes, a study of this sort of tractarian polemics would doubtless increase our understanding of the social history of Tantra.

No one has sorted out the different sorts of Advaita one finds in various sorts of Tantra. On the nondualist strands in various Śaiva and Śākta traditions, one may see Kundu (1964). Speaking of the *Jñānakhaṇḍa* of the *Tripurārahasya* (Vasavada 1965), a text expressing a position related to the Spanda and Pratyabhijñā schools of Śaivism, Goudriaan and Gupta (1981, 1.167) observes that its essential viewpoint, which is characteristically Śākta, is indeed Advaita, but of a particular sort: The world and the self are understood as nothing but a real manifestation (*abhāsa*) of the supreme Śakti itself.

THE SOCIAL AND RITUAL CONTEXT OF MANTRAŚĀSTRA

Tantric Mantraśāstra is never practiced in isolation. Even narrowly conceived, the concepts and practices of *tīrtha*, *pūjā*, *maṇḍala*, *mandir*, *mudrā*, *yātrā*, and *yantra* all shed light on each other and on the use of mantras. More broadly conceived, mantric utterance specifically presupposes the entire fabric of traditional Indian society and culture. To that extent, it is sui generis. In this portion of the Bibliography, I indicate some of the more obvious sources that illumine its socio-ritual setting.

Given the ubiquity of mantras in traditional India, the study of mantras historically would amount to the study of Indian culture historically. Therefore, it is difficult to single out a few works that shed light on the historical background against which the mantric tradition has grown. Somewhat arbitrarily, the following works seem to me to be helpful: on the especially interesting case of Assam, Gait (1963), Barua (1951), Neog (1965), and N. K. Basu (1970); on Nepal, Petech (1960) and Regmi (1965–66); on Bengal, Clark (1955); on the Deccan, Nandi (1973) and Handiqui (1949); on the emergence of Śaivism, Pathak (1960); of a general nature, N. Bhattacharyya (1975).

A number of Sanskrit literary works, some available in translation, provide significant insight into the social horizons in which Tantra emerged. Two of the most significant are Bāṇa's narrative, *Kādambarī* (early seventh century), for a translation of which see Kāle (1960) or Ridding (1896), and Bhavabhūti's lyric drama, *Mālati-Mādhava* (early eighth century), for a translation of which see Kāle (1967) or Devadhar and Suru (1935); for a summary of the portrayal of the Kāpālikas in works such as this, see Lorenzen (1972, 16–23, 48–63). Finally, the relevance of social scientific analysis and of a broadly Marxist perspective on the material basis of Indian religious life should not be underestimated. The point of departure for such reflection should undoubtedly be the too infrequently utilized six-volume survey of Ruben (1967–73), its Marxist perspective notwithstanding.

The Spatial Setting of Mantras

In contrast to the Semitic religions, which lay great stress on god's manifestation in time, that is to say, in history, the religious traditions of India emphasize god's manifestation in and as space. The cosmos is the visible manifestation (*darśan*) of god. In these terms, the metaphors of "seeing" and "hearing" intermingle freely: Ultimate reality refracts itself into a spatial complexity that can be seen and articulated. Mantras make sense to those who use them only because those individuals live as embodied beings in precisely the "Hindu" world; that is, in the world experienced and particularized in a precise way. By means of a variety of iconic, liturgical, and cosmological conventions and social institutions, traditional India domesticates space. To employ a nautical metaphor, mantras are one of the vessels by which men navigate through the spatial world that is understood theologically and mythically as the complex sea (or body) of god.

In this section of the Bibliography, material shedding light on the complex spatialization of mantric utterance is drawn together. In part, the subsections are artificial: These topics form a dense web in which each element both supports and is supported by all the others. This portion of the Bibliography opens up some of the most inviting aspects of South Asian culture. For preliminary orientation, the general reader might well begin with two recent texts, Eck (1981) and Waghorne and Cutler (1985). General orientation may also be provided by V. Das (1977; 1982), who attends directly to the spatial coordinates of Vedic and post-Vedic ritual.

Beyond the still indispensable Gopinatha Rao (1914–16), reference to the standard works on Indian art history and iconography is beyond the scope of this essay, but attention should be drawn to a few representative works dealing with Tantric art, if only to remind us that, as practiced, Tantra is neither as disembodied nor as text bound as yogis and Sanskritists, respectively, might imagine. To begin with, there is the popularizing but rather valuable works of Philip Rawson (1973a; 1973b). Both are based on a marvelous exhibition catalogue (Rawson, 1971) from the Hayward Gallery, London. In addition, Rawson (1966) is valuable in showing the degree to which Hindu art, like Hindu ritual, as a whole, in the general sense has been Tantricized. A. Moorkerjee (1967; 1971; 1975) has written three very well-illustrated "coffee-table" books on Tantra, which are well worth consulting. Caillat and Kumar (1981) is an equally lavish illustrated volume, which, moreover, deals with the neglected subject of the world-picture of the Jain tradition.

According to one strand of Tantric mythology (see pages 431–33) the universe emerges from and within god as an act of the progressive articulation of sound, phonemes, words, and sentences. One finds many diagrams that explicate this and that, thus, situate mantras within ritual, meditative, or cosmogonic space. To the best of my knowledge, no gallery or museum has mounted a show exclusively on this theme, but representative illustrations may be found scattered through the works just cited.

Evaluating the wealth of images available obviously presupposes some grasp of the way iconography is integrated symbolically with dance, theater, mythology, and ritual in traditional India. Here, a few standard references may provide orientation. From various perspectives and with differing foci see Kirfel (1920; 1959a; 1959b), Bosch (1960), and Moeller (1974). On the significance of specifically Tantric symbolism, there is Lauf (1974). For the general reader, Zimmer (1972) remains an engaging and sensitive introduction.

No one-to-one relationship exists between Tantric art and erotic art, but there is significant overlap. For a serious introduction to the Indian erotic tradition, see, in German, Fischer (1979; with bibliography 260–76); other studies include Anand (1958a) and (1958b), De (1959), Davidson (1960), Tucci (1969), and Desai (1975). There is a rather large literature concerning the famous temples of Khajurāho, for which see pages 407–408. There is a similarly large literature on the tradition of *mithuna* [or *maithuna*] (a couple, often embracing) in Indian sculpture and miniature painting, on this, see Ganguli (1925), B. Bhattacharya (1926); also

Ricci (1979), a volume by no means marketed exclusively for Indologists. I have not come across references to the use of mantra in post-Vedic *kāmaśāstra* but assume that, in this aspect of human life, too, they were pressed into service.

The overwhelming majority of mantras—certainly all of those that are cultic rather than "private"—have been uttered within an artificial zone demarcated through what might be called a sacred geometry. This is as true of Tantric Mantraśāstra as it is of the *Brāhmaṇas,* yet among recent scholars, only Staal has explored its significance. See Staal (1982) with further references, and the discussion related to the *Sāmaveda* on pages 343–45. Also relevant is the traditional Indian sense of geography; besides the works dealing with cosmology listed earlier, see Dube (1967). To understand all this, one must consider the canons of traditional Indian architecture and sculpture, see Gopinatha Rao (1920), P. N. Bose (1926), Kramrisch (1928), Bagchi (1943), Shukla (1958–60), Boner (1962), T. Bhattacharya (1963), Liebert (1976), Śivaramamurti (1978), and Boner, Sarma, and Baümer (1982); also Śivaramamurti (1955; and, on geographical factors in studying Indian iconography, 1950).

The most common terms for the sacralized space in which mantras are uttered include *cakra, yantra,* and *maṇḍala.* The last two terms have become well known in the West, but there is considerable confusion in the popular and secondary literature about their force and meanings. The remarks of Hoens (Gupta, Hoens, & Goudriaan 1979, 113) indicates some of the problems:

> In the existing literature yantra and maṇḍala are often considered to be synonyms. This is not correct, because *yantra* [in] general means an instrument, an implement. The yantra is often three-dimensional whereas the maṇḍala always is two-dimensional. Maṇḍala and yantra often have the same geometrical forms [i.e., squares, circles, triangles, half-circles], but the yantra may also have different forms. . . . The yantra is more worshipped than meditated upon. As far as the aims are concerned one can say that the yantra is more used for worldly purposes than for liberation, whereas the maṇḍala is used for both purposes.

It is tempting to contrast *yantras* as "magical" and *maṇḍalas* as "mystical" instruments, but that would be misleading. Both are used in what I have called quotidian and redemptive contexts. Moreover, they do have much in common. Both are constructions in space that depict a world whose inner fabric may be manipulated through meditation and mantric utterance, because it is understood to be a world woven—the metaphors vary—of *varṇas* and mantras. Hence, *bīja* and other mantras are regularly incised within them. Both allow an adept to utilize the inner forces that govern the cosmos by aligning the person with them.

Not many texts are devoted exclusively to *yantra*. Goudriaan and Gupta (1981, 1.158) mention the *Yantracintāmaṇi* of Dāmodara. Bharati (1965, 318) mentions a *Kāmyayantroddharā*, ascribed to a Bengali Tantric with the title Mahāmahopādhyāya Parivrājikācārya. The *Yoginīhṛdaya* is a work dealing largely with the Śrīcakra. A French translation has been prepared by Padoux. A combing of the manuscript literature would undoubtedly turn up other references, but not very many. Among secondary sources, on *yantra*, the monograph by Pott (1966) retains its interest in spite of the considerable progress made in our knowledge of Tantric texts and in Indian archeology in the past four decades. Rivière (1976), although dicey Indologically, illustrates the "ritual of Tantric magic" in terms of a French translation of a *Yantracintāmaṇi*, a manual of *yantras* to be used as aids in attaining various aims.* Earlier secondary works dealing with *yantras* have been superseded by a collection of essays (Padoux 1986b) that focuses on the interface between the use of mantras and ritual diagrams. On *maṇḍala*, Tucci (1961) remains a lively and readable introduction. One might compare its approach with that of Kramrisch (1946) and then Meister (1979b); see also L. Chandra (1969). On the *kṛṣṇamaṇḍala*, there is a fine monograph by Spink (1971), which is at once well illustrated, reliable, and appropriate for the general reader. For a sympathetic popularization of the *maṇḍala*, see Arguelles and Arguelles (1972), which is not of Indological value, however. For a similar treatment of *yantra*, see Khanna (1979). In interpreting *maṇḍalas* and *yantras* as instruments for sacralizing the human experience of space, one should consider the critique of the Eliadean analysis of sacred space in J. Z. Smith (1978).

The *yantra* and *maṇḍala* should be studied in light of the symbolism of the iconic—and, of course, the ritual—significance of the circle, more specifically the *cakra*. See, for example, Przlyuski (1920; 1936a), J. O. Schrader (1929), Masson-Oursel (1932), Coomaraswamy (1933–35), B. R. Sharma (1956), Horsch (1957), Auboyer (1965), Gowdra (1971), Begley (1973), and M. Johnson (1981, 102–25). I refrain from citing additional items on the widely discussed Buddhist wheel of life. On the cognate figure of the *svāstika*, see Deb (1921), who relates it to the cosmic symbolism of OṂ, and Freed and Freed (1980). A final motif, that of the "full pot" (*pūrṇaghaṭa*), deserves special attention, in particular as a counterpart to the conception of the world as a nondual sonic unity; on this see, for example, Gairola (1954) and Rosu (1961).

Maṇḍalas are one form of Indian ritual symbolism that have caught the imagination of certain twentieth century Westerners. Surveying the literature they have produced is well beyond the scope of this essay, but one may observe that Jung (1955) is at once seminal and representative of this appropriation of an Indian symbol. In this connection, one might also see Zimmer (1960).

**Several different texts are circulating under this name.*

Shrines and temples* are erected at *tīrthas* (points of transition) where power makes itself available. They are living *maṇḍalas, maṇḍalas* institutionalized. Besides being a setting *for* acts of meditation and mantric utterance, pilgrimages (*yātrā*) to them might be conceived of homologously as acts *of* meditation and mantric utterance. The study of the use of mantras in temple ritual and on pilgrimages should be undertaken in light of traditional Indian concepts of cosmos, architecture, drama, and geography, orientation to which has been provided earlier.

Today, the largest single subset of mantric utterances surely takes place in the course of the common pan-Hindu ritual of temple *pūjā*. There is a large anthropological literature on *pūjā*, but the clearest introduction I have come across is Babb (1975, 31–67). See also Charpentier (1926), Östör (1978) and, more generally, Saraf (1976). Gupta (Gupta, Hoens, & Goudriaan 1979, 121–62) provides a sequential description of *pūjā* in a Tantric setting.

On the Hindu temple, Kramrisch (1946) remains one of the landmarks in twentieth-century Indology, known especially for its treatment of the temple in terms of the important concept of the *vāstupuruṣa*, the prototype of the temple that is at once cosmic and geometric, and its conception of the temple as microcosm. It also deals in passing with the use of mantras in the construction and consecration of temples. For more recent work, see P. Chandra (1975) and Meister (1979a; 1979b); also Michell (1977); on the concept of *divyadeśa* ("divine ground"), see K. K. Young (n. a.). On pilgrimages, real and metaphorical, see Bharati (1963; 1970a), and Salomon (1979); also, a special issue of the Hindi periodical *Kalyan* (31.1 [1957]) was devoted to the subject of pilgrimage (*tīrtha*).

It is possible that in traditional India the person, the altar, the house, the temple, and the city were conceived of as organisms analogous to each other and to the cosmos as a whole. To the extent that this is so, mantras emerge, not least because of their use as premier instruments of consecration and purification, as the instruments by which persons may retain their spatial balance. Such an hypothesis will have to be tested in terms of our knowledge of Indian urban and domestic design. Recently, this has gained the attention of a number of scholars. To survey this important literature here would be quite impossible, but for a representative sample of the new holistic or "ecological" approach, I recommend three journals: *Beiträge und Studienmaterialien der Fachgruppe Stadt* 11 (Gutschow & Sieverts 1977), *Art and Archeology Research Papers* 16 and 17 (Jones & Michell 1979; Pieper 1980).

Perhaps the most exciting recent work has been done on Nepal, the Kathmandu valley, and especially Bhaktapur. Besides Tucci (1969) and Übach (1970), see Slusser (1980) and various works of Niels Gutschow (Gutschow & Auer 1974; Gutschow & Kölver 1975; Gutschow & Ba-

---

**This English term does duty for a large number of Sanskrit terms. They are surveyed in Kramrisch (1946, 1.130–38).*

jrācārya 1977). Two traditions of sacred space are especially relevant to the study of Tantra. First is the tradition of Śākta *pīṭhas,* see Sircar (1973), a carefully written study based on an edition and translation of the *Pīṭhanirṇaya.* Second, among the most important sacred sites of certain, primordial strands of Tantra, were cremation grounds; for background, see the discussion in Pott (1966, 76–101). The social significance of the cremation grounds as a locus of ritual activity is well brought out in Sanderson (1986), who comments (n. 110) "The distinction between Kula and Kaula traditions . . . is best taken to refer to the clan-structured tradition of the cremation-grounds . . . on the one hand and on the other its reformation and domestication through the banning of mortuary and all sect-identifying signs . . . and generally associated with Macchanda/Matsyendra." On the ritual of the "construction of the eight cremation grounds" in both Hindu Tantra and Tibetan Buddhism, see Meisezahl (1974).

Beyond this, the literature on the sacred cities and regions of the subcontinent is by now quite large. A selection of items I believe useful, arranged geographically, follows: for India as a whole, von Glasenapp (1900), but cf. Gutschow and Pieper (1978). On Vārāṇasī (Banaras, Kāśī), Eck (1982), with a useful bibliography, including sources in Hindi; on Gayā, Vidyarthi (1961); on Khajurāho, Anand and Kramrisch (1939), Anand, Fabri, and Kramrisch (1962), P. Chandra (1955–56), Goetz (1939; 1958), Deva (1959), Auboyer (1960), and cf. Meister (1979a; 1979b); on Purī, Rösel (1976; 1978); on South India, Mahalingam (1970); on Tamilnad, Clothey (1972) and B. Stein (1978); on Cidambaram, Kulke (1970); on Kāñcipuram, Dessigane, Pattabiramin, and Filliozat (1964). Finally, on Barabudur (Java), the most famous of all *maṇḍala*-inspired shrines, there is the classic study of Paul Mus (1935), which now has been supplemented by a collection of essays, Gomez and Woodward (1981), in which see especially Wayman (1981), who interprets Baradubur as a *maṇḍala.* Finally, Tambiah (1977b) employs the concept of "*maṇḍala* as cosmological topography" in order to explicate the "design of traditional Southeast Asian kingdoms," a coded design that he calls "galactic polity."

The utterance of a mantra is often accompanied by the use of those stylized ritual hand gestures known as *mudrā.* As Hoens (Gupta, Hoens, & Goudriaan, 1979, 116) puts it, "mudrās are undoubtedly physical presentations of mantras." The common Tantric ritual of *nyāsa,* the "seating" of a power in one's own body, utilizes mantra and *mudrā* simultaneously. In general, *mudrā* and *nyāsa* may be thought of as instruments of intended integration with forces that are thereby to be controlled. In the vocabulary of religious studies, they are understood to homologize a person to some powerful or, if one prefers, sacred reality or realities. The use of *mudrā* and *nyāsa* thus presupposes that powers, persons, and at times, the cosmos as a whole are related in a regular, manageable fashion. The person is a key to the cosmos and vice versa.

Gonda (1977a, 152) mentions a Vaikhānasa text, the *Ātmasūkta*, cited in the *Mantrasaṃhitā*, that "stresses the identity of the worshiper's body with the cosmos." Similarly the *KubjikāmataT* (KubjT) (Goudriaan & Gupta 1981, 1.54) speaks of the "continents" and sacred sites (*pīṭhas*) in the adept's body. The use of personal body metaphors to describe the cosmos and, conversely, the use of geographic and cosmic terms to describe the person merits investigation. I have not come across any study of this motif in Tantric literature, but on the nomenclature for the body and its parts and their religious significance in the ṚV and AV, see D. Srinivasan (1975; 1979), in the Vedic and post-Vedic *Upaniṣads*, G. W. Brown (1921); and cf. Coomaraswamy (1913–14). One place these intersecting personal/cosmic metaphors come into play is in the vocabulary of the subtle body and thus of *kuṇḍalinī* yoga, on which see page 429. See, too, the works on iconography and cosmology listed on pages 404–406.

Not many texts focus on *mudrā*. As an example, Goudriaan and Gupta (1981, 1.158) mention the *Mudrāprakāśa* of Rāmakiśora (Śarman). For secondary accounts, one may consult Franke (1892), Coomaraswamy (1928), Hommel (1931), Przyluski (1936b), Auboyer (1950–51), Haarh (1958), and Gonda (1972a); cf. Vogel (1919) and Auboyer (1949). Staal (1983d) discusses Vedic *mudrā*. Gonda (1980a, 52–81) discusses "gestures" in the *GṛhyaSū* and related texts. Note also, on *mudrā* in Japanese Buddhist iconography, Saunders (1960) with excellent notes and bibliography is something of a classic and, for a briefer statement by the same author, see Saunders (1957); on the use of *mudrā* among the Śaivite and Buddhist priesthoods of Bali, see de Kleen (1942). Presumably, there is some sort of continuity between the use of *mudrā* in ritual and in dance, but this is a subject on which I can offer no guidance; see, however, La Meri (1941), and Ikegami (1971). On Nandikeśvara's *Abhinayadarpaṇa*, see Michael (1985); also Coomaraswamy and Duggirāla Gopālakrishnāyya (1917) and M. M. Ghosh (1975); Jones (1983) lists the *mudrās* in Kathakali, on which, see Jones and Jones (1970).

There are two important scholarly studies of *nyāsa:* Bharati (1964), in German, has something of a sociological focus; Padoux (1980), in French, based upon a clear, painstaking collation of various texts, sheds particular light on the character of *nyāsa* as a tool for the transformation of consciousness, notably where the adept's goal is identification with the transcendental structure of the cosmos. As on so many other subjects, the most detailed discussion of *nyāsa* in English is provided by Diehl (1956).

The varieties of *nyāsa* are legion, and it would be difficult to provide an exhaustive list. Among others, Sircar (1973, 7, n. 1; this is quoted in Bharati 1965, 98, n. 4, but without citation) discusses *aṅganyāsa*, "touching limbs with the hand accompanied by appropriate *mantras*"; *ṣoḍhānyāsa*, "six ways of touching the body with mystical *mantras*"; and *pīṭhavinyāsa*. The last (Bharati 1965, 91, following the *Mantramahodadhi*) is particularly interesting: With it, one employs *mudrās* and mantras in order to appropriate the power (*śakti*) inherent in a sacred site by homologizing the limbs of one's own body with the limbs of Satī whose body, according to the well-known legend, had been established at various places that became centers of pilgrimage (*pīṭhas*).* Padoux (1980, 81–93) discusses what he identifies as the three most typical forms of Hindu *nyāsa,* those of the "seers" (*ṛṣādi-*), the "limbs" of the body (*āṅga* or *karāṅga-*), and the phonemes of the Tantric alphabet conceived of as "mothers" (*mātṛkā-*). Finally, Padoux (1980, 95–99) provides several representative lists of *nyāsa,* in which at least two dozen different sorts are mentioned.

The "Magical" Context of Tantric Mantraśāstra

Meditation is central to the practice of many religious specialists in India. Yoga is immensely popular. Why? A hermeneutics of suspicion must lead one to suppose that the sustained popularity with which the meditative traditions have been supported is due to the continuing conviction that meditation gets results. The pieties of apologists notwithstanding, without difficulty one can imagine that the generality of Indians have meditated in the hope of manifesting the *vibhūtis,* rather than in the hope of *mokṣa.* So, too, one may suppose, practical (that is, magical) concerns surely account for the overwhelming popularity of mantric utterance in traditional India. In this context, Goudriaan's observation (Goudriaan & Gupta 1981, 1.113) that "the popularity of the magical rites is reflected by the wide circulation of the magical Tantras even in regions where 'ordinary Tantras' are comparatively rare" need occasion no surprise.

Goudriaan's *Māyā Divine and Human* (1978) is a landmark in the study of Tantra as magic. As its subtitle indicates, it is "a study of magic and its religious foundations in Sanskrit texts, with particular attention to a fragment on Viṣṇu's Māyā preserved in Bali." For the purposes of this essay, let it suffice to indicate that this fragment of twenty-one verses and prose connectors "describes the supranormal effects of a meditation upon Viṣṇu's Māyā, . . . to be understood as that god's ability to change his appearance at will" (p. ix); that one who practices this meditation is "released from [the effects] all evil" (*sarvapāpāt pramucyate*), which is to say, attains the "pacification of all [evil forces]" (*sarvaprāyaścitta*); that the bulk of the fragment is concerned with the performance of the "Six Acts" (*ṣaṭ karmāṇi*), six paradigmatic acts of "magic" whereby the master of mantra and meditation controls the cosmos in all of its threatening

**Sircar (1973) makes the intriguing suggestion, which is worth following up, that the ritual convention may have preceded the (admittedly late) mythic convention: "The association of the limbs of the* sādhaka *with certain localities may have given rise to the belief regarding the Pīṭhas arising from particular limbs of the mother-goddess."*

diversity; that the heart of such "meditation" is the use of a series of mantras leading up to the Aghoramantra (pp. 136–62).*

Relying on Goudriaan's description, a few generalizations can be ventured concerning what I prefer to call the quotidian use of mantras. One cannot draw anything like a hard and fast line between "high" and "low" Tantra. Ultimate liberation and the "good life"—made possible by total control of a treacherous and untrustworthy cosmos—are the fruits of the same process. Thus, to a significant degree, what we wish to call magical is integral to Tantric *sādhanā* as such. As one would expect, mantric utterance is chief among the ritual instruments used in this "magical *sādhanā*." For appraising the magical use of mantras, Goudriaan (1978, 251–412), a detailed analysis of the "Six Acts" to control the cosmos, is especially important. Enumerations of the six include, for example, Attraction (*ākarṣaṇa*), Subjugation** (*vaśīkaraṇa*) ("the power to bewitch [creatures] to get work done by them, or to have desires fulfilled by them"); Immobilization (*stambhana*) (the power of stopping others in their tracks); Eradication (*uccāṭana*) ("the power to make enemies flee in shame and disgrace, also to explode houses and dwellings"); Sowing Dissension (*vidveṣaṇa*); Pacification (*prāyaścitta* or *śānti*) ("the power to remove diseases and yield protection from the influence of evil constellations, curses, and bad actions in some previous existence"); and Liquidation (*māraṇa*) ("the power of killing and maiming by *mantra*"). In evaluating Goudriaan's analysis, one should delve into the admittedly scattered and somewhat "unscientific" literature on Indian magic: for example, Gooneratne (1865–66), Hildburgh (1908), Wirz (1941), Dare (1947); on Indonesia(?), Hoens (1951) and Jacques (1966). Also, see the literature concerning "village" Hinduism and regional ethnography on pages 373–75.

Anand and Mookherjee (1977), which are to be used with caution, offer a general survey of Tantric magic. On sections of the written Tantras dealing with magic, see B. Bhattacharyya (1933); for a collection of brief magical Tantras on which Goudriaan draws frequently, see the *Indrajālavidyāsaṃgraha* (Vidyasagara 1915). One source that illustrates the close connection between practical and "spiritual" goals in the Indian meditative traditions is Narayanaswami Aiyar (1916). Partially informed by the vocabulary of the Theosophical Society, it deals with a set of

---

*Aghora *is one of the five faces/facets* (pañcamukha, pañcavaktra, pañcabrahma*) of Śiva; one version of the Aghoramantra (Goudriaan 1978, 155) is AGHOREBHYO 'THA GHOREBHYAḤ, GHORAGHORATAREBHYAŚ CA/ SARVATAḤ SARVASARVEBHYO NAMAS TE RUDRA RŪPEBHYAḤ, a mantra that can be translated, with Goudriaan: "To the Reassuring Ones who are also Awesome, who are even more awesome than the awesome, who are all and complete in all respects, honor to your manifestations, O Rudra."*

***In my definition of the six acts, I draw the phrases within quotation marks from Bharati (1965, 156, n. 36).*

meditations called *vidyās*, believed to be Upaniṣadic in origin and believed to have both mundane and redemptive effect. Central to these meditative exercises is an implicitly mantric *vidyā* on the Gāyatrī. If possible, this magical infrastructure on which soteric Mantraśāstra depends becomes even clearer in the vernacular literature of Tantrism. Thus, S. Gupta (Goudriaan & Gupta 1981, 205) reports "a vast body of magic formulae considered to be Tantric. Collectively these are called the Sāṃvarī Tantra . . . often accompanied by magic diagrams. They are mainly used . . . to cure various diseases and misfortunes such as possession by evil spirit, or to find lost property or to trace a lost person."

The Guru as Master of Mantravidyā

As Bharati (1965, 186f.) points out, the most succinct sociological definition of a guru is a person authentically capable of conferring initiation (*dīkṣā*). Since initiation, discussed on pages 426–27, invariably amounts to the imparting of the right mantra to the right person, it follows that, in this context, a guru, above all else, is a master of mantras.

Gonda (1965a, 229–83; with references) surveys the evolution of the figure of the guru, giving attention inter alia to the adjectival sense of guru as "weighty," parallel terms such as *ācārya*, *pūjārī* and *purohita*, Indo-European background, Jain and Buddhist conceptions, and the priestly office among Indian tribal groups. On the magic quality of "weight," also see Gonda (1947). On the evolution of the figure of the teacher in the Vedic age, one of the sources for the development of the Tantric guru, see pages 340–42.

Among numerous texts glorifying the guru are the *Gurugītā*, associated with the *SkandaP*, and the *Gurumāhātmya* of the Kabīrpanth (Gonda 1965, 280). Goudriaan (Goudriaan & Gupta 1981, 1.161) mentions a number of hagiographic works, in particular Umānanda's life of Bhāskararāya, the *Bhāskaravilāsa*, that presumably reflect the influence of the famous life of Śaṃkara, the *Śaṃkaradigvijaya*. To this, an immense regional and modern literature extolling the "saints" of Tamilnad, Maharashtra, and, of course, the Sikh gurus might be added. Once again, there is no doubt that surveys of the use of mantras both by such figures and in accounts of their lives could be useful in helping us build a composite picture for India as a whole. Literature on these regional gurus and saints—the Ālvārs, Nāyanārs, Sants and so forth—is beyond the scope of this essay, but see the discussion of Hindu theism on pages 364–66.

The guru is accepted as a figure of authority. But what does that really mean? The brief summary provided by Hoens (Goudriaan, Hoens, & Gupta 1979, 74–80) gives some of the ideological and social texture of a society that reveres the guru as master of the word. What strikes one above all else is the canny, practical dialectic involved. The disciple (*śiṣya*) must have confidence (*śraddhā*) in the guru and must be devoted to him. The guru is extolled as a god, nay as the highest god, and yet his also being human is taken for granted. Of course, it is recognized that different gurus have different "specialties" and that it is normal for an avid pupil to have a succession of gurus. The pupil is instructed to test the guru and among the guru's attributes; according to the *TantrarājaT* (Goudriaan, Hoens, & Gupta 1979, 76f.), he must be one "who does not give *yantra* and Tantra for sale" and one "who knows the difference between capable and incapable people." It is further recognized that there are bad gurus. In the words of the *KulārṇavaT* (KulāT) (Goudriaan, Hoens, & Gupta 1979, 77), the bad guru—the antiguru, one might say—is ugly, ungainly (has "extravagance of limbs"), sleepy, and dull. He gambles, is crooked, deceives others, and improperly reveals secret matters such as mantras. The emphasis on the appearance of the guru strikes me as particularly significant: The guru like the sacrificial animal, like the mantra itself, must be unblemished, which is to say, flawless in form. After all, as a civilization, India has long had a love affair with perfection of form (cf. Staal 1985a, 550, citing Renou).

It is important to recognize that the tradition oscillates between treatment of the guru as a real individual and as a type: The hagiography mediates between the real and the paradigmatic or "mythical" master. Perhaps, this is one of the reasons that the guru has sometimes fallen through the cracks in portraits of the Hindu tradition. He has been taken for granted by Indians, assimilated to types known in our society by Westerners. This could be either laudatory (the guru as charismatic, as psychopomp, e.g., in the fiction of Hermann Hesse) or censorious (the guru as fraud, e.g., according to most journalists), but in neither case did it encourage a sympathetic but dispassionate appraisal of an indigenous social institution that might well be as sui generis as the mantra itself.

In spite of the fact that Western culture has its own traditions of authoritative utterance (in religious communities, in the military, in athletic coaching) the guru as spokesman and culture hero has not been well received by scholars. The tradition of reliance on "verbal authority" (*śabda*),* as either a formal epistemological category or an informal social norm, has sometimes been thought embarrassing. It runs against the grain of our Enlightenment consensus. Yet, respect for the well-uttered word is central for traditional Indian culture. The concepts of guru, mantra, and *śabda*, the institutions of preceptorial authority, mantric utterance, and commentarial exegesis inform and support each other. Contemporary Western prejudices and preoccupations (for example, the hysteria against movements classified as cults) should not deflect one from a careful consideration of this nexus. The relationship between guru and disciple is neither trivial nor authoritarian. It is not for nothing

---

**To be sure, many of the formal philosophies, notably those of the Buddhist logicians, do not accept* śabda *as a formal* pramāṇa. *But even these schools share the general respect given by the culture to the testimony of classical, thus authoritative, precedents.*

that certain of the *GṛhyaSū* (cf. Gonda 1977b, 566) prescribe the same mantra to establish an intimate relationship between a husband and wife, on the one hand, and a master and a disciple, on the other. In India, the word of the guru—par excellence the mantra—has often been thought the most effective form of "truth-telling." See, in this regard, the section on Mīmāṃsā on pages 383–87.

One vocabulary that could be used in rethinking the reality of the guru is that of performance theory. Seen through that lens, the social reality of the guru presupposes a triad consisting of the guru (that is, the performer), the script, including the mantra itself conceived of as the text of the performance in kernel, and the disciples of the guru (that is, the audience). The constant social interaction between the guru and his disciples, mediated and made possible by the mantra, is the performance, an endless process in which the guru and the disciples both play active and passive roles. When the performance is real, when it works—carrying along master, disciples, and text—it might be thought of as the social correlate of *mantravīrya,* as the mantra's *social* efficacy. This does not say that Indian thought conceives of the guru in this way; it merely suggests the sort of experimental rethinking needed to stimulate a fresh look at a familiar subject. For a preliminary attempt to deal with issues of this sort, see Alper (1981), an essay that I expect to recast and expand for republication.

A final suggestion, the respect for the authority of the guru, the person who *is*—not merely has—the last word, must be studied in light of the psychology of authority and the family in Indian culture. Such work has barely begun in the rather controversial reflections of Spratt (1966) and J. M. Masson (1980), and in the more sympathetically received work of Kakar (1971; 1974; 1978). See, in this connection, Goldman (1978; 1982; 1985).

Mantra as Enigma

To a certain extent, Tantra is an esoteric tradition and *Mantraśāstra* is secret knowledge. For example, the *Yonigahvara* (Goudriaan & Gupta 1981, 1.78) speaks of a *vidyā* to secret to put into writing, it should be "as if written on water." Several motivations contributed to this. In the first place, Tantra exemplifies the well-known convention of setting the sacred apart from the profane. In emphasizing this separation, it was surely influenced by the Vedic precedent. Additional social factors doubtless came into play. Spritual masters would be well motivated to protect their monopoly of a sort of knowledge widely recognized by the cultures as practically and redemptively powerful. They would be enthusiastically abetted in this by their disciples, because they and their gurus together formed a "mystical elite" whose status was enhanced by their possession of knowledge not general to the society. Moreover, from the first, Tantra was the work of an "avant garde" out to scandalize and provoke the "respectable" classes. As the KulāT (9.83a, cited by Goudriaan & Gupta 1981, 1.96) expressed it in a well-known remark, "one should be a Kaula in one's heart, a Śaiva by external behavior and a Vaiṣṇava among the people." Secrecy protected those who practiced scandalous rituals. It also heightened the ill repute and, thus, the inverse prestige of those rites.

The penchant for mystification should not be overestimated. As with any esoteric religious tradition, the veiling and the unveiling of a higher truth went hand in hand, the desire for secrecy and publicity were always and of necessity in dialectic. One might have imagined that in India, as in China, the relatively small portion of the population that was literate would have meant that the very act of writing something down would serve to protect it from untoward disclosure. Writing something down, however, was not sufficient, perhaps because it was a question of obscuring Tantra precisely from the literate Brahmanical elite. The techniques for safeguarding mantras were relatively straightforward. The most common procedures for indicating a mantra that should not be expressed directly in writing simply involved writing it in reverse order (*vilomena, vyutkrameṇa*), "interchanging the syllables of a line (*vyākulitākṣara*)" (Schoterman 1982, 181), or paraphrasing it. This illustrates the tension between concealment and disclosure, for as Bharati (1965, 276, n. 69) observes, in reference to the exemplary *Saundaryalaharī*, the secret is open to anyone in a position to care.

In many instances, more elaborate precautions were taken to guard mantras. The most extreme involved various forms of encoding that required possession of a key, and knowledge of a procedure, before decoding would be possible. The best example of this about which I am aware are the devices known as *prastāra* and *gahvara*, which are specific to the tradition of the *Kulākikā-* or *Paścimāmnāya*, represented by the KubjT and the *Ṣaṭsāhasra Saṃ* (ṢaṭSaṃ). Schoterman (1982, 181–209) discusses them in an appendix to his translation of the first five chapters of the latter text. This involves secreting the mantra through something like a "substitution cipher." To get the mantra, one must first know how to construct the diagram in which the Sanskrit *akṣaras* are rearranged and know the terminology by which they are indicated.

Sometimes one gets the impression that the secrecy of Tantra became an end in itself, part of the game. For example, ṢaṭSaṃ 3.45ff. enumerates "sixteen different ways in which [its teachings are] veiled or handed down in a disguised form" (Schoterman 1982, 115). In any case, the subject of the encoding of mantras in such a manner clearly merits further study. One wonders whether these procedures are derived from Vedic precedents or were part of a continuous tradition of Indian cryptography. (On such a tradition, a standard history of codes and ciphers, Kahn (1967, 74), draws attention to the *Arthaśāstra*, the *Kāmasūtra*, and the *Lalitavistara.**) One wonders further whether the *prastāras* and *gahvaras* were ever used after being drawn either as *yantras* or as vehicles for mystical or meditative speculation. Such a use might seem natural since, for example, the *gahvara* is (Goudriaan & Gupta 1981, 1.76, citing the *Yonigahvara*), "considered the womb of all *mantras*". In this regard one is reminded of the magic squares, well known in China and the Islamic world, which have been studied by Cammann (1969, with further refs.). For lexica of Tantric "code language" see Goudriaan and Gupta (1981, 1.160f.). On possible folk precedents for, or analogues to, the esoteric aspects of *mantraśāstra* see Crooke (1919).

One of the most characteristic linguistic strategies, at least in Buddhist contexts, devised to protect Tantric *sādhanā* from use by the uninitiated (and, therefore, unprepared and unqualified) devotee, and conversely to protect the novice from tapping a power greater than he can control, is the use of a specific sort of indirect utterance, known variously as *saṃdhyā-*, *saṃdhā-*, or *saṃdhibhāṣā*. The first of these terms means twilight language. The latter terms might be translated (with Eliade and Bharati) intentional language, or alternatively allusive language, or code language (Goudriaan & Gupta 1981, 177). Bharati (1965, 182, n. 26) rightly observes that whether the "proper" term is *saṃdhā-* or *saṃdhyā-* makes little difference, for either easily could be used to refer to the linguistic usage in question. Wayman (1968a) presents evidence to show that several terms were used from the start.

Saṃdhābhāṣā is the systematically ambiguous use of a word in such a way that it can be taken literally by the unknowing while being read in its higher significance by the adept. Bharati (1965, 171) cites a memorable passage, "inserting his organ into his mother's womb, pressing his sister's breasts, placing his foot upon his *guru's* head, he will be reborn no more."** This statement, he adds, can be decoded to read "he practices mental penetration through the successive centres [*cakras*], and when he reaches the uppermost centre, he will not be reborn, as he thereby attained *nirvikalpa samādhi.*"

Bharati's discussion (1965, 164–84) provides orientation. He points out (p. 165) that, the assumption of many contemporary *paṇḍits* notwithstanding, "*sandhābhāṣā* has nothing [explicitly] to do with *mantra.*" At the same time, he recognizes that *saṃdhābhāṣā*, because of its enigmatic character, might be considered as "a specialized extension of mantric language" (p. 164). Few scholars have attempted to reflect systematically on *saṃdhābhāṣā* from the perspective of philosophy of language or

---

**A short list of fiction and nonfiction "skoobedoc" may be found in Dilys Winn,* Murder Ink, The Mystery Reader's Companion *(NY: Workman Publishing, 1977, 176); some think it contains mantras to protect one from mayhem.*

**Matriyonau liṅgaṃ kṣiptvā, bhaginiṣtanamardanam, gurur mūrdhni pādam dattvā, punar janma na vidyate. *According to Bharati (1965, 183, n. 35) the verse, attributed to Tarkālamkāra's commentary on the KT, is cited by Avalon in his introduction to KT (TT IX:10) and also circulates widely in many variant forms.*

literary criticism. Bharati (1965a, 173ff.) makes what is to my mind a very useful distinction between "afferent" and "efferent" use of intentional language. The former is the use of everyday terms to intend the ultimate; the latter is the use of ostensibly technical theological terms to intend everyday objects or situations. An example of each, taken from the *HevajraT*, when the word *ḍombī* (an untouchable washerwoman) is taken to imply *vajrakuli* (an adept of the *vajra*-class), it is being used as an afferent; when the word *bodhicitta* (consciousness awakened to the truth) is taken to imply *śukra* (semen), it is being used as an efferent. Perhaps, the common distinction between sign and symbol could help clarify the various usages. Both *saṃdhabhāṣā* and mantric utterance presuppose a rich tradition of religious metaphor. The former uses words invariably as signs, the latter never uses words as mere signs but in a variety of other ways.

For discussions, one may see Bannerji (1924), Bagchi (1930b), Dasgupta (1962, 413–24), Wayman (1968a), Eliade (1969, 149–54), Zbavitel (1976, 120ff.), Kvaerne (1977, 37–60); more broadly on language in Buddhist Tantra, see Elder (1976). It should be stressed that the use of "intentional language" in Tantra is a Buddhist convention, hence the work done on the *Dohās* and *Caryāpadas* of Bengal and Tibet, discussed on pages 439–40. The use of figurative or ambivalent language in general does not count as *saṃdhyābhāṣā*. An examination of parallel usages, if any, in Hindu and Jain texts would be useful.

TANTRIC TEXTS DEALING WITH MANTRA

Unfortunately, the critical editing, publication, and translation of Tantric texts is still in its infancy. There is no doubt that in the long run serious historical and phenomenological assessment of Tantra will depend upon a cooperative scholarly effort to sift through South Asian manuscript collections. Even delimiting the titles and contents of the surviving texts and their commentaries is not as simple as it might seem. Nonetheless, careful exegesis and reflection on the works already published, edited, and translated will go far in solidifying the place of Tantric studies within Indology. For those not limited to Western languages, Gopinath Kaviraj (1972) is an invaluable guide to the literature. For guidance in consulting manuscripts, see the list of catalogues in Goudriaan and Gupta (1981, 1.216f.). In this introductory survey, by and large, I limit myself to a selection of the texts that have attracted some degree of critical scholarly attention in Western languages. For further bibliography, see the general works listed on pages 392–94. For convenience vernacular works on mantra are discussed on pages 441–43 in relationship to the subject of neo-Hinduism.

The Āgamas

If a distinction between *āgama* and *tantra* makes any sense, it makes very rough social, or perhaps "geo-religious," sense: What in the Northern two thirds of India have come to be called *the* Tantras, tend in South India to be known as *the* Āgamas. Although it suggests an unrealistic division between North and South India, I shall follow the convention established in the HIL. Under *āgama,* I shall refer largely to the *Śaivāgamas* and the Pāñcarātra *saṃhitās* preserved in the South; under *Tantra* I shall refer largely to the parallel literature preserved in the North.

On the *Āgamas,* there is now Gonda (1977a), in which chapters 5–8 deal with the Pāñcarātra *Saṃhitās,* and chapters 11–12 deal with the *Śaivāgamas.* Appropriate background for assessing Gonda's account may be found in an important essay by Brunner (1975–76); but it is still useful to consult Filliozat (1961), who focuses on the South; with it one might compare Gnoli (1973) which deals with the survival of the Āgamic tradition in the North.

In recent decades, the most sustained and significant work on the Āgamic tradition has been done at the Institut Francais d'Indologie in Pondichéry, particularly by the Head Paṇḍit, N. R. Bhatt, and Hélène Brunner. Brunner's ongoing magnum opus is a lavishly annotated translation of the *Somaśambhupaddhati* (1963–77, with a fourth volume forthcoming), a South Indian Śaivāgamic ritual manual dating perhaps from the second half of the eleventh century. Each of the volumes is furnished with a synthetic introduction. Cumulatively, the volumes give a detailed view of the use of mantras in "le rituel quotidien" of southern Āgamic Śaivism; see especially the treatment of *dīkṣā* in the third volume.

In addition, Brunner has written a number of pioneering studies on particular Āgamic issues or texts. See her study (1965) of the *Kiraṇāgama,* her study (1967) of the *Suprabhedāgama,* and her translation (1985) of two sections of the *Mṛgendrāgama;* in this context, one should also see Bhatt (1977) on the *(Pūrva-)Kāmikāgama.* Brunner (1964) is a synthetic essay dealing with the treatment of "Vedic social categories" in southern Śaivism; see, in addition, her analysis (1977) of the mystical tradition of the Sanskritic (in distinction from the Tamil) *Śaiva Siddhānta* and her translation and analysis (1969) of an Āgamic fragment (dealing with the disputed propriety of eating the "leftovers" of offerings to Śiva), which appears in tte works of both Nīlakaṇṭha, the apparently fifteenth-century Vīraśaiva author of the *Kriyāsāra,* an Appaya Dīkṣita, the sixteenth–seventeenth century Smārta scholastic.

Of more general interest, Brunner (1975) is a study of the technical usage in the *Śaivāgamas* of the term *sādhaka* (disciple or adept, who is initiated into the *siddhis*), which contains a detailed discussion of the ritual process of becoming "someone who has realized the mantra" (*siddha-mantra*), "someone who possesses the mantra" (*mantrin*). Brunner (1974) presents a survey of the contents of the *NetraT,* a Śaivāgamic work on which Kṣemarāja, a successor of Abhinavagupta, wrote a commentary, and which focuses on one of the great Śaiva mantras, the *Mṛtyujit-* or Netramantra, (the "Conqueror of Death-" or "Eye-mantra"), OṂ JUṂ SAḤ.* Oberhammer (1977, 57–133) contains a detailed analysis of the meditative traditions of the *Mṛgendrāgama* (or *Tantra*) in comparison to the traditions of Sāṃkhya, as represented by the *Yuktidīpikā*, and the YSū. For comments on Oberhammer's treatment of Yoga, see page 429. Finally a translation of the *KumāraT*, a *Śaivāgama* recognized by the Śaiva Siddhānta of South India and dealing largely with mantras used in the ritual service of Skanda/Murugan (i.e., Kumāra), and not to be confused with a work of the same name mentioned earlier on page 391, has been provided in Zvelebil (1978). On the Vaiṣṇava *Pāñcarātrāgmas*, which are comparable to the *Śaivāgamas*, see the literature cited on page 371.

As is well known, the *Agamas* present themselves as "revelation," a Fifth Veda, *śruti* for the weak-willed folk of the Kali age. A study comparing their sense of revelation with that of the Vedic tradition, perhaps dealing with the evolving portrayal of the *ṛṣis*, might be interesting. After all, each mantra, like each Vedic *sūkta*, is assigned an *ṛṣi*. A broader comparison of the fate of the *Āgamas* with the fate of the Veda might go a long way toward illumining the function of canons in Indian religious life.

The "Classical" Tantras

My distinction between "classical" Tantras and "manuals" is a rough adaptation of Goudriaan's (Goudriaan & Gupta 1981, 1.4) between "Original Tantras" and "secondary works." His comparison merits attention, if only because it underscores that Tantra has a history:

> The "Original Tantras" are anonymous and written in dialogue form; their Sanskrit is often inferior, their style mediocre, sometimes even awkward; their method of presentation is repetitive, associative and nonsystematical. The digests are of known authorship; their language and style are much better; their set-up is more systematical; they abound in references to and quotations from older authorities. The authors were in overwhelming majority Brahmans, but other social groups are also represented, among them ruling aristocrats.

There is no reason to survey these texts here, for they are extensively treated by Goudriaan and, in any case, are largely inaccessible to the general reader. Among works dealing with individual Tantras or portions of Tantras, however, a few items should be noted.

The KulāT is one of the most famous Śākta Tantras of the Kula or Kaula tradition. (The varying technical senses of the terms *kula* and

---

**Bharati's comment (1965, 323) that the text "emphasized eye-cures and other healing magic centering on vision" should not mislead one into imagining that the* Netratantra *is a work of esoteric ophthalmology!*

*kaula** have not yet been adequately mapped. Goudriaan (Gupta, Hoens, & Goudriaan 1979, 45, n. 27) suggests that there are as many as twenty-four discrete meaning of the word *kula*!) It has been edited several times, in particular by Taranatha Vidyāratna with the assistance of Sir John Woodroffe (1917). There has been surprisingly little work on this major text, but one may see Carlstedt (1970; 1973–74, for translations of the "Jīvasthiti-" and "Kulamāhātmya-" *kathanas*, respectively; and 1974, for a content summary of those chapters). Unfortunately, all three items are in Swedish, but the last has a four-page English synopsis. It should be noted that Chakravarti (1931–32) apparently reports a different text of the same name.

The KubjT (Goudriaan & Gupta 1981, 1.53), a Kula text devoted to the goddess Kubjikā, the Curved One, a form of Kuṇḍalinī, discusses, among other related subjects, the Samayamantra** and the mythic origin of the Mālinī, discussed here on pages 431–32. On it and the related ṢaṭSaṃ, there is the important work by Schoterman (1982; 1977). It should be noted that the *KubjikāT*, especially popular in Bengal and commented on by Woodroffe, is a completely different text (Schoterman 1982, 7). In connection with the *MahānirvāṇaT*, a text probably written in the second half of the eighteenth century, see S. C. Banerji's survey (1977) of the Tantric traditions of Bengal; and see the comments on page 369. So, too, on the various texts and traditions that claim the authority of the legendary Nātha sages, see page 372.

Manuals of Mantraśāstra

As Goudriaan (Goudrian & Gupta, 1981, 1.130f.) summarizes, the greater part of Tantric literature amounts to a basically systematic set of "digests" that do not claim the status of revelation. A subgroup of this literature presents a more or less "orderly survey . . . of the origin, form, application and worship of the *mantras* of the gods which are taught in the Tantras." Each digest, Goudriaan continues, typically deals, in order, with at least five subjects, in my words: (1) the phonic emanation of the gods who are the cosmos; (2) the general norms concerning the utilization of mantras; (3) rituals of initiation (*dīkṣā*) enabling one to utilize mantras; (4) rituals preliminary to the use of a mantra (*puraścaraṇa*);† and (5) the "extraction" (*mantrodhhāra*) of the purposes for using particular mantras arranged according to deity (*devatā*).

The most famous of these digests are certainly the *Prapañcasāra* (PrpSā) and the *Śāradātilaka* (ŚārTlk), which Goudriaan and Gupta (1981,

---

*Kula *is a noun, literally meaning family, and* kaula *is an adjective derived from it, which can also serve as a noun.*

***It contains thirty-two* akṣaras: *NAMO BHAGAVATI ŚRĪKUBJIKĀYAI HRĀṂ HRĪṂ HROṂ ṄAÑAṆANAME AGORAMUKHI CHĀṂ CHĪṂ KIṆIKIṆI VICCE.*

†*Among the Pāñcarātrins, this term is used to refer collectively to the repetition of one's mantra in various rituals (Gonda 1977b, 71). In general, see the discussion on page 423.*

1.131) describe together as "authoritative and intellectualistic." Perhaps because it is anonymous the PrpSā was traditionally ascribed to Śaṃkarācārya, just as its commentary, the *Vivaraṇa* was ascribed to Śaṃkara's follower Padmapāda. Goudriaan judiciously concludes that "it is plausible that this outstanding and probably highly original description of Mantraśāstra was written at an early date by a member of one of the monastic communities founded by [Śaṃkara]," in any case, before the latter part of the eleventh century. The ŚārTlk is essentially a simplified replication of the PrpSā. It was written by Lakṣmaṇadeśika, reputedly a disciple of the Pratyabhijñā author Utpaladeva. The most significant commentary on the ŚārTlk is the *Padārthādarśa* of Rāghavabhaṭṭa, a learned fifteenth–sixteenth resident of Benares. Surprisingly little work has been done on these two texts. Sir John Woodroffe (1914; 1933) wrote introductions to his editions of the texts; Goudriaan calls his introduction to the PrpSā a "detailed but unbalanced survey." There are scattered references in all of the standard surveys of Tantra; on the PrpSā there is an essay by Ewing (1902) that Goudriaan (Goudriaan & Gupta 1981, 1.134) describes as suffering from prejudice; on Rāghavabhaṭṭa, see Pusalker (1960).

Among other digests of Mantraśāstra, Goudriaan (1.136–40) mentions the *Mantramuktāvalī* of Paramahaṃsa Pūrṇaprakāśa (no later than the early fifteenth century); the *Mantramahodadhi* of Mahīdhara with an autocommentary entitled *Naukā* (1588–89) that seems to be especially popular in the Hindi heartland of North India; the *Mantradevaprakāśikā* of Viṣṇudeva; the *Mantrakamalākara* by Kamalākara Bhaṭṭa, which Goudriaan (1.138) observes "can almost be characterized as a private collection of *mantra* lore probably meant for a restricted circle of people (presumably a family) whose chief object of worship was Rāma"; the *Mantraratnākara* of Yadunātha Cakravartin; the *Mantrārādhanadīpikā* of Yaśodhara (1566); the *Mantracandrikā* of Kāśīnātha Bhaṭṭa (seventeenth–eighteenth centuries); the *Mantrakalpadruma* attributed to Rajendra Vikrama Sāha, ruler of Nepal (1816–1847), which Goudriaan reports devotes special attention to a mantra concerning archery (*dhanurveda*); the *Mantramahārṇava* of Mādhava Rāya Vaidya (early twentieth century?), which has been especially popular in the West of India and on which see the content-summary in Bharati (1965, 123–28); and, finally, the famous *Tantrasāra* of Kṛṣṇānanda (probably seventeenth century), which has been especially popular in Bengal. Among Tantric lexica (Goudriaan & Gupta 1981, 1.160f.), one might notice the *Uddhārakośa* (Raghu Vira and Shodo Taki 1938) and the *Bījanighaṇṭu*. The latter has been edited with a number of cognate texts and translated in R. K. Rai (1978).

The significance of these little noticed works cannot be sufficiently stressed: If it is ever going to be possible to write a social history of the use of mantra, to portray and assess the role mantra plays in the life of the Hindu world today, in different regions and communities, this literature must be mastered and digested. It is often repetitious and inelegant. It can easily strike one as tiresome and insignificant. Therefore, the process of studying it has barely begun. Information on Sanskrit editions of these works is provided in Goudriaan's notes. (Special attention should be drawn to the fact that a single title often attaches to two or more entirely separate works.) Unfortunately, most of these works have not yet been discussed at any length by scholars and, accordingly, cannot be approached without Sanskrit. One exception is the *Mantramahodadhi,* which has been translated into Hindi and commented on by S. Chaturvedi (1981) and also put into English by a "board of scholars." See, too, Bharati's (1965, 142–50) very interesting content-summary of a modern North Indian Vaiṣṇava treatise, the *Mantramuktāvalī,* one of at least three works circulating under that name and not the fifteenth century text mentioned earlier.

MANTRAŚĀSTRA AND SĀDHANĀ

I think it is a safe generalization to say that all Tantric Mantraśāstra is at once ritualistic and meditative. Nonetheless, the balance between ritual and meditative elements varies according to the context. Two generalizations may be proposed as hypotheses for testing. The ritualistic component is most noticeable in what I have called a quotidian context, while the meditative predominates in what I have called a redemptive context. Similarly, it appears useful to contrast the practices that are preliminary to the use of a mantra, with the practices that follow those preliminaries. It seems to me that in the former the ritualistic element is central, while in the latter the meditative comes to the fore. To use an athletic metaphor, "warming up" is inherently more ritualistic than actually putting a ball into play. The former is more a highly stylized public event, the latter more a question of an inner journey. Reflecting this distinction, I have divided my remarks on mantra and *sādhanā* into two sections. First, I consider what I like to call preparatory moves in the game of playing mantras. The most significant of these is undoubtedly initiation. Second, I consider the meditative element in Mantraśāstra, broadly mantra and Yoga, the most significant element of which is undoubtedly *japa.* Note, however, that some of the material that could have been discussed here has been otherwise classified. On the important preliminary procedure known as *nyāsa,* see pages 408–10.

One caveat is in order, a single basic Indological imperative must govern future research on both the ritualistic and meditative sides of Mantraśāstra. To understand mantric utterance as it was meant to be practiced means deciphering the technical terminology in which is couched. The process of mapping this terminology has only just begun and what Goudriaan (Goudriaan & Gupta 1981, 1.26) says about the vocabulary of Tantra in general applies a fortiori to the vocabulary of mantra: "Tantric literature offers a jungle growth of specialized terminology rarely defined or paraphrased; of unexpected hidden meanings; of mutual intersection of fundamental ideas, categories or prescriptions."

Initiation and Other Preparatory Rites

There is agreement among all those who utilize mantras that mantric utterance can never be both casual and effective. It is always methodical. If mantric utterance is improperly launched, it will not work. It will be invalid, unsuccessful, or just not counting as mantric. Still, to the best of my knowledge, the Hindu Tantras provide nothing like a single list of preliminaries that are either necessary or sufficient for the successful use of a mantra. It would be helpful for someone to take one or two dozen representative Tantric texts and collate the terminology for mantric preliminaries. It would be similarly useful to do the same for lists of defects (*doṣa*) that render mantras inoperative and the procedures used to correct or nullify those defects. Until that has been done in an historical and textually scientific manner, any comment on these preliminaries must be considered suggestive and provisional.

The most general term for the preliminaries to successful mantric utterance seems to be *puraścaraṇa,* which refers, in Goudriaan's words (Goudriaan & Gupta 1981, 1.157), to "the preliminary ritual aiming at the [obtaining] of mastery over a *mantra.*" As with *dīkṣā,* it was not all that often made the subject of substantive and independent treatises. Goudriaan mentions the *Puraścaraṇabodhinī* (c. 1813) of Harakumāra Thākur, of the famous "Tagore" family of Calcutta, for example. The term *puraścaraṇa* appears to be used with both broad and narrow meanings. Gupta (Gupta, Hoens, & Goudriaan 1979, 161) indicates its basic elements. Narrowly construed, *puraścaraṇa* seems to amount to *mantrasādhanā,* a term that has been translated as the cult or worship of the mantra (cf. Padoux 1980, 93f.). What does this really involve? Is it a matter of etiquette, of psychology, of power? A phenomenological description of this ritual would be most desirable.

Hoens (Gupta, Hoens, & Goudriaan 1979, 107f.), citing the *Prāṇatoṣiṇī,* an early nineteenth-century manual (for a description, see Goudriaan & Gupta, 1981, 1.147), mentions twelve or thirteen rites introductory to successful utilization of a mantra's power (*vīrya*). (These rites are numbered in parentheses.) The list is interesting at least in that it shows that the distinction between external and internal acts, between ritual and meditation, is rather artificial. I would suggest that these preliminaries fall *roughly* into five classes.

First is what we might call spiritual/intellectual preparation. It has two elements: (1) *Mantracaitanya* (consciousness of the mantra), understood as the realization that the *mūlamantra* is one with *citśakti.* Notice that one way of doing this seems to involve *japa,* repeating a certain formula 108, 1008, or more times, thus making *japa* a necessary preliminary of *japa,* a situation that merits reflection. But it is typical, often a necessary condition for the utterance of one mantra is the prior utterance of another. On *japa* as a preliminary rite, see Padoux (1986a). (2) *Mantrārtha,* understanding the meaning (i.e., the object ?) of the mantra.

Second are four rites in which the recitation of a mantra is prepared for by the recitation of the appropriate *bījas.* These are called (3) *kulluka,* (4) *setu* (bridge), (5) *mahāsetu,* and (6) *nirvāṇa.* Third are two rites that I would describe as preparing the individual spatially for the utterance of the mantra: (7) *yonimudrāvibhāvana,* exhibiting the gesture known as the *yonimudrā,* and (8) *aṅganyāsa* (application of the mantra to the (six) limbs).

The third set of acts seems to be especially purificatory and include (9) *prāṇāyāma,* breath control; (10) *mukha-* or *jihvāśodhana,* the purification of the mouth or tongue; (11) *prāṇayoga,* disciplining the central breath; and sometimes, (12) *aśaucabhaṅga* (the destruction of impurity). Fourth and difficult to classify is (13) *dīpana* (or *dīpanī*), the "kindling" or lighting of the mantra, which is performed both before *and after* its utterance, however.

Closely related, conceptually and practically, to these preliminary rites are those designed to rectify a mantric process that has gone wrong. As Hoens (Gupta, Hoens, & Goudriaan 1979, 108f.) summarizes, "The older texts . . . mention a series of ten *saṃskāra* (ceremonies) which have to be performed in the case of faults (*doṣa*) in the mantra." He cites such a list from the ŚārTlk. These include (1) *janana,* "producing" the mantra, which has the technical meaning of "extricating" (*uddhāra*) the mantra out of the *mātṛkās* (the sequence of primal *akṣaras*); (2) *jīvana,* "vivifying" the mantra, which interestingly involves deconstructing its plain sense; (3) *tāḍana,* "striking" the written mantra *akṣara* by *akṣara* with sandal-water and the *bīja* YĀṂ; (4) *bodhana,* "awakening" the mantra by striking it with Oleander flowers and the *bīja* YĀṂ; (5) *abhiṣecana,* "consecration," a ritual in which the mantra is sprinkled with Aśvattha blossoms and the word NAMAḤ; (6) *vimalīkaraṇa,* a "purification" ritual through which the mantra is protected from evil (or inauspiciousness?) by means of the recitation of another mantra; (7) *āpyāyana* (causing to swell) and (8) *tarpaṇa* (refreshing by libation), two rituals that combine *japa* and sprinkling; (9) *dīpana,* "kindling" the mantra by the use of *bījas,* and (10) *gopana,* keeping the mantra secret. Conversely, there are concepts that articulate success in and the power of mantric utterance. The two most common are perhaps *mantrasiddhi* and *mantravīrya,* respectively. Both merit more attention than they have received.

In spite of the fragmentary nature of the evidence, certain generalizations may be offered. First, many of the elements in these mantric preliminaries are "borrowed" from other strata of Hindu ritual life: sprinkling with water and flowers from *pūjā;* the fear of impurity and the complementary confidence in rites of purification from the Vedic ritual system and, perhaps, also from village Hinduism; concern for the inner purification of the breaths from Yoga. Second, common to the tradition as a whole is the conviction that mantric utterance cannot be haphazard. Mantras do not count as mantras unless one follows some impersonal standard, some protocol proper to them. Precision is of the essence, even when there is no agreement on the content about which one is being precise. Third, not all of the ritual elements deployed in the preliminary practices strike one as equally central. However, the use of *mudrās, bījas,* and especially *nyāsa* seem to be indispensable, irrespective of nomenclature or ideological context. Fourth, there is a consensus that mantras cannot be recited "cold." Something special must be done to prime the officiant and to activate the mantras, thus signifying that they are mantras. In other words, a mantric performance demands a special decorum. Notice in this regard the proclivity of the tradition to utilize metaphors—awakening, vivifying, kindling, opening the eyes—to identify the key act by which a mantra is made efficacious. Fifth, mantric utterance might be characterized as incestuous. Mantras presuppose and feed upon other mantras. The drill seems to presuppose this to worship a god, one must be that god; to use a mantra, one must become that mantra.*

Standing somewhat outside of these mantric preliminaries are procedures equally, perhaps even more, important. Chief among these is undoubtedly *mantroddhāra,* the "selection" or "extraction" of mantras. These complex procedures employ a verbal mathematics, and accordingly they may be compared with at least three other aspects of Mantraśāstra: First, with the Vedic traditions according to which a mantra was systematically deformed so that they could be preserved and used, discussed on page 338; second, with the coding procedures by which mantras were secreted within "mystic" diagrams, e.g. *gahvara,* described on page 404; third, with the procedures for various sorts of "ornamented" *japa,* see page 430. Another exceedingly common preliminary ritual, for both Hindu and Buddhist Tantrics, is *bhūtaśuddhi.* Described by Bharati (1965, 112) as "a step-by-step dissolution of grosser into subtler elements in the cosmographical hierarchy" through the use of a set group of mantras and *mudrās,* in order to achieve a "visualized merger with whatever supreme being or state the particular tradition postulates." It is discussed by Wheelock in his essay in this volume.

Considering the significance and complexity of these mantric preliminaries, it is surprising how little scholarly reflection they have elicited. Standing virtually alone as a model for systematic, scientific reflection is a two-part study by Padoux, dealing first (1978a) with *mantroddhāra,* second (1980) with *nyāsa.* Comparing the two lists cited earlier, Hoens (Gupta, Hoens, & Goudriaan 1979, 109) recognizes that the ten *saṃskāras* "could originally have been a more general series of ceremonies introducing the practice of mantras. "Perhaps," he adds, "study of more texts can solve this riddle." Such study is surely necessary for clarifying

---

**Padoux (1980, 83, n. 2) makes much the same point more fully and more eloquently.*

the nature and function of the mantric preliminaries. One should add that it will bear the most fruit only if it is informed by a coherent theory of ritual action.

It is convenient to consider here not only Tantric initiation but some references to Vedic initiation and to initiation in classical and "sectarian" Hinduism in general. To begin with, on *dīkṣā* there is a marvelous monograph by Gonda (1965a, 315–462) with attention given to Indo-European background, possible central Asian/shamanic influence, practices among Indian tribal groups, and ethnographic parallels. On initiation preparatory to the Vedic sacrifice, see Lindner (1878); Heesterman (1957) provides a clear, well-documented, imaginative account of the Vedic "royal consecration" (*rājasūya*); on initiation and the symbolism of rebirth, see Lommel (1955). Von Glasenapp (1952–54) presents an account of Buddhist initiation in medieval Java. This, of course, should be thought through in the context of the large comparative literature concerning rituals of initiation, which cannot be surveyed here. For the classic approach of history of religions, see van Gennep (1960), Bleeker (1965), and Eliade (1965), which are representative. For orientation to the treatment of initiation among anthropologists, see the general remarks on the study of ritual on pages 331–32.

On Tantric *dīkṣā*, one may well begin with the brief survey by Hoens (Gupta, Hoens, & Goudriaan 1979, 71–89), with comments on the role of the guru. Another brief discussion is found in Bharati (1965, 185–98). As Bharati (185f.) stresses, mantric utterance is definitive of Tantric initiation:

> The dictionary [i.e., Monier-Williams] omits the most important aspect of *dīkṣā* . . . that its content must be a *mantra* of some sort, or that a *mantra* must be part of its content. A person may be initiated into the use, say, of a *maṇḍala*, a *yantra*, or into the performance of a *yajña* . . . , but along with it a *mantra* is invariably imparted.

Bharati's assertion is supported by the words of Kṛśṇānanda's *Tantrasāra* "initiation is the giving of mantra by the guru."* On the other hand, (analogically?) there are *dīkṣās* that do not seem to involve the passing on of a mantra. Bharati (1965, 190) refers to the *yogadīkṣā* of certain religious orders, such as the Nāthas, and to the conception, among the same groups, of *jñānadīkṣā*, where the mantra is Brahman, period. Even more striking is the widespread conviction that one can receive a valid *dīkṣā* in

**One might observe that this passage was established as defining* dīkṣa *in the scholarly literature by Woodroffe, when he quoted it in his 1913 introduction to the* Mahānirvāṇa Tantra *(rep.* Introduction to Tantra Śāstra *1973, 68). It has subsequently been cited by any number of writers, among them Gonda (1965a, 441) and Bharati (1965, 193). The latter speaks of this as if it were from Abhinavagupta's TS, thus falling foul of his own sound caution (p. 320) that the two are not to be confused.*

a dream. This tradition implicitly undercuts the indispensability of the guru, but his absence is often rationalized by the convention that the deity is serving as his or her own guru, something one would think twice about before criticizing. In this regard, one wonders how often mantras figure in dreams. For example, a Jain work, the *Riṣṭasamuccaya,* proposes a twofold classification of dreams. A dream told by a god is one in which a mantra is recited; the other sort lacks the mantric recitation (Wayman [1967] 1984, 402). On dreams, see Esnoul (1959) and O'Flaherty (1984). The interplay between liturgical and "spontaneous" initiations merits further investigation.

Just as in the case of mantric preliminaries and defects a list of types of *dīkṣā* would be useful. Hoens (Gupta, Hoens, Goudriaan 1979, 72–89) discusses several classifications drawn especially from the ŚārTlk and KulāT. To give some sense of the terminology, let me note that he mentions threefold classifications of *dīkṣās* appropriate to different levels of existence, in ascending order, *paśu, vīra* and *divya* or *sthūla, sūkṣma,* and *para* (72–74); a fourfold classification arranged ritualistically in terms, it seems to me, of ascending subtlety or ease of performance: *kriyāvatī-, varṇamayī-, kalāvatī-,* and *vedhamayīdīkṣā*. These terms barely scratch the surface. In a few pages, Hoens mentions at least ten other sorts of *dīkṣā* and, naturally, many subdivisions are possible.

While no scholar has yet written a general synthesis dealing with Tantric *dīkṣā,* one comparable to Gonda's synthesis focusing on the earlier material, the third volume of Hélène Brunner's *Somaśambhupaddhati* (1963–77), discussed on page 418 is exemplary. It provides a lavishly annotated French translation and analysis of the portion of the text that deals with initiation (pp. 1–538). The introduction contains a theoretical study of *dīkṣā* (pp. iii–xxvii), a description of the *dīkṣās* the text describes (pp. xxx–xliii)—Somaśambhu distinguishes between *samaya-, viśeṣa-, nirvāṇa-, tritattva-,* and *ekatattvadīkṣā*—as well as relevant remarks concerning the master and disciple (pp. xxvii–l) and ritual ablutions (*abhiṣeka*) (pp. xliii–xlvii). All in all, Brunner's work may be held up as a model of the sort of study without which further progress in understanding Tantric Mantraśāstra cannot be made.

It goes without saying that the right initiation was the one indispensable social preliminary to the effective use of a given mantra. Nonetheless, while initiation (*dīkṣā*) was typically discussed in every Tantric work, it does not seem to have been the subject of many independent treatises. Goudriaan (Goudriaan & Gupta 1981, 1.157) mentions only the *Kalādīkṣārahasyacarcā* and the *Kramadīkṣā* of Jagannātha. Hence, the documentation is especially scattered. Further study is obviously needed and, in so far as the evidence allows, it should coordinate textual, historical, and sociological perspectives, so that one can begin to get a picture of the kinds of initiations which were performed by various sorts of individuals under different circumstances.

Mantra and Meditation

A history of the use of mantras in the highly ritualized context of Tantric meditation would amount to a history of *sādhanā,* and such could not be written without clarifying the evolution of the family of meditative traditions that it has been conventional to label generically as *Yoga.* The extensive literature on Yoga is largely beyond the scope of this essay, but a few items may be noted. Obviously, many of the works cited earlier in the discussions of the ideology and context of Tantra are relevant to the study of Yoga. The closest we come to a general introduction to Yoga remains Eliade (1969). It offers less a history or an exegesis of texts than an imaginative interpretation written from the point of view of the *histoire des religions.* While Indologists do not always find it persuasive, its attempt to establish a broad interpretive context for the study of Yoga is invaluable. Of particular interest is the juxtaposition of discussions of Hindu and Buddhist yoga, and of Yoga and shamanism, a subject on which Eliade has also written extensively. The volume has a rich bibliography, which, however, should be supplemented with the bibliography of Schreiner (1979). With Eliade, one might compare a different but equally accessible interpretation of yoga, Zimmer (1960).

The obvious place to begin the study of mantras and Yoga in the post-Upaniṣadic age is the *YogaSū* and its commentaries. Especially relevant are *Sūtras* 1.27–28, "Īśvara is designated by the word OṂ. [One should] repeat the word OṂ and meditate on [Īśvara] to whom it refers";* and *Sūtra* 2.32, "The observances are cleanliness, contentment, self-denial (*tapas*), study (*svādhyāya*), and devotion to god," where *tapas* is understood by Vyāsa to include vows of silence (*ākāramauna*) and inexpressiveness (*kāṣṭhamauna*), and *svādhyāya* to include *praṇavajapa.*** The import of these sūtras can only be appreciated in context and in light of the commentaries. Among the numerous English translations, the general reader might consult Taimni (1961) and Hariharānanda Āranya Swāmi (1983). The standard commentary (*bhāṣya*) on the YSū is attributed to Vyāsa; however, it needs to be read in terms of its own commentaries. The oldest of these is the *Tattvavaiśāradī* of Vācaspatimiśra (ninth–tenth centuries), for which, see Woods (1914). Later, but of greater philosophical interest, is the *Yogavārttika* of Vijñānabhikṣu (late sixteenth–early seventeenth centuries). On this, we now have a (still incomplete) translation by Rukmani (1981–83), which contains what, all and all, is probably the best English translation of the YSū so far.

Read in translation, the YSū is a deceptively simple text. A serious assessment of what it has to say about mantric utterance must take into account the historical and systematic problems involved in its exegesis.

---

* *tasya vācakaḥ praṇavaḥ* (27)
tajjapas tadarthabhāvanam (28)

** *śaucasantoṣatapaḥsvādhyāyeśvarapraṇidhānāni niyamāḥ* (32)

The most recent and sophisticated reading is that of Oberhammer (1965; and especially 1977), which is in German. Oberhammer carefully disentagles what different portions of the text have to say about central terms for types of meditative experience; e.g., *samādhi, nirodha, samāpatti,* and *saṃyama* (very roughly: immersion, suppression, absorption, and concentration). He further attempts to sort out the complex relationship between Yoga and theism. It is in this context that one should consider his discussion (pp. 167–77) of OṂ, *japa,* and mantra in the YSū.

Central to the use of Mantraśāstra as an internal meditative discipline are the elaborate traditions of internal physiognomy, which are at least as old as the Vedic Upaniṣads. On the pivotal concept of the inner breaths and related matters, see Ewing (1901), G. W. Brown (1919), Falk (1939), Narahari (1944), Filliozat (1946), who speculates on the origins of *prāṇāyāma* in the late Vedic age, and Pensa (1969); and compare Wikander (1941) on Indo-Iranian concepts of wind. Compare these with the discussion of *mudrā* and *nyāsa* on pages 408–10.

It is abundantly evident that the cultivation of magical powers is a significant element in the social context that leads large numbers of people to take seriously both Mantraśāstra and Yoga. Therefore, an assessment of the intersection between Yoga and mantra necessitates grappling with the tradition of acquiring *siddhis* (or *vibhūtis*) (perfections, extraordinary powers) through mantric utterance allied with the discipline of meditation. It should be pointed out that this tradition is by no means limited to the movement of the Siddhas or the Nāthasaṃpradāya. On the contrary, as the *Vibhūti-* and *Kaivalyapādas* of the YSū—sections of the text too often rationalized or dismissed as peripheral by Western and neo-Hindu apologists—make plain, it is central. Hence, YSū 4.1, "The perfections (*siddhi*) arise innately, chemically, from mantra, from ascetic exercises (*tapas*) or from meditative trance (*samādhi*)." Vyāsa explicates forthrightly, "Through mantra one gains [powers such as] miniaturization and flying through the air."* On the *siddhis,* there is an important study by Lindquist (1935), in German. Bharati (1976a) presents a set of essays that place this tradition in its social context. See, too, Garbe (1903), A. Jacoby (1914), Hocart (1923), Hauer (1931), and in assessing this tradition, see Filliozat (1953).

Finally, two topics must be mentioned if only because they have received unwarranted and mystifying attention in the West, the imagery of *kuṇḍalinī,* which is connected with the whole notion of the subtle body and, related to it, *haṭhayoga,* a term that does not appear to lend itself to any single precise definition but which is connected to the tradition of the Nāthas discussed on page 372. A representative text dealing with the tradition of *kuṇḍalinīyoga* is the *Ṣaṭcakranirūpaṇa* of Pūrṇānanda, a translation of which appeared in Woodroffe (1918), *The Serpent Power.*

---

* janmauṣadhimantratapaḥsamādhijāḥ siddhayaḥ
mantraiḥ ākāśagamanāṇimādilābhaḥ.

Woodroffe's account strikes me as both clearer and sounder than that of his many imitators. Woodroffe's treatment is discussed in Pandit (1959). The most recent, up-to-date treatment of *kuṇḍalinīyoga* is by Silburn (1983), in French. Based largely on texts associated with the Śaiva traditions of Kashmir, it is a psychologically sensitive analysis giving special attention to the use of the mantra SAUḤ. See also Roesel (1928), Zimmer (1931), Risch (1951), and Dekker (1955). For the treatment of these two themes in Neo-Hinduism as preached in the West see pages 441–43.

At least from the age of the *Sāma-* and *Yajurvedas-*, it was taken for granted that to be effective a mantra, as a ritual instrument, must be uttered with mathematical exactitude. In post-Vedic India, this concern for precision characteristically expresses itself as a preoccupation with the frequency with which a mantra is repeated, although, generally speaking, repetition without counting does not count (Gonda [1963b] 1975b, 4.263). Hence the notion of *japa,* the repetitive murmuring of a mantra or of the name of a god. *Japa* is undoubtedly the central mode of uttering mantras in both the Tantric and devotional context. As Gonda (*ibid.*) notes, already *ViṣṇuDhŚās* 55.21 teaches that a Brahman attains perfection through *japa* alone. Yet *japa* is an open field to explore with the multitude of methodological strategies offered, for example, by linguistics, ritual studies, and theater. To the best of my knowledge, there is no single textually grounded, methodologically imaginative general essay on this vital subject. Bedekar (1964) deals with the exposition of *japa* in the *Mokṣadharmaparvan* of the Mhb and in the YSū. On the important topic of types of *japa,* see Padoux (1977, a brief discussion of the technical term *vidarbha;* as well as 1986a). On the use of a "rosary" as an aid in counting mantric repetitions, see Kirfel (1949). For a brilliant, highly personal neo-Hindu reinterpretation of *japa,* very broadly conceived see the works of Pratyagātmānanda Sarasvati cited on page 442.

THE WORLD OF SOUND

Vāc and Her Permutations

Tantric *Mantraśāstra* envisions ultimate reality as sonic, a primordial, ineffable trilling of infinite potentiality, comparable perhaps to the faint humming of bees.* The penultimate quotidian world, in all its messy complexity, is conceived of as the expression of this primordial sonic energy, although a variety of metaphors are used. Mantra is the privileged key to this reality. As Sanjukta Gupta (Gupta, Hoens, & Goudriaan 1979, 179) puts it, "mantras are the highest forms of manifest

---

**This metaphor is suggested by* Śivasaṃhitā *5.26–27 (Vasu [1914–15] 1979, 58), which states that when through gradual practice the primordial sound arises it is first comparable to a sound like that of intoxicated bees, the flute, and the vina;* nādaḥ saṃjāyate tasya krameṇābhyāsataś ca vai// mattabhṛṅgaveṇuvīṇāsadṛśaḥ prathamo dhvaniḥ/.

sound and are the perfect media for experiencing the supreme *Śabdabrahman.*"

For a brief introduction to this view of the cosmos, see Hoens (Gupta, Hoens, & Goudriaan 1979, 90–117). For a more thorough survey one must turn to Padoux (1963), in French, which, for some twenty years, has been a standard source. See especially Chapter 1, "Les premières spéculations sur les origines de la parole"; Chapter 3, "La manifestation du son," which includes treatments of *nāda, bindu,* and *Śabdabrahman;* and Chapter 4, "Les niveaux de la parole," dealing with the theory of fourfold speech: *parā-, paśyantī-, madhyamā-,* and *vaikharī vāk.* A revised and enlarged English edition of this work is in preparation. The general reader limited to English may still consult Woodroffe (1922), the *Garland of Letters,* a collection of essays on the theory and practice of Mantraśāstra. It lacks historical and textual discrimination but partially compensates for this by its accessibility. Indeed, a brief essay on "the theory and practice of the mantra," comparable to Tucci's essay on the *maṇḍala,* is a desideratum.

The Tantric "Alphabet"

Paralleling the concept of the four states of Vāc is a more complex scheme focusing on the refraction of Vāc in the fifty phonemes of the Sanskrit language. (For this purpose *kṣ* is considered an independent *akṣara* rather than a conjunct of *k* and *ṣ,* yielding fifty rather than forty-nine *varṇas.*) Although it is conventional to speak in this context of an "alphabet," this is somewhat misleading. Rather, one has an ordered cosmogonic procession of phonemes understood to be the eternal, primordial sounds that are the building blocks of the cosmos in its entirety. Utilized in cosmogonic, ritual, meditative, and mantric contexts, the alphabet is conceived of the primal matrix out of which the ordinary (*vyavahārika*) world emerges and to which the adept may return.

In some texts, it is thought of both in its usual order as *śabdarāśi* (literally, the mass of sound), and as Mālinī (Garland), in a special order from *na* to *pha,* hence called *nādiphāntarūpā.** Through this doubling of the fifty permutations of Vāc, we can glimpse something of the self-consciousness of Tantra. For example, the first sections of the KubjT describes the Mālinī as "a particular secret 'female' sequence of the letters of the alphabet and a 'womb' of *mantras,* conceived of as a re-creation of Devī out of Śiva's body" (Goudriaan & Gupta 1981, 1.53). In contrast, Śiva is "the usual 'male' arrangement of letters (*śabdaraśi*)." The "quarrel" between Śiva and Kubjikā, which the text reports, is really between the two arrangement of *akṣaras.* It reveals a characteristic dialectic: On the one hand is the world of social orthodoxy, the world of the Veda, masculinity, and ordinary language; over against it is an in-

*(*Having a form which begins with* na *and ends with* pha.)

verted realm, if you will, a "counterculture," the world of the *Āgamas*, femininity, and mantric utterance.

For a standard account of this material, see Chapter 5, "L'Émanation phonématique," in Padoux (1963, 183–260), which, among other topics, deals with *nāda*, *bindu*, *mātṛkā*, and *mālinī*. In English, there is a useful discussion in Appendix 2 in Schoterman (1982, 210–21) and a less technical summary by Hoens (Gupta, Hoens, & Goudriaan 1979, 90–101). From these accounts, one can get a sense of the elaborate sets of correlations between phonemes, constituents of reality (*tattvas*), "powers" (*śaktis*, *mātṛkās*), and parts of the body.

The general reader should keep in mind two caveats. Different texts present the evolutionary efflorescence of Vāc—and of Śiva and Śakti—differently. So, too, their understanding of basic concepts such as *nāda* and *bindu* vary. Popular accounts that speak as if there were a single Tantric system of "sonic mysticism" are grievously misleading. Second, the conceptual and historical priority can easily be misunderstood. The elaborate sonic mysticism found in the Tantras, as we saw earlier on pages 414–15, has Vedic precedents and presupposes the philosophy of Bhartṛhari. It is reasonable to hypothesize that it arose as an attempt to explain mantric utterance. In other words, it was taken for granted—experienced empirically—that mantras work. The Tantric speculation on Vāc explains how they work in such a way that more of them can be "created" and so they can be made to work more effectively. As Hoens (Gupta, Hoens, & Goudriaan 1979, 93) says, "The theory of sound and meaning probably originated in the speculation on the sacred syllables, particularly *Oṃ*, which . . . originated in the Veda and continues to be the main focus of Tantric sound symbolism."

Besides the KubjT and related texts, the Śrīvidyā/Śrīcakra tradition offers a rich source for systematic reflection on the cosmos as an organism woven of sound. Perhaps the most important speculative work in this tradition is the *Kāmakalāvilāsa*, "a learned exposition in 55 artfully composed Āryā stanzas of the principles of cosmogonic symbolism . . . geometrically represented in the Śrīcakra" (Goudriaan & Gupta 1981, 1.168f.). An English translation is found in Rawson (1973b). More thorough and more impressive is the *Yoginīhṛdaya*, a French translation of which by Padoux is forthcoming.

While I have generally excluded works dealing with the Śaiva traditions of Kashmir from this Bibliography, one cluster of studies are too significant to overlook. Important evidence concerning the Tantric alphabet and the *bīja* mantra SAUḤ is provided in an Āgamic fragment of approximately thirty-five verses attributed to the *RudrayāmalaT*.* Known as the *Parātrīśikā* (or *Parātriṃśikā*), it was commented upon twice by

**In a very Borgesian manner, this appears to be a* title—*to which some fifty independent and apparently unrelated texts have attached themselves—rather than a* text *see Goudriaan & Gupta 1981, 1.47).*

Abhinavagupta, in a *Laghuvṛtti* (also known as the *Anuttaratattvavimarśinī*) and a *Vivaraṇa* (also known as the *Tattvaviveka*). Both texts are rather obscure and have attracted considerable attention. The longer text was published in Volume 18 (M. R. Shastri 1918), the shorter in Volume 68 (J. Z. Shastri 1947) of the KSTS. The *Laghuvṛtti* has been translated into Italian by Gnoli (1965) and French, with extensive annotations, by Padoux (1975); for a critical response to the French translation, see Torella (1980). After a number of preliminary essays (1959a; 1959b; and 1960), Gnoli (1985) has also brought out an Italian translation of the *Vivaraṇa*. An English translation has been prepared by Jaidev Singh (forthcoming). For reflection on this literature from the perspective of religious studies, see Muller-Ortega (forthcoming).

On the function of the *akṣaras* of the Sanskrit alphabet as "mystical symbols" in non-Indian Buddhist circles, see Scherman (1947). This is a tradition that traveled with Buddhism to East Asia, where it was influenced by the indigenous importance of calligraphy; on the Siddha alphabet in Japan, see Etasu (1978). For a well-illustrated general account, Stevens (1981) may be recommended.

Bīja and Other Exemplary Mantras

The number of mantras is sometimes reckoned at seventy million. That means the tradition recognizes it as infinite. But, in fact, the number of mantras in regular use is finite (cf. Brunner 1963–77, I.xxx–xxxvi). Is it possible to decide which mantras are the most important or the most typical? Not with any certainty at this stage in the study of Mantraśāstra, but note the selection of some standard surveys: Hoens (Gupta, Hoens, & Goudriaan 1979, 110f.) very briefly discusses the Pādukāmantra PĀDUKĀṂ PŪJAYĀMI, the Haṃsa mantra SO HAṂ, the Gāyatrī, OM, and the Māyābīja HRĪṂ. Padoux (1963, 339–62) provides expositions of OṂ, AHAM, MAHA, SAUḤ, and the Piṇḍanātha, RKṢKHEṂ. Bharati (1965, 132–40) discusses more than a dozen mantras drawn from Jain and Buddhist as well as Hindu sources.

In the introduction to this volume and in my own essay, I argued that the function—and in that sense the "meaning"—of a mantra is radically context-dependent. To the extent that is the case, any list of exemplary mantras will have to be context or "sub-context" specific. At the very least, one would have to discriminate among the mantras that occur in the *Śrauta* ritual, in the *Gṛhya* ritual, in a Bhaktic and theistic setting, in Tantra, not to mention those situations we classify as "folk." For each identifiable strand of Indian religious life, then, an exemplary mantra would be one around which one might organize a portrayal of the ideology, ritual, and social order that together make-up its "support-structure." Implicitly, the tradition recognizes this. Many texts or movements designate a certain mantras, or group of mantras, as *mūla* mantras, "root" mantras. In each case, the term is intended to assert the metaphysical priority of a mantra. Seen sociologically, it suggests one way of identifying those mantras that functioned in a definitive way for each *saṃpradāya*.

The essays in this volume, as well as other sections of this Bibliography, will suggest numerous mantras that might be exegeted as exemplars. For the purpose of illustration, a few possibilities may be mentioned here. One of the distinguishing features of Śākta Tantra is the use of the Śrīvidyā (mantra) (Goudriaan & Gupta 1981, 1.58ff.). One of the chief texts devoted to it is the *Saundaryalaharī*, an illustrated edition of which has been edited and translated by W. N. Brown (1958). (It should be noted that the first forty-one verses of this text also circulate separately as the *Ānandalaharī*, on which, see Woodroffe (1961).) Allowing for certain variants, the *Śrīviydā* consists of sixteen syllables, fifteen of them "public," the sixteenth imparted by the guru to his *śiṣya* in secret, namely, *HASAKALAHṚṂ HASAKAHALAHṚṂ SAKALAHṚṂ ŚRĪṂ*.* This mantra is sometimes understood to be "an esoteric form of the Gāyatrī mantra, which is the quintessence of the Vedas and is identified with the [four Vedāntic] *Mahāvākyas* of the Upaniṣads" (Venkataraman 1956, 257). It is sometimes held to have originated from the mantra of ṚV 5.47.4a: *Catvāra īm bibhrati kṣemayantaḥ*. Literally, this means "Four support him (*īm*), desiring (his) rest." Sāyaṇa interprets it, "Four priests, desiring to protect themselves, support God (the Āditya) with offerings and praises." According to some interpreters of the Śrīkula the esoteric reading is, "that which contains the four *īms* and confers benefit," that is, the Śrīvidyāmantra (*ibid.*)**

Similarly, one might consider the Prāsāda- or Parāprāsādamantra—the *bīja* mantra SAUḤ—which is central to certain of the Śaivāgamas that were widely respected in the Trika, where, however, it is known as the *Hṛdayabīja* not the *prāsada;*† the twenty-two syllable *vidyā* of Dakṣiṇakālī, KRĪṂ KRĪṂ KRĪṂ HŪṂ HŪṂ HRĪṂ HRĪṂ DAKṢIṆE KĀLIKE KRĪṂ KRĪṂ KRĪṂ HŪṂ HŪṂ HRĪṂ HRĪṂ SVĀHĀ, which is discussed in the KāliT, (Goudriaan & Gupta 1981, 1.80); or the ten *akṣara* Bengali Vaiṣṇava mantra, GOPĪJANAVALLABHĀYA NAMAḤ, discussed in the first chapter of the *GautamīyaT* (Goudriaan & Gupta 1981, 1.106).

One phenomenon requires special attention. Central to Tantric mantraśāstra is the use of *bījas:* adamantine, unbreakable syllables lacking meaning outside a mantric context. Insofar as I know, no one has cata-

---

**This is based on verses 32f. of the* Saundaryalaharī *(W. N. Brown 1958, 93).*

***CATVĀRAḤ ṛtvijaḥ ĪM enam ādityaṃ KṢEMAYANTAḤ kṣemam ātmana icchantaḥ BIBHRATI dhārayanti havirbhiḥ stutibhiś ca (Sontakke and Kashikar reissue 1976, 875), this sort of imaginative exegesis is facilitated by the fact that the verse is enigmatic to start with and that the pronominal particle* īm *is not used in classical Sanskrit.*

†For some refs. see Goudriaan and Gupta (1981, I.81, 96); in fact the names of mantras vary from preceptorial tradition to preceptorial tradition; for some the Prāsādamantra is HAUḤ, cf. Brunner (1963–77, I.xxxii).

logued the textual descriptions of *bījas*. But Hoens (Gupta, Hoens, & Goudriaan 1979, 105) provides a useful definition. A *bīja* is "a mantra consisting of one syllable with no ordinary meaning and always ending in the *anusvara:* ṃ." The problem that is most vexing is that of the etiology of *bījas:* Where do they come from? Questions concerning their history and function will not be solved until the question of their origin, which should not be understood as a diachronic question, has been clarified. Bharati (1965, 113–18) outlined the problem over twenty years ago, but he does not seem to have addressed it in his subsequent work. The most fruitful approach, I suspect, will emerge from Staal's work in which mantra is analyzed in light of ethology—the study of animal behavior. See Staal (1984a; 1984b; 1985a), as well as his essay in this volume. See, further, on Vedic roots of the *bīja* tradition, the discussion of *stobha* on page 344, and C. W. Bolle (1959).

THE DIFFUSION OF MANTRAS

To treat the diffusion of mantras beyond the various modalities of Brahmanism, classical Hinduism, and Tantra stretches this essay beyond its central foci. Accordingly, this section of the Bibliography should be considered an appendix. It is meant only to suggest lines of inquiry. It is even more highly selective than the previous sections.

INDO-EUROPEAN BACKGROUND

I do not know whether anyone has systematically researched the possible existence of Indo-European technical vocabulary shedding light on the origin of the term *mantra*. But on the meaning of Indo-European *men-*, see, besides the standard etymological dictionaries, Meillet (1897). Equally important, when considering the structure of Vedic mantras, is their possible "precursors" in the poetic style of other Indo-European literature. On this, see, in general, Schmitt (1967), also Wüst (1969a; 1969b) and Benveniste (1968).

Gonda ([1963b] 1975b, 4.259) categorically states, "it may . . . safely be contended that from the prehistoric period of Indo-Iranian community onward the mantra concept—created no doubt by the mystery of speech as that which expresses thought—played an important role in the religious life and conceptions of the Āryan peoples." See Thieme (1957) and, on the Avestan *ma ra*, see the references in (Gonda [1963b] 1975, 258f.). Gonda (1963a, 259–65, with refs.) discusses Iranian cognates to *dhī*, on which, see also Molé (1960). On traditions of poetry/prophecy among other Indo-European peoples, see, for example, Runes (1926).

NON-HINDU AND QUASI-HINDU MANTRIC TRADITIONS WITHIN INDIA

Although anything like an exhaustive survey of mantras among strata of South Asian culture not usually considered Hindu is beyond the scope of this essay, certain readily available items may be mentioned for the convenience of the reader.

Just as most mantras are multifunctional, so many—but not all—of them can easily be made to work in mythologically and philosophically distinct traditions. Bharati (1965, 135) discusses this and notes, for example, that Śiva, in various guises, is "worshipped in Buddhist Tantric and partly even in Jaina Tantric discipline." Similarly, he observes (p. 136) that "the notion of *śūnya*, though be no means identical in philosophical import with Brahman, is sufficiently close in its numinosity to it to warrant *mantra* similarity." (In this regard, one might add that a comparative study of the concept of *śunya* in the *Śaivāgamas*, and especially in the Śaiva traditions of Kashmir, and Tantric, Indian and Tibetan, Buddhism might throw considerable light on the common religious milieu of South Asia in the second half of the first millenium.)

One of the subsidiary themes of this essay has been that mantra is a pan-Indian phenomenon and that, from the point of view of Mantraśāstra, the division of South Asian religious life into "religions" is artificial. The case should not be overstated, however. The significant overlap in practice between Hindu and Buddhist Tantra must not obscure the contrast between the ontological stance of the former tradition and the deontological stance of the latter. Much of the available literature on Buddhist thought stresses the difference. One brief essay that presents the Buddhist side, relevant to the study of Buddhist Tantric Mantraśāstra, is Guenther (1956).

The Use of Mantras Among "Tribal Groups"

Bharati (1965, 152), discussing the extent of mantric utterance in Indian initiation rituals, observes that according to Koppers (1948) the Bhils, the Santals, and the Mundas widely employ "partly intelligible, partly dyssemantic" sacred formulae. To a certain extent—I would suppose, both predominantly and increasingly—the use of mantras or, as some writers would have it, "mantralike" utterances in the tribal vernaculars reflects that process of acculturation to high-caste, pan-Indian practices and values, which Srinivas dubbed Sanskritization. Thus Bharati (1965, 186) reports that "the Todas in South India impart a regular *mantra* [in the Toda language] to their sons, in analogy to the *upanayana* (investiture with the sacred thread) ceremony of the twice-born Hindus."

Kakar (1982, 92–106) discusses an Oraon shaman, a *bhagat,* who uses mantras to repel cases of possession involving "lower-order" spirits. More powerful spirits require more elaborate treatments; e.g., *pūjā*. Here, too, mantras seem to be a prime vehicle of Sanskritization: When talking to the patient, the *bhagat* speaks Oraon, but his "communication with the divine, either through the mantra or prayer, are invariably in Hindi, stressing both the formality and the privilege of the *bhagat*'s position vis a vis the divine" (p. 103).

Examination of the ethnographic literature might reveal interesting instances of interaction between Hindu mantras and non-Hindu verbal formulae. However, I have not pursued this line of research and I cannot vouch for its fruitfulness. The place to begin is probably the survey of Hermanns (1964–73) and the *Encyclopedia Mundarica*, Hoffmann and van Emelen (1930–41); see, in addition, Jungblut (1943) on "magic songs" among the Bhils, Elwin (1944–54), Stiglmayr and Fodermayr (1970), Bhagvat (1972), and Mahapatra (1979) on Santal "invocation songs." In general, exploration of tribal priesthoods, rituals of possession, and rituals of healing might be most interesting, in regard to which, see the items on medicine on pages 391–92.

The Use of Mantras Among Muslims, Sikhs, and Jains

The evidence for the use of mantras among Indian Muslims—on the folk level, at popular shrines, perhaps in devotional poetry—must be culled from the ethnographic literature. Given the history of Indian Islam, the role of the Sufi orders in the conversion of large portions of the Hindu peasantry in certain regions, significant overlap between so-called Hindu and Muslim practices is not surprising. To give some idea of the possibilities, Bharati (1965, 186) reports a Dattātreyapīṭha in Mysore, where the officiant is a Muslim *mahant*, installed by a predecessor who imparts *dīkṣā* with a lengthy mantra of "garbled Sanskrit and Arabic" including, of course, both OṂ and BISMILLAHI. Gonda (1975b, 272) cites an instance of Muslims using verses from the Qur'an the way Hindus use Tantric mantras in amulets.* Sanjukta Gupta discusses Fakir Lalan Sah (Matilal Das and Mahapatra 1958). Her judgment (Goudriaan & Gupta 1981, 178) is germane, "The general technique of Tantra Yoga became so diffused amongst the mystics of India that even Muslim mystics borrowed it and used its terminology in their mystic lyric songs." Hence, it is exceedingly difficult to decide what to count as Tantric and what to exclude.

I assume that the literature, ritual traditions, and folk practices of the Sikhs would prove another rich source for the study of Mantraśāstra in a North Indian devotional context. It would seem likely that the importance of the divine name in both the Vaiṣṇava tradition and in Islam would be reflected in the *Ādi Granth* and later Sikh scriptures and that, perhaps through the intermediary of the Kabīrpanth, the Sikh tradition inherited much of the sonic mysticism of words and the Word one associates with Tantra. Gonda ([1963b] 1975b, 4.286), for example, cites *Ādi Granth* 1.2, "Everything connected with the three worlds is contained in the fifty-two letters." But the scientific study of the Sikh tradition has hardly begun, and I have come across no secondary literature devoted to its use of mantras or its theology of the Word. For orientation, see Juergensmeyer and Barrier (1979).

**Indeed, written with the blood of bats or moles!*

On Jain Mantraśāstra, there is Jhavery (1944), which, even more than Kiehl's *Instrument and Purpose,* is a remarkable and grievously underconsulted work. Bharati mentions in passing (1965, 121) that the principal Jain Tantra is the *Bhairavīpadmāvatīkalpa.* See also Shah (1947), and Bagchi (1921).

Mantras in Indian Buddhism

As general introductions to Buddhist Tantra, a variety of older works are still serviceable: Benoytosh Bhattacharyya (1927; 1932; 1956), S. B. Dasgupta (1950), Bagchi (1956a), and, in German, von Glasenapp (1936a; 1936b; 1940). Among popular accounts written by Westerners, Govinda (1970) strikes me as particularly helpful. For brief orientation, see R. Ray (1974), a review essay on Wayman (1973). The most thought-provoking, up-to-date introductions to Buddhist Tantra of which I am aware are found in various works of Alex Wayman and Herbert Guenther, both of whom, of necessity, draw upon both Sanskrit and Tibetan materials. The work of both scholars may conveniently be approached through collections of essays, Wayman (1973) and Guenther (1977). From them, one should to on the Lessing and Wayman (1968) and Wayman (1977), on the one hand, and Guenther (1959; 1963; 1969b), on the other. Among other editions and translations of Buddhist Tantric works into English, I would note the *Hevajra Tantra,* Snellgrove (1959); the *Samvarodaya Tantra,* Tsuda (1974); and the *SarvadurgatipariśodhanaT,* Skorupski (1983a). See, further, the references specific to Buddhism in Tibet on pages 439–41.

Bharati (1965, 104) argues that "there is evidence of a well-founded body of mantric texts in the Pāli scriptures" and cites the occurrence of *parittas* (protective *mantras*) in the *Nikāyas.* He goes on to note that later "the Mahāsanghikas had collections of quasi-mantric formulae called '*dhāraṇī*' or '*vidyādharapiṭaka,*'" as well as to argue that the *udānas* (solemn pronouncements) of the Theravāda tradition "could well be called *mantric.*" I am unaware of any studies that explore the possible evolution of Mantraśāstra in pre-Tantric Buddhism, but see J. Masson (1942) on early Buddhist popular religion in general. The contribution of non-Indian sources to the rise of Tantra has been the subject of some speculation, but less thought; for possible foreign elements in Indian Tantras, see Bagchi (1931).

The most abundant evidence and work has focused on the Tantric Buddhism of Bengal (and its survival in neighboring Tibet), for general information on which, see Benoytosh Bhattacharyya (1921), De (1938), and S. B. Dasgupta (1962). The most important expression of Buddhist Tantra in Bengal is a group of songs known as *dohās* or *cāryas.* Versions, presenting knotty textual and historical problems exist in Apabhraṃśa, old Bengali, and Tibetan. On the *Cāryapadas,* one may see for rapid orientation, Zbavitel 1976, 124–33). See further Shahidullah (1928, in French; 1940), Bagchi (1938), Mojumdar (1967), Guenther (1969a), which is an English translation from the Tibetan, and most recently, Kvaerene (1977). Among works in Bengali, note Sen (1956), Haraprasād Śāstrī (1916), M. Basu (1968); in Hindi, Sankṛtyāyana (1957). To this one should compare the material on the Vaiṣṇava Sahajiyā cult, as well as the material on Bengali folk religion listed on page 369. The discussion of the nature of language in Buddhist philosophical texts has been treated on page 390.

MANTRAS BEYOND INDIA

Śrī Laṅka, Indonesia, and Southeast Asia

In an important theoretical essay, Tambiah ([1968] 1985, 19ff.) discusses the use of mantras among Sinhalese Buddhists. He distinguishes between mantra (spell), *kannalavva,* a sequence in prose, and *kaviya* (verses). In spite of the fact that mantras are classified as the language of demons (*yakṣā bāsāva*), he argues against "a prevailing misconception . . . that Sinhalese *mantra* are unintelligible or even nonsensical" and he reports that the mantras make use of a "hierarchy of languages": Sanskrit, Pāli, Bengali, Tamil, Telugu, Malayalam, and Persian. Compare the other essays by Tambiah.

For a general account of the Indian religions in Indonesia, see Gonda (1975c). We are fortunate in having a detailed set of studies by Hooykaas (1964; 1966; 1973a; 1973b; 1974) and Goudriaan and Hooykaas (1971), which cumulatively discuss the context and lavishly document the use of mantras in the generally Tantric, Hindu, and Buddhist Indic traditions of Java and Bali. For a review article of recent work on the religion of Bali, see Goudriaan (1976); also Hooykaas (1983). Much of the prior work on these traditions has been done in Dutch; among others, Gonda ([1963b] 1975b, 4.298) cites Goris (1926); also de Zoete and Spies (1938), and the *Gaṇapatitattwa* (Singal 1958). On the *Jñānasiddhānta,* a Balinese Śaiva Tantra, Goudriaan (Goudriaan & Gupta 1981, 1.102) cites the theses of H. Saebadio (1971). On Buddhist Tantra in Bali and Java, see Prabodh Chandra (1931) and von Glasenapp (1952–54), which deals with a thirteenth century Javanese initiation ritual (*mantrānaya*) edited in Wulff (1935). De Kleen (1942) is a study of the use of *mudrā* among Balinese Śaivite and Buddhist priests. For a general account of Hinduism in Cambodia, see K. Bhattacharya (1961); on Tantra in Cambodia see Bagchi (1928; 1930a).

Tibet

Besides the works on Indian Buddhism mentioned above, I wish to draw attention to a few items dealing exclusively with Tibet, which are relevant for the study of mantras (Tib., *sngags*). Three, in particular, display something of the range of available material.

First, Nebesky-Wojkowitz (1956), focusing on the Tibetan cult of protective deities (Skr. *dharmapāla, dvārapāla;* Tib. *chos skyong*), provides a dense, detailed account of popular Tibetan ritual. The discussion of oracles, divination, weathermakers, and destructive magic is especially valuable. Second, Beyer (1973), focusing on the cult of the goddess Tārā, offers the most extensive sophisticated interpretation of Tibetan Buddhist ritual to date. Of special importance is the discussion of "worship" in Tibetan Buddhist context and of rituals of initiation. Third, Govinda (1959), written by a passionate Western advocate of Buddhism, uses the famous mantra OṂ MAṆIPADME HŪṂ as a device around which to organize the central themes of Tibetan Buddhist mysticism in general. Whatever its defects might be, it remains—at least for this reader—a powerful, engaging introduction to its subject. As is well known, OṂ MAṆIPADME HŪṂ, which appears to be associated with the *bodhisattva* Avalokiteśvara, is one of the most widespread of all mantras. As Bharati (1965, 133) recognized it does not mean "The jewel is in the lotus." It means "[Homage to thee] O Maṇipadmā", where *maṇipadme* is the vocative of Manipadmā, the name of a goddess (note the long *ā*); but for an alternative, non-Sanskritic, way of reading the mantra, see Wayman (1977, 76). Among other sources, on the social role of poetry in Tibetan culture, see Duncan (1955) and R. A. Stein (1959); for an invocation ritual, Lessing (1951); Skorupski (1983b) on *homa* (oblation) rites and the *maṇḍalas* used for them; also the works by Stablein.

For good reason, the Tantric Buddhism of Tibet sometimes styles itself *mantrayāna*. Within its ritual cosmos, a variety of mantric techniques have been created. Besides *bīja*, the terms that parallel *mantra* include *hṛdaya*, *vidyā*, and *dhāraṇī*. The last of these has received the most attention, and on it, one may see Waddell (1912; 1914), Hauer (1927a), with a strong comparative, Middle Eastern perspective, and Bernhard (1967). On Tibetan Tantric art, see Lauf (1976); on charms and amulets, see Douglas (1978), with which one might compare Tambiah (1984), who deals with the cult of amulets in Southeast Asia. Finally, it is well worth mentioning that the "infamous" prayer wheels of Tibet are properly called, in Sanskrit, *mantracakras*. They are "machines for *japa*" not for personal prayers. How typical that for Westerners, unaware of the metaphysical theory in whose terms they *might* make sense, it would be taken for granted that they were inappropriately mechanical vehicles for prayer.

China and Japan

Mantraśāstra enters China, and through China the entire Far East, through Buddhism. There it finds itself allied with cognate indigenous traditions that, for the sake of convenience, may be referred to collectively as Taoist. The literature on the transmission of Buddhism to China and then Japan, no less the bibliography on Taoism, is quite extensive. On the former, see, for example, Bagchi (1927–28; 1950). Among standard sources see Zürcher (1959) and, on Japan, de Visser (1928–35). After many decades of receiving little attention, Taoist ritual has recently been the subject of several penetrating studies. Welch (1957), a model of generalization, can well serve the general reader as an introduction. For a few recent studies, see Saso (1972; 1978), Saso and Chappell (1977, with bibliog. 123–48), and Welch and Seidel (1979). For further bibliographical guidance, see Thompson (1976). Strickmann (1983, with bibliog.) deals with the persistence of the Indian *homa* ritual in the Far East. Specifically on Chinese Tantra, one might begin with Chou-yi-liang (1945). On the "mantrayānic aspect of the horse-cult in China and Japan" is a well-known monograph by van Gulik (1935). Finally, I shall group together a few items relevant to the study of *mudrā, maṇḍala,* mantra, or the Siddha alphabet in the Far East: Demiéville (1930; 1980) relevant to the music of mantras, Schubert (1954), van Gulik (1956), Saunders (1960), Macdonald (1962), Nagao (1971), L. Chandra and S. Devi (1978), and Rambach (1979); Tajima (1959) and Kiyota (1968) both deal with *maṇḍalas* in Shingon, which word, by the way, is the Japanese counterpart to the Sanskrit *mantra.* Also see the works on *mudrā* and *maṇḍala* listed on pages 405–409.

Analogous Practices in Western Religions

While Mantraśāstra is arguably unique to the Indic cultural sphere, several traditions have been identified that are patently analogous to it. Typically, they focus on the repetition of the name of god in what would usually be accepted as a mystical context. Eliade (1969, 216–19), for example, discusses the Muslim mystical technique of *dhikr.* While the relevant literature can hardly be surveyed here, a few items may be mentioned as a convenience to the reader: For the older *Religionswissenschaftliche* literature, see Heiler (1961, 275ff.); for a general survey focusing on the significance of names in classical antiquity, see Hirzel (1916); for the comparative significance of names among the Indo-European peoples, Solmsen (1922); on the repetition of the divine name in the context of Muslim mysticism, see Massignon (1922; 1943–45), Horten (1927–28), Moreno (1946), Dermenghem (1953), and Gardet (1952–53; 1972). On Christian hesychism, see Hausheer (1927; 1956), Jugie (1931), Bloom (1948; 1953), Kadloubousky and Palmer (1951; 1954), Gouilliard (1953), Nölle (1954), Lossky (1957), and von Ivanka (c. 1974). If, by the way, one doubts the living potential of this tradition in the secularized postwar United States, one should reread J. D. Salinger's *Franny and Zooey.*

MANTRAS IN NEO-HINDUISM IN INDIA AND THE WEST

Anything like a final appraisal of the evolution of Mantraśāstra in the reformulated Hinduism of the last century and a half would be premature. Some useful and important theoretical work has, been done, however. Three essays of Hacker (1958; 1970; 1971), to whom we are indebted for the very concept of neo-Hinduism (*Neuhinduismus*), are indispensable. Halbfass (1981), in German but with an expanded English version (forthcoming), provides a thorough, well-documented, philosophically lively history of the interaction of Indian and Western cultures. See also, Ashby (1974a) and, for an important social scientific perspective on neo-Hinduism, Bharati (1970b; 1971; and 1972).

Many contemporary works in the Indian vernaculars straddle the lines between traditional scholarship, modern scholarship, and popularization. A complete assessment of the place of Mantraśāstra in Indian civilization would have to examine these works and assess how they fit Mantraśāstra into the modern, in part neo-Hindu, age: how, in other words they present Mantraśāstra as a practical "science." Besides the works of Gopinath Kaviraj mentioned on page 394, a representative work of this sort is Awasthi Shastri (1966).

Among writers interpreting mantric utterance, and sacred language more broadly, to the twentieth-century Indian audience the most intriguing and prolific might well be Swāmi Pratyagātmānanda Saraswatī (Pramathanātha Mukhopādhyāya), at one time a collaborator of Sir John Woodroffe. His magnum opus is *Japasūtram,* for an English summary see (1971). On his work, see Mukhopadhyaya (1963). For other examples, see Vajpeyi (1979), in English, and B. Sharma (1969) and Sethiyā (1969), both in Hindi.

Mantra is used in neo-Hinduism predominantly, if not exclusively, in the context of Yoga. In this regard, see the bibliography dealing with Yoga among contemporary movements in Schreiner (1979, 78–104), an annotated list of some three hundred items dealing *inter alia* with the following figures: Sri Ramakrishna (1836–1886), Yogi Ramacharaka (Wm. Walker Atkinson) (1862–1932), Swami Vivekananda (1863–1902), Swami Abhedananda (1866–1939), Sri Aurobindo (1872–1950), Swami Sivananda (1887–1963), Sri Ramana Maharshi (1879–1950), Paramahamsa Yogananda (1893–1952), Krishnamurti (1895–1986), Srila A. C. Bhaktivedanta Swami Prabhupada (1896–1977), Gopi Krishna (1903–), Swami Narayanandana (1902–), Swami Satyananda (1923–), Rajneesh (1931–), Swami Kuvalayananda, Maharishi Mahesh Yogi, and Anandamayi Ma. A complete study of mantra would have to deal with the ways in which figures such as these modified traditional Mantraśāstra to fit the modern world or vice versa.

A few movements and items may be noted. One well known item is Vivekananda (1962). On Sri Aurobindo, see K. W. Bolle (1962; 1965b). Of the neo-Hindu movements that have flourished in the West, mantras are probably most central to Maharishi Mahesh Yogi's Transcendental Meditation movement, TM; on this, see White (1976) and Russell (1976). The use of *japa* and the repetition of the divine name is probably most characteristic of Bhaktivedanta Swami Prahbhupada's International Society of Krishna Consciousness; on ISKCON, see Gelber (1983) with a well-balanced bibliography. Among the movements relatively less well known in the West, sonic mysticism is probably most central to the Radhasoamis; on which, see Fripp (1964) and Ashby (1974b). Some contemporary enthusiasts interpret mantra as music or use mantra as a key for understanding music. See, for instance, Marcotty (1980) and Keyserling (1972).

Is it correct to describe the practices in these neo-Hindu movements in the West as Mantraśāstra? Perhaps, it is too early to know. To the extent that they are authentically Hindu, the movements are often inspired by Bhakti. The rigor of traditional *sādhanā* at its best is relaxed, swallowed up in devotional latitude, as was already the case in the "neo-Śāktism" of the Bengali Ramakrishna (Gupta in Goudriaan & Gupta 1981, 200).

And, then, there is the knotty problem of pronunciation. Americans, after all, do not get the sound right. This is bound to be troubling. From the Vedic age to the present day, in mantras the sound is the thing. An apologist might respond, neither do Indians. The Vedic ideal notwithstanding, there is no single absolutely correct way to pronounce Sanskrit, as regional variations in pronunciation, not to mention the migration of mantras from India to Central Asia and East Asia, abundantly prove.

Hindu devotees may take consolation from the reasoning of the Buddhist convert, Govinda (1959, 27):

> If the efficacy of mantras depended on their correct pronunciation, then all mantras in Tibet would have lost their meaning and power, because they are not pronounced according to the rules of Sanskrit, but according to the phonetic laws of the Tibetan language (for instance not: OṂ MAṆI PADME HŪṂ, but 'OṂ MAṆI Péme HŪṂ').
>
> This means that the power and the effect of a mantra depend on the spiritual attitude, the knowledge and responsiveness of the individual. The *śabda* or sound of the mantra is not a physical sound (though it may be accompanied by such a one) but a spiritual one. It cannot be heard by the ears but only by the heart, and it cannot be uttered by the mouth but only by the mind.

Filtered through Brooklynese, uttered as a Bronx cheer, whispered in an East Texas drawl, OṂ is always OṂ—or it isn't.

BIBLIOGRAPHICAL LIST

Abbot, Justin Edwards. 1933. *The Keys of Power, A Study of Indian Ritual and Belief.* NY: E. P. Dutton [1932].

Abegg, Emil. 1914. "Die Lehre vom Sphoṭa im Sarvadarśanasaṃgraha." In *Festschrift für Ernst Windisch* (Leipzig: Harrassowitz).

———. 1923. "Die Lehre der Ewigkeit des Wortes bei Kumārila." In *Festschrift Wackernagel,* pp. 255–64. (Göttingen: Vandenhoeck and Ruprecht).

Abhyankar, Kasinath Vasudev, and J. M. Shukla. 1977. *A Dictionary of Sanskrit Grammar,* 2nd rev. ed.. (GOS 134) Baroda: Oriental Institute. Orig. 1961.

Ācārya, Jādavaji Trikamji, ed. 1941. *The Caraka Saṃhitā by Agniveśa, revised by Caraka and Dṛḍhabala, with the Āyurvedadīpikā Commentary of Cakrapāṇidatta.* Bombay: Nirnaya Sagar Press.

Ācārya, Jādavaji Trikamji, and Nārāyaṇa Rāma Ācārya "Kāvyatīrtha," eds. 1980. *The Suśruta Saṃhitā of Suśruta, with the Nibandhasaṃgraha Commentary of Ḍalhaṇācārya and the Nyāyacndrikā Pañjikā of Gayadāsācārya on Nidānasthāna. (Jaikrishnadas Āyurveda Series* 34) Varanasi: Chaukhamba Orientalia.

Āchārya, Narayan Ram, ed. 1948a. *Brahmasūtrabhāṣya of Śaṅkara.* Bombay: Nirnaya Sagar Press.

———. 1948b. *Īśādiviṃśatyuttaraśatopaniṣadaḥ,* 5th ed. Bombay.

Agnihotri, B. S. 1964. "The Implication of *OM* in Philosophy," JOIB 14, no. 1:70–74.

Agrawala, V. S. 1959. "Sanskrit, the Wish-fulfilling Mother of Wisdom and Culture," JBORS 45:31–35.

———. 1963. "Vision in Long Darkness, The Thousand-Syllabled Speech," *Prthivi Prakashan,* folio 1. Varanasi.

Ahirbudhnya Saṃhitā; see Krishnamacharya, Pandit V., ed., 1966.

Aithal, Pandit K. Parameśwara. 1969. *Stotrasamuccaya, A Collection of Rare and Unpublished Stortra-s,* 2 vols. (ALS 99) Adyar, Madras: ALRC.

Aklujkar, Ashok Narhar. 1970a. "Ancient Indian Semantics," ABORI 51:11–29.

______. 1970b. *The Philosophy of Bhartrhari's Trikāṇḍī.* Cambridge, Mass.: Diss. Harvard.

______. 1972. "The Authorship of the Vākyapadīya-vṛtti," WZKSOA 16:181–98.

Allen, William Sidney. 1953. *Phonetics in Ancient India (London Oriental Series* 1) London: OUP. Rep. 1963.

______. 1955. "Zero and Pāṇini," IL 16:106–113.

Alper, Harvey Paul. 1979. "Śiva and the Ubiquity of Consciousness: the Spaciousness of an Artful Yogi," JIPh 7:345–407.

______. 1981. "Re-Imagining Liberation: Reflections on the Existential Non-Existence of Moksa." In *Man and the Ultimate: A Symposium,* Edgar C. Polome, ed. (Austin, Texas: SW AOS), 22–38.

______. 1982. "What Sort of Speech Act Is the Uttering of a Mantra?" Paper read before the American Oriental Society (Austin, Texas).

______. 1983a. "Regression Towards the Real," *Parabola* 8, no. 3:72–81.

______. 1983b. "The Vocabulary of Consciousness in Utpaladeva's IPK-Vṛtti, the Evidence of the Jñānādhikara." Paper read at the 12th Univ. of Wisconsin South Asian Regional Studies Conference.

______. (1987). "Svabhāvam Avabhāsasya Vimarsam, 'Judgment' (Vimarsa) as a Transcendental Category in Utpaladeva's Śaivite Theology." In *Festschrift in Honor of Ludo Rocher.*

______. (forthcoming) *Approaching the Saivism of Kasmir.* Albany: SUNY Press.

Alston, William P. 1964. *Philosophy of Language.* (*Prentice-Hall Foundations of Philosophy Series*) Englewood Cliffs, N.J.: Prentice-Hall.

Anand, Mulk Raj. 1958a. *Kamakala—Some Notes on the Philosophical Basis of Hindu Erotic Sculpture.* NY: Nagel.

______. 1958b. "The Great Delight, An Essay on the Spiritual Background of the Erotic Sculpture at Konarak," *Marg* 12.

Anand, M. R., C. Fabri, and Stella Kramrisch. 1962. *Homage to Khajuraho,* 2nd ed. Bombay: *Marg.* 1st ed. 1960.*

Anand, M. R., and Stella Kramrisch. 1939. "Chandella Sculpture in Khajuraho," JISOA 1/2.

Anand, M. R., and A. Mookherjee. 1977. *Tantric Magic*. New Delhi.

Anantakrishna Sastri, R., ed. 1902. *Śivasahasranāma Stotra with Nīlakaṇṭha's Commentary*. Madras.

———. 1927. *Ucchiṣṭa Gaṇeśa Sahasranāmastava*, 2nd ed.. Adyar.

———. 1940. *Pāśupata-Sūtras with Pañcārthabhāṣya of Kauṇḍinya*. Trivandrum.

———. 1970. *Lalitāsahasranāma Stotra with Bhāskararāya's Commentary*, 4th ed. orig. 1899 (Madras).

Anjaneya Sarma, V. 1965. "The Śabda-brahman and the Prasthāna-traya," *Sri Venkateswara University Oriental Journal* (Tirupati) 18:31–35.

Āpadeva. *Mīmāṅsā Nyāya Prakāsa;* see Edgerton 1929.

Apate, V. S. 1929–34. *Mīmāṃsāsūtrabhāṣya of Śbara, with the Mīmāṃsāsūtra and Kumārilabhaṭṭa's Tantravārttika*, 6 vols.. (ASS 97) Poona.

Apel, Karl-Otto. 1973. "Das Apriori der Kommunikationsgemeinschaft und der Grundlagen der Ethik, Zum Problem einer rationalen Begründung der Ethik im Zeitalter der Wissenschaft." In *Transformation der Philosophie*, 358–435 (Frankfurt); Eng. tr: Glyn Adey and David Frisby, trs., "The a Priori of the Communication Community and the Foundation of Ethics: The Problem of a Rational Foundation of Ethics in the Scientific Age," in *Transformation of Philosophy* (London: RKP, 1980), 225–300.*

Apte, P. P. 1974. "Pāñcarātra: Name and Origin." In *Center for Advanced Studies in Sanskrit*, 2, R. N. Dandekar, ed., pp. 83–110. (Poona: Univ. of Poona.)

Apte, R. N. 1926. "Constructive Geometry of Vedic Altars," ABORI 7:14ff.

Apte, Vinayak Mahadev. 1939–40. "The Ṛgveda Mantras in Their Ritual Setting in the Gṛhyasūtras," BDCRI 1:14, 127.

———. 1940–41. "Non-Ṛgvedic *Mantras* Rubricated in the Āśvalāyana-Gṛhyasūtra, Their Sources and Interpretation," NIA 3:49, 101, 144.

———. 1941. "Ṛgveda Citations in the Mahābhārata." In *Kane Commemorative Volume* (Poona).

———. 1942–43. "The Spoken Word in Sanskrit Literature," BDCRI 4.

———. 1946. "Mantra Rubrics in Ritual Literature, New Lines of Investigation." In C. *Kunhan Raja Commemorative Volume* (Adyar), 233–40.

———. 1954. *Social and Religious Life in the Gṛhyasūtras*, 2nd ed. Bombay; orig. 1939.

Apte, Vaman Shivram. 1957–59. *The Practical Sanskrit-English Dictionary* (rev. ed., 3 vols.), P. K. Gode and C. G. Karve, eds. Poona: Prasad Prakashan.

***D'Aquili, Eugene D.,* et al.** 1979. *The Spectrum of Ritual: A Biogenetic Structural Analysis*. NY: ColUP.

Arguelles, J., and M. Arguelles. 1972. *Maṇḍala.* Berkeley, Calif.: Shambala.

Arnold, E. Vernon. 1905. *Vedic Metre in Its Historical Development.* Cambridge: CUP.

Ashby, Philip H. 1974a. *Modern Trends in Hinduism.* (*Lectures on the History of Relgions* 10) NY: ColUP.

———. 1974b. "Popular Esoteric Religion: Rādhā Soāmī Satsang." In Asbhy 1974a, 71–91.

Auboyer, Jeannine. 1949. Le trône et son symbolisme dans l'Inde ancienne. (*Annales du Musée Guimet, Bibliothèque d'études* 55) Paris: PUF.

———. 1950–51. "Moudrā et hasta ou le langage par signes," OA 3:153–61.

———. 1960. *Khajuraho.* The Hague: Mouton.

———. 1965. "Quelques réflexions à propos du cakra, arme offensive," *Arts Asiatiques* 11, no. 1:119–30.

Aurobindo [Ghose]. 1956. *On the Veda.* Pondichéry: Sri Aurobindo Ashram Press.

Austin, J. L. 1961. "Performative Utterances." In *Philosophical Papers,* pp. 233–52. Oxford: OUP.

———. 1962. *How to Do Things with Words* ("The William James Lectures," Harvard Univ., 1955), 2nd. ed. Cambridge: HUP. (NY: OUP, Galaxy Books, 1965); reissued 1975, 1978.

Awasthi Shastri, Shiv Shankar. 1966. *Mantra aur mātṛkāon kā Rahasya* (*Significance of Mantra and Mātṛkās*). Varanasi: Chowkhamba Vidyabhavan.

Babb, Lawrence A. 1975. *The Divine Hierarchy: Popular Hinduism in Central India.* NY: ColUP.

Bag, A. K. 1971. "The Knowledge of Geometrical Figures, Instruments, and Units in the Śulbasūtras," EW 21, nos. 1–2:111–19.

Bagchi, Prabodh Chandra. 1921. "Primitive Elements in Jainism," JDLCU 5:349–64.

———. 1927–28. *Le Canon bouddhique en Chine: les traducteurs et les traductions* 2 vols. Paris: Geuthner.

———. 1928. "On Some Tantrik Texts Studied in Ancient Kambuja," IHQ 4:754–69. Rep. Bagchi 1939, 1–15.

———. 1930a. "Further Notes on Tantrik Texts Studied in Ancient Kambuja," IHQ 6, no. 1:97–107. Rep. Bagchi 1939, 16–26.

———. 1930b. "The Sandhābhāṣā and Sandhāvacana," IHQ 6, no. 2:289–96. Rep. Bagchi 1939, 27–33.

______. 1931. "On Foreign Elements in the Tantras," IHQ 7, no. 1:1–16. Rep. Bagchi 1939, 45–55.

______. 1934. *Kaulajñānanirṇaya and Some Minor Texts of the School of Matsyendranātha.* (CSS 3) Calcutta: Metropolitan Printing and Publishing House.

______. 1938. "Materials for a Critical Edition of the Old Bengali Caryāpadas: A Comparative Study of the Text and Tibetan Translation," JDLCU 30.

______. 1939. *Studies in the Tantras.* Calcutta: Calcutta Univ. Press.

______. 1943. "On the Canons of Image-making: *Piṅgalāmata,* Chapter IV," JISOA 11:9–31.

______. 1950. *India and China: A Thousand Years of Cultural Relations* 2nd ed. Bombay.

______. 1956a. "Evolution of the Tantras." In CHI 4.211–226.

______. 1956b. "The Cult of the Buddhist Siddhācāryas." In CHI 4.273–79.

Bake, A. A. 1934. "Different Aspects of Indian Music," *Indian Art and Letters* (London) 8.

______. 1935. "The Practice of Sāmaveda," PAIOC 7:143–55.

______. 1948. "Some Aspects of Indian and Western Music," *Prabuddha Bharata* (Almora) 53, no. 2:71–77.

Baker, G. P., and P. M. S. Hacker. 1980. *Wittgenstein, Understanding, and Meaning* (*An Analytical Commentary on the Philosophical Investigations,* vol. 1). Chicago: UChP.

Bakshi, Mukunda Jhā. 1963. *Śāradātilaka Tantra [of Lakṣmaṇdeśika] with Rāghavabhaṭṭa's Commentary,* 2nd ed.. (KSS 107) Varanasi.

Balfour, Henry. 1897. "The Life History of an Aghorī Fakir," *Journal of the Anthropological Institute* (London) 26:340–57.

Banerjea, Akshaya Kumar. 1962. *Philosophy of Gorakhnath with Goraksha-Vacana-Sangraha.* Gorakhpur: Mahant Dig Vijai Nath Trust.

Banerjea, Jitendra Nath. 1938. "Some Folk Goddesses of Ancient and Mediaeval India," IHQ 14, no. 1:101–109.

Banerji, Suresh Chandra. 1962. *Dharma-Sūtras: A Study in Their Origin and Development.* Calcutta: Punthi Pustak.

______. 1977. *Tantra in Bengal; A Study in Its Origin, Development, and Influence.* Calcutta: Naya Prokash.

Bannerji, P. K. 1924. "Sandhyābhāṣā," *Viśvabhāratī Quarterly* (Santiniketan).

Barrow, H. W. 1893. "On Aghorīs and Aghorapanthīs," *Proceedings of the Anthropological Society of Bombay* 3:197–251.

Barthwal, Pitambar Datta, ed. 1971. *Gorakh Bani.* Allahabad: Hindustani Academy.

Barua, Birinchi Kumar. 1951. *A Cultural History of Assam.* Gauhati: Lawyer's Book Stall. 2nd ed., 1959.

Basham, A. L. 1954. *The Wonder That Was India, A Survey of the Culture of the Indian Sub-Continent Before the Coming of the Muslims.* NY: Macmillan, Rep. 1959 (NY: Grove Press, *Evergreen Encylopedia* 1).

Basu, Arabinda. 1956. "Kashmir Saivism." In CHI 4:79–98.

Basu, Jogiraj. 1969. *India in the Age of the Brāhmaṇas.* Calcutta: Sanskrit Pustak Bhandar.

Basu, Manīndramohan. 1968. *Caryāpad.* Calcutta.

Basu, Nirmal Kumar. 1970. *Assam in the Ahom Age, 1228–1826; Being Politico-Economic and Socio-Cultural Studies.* Calcutta: Sanskrit Pustak Bandar.

Bauman, Richard. 1973. "Verbal Art as Performance," AAnth 77, no. 2:290–311.

Bauman, R., and J. Sherzer. 1974. *Explorations in the Ethnography of Speaking.* London: CUP.

Beane, Wendell C. 1977. *Myth, Cult, and Symbols in Śākta Hinduism: A Study of the Indian Mother Goddess.* Leiden: E. J. Brill.

Bechert, Heinz, and Georg von Simson, eds. 1979. *Einführung in die Indologie, Stand, Methoden, Aufgaben.* Darmstadt: Wissenschaftliche Buchgesellschaft.

Bedekar, V. M. 1964. "The Place of Japa in the Mokṣadharmaparvan (12.189–93) and the Yogasūtras. A Comparative Study," ABORI 44:63–74.

Begley, W. E. 1973. *Viṣṇu's Flaming Wheel: The Iconography of the Sudarśana-Cakra.* NY: NYU Press for the College Art Assoc. of Amer.

Belvalkar, Sripad Krsna. 1915. *An Account of Different Existing Systems of Sanskrit Grammar.* Poona: the author.

______. 1922. "Literary Strata in the Ṛgveda," PAIOC 2:11–34.

Benfey, T. 1848. *Die Hymnen des Sāma-Veda.* Leipzig. Rep. 1968–69.

Benveniste, E. 1968. "Phraséeologie poétique de l'indo-iranien." In Renou 1968, 73–79.

Bergaigne, Abel. 1889. "Recherches sur l'histoire de la liturgie védique," JA 5–32.

______. 1934–35. "Syntax of Vedic Comparisons," ABORI 16:232–61.

______. 1935–36. "Some Observations on the Figures of Speech in the ṚgVeda," ABORI 17:61–83, 259–88.

Berger, Peter L. 1968. *The Sacred Canopy, Elements of a Social Theory of Religion.* Garden City, N.Y.: Anchor Books, Doubleday and Co.

Bernhard, F. 1967. "Zur Entstehung einer Dhāraṇī," ZDMG 117:148–68.

Beyer, Stephan. 1973. *The Cult of Tārā, Magic and Ritual in Tibet.* Berkeley: UCaP.

———. 1977. "Notes on the Vision Quest in Early Mahāyāna." In Lancaster and Gomez 1977, 329–40.

Bhagvat, Durga. 1965. *The Riddle in Indian Life, Lore and Literature.* Bombay: Popular Prakashan.

———. 1972. "Dances and Charms of the Tribes of Central India," *Asian Folklore Studies* (Nagoya) 31, no. 1:41–70.

Bhandarkar, Sir Ramakrishna Gopal. 1913. *Vaiṣṇavism, Śaivism and Minor Religious Systems.* (*Grundriss der Indo-Arischen Philologie und Altertumskunde* 3.6) Strassburg. Rep. 1929 (*Collected Works,* N. B. Utgikar, ed. Poona: BORI, 4); 1965 (Varanasi: Indological Book House).

Bhandu; see Vishna Bhandu.

Bharati, Agehananda. 1963. "Pilgrimage in the Indian Traditions," HR 3, no. 1:135–67.

———. 1964. "Symbolik der Berührung in der hinduistisch-buddhistischen Vorstellungswelt," *Studium Generale* (Heidelberg) 17, no. 10:609–20.

———. 1965. *The Tantric Tradition.* London: Rider and Co. Rep. 1970 (Garden City, N.Y.: Anchor Books); 1975 (NY: Samuel Weiser).

———. 1970a. "Pilgrimage Sites and Indian Civilization." In *Chapters in Indian Civilization,* Joseph W. Elder, ed., pp. 83–126. rev. ed. (Dubuque: Kendall, Hunt).

———. 1970b. "The Hindu Renaissance and Its Apologetic Patterns," JAS 29, no. 2:267–88.

———. 1971. "Hinduism and Modernization." In *Religion and Change in Contemporary Asia,* R. F. Spencer, ed., pp. 67–104. Minneapolis: U. Minn. Press.

———. 1972. *The Asians in East Africa: Jayhind and Uhuru.* Chicago: Nelson-Hall.

———. 1976a. *The Light at the Center: Context and Pretext of Modern Mysticism.* Santa Barbara, Calif.: Ross-Erikson Publications.

———. 1976b. *The Realm of the Extra-Human.* The Hague: Mouton.

Bhardwaj, S. M. 1973. *Hindu Places of Pilgrimage in India, A Study in Cultural Geography.* Berkeley: UCaP.

Bhargava, Purushottam Lal. 1971. *India in the Vedic Age: A History of Aryan*

Expansion in India (rev. ed). Lucknow: Upper India Publishing House. 1st ed., 1956.

Bhatt, Govardhan P. 1962. *Epistemology of the Bhāṭṭa School of Pūrva Mīmānsā.* (ChowSSt 17) Varanasi: ChowSSe Office.

Bhatt, N. R. 1977. "Analyse du Pūrvakāmikāgama," *Bulletin of* ÉFEO 64:1–38.

Bhatta, Laksmi Narasimha, ed. 1972. *Viṣvakṣena Saṃhitā.* Tirupati: Kendriya Sanskrit Vidyapeetha.

Bhattacharji, Sukumari. 1970. *The Indian Theogony: A Comparative Study of Indian Mythology from the Vedas to the Purāṇas.* Cambridge: CUP.

Bhattacharya, Bishnupada. 1956. "Philosophical Data in Patañjali's Mahābhāṣya," *Our Heritage (Bulletin of the Dept. of Post-Graduate Training and Research)* (Calcutta) 4:51–65.

———. 1958. *Yāska's Nirukta and the Science of Etymology: An Historical and Critical Survey.* Calcutta: Mukhopadhyay.

———. 1962. *A Study in Language and Meaning (A Critical Examination of Some Aspects of Indian Semantics).* Calcutta: Progressive Publishers.

Bhattacharya, Dipak. 1978. "The Doctrine of Four in the Upaniṣads," JIPh 6:1–34.

Bhattacharya, Gaurinath. 1937. "A Study in the Dialectics of Sphoṭa," JDLCU 29, no. 4:1–115.

Bhattacharya, Kamaleswar. 1961. *Les Religions brahmaniques dans l'ancien Cambodge.* (PÉFEO 49) Paris.

Bhattacharya, P. 1983. *Tārābhaktisudhārṇava.* New Delhi: BVB.

Bhattacharya, Tārakanātha. 1946. *Gāyatrītantra.* (KSS, Tantraśāstra section, 2) Varanasi.

Bhattacharya, Tarapada. 1963. *The Canons of Indian Art, or a Study of Vastuvidyā,* 2nd ed. Calcutta: KLM. 1st ed, 1947.

Bhattacharyya, Benoytosh. 1921. "The Buddhists in Bengal," *The Dacca Review* 2, no. 7:91–104.

———. 1926. "Some Notes on Mithuna in Indian Art," *Rupam* (Calcutta) 1.

———. 1927. "Origin and Development of Vajrayāna," IHQ 3, no. 4:733–46.

———. 1932. *An Introduction to Buddhist Esoterism.* London: OUP. Rep. 1964 (Varanasi: ChowSSe 46), with new preface, 3–23.

———. 1933. "The Cult of Bhūtaḍamara," 6th AIOC (1930, Patna), Proc. 349–70.

______. 1956. "Tantrika Culture Among the Buddhists." In CHI 4.260–72.

Bhattacharyya, Benoytosh, and Vraj Vallabha Dviveda, eds. 1932–79. *Śaktisaṃgamatantra.* (GOS 61, 91, 104, 166) Baroda: Oriental Institute.

Bhattacharyya, D., ed. 1960. *Brāhmaṇa-sarvasva.* Calcutta.

Bhattacharyya, Haridas, ed. 1956. *The Cultural Heritage of India, IV: The Religions,* 2nd ed. Calcutta: The Ramakrishna Mission Institute of Culture.

Bhattacharyya, Narendranath. 1974. *History of the Śākta Religion.* Delhi: Munshiram Manoharlal.

______. 1975. *Ancient Indian Rituals and Their Social Contents.* London: Curzon Press.

______. 1982. *History of the Tantric Religion (A Historical, Ritualistic and Philosophical Study).* New Delhi: Manohar.

Bhattacharyya, Viman Ch. 1959. "Magical Kāmya-rites in the Sāmavidhāna-Brāhamaṇa," IHQ 35, no. 4:312–26.

Bhawe, S. S. 1950. "The Conception of a Muse of Poetry in the Ṛgveda," JBU 19, no. 2:19–27.

______. 1955. "An Interpretation of ṚV 10.109 (*Brahma-Kilbisa*)." In *Kirfel Commemorative Volume,* 17–26.

______. 1957–62. *The Soma Hymns of the Ṛgveda: A Fresh Interpretation* (3 vols.). (M. S. Univ. Res. Series 3, 5, and 6) Baroda: Oriental Institute.

______. 1959. "Recent Trends in Vedic Research," PAIOC 20:29–30.

Bhise, Usha R. 1969. "The Importance of *Nāman* in the Ṛgveda," AIOC (Summary of Papers) 25:2–3.

Biardeau, Madeleine. 1958. *Sphoṭa siddhi (La Démonstration du Sphoṭa) par Maṇḍana Miśra, introduction, et commentaire par Madeleine Biardeau, texte établi par N. R. Bhatt avec la collaboration de T. Ramanujam.* (PIFI 13) Pondichéry: IFI.

______. 1964a. *Théorie de la connaissance et philosophie de la parole dans le brahmanisme classique.* (ÉPHE *Le Monde d'outre-mer passe et present* 1.23) Paris: Mouton.

______. 1964b. *Bhartṛhari, Vākyapadīya brahmakāṇḍa avec le vṛtti de Harivṛṣabha: texte reproduit de l'édition de Lahore; traduction, introduction et notes* (PICI 24). Paris: Boccard.

______. 1968. "Some More Considerations About Textual Criticism," *Purāṇa* 10:115–23.

Biardeau, Madeleine, and Charles Malamoud. 1976. *Le sacrifice dans l'Inde ancienne.* (BÉHE, Section des sciences religieuses [Centre de Recherche comparees sur les Societes anciennes] 79) Paris: PUF.

Birdwhistell, Ray L. 1970. *Kinesics and Context: Essays on Body Motion Communication.* Philadelphia: Univ. Penn. Press.

Biswas, S. N. 1955. *Vrātyastoma.* Berlin: Dissertation, Freie Univ.

———. 1959. "Kritik der rituellen bemerkungen Sāyaṇas über die Hymnen des Ṛgveda," in *Akten 24. Orient. Kong. München 1957* (Wiesbaden).

———. 1955. "Über das Vrātya-problem in der vedischen Ritualliteratur," ZDMG 105:53.

Bleeker, C. J., ed. 1965. *Initiation.* (*Int. Assoc. for the History of Religions*) Leiden: E. J. Brill.

Bloom, A. 1948. "Contemplation et ascèse, contribution orthodoxe," *Études carmélitaines* ("Technique et contemplation") 48ff.

———. 1953. "L'Hésychasme, Yoga Chrétien?" In *Yoga, science de l'homme intégral,* Jacques Masui, ed. pp. 177–95. Paris.

Bloomfield, Maurice. 1889. "On the Etymology of the Particle Om," Proc. AOS.

———. 1890. *The Kauśikasūtra of Atharva-Veda, with Extracts from the Commentaries of Dārila and Keśava.* (JAOS 14) New Haven; Rep. Delhi: 1972.

———. 1899a. *The Artharva-Veda and the Gopatha-Brāhmaṇa.* (*Grundriss der Indo-Arischen Philologie und Altertumskunde* II.1.B) Strassburg: Verlag von Karl J. Trübner. Rep. 1978 (New Delhi: Asian Publication Services).

———. 1899b. "Position of the Gopatha-Brāhmaṇa in Vedic Literature," JAOS 19, no. 2:1–11.

———. 1906. *A Vedic Concordance.* Cambridge, Mass.: HUP. Rep. 1964 (New Delhi: MB).

———. 1916. *Rig-Veda Repetitions* (2 vols. in 3 pts, HOS 20, 24). Cambridge, Mass.: HUP.

———. 1919. "The Mind as Wish-Car in the Veda," JAOS 39:280–82.

Bloomfield, Maurice, Franklin, Edgerton, and M. B. Emeneau. 1930–34. *Vedic Variants,* 3 vols. Philadelphia: Univ. Penn. Press.

Bodewitz, H. W. 1976. *The Daily Evening and Morning Offering (Agnihotra) According to the Brāhmaṇas.* Leiden: E. J. Brill.

Boeles, J. J. 1947. "The Migration of the Magic Syllable OM." In *India Antiqua* (Fest. J. Ph. Vogel) (Leiden), 40–56.

Böhtlingk, Otto. 1887. *Pāṇini's Grammatik, herusgegeben, übersetzt, erlutert und mit verschiedenen Indices versehen.* Leipzig: Haessel. Rep. 1964 (Hildeshiem: Olms).

Bolle, C. W. 1959. "Remarks on the Pre-History of Tantric Bījas," PAIOC Bhubaneshwar.

Bolle, Kees W. 1962. "Tantric Elements in Śrī Aurobindo," *Numen* 9:128ff..

———. 1965a. "Devotion and Tantra." In *Studies of Esoteric Buddhism and Tantrism* (Koyasan Univ.).

———. 1965b. *The Persistance of Religion, An Essay on Tantrism and Sri Aurobindo's Philosophy.* (*Studies in the History of Religions* 8) Leiden: E. J. Brill. Rep. 1971.

Boner, Alice. 1962. *Principles of Composition in Hindu Sculpture.* Leiden: E. J. Brill.

Boner, Alice, Sadāśiva Rath Śarmā, and Bettina Bäumer. 1982. *Vāstusūtra Upaniṣad, The Essence of Form in Sacred Art, Sanskrit Text, English Translation and Notes.* Delhi: MB.

Bosch, F. D. K. 1960. *The Golden Germ: An Introduction to Indian Symbolism.* (*Indo-Iranian Monographs* 2) The Hague: Mouton.

Bose, Manindra Mohan. 1927. "An Introduction to the Study of the Post-Caitanya Sahajia Cult," JDLCU 16:1–162.

———. 1930. *The Post-Caitanya Sahajia Cult of Bengal.* Calcutta: Calcutta Univ. Press.

Bose, Phanindra Nath. 1926. *Principles of Indian Śilpaśāstra.* (*Punjab Oriental Series* 11) Lahore: Punjab Sanskrit Book Depot.

Bowra, Sir Cecil Maurice. 1952. *Heroic Poetry.* London: Macmillan.

———. 1966. "Dance, Drama, and the Spoken Word." In Huxley 1966, 387–92.

Brand, Gerd. 1979. *The Essential Wittgenstein,* Robert E. Innis, tr. NY: Basic Books. Orig. *Die Grundlegenden Texte von Ludwig Wittgenstein* (Frankfurt: Suhrkamp Verlag, 1975); UK: Basil Blackwell, 1979.

Briggs, George Weston. 1938. *Gorakhnāth and the Kānphaṭa Yogīs.* Calcutta: YMCA Publishing House. Rep. 1973 (Delhi: MB).

Brough, John. 1951. "Theories of General Linguistics in the Sanskrit Grammarians," *Trans. of the Philological Soc.* (London) 1951:27–46. Rep. Staal 1972, 402–14.

———. 1953. *The Early Brahminical System of Gotra and Pravara, a Translation of the Gotra-pravara-mañjarī.* Cambridge: CUP.

———. 1971. "Soma and Amanita Muscaria," BSOAS 34:331–62.

———. 1973. "I-Ching on the Sanskrit Grammarians," BSOAS 36:248–60.

Brown, Cheever Mackenzie. 1974. *God as Mother: A Feminine Theology in India,*

An Historical and Theological Study of the Brahmavaivarta Purāṇa. Hartford, Vt.: Claude Stark.

Brown, George W. 1919. "Prāṇa and Apāna," JAOS 39:104–12.

———. 1921. *The Human Body in the Upaniṣads*. Jubbulpore: The Christian Mission Press. orig. diss. Johns Hopkins Univ.

Brown, W. Norman. 1931. "The Sources and Nature of *Puruṣa* in the Puruṣasūkta," JAOS 51:108–18. Rep. R. Rocher 1978, 5–10.

———. 1958. *The Saundaryalaharī or Flood of Beauty Traditionally Ascribed to Saṅkarācārya, Edited, Translated, and Presented in Photographs*. (HOS 43) Cambridge, Mass.: HUP.

———. 1962. *Indological Studies in Honor of W. Norman Brown*. Ernest Bender, ed. (*American Oriental Series* 47) New Haven, Conn.: AOS.

———. 1963. "Ṛg Veda 10.34 as an Act of Truth," *Bharatīya Vidyā* 20–21 (*Munshi Indological Felicitation Volume*):8–10.

———. 1965. "Theories of Creation in the Rig Veda," JAOS 85:23–34. Rep. R. Rocher 1978, 40–52.

———. 1968a. "Agni, Sun, Sacrifice, and Vāc: A Sacerdotal Ode by Dīrghatamas (Rig Veda 1.164)," JAOS 88:199–218. Rep. R. Rocher 1978, 53–78.

———. 1968b. "The Creative Role of the Goddess Vāc in the Rig Veda." In *Pratidānam, Indian, Iranian, and Indo-European Studies Presented to F. B. J. Kuiper*, 393–97. The Hague: Mouton, 1968. Rep. R. Rocher 1978, 75–78.

———. 1968c. "The Metaphysics of the Truth Act (**Satyakriya*)." In Renou 1968, 171–77.

———. 1972a. "Duty as Truth in the Rig Veda." In *India Maior, Congratulatory Volume Presented to J. Gonda*, J. Ensink and P. Gaeffke, eds., pp. 57–67. Leiden: E. J. Brill.

———. 1972b. "Duty as Truth in Ancient India," *Proc. of the American Philosophical Society* 116:252–68. Rep. R. Rocher 1978, 102–19.

Brunner(-Lachaux), Hélène. 1963–77. *Somaśambhupaddhati, Rituels occasionels dans le tradition śivaïte de l'Inde du Sud selon Somaśambhu, texte, traduction et notes*, 3 vols. (PIFI 25) Pondichéry: PIFI.

———. 1964. "Les catégories sociales védiques dans le śivaïsme du sud," JA 252:451–72.

———. 1965. "Analyse du Kiraṇāgama," JA 253:309–28.

———. 1967. "Analyse du Suprabhedāgama," JA 255:31–60.

———. 1969. "De la consommation du *nirmālya* de Śiva," JA 257:214–63.

———. 1974. "Un Tantra du nord: *le Netra Tantra,*" *Bulletin of* ÉFEO 61:125–97.

———. 1975. "Le *sādhaka,* personnage oublié du śivaïsme du sud," JA 263:411–43.

———. 1975–76. "Importance de la littérature āgamique pour l'etude des religions vivantes de l'Inde," IT 3–4:107–24.

———. 1977. "Le mysticisme dans les āgama śivaïtes," *Studia Missionalia* 26:287–314.

———. 1985. *Mṛgendrāgama, carya et kriyāpada, section des rites et du comportement, avec la Vṛtti de Bhaṭṭanārāyaṇa.* (PIFI 69) Pondichéry: PIFI.

———. 1986. "Les membre de Siva." *Asiatische Studien/Etudes Asiatiques* 40, no. 2:89–132.

van Buitenen, J. A. B. 1955a. "Notes on Akṣara," BDCRI 17, no. 3:204–15.

———. 1955b. "Vācārambhaṇam." In *Suniti Kumar Chatterji Commemorative Volume,* B. P. Mallik, ed., pp. 157–62. Burdwan: Univ. of Burdwan.

———. 1956. *Rāmānuja's Vedārthasaṇgraha.* (*Deccan College Monograph Series* 16) Poona: Deccan College Postgraduate and Research Center.

———. 1958. "*Vācārambhaṇam* Reconsidered," IIJ 2:296–305; 4:67.

———. 1959. "Akṣara," JAOS 79:176–87.

———. 1968a. *The Pravargya: An Ancient Indian Iconic Ritual Described and Annotated.* Poona: Poona College Postgraduate and Research Institute.

———. 1968b. "The Speculations on the Name "Satyam" in the Upaniṣads." In *Studies in Indian Linguistics* (*Professor M. B. Emeneau Ṣaṣṭipūrti Volume*), Bhadiraju Krishnamurti, ed., pp. 54–61. Poona: Center of Advanced Study in Linguistics, Deccan College.

———. 1973. *The Mahābhārata: I. The Book of the Beginning.* Chicago: UChP.

Burkert, Walter. 1979. *Structure and History in Greek Mythology and Ritual.* (*Sather Classical Lectures* 47) Berkeley: UCaP.

———. 1983. *Homo Necans, The Anthropology of Ancient Greek Sacrificial Ritual and Myth,* Peter Bing, tr. (Berkeley: UCaP). Orig. Ger. ed., 1972 (Berlin: Walter de Gruyter).

Burlingame, E. W. 1917. "The Act of Truth (Saccakriyā): A Hindu Spell and Its Employment as a Psychic Motif in Hindu Fiction," JRAS 429–67.

Burne, Charles S. 1910. "Occult Powers of Healing in the Panjab," *Folk-Lore* 21:313ff.

Caillat, Colette. 1964. "L'asceticisme chez les Jaina," *Archives de sociologie des religions* 9, no. 18:45–53.

Caillat, Collette, and Ravi Kumar. 1981. *The Jain Cosmology.* Basel: Ravi Kumar Pub.

Caland, Willem. 1888. *Über Totenverehrung bei einige der Indo-germanischen Völker.* Amsterdam: VKNAW, J. Müller.

———. 1893. *Altindischer Ahnenkult,das Śrāddha nach den verschiedenen Schulen mit Benutzung handschriftlicher Quellen dargestellt.* Leiden: Brill.

———. 1896. *Die altindischen toten- und Bestattungsgebräuche.* (VKAWA) Amsterdam: Amsterdam Academy, J. Müller.

———. 1900. *Altindisches Zauberritual, Probe einer Übersetzung der wichtigsten Teile des Kauśika Sūtra.* (VKAWA n. s. 3.2) Amsterdam. Rep. 1967 (Wiesbaden: Martin Sändig).

———. 1903. *Über das rituelle Sūtra des Baudhāyana.* (AKM) Leipzig. Rep. 1966.

———. 1904–24. *The Baudhāyana Śrauta Sūtra Belonging to the Taittirīya Saṃhitā.* (BI 163) Calcutta: Baptist Mission Press.

——— . 1907a. *Die Jaiminīya-Saṃhitā mit einer Einleitung über die Sāmavedaliteratur.* (*Indische Forschungen* 2) Breslau.

———. 1907b. *De Wording van den Sāmaveda.* (VKNAW) Amsterdam. Eng. Tr., Nilakantha Sastri (1935).

———. 1908a. *Altindische Zauberei, Darstellung der altindischen Wunschopfer.* (VKNAW n. s. 10.1) Amsterdam: J. Muller.

———. 1908b. "Zum altindischen Würfulspiel," ZDMG 62:123–28.

———. 1908c. "Zur Frage über die Entstehung des Sāmaveda," WZKM 22:436.

———. 1919. *Das Jaiminīya-Brāhmaṇa in Auswahl.* (VKNAW 61.4) Amsterdam: Johannes Müller. Rep. 1970 (Wiesbaden: Dr. Martin Sändig).

———. 1921–28. *Das Śrauta Sūtra des Āpastamba* (3 vols.). (VKNAW) Göttingen; Leipzig; Amsterdam: Vandenhoeck and Ruprecht; J. C. Hinrrichs. Rep. 1969 (Wiesbaden).

———. 1928. *On the Sacred Books of the Vaikhānasas.* Amsterdam: Academy.

———. 1929. *Vaikhānasasmartasūtram.* Calcutta [1927].

Caland, W., and V. Henry. 1906. *L'Agniṣṭoma: description complète de la forme normale du sacrifice de Soma dans le culte védique,* 2 vols. Paris: Société Asiatique, E. Leroux.

Cammann, Schuyler van Rensselaer. 1969. "Islamic and Indian Magic Squares," HR 8, nos. 3–4:181–209, 271–99.

Canfield, John V. 1981. *Wittgenstein, Language and World.* Amherst: Univ. Mass. Press.

Caraka Saṃhitā; see Jādavaji Trikamji Ācārya, ed. 1941.

Cardona, George. 1976. *Pāṇini, A Survey of Research.* (*Trends in Linguistics, State-of-the-Art Reports* 6) The Hague: Mouton.

______. 1983. *Linguistic Analysis and Some Indian Traditions.* (*Post-graduate and Research Dept. Series* 20 (*Pandit Shripad Shastri Deodhar Memorial Lectures* 1)) Poona.

Carlstedt, Gunnar. 1970. "Hinduistik livssyn, Jīvasthitikathana ur Kulārṇava Tantra," *Kungl. Vetenskapssamhällets i Uppsala* 14. Uppsala: Almqvist and Wiksell.

______. 1973–74. "Till kulas lov. Kulamāhātmyakathana ur Kulārṇava-tantra," *Kungl. Humanistiska Vetenskaps-Samfundet i Uppsala.* Uppsala: Almqvist and Wiksell.

______. 1974. "Studier i Kulārṇava-tantra," *Skrifter Utgivna av Religionshistorika Institutionen i Uppsala.* Uppsala: Almqvist and Wiksell.

Carman, John Braisted. 1974. *The Theology of Rāmānuja, An Essay in Interreligious Understanding.* (*Yale Publications in Religion* 18) New Haven, Conn.: YUP.

Carpenter, Joseph Estlin. 1921. *Theism in Medieval India.* London: Williams and Norgate.

Cassirer, Ernst. 1953. *Language and Myth.* NY: Dover.

Cavell, Stanley. 1962. "The Availability of Wittgenstein's Later Philosophy," *Philosophical Review* 71:67–93.

Chadwick, H. Munro, and N. Kershaw. 1932–40. *The Growth of Literature* (3 vols.). Cambridge: CUP.

Chakraborti, Haripada. 1970. *Pāsupata Sūtram with Pañcārthabhāṣya of Kauṇḍinya, Translated with an Introduction on the History of Śaivism in India.* Calcutta: Academic Publishers.

______. 1973. *Asceticism in Ancient India in Brahmanical, Buddhist, Jaina and Ajivika Societies.* Calcutta: Punthi Pustak.

Chakravati, Chintaharan. 1930. "The Cult of Bāro Bhāiyā of Eastern Bengal," JRASBe 26:379–88.

______. 1931–32. "Kulārṇava Tantra: Its Extent and Contents," ABORI 13:206–11.

______. 1932. "The Soma or Sauma Sect of the Śaivas," IHQ 8, no. 1:221–23.

______. 1952. "Application of Vedic *Mantras* in Tantric Rites," JASBe 18.2.

______. 1956. "Śakti-Worship and the Śakta Saints," in CHI 4.408–18.

______. 1957. "Kālī Worship in Bengal," ALB 21:296–303.

______. 1963. *Tantras, Studies on Their Religion and Literature.* Calcutta: Punthi Pustak.

Chakravarti, Prabhat Chandra. 1926. "Patañjali as He Reveals Himself in the Mahabhāṣya," IHQ 2:67–76, 262–89, 464–94, 738–60.

———. 1930. *The Philosophy of Sanskrit Grammar*. Calcutta: Calcutta University.

———. 1933. *The Linguistic Speculations of the Hindus*. Calcutta: Univ. of Calcutta.

———. 1934. "Spiritual Outlook of Sanskrit Grammar," JDLCU 25, no. 1:1–11.

———. 1940. *Doctrine of Śakti in Indian Literature*. Calcutta: General Printers and Publishers Limited.

Chandra, L. 1969. *Maṇḍales of the Tantrasamuccaya*. Delhi.

Chandra, Lokesh, and Sharada Devi. 1978. *Mudrās in Japan*. New Delhi.

Chandra, Pramod. 1955–56. "The Kaula-Kāpālika Cults at Khajuraho," *Lalit Kala* 1–2:98–107.

———. 1975. *Studies in Indian Temple Architecture: Papers Presented at a Seminar Held in Varanasi, 1967*. New Delhi: AIIS.

Charpentier, Jarl. 1926. "Über den Begriff und die Etymologie von pūjā." In *Beiträge zur Literaturwissenschaft und Geistesgeschichte Indiens* (*Fest. Jacobi*), pp. 276–97. Eng. tr, IA 56 (1927, 93–99, 130–36).

———. 1931. *Brahman: Eine sprachwissenschaftlich-exegetisch-religionsgeschichtliche Untersuchung I–II*. Uppsala: Univ. of Uppsala.

Chatterji, C. C. 1935. "The Concept OM," *Prabuddha Bharati* 40.

Chatterji, Jagdish Chandra. 1911. *The Śiva Sūtra Vimarshinī, being the Sūtras of Vasu Gupta with the Commentary called Vimarshinī by Kshemarāja*. (KSTS 1) Srinagar: Research and Publication Dept., Jammu and Kashmir State; printed, Bombay: Nirnaya Sagar Press.

———. 1916. *The Shiva Sūtra Vārttika by Bhāskara*. (KSTS 4) Srinagar: Research and Publication Dept., Jammu and Kashmir State; printed, Allahabad: Indian Press. Orig. 1914.

———. 1962. *Kashmir Shaivism*. (KSTS 2 [?]) Srinagar: Research and Publication Dept., Jammu and Kashmir State; printed, New Delhi: Services Press. Orig. 1914.

Chatterji, Kshitish Chandra. 1964a. *Technical Terms and Technique of Sanskrit Grammar*. Calcutta: Calcutta University.

———. 1964b. *Patañjali's Mahābhāṣya: Paspaśāhnika* (Introductory Chapter). (*Usha Memorial Series* 7) Calcutta: A. Mukherjee. 2nd ed. 1957, 3rd ed. 1964.

Chattopadhyay, D. P. 1959. *Lokāyata—A Study in Ancient Indian Materialism*. New Delhi: People's Publishing House.

Chattopadhyaya, Aparna. 1967. "Some Social Aspects in the Āpastambagṛhyasūtra," IA 3rd ser. 1, no. 3:37–42.

Chattopadhyaya, Ksetresa Chandra. 1935. "The Place of the Rigveda-Saṃhitā in the Chronology of Vedic Literature," PAIOC 8:31–40.

Chaturvedī, Shukadeva. 1981. *Mahīdhara's Mantramahodādhi, With His Own Nauka Sanskrit Commentary, Translated into Hindi with Mohinī \hindi Commentary.* (*Tantra Granthamālā* 2) Varanasi: Prācya Prakāśan.

Chemparathy, George. 1982. "The Veda as Revelation," *J. of Dharma* (Dharma Research Assoc., Center for the Study of World Religions, Dharmaram College, Bangalore) 7, no. 3:253–74.

———. 1983. *L'Autorité du Veda selon les Nyāya-Vaiseṣikas.* (*Conférences et Trauvaux* 2) Louvain-la-neuve: Centre d'Histoire des Religions.

Chintamani Dikshit, T. R. 1929. *The Samnyasa Upanishads with the Commentary of Sri Upanishad-Brahma-Yogin.* (ALS 12) Madras: Theosophical Society/ Adyar Library. Rep. 1966.

Chomsky, Noam. 1964. *Current Issues in Linguistic Theory.* The Hague: Mouton.

———. 1966. *Cartesian Linguistics, A Chapter in the History of Rationalist Thought.* NY and London: Harper and Row.

———. 1968. *Language and Mind.* NY: Harcourt, Brace, and World.

———. 1975. *Reflections on Language.* NY: Pantheon.

Chomsky, N., and Morris Halle. 1978. *The Sound Patterns of English.* NY: Harper.

Chou-yi-liang. 1945. "Tantrism in China," HJAS 8:241–332.

Choudhary, R. K. c. 1953. "Some Aspects of Social History as Gleaned Through Jaiminīya-Gṛhyasūtra," JOIB 3, no. 4:391–402.

Clark, T. W. 1955. "Evolution of Hinduism in Medieval Bengali Literature," BSOAS 17:503–18.

Clothey, Fred W. 1972. "Pilgrimage Centers in the Tamil Cultus of Murukan," JAAR 40, no. 1:79–95.

Coburn, Thomas B. 1980. "The Study of the Purāṇas and the Study of Religion," *Religious Studies* 16:341–52.

———. 1984a. *Devī-Māhātmya, The Crystallization of the Goddess Tradition.* Delhi: MB.

———. 1984b. "'Scripture' in India: Towards a Typology of the Word in Hindu Life," JAAR 52, no. 3:435–59.

Cole, Peter, and Jerry Morgan, eds. 1975. *Speech Acts.* (*Syntax and Semantics,* John Kimball, ed. [NY: Academic Press], v. 3).

Coomaraswamy, A. K. 1913–14. "Hands and Feet in Indian Art," *Burlington Magazine* (London) 24:204–11.

———. 1928. "Mudrā, Muddā," JAOS 48:279–81.

———. 1928–31. *Yakṣas.* Washington, D. C: Smithsonian Institute. Rep. 1971 (Delhi: Munshiram).

———. 1933–35. "*Kha* and Other Words Denoting 'Zero' in Connection with the Metaphysics of Space," BSOAS 7:487–97.

Coomaraswamy, A. K., and Duggirāla Gopālakrishnāyya. 1917. *The Mirror of Gesture, Being the Abhinaya Darpaṇa of Nandikeśvara.* Cambridge. 2nd ed. 1936 (NY: Weyhe), Rep. 1970 (ND: Munshiram).

***Coope, Christopher,* et al.** 1970. *A Wittgenstein Workbook.* Berkeley: UCaP.

Coward, Harold. 1980. *Sphoṭa Theory of Language.* Delhi: MB.

Coward, Harold, and Krishna Sivaraman, eds. 1977. *Revelation in Indian Thought.* Emeryville, Calif.: Dharma Publishing.

Cox, Harvey. 1969. *The Feast of Fools.* NY: Harper and Row.

Crooke, William. 1919. "Secret Messages and Symbols Used in India," JBORS 5:451–62.

D'Sa, Francis X. 1974. "Revelation Without a God, Kumārila's Theory of Śabdapramāṇaṃ." In *Research Seminar on Non-Biblical Scriptures,* D. S. Amalorpavadass, ed. (Bangalore).

———. 1980. *Śabdaprāmānyam in Śabara and Kumārila: Towards a Study of the Mīmāṃsā Experience of Language.* (DeNRL 7) Wien.

Dalal, Chimanlal D. 1920. *Gaṇakārikā od Ācārya Bhāsarvajña, with four appendices including the Kāravaṇa-Māhātmya.* (GOS 15) Baroda: Oriental Institute. Rep. 1966.

Dallmayr, Fred. R., and Thomas A. McCarthy, eds. 1977. *Understanding and Critical Inquiry.* Notre Dame, Ind.: Univ. of Notre Dame Press.

Dandekar, R. N. 1946–73. *Vedic Bibliography* (3 vols.). Poona: 1, Karnatak Publishing House; 2, Univ. of Poona; 3, BORI.

———. 1969. "Vasiṣṭha as Religious Conciliator." In *K. R. Cama Oriental Institute Golden Jubilee Volume* (Bombay). K. R. Cama Oriental Institute.

———. 1970. "Varuṇa, Vasiṣṭha and *Bhakti.*" In *Añjali, O. H. de A. Wijesekara Felicitation Volume,* J. Tilakasiri, ed. (Peradeniya: Univ. of Ceylon).

Dandekar, R. N., C. G. Kashikar,* et al., *eds. 1958–73. *Śrautakośa, Encyclopedia of Vedic Sacrificial Ritual.* Poona: Vaidika Saṃśodhana Maṇḍala.

Daniélou, Alain. 1964. *Hindu Polytheism.* (*Bollingen Series* 73) NY: Pantheon Books, orig. Fr. ed 1960.

Dare, Paul. 1947. *Magie blanche et magie noire aux Indes.* Paris: Payot.

Das, Nilakantha. c. 1958. "Om," *Orissa Hist. Res. J.* 7, no. 3–4:149–67.

Das, U. K. 1966. *Bhāratīya Śaktisādhana,* 2 vols.. Santiniketan.

Das, Veena. 1977. "On the Categorization of Space in Hindu Ritual." In *Text and Context, the Social Anthropology of Tradition,* Ravindra Jain, ed., pp. 9–27. (Philadelphia: Institutue for the Study of Human Issues.)

———. 1982. *Structure and Cognition: Aspects of Hindu Caste and Ritual,* 2nd ed. Delhi: OUP. 1st ed. 1977.

Dasgupta, Shashi Bhushan. 1950. *An Introduction to Tantrik Buddhism.* Calcutta: Calcutta Univ. Press.

———. 1956. "Some Later Yogic Schools," in CHI 4.291–99.

———. 1961. *Bhārater Śakti-sādnana o Sāhitya* (*The Literature and Teachings of Indian Śaktism*). Calcutta: Sāhitya Saṅgsad.

———. 1962. *Obscure Religious Cults,* 2nd ed. Calcutta: Firma K. L. Mukhopadhyay. Orig. 1946, 3rd ed. 1969.

———. 1956. "The Role of Mantra in Indian Religion," *Bulletin of the Ramakrishna Mission Institute of Culture* (Calcutta) 7, no. 3:49–57.

Dasgupta, Surendranath N. 1955. *A History of Indian Philosophy,* V: *The Southern Schools of Śaivism.* Cambridge: CUP. Rep. 1962, 1969.

Dave, T. N. 1966. "Śrī Śaṅkarāchārya and Sphoṭa," *Śāradā Pīṭha Pradīpa* (Biannual of the Indological Res. Inst.) (Dwaraka) 6:19–27.

Davidson, J. Le Roy. 1960. "Mannerism and Neurosis in the Erotic Art of India," *Oriental Art* 6.

De, Sushil Kumar. 1938. "The Buddhist Tantric Literature (Sanskrit) of Bengal," NIA 1, no. 1:1–23.

———. 1959. *Ancient Indian Erotics and Erotic Literature.* Calcutta: K. L. Mukhopadhyay.

———. 1960. *History of Sanskrit Poetics,* 2nd rev. ed. (2 vols.). Calcutta: Firma K. L. Mukhopadhyay, orig. 1923.

———. 1961. *Early History of the Vaisnava Faith and Movement in Bengal, From Sanskrit and Bengali Sources,* 2nd ed. Calcutta: Firma K. L. Mukhopadhyay. orig. 1942.

Deb, H. K. 1921. "The Svastika and the Oṃkāra," JASBe n. s. 17:31–247.

Dekker, Gerbrand. 1955. "Der Kuṇḍalinī-Yoga," *Asiatische Studien* (Bern) 9:45ff..

Demiéville, Paul. 1930. "Bombai." In *Hôbôgirin, Dictionaire encyckopédique du bouddhisme d'après les sources chinoises et japonaises* 1.93–113. Also Tokyo: Maison Franco franco-japonais 1929. Rep. 1974.

______. 1980. "Notes on Buddhist Hymnology in the Far East." In *Buddhist Studies in Honor of Walpola Rahula,* S. Balasooriya, *et al.,* eds. (London and Śrī Laṅka.)

Deo, Shantaram Balachandra. 1956. *History of Jaina Monachism From Inscriptions and Literature.* (*Deccan College Diss. Series* 6) Poona: Deccan College.

Deppert Joachim. 1977. *Rudras Geburt, systematische Untersuchungen zum Inzest in der Mythologie der Brāhmaṇas.* (*Beiträge zur Südasien-Forschung* [Südasien-institut Universität Heidelberg] 28) Wiesbaden: Franz Steiner Verlag.

Dermenghem, Émile. 1953. "Techniques d'extase en Islam." In *Yoga, science de l'homme intégral,* Jacques Masui, ed. (Paris), 274–83.

Derrett, J. Duncan M. 1974. "Modes of Snnyāsīs and the Reform of a South Indian Maṭha Carried Out in 1584," JAOS 94:65–72. Rep. 1976: *Essays in Modern Hindu Law,* J. D. M. Derrett, ed. pp. 111–19. (Leiden: E. J. Brill.)

______. 1977. "A Juridical Fabrication of Early British India: The Mahānirvāna-Tantra." In *Essays in Classical and Modern Hindu Law* Vol. 2, pp. 197–242. (Leiden: E. J. Brill.)

Desai, Devangana. 1975. *Erotic Sculpture of India.* New Delhi: Tata McGraw-Hill.

Dessigane, R., P. Z. Pattabiramin, and Jean Filliozat. 1964. *Les Légendes çivaītes de Kāñcipuram, Analyse de textes et iconographie.* (PIFI 27) Pondichéry.

Deussen, Paul. 1921. *Sechzig Upanishad's des Veda,* 3rd ed. Leipzig. Rep. 1963 (Darmstadt); Eng. tr. 1980 (*Sixty Upaniṣads of the Veda,* V. M. Bedekar and G. B. Palsule, trs. Delhi: MB, 2 vols.).

Deva, K. 1959. "The Temples of Khajuraho in Central India," *Ancient India* (*Bulletin of the Archeological Survey of India*) (New Delhi) 15:43–65.

Devadhar, C. R., and N. G. Suru. 1935. *Mālatī-Mādhava.* Poona: By the editors.

Devasthali, Govind Vinayak. 1965. *Religion and Mythology in the Brāhmaṇas.* Poona: Univ. of Poona.

Diamond, Malcolm L., and Thomas V. Litzenberg, Jr. 1975. *The Logic of God, Theology and Verification.* Indianapolis: Bobbs-Merrill.

Diehl, Carl Gustav. 1956. *Instrument and Purpose, Studies on Rites and Rituals in South India.* Lund (Sweden): CWK Gleerup.

Dikshitar, V. R. 1942. *The Lalitā Cult.* Madras: Monograph of the Bulletin of the Dept. of Indian History and Archaeology, University of Madras.

Dimock, Edward C., Jr. 1966. *The Place of the Hidden Moon, Erotic Mysticism in the Vaiṣṇava-Sahajiyā Cult of Bengal.* Chicago: UChP.

Douglas, Mary. 1978. *Purity and Danger: An Analysis of Concepts of Pollution and Taboo.* Boston: Routledge.

Douglas, Nik. 1978. *Tibetan Tantric Charms and Amulets.* NY: Dover.

Dube, Bechan N. 1967. *Geographical Concepts in Ancient India.* Varanasi: National Geographical Society of India.

Ducrot, Osvald, and Tzvetan Todorov. 1979. *Encyclopedic Dictionary of the Sciences of Language.* Catherine Porter. tr. Baltimore: The Johns Hopkins Univ. Press. Orig. *Dictionnaire encyclopédique des sciences du langage* (Paris: Éditions du Seuil, 1972).

Dumont, Lois. 1960. D. F. Pocock and R. G. Lienhardt, trs. "World Renunciation in Indian Religions," CIS 4:33–62. Orig. Fr. ed. *Archives de Sociologie des Religions* 7 (1959):45–69. Rep. Dumont 1970, 33–60 and Dumont 1980, 267–86.

______. 1970. *Religion/Politics and History in India, Collected Papers in Indian Sociology.* (ÉPHE: *Le Monde d'outre-mer passé et présent* 1.34) Paris: Mouton.

______. 1980. *Homo Hierarchicus, The Caste System and Its Implications,* complete and rev. ed.. Chicago: UChP. Orig. Fr. ed. 1966 (Paris: Gallimard); 1st Eng. ed. 1970.

Dumont, Paul Émile. 1927. *L'Aśvemedha, description du sacrifice solennel du cheval dans le culte védique d'après les textes du Yajurveda blanc.* Louvain, Paris: Geuthner.

______. 1933. *L'Īśvaragītā, le chant de Śiva, texte eduit du Kūrma-pūraṇa.* Paris: Librairie Paul Geuthner.

______. 1939. *L'Agnihotra, description de l'agnihotra dans le rituel védique.* Baltimore: The John Hopkins Univ. Press.

Duncan, Marion Herbert. 1955. *Harvest Festival Dramas of Tibet.* Hong Kong: Orient Pub. Co.

Dviveda, Vraj Vallabha. 1968. *Nityāṣoḍaśikārṇava, with Two Commentaries: Ṛjuvimarśinī by Śivānanda and Artharatnāvalī by Vidyānanda.* (*Yoga-tantra-granthamālā* 1) Varanasi: Varasaneya Sanskrit Viśvavidyālaya University Press.

______. 1972. *Mahārthamañjarī.* Varanasi.

______. 1978. "Āgama evaṃ tantraśastra ko Kavirājajī kī den (The Contribution of (Gopinath) Kaviraj to the Study of Tantra and Āgama) (?)," *Pariṣadpatrikā* 18, no. 2:17–36.

———. 1982a. *Satvatā Saṃhitā.* Varanasi: The Yoga Tantra Department of the Sampūrṇānanda Sanskrit University.

———. 1982b. *Tantrayātrā.* Varanasi: Ratna Publications.

Dvivedi, Hazari Prasad, ed. 1957. *Nāth Siddhoṃ kī Bāniyāṃ.* Banaras: Nagari Pracharini Sabha.

———. 1966. *Nāth Sampradāya.* Varanasi: Naivedya Niketan.

Dvivedi, Kapila Deva. 1951. *Arthavijñāna aur vyākaraṇadarśana* (*Semantics and Philosophy of Grammar*). Allahabad: Hindusthani Academy.

Eck, Diana L. 1981. *Darśan, Seeing the Divine Image in India.* Chambersburg, Penn.: Anima Books.

———. 1982. *Banaras, City of Light.* NY: Alfred A. Knopf.

Edgerton, Franklin. 1928. "Some Linguistic Notes on the Mīmāṃsā System," *Language* 4:171–77.

———. 1929. *Mīmāṅsā Nyāya Prakāsa or Āpadevī: A Treatise on the Mīmāṅsā System by Apadeva, Translated into English, With an Introduction, Transliterated Sanskrit Text, and Glossarial Index.* New Haven, Conn.: YUP.

Eggeling, Julius. 1882–1900. *The Śatapatha—Brāhmaṇa, According to the Text of the Mādhyandina School,* 5 vols. (SBE 12,26,41,43,44) Oxford: Clarendon Press. Rep. 1963 (Delhi: MB).

Ehrmann, Jacques. 1971. *Game, Play, and Literature.* Boston; Beacon.

Ekvall, Robert B. 1964. *Religious Observances in Tibet: Patterns and Functions.* Chicago: UChP.

Elder, G. R. 1976. "Problems of Language in Buddhist Tantra," HR 15, no. 3:231–50.

Eliade, Mircea. 1965. *Rites and Symbols of Initiation: The Mysteries of Birth and Rebirth.* Willard R. Trask, tr. NY: Harper. Orig. Fr. Ed., *Naissances mystiques, essais sur quelques types d'initiation* (Paris: Gallimard, 1959); 1st Eng. ed., *Birth and Rebirth, The Religious Meaning of Initiation in Human Culture* (NY: Harper, 1958 [?]).

———. 1969. *Yoga: Immortality and Freedom,* 2nd ed. (*Bollingen Series* 56) Princeton: Princeton Univ. Press. Fr. ed. 1945; 1st Eng. ed. 1958.

Elwin, Verrier. 1944–54. *Specimens of the Oral Literature of Middle India,* I: *Folk Tales of Mahakoshal,* II: *Folk-songs of the Maikal Hills,* III: *Folk-songs of Chattisgarh,* IV: *Myths of Middle India,* V: *Tribal Myths of Orissa.* London: OUP.

Emeneau, Murray B. 1955. "India and Linguistics," JAOS 75:145–53.

Ernout, A., and A. Meillet. 1959. *Dictionnaire étymologique de la langue latine, histoire des mots,* 4th ed.. Paris: Librairie C. Klincksieck.

Esnoul, Anne Marie. 1959. "Les Songes et leur interpretation dans l'Inde." In

Les Songes et leur interpretation: Sources orientales, A. M. Esnoul *et al.*, eds., vol. 2, pp. 208–47.

Essers, B. 1952a. *Vāc, Het woord als godsgestalte in de Vega.* Groningen: Thesis.

______. 1952b. *Een oudindische symbolik van het geluid.* (*Philosophia Religionis* 4) Assen: van Gorcum and Co.

Esteller, A. 1962. "A 'Brahmodya' or a Palimpsest?," JAS (Bombay) 34–35:102–19.

Evans-Pritchard, Edward E. 1929. "The Morphology and Function of Magic: A Comparative Study of Trobriand and Zande Ritual and Spells," AA 31:619–41.

Evola, Giulio Cesare Andrea. 1949. *Lo Yoga della potenza (Saggio sui tantra) (The Yoga of Power, An Essay on the Tantras).* Milano: Mailard (?); rep. Roma: Mediteranee, 1968.

Ewing, Arthur H. 1901. "The Hindu Conception of the Functions of the Breath," JAOS 22:249–308.

______. 1902. "The Śāradātilaka Tantra," JAOS 23:65–76.

Faddegon, Barend. 1927. "Ritualistic Dadism," ActaOr 5:177–95.

______. 1951. *Studies on the Sāmaveda.* (VKNAW 57.1) Amsterdam.

Falk, Maryla. 1939. *Il Mito psicologico nell'India antica.* (*Reale Academia nazionale dei Lincei* 6.8.5) Roma: Accaemia nazionale dei Lincei, G. Bardi.

______. 1943. *Nāma-rūpa and Dharma-rūpa.* Calcutta: Univ. of Calcutta.

Farquhar, J. N. 1967. *An Outline of the Religious Literature of India.* Delhi: MB. Orig. 1920.

Ferro-Luzzi, Gabriella Eithinger. 1977. "Ritual as Language: The Case of South Indian Food Offerings," CA 15:119–45.

Filliozat, Jean. 1937. *Étude de démonologie indienne, Le Kumāratantra de Rāvaṇa, et les textes parallèles indiens, tibétains, chinois, cambodgien et arabe.* (*Cahiers de Société Asiatique* 1.4) Paris: Imprimerie nationale.

______. 1940. "Nāgārjuna et Agastya, médecins, chimistes et sorciers." *Actes du XXe Congrès Inter. des Orientalistes,* pp. 228–29. Brussells. Rep. Filliozat 1974, 210–11.

______. 1943. *Magie et médecine.* (*Coll. Mythes et Religions*) Paris: Presses Universitaires.

______. 1946. "Les Origines d'une technique mystique indienne," RevPhil 6, no. 136:208–20.

______. 1949. *La Doctrine classique de la médecine indienne, Ses Origines et ses parallèles grecs.* Paris: Imprimerie nationale.

———. 1952. "Pronostics médicaux akkadiens, grecs, et indiens," JA 240:299–321. Rep. Filliozat 1974, 243–65.

———. 1953. "Les limites des pouvoirs humains dans l'Inde," *Études carmélitaines (Limites de l'humain)*, 22–38.

———. 1954. "A propos de la religion de Bhartṛhari." In *Silver Jubilee Volume of the Zinbun Kagaku Kenkyusyo*, pp. 116–20. Kyoto: Kyoto Univ.

———. 1961. "Les Āgama çivaītes." (PIFI 18) in *Rauravāgama*, N. R. Bhatt, ed. vol. 1, pp. v–xv. Pondichéry.

———. 1974. *Laghu-Prabandhāḥ, Choix d'articles d'indologie*. Colette Caillat, Bruno Dagens, François Gros, and Ludwik Sternbach, eds., Leiden: Brill.

Finch, Henry Leroy. 1971. *Wittgenstein—the Early Philosophy, An Exposition of the 'Tractatus.'* NY: Humanities Press.

———. 1977. *Wittgenstein—the Later Philosophy: An Exposition of the 'Philosophical Investigations'*. Atlantic Highlands, N.J.: Humanities Press.

Findly, Ellison Banks. 1981. "Jātavedas in the Ṛgveda: The God of Generations," ZDMG 131, no. 2:349–73.

Finnegan, Ruth. 1969. "How to Do Things with Words: Performative Utterances Among the Limba of Sierra Leone," *Man* n. s. 4, no. 4:537–51.

Firth, J. R. 1957. "Ethnographic Analysis and Language with Reference to Malinowski's Views." In *Man and Culture*, R. Firth. ed. (London: RKP).

Firth, Raymond. 1973. *Symbols: Public and Private*. Ithaca. NY: Cornell Univ. Press.

Fischer, Klaus. 1979. *Erotik und Askese in Kult und Kunst der Inder*. Köln: Dumont Bucherverlag.

Fiser, Ivo. 1966. *Indian Erotics of the Oldest Period*. (*Acta Universitatis Carolinae Philologica Monographia* 14) Praha (Prague): Universita Karlova.

Fort, Andrew O. forthcoming. *The Self and Its States: A State of Consciousness Doctrine in Advaita Vedānta*.

Franke, R. Otto. 1892. "Mudrā = Schrift (oder Lesekunst)?," ZDMG 46:731–34.

Fraser, Russell. 1977. *The Language of Adam*. NY: Col. UP.

Frauwallner, Erich. "Beiträge zur Apohalehre, I: Dharmakīrti, II: Dharmottara," WZKM 37:259–83; 39:247–85; 40:51–94; 42:93–102; 44:233–87. Rep. KS:367–459, 582–637.

———. 1938. "Bhāvanā und Vidhiḥ bei Maṇḍanamiśra," WZKM 45:212–52.

———. 1960a. "Das Eindringen des Sprachtheorie in die indischen philosophischen systeme." In *Indologen-Tagung 1959; Verhandlungen der indologischen*

Arbeitstagung in Essen-Bredeney, Ernst Waldschmidt, ed., pp. 239–43 (Göttingen). Rep. KS:279–83.

———. 1960b. "Sprachtheorie und Philosophie im Mahābhaṣyam des Patañjali," WZKSO 4:92–118. Rep. KS:284–310.

———. 1961. "Mīmāṃsāsūtram 1.1.6–23," WZKSO 5:113–24. Rep. KS:311–22.

———. 1968. *Materialien sur áltesten erkenntnislehre der Karmamīmāṃsā.* (VKSKS 9 (=OAW Sitzungbericht 259.2)) Wien.

———. 1982. *Kleine Schriften.* Gerhard Oberhammer and Ernst Steinkellner, eds. (*Glasenapp-Stiftung* 22) (Wiesbaden: Franz Steiner Verlag.

Freed, Ruth S., and Stanley A. Freed. 1962. "Two Mother-Goddess Ceremonies of Delhi State in the Great and Little Traditions," *Southwestern J. of Anthro.* 18:246–77.

———. 1980. "Origin of the Swastika: Ceremonies in India Have Shed New Light on an Ancient Symbol," *Natural History* 89, no. 1:68–75.

Frick, H. 1931. *Ideogram. Mythologie und das Wort.* (*Marburger Theol. Stud.* 3) Marburg.

Fripp, P. 1964. *The Mystic Philosophy of Sant Mat as Taught by the Present Spiritual Master at the Radha Soami Colony at Beas.* London: Spearman.

Gächter, Othmar. 1983. *Hermeneutics and Language in Pūrva Mīmāṃsā, A Study in Śābara Bhāṣya.* Delhi: MB.

Gairola, C. K. 1954. "Évolution du pūrṇa ghaṭa (vase d'abondance) dans l'Inde et l'Inde extérieure," *Arts Asiatiques* (Paris) 1:209–26.

Gait, Edward Albert. 1963. *A History of Assam,* 3rd ed.. rev. by B. K. Barua and H. V. S. Murthy Calcutta: Thacker Spink. 1st ed, 1905, 2nd ed. 1926.

Gajendragadkar, A. B., and R. D. Karmarkar, eds. 1934. *The Arthasaṃgraha of Laugākṣi Bhāskara.* Bombay. Rep. 1984 (Delhi: MB).

Gampert, Wilhelm. 1939. *Die Sühnezeremonien in der altindischen Rechtsliteratur.* Prague: Orientalisches Insitut.

Ganguly, O. C. 1925. "The Mithuna in Indian Art," Calcutta: *Rupam* 22–23.

Garbe, Richard, ed. 1882–1902. *Āpastamba Śrauta Sūtra.* (BI 42) Calcutta: Asiatic Society.

———. 1903. "Über den willkürlichen Scheintod indischer Fakire," in *Beiträge zur indischen Kulturgeschichte* (Berlin), 199ff.

Gardet, Louis. 1952–53. "La Mention du nom divin (*dhikr*) dans la mystique musulmane," *Revue Thomiste* (Paris) 52:642–79; 53:197–216.

———. 1972. *Études de philosophie et mystique compar'és.* Paris: Vrin.

Garge, Damodar Vishnu. 1940. "A Revised and Enlarged Version of the Nirukta," BDCRI 2.

———. 1941. "The Contribution of the Śābharabhāṣya to Ṛgveda-Exegesis," PAIOC (Hyderabad) 11. Poona: Deccan College.

———. 1942. "Śābarabhāṣya and the Ṛgveda-Exegesis," BDCRI 3, no. 4:531–46.

———. 1943. "The Contribution of the Śābara-Bhāṣya to Ṛgveda-Exegesis," BDCRI 4.

———. 1949. "Jaimini—Śabara and the Science of Grammar," ABORI 30:254–62. Rep. Garge 1952, 236–42.

———. 1952. *Citations in Śābara-Bhāṣya.* (*Deccan College Dissertation Series* 8) Poona: Deccan College.

Gaur, Albertine. 1979. *Writing Materials of the East.* (*British Library Booklets*) London: The British Library.

Gaurinath Sastri. 1939. "The Doctrine of Śabdabrahman—A Criticism by Jayantabhaṭṭa," IHQ 15:441–53.

———. 1959. *The Philosophy of Word and Meaning: Some Indian Approaches with Special Reference to the Philosophy of Bhartṛhari.* (*Calcutta Sanskrit College Research Series* 5) Calcutta: Sanskrit College.

———. 1968–69. "Monism of Bhartṛhari," in *Beiträge zur Geschichte Indiens: Fest. für Erich Frauwallner*, G. Oberhammer, ed., (WZKSOA 12–13), pp. 319–22.

Gay, Volney. 1979. *Freud on Ritual: Reconstruction and Critique.* Missoula, Montana: Scholar's Press.

Gelber, Steven J., ed. 1983. *Hare Krishna, Hare Krishna, Five Distinguished Scholars on the Krishna Movement in the West.* NY: Grove Press.

Geldner, Karl Friedrich. 1951–57. *Der Rig-Veda.* 4 vols. (HOS 33–36) Cambridge, Mass.: HUP.

van Gennep, Arnold. 1960. *The Rites of Passage*, Monika B. Vizedom and Gabrielle L. Caffee, trs. Chicago: UChP. Orig. Fr. ed. 1909.

Gerow, Edwin. 1977. *A History of Indian Poetics.* (HIL 5.3) Wiesbaden: OH.

Getty, Alice. 1914. *The Gods of Northern Buddhism.* Oxford.

Ghirshman, R. 1977. *L'Iran et la migration des Indo-Aryens et Iraniens.* Leiden.

Ghosh, Atal Behari. 1956. "The Spirit and Culture of the Tantras." In CHI 4:241–51.

Ghosh, Batakrishna. 1941–42. "The Hindu Ideal of Life According to the Gṛhyasūtras," *Indian Culture* 8:219.

Ghosh, M. M. 1975. *Nandikeśvara's Abhinayadarpanam: A Manual of Gesture and*

Posture Used in Ancient Indian Dance and Drama, 3rd rev. ed.. Calcutta: Manisha Granthalaya.

Ghurye, K. G. 1950. *The Preservation of Learned Tradition in India.* Bombay: The Popular Book Depot.

Gier, Nicholas F. 1981. *Wittgenstein and Phenomenology, A Comparative Study of the Later Wittgenstein, Husserl, Heidegger, and Merleau-Ponty.* Albany: SUNY.

Gill, Sam D. 1977. "Prayer as Person: The Performative Force in Navaho Prayer Acts," HR 17, no. 2:143–57.

Girard, Rene. 1977. *Violence and the Sacred.* Patrick Gregory, tr. Baltimore: The Johns Hopkins Univ. Press. Orig. Fr. ed., *Violence et la sacré* (Paris: Éditions Bernard Grasset, 1972).

von Glasenapp, Helmuth. 1900. *Heilige Stätten Indiens.* Jena: Diederich.

______. 1936a. "Die Entstehung des Vajrayāna." ZDMG 90:546–72.

______. 1936b. "Tantrismus und Śaktismus," *Ostasiatische Zeitschrift* (Berlin), n. s., 12:120–33.

______. 1940. *Buddhistische Mysterien, Die geheimen Lehren und Riten des Diamant-Fahrzeugs.* Stuttgart: W. Spemann.

______. 1952–54. "Ein buddhistische Initiationsritus der javanischen Mittelalters," *Tribus* (Stuttgart) n. s. 2–3:259–74.

Gnoli, Raniero. 1959a. "Miscellanea Indica: Corrections and Emendations to the Text of the *Paratriṃśikāvivaraṇa,*" EW 10, no. 3:192–212.

______. 1959b. "Passi scelti e tradotti del *Parātriṃśikāvivaraṇa,*" RSO 163–82.

______. 1960. "Passi scelti e tradotti del *Parātriṃśikāvivaraṇa* (continuazione)," RSO 63–83.

______. 1965. *La Trentina della Suprema (Parātriṃśikālaghuvṛtti).* Torino: Boringhieri.

______. 1973. "Gli Āgama scivaiti nell'India settentrionale (The Śivite Āgamas in Northern India)," IT 1:61–69.

______. 1985. *Il Commento di Abhinavagupta alla Parātriṃśikā (Parātriṃsikāvivaraṇa)* (SOR 58) Rome.

Goetz, Heinrich. 1939. "Khajurāho," *Maandblad voor beeldende kunsten (Vereeniging van vrienden der Aziatische Kunst)* (Amsterdam) 16:210–17 (?).

______. 1958. "The Historical Background of the Great Temples of Khajurāho," ArAs 5, no. 1:35–47. Rep. (1) 1961 *Roopa-Lekhā, An Illustrated Quarterly Journal of Indian Arts and Crafts* (New Delhi: The All-India Fine Art and Crafts Society) 32, no. 2:59–79; (2) Goetz 1974, 108–21.

______. 1974. *Hermann Goetz: Studies in the History, Religion and Art of Classical and Mediaeval India*, Hermann Kulke, ed. Wiesbaden: Franz Steiner.

Gold, Daniel, and Ann Grodzins Gold. 1984. "The Fate of the Householder Nath," HR 24, no. 2:113–32.

Goldman, Robert P. 1978. "Fathers, Sons, and Gurus: Oedipal Conflict in the Sanskrit Epics," JIPh 6:325–92.

______. 1982. "Matricide, Renunciation, and Compensation in the Legends of Two Warrior-Heroes of the Sanskrit Epics," IT 10:117–31.

______. 1985. "Karma, Guilt, and Buried Memories: Public Fantasy and Private Reality in Traditional India," JAOS 105, no. 3:413–25.

Gomez, Luis O., and Hiram W. Woodward, Jr. 1981. *Barabuḍur, History and Significance of a Buddhist Monument*. (*Berkeley Buddhist Studies Series* 2) Berkeley, Calif.: Asian Humanities Press.

Gonda, Jan. 1939a. *Remarks on Similes in Sanskrit Literature*. Wageningen. Rep. 1949 (Leiden: Brill, ORT 1).

______. 1939b. "The Meaning of the Word *alaṃkāra*," in *A Volume of Eastern and Indian Studies in Honour of F. W. Thomas*, S. M. Katre and P. K. Gode, eds. (NIA, extra series I) (Bombay), pp. 97–114. Rep. Gonda 1975b, 2:258–74.

______. 1941. "Ein Neues Leid," WZKM 48:275–90. Rep. Gonda 1975b, 4.144–59.

______. 1947. "A propos d'un sens magico-religieux de Skt. *guru-*," BSOAS 12:124–31. Rep. Gonda 1975b, 2.295–302.

______. 1950. *Notes on Brahman*. Utrecht: J. L. Beyers.

______. 1951. *The Ṛgvidhāna, English Translation With an Introduction and Notes*. Utrecht: Osthoek.

______. 1956. "The Sīmantonnayana as Described in the Gṛhyasūtras," EW 7:12–31. Rep. Gonda 1975b, 4.186–205.

______. 1957. "The Vedic Concept of Aṃhas," IIJ 1:33–60. Rep. Gonda 1975b, 2.58–85.

______. 1959a. *Epithets in the Ṛgveda*. (DRT 4) The Hague: Mouton and Co.

______. 1959b. *Stylistic Repetition in the Veda*. (VNAW 65.3) Amsterdam: North Holland Publishing Co.

______. 1960. *Ellipsis, Brachyology, and Other Forms of Brevity in Speech in the Ṛgveda*. (VNAW 67.4) Amsterdam.

______. 1960–63. *Die Religionen Indiens* (2 vols.). Stuttgart: W. Kohlhammer Verlag.

———. 1961a. "Some Notes on the Study of Ancient Indian Religious Terminology," HR 1:243–73. Rep. Gonda 1975b, 2.1–31.

———. 1961b. "Ascetics and Courtesans," ALB 25:78–102. Rep. Gonda 1975b, 4.223–47.

———. 1963a. *The Vision of the Vedic Poets.* The Hague: Mouton and Co.

———. 1963b. "The Indian Mantra," *Oriens* 16:244–97. Rep. Gonda 1975b, 4.248–301.

———. 1965a. *Change and Continuity in Indian Religion.* (DRT 9) The Hague: Mouton and Co.

———. 1965b. *The Savayajñas (Kauśikasūtra 60–68. Translation, Introduction, Commentary).* (VKNAW 71:2) Amsterdam, N. V. Noord-Hollandsche Uitgevers Maatschappij.

———. 1966. *Loka, World and Heaven in the Veda.* (VKNAW 73.1) Amsterdam: North-Holland Publishing Co.

———. 1967. *The Meaning of the Sanskrit Term Dhāman.* (VKNAW 73.2) Amsterdam: Noord-Hollandsche Uitgevers Maatschappu.

———. 1969. *Eye and Gaze in the Veda.* (VKNAW 75.1) Amsterdam: North-Holland Publishing Co.

———. 1970a. *Notes on Names and the Name of God in Ancient India.* (VNAW 75.4) Amsterdam: North Holland Publishing Co.

———. 1970b. *Viṣṇuism and Śivaism, A Comparison.* London: Univ. of London, Athlone Press.

———. 1971. *Old Indian.* (HO 2.1.1) Leiden: E. J. Brill.

———. 1972a. "Mudrā," in *Ex orbe religionum, Studia G. Widengren,* II Leiden: Brill.

———. 1972b. "The Use of Vedic *Mantras* in the Ritual Texts of the Vaikhānasa," IIJ 14.

———. 1975a. *Vedic Literature (Saṃhitās and Brāhmaṇas).* (HIL I.1) Wiesbaden: OH.

———. 1975b. *Selected Studies, Presented to the Author by the Staff of the Oriental Institute, Utrecht University, on the Occasion of his 70th Birthday* (4 vols.). Leiden: E. J. Brill.

———. 1975c. "The Indian Religions in Pre-Islamic Indonesia and Their Survival in Bali." In HO 3.2.1 (*Indonesien . . . Religionen,* H. Kähler, ed., pp. 1–54. Leiden: Brill).

———. 1977a. *Medieval Religious Literature in Sanskrit.* (HIL II.1) Wiesbaden: OH.

______. 1977b. *The Ritual Sūtras.* (HIL 1.2) Wiesbaden: OH.

______. 1977c. "Religious Thought and Practice in Vaikhānasa Viṣṇuism," BSOAS 40:550–557.

______. 1980a. *Vedic Ritual: The Non-solemn Rites.* (HO II.IV.1) Leiden: E. J. Brill.

______. 1980b. "The Śatarudriya." In *Sanskrit and Indian Studies, Essays in Honour of Daniel H. H. Ingalls,* M. Nagatomi, *et al.*, eds., pp. 75–91. (Dordrecht: D. Reidel Publishing Co., 1980.)

______. 1980c. *The Mantras of the Agnyupasthāna and the Sautrāmaṇī.* Amsterdam: North-Holland Publishing Co..

Goody, Jack. 1961. "Religion and Ritual: The Definitional Problems," *British J. of Sociology* 12, no. 2:142–64.

______. 1968. *Literacy in Traditional Socieities.* Cambridge: CUP.

______. 1977. *The Domestication of the Savage Mind.* Cambridge: CUP.

Gooneratne, D. de Silva. 1865–66. "On Witchcraft and Demonology in Ceylon," JCyBRAS 4:1–118.

Gopal, Ram. 1959. *India of Vedic Kalpasūtras.* Delhi: National Publishing House, rep. MB, 1983.

Gopinath Kaviraj. 1924. "The Doctrine of Pratibhā in Indian Philosophy," ABORI 5:1–18, 113–32. Rep. G. Kaviraj, *Aspects of Indian Thought* (Burdwan: Univ. of Burdwan, 1966), 1–44.

______. 1963a. *Tantra o Āgamaśāstrer Digdarśan (A General Introduction to Tantra and Āgamaśāstra).* (*Calcutta Sanskrit College Res. Series* 25) Calcutta: Sanskrit College.

______. 1963b. *Tāntrika Vāṅmaya mem Śāktadṛṣṭi* (*The Śākta Perspective in Tantric Literature.*). Patna: Bihar Rastrabhasa Parishad.

______. 1963–64. *Bhāratīya Saṃskṛti aur Sādhanā* [= *Indian Culture and Spiritual Discipline*], 2 vols. Patna: Bihar Rastrabhasa Parisad.

______. 1972. *Tantrika Sahitya* (*Tantric Literature*) (A Descriptive Catalogue). Lucknow: Hindi Samiti.

Gopinatha Rao, T. A. 1914–16. *Elements of Hindu Iconography,* 2 vols. in 4 parts. Madras. Rep. 1968 (NY: Paragon).

______. 1920. *Talamana: or, Iconometry, Being a Concise Account of the Measurements of Hindu Images as Given in the Āgamas and Other Authoritative Works.* (*Archeological Survey of India* Memoir 3) Calcutta, Rep. 1977 (New Delhi: Indological Book House).

Goris, Roelof. 1926. *Bijdrage tot de kennis der Oud-Javaansche en Balineesche Theologie.* Leiden: Dissertation, A. Vros.

Goswami, M. L. 1978. *Vidhiviveka of Maṇḍanamisra with the Nyāyakaṇikā of Vācaspatimiśra.* Banares: Tara Publications.

Goudriaan, Teun. 1965. *Kāśyapa's Book of Wisdom, (Kāśyapa-Jñānakāṇḍaḥ), A Ritual Handbook of the Vaikhānasas.* The Hague: Mouton.

———. 1970. "Vaikhānasa Daily Worship," IIJ 12.

———. 1973. "Tumburu and His Sisters," WZKSA 17:49–95.

———. 1976. "Some Recent Publications on Balinese Religion," *Review of Indonesian and Malaysian Affairs* 10:121–32.

———. 1977. "Khaḍgarāvaṇa and His Worship in Balinese and Indian Tantric Sources," WZKSA 21:143–69.

———. 1978. *Māyā Divine and Human. A Study of Magic and Its Religious Foundations in Sanskrit Texts, with Particular Attention to a Fragment on Viṣṇu's Māyā Preserved in Bali.* Delhi: MB.

Goudriaan, Teun, and C. Hooykaas. 1971. *Stuti and Stava (Bauddha, Śaiva and Vaiṣṇava) of Balinese Brahman Priests.* (VKNAW 76) Amsterdam.

Goudriaan, T., and Sanjukta Gupta. 1981. *Hindu Tantric and Śākta Literature.* (HIL 2.2) Wiesbaden: OH.

Gough, Kathleen. 1968a. "Implications of Literacy in Traditional China and India." In Goody 1968, 69–84.

———. 1968b. "Literacy in Kerala." In Goody 1968, 132–60.

Gouillard, Jean. 1953. *Petite Philocalie de la prière du coeur.* Paris: É. du Seuil.

Govinda, [Lama] Anagarika [Brahmacari] (Anangavajra Khamsum-Wangchuk). 1934. "Some Aspects of Stūpa Symbolism," *J. of Indian Society of Oriental Art.*

———. 1950–51. "The Significance of OṂ and the Foundation of Mantric Lore," *Stepping Stones* (Kalimpong, Sikkim) 17–47.

———. 1959. *Foundations of Tibetan Mysticism, According to the Esoteric Teachings of the Great Mantra.* London: Rider and Co. Rei. 1962, 1967.

———. 1970. *The Way of the White Clouds, A Buddhist Pilgrim in Tibet.* (*Clear Light Series*) Berkeley, Calif.: Shambala Publications. UK 1966.

Gowdra, Gurumurthy K. 1971. "Ritual Circles in a Mysore Village," *Sociological Bulletin* 20, no. 1:24–38.

Graham, William A. 1984. "Qur'ān as Spoken Word: An Islamic Contribution to Scripture." In *Islam and the History of Religions,* Richard C. Martin, ed. (Tucson: Univ. of Arizona Press).

Granoff, Phyllis E. 1978. *Philosophy and Argument in Late Vedānta: Śrī Harṣa's Khaṇḍanakhaṇḍakhādya.* (*Studies of Classical India* 1) Dordrecht: D. Reidel.

Gray, E. B. 1959. "An Analysis of Ṛgvedic Recitation," BSOAS 22:86–94.

Gren-Eklund, G. 1978–79. "Un Upaniṣad of Sāman," *Orientalia Suecana* 27–28, 148–58 (?).

Grimes, Ronald L. 1982. *Beginnings in Ritual Studies.* Washington, D.C.: University Press of America.

———. 1985. *Research in Ritual Studies, A Programmatic Essay and Bibliography.* (*American Theological Library Association Series* 14) Metuchen, N.J.: The Scarecrow Press.

Grünwedel, Albert. 1916. "Die Geschichte der vierundachtzig Zaubereer (Mahasiddhas) aus dem Tibetischen übersetzt," *Baessler Archiv* (Leipzig) 5:137–228.

Guenther, Herbert V. 1956. "The Concept of Mind in Buddhist Tantra," *J. of Oriental Studies* (Hong Kong) 3:261ff. Rep. Guenther 1977, 36–56.

———. 1959. *Jewel Ornament of Liberation.* London: Rider and Co.. Rei. 1971 (*The Clear Light Series,* Berkeley: Shambala Publications).

———. 1963. *The Life and Teaching of Nāropa, Translated from the Original Tibetan with a Philosophical Commentary Based on the Oral Transmission.* Oxford: Clarendon Press.

———. 1969a. *The Royal Song of Saraha: A Study in the History of Buddhist Thought.* Seattle: Univ. of Washington Press.

———. 1969b. *Yuganaddha, The Tantric View of Life,* 2nd ed. (ChowSSt 3) Varanasi: ChowSSe Office. Orig. 1952.

———. 1977. *Tibetan Buddhism in Western Perspective.* Emeryville, Calif.: Dharma Publishing.

van Gulik, Robert Hans. 1935, *Hayagrīva, the Mantrayānic Aspect of the Horse-Cult in China and Japan.* Leiden: Brill.

———. 1956. *Siddham: An Essay on the History of Sanskrit Studies in China and Japan.* (*Sarasvati Vihara Series* 36) Nagpur: Int. Acad. of Indian Culture. Rep. 1980 (New Delhi: Mrs. Sharada Rani).

Güntz, T. 1861. *Der Geisteskranke in seinen Schriften.* Thonberg bei Leipzig.

Gupta, Sanjukta. 1971. "Caturvyūha and the Viśākhayūpa," ALB 35.

———. 1972. *Lakṣmī Tantra: A Pāñcarātra Text, Translation and Notes.* Leiden: E. J. Brill.

Gupta, S., Dirk Jan Hoens, and Teun Goudriaan. 1979. *Hindu Tantrism.* (HO 2.4.2) Leiden: E. J. Brill.

Gutschow, Niels, and Gerhard Auer. 1974. *Bhaktapur: Gestalt, Functionen und* *religiöse Symbolik einer nepalesischen Stadt im vorindustriellen Entwicklungsstadium.* Darmstadt: Lehrdruckerei der technische Hochschule.

Gutschow, Niels, and Manabajra Bajrācārya. 1977. "Ritual as Mediator of Space in Kāṭhmāṇḍu/Nepal." In *Nepal Research Center Publication* 2:1–10. Wiesbaden: Franz Steiner.

Gutschow, Niels, and Bernhard Kölver. 1975. *Ordered Space: Concepts and Functions in a Town of Nepal.* (*Nepal Research Center Publication* 1) Wiesbaden.

Gutschow, Niels, and Jan Pieper. 1978. *Indien: von den Klöstern im Himalaya zu den Templestädten Südindiens, Bauformen und Stadtgestalt einen bestandigen Tradition.* Köln: Dumont.

Gutschow, Niels, and Thomas Sieverts, eds. 1977. *Stadt und Ritual, Beiträge eines internalionalen Symposiums zur Stadtgeschichte Süd- u. Ostasiens/ = Urban Space and Ritual, Proceedings of an International Symposium on Urban History of South- and East-Asia.* (*Beiträge und Studienmaterialien der Fachgruppe Stadt* 11) Darmstadt.

Haarh, Erik. 1958. "Contributions to the Study of Maṇḍala and Mudrā," ActaOr (Leiden) 23:57–91.

Haas, E. 1862. "Dir Heiratsgebrauche der alten Inder nach den Gṛhyasūtra." In IS 5:267.

Hacker, Paul. 1950. "Eigentümlichkeiten der Lehre und terminologie Śaṅkaras: Avidyā, Nāmarūpa, Māyā, Īśvara," ZDMG 100:246–86. Rep. KS:69–109.

______.1953. *Vivarta: Studien zur Geschichte der illusionistischen Kosmologie und Erkenntnistheorie der Inder.* (*Abh. der Akademie der Wissenschafter und der Literatur* 1953. 5:185–242) Mainz: Verlag der Akademie der Wissenschaften und Literatur in Mainz.

______. 1958. "Die Dharmabegriff des Neuhinduismus," *Z. für Missionswissenschaft und Religionswissenschaft* (Münster) 42:1–15. Rep. KS:510–24.

______. 1960. *Prahlāda, Werden und Wandlungen einer Idealgestalt, Beiträge zur Geschichte der Hinduismus;* I: *Die Entstehung der Legende; die Prahlāda-Legenden des Viṣṇupurāna und des Bhāgavatapurāṇa,* II: *Weiterentwicklungen nach dem Bhāgavatapurāṇa, Nebenentwicklungen.* (*Abh. der Akad. der Wissenschaften und der Literatur Mainz* 1959, 9:517–663; 13:889–993). Mainz: Steiner.

______. 1961. "The Sāṅkhyization of the Emanation Doctrine, Shown in a Critical Analysis of the Texts," WZKSO 5:75–112. Rep. KS:167–204.

______. 1970. "Aspects of Neo-Hinduism as Contrasted with Surviving Traditional Hinduism." London: Discussion paper: Univ. of London. Rep. KS:580–608.

______. 1971. "Der religiöse Nationalismus Vivekānandas," *Evangelische Missionszeitschrift* 28:1–15. Rep. KS:565–579.

______. 1972. "Notes on the Māṇḍūkyopanisad and Śaṅkara's Āgamaśāstra-vivarana." In *India Maior, Congratulatory Volume Presented to J. Gonda,* J. Ensink and P. Gaeffke, eds., pp. 115–32. (Leiden: Brill.) Rep. KS:252–69.

______. 1978. *Kleine Schriften.* Lambert Schmithausen, ed. (*Glasenapp-Stiftung* 15) Wiesbaden: Franz Steiner Verlag.

Halbfass, Wilhelm. 1980. "Karma, *Apūrva* and 'Natural' Causes: Observations on the Growth and Limits of the Theory of Saṃsāra." In *Karma and Rebirth in Classical Indian Traditions,* W. D. O'Flaherty, ed., pp. 268–302. (Chicago: UChP).

______. 1981. *Indien und Europa, Perspektiven ihrer geistigen Begegnung.* Basel: Schwabe. Rev. Eng. ed., forthcoming (Albany: SUNY Press).

______. 1983. *Studies in Kumārila and Śaṅkara.* (*Studien zur Indologie und Iranistik*) Reinbeck: Dr. Inge Wezler, Verlag Für Orientalische Fachpublikationen.

Hallett, Garth. 1967. *Wittgenstein's Definition of Meaning and Use.* NY: Fordham Univ. Press.

Hamm, Frank-Richard. 1968–69. "Chāndogyopaniṣad VI, Ein erneuter Versuch," WZKSA 12–13:149–60.

Handiqui, Krishna Kanta. 1949. *Yaśastilaka and Indian Culture, or Somadeva's Yaśastilaka and Aspects of Jainism and Indian Thought and Culture in the Tenth Century.* (*Jīvarāja Jaina Granthamālā* 2) Sholapur: Jaina Saṃskṛti Samrakshaka Saṅgha. Rep. 1968.

Harāṇacandra Śāstrī. 1937. "Śabdabrahmavādaḥ," in *Jha Commemoration Volume, Essays on Oriental Subjects Presented to Vidyāsāgara Mahāmahopādhyāya Paṇḍita Gangānātha Jhā on His Completing His 60th Year* (POS 39), K. Chaṭṭopādhyāya, *et al.* eds., pp. 89–96. (Poona: Oriental Book Agency.)

Haraprasād Śāstrī. 1916. *Hājār bacharer purāṇa Bāṅgālā Bauddha gān o dohā.* Calcutta: Vangiya Sahitya Parisad. 2nd ed. 1959.

Hardy, Friedhelm. 1983. *Viraha-bhakti, The Early History of Kṛṣṇa Devotion in South India.* New Delhi: OUP.

Haridatta Śāstrī. 1971. "Śabdādvaitavādaḥ." In Rajeshwar Shastri Dravid 1971, philosophy section, 8–11.

Hariharānanda Āraṇya Swāmi. 1983. *Yoga Philosophy of Patañjali,* P. N. Mukherji, tr. Albany: SUNY Press. Orig. 1963 (Calcutta: Calcutta Univ. Press), Rei. 1977, 1981.

Harries, Karsten. 1968. "Two Conflicting Interpretations of Language in Wittgenstein's Investigations," *Kant Studien* 59:397–409.

Hartmann, C. G. 1969. *Aspects de la déesse Kālī dans son culte et dans la littérature indienne.* Helsinki.

Hartmann, Gerda. 1933. *Beiträge zur Geschichte der Göttin Lakṣmī.* Kiel: Thesis.

Hauer, Jakob Wilhelm. 1927a. *Die Dhāraṇī im nördlichen Buddhismus und ihre Parallelen in der sogennante Mithrasliturgie.* Stuttgart: Kohlhammer.

______. 1927b. *Der Vrātya, Untersuchungen über die nichtbrahmanische Religion Altindiens,* I: *Die Vrātya als nichtbrahmanische Kultgenossenschaften arischer Herkunft.* Stuttgart: Kohlhammer.

______. 1931. "Das IV. Buch des *Yogasūtra.* Ein Beitrag zu seiner Erklärung und Zeitbestimmung." In *Studia Indo-Iranica, Ehrengabe für Wilhelm Geiger,* Walther Wüst, ed., pp. 122–33. (Leipzig).

______. 1958. *Der Yoga, ein indischer Weg zum Selbst.* Stuttgart: Kohlhammer.

Haug, M. 1875. *Vedische Rätselfragen und Rätselsprüche.* (*Sitzungsberichte der Bayerische Akademie der Wissenschaften*) München.

Hausheer, Irenée. 1927. *La Méthode d'oraison hésychaste.* Rome: *Orientalia Christiana* 9.2.

______. 1956. "L'Hésychasme, étude de spiritualité," *Orientalia Christiana Periodica* (Rome) 22:5–40, 247–85.

Hawley, John S., in association with Srivatsa Goswami. 1981. *At Play with Krishna: Pilgrimage Dramas from Brindavan.* Princeton: Princeton Univ. Press.

Hawley, John Stratton, and Donna Marie Wulff, eds. 1982. *The Divine Consort: Rādhā and the Goddesses of India.* Berkeley: Berkeley Religious Studies Series, GTU.

Hazra, H. C. 1940. *Studies on the Purāṇic Record on Hindu Rites and Customs.* Dacca: Dacca Univ..

Heesterman, J. C. 1957. *The Ancient Indian Royal Consecration, The Rājasūya Described According to the Yajus Texts and Annoted.* (DRT 2) The Hague: Mouton.

______. 1962. "Vrātya and Sacrifice," IIJ 6:1–37.

______. 1964. "Brahmin, Ritual and Renouncer," WZKSO 8:1–31; rep. 1985, 26–44.

______. 1967. "The Case of the Severed Head," WZKSO 11:22–43; rep. 1985, 45–58.

______. 1968. "On the Origin of the *Nāstika,*" WZKSA 12–13:171–85; rep 1985, 70–80.

______. 1974. "Die Authorität des Veda." In Oberhammer 1974, 29–40.

______. 1985. *The Inner Conflict of Tradition, Essays in Indian Ritual, Kingship, and Society.* Chicago: UChP.

Heiler, Friedrich. 1923. *Das Gebet, Eine religionsgeschichtliche und religionspsychologische Untersuchung* 5th ed. rev. München: Ernst Reinhardt. 1st ed. 1918;

Rep. with add. bibliog. 1969; Eng. tr: *Prayer, a Study in the History and Psychology of Religion,* Samuel McComb, tr. (NY: OUP, 1932, 1958).

———. 1961. *Erscheinungsformen und Wesen der Religion.* (*Die Religionen der Menschheit* 1) Stuttgart: W. Kohlhammer Verlag.

Heilmann, L. c. 1944. "Linguistica e filosofia," *Quaderni* (Bologna Univ.) 2:3–19.

Heimann, Betty. 1941. "Sphoṭa and Artha." In *A Volume of Studies in Indology Presented to Professor P. V. Kane on His 61st Birthday,* S. M. Katre and P. K. Gode, eds., pp. 222–27. (Poona: Oriental Book Agency.)

Hein, Norvin J. 1972. *The Miracle Plays of Mathura.* New Haven, Conn.: YUP.

Held, G. J. 1935. *The Mahābhārata, An Ethnological Study.* London/Amsterdam: KPTT.

Henry, V. 1909. *La Magie dans l'Inde antique,* 2nd ed., (*Les Religions des peuples civil* 1) Paris: E. Nourry, orig. 1904.

Herman, A. L. 1962–63. "Sphoṭa," JGJRI 19:1–21.

Hermanns, Matthias. 1964–73. *Die religiös-magische Weltanschauung der Primitivstämme Indiens,* I: Die *Bhagoria Bhil,* II: *Die Bhilala, Korku, Gond, Baiga,* III: *Die Oraon.* Wiesbaden: Franz Steiner.

Hesse, Mary B. 1961. *Forces and Fields: The Concept of Action at a Distance in the History of Physics.* London: Nelson.

High, Dallas M. 1967. *Language, Persons, and Belief.* NY: OUP.

———. 1969. *New Essays on Religious Language.* NY: OUP.

Hildburgh, W. L. 1908. "Notes on Singhalese Magic," JRAI 38:148–205.

Hilgenberg, Louise, and Willibald Kirfel, trs. 1941. *Vāgbhaṭa's Aṣṭāṅgahṛdayasaṃhitā.* Leiden: Brill.

Hill, W. D. P. 1952. *The Holy Lake of the Acts of Rāma, a Translation of Tulasī Dās's Rāmacaritamānasa.* Oxford: OUP. Rep. Bombay: 1971.

Hillebrandt, Alfred. 1880. *Das altindische Neu- und Vollmondopfer.* Jena: G. Fischer [1879].

———. 1897. *Ritualliteratur—Vedische Opfer und Zauber.* (*Grundriss der Indoarischen Philologie und Altertumskunde,* Geo. Bühler, ed., 3.2) Strassburg: K. J. Trübner.

Hirzel, A. 1890. *Gleichnisse und Metapherm im Ṛgveda in cultur-historischer Hinsicht zusammengestalt.* Leipzig: Thesis. Eng. tr., H. D. Velankar, JUB, n. s., 7.2 (1938); 9.2 (1940):126.

Hirzel, Rudolf. 1916. *Der Name, Ein Beitrag zu seiner Geschichte im Altertum und* *besonders bei den Greichen.* (*Abh. d. Sächs. Ges. d. Wiss.* 36.2) Leipzig: B. G. Teubner. (1918, 1921 ?).

Hitchcock, John T., and Rex. L. Jones. 1976. *Spirit Possession in the Nepal Himalayas.* Warminster, England: Aris and Phillips.

Hocart, Arthur Maurice. 1923. "Flying Through the Air," *Indian Antiquary* 52:80–82.

Hoens, Dirk Jan. 1951. *Śānti, A Contribution to Ancient Indian Religious Terminology.* Utrecht/ the Hague.

Hoffmann, J., and A. van Emelen. 1930–41. *Encyclopaedia Mundarica* (13 vols.). Patna: Supt., Government Printing Office. Rep. 1950.

Holdcraft, David. 1978. *Words and Deeds: Problems in the Theory of Speech Acts.* London: OUP.

Hommel, Fritz. 1931. "Pali *muddā* = Babylonisch *musarū* und die Herkunft der indischen Schrift," in *Studia Indo-Iranica, in Honor of the 75th Birthday of Wilhelm Geiger,* Walter Wüst, ed., pp. 73–84. (Leipzig: OH).

van der Hoogt, J. M. 1930. *The Vedic Chant Studied in Its Textual and Melodic Form.* Wageningen (Thesis.) H. Veenman.

Hooykaas, C. 1964. *Āgama Tīrtha, Five Studies in Hindu-Balinese Religion.* (VKNAW 70) Amsterdam: Noord-Hollandsche Uitgevers Maatschappij.

———. 1966. *Sūrya Sevanā, The Way to God of a Balinese Śiva Priest.* (VKNAW 72–73) Amsterdam.

———. 1973a. *Balinese Bauddha Brahmans.* (VKNAW 80) Amsterdam: North Holland Publishing Company.

———. 1973b. *Religion in Bali.* (*Iconography of Religions* 13.10, Institute of Religious Iconography, State Univ. of Groningen) Leiden: Brill.

———. 1974. *Cosmogony and Creation in Balinese Tradition.* (*Bibliotheca Indonesica* 9) The Hague.

———. 1983. "Agni Offerings in Java and Bali." In Staal 1983a, 382–402.

Hopkins, Edward Washburn. 1901. "Yoga-Technique in the Great Epic," JAOS 22:333–79.

———. 1908. "Gods and Saints of the Great Brāhmaṇa," *Trans. Connecticut Academy* 15:23.

Horsch, Paul. 1957. "The Wheel: An Indian Symbol of World-Interpretation." In *Liebenthal Festschrift,* Ksitis Roy, ed., pp. 62–79. (Santiniketan: Visvabharati.)

Horten, Max. 1927–28. *Indische Strömmungen in der islamischen Mystik,* 2 vols. Heidelberg: OH.

Horton, Robin, and Ruth Finnegan, eds. 1973. *Modes of Thought, Essays on Thinking in Western and Non-Western Societies.* London: Faber and Faber.

Howard, Wayne. 1977. *Sāmavedic Chant.* New Haven, Conn.: YUP.

———. 1983. "The Music of Nambudiri Unexpressed Chant (aniruktagāna)." In Staal 1983a, 2.311–42.

Hudson, W. Donald. 1968. *Ludwig Wittgenstein, the Bearing of His Philosophy upon Religious Belief.* Richmond: John Knox Press.

———. 1975. *Wittgenstein and Religious Belief.* NY: St. Martin's Press.

Huizinga, Johan. 1955. *Homo Ludens: The Play Element in Culture.* NY: Beacon Press. Orig. Dutch ed. Haarlem, 1938; UK: London 1949.

Hunter, J. F. M. 1971. " 'Forms of Life' in Wittgenstein's Philosophical Investigations." In *Essays on Wittgenstein,* E. D. Klemke, ed., pp. 273–97. (Urbana: Univ. of Illinois Press.)

Hutch, Richard. 1980. "The Personal Ritual of Glossolalia," JSSR 19, no. 3:255–66.

Huxley, Sir Julian. 1966. "A Discussion on Ritualization of Behavior in Animals and Man," *Philosophical Transactions of the Royal Society of London* Series B, no. 772, 251:247–526.

Ikari, Yasuke. 1983. "Ritual Preparation of the Mahāvīra and Ukhā Pots." In Staal 1983a, 168–77.

Ikegami, Y. 1971. "A Stratification Analysis of the Hand Gestures in Indian Classing Dancing," *Semiotica* 4, no. 4:365–91.

Inden, Ronald B. 1976. *Marriage and Rank in Bengali Culture. A History of Caste and Clan in Middle-Period Bengal.* Berkeley: UCaP.

Ingalls, Daniel H. H. 1959. "The Brahman Tradition." In *Traditional India: Structure and Change,* Milton Singer, ed., pp. 3–9. (Philadelphia: the Amer. Folklore Society.)

———. 1971. "Remarks on Mr. Wasson's Soma," JAOS 91:188–91.

von Ivanka, E. c. 1974. "Byzantinische Yogis?," ZDMG 52:234–49.

Iyer (Gayatonde) Shakuntala. 1962–63. "The Sāmans," JUB 31:35–62; 32:89–126.

Izutsu, T. 1956. *Language and Magic.* Tokyo: Keio Institute of Philological Studies.

Jackson, Anthony. 1968. "Sound and Ritual," *Man* n. s. 3, no. 2:293–99.

Jacoby, Adolf. 1914. "Zum Zerstückelungs- und Wiederbelebungswunder der indischen Fakire," ARW 17:455–75.

Jacques, Claude. 1966. "Le Monde du sorcier en Inde." In *Le Monde du sorcier* (*Sources orientales* 7) pp. 234–80. (Paris: Seuil.)

***Jagannathan, Y,* et al.** 1958. "On nāmakīrtan (?)," *Indian Philosophy and Culture* (Vṛndaban).

Jaini, Padmanabh S. 1959. "The Vaibhaṣika Theory of Words and Meanings," BSOAS 22:95–107.

Jaiswal, Suvira. 1967. *The Origin and Development of Vaiṣṇavism, Vaiṣṇavism From 200 B. C. to A. D. 500.* Delhi: Munshiram Manoharlal.

Jakobson, Roman, and M. Halle. 1960. *Grundlagen der Sprache.* Berlin.

James, William. 1902. *The Varieties of Religious Experience.* NY: Random House, Modern Library.

Jamison, Stephanie W. 1979. "Remarks on the Expression of Agency With the Passive in Vedic and Indo-European," *Z. für vergleichende Sprachforschung* 93, 2:196–219.

Jarvie, I. C. 1976. "On the Limits of Symbolic Interpretation in Anthropology," CA 17:687–701.

Jayākhya Saṃhitā; see Embar Krishnamacarya, ed. 1931.

Jayanta Bhaṭṭa. *Āgamaḍḍambara;* see V. Raghavan and Anantalal Thakur, eds. 1964.

Jayatilleke, K. N. 1963. *Early Buddhist Theory of Knowledge.* London: George Allen and Unwin. Rep. 1980 (Delhi: MB).

Jethībhāi Kavi, Sankardān, ed. 1891. *Deviyāna.* Limblī.

Jha, Ganganath. 1900–09. *Ślokavārttika, Translated With Extracts From Pārthasārathi Miśra's Nyāyaratnākara and Sucaritamisra's Kāśikā.* (BI 146) Calcutta.

———. 1903–24. *Tantravārttika, A Commentary on Śavara's Bhāṣya on the Pūrvamīmāṃsā Sūtras* (2 vols.). (BI 161) Calcutta. Rep. 1983 (New Delhi: Sri Satguru Publications).

———. 1911. *The Prabhākara School of Pūrva-Mīmāṃsā.* Allahabad. Rep. 1978 (Delhi: MB).

———. 1933. *Śābara-bhāṣya* (3 vols.). (GOS 66, 70, 73) Baroda: Oriental Institute. Rep. 1973–74.

———. 1942. *Pūrva-Mīmāṃā in Its Sources.* Varanasi: BHU. 2nd ed. 1964.

Jhalkikar, Bhimacarya, and Vasudev Sahastri Abhyankar. 1928. *Nyāyakośa or Dictionary of Technical Terms of Indian Philosophy,* 3rd. ed.. (BSPS 49) Poona: BORI. Rep. 1978; Eng tr. announced.

Jhavery, Mohanlal Bhagawandas. 1944. *Comparative and Critical Study of Mantraśāstra, with Special Treatment of Jain Mantravāda, Being the Introduction to Śrī*

Bhairava Padmāvatī Kalpa, with Text by V. K. Abhyankar. Ahmedabad: Sarabhai Manilal Nawab.

Johannson, Karl Ferdinand. 1917. *Die altindischen Göttin Dhiṣaṇa und Verwandtes, Beiträge zum Fruchtbarkeitskultus in Indien*. Uppsala/ Leipzig.

Johnson, Mark. 1981. *Philosophical Perspectives on Metaphor*. Minneapolis: Univ. of Minn.

Johnson, Willard. 1976. "On the Rig Vedic Riddle of the Two Birds in the Fig Tree (ṚV 1.164.20–2) and the Discovery of the Vedic Speculative Symposium," JAOS 96, 2:248–58.

———. 1980. *Poetry and Speculation of the Ṛg Veda*. Berkeley: UCaPress.

Jolly, J. 1903. "Über einige indische Hochzeitsgebräuche." In *Album H. Kern* (Leiden).

Jones, Clifford R. 1983. "Notes on Comparison of Vedic Mudras With Mudras as Used in Kūṭiyāṭṭam and Kathakali." In Staal 1983a, 2.380–81.

Jones, Clifford R., and B. T. Jones. 1970. *Kathakali*. San Francisco: Amer. Soc. for Eastern Arts.

Jones, Dalu, and George Michell. 1979. *Mobile Architecture in Asia: Ceremonial Chariots, Floats and Carriages*. (AARP 16) London.

Joshi, Rasik Vihari. 1959. *Le Rituel de la dévotion Kṛṣṇaite, préface par Jean Filliozat*. (PIFI 17) Pondichéry.

Joshi, S. 1969. "Gold in Hindu saṃskāras," PAIOC 25:251ff.

Joshi, Shivaram Dattatray. 1967. *The Sphoṭanirṇaya (Chapter xiv of the Vaiyākaraṇabhūṣaṇasāra) of Kauṇḍaṭṭa, Edited With Introduction, Translation, and Critical and Exegetical Notes*. (*Publications of the Centre of Advanced Study in Sanskrit* C 2) Poona: Univ. of Poona.

Juergensmeyer, Mark, and N. Gerald Barrier, eds. 1979. *Sikh Studies, Comparative Perspectives on a Changing Tradition*. (*Berkeley Religious Studies Series*) Berkeley: GTU.

Jugie, Martin. 1931. "Les Origines de la méthode d'oraison des hésychastes," *Echos d'Orient* (Paris) 30, 162:179–85.

Jung, Carl G. 1955. "On Mandala Symbolism." In *Archetypes and the Unconscious*, R. F. C. Hull, tr. London.

Jungblut, Leonard J. 1943. "Magic Songs of the Bhils of Jhabua State, C. I.," *Intern. Archiv für Ethnographie* 43:1–136.

Kadloubousky, E., and G. E. H. Palmer. 1951. *Writings From the Philokalia On Prayer of the Heart*. London: Faber and Faber.

———. 1954. *Early Fathers from the Philokalia, Together With some Writings of St.*

Abba Dorotheus, St. Isaac of Syria and St. Gregory Palamas, Selected and Translated From the Russian Text Dobrotolubiye. London: Faber and Faber.

Kahn, David. 1967. *The Codebreakers, The Story of Secret Writing.* NY: Macmillan.

Kakar, Sudhir. 1971. "The Theme of Authority in Social Relations in India," *J. of Social Psychology* 84:93–101.

———. 1974. "Aggression in Indian Society: An Analysis of Folk Tales," *Indian J. of Psychology* 49:119–26.

———. 1978. *The Inner World: A Psycho-Analytic Study of Childhood and Society in India.* Delhi: OUP.

———. 1982. *Shamans, Mystics, and Doctors, A Psychological Inquiry into India and Its Healing Traditions.* NY: Alfred A. Knopf.

Kakati, Bani Kanta. 1948. *The Mother Goddess Kāmākhyā; or, Studies in the Fusion of Aryan and Primitive Beliefs of Assam.* Gauhati: Lawyer's Book Stall. Rep. 1967.

Kāle, M. R., ed. and tr. 1960. *Bāṇa's Kādambarī,* 4th ed. Bombay: Jaico.

———. 1967. *Mālatīmādhava, with the Commentary of Jagadhara,* 3rd ed. ND: MB.

Kalia, Ashok Kumar. 1977. *Lakṣmītantra, dharma aur darśan* (*The Religion and Philosophy of the Lakṣmī Tantra*). Lucknow: Akhila Bhāratīya Saṃskṛt-pariṣad.

Kane, Pandurang Vaman. 1924. *Brief Sketch of the Pūrva-Mīmāṃsā System.* Poona.

———. 1930–62. *History of Dharmaśāstra* (5 vols. in 7 pts). 2nd ed., 5 vols in 8 pts, 1968–74 Poona: BORI.

———. 1961. *History of Indian Poetics,* 3rd ed. Delhi: MB.

Kapāli Śāstry, T. V. 1971. *Sidelights on the Tantra.* Pondichéry: Dipti Pubs.

Kapera, Constance. 1966. *The Worship of Kali in Banaras: An Inquiry.* Delhi: MB.

Kapil Deva Shastri. 1964a. "Bhartṛhari's Discussion on Sāmānādhikaraṇya," ALB 28:41–54.

———. 1964b. "Bhartṛhari's Discussion on the Relation Between Upamāna and Upameya in his Vākyapadīya." In *Babruam Saksena Felicitation Volume* (*Indian Linguistics* 25) 229–33. (Poona.)

———. 1964c. "Bhartṛhari on the Relation Between Upamāna and Upameya," VIJ 2:87–92.

———. 1965. "Upamāna, Upameya and Sāmānyavacana According to the Vākyapadīya of Bhartṛhari," VIJ 3:19–28.

———. 1966. "'Catvāri vākparimitā padāni' ity atra Bhartṛhariḥ (Bhartṛhari on ṚV 1.164.45)," *Viśvasaṃskṛta* (Hoshiarpur) 3:144ff..

———. 1967. "Vaiyākaraṇānāṃ sphoṭavādaḥ," *Viśvasaṃskṛta* (Hoshiarpur) 4:40–51, 68.

Karambelkar, Vinayak Waman. 1961. *The Atharva-Veda and the Āyur-Veda.* Nagpur.

Kashikar, Chintaman G. 1958. "The Present-Day Vedic Rituals in India." In *Shastri Rewashanker Becharbhav Trivedi,* pp. 56–64. (Madras: Abhinandana Grantha.)

———. 1960a. "A Critical Study of the Ritualistic Sūtras, Baudhāyana Śrautasūtra, Praśnaa I–V, XX, XXIII–XXIX." In *Gode Commemorative Volume,* pp. 203–10.

———. 1960b. "A Critical Study of the Ritualistic Sutras: Bhāradvāja Śrauta Sūtra," ABORI 40 (1959):56–62.

———. 1961. "A Critical and Exegetical Study of the Vārāha Śrauta Sūtras 1.1–3," ALB 25:229–41.

———. 1964. "The Vedic Sacrificial Rituals through the Ages," IA 3rd ser., 1, no. 2:77–89.

———. 1972. "A Critical and Exegetical Study of the Ritualistic Sūtras: Vārāha-Śrautasūtra 1.4–5," *Vimarśa* 1, no. 1:85–88.

Kashikar, C. G., and R. N. Dandekar. 1958–70. *Śrautakośa, Encyclopaedia of Vedic Sacrificial Ritual* (4 vols.) (?). Poona: Vaidika Saṃśodhana Maṇḍala.

Kashikar, C. G., and Asko Parpola. 1983. "Śrauta Traditions in Recent Times." In Staal 1983a, 199–251.

Kashikar, S. 1966. "A Survey of the Śrautasūtras," JUB 35 (n. s.).2. Arts 41; also separately, 1968 (Bombay: Univ. of Bombay).

Kāśinātha Bhaṭṭa Bhaḍa (Śivānandanātha). 1840. *Durjanamukhacapeṭikā (Slap in the Face of the Wretches).* In *Le Bhāgavata Purāṇa,* Eugène Burnouf, tr., pp. lxxix–lxxxix. (Paris: Imprimerie royale.).

———. 1939. *"Vāmācāramatakhaṇḍana,"* JRAS Bengal 4:455ff. (?).

Katz, Steven T. 1978. *Mysticism and Philosophical Analysis.* NY: OUP.

———. 1983. *Mysticism and Religious Traditions.* Oxford: OUP.

Keightley, Alan. 1976. *Wittgenstein, Grammar, and God.* London: Epworth Press.

Keith, Arthur Berriedale. 1908. "The Game of Dice," JRAS 823–28.

———. 1914. *The Veda of the Black Yajus School Entitled Taittirīya Sanhitā* (2 vols.). (HOS 18–19) Cambridge, Mass.: HUP. Rep. Delhi: MB 1967.

———. 1921. *Karmamīmāṃsā*. London: OUP.

Kelber, Werner. 1983. *The Oral and the Written Gospel, the Hermeneutics of Speaking and Writing in the Synoptic Tradition, Mark, Paul, and Q*. Philadelphia: Fortress Press.

Kevalānandasarasvatī, ed. 1952–66. *Mīmāṃsākoṣa*, 7 vols. (PPMGM 4, variously numbered) Wai: Prajñā Pāṭhshālā Maṇḍala.

Keyserling, Arnold. 1972. *Chakrale Musik*. Wien: Verlag der Palme.

Khanna, Madhu. 1979. *Yantra*. London: Thames and Hudson.

Kinsley, David R. 1975. *The Sword and the Flute, Kālī and Kṛṣṇa, Dark Visions of the Terrible and the Sublime in Hindu Mythology*. Berkeley: UCaP.

Kirfel, Willibald. 1920. *Die Kosmographie der Inder nach Quellen dargestellt*. Bonn: Kurt Schroeder. Rep. 1967 (Hildesheim: Georg Olms Verlagsbuchhandlung).

———. 1949. *Der Rosenkranz, Ursprung und Ausbreitung*. (*Beiträge zur Sprach- und Kulturgeschichte des Orients* 1) Walldorf-Hessen: Verlag für Orientkunde, Dr. H. Vorndran.

———. 1959a. *Symbolik des Buddhismus*. (*Symbolik der Religionen* 5) Stuttgart: Anton Hiersemann.

———. 1959b. *Symbolik des Hinduismus und Jinismus*. (*Symbolik der Religionen* 4) Stuttgart: Anton Hiersemann.

Kiyota, Minoru. 1968. "Shingon Mikkyo Maṇḍala," HR 8, no. 1:31–59.

de Kleen, Tyra. 1942. *Mudrās: The Ritual Hand-Poses of the Buddha Priests and the Shiva Priests of Bali*, 2nd ed. London: Kegan Paul. Orig. 1924.

Kliever, Lonnie D. 1981. *The Shattered Spectrum, A Survey of Contemporary Theology*. Atlanta: John Knox Press.

Klostermaier, Klaus. 1977. "Man Carries the Power of All Things in His Mouth." In Coward and Sivaraman 1977.

Knipe, David M. 1977. "Sapiṇḍīkaraṇa: The Hindu Rite of Entry Into Heaven," in *Religious Encounters With Death*, Frank E. Reynolds and Earle H. Waugh, eds., pp. 111–24. (University Park: Pennsylvania State Univ. Press.).

Konow, Sten. 1893. *Das Sāmavidhānabrāhmaṇa, ein altindisches Handbuch der Zauberei, eingeleitet und übersetzt*. Halle: Thesis.

———. 1926. "Zur Frage nach den Asuras." In *Beiträge zur Literaturwissenschaft und Geistesgeschichte Indiens* (*Festgabe Hermann Jacobi*) 259–64. (Bonn).

van Kooij, K. R. 1972. *Worship of the Goddess According to the Kalikapurāṇa, part I, a Translation with an Introduction and Notes of Chapters 54–69*. (ORT 14) Leiden: Brill.

Koppers, Wilhelm. 1948. *Die Bhils von Zentralindien* (?) (*Wiener Beiträge zur Kulturgeschichte und Linguistik* 7). Horn (Austria): F. Berger.

Kramrisch, Stella. 1928. *The Vishnudharmottara (part III), a Treatise on Indian Painting and Image-making*, 2nd rev. ed., Calcutta: Calcutta University Press. 1st ed. 1924.

———. 1946. *The Hindu Temple.* Calcutta: The University of Calcutta. Rep. 1976, 1980 (Delhi: MB); with photographs by Raymond Burnier.

———. 1975. "The Indian Great Goddess." HR 14, no. 4:235–65.

Krishna Lal. c. 1958. "A Historical Study of the Saptapadī Mantras," *Orissa Hist. Res. J.* 7, no. 3–4:168–74.

———. 1967. "Mantras Employed in the Gṛhyasūtras for Placing the Fuel Sticks in the Fire in Upanayana Ritual," JOIB 17, no. 2:129–36.

———. 1970. *Gṛhyamantra aur unakā viniyoga* (*A Critical Study of Gṛhya Mantras With Special Reference to their Ritual Application*). Delhi: National Publishing House.

———. 1972. "Sāvitrī—From Saṃitās to Gṛhyasūtras," ABORI 52 (1971):225–29.

Krishna Warrier, A. G., tr. 1967. *The Śākta Upaniṣads, Translated into English.* (ALS 89) Adyar: ALRS.

Krishnamacarya, Embar, ed. 1931. *Jayākhya Saṃhitā.* (GOS 54) Baroda: Oriental Institute.

Krishnamacharya, Pandit V., ed. 1946. *Sphoṭavāda by Nagesa Bhaṭṭa, Edited by Vyākaraṇaśiromaṇi with His Own Commentary Subodhinī.* (ALS 55) Adyar: ALRC.

———. 1959. *Lakṣmī Tantra, A Pāñcarātra Āgama.* (ALS 87) Madras:Adyar Library. Rep. 1975.

———. 1966. *Ahirbudhnya Saṃhitā*, 2 vols. Madras: Adyar Library. Orig. 1916 (M. D. Rāmānujāchārya).

Kuiper, Franciscus Bernardus Jacobus. 1957. "Vācārambhaṇam," IIJ 1:155–59.

———. 1958. "Vācārambhaṇam (II)," IIJ 2:306–10.

———. 1960. "The Ancient Indian Verbal Contest," IIJ 4, no. 4:217–81.

———. 1968. *Pratidānam, Indian, Iranian, and Indo-European Studies Presented to Franciscus Bernardus Jacobus Kuiper on his Sixtieth Birthday*, J. C. Heesterman, G. H. Schokker, and V. I, Subrahmoniam, eds. (*Janua Linguarum, Studia Memoriae Nicolai van Wijk Dedicata* 34) The Hague: Mouton.

———. 1970. "Review of Wasson (1968)," IIJ 12:279–85.

———. 1974. "Vi Dayate and Vidatha-," IT 2:129–32.

Kulke, Hermann. 1970. *Cidambvaramāhātmya, Eine Untersuchung der religionsgeschichtlichen und historischen Hintergründe für die Entstehung der Tradition einer südindischen Tempelstadt.* Wiesbaden: OH.

Kumar (Sharma), Pushpendra. 1974. *Śakti Cult in Ancient India (With Special Reference to the Purāṇic Literature).* Varanasi: Bharatiya Publishing House.

Kumari Devi, Akshaya. c. 1920. *Female Seers of Ancient India.* Calcutta: Vijaya Krishna Brothers.

Kumārila. *Tantravārttika;* see V. S. Apate 1929–34.

Kundu, Nunda Lall. 1964. *Non-Dualism in Shaiva and Shakta Philosophy.* Calcutta: Sri Sri Bhairabi Jogeswari Math.

Kunhan Raja, Chittenjoor. 1941. *Sāmaveda Saṃhitā With Commentaries of Mādhava and Bharatasvāmin.* (ALP 26) Madras.

———. 1956. *Asya Vāmasya Hymn, with the Commentaries of Sāyaṇa and Ātmānanda.* Madras.

———. 1963. *Poet Seers [Philosophers] of the Ṛgveda.* Madras: Ganesh and Co.

Kunhan Raja, C., and S. S. Suryanarayana Sastri. 1933. *Mānaneyodaya of Nārāyana, An Elementary Treatise on the Mīmāṃsā.* (ALS 105) Adyar, Madras: Adyar Library and Research Center. Rep. 1975.

Kunjunni Raja, K. 1969. *Indian Theories of Meaning,* 2nd ed. Madras: Adyar Library and Research Center. Orig. 1963.

Kuroda, S.-Y. 1975. "Réflexions sur les fondements de la théorie de la narration." In *Langue, discours, société: Pour Émile Benveniste* (Paris). Eng. tr. "Reflections on the Foundations of Narrative Theory," *Pragmatics of Language and Literature,* T. A. can Dijk, ed., pp. 107–40. (Amsterdam.).

———. 1979. "Some Thoughts on the Foundations of Language Use," *Linguistics and Philoosphy* 3:1–17.

Kuvalayānanda, Swami, and S. A. Shukla. 1974. *Gorakṣaśatakaṃ,* 2nd ed. Lonavla. 1st ed. 1958.

Kvaerne, Per. 1977. *An Anthology of Buddhist Tantric Songs: A Study of the Caryāgiti.* (*Det Norske Videnskaps-Ak. Skrifter* II, n. s. 14) Oslo; also Irvington-on-Hudson, NY: ColUP.

Kwella, P. 1973. *Flussüberschreitung im Rigveda, ṚV III,33 und Verwandtes.* Wiesbaden: OH.

Ladriere, J. 1973. "The Performativity of Liturgical Language," *Concilium* 2.9:50–62.

Lakoff, George, and Mark Johnson. 1980. *Metaphors We Live By.* Chicago: UChP.

Lakshminarasimhia, M. c. 1943. "The Phonetics of Om," *Half-Yearly J. of Mysore Univ.* 4, no. 2:83–92.

Lakṣmī Tantra; see Pandit V. Krishnamacharya, ed.. 1959.

Laksman Sarup, ed. and tr. 1927. *Nirukta of Yāska With the Nighaṇṭu.* Lahore: Univ. of the Panjab.

Lalitāsahasranāma. 1935. *Lalitāsahasranāma with the Saubhāgyabhāskara of Bhāskararaya.* Bombay: Nirnaya Sagar Press.

La Meri (Russell Meriwether Hughes). 1941. *The Gesture Language of the Hindu Dance.* NY: Columbia Univ. Press.

Lamotte, Étienne. 1966–76. *Le Traité de la grande vertu de sagesse de Nāgārjuna (Mahāprajñāpāramitāśāstra)*, 4 vols. Louvain: vols. 1 and 2, Orig. 1944–49.

Lancaster, Lewis. 1979. "Buddhist Literature: Its Canons, Scribes, and Editors." In O'Flaherty 1979, 215–29.

Lancaster, Lewis, and Luis O. Gomez. 1977. *Prajñāpāramitā and Related Systems, Studies in Honor of Edward Conze.* (*Berkeley Buddhist Studies Series* 1) Berkeley: Center for South and Southeast Asian Studies, Univ. of California.

Lanczkowski, Günter. 1961. *Sacred Writings: A Guide to the Literature of Religions,* Stanley Goodman, tr. (NY: Harper and Row.)

Larock, V. 1930. "Essai sur la valeur sacrée et la valeur sociale des noms des personnes dans les sociétés inférieures," RHR 51 (101).

Lauf, Detlef-Inge. 1973. *Das Bild als Symbol im Tantrismus, Indische Tantras als praktische Führer zur seelischen Ganzheit des Menschen.* München: H. Moos.

———. 1976. *Tibetan Sacred Art: The Heritage of Tantra.* Berkeley, Calif.: Shambhala.

Laugakṣī Bhāskara. *Arthasaṃgraha;* see Thibaut 1882.

Leach, Edmund R. 1958. "Magical Hair," *J. of the Royal Anthropological Institute* 88:147–64.

———. 1964. "Anthropological Aspects of Language: Animal Categories and Verbal Abuse." In *New Directions in the Study of Language,* Eric. H. Lenneberg, ed. (Cambridge, Mass: MIT Press).

van der Leeuw, Gerardus. 1963. *Sacred and Profane Beauty, The Holy in Art,* David E. Green, tr. (NY: Holt, Rinehart and Winston.)

———. 1967. *Religion in Essence and Manifestation,* 2 vols, J. E. Turner, tr., appendices by Hans H. Penner. (Gloucester, Mass: Peter Smith.).

Leidecker, K. F. 1954. "The Philosophical Significance of Similes in Ancient Indian Thought," *The Aryan Path* 25:231.

Leroy, Olivier. 1928. *La Lévitation.* Paris. Eng. tr., London: Burns, Oates and Washbourne, 1928.

______. 1931. *Les Hommes salamandres, recherches et réflexions sur l'incombustibilité du corps humain.* Paris: Desclée, de Brouwer, et cie.

Lessing, Ferdinand. 1951. "Calling the Soul, A Lamaist Ritual," *Semitic and Oriental Studies* (*Univ. of California Publications in Semitic Philology*) 11:263–84.

Lessing, F. D., and A. Wayman. 1968. *Introduction to the Buddhist Tantric Systems, Translated from Mkhas Grub Rje's Rgyud Spyiḥi rnam par gzag pa rgyas par brjod, with Original Texts and Annotation.* (*Indo-Iranian Monographs* 8) The Hague. 2nd ed. 1978 (New Delhi: MB).

Lévi, Sylvain. 1898. *La doctrine du sacrifice dans les "Brāhmaṇas."* Paris: Ernest Leroux. Rep. 1966 (Paris: PUF).

______. 1936. "On a Tantric Fragment from Kucha," IHQ 12:197–214.

Liebert, Gösta. 1976. *Iconographic Dictionary of the Indian Religions: Hinduism-Buddhism-Jainism.* Leiden: Brill.

Liebich, Bruno. 1923. "Über den Sphoṭa (ein Kapital über die Sprachphilosophie der Inder)," ZDMG 77:208–19.

Lienhard. S. 1968. "Einige Bemerkungen über Śabdabrahman und vivarta bei Bhavabhūti," WZKSO 12:216–19.

Limaye, V. P., and R. D. Vadekar, eds. 1958. *Eighteen Principle Upanisads.* Poona: Vaidika Samsodhana Mandala.

Lin, Li-kouang. 1935. "Puṇyodaya (Na-T'i), un propagateur du tantrisme en Chine et au Cambodge à l'époque de Hiuan-tsang," JA 227:83–100.

Lincoln, Bruce. 1977a. "Two Notes on Modern Rituals," JAAR 45, no. 2:147–60.

______. 1977b. "Treatment of Hair and Fingernails," HR 16:351ff.

______. 1981. *Priests, Warriors, and Cattle: A Study in the Ecology of Religions.* Berkeley: UCaP.

Lindner, Bruno. 1878. *Die Dīkṣā oder Weihe für das Somaopfer.* Leipzig: OH.

Lindquist, Sigurd. 1935. *Siddhi und Abbiññā, eine Studie über die klassischen Wunder der Yoga.* Uppsala: Lundequistska bokhandelm, Uppsala Univ.

Lommel, H. 1932. "Eine arische Form magischer Gottesanrufung," ActaOr 10.

______. 1955. "Wiedergeburt aus embyonalem Zustand in der Symbolik des altindischen Rituals," in *Tod, Auferstehung, Weltordnung,* (C. Hentze, ed. Zürich) 1.107.

______. 1958. "Baumsymbolik beim altindischen Opfer," *Paideuma* 6:490–99.

Lorenzen, David N. 1972. *The Kāpālikas and Kālāmukhas, Two Lost Śaivite Sects.* Berkeley: UCaP.

Lossky, Vladimir. 1957. *The Mystical Theology of the Eastern Church.* London: James Clarke and Co.

Losty, Jeremiah P. 1982. *The Art of the Book in India.* London: The British Library.

Lucier, Pierre. 1973. "Le Statut du langage religieux dans la philosophie de Ludwig Wittgenstein," *Sciences religieuses (Studies in Religion)* 3, no. 1:14–28.

Lüders, Heinrich. 1907. "Das Würfelspiel im alten Indien," AGGW (*Philologica Indica*).

______. 1959. "Die Satyakriyā." In *Varuṇa,* 2. *Varuṇa und das Ṛta* Ludwig Alsdorf, ed., pp. 486–509. (Göttingen: Vandenhoeck and Ruprecht.)

Lupsa, Michèle. 1967. *Chants à Kālī de Rāmprasād, Introduction, Traduction et Notes.* (PIFI 30) Pondichéry: PIFI.

Macdonald, Ariane. 1962. *Le Maṇḍala du Mañjusrimūlakalpa.* Paris: A. Maisonneuve.

Macdonell, A. A. 1897. *Vedic Mythology.* Strassburg: K. J. Trubner.

______. 1900. *A History of Sanskrit Literature.* London: William Heineman Ltd.

______. 1916. *A Vedic Grammar for Students.* London: OUP.

Madhava Krishna Sarma, K. 1943. "Vāk Before Bhartṛhari," *The Poona Orientalist* 8:21–36.

Mahābhārata; see V. S. Sukthankar, S. K. Belvalkar, P. L. Vaidya, *et al.* 1927–66.

Mahadeva Śāstri, Allādi, tr. and ed. 1920. *Yoga Upaniṣads With the Commentary of Srī Upaniṣad-Brahma-Yogin.* (ALS 6) Adyar: Theosophical Society.

______. 1921. *The Sāmānya Vedānta Upaniṣads.* (ALS 7) Adyar: ALRS.

______. 1923. *The Vaiṣṇava Upaniṣads.* (ALS 8) Adyar: ALRS. Rep. 1953.

______. 1925a. *The Śākta Upaniṣads.* (ALS 10) Adyar: ALRS. Rep. 1950.

______. 1925b. *The Śaiva Upaniṣads.* (ALS 9) Adyar: ALRS. Rep. 1950.

Mahalingam, T. V. 1970. *Studies in the South Indian Temple Complex.* Dharwar: Kannada Research Institute, Karnatak Univ.

Mahapatra, S. 1979. *Bakhen: Ritual Invocation Songs of a Primitive Community.* New Delhi: Prachi Prakashan.

Mainkar, T. G. 1956. *Some Poetical Aspects of the Rigvedic Repetitions.* (Poona) Univ. of Poona.

Mair, Lucy. 1969. *Witchcraft.* NY: McGraw-Hill, World University Library. Rep. 1973.

Majumdar, R. C., ed. 1981. *The Classical Accounts of India.* Calcutta: Firma KLM.

Malamoud, Charles. 1975. "La Brique percée, sur le jeu du vide et du plein dans l'Inde brāmanique," *Nouvelle revue de psychanalyse* 11:205–22.

———. 1976. "Village et forêt dans l'ideologie de l'Inde brahmanique," *Archives euopéennes de sociologie* 17, no. 1:3–20.

———. 1983. "Exégèse de rites, exégèse de textes," *Puruṣārtha* 7:17–38.

Malaviya, Maya. 1967. *Atharvaveda Śātipuṣṭikarmāṇi.* (*Saraswati Bhavana Studies* 17) Varanasi.

Malinowski, Bronislaw Kaspar. 1923. "The Problem of Meaning in Primitive Languages." In Ogden and Richards 1923, suppl. 1, 451–510; NY ed., 296–336.

Mallik, Kalyani. 1950. *Nāthsāmpradāyer Itihās, darśan, o sādhana.* Calcutta.

———. 1954. *Siddhasiddhāntapaddhati and Other Works of the Nātha Yogīs.* Poona: Oriental Book House.

Maṇḍanamisra. *Vidhiviveka;* see M. L. Goswami 1978.

Mandelbaum, David. 1966. "Transcendental and Pragmatic Aspects of Religion," AA 68:1174–91.

Mantrasaṃhitā. 1926. *Vaikhānasamantrapraśnaṃ [= Mantrasaṃhitā].* (*Vaikhānasagranthamālā* 14) Akulamannadu.

Marcotty, Thomas. 1980. *The Way of Music: How to Conjure With Sounds, The Theory and Technique of Tantric Music* (with accompanying cassette). Lugano, Switz: Decisio Editrice.

Marulasiddiah, G. c. 1951. "Nature and Scope of Vṛttis," *Half-Yearly J. of the Mysore Univ.* 12, no. 1:59–74.

Masani, Rustom Pestonji. 1932. "Customs, Ceremonies, and Superstitions Connected with the Naming of Children in India," *Actes de XVIIIe Congrès intern. des Orientalistes,* 1931, 147ff., Leiden.

———. 1966. *Folk Culture Reflected in Names.* Bombay: Popular Prakashan.

Massignon, Louis. 1922. *Essai sur les origines de lexique technique de la mystique musulmane.* Paris: P. Geuthner.

———. 1943–45. "Le Souffle dans l'Islam," JA 234:436–38.

Masson, J. Moussaieff. 1974. "Sex and Yoga: Psychoanalysis and the Indian Religious Experience," JIPh 2, nos. 3–4:307–20.

———. 1976. "The Psychology of the Ascetic," JAS 35, no. 4:611–25.

______. 1980. *The Oceanic Feeling, The Origins of Religious Sentiment in Ancient India* (*Studies of Classical India* 3) Dordrecht: D. Reidel.

Masson, Joseph. 1942. *La Religion populaire dans le canon bouddhique pāli.* (*Le Muséon Bibliothèque* 15) Louvain: Oriental Institute.

Masson-Oursel, P. 1932. "La Noria, prototype du saṃsāra, et son rapport au dharmacakra." In *Études d'orientalisme publiees par le Musée Guimet à la mémoire de Raymonde Linoissier,* 2.419–21. (Paris: Librarie Ernest Leroux.)

Matilal, Bimal Krishna. 1973. "The Notion of Substance and Quality in Ancient Indian Grammar," *Oriental Studies* II.2 (I. Konks, *et al.* eds., Tartu [Estonia, USSR]: Tartu University) (*Acta et communicationes Universitatis Tartuensis*), 384–405.

______. 1977. *The Logical Illumination of Indian Mysticism.* Oxford: Clarendon Press.

Matilal Das and Pijuskanti Mahapatra, eds. 1958. *Fakir Lālan Sāh, Lālangītikā.* Calcutta: Calcutta University.

May, L. C. 1956. "A Survey of Glossolalia and Related Phenomena in Non-Christian Religions," AA 58:75–96.

Mayeda, Sengaku. 1979. *A Thousand Teachings, the Upadeśasāhasri of Śaṅkara, Translated, with Introduction and Notes.* Tokyo: Univ. of Tokyo Press.

Mazumdar, B. C. 1906–07. "Durgā: Her Origin and History," JRAS 38:355–58.

Mazumdar, P. K. 1977. *The Philosophy of Language: In the Light of Pāṇinian and the Mīmāṃsāka Schools of Indian Philosophy.* Calcutta: Sanskrit Pustak Bhandar.

McCormack, William Charles. 1957. "The Forms of Communication in Vīraṣaiva Religion." In *Traditional India: Structure and Change,* Milton Singer, ed. pp. 119–29. (Philadelphia: American Folklore Soc.)

McDermott, A. C. S. 1975. "Towards a Pragmatics of Mantra Recitation," JIPh 3:283–98.

Mehta, N. D. 1916. "Evolution of the Conception of Praṇava or Oṃ in Sanskrit Literature," *Sanskrit Research* (Calcutta?) 1:213–40.

Meillet, A. 1897. *De indo-eur. radice *MEN- "mente agitare."* Paris: Thesis, Aemilium Bibliopolam.

Meinhard, Heinrich. 1928. *Beiträge zur Kenntnis des Śivaismus nach den Purāṇa's.* (Diss: Rheinischen Friedrich-Wilhelms-Univ. zu Bonn) Berlin: Dietrich Reimer (Ernst Vohsen).

Meisezahl, R. O. 1974. "Śmaśānavidhi des Lūyī," *Zentralasiatische Studien* 8:9–127.

Meister, Michael. 1979a. "Juncture and Conjunction. Punning and Temple Architecture," ArAs 41:226–35.

______. 1979b. "Maṇḍala and Practice in Nāgara Architecture in North India," JAOS 99, no. 2:204–19.

Mencher, J. 1966. "Namboodiri Brahmins: An Analysis of a Traditional Elite in Kerala," JAAS 1:7–20.

Menon, C. A. 1959. *Kālī Worship in Kerala*, 2nd ed. Madras.

Mensching, Gustav. 1926. *Das heilige Schweigen, eine religionsgeschichtliche untersuchung.* Geissen: A. Topelmann.

Meyer, Johann Jakob. 1937. *Trilogie altindischer Mächte und Feste der Vegetation, ein beitrag zur vergleichenden religions- und kulturgeschichte, fest- und volkskunde,* 3 vols. Zürich/Leipzig: Max Niehan.

Michael, Tara. 1974. *Haṭayogapradīpikā, Traité Sanskrit de Haṭha-yoga, traduction, introduction et notes, avec extraits do commentaire de Brahmānanda.* (*Documents spirituels* 11) Paris: Fayard.

______. 1985. *The Symbolism of Hand-gestures (hasta or mudrā) According to the Abhinnaya Darpana.* Paris: É. Sémaphore.

Michaels, Axel. 1978. *Beweisverfahren in der vedischen Sakralgeometri. Ein Beitrag zur Entstehungsgeschichte von Wissenschaft.* Wiesbaden: F. Steiner.

Michell, G. 1977. *The Hindu Temple: An Introduction to Its Meaning and Forms.* London: Elek.

Miller, David L. 1973. *Gods and Games.* NY: Harper and Row.

Miller, G. A., and N. Chomsky. 1963. *Handbook of Mathematical Psychology,* II. NY.

Minard, Armand. 1949–56. *Trois enigmes sur les cent chemins, recherches sur le Śatapatha-Brāhamaṇa,* 2 vols. (I: *Annales du l'Univ. de Lyon (Les Belles lettres)* 17; II: PICI 3) Paris: E. de Boccard.

Miśra, Ganeswar. 1971. *Analytical Studies in Indian Philosophical Problems.* Bhubhaneshwar. Utkal Univ. Press.

Mishra, Kamalakar. 1981. *Significance of the Tantric Tradition.* Varanasi: Ardhanarisvara Publications.

Mishra, Umesha. 1926. "Physical Theory of Sound and Its Origin in Indian Thought," AUS 2.

______. 1942. "Critical Bibliography (Mīmāṃsākusumāñjali)." In Jha 1942, Appendix, 1–75.

______. 1945. *Index to the English Translation [by G. Jha] of Shabara Bhāṣya.* (GOS 103) Baroda.

Miśra, Vidya Niwas. 1967. "Vāk Legends in the Brāhmaṇas." In *Kaviraj Felicitation Volume*, 20–28.

Mitra, Rājendralāla. 1872. *Gopatha Brāhmaṇa.* Calcutta.

Mitra, Sarat Chandra. 1927. "On the Cult of Gorakṣanātha in Eastern Bengal," JDLCU 15:1–41.

Moberly, A. N. 1906. "Amulets as Agents in the Prevention of Disease in Bengal," *Memoirs, Asiatic Soc. of Bengal* 1.

Modi, P. M. 1932. *Akṣara, A Forgotten Chapter in the History of Indian Philosophy.* (*Sri Garib Das Oriental Series* 30) Baroda. Rep. 1895.

Moeller, Volker. 1974. *Symbolik des Hinduismus und des Jainismus, Tafelband.* (*Symbolik des Religionen* 19) Stuttgart: Anton Hiersemann.

Moghe, S. G. 1971. "Śāṅkarācārya and Pūrvamīmāṃsā," *Mysore Orientalist* 4:79–89.

Mohan Singh. 1937. *Gorakhnath and Medieval Hindu Mysticism.* Lahore.

Mojumdar, Atindra. 1967. *The Caryāpadas.* Calcutta.

Molé, M. 1960. "Daenā, le pont Cinvat et l'iniitiation dans le Mazdéisme," RHR 19:155ff.

Mookerjee, Ajit. 1967. *Tantra Art, Its Philosophy and Physics.* New Delhi: R. Kumar.

———. 1971. *Tantra Asana.* Basel: Ravi Kumar.

Mookerjee, Ajit, with a contribution by Philip Rawson. 1975. *Yoga Art.* Boston: New York Graphic Society (Little Brown).

Moreno, Martino Mario. 1946. "Mistica Musulmana e mistica indiana," *Annali Lateranensi* (Vatican City) 10:103–212.

Morgenroth, Wolfgang. 1970. "Die Lehre des Uddālaka Āruni, *Ch. Up.* VI: Bemerkungen zur Textkritik und Interpretation," ArchOr 38, no. 1:33–44.

Mukhopadhyaya, P. N. 1963. *Sadhana for Self-realisation; Mantras, yantras, and tantras, by Pratyagatmananda Saraswati and Sir John Woodroffe.* Madras: Ganesh.

Muktananda, Swami. 1972. *Śrī Gurugītā. Transliteration and English Translation.* Ganeshpuri, Maharashtra: Gurudev Siddha Peeth.

Muller-Ortega, Paul. Forthcoming. *The Triadic Heart of Śiva.* Albany: SUNY Press.

Murti, T. R. V. 1955. *The Central Philosophy of Buddhism.* London: Allen and Unwin.

———. 1974. "Some Comments on the Philosophy of Language in the Indian Context," JIPh 2:321–31.

Murty, K. Satchidananda. 1959. *Revelation and Reason in Advaita Vedānta.* NY: ColUP. Orig. Ind. ed. (Waltair: Andhra Univ. Press). Rep. 1974 (Delhi: MB).

Mus, Paul. 1935. *Barabuḍur: Esquisse d'une histoire du Bouddhisme fondée sur la critique archéologique des textes,* 2 vols.. Hanoi: Imprimerie, d'Extrême-Orient. Orig. ed. 1932–34 (Bulletin of EFEO 32:269–439, 33:577–980, 34:175–400).

———. 1962. "Du nouveau sur Ṛgveda, 10–90? Sociologie d'une grammaire." In W. Norman Brown 1962, 165–85.

———. 1968. "Ou finit puruṣa?" In Renou 1968, 539–63.

Mylius, Klaus. 1968. "Die Identifikationen der Metren in der Literatur des Ṛgveda," *Wissenschaftliche Z. der Martin Luther Univ.* (Halle) 17, no. 2–3:267–73.

Nagao, Gadjin. 1971. "Siddham and Its Study in Japan," *Acta Asiatica* 21:1–2.

Nagendra, S. P. 1971. *The Concept of Ritual in Modern Sociological Theory.* New Delhi: Academic Journals of India.

Nakamura, Haijme. 1955. "Tibetan Citations of Bhartṛhari's Verses and the Problem of His Date," in *Indology and Buddhology* (*S. Yamaguchi Commemoration Volume*) pp. 122–36. (Kyoto.)

Nandi, Rajendra Nath. 1973. *Religious Institutions and Cults in the Deccan, c. A. D. 600–A. D. 1000.* Delhi: MB.

Nandimath, S. C. 1942. *A Handbook of Vīraśaivism.* Dharwar: 2nd rev. ed. 1979 (Delhi: MB).

Narahari, H. G. 1944. *Ātman in Pre-Upaniṣadic Vedic Literature.* Adyar: Theosophical Society.

Narasimhachar, V., ed. 1944. *Āpastamba Śrauta Sūtra.* Mysore.

Narayana Pillai, P. K. 1958. *Non-Ṛgvedic Mantras in the Marriage Ceremonies,* with a foreword by Louis Renou. Trivandrum.

Narayanan, Vasudha. 1982. "The Goddess Śrī: The Blossoming Lotus and Breast Jewel of Viṣṇu." In Hawley and Wulff 1982, 224–37.

Narayanan, M. G. S., and Kesavan Veluthat. 1983. "A History of the Nambudiri Community in Kerala." In Staal 1983a, 256–78.

Narayanasvami Aiyar, K. 1914. *Thirty Minor Upanishads, Including the Yoga Upanishads.* Madras. Rep. 1980 (El Reno, Oklahoma: Santarasa Publications).

———. 1916. *The Thirty-Two Vidya-s.* (ALS 90) Adyar, Madras: Adyar Library and Research Center. 2nd ed. 1962, 3rd ed. 1975.

Nazari, Oreste. 1897. *Bhūr, bhuvaḥ, svaḥ, formola sacrificiale indiana.* Torino.

Neale, Robert E. 1969. *In Praise of Play.* NY: Harper.

de Nebesky-Wojkowitz, Réne. 1956. *Oracles and Demons of Tibet, The Cult of Tibetan Protective Deities.* The Hague: Mouton.

Needham, Rodney. 1967. "Percussion and Transition," *Man* n. s. 2:606–14.

Neog, Maheśwar. 1965. *Śaṅkaradeva and His Times, Early History of Vaiṣṇava Faith and Movement in Assam.* Gauhati: Gauhati University.

Nettl, B. 1953. "Observations on Meaningless Peyote Song Texts," *J. of Amer. Folklore* 66:161–64.

Neumann, Erich. 1963. *The Great Mother: An Analysis of the Archetype,* 2nd ed., Ralph Manheim, tr. (*Bollingen Series* 47) NY: Pantheon.

Nicholas, Ralph. 1982. "Shraddha, Impurity, and Relations Between the Living and the Dead." In *Way of Life: King, Householder, Renouncer,* T. N. Madan, ed., pp. 367–79. (Delhi: Vikas.)

de Nicolas, Antonio. 1976. *Four-Dimensional Man: Meditations Through the Ṛg Veda.* Stony Brook, NY: Nicolas Hays.

Nielsen, Kai. 1967. "Wittgensteinian Fideism," *Philosophy* 42:191–209.

———. 1973. "The Challenge of Wittgenstein: An Examination of his Picture of Religious Belief," *Sciences religieuses* (*Studies in Religion*) 3, no. 1:29–46.

Nijenhuis, E. T. 1974. *Indian Music: History and Structure.* Leiden: Brill.

Nilakantha Sastri, K. A. 1935. "The Origin of the Sāmaveda," JOR 9.

Nölle, W. 1954. "Hesychasmus und Yoga," *Byzantinische Zeitschrift* (Leipzig) 47:95–103.

Nottebohm, F. 1970. "Ontogeny of Bird Song," *Science* 167:950–56.

Novak, Michael. 1976. *The Joy of Sports.* NY: Basic Books.

Nowotny, Fausta. 1957. "Das Pūjāvidhinirūpaṇa des trimalla," IIJ 1:109–54.

———. 1958. *Eine durch Miniaturen erläuterte Doctrina Mystica aus Srinagar.* The Hague: Mouton.

———. 1976. *Das Gorakṣaśataka.* (*Dokumente der Geistesgeschichte* 3) Köln: Dr. Karl A. Nowotny.

O'Flaherty, Wendy Doniger. 1979. *The Critical Study of Sacred Texts.* (*Berkeley Religious Studies Series*) Berkeley: GTU.

———. 1980. *Women, Androgynes, and Other Mythical Beasts.* Chicago: UChP.

———. 1981. *The Rig Veda.* NY: Penguin Books.

———. 1984. *Dreams, Illusions, and Other Realities.* Chicago: UChP.

———. 1985. *Tales of Sex and Violence: Folklore, Sacrifice, and Danger in the Jaiminīya Brāhmaṇa.* Chicago: UChP.

O'Keefe, Daniel L. 1982. *Stolen Lightning: The Social Theory of Magic.* NY: Continuum.

Oberhammer, Gerhard. 1965. "Meditation und Mystik im Yoga des Patañjali," WZKSO 9:98–118.

———. 1974. *Offenbarung, geistige Realität des Menschen, Arbeitsdokumentation eines Symposiums zum Offenbarungsbergriff in Indien.* (DeNRSL 2) Wien: DeNRS.

———. 1977. *Strukturen yogischer Meditation, Untersuchungen zur Spiritualität des Yoga.* (VKSKS 13) (OAW phil-hist kl. 322) Wien: Verlag der OAW.

———. 1978. *Transzendenzerfahrung, Vollzugshorizont des Heils.* (DeNRL 5) Wien: Institut für Indologie der Univ. Wien.

———. 1982. *Epiphanie des Heils, zur Heilsgegenwart in Indischer und Christlicher Religion, Arbeitsdokumentation eines Symposiums.* (DeNRL 9) Wien: Institut für Indologie der Univ. Wien.

———. 1984. *Wahrheit und Transzendenz, Ein Beitrag zur Spiritualität des Nyāya.* (VKSKS 18) (OAW phil-hist kl. 424) Wien: Verlag der OAW.

Oberhammer, G., with Hans Waldenfels. 1980. *Überlieferungsstruktur und Offenbarung, Aufriss einer Reflexion des Phänomens im Hinduismus mit theologischen Anmerkungen.* (DeNRL, *Occasional Papers* 1) Wien: Institut für Indologie der Univ. Wien.

Obeyesekere, Gananath. 1981. *Medusa's Hair, An Essay on Personal Symbols and Religious Experience.* Chicago: UChP.

Oertel, Hanns. 1930. *Zur indischen Apologetik.* (*Beiträge zur Sprachwissenschaft und Religionsgeschichte* 5) Stuttgart: Kohlhammer.

Ogden, C. K., and I. A. Richards. 1923. *The Meaning of Meaning.* London: Kegan, Paul, Trench, Trübner.

Oldenberg, Hermann. 1888. "Über die Liedverfasser des Rigveda," ZDMG 42:199–247.

———. 1919. *Vorwissenschaftliche Wissenschaft, Die Weltanschauung der Brāhmaṇa Texte.* Göttingen.

Olivelle, Patrick. 1974a. "The Notion of Āśrama in the Dharmasūtras," WZKS 18:27–35.

———. 1974b. *The Origin and Early Development of Buddhist Monarchism.* Columbo (Śrī Laṅka): M. D. Gunasena.

———. 1975. "A Definition of World Renunciation," WZKS 19:75–82.

———. 1976–77. *Vāsudevāśrama Yatidharmaprakāsa, A Treatise on World Renunciation, Critically Edited with an Introduction, Annotated Translation and Appendices,* 2 vols.. (DeNRL 4) Vienna: Indologisches Institut der Univ. Wien.

———. 1978. "Ritual Suicide and the Rite of Renunciation," WZKS 22:19–44.

———. 1981. "Contributions to the Semantic History of Saṃnyāsa," JAOS 101, no. 3:265–74.

———. 1984. "Renouncer and Renunciation in the Dharmaśāstras," in *Studies in the Dharmaśāstra*, Richard W. Lariviere, ed., pp. 81–152. (Calcutta: Firma KLM.)

Ong, Walter J. 1977. "African Drums and Oral Noetics," *New Literary History* 8, no. 411–29.

Orenstein, H. 1968. "Toward a Grammar of Defilement in Hindu Sacred Law." In *Structure and Change in Indian Society*, M. Singer and B. S. Cohn, eds. (Chicago: Aldine.)

Östör, Akos. 1978. "Puja in Society, an Methodological and Analytical Essay on an Ethnographic Category," *Eastern Anthropologist* (Lucknow) 31, no. 2:119–76.

———. 1980. *The Play of the Gods, Locality, Ideology, Structure, and Time in the Festivals of a Bengali Town*. Chicago: UChP.

Padmanabha, Seetha, ed. 1969. *Śrīpraśna Saṃhitā*. Tirupati: Kendriya Sanskrit Vidyapeetha.

Padoux, André. 1963. *Recherches sur la symbolique et l'énergie de la parole dans certains textes tantriques*. (PICI 21) Paris: Éditions de Boccard. 2nd ed. 1975; Rev. Eng. ed. forthcoming.

———. 1975. *La Parātrīśikālaghuvṛtti de Abhinavagupta, texte traduit et annoté*. (PICI 38) Paris: Éditions de Boccard.

———. 1977. "Un Terme technique du *mantraśāstra: vidarbha*," JA 345–49.

———. 1978a. "Contributions à l'étude du mantraśāstra: I, La sélection des *mantra* (*mantroddhāra*)," BEFEO 65:65–85.

———. 1978b. "Some Suggestions on Research into Mantra," IT 6:235–39.

———. 1978c. "On Mantras and Mantric Practices in the Agni-Purāṇa," *Purāṇa* 20, no. 1:57–65.

———. 1980. "Contributions à l'étude du mantraśāstra: II *nyāsa:* l'imposition rituelle des *mantra*," BEFEO 67:59–102.

———. 1981. "A Survey of Tantric Hinduism for the Historian of Religion," HR 20, no. 4:345–60.

———. 1986. *Mantras et diagrammes rituels dans l'hindouisme*, André Padoux, ed. Paris: CNRS.

Pandey, Shri Janardhan Shastri, ed. 1978. *Gorakṣ Saṃhitā*. Varanasi: Sampūrṇānanda Sanskrit Univ.

Pandey Kanti Chandra. 1954. *Bhāskarī. Vol. III: An English Translation of the Īśvara Pratyabhijñā Vimarśinī in the Light of the Bhāskarī With an Outline of [the] History of Śaiva Philosophy. (The Princess of Wales Saraswati Bhavana Texts* 84) Lucknow: Superintendent, Printing and Stationery, U. P.

Pandey, Raj Bali. 1969. *Hindu Saṃskāras (Socio-religious Study of the Hindu Sacraments).* Delhi: MB.

Pandey, Ram Chandra Sharma. 1963. *The Problem of Meaning in Indian Philosophy.* Delhi: MB.

Pandit, M. P. 1959. *Kundalinī Yoga, A Brief Study of Sir John Woodroffe's "The Serpent Power".* London: Luzac.

Pannikar, Raimundo. 1964. "Die Begründung des hermeneutischen Pluralismus im Hinduismus," *Kerygma und Mythos* 6.2 (*Entmythologisierung und Bild*): 119–36.

Panse, G. M. 1968. "Significance of Water in Indian Rituals," *Śaradāpīṭhapatrikā* (Dwarka) 8:18ff.

Parab, B. A. 1949. "Human Miracles and Hymns of Will-Power in the Rigveda," AIOC 15.

———. 1952. *The Miraculous and Mysterious in Vedic Literature.* Bombay: Popular Book Depot.

Paranjpe, Vāsudeva Gopāla. 1922. *Le Vārtika de Kātyāyana: une étude du style, du vocabulaire et des postulats philosophiques.* Heidelberg: Weiss.

Parpola, Asko. 1968. "On the Quotations of Ritualistic Teachers in the Śrautasūtras of Lāṭyāyana and Drāhyāyana." In *Raghu Vira Memorial Volume*, D. Sinor, ed. (New Delhi.)

———. 1973. *The Literature and Study of the Jaiminīya Sāmaveda in Retrospect and Prospect.* Helsinki: Helsinki Academy.

———. 1981. "On the Primary Meaning and Etymology of the Sacred Syllable OM," *Proc. of the Nordic South Asian Conference* (Helsinki, 1980).

———. 1983a. "The Pre-Vedic Indian Background of the Śrauta Ritual." In Staal 1983a, 41–75.

———. 1983b. "Jaiminīya Śrauta Sūtra on the Agnicayana, with Bhavatrāta's Commentary," in Staal 1983a, vol. 2, 700–36.

Parthasarathy, K. E. 1966. *Śrī Viṣṇu Sahasranāmam.* Madras.

Patel, Manilal. 1930. *Die Dānastuti's des Rigveda.* Leipzig. Eng. tr., B. H. Kapadia, Vallabh Vidyanagar, 1961.

———. 1938. "A Study of ṚV 10.71," *Visvabharati Quarterly* 4.

Pathak, V. S. 1960. *History of Śaiva Cults in Northern India From Inscriptions (700 A. D. to 1200 A.D.).* Varanasi: Ram Naresh Varma.

Patyal, H. C. 1976. "The Saptapadī Rite," BDCRI 35:104.

Payne, Earnest A. 1933. *The Śāktas: An Introductory and Comparative Study (The Religious Life of India)* Calcutta: YMCA Publishing House.

Pensa, Corrado. 1969. "On the Purification Concept in Indian Tradition with Special Regard to Yoga," EW 19:194–228.

———. 1972. "Some Internal and Comparative Problems in the Field of Indian Religions," in *Problems and Methods of the History of Religions (E. O. James Festschrift,* U. Bianchi, ed.) pp. 102–22. (Leiden: E. J. Brill.)

———. 1974. "Considerazioni sul tema della bipolarità nelle religioni indiane." In *Gururājamañjarikā, Studi in onore di Giuseppe Tucci* (Napoli.), 2.379–409.

Pepper, Stephen C. 1942. *World Hypotheses, A Study in Evidence.* Berkeley: UCaP.

Péri, Noël, 1917. "Hārītī, la mère-de-démons," BEFEO 17:1–102.

Periveṅkateśvara Śāstrī. 1971. "Pāṇinīyaśabdānuśāsane sphoṭabrahmanirūpaṇaṃ (Description of Sphoṭabrahman in Pāṇinian Grammar)." In Rajeshwar Shastri Dravid 1971, grammar section, 34–39.

Petech, L. Luciano. 1960. *History of Medieval Nepal.* Rome: Serie Orientale Roma.

Pettazoni, Rafaele. 1956. *The All-Knowing God, Researches into Early Religion and Culture.* London: Methuen and Co. Orig. Ital ed., *L'Onniscienza di Dio,* 1956 (Torino: Einaudi).

Phillips, D. Z. 1970. *Faith and Philosophical Enquiry.* London: RKP.

Pieper, Jan. 1980. *Ritual Space in India: Studies in Architectural Anthropology.* (AARP 17) London: Max Mueller Bhavan, Bombay/The Goethe Institute, Munich.

Piet, John H. 1952. *A Logical Presentation of the Śaiva Siddhānta Philosophy.* (*Indian Research Series* 8) Madras: The Christian Literature Society for India.

Pitt-Rivers, Julian. 1967. "Words and Deeds: the Ladinos of Chiapas," *Man* n. s. 2:71–86.

Poddar, Hanuman Prasad, and Chimanlal Goswami, eds. 1934. "Śaktyaṇka (Gorakhpu: Gita Press)," *Kalyāṇa* 97.1.

Pollack, Sheldon. 1985. "The Theory of Practice and the Practice of Theory in Indian Intellectual History," JAOS 105, no. 3:499–519.

Popkin, Richard H. 1979. *The History of Scepticism, from Erasmus to Spinoza.* Berkeley: UCaP.

Potdar, K. R. 1953. *Sacrifice in the Ṛgveda, It's Nature, Influence, Origin and Growth.* (BVS 16) Bombay: BVB.

Pott, Pieter Hendrik. 1966. *Yoga and Yantra, Their Interrelations and Their Significance for Indian Archaeology.* Rodney Needham, tr. (Koninklijk instituut voor taal-, land-, en volkenkunde, translation series 8) The Hague: Martinus Nijhoff.

Potter, Karl H. 1963. *Presuppositions of India's Philosophies.* Englewood Cliffs, N.J.: Prentice-Hall. Rep. 1972, pap. 1976 (Westport, Connecticut: Greenwood Press).

———. 1970. *Bibliography of Indian Philosophies.* (EIPh [1]) Delhi: MB.

———. 1981. *Advaita Vedānta up to Śaṃkara and His Pupils.* (EIPh [3]) Princeton: Princeton Univ. Press.

Prabodh Chandra. 1931. "Le Bouddhisme tantrique à Bali d'aprés une publication récente," JA 218:159–67.

Pratyagātmānanda (Sarasvatī), Swami (Pramathanatha Mukhopadhyaya). 1956. "Tantra as a Way of Realization." In CHI 4:227–40.

———. 1966. *Japasūtram,* (Prathamakhaṇḍaḥ). Varanasi: Bhāratīya Vidyā Prakāśan.

———. 1971. *Japasūtram, The Science of Creative Sound* (Eng. tr. and condensation of the six volume Bengali and Sanskrit work of the same name). Madras: Ganesh and Co.

Przyluski, Jean. 1920. "La Roue de la vie à Ajaṇṭā," JA 16:313–31.

———. 1934. "The Great Goddess in India and Iran," 10:405–30.

———. 1936a. "The Solar Wheel of Sārnāth and in Buddhist Monuments," JISOA 4, no. 1:45–51.

———. 1936b. "Mudrā," *Indian Culture* (Calcutta) 2:715–19.

———. 1938. "From the Great Goddess to Kalā," IHQ 14:267–74.

Pulsule, Gajanan Balakrishna. 1969. "Patañjali's Interpretation of ṚV 10.71.2," Bombay: *Professor R. N. Dandekar Felicitation Volume* (G. V. Devasthali, ed., Bombay: Popular Prakashan) (Indian Antiquary, 3rd ser., 3), 27–29.

Pusalker, A. D. 1960. "Literary Background of Rāghavabhatta, Author of Padārthādarśa . . . and Arthadyotanikā . . . (?)" ABORI 41:29–48.

Raghava Varier, M. R. 1983. "The Nambudiri Ritual Tradition (with Special Reference to the Kollengode Archives)." In Staal 1983a, 279–99.

Raghavan, T. S. c. 1956. "The Concept Om," *The Vedanta Kesari* (Mylapore, Madras), 43, no. 11:464–67.

Raghavan, V. 1942. *Studies on Some Concepts of the Alaṅkāra Śāstra.* Adyar: ALRC. Rep. 1973.

———. 1953. "The Viṣṇusahasranāmastotra," *The Indian Heritage* (Bangalore) 421ff.

———. 1957. "Present Position of Vedic Chanting and Its Future," *Bulletin of the Institute of Traditional Cultures* (Madras) 48–69.

———. 1959. "Methods of Popular Religious Instruction in South India." In Singer 1959, 117–24.

———. 1962a. *The Present Day Position of Vedic Recitation and Vedic Sakhas.* Kumbhakonam: Veda Dharma Paripala Sabha.

———. 1962b. "Sāma Veda and Music," *J. of the Music Academy* (Madras) 33:127–33.

———. 1965. "The Name Pāñcarātra, With an Analysis of the Sanatkumāra-Saṃhitā in Manuscript," JAOS 85:73–79.

Raghavan, V., and Anantalal Thakur, eds. 1964. *Āgamaḍdambara Otherwise Called Ṣaṇmatanāṭaka of Jayanta Bhaṭṭa.* Dharbhanga.

Raghu Vira. 1938. *Sāma-Veda of the Jaiminīyas.* (*Sarasvati Vihara Series* 3) Lahore.

Raghu Vira and Shodo Taki, eds. 1938. *Dakṣiṇamrti: Uddhārakośa, A Dictionary of the Secret Tantric Syllabic Code.* Lahore. Rep. New Delhi: 1978.

Raghunātha Śarmā. 1964a. *Citranibandhāvaliḥ* (Vividhaśāstrīyanibandhānāṃ *Saṃgrahaḥ*) (*A Collection of Various Learned Papers*). Delhi: MB.

———. 1964b. "Śabdādvaitavimarśah (On the Concept of Śabdādvaita)." In Raghunātha Śarmā 1964a, 27–42.

———. 1964c. "Pratibhāvimarsaḥ (On the Cocept of Prqatibhā)." In Raghunātha Śarmā 1964a, 193–215.

Rahner, Hugo. 1972. *Man at Play.* NY: Herder and Herder.

Rahurkar, V. G. 1956–57. "The Word *ṚṢi* in the Veda." In *Irach Jehangir Sorabji Tarporewala Memorial Volume* (BDCRI 18), 55–57.

Rai, Amita. 1960. "House-Building Rituals in Ancient India." In *Jitendra Nath Banerjea Volume* (Calcutta), 298ff.

Rai, Ram Kumar. 1976. *Mantrayogasaṃhitā.* Varanasi.

———. 1978. *Dictionaries of Tantra Śāstra or the Tantrāabhidhāna, Containing: Texts and English Translations of Mantrārthābhidhānam, Prakārāntara Mantrāabhidhānam, Ekākṣarkoṣa, Bījanighaṇṭu, Mātṛkānighaṇṭu, Prakārāntara Mātṛkānighaṇṭu, I, Prakārānta Mātṛkānighaṇṭu II, Prakārānta Varṇanighaṇṭu, Bījābhidhāna, Mantrārthābhidhāna of Varadā Tantra, Mudrānighaṭu, and Varṇabījakoṣa.* (*Indological Reference Series* 2) Varanasi: Prachya Prakashan.

Rajagopala Aiyar, T. K. 1949. "The Music of the Sāmaveda Chants," *J. of the Music Academy* (Madras) 20:144–51.

Rajeshwar Shastri Dravid. 1971. *Ṛṣikalpanyāsaḥ*. Devadatta Śāstrī, ed. Prayāg (Allahabad): Bharati Parisad.

Rama Sastry, R. 1960–61. *Viṣṇusahasranāmastotra [with Śaṃkara's and other CC]*, 2 vols. Mysore.

Rāma Sureśa Tripāṭhī. 1972. *Saṃskṛta Vyākaraṇadarśana [= Philosophy of Sanskrit Grammar]*. Delhi: Rajkamal.

Ramakrishna Dikshithar, Pandit Sri A., and Pandit Sri K. Ramachandra Sarma, eds. 1980. *Collection of Stotras by Srimad Appayya Dikshitendra with own Commentaries*. (*Srimad Appayya Dikshitendra Granthavali* Series-3) Secunderabad, A. P.: Srimad Appayaya Dikshitendra Granthavali.

Ramana Sastri, V. V. 1956. "The Doctrinal Cultue and Tradition of the Siddhas." In CHI 4.300–308.

Rāmanārāyaṇa Tripāṭhī. 1971. "Vyākaraṇasya darśanatvam (On Grammar as a Philosophy). In Rajeshwar Shastri Dravid 1971, grammar section, 67–77.

Rāmanātha Śāstrī. 1931. *The Sphoṭa Siddhi of Ācārya Maṇḍanamiśra with the Gopālikā of ṛṣiputra Parameśvara*. (MUSS 6) Madras: Univ. of Madras.

Ramanujacariyan. n.d. *Śrī-Viṣṇu-Sahasra-Nāma-Stotra*.

Ramanujan, A. K. 1973. *Speaking of Śiva*. Baltimore: Penguin Books.

Rāma Prasāda Tripāṭhī. 1971. "Vyākaraṇadarśane sṛṣṭiprakriyā (Creation According to the Philosophy of Grammar)." In Rajeshwar Shastri Dravid 1971, philosophy section, 131–40.

______. 1972. *Pāṇinīyavyākaraṇe pramāṇasamīkṣā (A Critical Study of Pramāṇa in the Grammatical System of Pāṇini)* (*Sarasvatī Bhavana Adhyayanamālā* 20) Varanasi: Vārāṇaseya Saṃskṛta Viśvavidyālaya (Banaras Sanskrit Unviersity).

Ramaswami, Sastri, V. A. 1932–33. "The Doctrine of Sphoṭa," *Annamalai Univ. J.* (Annamalainagar) 1:231–40; 2:109–20.

______. 1936–37. "Bhartṛhari a Bauddha?," *Annamalai Univ. J.* (Annamalainagar) 6:65–69. Rep. 1937, PAIOC 8:254–57 (Mysore 1935).

______. 1938. "Bhartṛhari a Pre-Saṅkara Advaitin," *Annamalai Univ. J.* (*Annamalainagar*) 8:42–53.

______. 1952. "Bhartṛhari as a Mīmāṃsaka," BDCRI 14:1–15.

Rambach, Pierre. 1979. *The Art of Japanese Tantrism*. London: Macmillan.

Ramjan Singh. 1974. *The Jaina Concept of Omniscience*. Ahmedabad: L. D. Institute of Indology.

Rangachari, K. 1931. *The Śrī Vaiṣṇava Brahmans.* (*Bulletin of the Madras Government Museum*, n. s., gen. sect., II.2) Madras.

Rappoport, Roy A. 1979. *Ecology, Meaning, and Religion.* Richmond, Calif.: North Atlantic Books.

Rastogi, Navjivan. 1979. *The Krama Tantricism of Kashmir, Historical and General Sources*, vol. 1. Delhi: MB.

Rau, Wilhelm. 1957. *Staat und Gesellschaft in alten Indien nach den Brāhmaṇa Texten Dargestellt.* Wiesbaden: OH.

———. 1971. *Die handschriftliche Überlieferung des Vākyapadīya und seiner Kommentare* (*Abhandlungen der Marburger Gelehrten Gesellschaft* 1971.1). München: Fink.

Rawson, Phillip S. 1966. *Indian Sculpture.* NY. E. P. Dutton and Co.

———. 1971. *Tantra.* London: Arts Council of Great Britain/ Hayward Gallery.

———. 1973a. *Tantra, the Indian Cult of Ecstasy.* NY: Bounty Books (Crown Publishers). Orig. ed. Thames and Hudson.

———. 1973b. *The Art of Tantra.* NY: OUP.

Ray, Benjamin. 1972. "'Performative Utterances' in African Rituals," HR 13, no. 1:16–35.

Ray, Prafulla Chandra. 1902–09. *A History of Hindu Chemistry from the Earliest Times to the Sixteenth Century*, 2 vols. London: Williams, and Norgate.

Ray, Priyada Rajan. 1956. *History of Chemistry in Ancient and Medieval India.* Calcutta: Indian Chemical Society.

———. 1967. "Origin and Tradition of Alchemy," IJHS 2, no. 1:1–21.

Ray, Reginald. 1974. "Understanding Tantric Buddhism," JAS 34, no. 1:169–75.

Regmi, Dilli Raman. 1965–66. *Medieval Nepal.* Calcutta: KLM.

Regnaud, P. 1905. "Recherches sur le point de départ des noms de poètes védiques," JA 10.5.

Renou, Louis. 1931. *Bibliographie Védique.* Paris: Adrien Maisonneuve.

———. 1939. "L'ambiguïté du vocabulaire du Ṛgveda," JA 231:161.

———. 1940. "Aperçu de la littérature grammaticale en sanskrit." In *La Durghaṭavṛtti de Śaraṇadeva, Traité grammatical en Sanskrit du xiie siècle* (*Collection Émile Senart* 61) (Paris. Société d'édition "Les Belles Lettres," 1941–56), 1.1.5–44.1940.

———. 1941–42. "Les connexions entre le ritual et la grammaire en Sanskrit," JA 233:105–65. Rep. Staal 1972, 434–69.

______. 1942. *Terminologie grammaticale du sanskrit*, 3 vols. (BÉPHÉ 280–82) Paris: Champion. Rep. 1 vol. 1957.

______. 1947. *Les écoles védiques et la formation du Veda*. (*Cahiers de la société asiatique* 9) Paris.

______. 1948–49. "Sur la notion de Brahman" (in collaboration with L. Silburn), JA 236–37:7–46.

______. 1948–54. *La grammaire de Pāṇini traduite du sanskrit avec des extraits des commentaires indigènes*, 3 fasc. Paris: Klincksieck. rev. ed., 2 vols., 1966 (Paris: ÉFEO).

______. 1949a. "La valeur du silence dans le culte védique," JAOS 69:11–18.

______. 1949b. "Un Hymne à énigmes du Ṛgveda [1.152]" (in collaboration with L. Silburn), *J. de psychologie normale et pathologique* 42:266–73.

______. 1949c. "Considerations on Ṛgveda I,152" (and L. Silburn), BV 10:133–39.

______. 1949d. "Cérémonies védiques dans l'Inde contemporaine," *Séance annuelle des Cinq Académies* 1–8. Paris: Institut de France.

______. 1952. "Études védiques: 1. Les Versets du Sāmaveda d'origine non ṛgvédique," JA 240:133–41.

______. 1953a. "Le passage des Brāhmaṇa aux Upaniṣad." JAOS 73:138–44.

______. 1953b. "Études védiques 3.e: Kavi," JA 241:180–83.

______. 1953c. "Les Débuts de la spéculation indienne," *Revue philosophique* 143:334–41.

______. 1954a. "Les vers insérés dans la prose védique." In *Asiatica, Festschrift Friedrich Weller*, 528–34.

______. 1954b. "Les pouvoirs de la parole dans les hymnes védiques," *Samjna-Vyakarana* (*Studia Indologica Internationalia*) 1:1–12.

______. 1954c. *Vocabulaire du rituel védique*. (*Collections de vocabulaires techniques du Sanskrit* 1) Paris: Librairie C. Klincksieck.

______. 1954d. "Nirukta and Anirukta in Vedic" (in collaboration with L. Silburn). In *Sarupa-Bhāratī*, (*Lakṣman Sarup Memorial Volume*) pp. 68–79. (Hosiarpur: VVRI.)

______. 1955. "Les pouvoirs de la parole dans le Ṛgveda." In ÉVP 1.1–27.

______. c. 1955. "Dhiṣaṇā in the Ṛgveda," *Oriental Thought* (Nasik) 2, no. 1:17–21.

______. 1955–69. *Études védiques et pāṇinéennes*, 17 fascs. (PICI 1–2, 4, 6, 9–10, 12, 14, 16–18, 20, 22–23. 26–27, 30) Paris: É. E. de Boccard.

———. 1956. "Études sur quelques hymnes spéculatifs." In EVP 2:55–59.

———. 1957. "Introduction générale." In 1–125, preface to the first volume of Jacob Wackernagel [and Albert Debrunner], *Altindische Grammatik* (Göttingen: Vandenhoeck and Ruprecht).

———. c. 1957. "[Reviews of] 'Ṛgveda-Mantras in their Ritual Setting in Gṛhyasūtras' and 'Non-Ṛgvedic Mantras in the Āśvalāyana-Gṛhya-sūtra' by V. M. Apte," JA 236:132.

———. 1958. *Études sur le vocabulaire du Ṛgveda*, première série. (PIFI 5) Pondichéry. IFI.

———. 1960a. *Le destin du Veda dans l'Inde.* (ÉVP 6 [PICI 10]) Paris: É. E. de Boccard.

———. 1960b. "The Enigma in the Ancient Literature of India," *Diogenes* 29 (Spring):32–41.

———. 1962. "Recherches sur le rituel védique: la place du Rig-Vedique dans l'ordannance du culre," JA 250, no. 2:161–84.

———. 1968. *Mélanges d'Indianisme à la mémoire de Louis Renou.* (PICI 28) Paris: É. E. de Boccard.

———. 1969. "Pāṇini." In *Current Trends in Linguistics* 5 (*Linguistics in South Asia*, T. A. Sebeok, *et al.*, eds.) pp. 481–98. (The Hague: Mouton.)

***Renou, L., Jean Filliozat,* et al.** 1947–53. *L'Inde classique, manuel des études indiennes* (2 vols.). I: Paris; II: Hanoi: I: Payot; II: EFEO. Rep. 1986.

Ṛgvedabhāṣya. 1972. *Ṛgveda-saṃhitā śrimatsāyaṇācārya viracita-bhāṣyasameta.* Poona: Vaidika-samsodhana mandala.

Ṛgveda Saṃhitā, bhāṣya, *and* khila; see Sonatakke, N. S., and C. G. Kashikar, eds. 1933–51.

Ricci, Fanco Maria, with Ravi Kumar and Gabriele Mandel. 1979. *Tantra, Rites of Love.* NY: Rizzoli.

Ricoeur, Paul. 1977. *The Rule of Metaphor, Multi-disciplinary Studies of the Creation of Meaning in Language.* Robert Czerny with Kathleen McLaughlin and John Costello, trs. Toronto: Univ. Toronto Press. Orig. Fr. ed. 1975, *La Métaphor vive* (Paris: Éditions de Seuil); pap. ed. 1981.

Ridding, C. M., tr. 1896. *Kādambarī.* London: Royal Asiatic Society. Rep. 1974.

Rilke, Rainer Maria. 1938. *Briefe aus den Jahren 1914 bis 1921.* Ruth Sieber-Rilke and Carl Sieber, eds. Leipzig: Insel-Verlag.

Risch, Hubert. 1951. *Le Haṭha Yoga, Exposé sommaire de la méthode, quelques expériences physiologiques et applications thérapeutiques.* Paris: Diss., Faculté de Médecine.

Rivière, Jean Marquès. 1976. *Rituel de magie tantrique Hindoue, Yantra Chintāmani (Le Joyau des Yantras).* Milano: Archè, Bibliothèque de l'unicorne, *La Tradition: textes et études, série française* 5.

Robinson, James B. 1979. *Buddha's Lions: The Lives of the Eighty-Four Siddhas.* Berkeley, Calif.: Dharma Publishing.

Robson, E. I. 1958. *Arrian,* vol. 2. (Loeb edition). Cambridge, Mass.: HUP.

Rocher, Ludo. 1986. *The Purāṇas.* (HIL 2.3) Wiesbaden: OH.

Rocher, Rosane. 1975. "India." In *Current Trends in Linguistics* 13 (*Historiography of Linguistics,* pt. 1) Thomas A. Sebeok, ed., pp. 3–67. (The Hague: Mouton.)

______. 1978. *India and Indology, Selected Articles by W. Norman Brown.* Rosane Rocher, ed. Delhi: MB for the AIIS.

Roesel, Richard. 1928. *Die Psychologischen Grundlagen der Yogapraxis.* Stuttgart.

Rolland, Pierre. 1971. *Un rituel domestique védique, Le Vārāhagṛhyasūtra.* Aix-en-Provence: Univ. de Provence.

______. 1973. *Le Mahāvrata: contribution à l'étude d'un rituel solennel védique.* Göttingen: Vandenhoeck und Ruprecht.

______. 1975. *Compléments au rituel domestique védique, Le Vārāhagṛhyapuruṣa et autres extraits des Vārāhapariśista à caractère domestique.* (*Études indiennes* 3) Aix-en-Provence: Univ. de Provence.

Rorty, Richard. 1967. *The Linguistic Turn, Recent Essays in Philosophical Method.* Chicago: UChP.

Rosaldo, Michelle Zimbalist. 1975. "It's All Uphill: The Creative Metaphors of Ilongot Magical Spells." In Sanches and Blount 1975.

Rösel, J. 1976. "Pilger und Tempelpriester: indische Wallfahrtsorganization, dargestellt am Beispiel der südost-indischen Tempelstadt Puri," *Internationales Asienforum* (Munich) 7:322–54.

______. 1978. "Über die Bedeutung von Tempelstädten für Entstehen und Bestand indische Regionalreiche—Der Jaggannāth-Temple und das Regionalreich von Orissa," *Internationales Asienforum* (Munich) 9:41–59.

Rosu, Arion. 1961. "Pūrṇaghaṭa et le symbolisme du lotus dans l'Inde," ArAs 8, no. 3:163–94.

Roy, Satindra Narayan. 1927/28–31. "The Witches of Orissa," JASB 14:185–200.

Ruben, Walter. 1967–73. *Die Gesellschaftliche Entwicklung im alten Indien,* I: *Die Entwicklung der Produktionsverhältnisse,* II: *Die Entwicklung von Staat und Recht, III: Die Entwicklung der Religion,* IV: *Die Entwicklung der Philosophie,* V: *Die Entwicklung* *der Dichtung*, VI: *Die Entwicklung der Gangesgesellschaft*. (*Veröffentlichungen des Instituts für Orientforschung* (DAWB) 67) Berlin: Akademie-Verlag.

Ruegg, David Seyfort. 1955. "Védique *addhā* et quelques expressions parallèles à *tathāgata-*," JA 243:163–70.

———. 1958. "The Term *Buddhi-viparinama*," IIJ 2:271–83.

———. 1959. *Contributions à l'histoire de la philosophie linguistique indienne*. (PICI 7) Paris: É. E. de Boccard.

———. 1969. *La théorie de Tathāgatagrabha et du gotra*. (PÉFEO 70) Paris.

———. 1973. *Le traité du Tathāgatagarbha de Bu ston Rin chen grub*. (PÉFEO 88) Paris.

Rukmani, T. S. 1981–83. *Yogavārttika of Vijñānabhikṣu, Text With English Translation and Critical Notes Along With the Text and English Translation of the Pātañjala Yogasūtras and Vyāsabhāṇṣya*. I: *Samādhipāda*, II: *Sādhanapāda*. Delhi: Munshiram Manoharlal.

Runes, M. 1926. "Geschichte des Wortes *vates*," in *Festschrift P. Krertschmer* (Berlin), 202ff.

Russell, Peter. 1976. *The TM Technique, An Introduction to Transcendental Meditation and the Teachings of Maharishi Mahesh Yogi*. London: RKP.

Śabara. *Mīmāṃsāsūtrabhāṣya;* see V. S. Apate 1929–34; Ganganath Jha 1933.

Sadasivaiah, H. M. 1967. *A Comparative Study of Two Vīraśaiva Monasteries*. Mysore: Prasaranga Univ. of Mysore.

Saebadio Haryati. 1971. *Jñānasiddhānta, Secret Lore of the Balinese Śaiva-priest, Introduction, Text, and Translation*. The Hague: Thesis. Amsterdam.

Salomon, Richard. 1979. "Tīrtha-pratyāmnāyāḥ: Ranking of Hindu Pilgrimage Sites in Classical Sanskrit Texts," ZDMG 129, no. 1:102–28.

Samarin, William J., ed. 1976. *Language in Religions Practice*. Rowley, Mass.: Newbury House.

Śaṅkara *Brahmasūtrabhāṣya;* see Narayan Ram Āchārya, ed., 1948a.

Sāmkṛtyāyana, Rahul. 1957. *Siddha Sarahapādakṛta Dohakośa*. Patna: Bihar Rastrabhasa Parisad.

Sanches, Mary, and B. G. Blount, eds. 1975. *Sociocultural Dimensions of Language Use*. NY: Academic Press.

Sanderson, Alexis. 1986. "Purity and Power Among the Brahmans of Kashmir." In *The Category of the Person: Anthropological and Philosophical Perspectives*, Michael Carrithers, Steven Collins, and Steven Lukes, eds. (Cambridge: CUP.)

Santucci, James A. 1976. *An Outline of Vedic Literature.* (*The Ameri. Acad. of Rel. Aids to the Study of Religion Series* 5) Missoula, Montana: Scholars Press.

Sapir, J. David, and J. C. Crocker. 1977. *The Social Use of Metaphor: Essays in the Anthropology of Rhetoric.* Philadelphia: Univ. of Pennsylvania Press.

Saraf, S. 1969. "The Hindu Ritual Purity-Purification Complex," *Eastern Anthropologist* 22:161ff.

______. 1974. "The Tantric Tradition," *Eastern Anthropologist* (Lucknow) 27, no. 2:99–156.

______. 1976. "Hindu Ritual Idiom: Cosmic Perspective and Basic Orientations." In Bharati 1976a, 151–64.

Saraswati, B. 1972. "Traditional Modes of Learning in Indian Civilization," in *Aspects of Indian Culture and Society,* S. Sinha, ed., pp. 153–69. (Calcutta: Indian Anthropological Society.)

Śarma, K. Madhava Krishna. 1943. "Vāk Before Bhartṛhari," *Poona Orientalist* 8.1–2.

Śarmā, Rāmprasād. 1977. *Śakti Tattva Darśan.* Birlagram, Madhya Pradesh: Śivatattva Darśan Granth Prakasan Samiti.

Sarup, Laksman. 1927. *The Nighaṇṭu and the Nirukta, the Oldest Indian Treatise on Eytmology, Philology, and Semantics.* Lahore: Univ. of the Panjab. Rep. 1967 (ND: MB).

Saso, Michael R. 1972. *Taoism and the Rite of Cosmis Renewal.* Pullman; Washington State Univ. Press.

______. 1978. *The Teachings of Taoist Master Chuang.* New Haven, Conn.: YUP.

Saso, M. R., and David W. Chappell, eds. 1977. *Buddhist and Taoist Studies I.* (*Asian Studies at Hawaii* 18) Honolulu: Univ. Press of Hawaii.

Satvatā Saṃhitā; see Vraj Vallabha Dviveda 1982.

Saunders, E. Dale. 1957. "Symbolic Gestures in Buddhism," *Artibus Asiae* 21.

______. 1960. *Mudrā, A Study of Symbolic Gestures in Japanese Buddhist Sculpture.* (*Bollingen Series* 58) NY: Pantheon Books.

Scharbau, Carl Anders. 1932. *Die Idee der Schöpfung in der vedischen Literatur: Eine religionsgeschichtliche Untersuchung über den fruhindischen Theismus.* Stuttgart: Kohlhammer.

Scharfe, Hartmut. 1961. *Die Logik im Mahābhāṣya.* (DAWIO 50) Berlin: Akademic Verlag.

Schayer, Stanislav. c. 1917. "Die Weltanschauung der Brāhmaṇa Texte," RO 3:57.

———. 1925. "Die Struktur der magischen Weltanschauung nach dem Atharva Veda und den Brāhmaṇa-Texten," *Z. für Buddhismus* 6:259–277 (?).

Schechner, Richard. 1977. *Essays on Performance Theory, 1970–76.* NY: Drama Books.

Schechner, Richard, and Linda Hess. 1977. "The Ramlila of Ramnagar [India]," *The Drama Review* 2:51–82.

Schechner, R., and Mady Schuman, eds. 1976. *Ritual, Play, and Performance: Readings in the Social Sciences/Theatre.* NY: Seabury.

Scheftelowitz, Isidor. 1906. *Die Apokryphen des Ṛgveda* [=*Indische Forschungen* 1]. Breslau: Marcus.

———. c. 1914. "Die Sündentilgung durch Wasser," ARW 17:353ff.

Scherman, Lucian. 1947. "Siddha, Sanskrit Letters as Mystical Symbols in Later Buddhism Outside India," in *Art and Thought, Fest. in Honor of Dr. Ananda Coomaraswamy on the Occasion of his 70th Birthday,* K. Bharatha Iyer, ed., pp. 55–62. (London: Luzac).

Scheuer, Jacques. 1982. *Śiva dans le Mahābhārata.* (BÉHÉ, Sciences religieuses 84) Paris: PUF.

Schmidt, Hanns-Peter. 1959. "Review of Renou, EVP 1–2," ZDMG 109:442–49.

———. 1968. "The Origins of Ahiṃsā." In Louis Renou 1968, 626–55.

Schmidt, Richard. 1908. *Fakire und Fakirtum in alten und modernen Indien nach den indischen originalquellen dargestellt.* Berlin: H. Barsdorf [1907].

Schmidt, Toni. 1958. *The Eighty-Five Siddhas* (*Sino-Swedish Expedition Publication* 42). Stockholm: Statens etnografiska museum.

Schmithausen, Lambert. 1965. *Maṇḍanamisra'a Vibhramavivekaḥ.* (OAW 247.2) Wien.

Schmitt, Rüdiger. 1967. *Dichtung und Dichtersprache in indogermanischer Zeit.* Wiesbaden: OH.

Schoterman, J. A. 1977. "Some Remarks on the Kubjikāmatatantra," ZDMG suppl. 3.2:932–40.

———. 1982. *The Ṣaṭsāhasra Saṃhitāa, Chapters 1–5.* (ORT 27) Leiden: E. J. Brill.

Schrader, Friedrich Otto. 1912. *The Minor Upaniṣads,* I: *Sāṃyasa Upaniṣads.* (ALS 12) Adyar, Madras: Theosophical Society/ ALRC.

———. 1916. *Introduction to the Pāñcarātra and the Ahirbudhnya Saṃhitā.* (ALS 5) Adyar. Rep. 1973.

Schrader, J. Otto. 1929. "The Sacrificial Wheel Taught in the Bhagavadgītā," IHQ 5, no. 2:173–81.

Schreiner, Peter. 1979. *Yoga, Grundlagen, Methoden, Ziele: Ein Bibliographischer Überblick.* (*Arbeitsmaterialien zur Religionsgeschichte* 4) Köln: Brill.

von Schroeder, Leopold. 1887. *Indiens Literatur und Cultur in historischer Entwicklung.* Leipzig: H. Haessel.

———. 1908. *Mysterium und Mimus im Rigveda.* Leipzig: H. Haessel.

Schubert, Johannes. 1954. "Das Reis-Maṇḍala." In *Asiatica, Festschrift Friedrich Weller,* J. Schubert and U. Schneider, eds., pp. 584ff. (Leipzig: OH.)

Schulz, Friedrich August. 1958. *Die philosophisch-theologischen Lehren des Pāśupata-Systems nach dem Pañcārthabhāṣya und der Ratnaṭīkā.* Walldorf-Hessen: Verlag für Orientkunde Dr. H. Vorndran.

Schwab, Julius. 1886. *Das altindische Thieropfer.* Erlangen: A. Deichert.

Searle, John R. 1969. *Speech Acts: An Essay in the Philosophy of Language.* Cambridge: CUP.

———. 1971a. "What is a Speech Act?" In Searle 1971b, 39–53.

———. 1971b. *The Philosophy of Language.* Oxford: OUP.

———. 1979a. "A Taxonomy of Illocutionary Acts." In Searle 1979b, 1–29.

———. 1979b. *Expression and Meaning.* Cambridge: CUP.

Sehgal, S. R. 1960. *Śāṇkhāyana Gṛhya Sūtra.* Delhi: Manoharlal.

Seidenberg, A. 1962. "The Ritual Origin of Geometry," *Archive for History of Exact Sciences* (Berlin/NY) 1.

———. 1978. "The Origin of Mathematics," *Archive for History of Exact Sciences* (Berlin/NY) 18.

———. 1981. "The Ritual Origin of the Circle and the Square," *Archive for History of Exact Sciences* (Berlin/NY) 25.

———. 1983. "The Geometry of the Vedic Rituals." In Staal 1983a, 95–126.

Sen, Chitrabhanu. 1963. "Vrātyas and Vedic Society," JOIB 12:288.

Sen, Sukumar. 1956a. *Caryāgiti-padābalī.* Calcutta.

———. 1956b. "The Nātha Cult." In CHI 4.288–90.

Sethiyā, Karanidan. 1969. *Mantravidyā.* Calcutta: Karanidan Sethiya (*samvat* 2033).

Shah, U. P. 1947. "A Peep Into the Early History of Tantra in Jaina Literature," *Bharata Kaumudi* (Allahabad) 2.

Shahidullah, Muhammad. 1928. *Les Chants mystiques de Kāṇha et de Saraha; les*

Dohā-koṣa et les Caryā. (Paris: Adrien-Maisonneuve.) Rep. and ed. by L. Misch, Library of Congress, 1958.

———. 1940. *Buddhist Mystic Songs, Āścara-caryācarya (Oldest Bengali and Other Eastern Vernaculars from 700 to 1100 A. D.).* (*Dacca Univ. Studies* 4.2) Dacca: Dacca Univ.

Sharma, Bhadrashila. 1969. *Mantrasiddhi kā upāya.* Prayag: Kalyan Mandir (*samvat* 2026).

Sharma, B. R. 1956. "Cakra in Brahmanical and Buddhist Scriptures," JBiRS, Buddha Jayanti Special Issue, 1:218–44.

———. 1972. "On Mati—In the Ṛgveda," *Virmarśa* 1, no. 1:37–44.

Sharma, Narendra Nath, ed. and tr. 1979. *Kalpacintāmaṇi of Dāmodara.* Delhi: Eastern Book Linkers.

Shastri, Dharmendra Nath. 1964. *Critique of Indian Realism, A Study of the Conflict Between the Nyāya-Vaiśeṣika and the Buddhist Dignāga School.* Agra: Agra University.

Shastri, Dakshina Ranjan. 1963. *Origin and Development of the Rituals of Ancestor Worship in India.* Calcutta.

Shastri, Jagaddhara Zādoo. 1947. *The Paratriśikā Lāghuvritti by Abhinavagupta.* (KSTS 68) Srinagar: Mercantile Press for the Research Dept. of Jammu and Kashmir State.

Shastri, Madhusudan Kaul, ed. 1921–35. *The Swacchanda-Tantra with Commentary by Kshemaraja,* 6 vols. in 7 parts, (KSTS 31, 37, 44, 48, 51, 56). Bombay: Nirnaya Sagar Press.

———. 1925. *The Shivasūtra-Vārtikam by Varadarāja.* (KSTS 43) Srinagar: Kashmir Pratap Steam Press.

———. 1926–39. *The Netra Tantra* (KSTS 000) Srinagar: Kashmir Pratap Steam Press.

Shastri, Mukunda Rāma. 1918. *The Parā-Trimshikā with Commentary, the Latter by Abhinava Gupta.* (KSTS 18) Bombay: Tatva-Vivechaka Press for the Research Dept., Jammu and Kashmir State.

Shastri, Pashupatinath. 1923. *Introduction to the Pūrva-Mīmāṇsā.* Calcutta: A. N. Bhattacharya.

Shastri, P. S. 1948. "The Imagery of Ṛgveda," ABORI 29:152–96.

———. c. 1955. "Meaning and the Word," *Oriental Thought* (Nasik) 2:99–130.

———. 1957. "The Vision of Dīrghatamas," *Prabuddha Bhārata* (Calcutta) 62:63–6.

Shaughnessy, James, ed. 1973. *The Roots of Ritual.* Grand Rapids, Michigan: Wm. B. Eerdmans.

Shende, N. J. 1949. *The Foundations of the Atharvanic Religion.* Poona.

______. 1952. *The Religion and Philosophy of the Atharvaveda.* (BOS 8) Poona: BORI.

______. 1963. "The Hotṛ and Other Priests in the Brāhmaṇas of the Ṛgveda," *J. Bombay Univ.* n. s. 32.2 (Sept.):48–88.

______. 1965. "Teachers and Their Views on the Ṛgveda Brāhmaṇas." In *Velankar Felicitation Volume,* 133–53.

______. 1967. *Kavi and Kāvya in the Atharvaveda.* Poona: Univ. of Poona.

Sherry, Patrick. 1977. *Religions, Truth and Language-Games.* NY: Harper.

Shrinivas Iyengar, P. T. 1912. *The Shiva-Sutra-Vimarsini of Ksemaraja.* (*Indian Thought Series* 2) Allahabad: Indian Thought.

Shukla, Dvijendra Nāth. 1958–60. *Vāstu-śāstra,* I: *Hindu Science of Architecture,* II: *Hindu Canons of Iconography and Painting.* (*Bhāratīya Vāstu-śāstra Series* 9) I: Chandigarh (1960), II: Lucknow (1958).

Siauve, Suzanne. 1959. *Les Noms Védiques de Viṣṇu dans l'Anuvyākhyāna de Madhva (Brahma-Sūtra I, 1, adhikaraṇa 2 à 12).* (PIFI 14) Pondichéry.

Siddheswar Varma. 1953. "The Vedic Concept of Metres," PAIOC (Lucknow) 16:10–19.

Sierksma, F. 1964. "Rtsod-pa: The Monachal Disputations in Tibet," IIJ 9:130–51.

Silburn, Lilian. 1961. *Le Vijñāna bairava, texte traduit et commenté.* (PICI 15) Paris: É. E. de Boccard.

______. 1980. *Études sur le śivaïsme du Cachemire, École, Spanda: Śivasūtra et Vimarśinī de Kṣemarāja.* (PICI 47) Paris: É. E. de Boccard.

______. 1983. *La Kuṇḍalinī, ou l'énergie des profondeurs, Étude d'ensemble d'après les textes du Śivaīsme du Kaśmir.* Paris: Les Deux Océans.

Singal, Sudarshana Devi, ed. 1958. *Gaṇapatitattwa.* New Delhi.

Singer, Milton. 1959. *Traditional India: Structure and Change.* Philadelphia: American Folklore Society.

______. 1961. "Text and Context in the Study of Contemporary Hinduism," ALB 25:274–303. Rep. Singer, *When a Great Tradition Modernizes* (NY: Praeger, 1972), 39–54.

Singh, Jaideva. 1979. *Śiva Sūtras, the Yoga of Supreme Identity.* Delhi: MB.

———. 1980. *Spanda-Kārikās, the Divine Creative Pulsation, the Kārikās and the Spanda-nirṇaya translated into English*. Delhi: MB.

———. Forthcoming. [*The Parātriṃśikā Vivaraṇa*]. Delhi: MB.

Singh, Lalan Prasad. 1976. *Tantra—Its Mystic and Scientific Basis*. Delhi: Concept Publishing Co.

Sinha, Jadunath. 1966. *Shakta Monism: The Cult of Shakti*. Calcutta: Sinha Publishing House.

Sircar, D. C. 1967. *The Śakti Cult and Tārā*. Calcutta: Univ. of Calcutta Press.

———. 1972–73. "Tantrasāradhṛta Dhyānamālā," JAIH 6:186–278.
———. 1973. *The Śākta Pīṭhas*, 2nd rev. ed. Delhi: MB.

Śivadatta Miśra. 1969. *Gāyatrī Tantra, With Hindi Commentary*. Varanasi.

Śivanārāyaṇa Shastri. 1972. *Vaidika vāṅmaya meṃ bhāṣācintana (Reflection on Language in Vedic Literature)*. Varanasi: Indological House.

Śivaramamurti, C. 1950. "Geographical and Chronological Factors in Indian Iconography," *Ancient India* 6:21ff.

———. 1955. "Parallels and Opposites in Indian Iconography," JAS 21.2:77ff.

———. 1976. *Śatarudrīya: Vibhūti of Śiva's Iconography*. New Dehli: Abhinav Publications.

———. 1978. *Chitrasūtra of the Vishnudharmottara*. New Delhi: Kanak.

Sivaraman, K. 1973. *Śaivism in Philosophical Perspective, A Study of the Formative Concepts, Problems and Methods of Śaiva Siddhānta*. Delhi: MB.

Skorupski, Tadeusz. 1983a. *The Sarvadurgatipariśodhana Tantra, Elimination of All Evil Destinies, Sanskrit and Tibetan Texts with Introduction, English Translation and Notes*. Delhi: MB.

———. 1983b. "Tibetan Homa Rites." In Staal 1983a, 403–17.

Slusser, Mary Shepherd. 1980. *Nepal Mandala: A Cultural Study of the Kathmandu Valley*. Princeton: Princeton Univ. Press.

de Smet, Richard V. 1953. *The Theological Method of Śaṃkara*. Rome: thesis, Pontifical Gregorian University.

———. 1954. "Langage et connaissance de l'absolue chez çaṃkara," *Revue philosophique de Louvain* 52:31–74.

———. 1960. "Language and Philosophy in India," *Proc. of the International Congress of Philosophy* 10 (Venice 1958):47–54.

Smith, H. Daniel. 1963. "Some Notes on the Canonical Identification of a Pāñcarātrāgama Text," ALB 27:1–17.

———. 1966. "Prāyaścitta in the Canonical Works of the Pāñcarātrāgama," ALB 30.

———. 1972. "The "Three Gems" of the Pāñcarātra Canon, a Critical Appraisal." In *Ex Orbe Religionum,* C. J. Bleeker, ed., pp. 42–51. (Leiden: Brill.)

———. 1973. "A Typological Survey of Definitions: the Name 'Pāñcarātra'," JOR (Madras) 34–35:102–17.

———. 1975–80. *A Descriptive Bibliography of the Printed Texts of the Pāñcarātrāgama,* 2 vols. (GOS 158, 168) Baroda.

———. 1978. *The Smith Āgama Collection: Sanskrit Books and Manuscripts Relating to Pāñcarātra Studies: A Descriptive Catalog.* (*Foreign and Comparative Studies/South Asian Special Publication* 2) Syracuse, NY: Maxwell School of Citizenship and Public Affairs.

Smith, Jonathan Z. 1978. *Map is Not Territory: Studies in the History of Religions.* Leiden: Brill.

Smith, Wilfrid Cantwell. 1980. "The True Meaning of Scripture: An Empirical Historian's Nonreductionist Interpretation of the Qur'an," *International J. of Middle Eastern Studies* 11:487–505.

Snellgrove, D. L., ed. and tr. 1959. *The Hevajra Tantra, A Critical Study,* 2 vols. (*London Oriental Series* 6) London: OUP.

Solmsen, Felix. 1922. *Indogermanische Eigennamen als Spiegel der Kulturgeschichte.* Heidelberg: Carl Winter.

Somayajipad, C. V., M. Itti Ravi Nambudiri, and Erkkara Raman Nambudiri. 1983. "Recent Nambudiri Performances of Agniṣṭoma and Agnicayana." In Staal 1983a, 252–55.

Sontakke, N. S., and C. G. Kashikar, eds. 1933–51. *Ṛgveda Saṃhitā With the Commentary of Sāyaṇācārya,* 5 vols., rei. 1972–78. Poona: Vaidika Samsodhana Mandala (Vedic Research Institute).

———. 1946. *Ṛgvedakhila.* Poona: Vaidika Samsodhana Mandala.

Specht, Ernst Konrad. 1969. *The Foundations of Wittgenstein's Late Philosophy.* D. E. Walford, tr. NY: Barnes and Noble [Ger. ed. 1963].

Sperber, Dan. 1975. *Rethinking Symbolism.* Alice L. Merton, tr. Cambridge: CUP.

Spink, Walter M. 1971. *Krishnamandala, A Devotional Theme in Indian Art.* (*Special Publications* 2) Ann Arbor, Michigan: The Center for South and Southeast Asian Studies, Univ. of Michigan.

Spratt, Philip. 1966. *Hindu Culture and Personality, A Psycho-Analytic Study.* Bombay: Manaktalas.

Sprung, Mervyn, ed. 1973. *The Problem of Two Truths in Buddhism and Vedānta.* Dordrecht: Reidel.

Sreekantaiya, N. 1937. "Imagination in Indian Poetics," IHQ 13:59ff.

Sreekrishna Sarma. 1957. "The Words *ākṛti and jāti* in the *Mahābhāṣya,*" ALB 21:54–65.

Srīnivāsa Ayyaṇgar, T. M. 1893. *Haṭhayogapradīpikā of Svātmārāma Svāmin.* Bombay.

Śrīnivāsa Ayyaṅgār, T. R. 1938. *Yoga Upaniṣads, Translated into English.* Adyar, Madras: Theosophical Society, ALRC. 2nd ed. 1952.

———. 1941. *Sāmānya Vedānta Upaniṣads, Translated into English.* Adyar, Madras: Theosophical Society, ALRC.

———. 1945. *Vaiṣṇava Upaniṣads, Translated into English.* Adyar, Madras: Theosophical Society, ALRC. 2nd ed. 1949.

———. 1953. *Śaiva Upaniṣads, Translated into English.* Adyar, Madras: Theosophical Society, ALRC.

———. 1972. *The HaṭhayogapradĪpikā of Svātmārāma, with the Commentary Jyotsnā of Brahmānanda and English Translation.* Adyar: Adyar Library and Research Center. Orig. 1893, Rep. 1975.

Srinivasan, Doris. 1975. "The Religious Significance of Multiple Bodily Parts to Denote the Divine: Findings from the Rig Veda," *Asiatische Studien* (Bern) 29, no. 2:137–79.

———. 1979. "The Religious Significance of Divine Multiple Body Parts in the Atharva Veda," *Numen* 25, no. 3.

Śrīpraśna Saṃhitā; see Seetha Padmanabha, ed. 1969.

Staal, J. Frits. 1958. "Notes on Some Brahmin Communities of South India," *Arts and Letters, J. of the Royal India, Pakistan and Ceylon Society* 32:1–7.

———. 1959. "Uber die Idee der Toleranz im Hinduismus." *Kairos. Zeitschrift für Religionwissenschaft und Theologie* 1:215–18.

———. 1960. "Review of Ruegg (1959)," PEW 10:53–57.

———. 1961. *Nambudiri Veda Recitation.* The Hague: Mouton.

———. 1963a. "Report on Vedic Rituals and Recitations," *Year Book of the American Philosophical Society:* 607–11.

———. 1963b. "Review of Scharfe (1961)," JAOS 83:252–56.

———. 1966. "Indian Semantics, I," JAOS 86:304–11.

———. 1967. *Word Order in Sanskrit and Universal Grammar.* (*Foundations of Language, Supplementary Series* 5) Dordrecht: D. Reidel.

———. 1968. "The Twelve Ritual Chants of the Nambudiri Agniṣṭoma." In Kuiper 1968, 409–29.

———. 1969. "Sanskrit Philosophy of Language." In *Current Trends in Linguistics* 5, *Linguistics in South Asia,* T. A. Sebeok, *et al.*, eds., pp. 449–531. (The Hague: Mouton.)

———. 1972. *A Reader on The Sanskrit Grammarians.* (*Studies in Linguistics* 1) Cambridge, Mass.: MIT Press.

———. 1975a. "The Concept of Metalanguage and Its Indian Background," JIPh 3:215–54.

———. 1975b. *Exploring Mysticism: A Methodological Essay.* Berkeley: UCaPress.

———. 1976. "Sanskrit Philosophy of Language." In *History of Linguistic Thought and Contemporary Linguistics,* H. Parret, ed., pp. 102–36. (Berlin: Walter de Gruyter.)

———. 1977. "Rigveda 10.71 on the Origin of Language." In Coward and Sivaraman 1977.

———. 1978. "The Ignorant Brahmin of the Agnicayana," ABORI 59:337–48.

———. 1979a. "The Meaninglessness of Ritual," NUMEN 26, 1:2–22.

———. 1979b. "The Concept of Scripture in the Indian Tradition." In Jeurgensmeyer and Barrier 1979, 121–24.

———. 1979c. "Oriental Ideas on the Origin of Language," JAOS 99:1–14.

———. 1980. "Ritual Syntax," in *Sanskrit and Indian Studies, Essays in Honor of Daniel H. H. Ingalls* (*Studies of Classical India* 2), Masatoshi Nagatomi *et al.*, eds., pp. 119–42. (Dordrecht: D. Reidel.)

———. 1982. *The Science of Ritual.* (*Post-graduate and Research Department Series* 15 [*Prof. P. D. Gune Memorial Lectures,* first series]) Poona: BORI.

———. 1983a. *Agni, The Vedic Ritual of the Fire Altar* (in collaboration with C. V. Somayajipad and M. Itti Ravi Nambudiri), 2 vols. Berkeley, Calif.: Asian Humanities Press.

———. 1983b. "Moon Chants, Space Fillers and Flow of Milk." In *Felicitation Volume Professor E. R. Sreekrishna Sarma,* pp. 17–30. (Madras: Kalakshetra Publications Press.). Rep. this volume, Chapter Two.

———. 1983c. "Ritual Structure." In Staal 1983a, 127–34.

———. 1983d. "Vedic Mudras." In Staal 1983a, 359–75.

———. 1984a. "Ritual, Mantras and the Origin of Language." In *Amṛtadhārā, Professor R. N. Dandekar Felicitation Volume,* pp. 403–25. (Poona).

———. 1984b. "The Search for Meaning: Mathematics, Music, and Ritual," *Amer. J. of Semiotics* 2, no. 4:1–57.

———. 1985a. "Mantras and Bird Songs," JAOS 105, no. 3:549–58.

———. 1985b. "Substitutions de paradigmes et religions d'Asie." *Cahiers d'Extrême-Asie* 1:21–57.

———. 1987. "The Sound of Religion." *Numen* 33:33–64, 185–224.

———. 1988a. *Rules Without Meaning. Essays on Rituals, Mantras and the Science of Man.* NY: Peter Lang.

———. 1988b. *Jouer avec le feu, Pratique et théorie du rituel védique.* Paris: PICI.

———. 1988c. *Universals. Studies in Indian Logic and Linguistics.* Chicago: UChP.

Stablein, William George. 1973. "A Medical-Cultural System Among the Tibetan and Newar Buddhists: Ceremonial Medicine," *Kailash: A Journal of Jimalayan Studies* (Kathmandu) 1, no. 3:193–203.

———. 1976. *The Mahakālatantra: A Theory of Ritual Blessings and Tantric Medicine.* NY: Dissertation, Columbia Univ.

Stace, W. T. 1961. *Mysticism and Philosophy.* London: Macmillan.

Stahl, Abraham. 1979. "Ritualistic Reading Among Jews," *Anthropological Quarterly* 52, no. 2:115–20.

Stasiak, Stefan. 1929. "Fallacies and Their Classification According to the Early Hindu Logicians," *Rocznik Orientalistyczny* (Lwow) 6:191–97.

Stein, Burton. 1978. *South Indian Temples: An Analytical Reconsideration.* New Delhi: Vikas.

Stein, R. A. 1959. *Recherches sur l'épopée et le barde au Tibet.* Paris: Presses universitaires de France.

Steinkellner, Ernst. 1978a. "Yogische Erkenntnis als Problem im Buddhismus." In Oberhammer 1978, 121–34.

———. 1978b. "Remarks on Tantric Hermeneutics." In *Proc. of the Csoma de Koros Memorial Symposium*, L. Liget, ed, pp. 445–58. (Budapest.)

Sternbach, Ludwik. 1974. *Subhāṣita, Gnomic and Didactic Literature.* (HIL 4.1.1) Wiesbaden: OH.

Stevens, John. 1981. *Sacred Calligraphy of the East.* Boulder, Colo.: Shambhala.

Stiglmayr, E., and F. Fodermayr. 1970. *The Barela-Bhilala and Their Songs of Creation: Musical Analysis of the Songs.* Vienna: Englbert Stiglmayr.

Starthern, Andrew, and Marilyn Strathern. 1968. "Marsupials and Magic: A Study of Spell Symbolism Among the Mbowamb." In *Dialectic in Practical Re-*

ligion, E. R. Leach, ed., (*Cambridge Papers in Social Anthropology* 5) (Cambridge: CUP).

Strauss, Otto. 1927a. "Altindischen Spekulationen über die Sprache und ihre Probleme," ZDMG 81:99–151.

———. 1927b. "Mahābhāṣya ad Pāṇini 4,1,3 und seine Bedeutung für die Geschichte der indischen Logik," in *Aus Indiens Kultur: Festgabe für Richard von Garbe* (*Veröffentlichungen des Indogermanischen Seminars der Universität Erlangen* 3), J. Negelein, ed., pp. 84–94. (Erlangen: Palm und Ecke.)

Strawson, P. F. 1966. "Review of PI," in *Wittgenstein, the Philsophical Investigations, A Collection of Critical Essays*, George Pitcher, ed. (Garden City, N.Y.: Anchor Books). Orig. 1954.

Strickmann, Michel. 1983. "Homa in East Asia." In Staal 1983a, 418–55.

Subha Rao, Veluri. 1969. *The Philosophy of a Sentence and Its Parts*. New Delhi: Munshi Ram Manoharlal.

Subramania Iyer, K. A. 1937. "Who Are the Anityasphoṭavādinaḥ," PAIOC [Mysore 1935] 8:258–63.

———. 1941. "Pratibhā as the Meaning of a Sentence," PAIOC [Tirupati 1940] 10:326–32.

———. 1942. "The Conception of Guṇa Among the Vaiyākaraṇas," NIA 5:121–30.

———. 1947. "The Doctrine of Sphoṭa," JGJRI 5:121–47.

———. 1948. "The Point of View of the Vaiyākaraṇas," JOR 18:84–96. Rep. Staal 1972, 393–400.

———. 1950–51. "The Concept of Action Among the Vaiyākaraṇas," JGJRI 8:165–88.

———. 1964. "Bhartṛhari on Vyākaraṇa as a Means of Attaining Mokṣa," ALB 28:112–31.

———. 1965a. *The Vākyapadīya of Bhartṛhari with the Vṛtti, Chapter I: Translation* (*Deccan College Building Centenery and Silver Jubilee Series* 26). Poona: Deccan College.

———. 1965b. "Bhartṛhari on Dhvani," ABORI 46:49–65.

———. 1966. *Sphoṭasiddhi of Maṇḍana Miśra (English Translation)* (*Deccan College Building Centenery Series* 25). Poona: Deccan College.

———. 1969. *Bhartṛhari, a Study of the Vākyapadīya in the Light of Ancient Commentaries* (*Deccan College Building Centenery and Silver Jubilee Series* 68). Poona: Deccan College.

Subramanya Sastri, K. S. n. a. *Mantraśāstramātṛkāgranthānām Vivaraṇātmikā*

Sūcikā (A Descriptive Index of the Texts of Mātṛka and the Science of Mantra). Varanasi.

***Sukthankar, V. S., S. K. Belvalkar, P. L. Vaidya,* et al.** 1927–66. *The Mahābhārata, for the First Time Critically Edited*, 19 vols., in 22 parts. Poona: BORI.

Sukul, Kuber Nath. 1964. "Report on Vedic Ritual and Recitations," *Yearbook of the American Philosophical Society* (Philadelphia) 1964:607–11.

Sureshcandra, Babu. 1940. *Le Culte des ancêtres (pitṛ) dans l'Inde antique d'après les Purāṇa*. Paris: Adrien-Maisonneuve.

Suśruta Saṃhitā; see Jādavaji Trikamji Ācārya and Nārāyaṇa Rāma Ācārya "Kāvyatīrtha," eds., 1980.

Swamy, B. G. L. 1976. "Sources for a History of Plant Sciences in India: II, the Rig Vedic Soma Plant," IJHS 11, no. 1:11–48.

Taber, John. 1983. "Review of D'Sa (1980)," PEW 33, no. 4:407–10.

______. 1983. "Review of Gächter (1983)," PEW 35, no. 2:215–17.

Taimni, I. K. 1961. *The Science of Yoga*. Wheaton, Ill.: The Theosophical Publishing House.

Taittirīya Saṃhitā; see Keith 1914.

Tajima, Ryujun. 1959. *Les deux grands maṇḍalas et la doctrine de l'ésoterisme Shingon*. (*Bulletin de la Maison Franco-Japonaise* n. s. 6). Tokyo: Kasai; Paris: Presses universitaires de France.

Tambiah, Stanley Jeyaraja. 1968a. "The Magical Power of Words," *Man* 3, no. 2:175–208. Rep. Tambiah 1985, 17–59.

______. 1968b. "Literacy in a Buddhist Village in North-East Thailand." In Goody 1983, 85–131.

______. 1977a. "The Cosmological and Performative Significance of a Thai Cult of Healing Through Meditation," *Culture, Medicine, and Psychiatry* 1:97–132. Rep. Tambiah 1985, 87–122.

______. 1977b. "The Galactic Polity: The Structure of Traditional Kingdoms in South East Asia." In *Anthropology and the Climate of Opinion*, Stanley Freed, ed., pp. 69–97. (NY: New York Academy of Sciences.). Rep. Tambiah 1985, 252–86.

______. 1981. "A Performative Approach to Ritual," *Proceedings of the British Academy* 65:113–69. Rep. Tambiah 1985, 123–66.

______. 1984. *The Buddhist Saints of the Forest and the Cult of Amulets, A Study in Charisma, Hagiography, Sectarianism, and Millennial Buddhism*. Cambridge: CUP.

______. 1985. *Culture, Thought, and Social Action: An Anthropological Perspective*. Cambridge, Mass.: HUP.

Tedlock, Dennis. 1983. *The Spoken Word and the Work of Interpretation.* (*Univ. of Pennsylvania Publications in Conduct and Communication*) Philadelphia: Univ. Penn. Press.

Thapar, Romila. 1983. "The Archeological Background in the Agnicayana Ritual." In Staal 1983a, 3–40.

Thibaut, G. 1870. *Das Jaṭāpaṭala, Lehrbuch des Jatāpāṭha für den Rigveda, nebst dem Abschnitt der Prātiśākhyajyotsnā über die Vikṛti des Kramapāṭha.* Leipzig: F. A. Brockhaus.

———. 1882. *Arthasaṃgraha of Laugakṣī Bhāskara.* (BeSS 4) Varanasi.

Thieme, Paul. 1931. "Grammatik und Sprache, ein Problem der altindischen Sprachwissenschaft," ZII 8:23–32. Rep. KS:524–27.

———. 1935. *Pāṇini and the Veda; Studies in the Early History of Linguistic Science in India.* Allahabad: Globe Press.

———. 1938. *Der Fremdling im Ṛgveda.* (ABh. DMG 23) Leipzig.

———. 1949. "Das Rätsel vom Baum," (*Hallische Monographien* 7) in *Untersuchungen zur Wortkunde und Auslegung des Rigveda* (Halle: Max Niemeyer Verlag), 55ff.

———. 1952. "Brahman," ZDMG 102:91–129.

———. 1956. "Paṇini and the Pāṇinīas (Review of Renou's tr. of Pāṇini's Aṣṭādhyāyī)," JAOS 77:51–56. Rep. KS:596–611.

———. 1957a. "Review of Renou, EVP (1955–69)," JAOS 77:51–56.

———. 1957b. "Vorzarathustrisches bei den Zarathustriern und bei Zarathrustra," ZDMG 107:67–104.

———. 1964. "Patañjali über Varuṇa und die sieben Ströme." In *Indo-Iranica: mélanges présentés à Geor Morgenstierne à l'occasion de son soixante-dixième anniversaire,* G. Redard. ed., pp. 168–73. (Wiesbaden: OH.)

———. 1967. "Vedisch *manīsā.*" In *Beiträge zur Indogermanistik und Keltologie Julius Pokorny zum 80. Geburtstag gewidmet,* W. Meid, ed. (Innsbruck: Sprachwissenschaftliches Institut der Universität) (Innsbrucker Beiträge zur Kulturwissenschaft 13). Rep KS:259–67.

———. 1971. *Kleine Schriften,* 2 vols. (*Glasenapp-Stiftung* 5.1–2), Georg Budruss, ed. (Wiesbaden: Franz Steiner Verlag.)

Thirugnanasambandhan, P. 1973. *Śataratnasaṃgraha.* Madras: Univ. Press.

Thite, G. 1972. "Magico-Religious Application of the White Yajurveda," CASS Studies 1:65–81.

Thompson, Laurence G. 1976. *Studies of Chinese Religion: A Comprehensive and*

Classified Bibliography of Publications in English, French, and German Through 1970. Encino, Calif.: Dickenson.

Thompson, E. J., and A. M. Spencer. 1923. *Bengali Religious Lyrics: Śākta.* "Calcutta," YMCA Press 1923.

Thorpe, W. H. 1966. "Ritualization in Ontogeny, II: Ritualization in the Individual Development of Bird Song." In Huxley 1966, 351–58.

Tiwari, Jagdish Narain. 1985. *Goddess Cults in Ancient India, With Special Reference to the First Seven Centuries A. D..* Delhi: Agam Prakashan.

Torella, Raffaele. 1979. *Śivasūtra con il commento di Kṣemarāja, traduzione dal sanscrito, introduzione e note.*

———. 1980. "Una Traduzione francese della *Parātriṃśikālaghuvṛtti* di Abhinavagupta," RSO 54:171–200.

Toulmin, Stephen. 1969. "Ludwig Wittgenstein." *Encounter* 32, no. 1:58–71.

Trigg, Roger. 1973. *Reason and Commitment.* Cambridge: CUP.

Suda, Shinichi. 1974. *The Saṃvarodayatantra, English, Tibetan, and Sanskrit.* Tokyo: Hokuseido Press.

Tucci, Giuseppe. 1929–30. "Note indologichi: Tracce di culto lunare in India," RSO 12:419–27.

———. 1930. "Animadversiones Indicae," JRASB n. s. 26:125–60.

———. 1961. *The Theory and Practice of the Maṇḍala, with Special Reference to the Modern Psychology of the Subconscious,* Alan Houghton Brodrick, tr. London: Rider and Co. Orig. Ital. 1949, *Teoria e practica del maṇḍala;* pap. 1969.

———. 1969. *Ratilīlā: An Interpretation of the Tantric Imagery of the Temples of Nepal,* James Hogarth, tr. Geneva: Nagel.

Turner. Victor W. 1967. *The Forest of Symbols.* Ithaca, N.Y.: Cornell Univ. Press.

———. 1969. *The Ritual Process.* Chicago: Aldine.

———. 1974. *Dramas, Fields, and Metaphors.* Ithaca, N.Y.: Cornell Univ. Press.

———. 1979. *Process, Pilgrimage, and Performance: A Study in Comparative Symbology.* New Delhi: Concept.

Übach, Helga. 1970. *Das Nepālamahātmyam des Skandapurāṇam. Legenden um die hinduistischen Heiligtümer Nepals.* München: Münchener Universitäts Schriften.

Unbescheid, Günter. 1980. (*Beiträge zur Südasien-Forschung* (Südasien-Institut, Universität Heidelberg) 63) Wiesbaden: Franz Steiner Verlag.

Upadhyaya, Nagendranath. 1976. *Gorakṣnāth: Nāth Sampradāya ke Pripreksya meṃ.* Varanasi: Kashi Nagari Pracharini Sabha.

Upadhyaya, Suresh A. 1961. "The Word Manīṣā in the Ṛgveda," PAIOC 21:21–30.

Vācaspatimiśra. *Nyāyakaṇikā;* see M. L. Goswami 1978.

Vajpeyi, Kailash. 1979. *The Science of Mantras, A Manual for Happiness and Prosperity.* New Delhi: Arnold Heineman.

Vansina, Jan. 1965. *Oral Tradition.* London: RKP.

Varenne, Jean. 1960. *La Mahā Nārāyaṇa Upaniṣad, édition critique, avec une traduction française, une étude, des notes er en annexe, La Prāṇāgnihotra Upaniṣad,* 2 vols. (PICI 13) Paris: E. de Boccard.

______. 1977. *Le Tantrisme, la sexualité transcendée. (Bibliothèque de l'irrationnel et des grands mystères, le domaine invisible)* Paris: Retz.

Varmā, Satyakāma. 1970. *Vākyapadīyam (Brahmakāṇḍa) of Shrī Bhartṛhari, the Great Linguist and Grammarian, with Trilingual Commentary.* New Delhi: Munshiram Manoharlal.

______. 1971. *Vyākaraṇa kī dārśanike bhūmikā (Bhartṛhari par mukhyataḥ ādhārita); The Philosophy of Grammar According to Bhartṛhari.* Delhi: Munshiram Manoharlal.

Vasavada, A. U., tr. 1965. *Tripurārahasya: Jñānakhaṇḍa.* (ChSSt 50) Varanasi.

Vasu, Rai Bahadur Srisa Chandra. 1914–15. *The Śiva Saṃhitā.* Allahabad: Panini Office. Rep. 1979 (New Delhi: Oriental Books Reprint Corporation).

Vaudeville, Charlotte. 1968–69. "The Cult of the Divine Name in the Haripāṭh of Dñandev," WZKS 12–13:395–406.

______. 1969. *L'Invocation, le Haripāṭh de Dñyāndev.* Paris: BEFEO.

Velankar, H. D. 1938. "Ṛgvedic Similes, I: Similes of the Vāmadevas (ṚV Maṇḍala IV)," JBombayBrRAS 14:1–47.

______. 1940. "Ṛgvedic Similes, II: Similes of the Atris (ṚV Maṇḍala V)," JBombayBrRAS 16:1–42.

______. 1954. "Magicians in the Ṛgveda." In *Laksman Sarup Commemorative Volume,* pp. 85–92. (Hoshiarpur.)

______. 1963. "Similes in the Atharvaveda," *J. of the Asiatic Soc. of Bombay* 38:19–43.

______. 1963–68. *Ṛgveda Maṇḍala VII; Ṛgveda Maṇḍala II; Ṛgveda Maṇḍala III.* (VII: BVS 23) Bombay: VII; BVB; II–III: Univ. of Bombay.

______. 1965. "Emotional Simile in the Ṛgveda and the Concept of Bhakti," *Bhāratīya Vidyā* 25:1–43.

______. 1966. "Kavi and Kāvya in the Ṛgveda," PAIOC 22:253–58.

______. 1969. "World Economy and Ṛgvedic Interpretation." In *Proc. 26th*

International Congress of Orientalists, 1964, 139–45. Wiesbaden. Also, ABORI 45 (1964):1–18.

———. 1972. *Ṛksūktaśatī, Selected Hymns from the Ṛgveda with Important Padapāṭha, English Translation, Critical Notes, Select Glossary and Indices.* (BVS 20) Bombay: BVB.

Venkatachari, K. K. A. 1978. *Śrīvaiṣṇava Maṇipravāla.* (*Ananthacharya Research Institute Series* 3) Bombay.

Venkatarama Sarma, V. 1966–67. "Paspaśāśayaprakāśaḥ (Light on the Introduction to Patañjali's Mahābhāṣya)," *Viśvasaṃskṛta* (Hoshiarpur) 4:3–11, 124–30, 135.

Venkataraman, K. R. 1956. "Śakti Cult in South India." In CHI 4.252–59.

Venkatasubbiah, A. 1940. "The Act of Truth in the Ṛgveda," JOR 14:133–65.

Venkatasubramania Sastri, V. S., and C. Raja Rajeswara Sarma, eds. 1977. *Bhelasaṃhitā.* New Delhi: Central Council for Research in Indian Medicine and Homeopathy.

Venkateswaran, T. K. 1968. "Rādhā-Krishna *Bhajanas* of South India: A Phenomenological, Theological, and Philosophical Study." In *Krishna: Myths, Rites, and Attitudes,* Milton Singer, ed., pp. 139–72. (Chicago: UChP.)

Vesey, G. N. A. 1969. *Talk of God* (*Royal Institute of Philosophy Lectures* 2 (1967–68) London: Macmillan.

Vidusekhar Bhattacharya Sastri. 1928. "Sandhabhasa," IHQ 4, 2:287–96.

Vidyaratna, R., ed. 1874. *Āśvalāyana Śrautasūtra.* (BI n. s. 49) Calcutta: Baptist Mission and Valmiki Presses.

Vidyarnava (Vasu?), Rai Bahadur Śrisa Chandra. 1918. *The Daily Practice of the Hindus, Containing the Morning and Midday Duties,* 3rd rev. ed. Allahabad: Panini Office. Rep. 1979 (New Delhi: Oriental Books Reprint Corporation).

Vidyarthi, Lalita Prasad. 1961. *The Sacred Complex in Hindu Gayā.* London: Asia Publishing House.

Vidyasagara, J.'s sons, eds. 1915. *Indrajālavidyāsaṃgraha.* Calcutta.

Vishva Bandhu. 1935–76. *A Vedic Word Concordance (Vaidika-padānukrama-kośa).* 5 vols. in 16 pts. Hoshiarpur: VVRI Publications, *Santakuti Vedic Series.* 2nd rev. eds: vols. 2.1–2, 1973 [1935–36]; vol. 1.1 1976 [1942].

———. 1967. "Vedic Textuo-linguistic Studies, 4: Atharvaveda I.1," VIJ 5,1:13–24.

de Visser, Marinus Willem. 1928–35. *Ancient Buddhism in Japan,* 2 vols. Paris.

Viṣvakṣena Saṃhitā; see Laksmi Narasimha Bhatta, ed., 1972.

Viśvanātha Miśra. 1971. "Vaiyākaraṇasampradaye sphoṭaparamparā

(Sphoṭa in the Grammatical Tradition)." In Rajeshwar Shastri Dravid 1971, grammatical section, 40–47.

Vivekananda, Swami. 1962. "On Mantra and Mantra-Chaitanya." In *Complete Works* (Calcutta [?]: Mayavati Memorial Edition), 7:407ff..

Vogel, Jean Phillipe. 1919. *The Sign of the Spread Hand or "Five Finger Token" (Pañcāṅulika) in Pali Literature.* Amsterdam.

de Vreese, K. 1948. "The Game of Dice in Ancient India." In *Orientalia Neerlandica: A Volume of Oriental Studies,* pp. 349–62. (Leiden: Sijthoff.).

Wackernagel, Jacob. 1954. *Alindisches Grammatik* 2.2. Gottingen: Vandenhoeck and Ruprecht.

Waddell, Laurence Austine. 1912. "The Dhāranī Cult in Buddhism, Its Origins, Deified Literature and Images," OAZ 1:155–95.

______. 1914. "Dhāraṇī, or Indian Buddhist Protective Spells," IA 43:37–42, 49–54, 92–93.

Waghorne, Joanne Punzo, and Norman Cutler, in association with Vasudha Narayanan. 1985. *Gods of Flesh, Gods of Stone, The Embodiment of Divinity in India.* Chambersburg, Penn.: Anima.

Walleser, Max. 1923. "The Life of Nāgārjuna from Tibetan and Chinese Sources." In *Hirth Anniversary Volume,* B. Schindler, ed. pp. 421–55. (London.).

Walter, Hermann. 1893. *Svātmārāma's Haṭhayogapradīpikā, Die Leuchte des Haṭhayoga, aus dem Sanskrit übersetzt.* Munich: Dissertation.

Ware, James H., Jr. 1981. *Not with Words of Wisdom: Performative Language and Liturgy.* Washington, D.C.: University Press of America.

Wasson, R. Gordon. 1968. *Soma, Divine Mushroom of Immortality.* (*Ethno-mycological Studies* 1) NY: Harcourt Brace Jovanovich.

______. 1970. "Soma: Comments Inspired by Professor Kuiper's Review," IIJ 12:286–98.

______. 1971. "The Soma of the Rig-Veda: What Was It?" JAOS 91:169–87.

______. 1972. *Soma and Fly-Agaric: Rejoinder to Professor Brough.* Cambridge, Mass.

______. 1979. "Soma Brought Up-to-Date," JAOS 99, no. 1:100–105.

Wayman, Alex. 1962. "Female Energy and Symbolism in the Buddhist Tantras," HR 2, no. 1:73–111. Rep. Wayman 1973, 164–201.

______. 1967. "The Significance of Dreams in India and Tibet," HR 7, no. 1:1–12. Rep. Wayman 1984, 399–411.

______. 1968a. "Concerning *saṃdhā-bhāṣā/saṃdhi-bhāṣā/saṃdhyā-bhāṣā,*" *in*

Mélanges d'Indianisme, à la mémoire de Louis Renou (PICI 28, Paris: Éditions E. de Boccard), 786–96.

———. 1968b. "The Hindu-Buddhist Rite of Truth—An Interpretation." In *Studies in Linguistics* (Emeneau Festschrift) pp. 365–69. (Poona: Linguistic Society of India.) Rep. Wayman 1984, 391–97.

———. 1973. *The Buddhist Tantras, Light on Indo-Tibetan Esotericism.* NY: Samuel Weiser.

———. 1974. "Two Traditions of India—Truth and Silence," PEW 24, no. 4:389–403. Rep. Wayman 1984, 370–89.

———. 1976. "The Significance of Mantras, from the Veda Down to Buddhist Tantric Practice," IT 3:483–97. Orig. ALB 39 (1975):65–89. Rep. Wayman 1984, 413–30.

———. 1977. *Yoga of the Guhyasamājatantra, The Arcane Lore of Forty Verses.* New Delhi: MB. Rep. 1980 (NY: Samuel Weiser).

———. 1981. "Reflections on the Theory of Barabuḍur as a *Maṇḍala.*" In Gomez and Woodward 1981, 139–72.

———. 1984. *Buddhist Insight, Essays by Alex Wayman.* George Elder, ed. (*Religions of Asia Series* 5) Delhi: MB.

Weber, Albrecht Friedrich. c. 1855. "Vedische Hochzeitssprüche." In IS 5:177.

———. 1858. *Zwei vedische Texte über Omina und Portenta.* Berlin: Berlin Acad.

———. 1865. "Vāc und Logos." In IS 9:473–80.

Weir, Roth Hirsch. 1970. *Language in the Crib.* The Hague: Mouton.

Welch, Holmes. 1957. *Taoism and the Parting of the Way.* Boston: Beacon Press. Rev. ed 1965.

Welch, Holmes, and Anna Seidel, eds. 1979. *Facets of Taoism, Essays in Chinese Religion.* New Haven, Conn.: YUP.

Weller, H. 1927. "Vergleichungen im Rigveda." In *Festgabe von Garbe,* 54.

Wheelock, Wade T. 1980. "A Taxonomy of the Mantras in the New- and Full-Moon Sacrifice," HR 19, no. 4:349–69.

———. 1982. "The Problem of Ritual Language: From Information to Situation," JAAR 50, no. 1:49–71.

———. 1984. "The Mass and Other Ritual Texts: A Computer Assisted Approach," HR 24, no. 1:49–72.

White, John. 1976. *Alles über TM, Transzendentale Meditation, Mantra, Mystik, Tecknik, Philosophie, Bewusstseinserweiterung; die neue Lehre des Maharishi Mahesh Yogi.* Munich: Heyne.

Whittaker, John H. 1978. "Wittgenstein and Religion: Some Later Views of His Later Work," RSR 4, no. 3:188–93.

Wikander, Stig. 1941. *Vāyu, Texte und Untersuchungen zur Indo-iranischen Religions-geschichte.* Uppsala: Lundeqvistska Bokhandeln.

Wilson, Bryan, ed. 1970. *Rationality.* (*Key Concepts in the Social Sciences*) NY: Harper and Row. UK: Basil Blackwell.

Winch, Peter. 1976. *The Idea of a Social Science and Its Relation to Philosophy.* London: RKP. Orig. 1958.

Winternitz, M. 1892. *Das altindische Hochzeitsrituell nach dem Āpastambīya-Gṛhyasūtra und einigen anderen verwandten Werken, mit Vergleichung der Hochzeitsgebrauche bei den übrigen indogermanischen Volkern.* (*Denkschriften Akad. Wien* 40) Wien.

———. 1897. *The Mantrapāṭha or the Prayer Book of the Āpastabins.* Oxford.

Wirz, P. 1941. *Exorzismus und Heilkunde auf Ceylon.* Bern. Eng. tr. 1954, *Exorcism and the Art of Healing in Ceylon* (Leiden: Brill).

Wittgenstein, Ludwig. 1953. *Philosophische Untersuchungen/Philosophical Investigations.* G. E. M. Anscombe, tr. NY: London.

———. 1965. *The Blue and Brown Books.* NY: Harper. Orig. 1958.

———. 1966. *Lectures and Conversations on Aesthetics, Psychology and Religious Belief,* Cyril Barrett, ed. Berkeley: UCaP.

———. 1967a. "Beremrkungen über Frazers 'The Golden Bough'," *Synthese* 17:233–53.

———. 1967b. *Zettel,* G. E. M. Anscombe and G. H. von Wright, eds., G. E. M. Anscombe, tr. Berkeley: UCaP.

———. 1972. *Über Gewissheit* (*On Certainty*), G. E. M. Anscombe and G. von Wright, eds., Paul Denis and G. E. M. Anscombe, trs., NY: Harper. Orig. 1969.

Woodroffe, Sir John George. [Note: The publication history of the works of John Woodroffe (Arthur Avalon) is complex. Imprints vary.] 1913. *Hymns to the Goddess.* Madras: Ganesh and Co. Rep. 1973.

———. 1914. *Prapañcasāra Tantra of Śaṅkarācārya with the Commentary Vivaraṇa by Padmapādācarya and Prayogakramadīpikā—a Vṛtti on the Vivaraṇa,* Taranatha Vidyaratna, ed. (TT 3) Calcutta: Sanskrit Press Depository. Reissued 1935 (TT 18–19), "revised and documented with exhaustive introduction" by Woodroffe, Aṭalānanda Sarasvatī, ed. (Madras: Ganesh and Co.).

———. 1917. *Kulārṇava Tantra.* Tārānātha Vidyāratna, ed. (TT 5). reissed 1965 (Madras: Ganesh), 1975 (New Delhi: MB).

———. 1918. *The Serpent Power, Being the Ṣaṭcakranirūpaṇa and Pādukāpañcaka, Two Works on Laya-yoga, Translated from the Sanskrit with Introduction and Commen-*

tary. Rev. eds. 2nd: 1922, 3rd: 1928, 5th: 1953, 6th: 1958. Madras: Ganesh and Co.

———. 1922. *Kaula and Other Upaniṣads*, Sītārāma Shāstrī, ed. (TT 11) Calcutta.

———. 1933. *Sāradā-tilaka Tantram*, Atalananda Sarasvati, ed. (TT 16–17) Calcutta: Agamanusamdhana Samiti.

———. 1959. *Shakti and Shakta*, 5th ed. Madras: Ganesh and Co. 3rd ed. 1929.

———. 1961. *Wave of Bliss (Ānandalaharī)*. Madras: Ganesh and Co.

———. 1963. *The Garland of Letters*, 4th ed. Madras: Ganesh and Co.

———. 1971. *Tantrarajatantra, A Short Analysis with a Preface by Yogi Shuddhananda Bharati; Kama-Kala-Vilasa by Punyananda-natha with the Commentary of Natanananda-natha*, (TT 8–9). Madras: Ganesh and Co. Orig. ed. 1920.

———. 1972. *Tantra of the Great Liberation*, 5th ed. Madras: Ganesh and Co. tr: 1913, 1927, 1971; text: Calcutta and London 1929 (TT 13). Rep. Delhi 1977; the introduction to the translation was issued separately as "Introduction to Tantra Sastra" (Madras), numerous eds. 6th 1933.

Woods, James Houghton, tr. 1914. *The Yoga System of Patañjali*. (HOS 17) Cambridge, Mass.: HUP. Rep. 1966 (Delhi: MB).

Wulff, Kurt, ed. 1935. *Sang Hyang Kamahāyanam Mantrānaya, Ansprache bei der weihe buddhistischer mönche, aus dem alt javanischen übersetzt und sprachlich erläutert*. Copenhagen: Levin and Munksgaard.

Wüst, W. 1969a. "Von indogermanischer Dichtersprache," *Rhèma* (?) 12. München.

———. 1969b. "Zum Problem einer indogermanischer Dichtersprache." In *Stúdia A. Pagliaro* III (Rome), 251ff.

Yāska. *The Nighaṇṭu and the Nirukta*; see Laksman Sarup 1927.

Young, Katherine K. n. a. *The Concept of Divine Place (divyadeśa) in Śrī Vaiṣṇava Literature from the 6th to 13th Centuries*. Thesis, Univ. of Montreal.

Young, Richard Fox. 1981. *Resistant Hinduism: Sanskrit Sources on Anti-Christian Apolgetics in Early Nineteenth-Century India*. (DeNRL 8) Wien: Institut für Indologie der Universität Wien.

Yudhiṣṭhira Mīmāṃsaka. 1973. *Samskṛta, vyākaraṇaśāstra kā itihāsa (History of Sanskrit Grammar)*, 3 vols, (vol. 1, 3rd ed; vol. 2, 2nd ed). Sonipat: Rama Lal Kapur Trust.

Zangenberg, F. 1962. "Śabaraḥ und seine philosophischen Quellen," WZKSO 6:60–77.

Zbavitel, Dusan. 1976. *Bengali Literature*. (HIL 9.3) Wiesbaden: OH.

Zelliot, Eleanor. 1976. "The Medieval Bhakti Movement in History: An Essay on the Literature in English." In *Hinduism: New Essays in the History of Religions* (*Studies in the History of Religions* 33), B. L. Smith, ed., pp. 143–68. (Leiden: Brill.)

Zemach, Eddy. 1964–65. "Wittgenstein's Philosophy of the Mystical," *Review of Metaphysics* 18:35–57.

Zimmer, Heinrich. 1931. "Lehren des Haṭhayoga, Lehrtexte," *Yoga* (Harburg-Wilhelmsburg) 1:45–62.

———. 1938. "Die Indische Weltmutter," *Eranos Jahrbuch* 6:175–220.

———. 1956. Joseph Campbell, ed. "Four Episodes from the Romance of the Goddess." In *The King and The Corpse, Tales of the Soul's Conquest of Evil* (*Bollingen Series* 11) pp. 239–306. (Princeton: Princeton Univ. Press, 2nd ed.)

———. 1960. "On the Significance of the Indian Tantric Yoga." In *Spiritual Disciplines* (*Papers from the Eranos Yearbooks* 4; *Bollingen Series* 30.4), Ralph Manheim, tr. (NY). Orig. Ger. ed., "Zur Bedeutung der indischen Tantra-Yoga," 1933 (*Eranos Jahrbuch* 1:9–94).

———. 1972. *Myths and Symbols in Indian Art and Civilization,* Joseph Campbell, ed. (*Bollingen Series* 6). Princeton: Princeton Univ. Press.

de Zoete, Beryl, and Walter Spies. 1938. *Dance and Drama in Bali.* London: Faber and Faber. Rep. 1952.

Zürcher, Erik. 1959. *The Buddhist Conquest of China.* Leiden: Brill.

Zvelebil, Kamil Veith. 1978. "Kumāratantra," ALB 42:169–220.

Zysk, Kenneth G. 1983. "Fever in Vedic India." JAOS 103, no. 3: 617–21.

———. 1985a. "Towards the Notion of Health in the Vedic Phase of Indian Medicine." ZDMG 135, no. 2:312–18.

———. 1985b. *Religious Healing in the Veda.* Philadelphia: American Philosophical Society.

———. 1986. "The Evolution of Anatomical Knowledge in Ancient India, with Special Reference to Cross-Cultural Influences." JAOS 106, no. 4:687–705.

———. (forthcoming.) *Early Buddhist Monastic Medicine.*